Human abilities in cultural context

Human abilities
in cultural context

Edited by

S. H. IRVINE
Department of Psychology
Plymouth Polytechnic

AND

J. W. BERRY
Psychology Department
Queen's University, Ontario

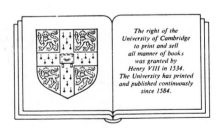

The right of the
University of Cambridge
to print and sell
all manner of books
was granted by
Henry VIII in 1534.
The University has printed
and published continuously
since 1584.

CAMBRIDGE UNIVERSITY PRESS

Cambridge
New York   New Rochelle   Melbourne   Sydney

Essay Index

Published by the Press Syndicate of the University of Cambridge
The Pitt Building, Trumpington Street, Cambridge CB2 1RP
32 East 57th Street, New York, NY 10022, USA
10 Stamford Road, Oakleigh, Melbourne 3166, Australia

First published 1988

Printed in the United States of America

Library of Congress Cataloging-in-Publication Data
Human abilities in cultural context.
Includes indexes.
1. Ability – Cross-cultural studies.   2. Ability –
Testing.   3. Psychological tests for minorities.
I. Irvine, S. H.   II. Berry, John W.
BF431.H747   1988   153.9   87–13230

British Library Cataloguing in Publication Data
Human abilities in cultural context.
1. Psychological tests   2. Ethnopsychology
I. Irvine, S. H.   II. Berry, John W.
150′.28′7   BF176

ISBN 0 521 34482 4

For Craig, Heather, John, Michael, and Susan

Contents

vii

Contributors

J. W. Berry
Psychology Department
Queen's University
Kingston
Ontario
Canada X7L 3N6

J. W. C. Chan
Educational Research
    Establishment
Education Department
Lee Gardens
Causeway B
Hong Kong

J. P. Das
Department of Educational
    Psychology
University of Alberta
Edmonton
Alberta
Canada T6G 2E1

H. J. Eysenck
Department of Psychology
Institute of Psychiatry
De Crespigny Park
Denmark Hill
London SE5 8AF
United Kingdom

Knut A. Hagtvet
Institute for Psychometrics
University of Bergen
Sydenplass 13
N-5000 Bergen
Norway

S. H. Irvine
Department of Psychology
Plymouth Polytechnic
Plymouth PL4 8AA
United Kingdom

Saburo Iwawaki
Graduate School of Education
Hyogo Kyoiku Daigaku
Yashirocho, Katogun
Hyogo 673-14
Japan

Douglas N. Jackson
Department of Psychology
University of Western Ontario
London
Ontario
Canada N6A 5C2

Arthur R. Jensen
Institute for Human Learning
University of California
Berkeley
California 94720
USA

Cigdem Kagitcibasi
Psychology Department
Bogazici University
PK 2 Bebek-Istanbul
Turkey

Daphne M. Keats
Psychology Department
University of Newcastle
Newcastle
New South Wales 2308
Australia

John A. Keats
Psychology Department
University of Newcastle
Newcastle
New South Wales 2308
Australia

I. M. Kendall
Australian Council for Educational
  Research
P.O. Box 210, Hawthorn
Melbourne
Victoria 3122
Australia
formerly of National Institute for
  Personnel Research
Port Elizabeth
South Africa

Amulya Kanti Satpathy Khurana
Health and Social Sciences
  Department
Indian Institute of Technology
Hauz Khas
New Delhi 110016
India

L. Z. Klich
Centre for Behavioural Studies
University of New England
Armidale
New South Wales 2351
Australia

Paul Kline
Department of Psychology
Singer Laboratories
University of Exeter
Exeter
Devon
United Kingdom

Damian McShane
UMC 28 College of Education
Utah State University
Logan
Utah 84322
USA

Samuel Messick
Research Division
Educational Testing Service
Princeton
New Jersey 08541
USA

Ype H. Poortinga
Department of Psychology
Tilburg University
Tilburg
225 Hogeschoolaan
Netherlands

R. J. Prinsloo
Institute for Psychological and
  Edumetric Research
Human Sciences Research Council
Private Bag X41
Pretoria
South Africa

Helmut Reuning
5 Welgelegen
28, 10th Street
Melville – Johannesburg 2090
South Africa

Joseph R. Royce
8911, 117th Street
Edmonton
Alberta
Canada

Isik Savasir
Department of Psychiatry
Hacettepe University
Ankara
Turkey

Robert J. Sternberg
Department of Psychology
Yale University
New Haven
Connecticut 06520
USA

Johan O. Undheim
Department of Psychology
University of Trondheim
N-7055 Dragvoll
Norway

Henk van der Flier
Nederlands Spoorwegen
Postbus 2025
3500 Ha Utrecht
Netherlands

Gajendra K. Verma
Faculty of Education
University of Manchester
Oxford Road
Manchester M13 9P
United Kingdom

Philip E. Vernon
late of University of Calgary
Alberta
Canada

Philip Anthony Vernon
Psychology Department
University of Western Ontario
London
Ontario
Canada N6A 5C2

J. M. Verster
National Institute for Personnel
    Research
Human Sciences Research Council
Box 32410 Braamfontein
Johannesburg 2017
South Africa

Mary Ann Verster
National Institute for Personnel
    Research
Human Sciences Research Council
Box 32410 Braamfontein
Johannesburg 2017
South Africa

J. W. Von Mollendorf
Institute for Psychological and
    Edumetric Research
Human Sciences Research Council
Private Bag X41
Pretoria
South Africa

Preface

Any collection runs the risk of becoming a collage that admits no firm focus. At the outset, therefore, we pursue the sharpness of image that all our contributors deserve as a setting for their own work. Consequently, the conceptual frames for the book are to be found in the first chapter, whose title, "The Abilities of Mankind," deliberately echoes Charles Spearman. Although that choice of words may provoke comparison with Spearman's great work *The Abilities of Man*, we beg to limit comparison to one aspect only. Spearman's book was restricted by its data base: Ours is expanded by it. The challenges he set 60 years ago have filled the scholarly journals with data from every continent. The richness and diversity of human ability have been demonstrated in every culture, but the literature is scarcely better known to the great majority of students of human abilities than it was to Spearman himself.

The work of the authors of this volume owes much to empirical sources that are unknown, neglected, and ignored in "mainstream" psychology. A realistic theory of the abilities of man can be founded only on evidence from all of mankind, not from one subgroup. Moreover, the pursuit of scientific truth in any field that has lacked theoretical closure and has consequently suffered an overabundance of speculation is not straightforward: But the effort has to be made if the measurement of individual differences in cognitive skills and abilities is to remain a psychological enterprise worthy of sustained scientific attention. This book is offered to students of human assessment as a contribution to the progress that must be registered when differential psychology comes to terms with both cultural context and cognitive theory: if not this century, then the next.

Early explanation of the structure and emphasis of the book's three parts and their individual chapters is certainly the reader's due, even if providing it proves to be a mild form of self-indulgence. This includes the perspective we sought when we first sketched the project some four years ago. None of our colleagues will be surprised to learn that it began with an ideal – that of having psychologists from all over the world contribute chapters about what they knew had been accomplished in their own countries, or in their own special frameworks, by measuring human abilities. We were able to count on people we had worked with in the field of cross-cultural psychology. We openly approached others whose theoretical advances we knew were relevant to the appraisal, growth, and survival of tests and testing, even if we had been numbered among their critics. Consequently, many different avenues of research are brought together at last in one volume. Perhaps that uniqueness is its justification, but there is one other that we can think of. A gathering together of diverse points of view, often strongly held and from all over the world, presupposes scientific tolerance. All of our authors, irrespective of citizenship, ethnic origin, or scientific leaning, contribute to that ethos by agreeing to write alongside even those with whom they have sharply disagreed. We ask nothing of our readers except the exercise of that same spirit in their appraisal of the material.

Unfortunately, gaps in our regional coverage were forced on us; and we are well aware of them. There is no Eastern European author, and no South American contribution. These were sought, but eluded us for a number of reasons. But we did try. Moreover, the last manuscript arrived on my desk some considerable time after the first. The result is an unavoidable time warp in the material.

In the end, after tempering idealism with publishing foresight and exercising unaccustomed patience with latecomers, I count myself privileged to be able to work with so many able and original scientists. Above all, I have been fortunate to share the editorial burden with John Berry, whose efforts will be observed, by those who know him, in every part of the book. Much as I value his role as a partner, his friendship over the past twenty years has been irreplaceable.

As co-editors, we decided to present the contents in three sections. The first of these divisions included our attempt at integration: and that effort had to take an early position in support of the title *Human Abilities in Cultural Context*. Hence, in the very first chapter, we provide a revaluation of theory, setting our rationale to work by constructing a taxonomy of empirical data types. We then use it for systematic appraisal of findings. We describe this revaluation as a "metatheory," a set of *prescriptions* for theory construction to be applied whenever comparisons of human performance on tests or tasks is part of the database. In demonstrating how to apply a taxonomic approach to existing data we have tried to be as demanding of our own work as we have of others'.

Central to our argument is the proposition that *Spearman's law of positive correlation* among all intellective tasks has to be reconciled with *Ferguson's law of cultural differentiation*. Ferguson's law predicts differences in human performance that are functions of ecological press to learn skills and strategies of adaptation. We consider the definition of ability to be incomplete without accounting for cultural and biological differences; and we judge the systematic analysis of the data we have at hand to be a major requirement in that definition.

Robert Sternberg's chapter on triarchic theory accompanies, and illuminates, that part of the volume given to holistic theory construction. Holistic theories stress the need to understand the logic of ability constructs. Hence, Sternberg's latest attempt to relate his own contributions to cross-cultural contexts is an important recognition that as we approach the end of the twentieth century, mental measurement has at long last had to accommodate cultural pluralism. Context has come in from the cold.

Part I has two further emphases. One of these, provided by Arthur Jensen and Hans Eysenck, is called *biometric fundamentalism* because it represents a consistent quest for a set of measures of ability with an emphasis on physiological functions. Both writers seek to extend the range of measures of ability by assessing the speed of information transmission in the cortex. This focus, exemplified by Jensen and Eysenck but by no means unique to them, on physiological measures has been controversial and not without emotion. We contribute to the discussion by juxtaposing paradigm and inferential differences in a fast-growing field where resolution can be achieved by considering the evidence on its scientific merits, and only on its merits. The target of those who pursue physiological paradigms is an *alternative method* of measuring intelligence; and a multimethod frame is a prerequisite of construct validity. A verdict on present claims for the success of any new method will take time and patient science.

The rest of the theoretical section is devoted to psychometric explanations of how intellect structures have been mapped. We are much indebted to a comprehensive essay on the traditional factor-analytic approach to abilities by Joseph Royce. The reliance on domain studies that have used factor analysis has characterised theory construction since Spearman and Thurstone first debated the meaning of correlation matrices. One could hardly hope to have a more scholarly explanation of the strengths and weaknesses of inference from correlations. Ype Poortinga also outlines a structuralist approach to test use by concentrating not on test totals but on *test items as stimuli*. On the surface, the chapter on *item bias* is about items that fail to behave consistently. Across cultures and within them, the identification of "rogue" items becomes an implicit statement about cognitive differences. The goal is to turn that implication into an explicit cognitive theory. In that pursuit, Poortinga and van der Flier represent a distinguished Dutch school of psychometrics in which the names of Martin Ippel, Cees Groot, Gideon Mellenbergh, and Fons van de Vijver are well known.

Significantly, Poortinga began his investigations into item behaviour in Southern Africa, and, note well, on *choice reaction times* long before their present vogue. That he did so is no small tribute to the vision, steadfastly held, of one of his mentors, Helmut Reuning, whose laboratory housed Poortinga's definitive work. Reuning's experimental rigour is apparent in Chapter 17 on Kalahari Bushmen, which appears in Part III. Their early awareness of the complexity of the "simplest" stimuli has been marked by a sensitivity to the pitfalls of psychometric measurement that one wishes could be transferred to every test user in every culture. Poortinga's unheralded African work on reaction times and item bias is today no longer a curiosity: It is a paradigm for theory construction based on the precise identification of any stimuli for which equivalence between groups may not be assumed.

A movement from theoretical frames of reference to *operational defini-*

tions can be observed in Parts II and III. In Part II the emphasis is on *the mainstream response to testing on a regional or national basis*. Paul Kline attempts to assess the rise and fall of a scientific subculture exerting strong influence on psychometrics in Britain; and he realistically asks where the psychologists of today are to be trained in the skills of human assessment if the major departments of psychology in his country hardly acknowledge its existence. In a psychological world exclusively of cognitive experiments, individual differences are consigned to the error term. Tony Vernon, with Douglas Jackson and Sam Messick, traces the thinking that has defined the American approach to culture in testing. No neglect of individual differences research has been witnessed there. One realises that the centre of gravity of North American cultural studies has been in what we call "enclave" research. The main difference between this and cross-cultural testing is the application of unaltered or unadapted instruments to enclaves. In cross-cultural test studies the major effort of the investigator is directed at altering standard methods or devising new ones in pursuit of construct validity. Meanwhile, the United States remains the world's largest user, and exporter, of tests and test products.

The technology that was perfected within the limits of postwar theory has dominated the world's operational use of tests. One of the most apt examples of the dependence of the rest of the world on American technology is available in the chapter by Hagtvet and Undheim on the Norwegian experience of testing. Wechsler has become a household word among Norway's psychometricians. Scientific enquiry proceeds, nevertheless, almost in spite of its instruments. When they break down in translation, theory is put at risk. As theoretical clarification has been sought in the modification of imported tests, the Norwegian work has given cautious definition to modern cultural contexts that qualify the meaning of test scores in cross-national comparisons.

From the North Sea to the Bosphorus, the American influence is dominant, only Piagetian enquiry emerging as a different, and consistently European, accent. The Norwegian and Mediterranean cultural heritages and ecologies are very different, but they are linked by their reliance on North American tests. In a chapter of meticulous scholarship and balance, Cigdem Kagitcibasi and Isik Savasir have, perhaps wisely, invoked Piaget as often as Wechsler in the first fully comprehensive account of work in the Eastern Mediterranean. This developmental approach is nicely contrasted with classical psychometrics in the chapter by Daphne and John Keats, whose account of developments in Australia adds to the already formidable contribution of Australian psychology. An identity, perhaps even a positive self-concept, is emerging in a subcontinent whose very size will dictate an adaptation of the tools of testing to its regional needs and ethnic pluralism. Those who wish to complete this picture of Australian progress should read Chapter 16, by Zpys Klich, on psychological research among Australian aborigines.

The contribution of research among Africa's peoples south of the Sahara to defining the limits of psychological measurement has already been marked, although much of it initially stemmed from the interests of expatriates. A vast natural laboratory of custom, language, habitat, and tribal migrations, Africa has nurtured for centuries an extended range of human variability. This heterogeneity has been captured in the publications of those who have used tests and tasks on that continent. So extensive is the African bibliography on ability testing that current problems in measurement among minorities in America and Europe can be seen to have surfaced in Africa decades ago, with sustained attempts at resolution that have been ignored or overlooked.

Because of this extensive but sparsely acknowledged legacy of work in measurement, Ian Kendall, Mary Ann Verster, and Jorrie Von Mollendorf have been able, in their chapter on the abilities of the peoples of Africa south of the Sahara, to create a work of significance for psychology as a whole. They show that when industrial technology has been exported from the West, the test technology that predicts worker success in that industrial context always transfers across cultures. Field-tested adaptations to test procedures and renorming are usually needed; but the test constructs survive transplantation. This finding says as much about western work organisations and school systems as it does about the nature of human abilities. And with clarity of hindsight from literature that goes back seventy years, Kendall reminds the reader that one should not seek to explain test results as if they were unalloyed functions of basic human skills in Africa, or indeed any other place. The social context of assessment is central to the meaning of the test score.

No book on human abilities written since 1940 could be said to be complete without reference to, or better still a contribution from, the late Philip Vernon. Testimony to his complete range of interests and powers of synthesis can be found in his collaboration with the distinguished Japanese psychologist Saburo Iwawaki, and also with Jimmy Chan, whose influence on assessment in Hong Kong has been consistent and pervasive. The result of these partnerships is a comprehensive statement of the consequences of administering psychological tests to dominant Asian cultures that have undergone swift technological change. The consistencies in the outcomes of testing Chinese and Japanese subjects underline the need for sound theory construction when replications survive experimental idiosyncracies to merit a causal explanation.

Part III deals with the outer limits of testing, in minorities or in groups threatened by cultural extinction who have survived through group maintenance rather than incorporation by the majority. Cross-cultural psychologists have come to realise that standard western psychological tests are not good fits for the psychology of the groups undergoing ecological threat. They represent attempts by psychologists to construct a cognitive universe with a limited sample of measures, on groups whose adaptation to stressful environments has demanded behavioural patterns that stretch the limits of human survival. Thus stated, it reads like weak science. Nevertheless, the chapters given to us in Part III do show one consistent trend. Minority cultures, or cultures for whom test adaptations or translations have to be made, always reveal "deficits" when test averages are compared. Although this may not be out of the ordinary when minority status is confounded with clear ethnic differences, Chapter 20, by John Verster and Roelf Prinsloo, shows that the Afrikaans-speaking minority test performance was not always on a par with that of its English-speaking peers, and for no obvious reason. Almost a mini-book by itself, Part III is perhaps the most powerful scientific commentary in print dealing with the common practice of equating deficits with differences in test performance by indigenous and migrant minorities.

Although all minorities seem to suffer when their test scores are compared with those of majorities, native, or indigenous, cultures are particularly vulnerable. Chapter 15, by Damian McShane and John Berry, is comprehensive and to the point. Their exhaustive review of the research into North American Native test performance shows that any group failure to approach the Euramerican norms provided in the test manual has been interpreted as part of a generalised "D" or deficit model, implying a lack of cognitive competence for a variety of reasons. The assumptions that lead to "D" models of Native achievement are never stated, let alone satisfied, in the design of the experiments themselves. Consequently, McShane and Berry set no great store by many of the published sources as hard evidence for theory construction: and they are not alone in their vote of no confidence in much of the enclave research conducted in America and Europe. Inferential leaps from performance differences to cognitive deficits have been made in the literature routinely and erroneously.

Almost all of the chapters in Part III are written by psychologists with "insider" experience of the groups they represent, either by membership or through long periods of fieldwork and training in the cultures they write about. J. P. Das and Amulya Kanti Satpathy Khurana give first-hand accounts of their recent work on caste and cognition in India; and Gajendra Verma surveys, as a long-time resident in Britain, the social and educational contexts of the achievements of migrants from the subcontinent of India and from the Caribbean. Zpys Klich, in spite of a heavy field commitment, provides a key statement on the claims for specialised aptitudes among Australian Aborigines. His direct and readable chapter portends lively debate in the resolution of the issues he raises. In similar vein, there is a retrospective by Helmut Reuning on the experimental programme he pioneered among the Kalahari Bushmen. His rigorous approach, without equal in the cognitive literature on vanishing groups of mankind, has been in print for almost a quarter of a century but has yet to be integrated into theories of ability through exposure in prestigious journals. His achievements, and their challenges, speak for themselves.

We welcome just as keenly the sober and balanced critique and review of the literature on the testing of white minorities in South Africa by John Verster and Roelf Prinsloo. The bitter scientific debates of the 1950s and 1960s within South Africa about the material they so cogently present should remind us all that time has to pass before the wounds that science may inadvertently inflict on society heal well enough for progress to be made. The United States is still too close to the anti-test sentiment aroused by publicity given to minority testing in the late 1960s and early 1970s for a dispassionate evaluation of the work carried out in those years. The time will soon be ripe, nevertheless; and one suspects that a judgment on that decade is already forecast in Verster's conclusions about the South African controversies.

Our own fieldwork and background predispose us to a general (and probably biased) conclusion. The African experience of tests, since the early years of the century, is a microcosm of what the rest of the world endures whenever testing becomes too closely allied with power to decide the education and work prospects of the citizens of any country. The late Alec Rodger concluded that tests had to be technically sound, administratively convenient, and politically defensible. While scientific efforts are directed towards satisfying the first of these criteria, people judge tests by whether they exercise undue political control over their opportunities and aspirations. The evidence from the book's comprehensive coverage of test use in enclaves and minorities requires that test use in groups who have no power to moderate the political consequences of testing be fully justified. That has not always happened in the past. We can only hope that future research in cultural contexts will be more enlightened.

Finally, we have dedicated this book to five grown-ups whom only yesterday we thought of as our children. Thus we complete the family circle, a context that we emphasised above all when we dedicated our first joint volume, *Human Abilities and Cultural Factors*, to Margaret and Joan.

S.I. and J.B.
Plymouth, Devon
March 1988

Acknowledgments

We first want to thank Susan Milmoe and Penny Carter of the Cambridge University Press for their enthusiastic support of this manuscript. Without their confidence we would be authors in search of strength of character. Next, many hours of work from Margaret Irvine ensured that the manuscript was delivered in as good a shape as the original contributors would have wished, had they written and proofread every chapter up to their own high standards. We know how much of the detailed checking was completed by her patience. Finally, our production team at Cambridge, Janis Bolster and Nancy Landau, have been outstanding in their attention to detail and efficiency. It has been a pleasure to work with them.

We wish to acknowledge permission to use figures and to quote from sources in Chapter 5, by Joseph Royce. The following figures are reproduced by permission of The Society of Multivariate Behavioral Research: *Figure 5.2* is from J. P. Guilford (1981), Higher-order structure-of-intellect model abilities, *Multivariate Behavioral Research, 16*, 91–111. *Figure 5.4* is from S. Diamond and J. R. Royce (1980), Cognitive abilities as expressions of three "ways of knowing," *Multivariate Behavioral Research, 15*, 31–58. *Figure 5.5* is reproduced by permission of Swets & Zeitlinger from E. E. Werner (1979), Subcultural differences in ability, achievement, and personality factors among Oriental and Polynesian children on the Island of Kauai, Hawaii, in L. Eckensberger, W. Lonner, and Y. H. Poortinga (Eds.), *Cross-cultural contributions to psychology* (Lisse: copyright Swets & Zeitlinger). *Figure 5.6* is reproduced by permission of the American Psychological Association from E. A. Fleishman and W. E. Hempel, Jr. (1955), The relation between abilities and improvement with practice in a visual discrimination reaction task, *Journal of Experimental Psychology, 49*, 301–312 (copyright APA).

The following permissions to quote, in Chapter 5, by Joseph Royce, from original manuscripts are acknowledged: from Martinus Nijhoff, Dordrecht, the Netherlands, to quote from pp. 614 and 619 of J. R. Royce and L. P. Mos (1979), *Theoretical advances in behavior genetics*, originally published by Sitjhoff & Noordhoff (copyright Martinus Nijhoff); from The University of Chicago Press, Chicago, Ill., to quote from pp. vi and vii of E. L. Thurstone (1947), *Multiple factor analysis*; and from John Wiley & Sons, Chichester, England, to quote from pp. 352–353 of J. McV. Hunt (1961), *Intel-*

ligence and experience, first published by Ronald Press (copyright © John Wiley & Sons).

Much of the gratitude we wish to express is implicit in what has been already been written in the Preface by way of introduction to our authors. We thank our contributors from all five continents for their patience over the past four years. Without their efforts we could not have realised our aim of letting them write for themselves about the abilities of mankind. They take any credit that is due, and we willingly accept blame for any errors in representing them to their readers.

It is no accident, either, that this volume has been produced in a supportive and tolerant Department of Psychology within an institution of higher technological education committed to promoting the discipline in spite of hard times in the social sciences. My colleagues in Plymouth Polytechnic have received no mention until now, but I hope they will have good reason to believe that my desire to publish has neither damned their reputation nor perished their kindness.

S.I. and J.B.
March 1988

Part I

Human abilities in theoretical cultures

Holistic theories

1   The abilities of mankind: A revaluation

S. H. Irvine and J. W. Berry

The law of cultural differentiation

Although standard measures of mental capacity have been used by psychologists for almost a hundred years, a unified theory of intellect has not emerged. In pursuit of that theory, many approaches have been tried and rejected. One of the most hardy has been the practice of comparing the performance of groups of subjects. Typically, the averages from cognitive tests have indexed cognitive differences between sexes, nationalities, ethnic and tribal groups, social classes and creeds, and even generations. For the purpose of data analysis, group membership acts as if it were a manipulated or *independent* variable, and the test score becomes the *dependent* or outcome variable. When significant variation exists between groups, meaning can be attached to the tests. Construct validation traditionally proceeds by accounting for performance differences by the characteristics that distinguish the groups from each other. In this guise, group membership has survived as a real-life projection of the need for laboratory control on batches of subjects in order to specify cause. A distant analogy to the principle of treatment variation in controlled settings, this line of enquiry and its conclusions have seldom had ready acceptance from within the discipline. On the fringes, and in the popular science journals, no single issue in human assessment has produced more debate and provoked more acrimony than the use of group performance in the construction of a theory of intellect. If this is so, why has the practice endured?

In the quasi-experimental use of group membership as a precursor to causal inference, another paradox exists. Although groups have served the same scientific purpose, they are often quite different from each other, as a little thought will determine. Nevertheless, such diverse categories are used to examine performance on cognitive tasks. They are all likely to reveal significant main effects, and occasional interactions, in the partitioning of variance between groups, and, of course, on the means of the test scores. This variation *between* groups, whatever the nature of the group chosen by the experimenter, has become a seductive constant in almost a century of research. If not quite as important an aspect of intelligence theory as Spearman's law of positive correlation *within* groups, it has persisted for

3

just as long. We consider that the consistency of the law of positive correlation within groups, and the ease with which between-group differences
can be observed post hoc or created experimentally, point to a number of
causes operating within a general law of nature. We propose to call this *the
law of cultural differentiation*, or Ferguson's law, after its statement in general form in Ferguson's (1956) essay on transfer and the abilities of man:
"Cultural factors prescribe what shall be learned and at what age; consequently different cultural environments lead to the development of different
patterns of ability" (p. 121).

Although we have not previously formulated our thinking in the form of
a law, the development of the construct is visible in our published work
since 1960. It emerges from empirically based work by Irvine (1965, 1969a,
1969b). From African data he determined a model for the sources of variance
in test scores when tests are used cross-culturally, resulting in what he
termed X scores. Having determined that the variance in a test score had
many components that were systematic across cultures, Irvine observed that
the variance components were not necessarily those that the experimenter
had predicted. He thereafter demanded proof of the nature of test score
variance before comparisons were made. Until such proof were presented,
all scores from tests administered cross-culturally became unknowns, or X
scores. Berry's early work (Berry, 1966, 1969, 1971) independently led him
to the same conclusions about traditional, unmodified ability tests as comparative instruments. At that time he advanced the proposition of "radical
cultural relativism" (Berry, 1972) to describe the relativity of the rituals and
methods of intelligence testing. If intelligence, as it is *operationalised* in
standard western instruments is a socially sanctioned set of skills, argued
Berry, it follows that one version cannot be used to assess all of mankind.
More complete arguments, with the advantage of confirmatory evidence
from other laboratories, are available in Irvine (1970, 1979) and Berry (1980).

The law of cultural differentiation first assumes that abilities are behaviours that reach stable levels through the adaptation of cerebral structures
to ecological demand. This functional approach to what shall be learned by
whom over what time emerges from a second assumption. Abilities develop
in response to ecological demands that themselves are modified by skill
acquisition. A basic mutability, or dynamic change in the environment will
continuously modify what is learned and is valued. Berry's development of
these ideas is captured by Figure 1.1. The top line of the illustration implies
that as cultures vary with the demands of habitats, so abilities evolve to
modify these demands to a tolerable level. The lower line of the figure reveals
that new cultural forms and new alignments of skills must attend these newly
created adaptations. These two viewpoints dictate different questions for
the psychologist. The first demands an "ecological analysis" (Berry, 1980)
of what sorts of behaviours are necessary for making a living in a particular
habitat: Ecology sets life problems for man that must be solved. Then an
examination is made of the traditional cultural exchanges that characterise

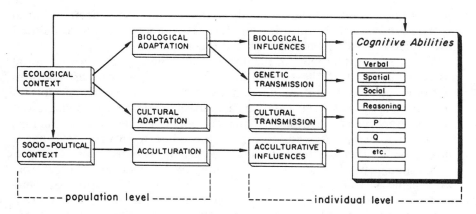

Figure 1.1. Theoretical mechanisms for the law of cultural differentiation (Berry, 1987).

a particular setting. The system assumes that the structural aspects of society and the habitat are concordant. For example, marginal climates, such as those identified by water shortage, extremes of temperature, and seasonal movements of animals are likely to predispose the population to hunting and gathering as a way of life. This in turn tends to be accompanied by a nomadic lifestyle, low population density, and minimal social stratification in its traditional form. Given these observations, one may ask what sorts of psychological coping skills and dispositional qualities are likely to ensure survival in such a setting. An answer to this question begins in a set of hypotheses about the behaviour to be found. As we shall see in Chapter 15, by McShane and Berry, this particular setting calls for the use and development of certain perceptual and spatial abilities.

The bottom of the figure reveals the interaction of the learned skill habits with factors that compel change in the society itself. Acculturative influences in the form of schooling, cash cropping, labour migration and urbanisation, and religious, linguistic, and political changes may affect behaviour, particularly the values that prescribe what shall be learned by a single generation. At any one period, an analysis of the forces of social change will inform the mode and emphasis of assessment. This very analysis can be performed on the thinking of psychologists who were formulating theory in the first quarter of the century, as we shall demonstrate.

Our primary concern is with human abilities in cultural context, and we recognise the primary task set by Ferguson (1954, p. 104), to be that of describing the patterns of ability that are considered characteristic of being reared in one environment or another. The second step – predicting what abilities and skills must be fostered in any one environment – is possible for some contexts, where descriptions are adequate, but not in those locales that have been poorly documented. Although writers from various parts of the world contribute greatly to this first systematic attempt at an assay of these abilities, there are gaps not only in description and collection, but in theory itself. Our first concern, therefore, is to apply the law of cultural differentiation to the revaluation of that theory.

We argue, first, that most of the debate about the implicit law of cultural differentiation as it manifests itself in the explicitly observed test performance of groups has been ill-founded, notwithstanding the persistence of differences. Debate has been based on imperfect theory; on inadequate operation of theory in its instruments; on incorrect inferences from correlations and variance estimates; and, above all, on failure to incorporate what is known about cultural differences into the design of experiments.

This summary is based on careful scrutiny of the evidence amassed from two decades of work in cross-cultural cognition. Our reservations on using test scores to assess the achievements of membership groups have been well documented in our earliest publications (Irvine, 1966, 1969a, 1969b; Berry, 1972), and have recently been explicitly restated (Irvine, 1983c, 1983d) in response to the cyclic reappearance of the issues (Flynn, 1982; Lynn 1982). Our mature judgment is that most attempts to use test scores as operational measures of the mental status of groups or populations have little claim to scientific credibility (Irvine & Berry, 1983). The aim of this chapter is to explore the scientific status of cross-cultural evidence for the nature, development, and function of abilities.

A revaluation

It might seem tendentious to call for a revaluation of theory construction methods in individual differences, a branch of enquiry that is as old as psychology itself. Nevertheless, there are two cogent reasons for a new approach. First, the insularity of early psychological research in human abilities denied it referents from exotic[1] contexts. The results of testing minority groups in cultural enclaves made no impact on theory specification except to reveal that categorisation of adult population samples into groups, particularly those of social class and race, produced group means that differed from each other – facts that seemed to find a permanent place in influential textbooks, American (Woodworth, 1940, pp. 123–129) as well as British (Knight, 1946, pp. 70–74) by World War II. Woodworth was, though, able to qualify such findings for children: "The tests are fairly successful in tapping what is common to the children in the same culture group, but are not adapted for comparing radically different groups" (p. 131). For adult comparisons, however, no such restraints were specified. Similarly, Nissen, Machover, and Kinder (1935), having also administered tests in West Africa to

---

[1] The term exotic is used in the original Greek sense of "external to" or "alien." It is also meant to carry the connotation of a specimen, as in "exotic" plant, which is imported and for which there is no indigenous substitute, and allows no scientific comparison. It should be contrasted with the term *cross-cultural*, reserved for empiricism that is not just an exotic specimen but that has a specified theoretical reference.

children, were convinced that group comparisons on "standard" instruments could not be made: "We are not warranted in assuming interpretations which have been found to be valid for groups whose . . . culture and environmental background differ from those of our subjects" (p. 310). By the time Nissen's article appeared, it was no new issue in Africa. The debate about such comparisons had begun in South Africa with Loram (1917), continued in East Africa with Oliver (1932, 1933, 1934), come to the surface again in South Africa in Fick (1939), and at last come under sustained scientific scrutiny from Biesheuvel (1943) in his portentous and much neglected book *African Intelligence*. Not much mention of this or indeed any other early cross-cultural work found its way into the literature on test theory before 1945. The classical published study of test technology transfer to India by Bhatia (1955) seems to have attracted the attention of its mentor, Godfrey Thomson, but arrived too late to modify Thomson's (1951) prescient step forward into general group factor theory. And even now, the most recent attempt to produce a synthetic theory of intelligence, Sternberg's (1985a) triarchic theory, "reviews" cross-cultural research in 2 or at most 3 out of almost 400 pages. A case has still to be made, apparently, for paying sustained and enlightened attention to findings from other cultures. Major theorists have ignored or only nodded in passing to them in theory construction and in data collection (Berry, 1984; Irvine 1984). By definition, from the law of cultural differentiation, such theory can expect confirmation only within its own culture, because it is equipped for that purpose and no other. Theory that does not encompass cross-cultural empiricism has no a priori claim to universality.

A membership group, nevertheless, might yet mediate theoretical changes. Since 1960, a cadre of cross-cultural psychologists has emerged. They have specified the aims of enquiry in exotic contexts so that results would cease to be simply "oddities" but would have to be integrated with mainstream thought. Brislin's (1983) review of cross-cultural psychology and Hui and Triandis's (1985) essay on the problems of measurement in exotic groups are the latest of a series that provides evidence of growing penetration of methods and ideas that were the property of only a few at the start, and now are shared by many. Malpass (1977) in a seminal discussion, perceives scientific enquiry across cultures as a *discipline of verification*. If the empiricism from exotic contexts is not theoretically oriented from the start, it cannot contribute to science. Even if it begins from theory, and that theory is itself imperfect, such empiricism probably contributes nothing. Harsh words by Malpass, perhaps, but not without their implications for the state of cross-cultural psychology. Here another paradox emerges. If a scientist is a functionary of imperfect theory, and this is carried forward in the operation of research across cultures, how can empiricism on mankind, as distinct from Euramericans,[2] produce other than poor science? As we shall

---

[2] *Euramerican* is a package word to describe the western, technological education and social backgrounds of those to whom it refers.

demonstrate, resolution may come only when substantive differences between cultures exist and remain constant over periods of time, and, perhaps even more critical, over cohorts of experimenters. Not only that, but the use of cultural variables to predict these differences elsewhere is a prior condition. Nevertheless, the task of interpreting observed differences in the literature remains, assuming that no trivial, experimenter-induced cause can be found for them.

The taxonomy

In our quest for better science, we begin by building a framework for the understanding and evaluation of cross-cultural empiricism. A taxonomy of data types is produced from a rationale that has emerged from cross-cultural psychology itself. We realise that the emerging framework is itself a definition of abilities, in the sense that Miles (1957) describes as "*a key to understanding*" (our italics). The other definition of abilities that comes from this book is an *ostensive* one, because the reports and reviews of the abilities of mankind that are produced by residents from every continent point empirically to what they are. We particularly try to avoid *stipulative* definitions that arise out of intemperate use of instruments outside the strict controls exercised by a theory of knowledge itself. In the end we anticipate that the use of this frame of reference will lead to the creation of instruments that provide systematic *operational* definition of the abilities of mankind.

By pursuing all these different types of definition at one and the same time, we determine a *metatheory*, because we attempt a set of ground rules for the use of groups in theory construction. We do not present a finished theory of human abilities as much as state what must be done to provide one. Until all our prescriptions are met, and probably more besides, it will not be possible to devise a theory of intellect that is adequate for all of mankind.

The first step on the road to understanding what test scores contribute to science is a specialised theory of knowledge. We consider that the appreciation of the logical constraints of separate conventional approaches to collecting cognitive data has priority. The taxonomy we propose postulates three lines of enquiry that are distinct in their assumptions about the nature and measurement of abilities. These are labelled *psychometric*, *piagetian*, and *cognitive information-processing*. These paradigms all produce different kinds of outcome or *dependent variables*. They are briefly described, with examples, in Table 1.1, while Figure 1.3, in the section on causal explanations, provides an overview of all the categories in the taxonomy. Why these are more than labels of convenience is explained now.

The psychometric paradigm

The Abilities of Man. Spearman's (1927) classic book on the nature and measurement of intelligence was entitled *The Abilities of Man*. In that work,

Table 1.1. *Three types of dependent variable in current use*

Psychometric	Test scores, examination results, grades, based upon group averages, and all transformations of these scores (IQs, factor scores, etc.)
Piagetian	Age in months when success in the item type that defines a "mental stage" is registered
Information-processing	Latency (time) to respond to given stimulus; speed of information transfer estimated from wave patterns in brain (averaged evoked potentials)

with its self-confident title, the foundations of psychometrics were laid down. Every work thereafter has had to come to terms with its assumptions and technology, which are, respectively, the implicit and explicit structures in a model of man's abilities. Spearman's empirical base for his model was necessarily a restricted one. He had no evidence, such as we inherit today from psychologists working outside North America and Europe, to challenge or to confirm his definitions. From the turn of the century he pursued a theory that satisfied the general mathematical laws derived from correlations in special relationship to each other. That special relationship is best described as *the tendency for all tests of ability to be positively correlated.* From the patterns made by these correlations, Spearman deduced that a fundamental source of energy was at work in mental test performance: ". . . all the mental activity, just like the physical, consists in ever varying manifestations of one and the same thing, to which may be given the name of energy" (p. 133). This pervasive energy "factor" he called *g* because of its general nature. For all its insularity, the theory has survived as one that always remains to be set against each acquisition of data from exotic cultures. New theories of the abilities of mankind must first test the limits of the trend to positive correlation, whatever the cultural heritage of the sample. This challenge is apparent in the response of those who questioned what that trend implied, notably Thurstone (1938), Thomson (1951), Guilford (1967), Cattell (1971), Carroll (1976), Eysenck (1982), and Sternberg (1985a). Such challenges have always had to come to terms with *g*.

Theories of abilities, whatever their outward appearance, tend to be like onions. The removal of an outer layer reveals a smaller, but critical centre. So far, only the obvious aspect of Spearman's model has been uncovered. That skin contains a more fundamental notion still: an inner-core *psychophysical* model for man's abilities that is independent of empiricism from other cultures. In fact, it controls, perhaps unknown to the scientists who carry out the research, the nature and limits of the enquiry itself. Awareness of the power of Spearman's technological legacy comes slowly. It begins in the realisation that Spearman's book synthesises not only empiricism but a

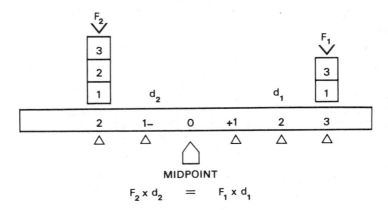

Figure 1.2. Moments around a fixed point (after Loney).

theory of knowledge formed over a 30-year period. In that time, physics was the premier science, and energy its preoccupation.

In producing a new universe of discourse, Spearman made no naive metaphoric attempt to link mental events with the physical world. His analogy between physics and mental life depended on the existence and use of a mathematical technology that manifested the parallel. By the turn of the century, it was there in the shape of an index of agreement among measures applied to the same set of individuals. Pearson, who developed the correlation coefficient upon which Spearman's theory was founded, called his index of common variation between two measures the *product–moment* correlation. It requires that the covariation of individual differences in more than a single measure of mental activity be calculated as a product of moments around a point: specifically, deviations from the mean of each measure. The mean is thereby a fixed point, or fulcrum, of a distribution of scores. How does this relate to the physics of Spearman's era?

Perhaps the most famous Victorian schoolboy textbook of physics to deal with measurements of forces *around a fixed point* is Loney's (1890), on statics. By 1964 the book had gone through 5 editions and 33 printings. Statics is the study of forces on bodies at rest, or in equilibrium. Loney describes moments very meticulously, and page 61 has a diagram showing that a system is in equilibrium around a fixed point when the sum of the products of force times distance from the fixed point are zero ($F_2 \times d_2 = F_1 \times d_1$). That diagram, whose essence is reproduced here as Figure 1.2, is, in fact, an illustrative introduction to the whole concept of the correlational technology of tests and testing. The idea of mental energy for an individual can be captured in terms of a test score's *relative* distance from a group mean. It is a moment around a point, as in physics. All the deviations from the mean of a test score distribution sum to zero. More than that, the deviation score in standard form was the building block of a quantum theory of human abilities, standing in relation to the mind as moments of forces around a point did to the physical world of energy, mass, and inertia. The correlation coefficient begins with individual deviations from an average score; and it is itself an average value, specifically of the amount of consistent deviation from the means that the same set of persons show when measured twice.

Spearman's concept of the abilities of man, and those variations introduced by his rivals and successors, are difficult to understand unless one grasps the power and the constraints of the method of measurement that takes physics and moments around a point not just as an analogue, but as a model for an exact science of the mind. At the very start of his theory construction (1904), Spearman stressed what his theory required, and what the Pearson coefficient appeared to give it, "the first fundamental requisite of correlation, namely, a *precise quantitative expression*" (p. 202).

To conceive of this as the only possible measure of man's capabilities would be incorrect, but to claim its heuristic potential for good as well as bad science is perhaps too easy a victory. Since Spearman's famous book appeared in 1927, one theory of abilities every ten years – and all of them based on the correlation coefficient – has been hatched in psychological laboratories in America and Europe (Irvine, 1983b). Some of the protagonists of these theories have already been brought to notice in the preface. It is unlikely that each one of these theories was closely conscious of its epistemological legacy; but in that dependence on the assumptions of the correlation coefficient they are identical. They have somewhat inaccurately been called *structuralist* theories. They are also, as the book by Loney reminds us, *static*, and not dynamic, theories of cognition.

Piagetian data

The names of Rutherford and the Cavendish laboratory in Cambridge had by 1927 become permanently linked with the knowledge that the atom could be fissioned, and that old models of energy had to be accommodated to the mathematics of atomic physics. The previous year witnessed the publication in English of Piaget's book on language and thought in the young child (Piaget, 1926). It was totally different from Spearman's in ethos, and in operation. For many, it was as revolutionary as Rutherford's work in physics. It produced a new universe of discourse about mental life.

Piaget's approach to science was, as he and his students have insisted, that of *genetic epistemology*. To add to the many attempts to define this grandiloquent but complex phrase would serve only to reveal the present writers' prejudices. Piaget has been elevated to Aristotelian status by his commentators, in that far many more books have been written about him than by him. For the key perspective on the abilities of mankind, the important aspects of piagetian[3] research are its origins, aims, and methods.

---

[3] The term *piagetian* is reserved for that work carried out in exotic contexts, laying claim to Piaget's theory, or piagetian instruments. By implication, the term *piagetian* implies qualifications about the meaning of such work.

Observations are not engendered as much from physics as from biology; not from energy as much as from growth: "Every psychological explanation comes sooner or later to lean either on biology or logic" (Piaget, 1950, p. 1). The necessary aim of experiments using piagetian cognitive tasks is to define universal progressions in the use of thought for making sense out of the environment. To do this, the scientist requires absolute scales of measurement against which individuals can be first measured and then, after clinical interview, understood. Thus, Piaget offers a theory of knowledge arising not from physics but out of the species itself – out of man's biological nature. The science of embryology has as much to offer as a key to understanding Piaget's emphases as physics has to realising the point of Spearman's arguments. Each stage of mental life is irreversible, just as the embryo cannot reverse to one of its earlier forms. There is no going back.

A steady body of research in Europe and America from 1950 onwards speaks to the pervasive influence of Piaget's interview methods. There are some quite obvious differences between psychometric approaches whose empiricism is to produce a correlation, and those whose prime function is a clinical judgment of the subject's use of logical tools based on a standard form of interview. First, the result of the application of a small number of tasks to a single subject is designed to illuminate the processes of thought of the embryonic adult. Next, there is no *mean* by which to fix a deviation, positive or negative. A scale of mental life, analogous to egg, tadpole, and frog, assures all of adult thinking status if they survive environmental hazards and censors. In Piaget's theory, normality *is* progression. Rough age limits for the biological anchoring of the thought system are offered, but no one worries overmuch about precocity or lag. We will all get there in the end. That is the genetic element, since invariant, or fixed pattern, behaviour in processing defines man as a species. And, with uncertainty about the arrival and timing of skills in different modes of thought taken care of by Piaget's convenient notion of *horizontal décalages* (of which more in the section on conservation across cultures), the emphasis on an *absolute process progression* is quite different from a deviation about a mean defining a moment of energy that is a *relative product* measure.

One must be careful to link and distinguish the two most influential schools of mental measurement in educational contexts in one other way. First, there are obvious differences of scale. The application of group tests of abilities to large numbers of subjects adds a dimension that individual tests of intelligence, piagetian tasks, and laboratory measures of mental functions cannot match. Individuals are assessed by trained psychologists on a one-to-one basis except when group tests, which are self-report questionnaires in highly mechanised form, are administered. Far many more people have taken standardised group tests than have been subjects of piagetian or laboratory experiments in cognition. On the other hand, all forms of individual assessments resemble group tests in their quest for standard procedures. Piagetian research is no exception. Apart from differences of scale that affect the sensitivity of a system for detecting sources of variation, there is one important logical constraint on empirical observations, *the condition of stimulus identity*. Consequently, all test and laboratory manuals stress the need for homogeneity in methods of assessment.

This effort to control as much as possible derives from the emergence of differential psychology from the laboratories of the hard sciences. Replication without standardisation is impossible, unless the effect is so robust that the stimulus is inconsequential. Cronbach (1957) drew attention to a split in psychology between those who exercise control over the dependent variable in the laboratory, and those who let the subject do what he must. Yet both test and laboratory cultures in the discipline pursue stimulus identity as a logical starting point. Without identical stimuli for each group of subjects, observed differences are hard, if not impossible, to interpret. In social contexts, particularly those involving mental measurement, the disappearance of identical stimuli for scientific purposes is bound to evoke suspicion of lack of fairness, although that conclusion may not be a logical one. All seem agreed on that point. What happens after that is the watershed.

Information processing

Others prefer to travel along a third highway – leading to the doorstep of Wundt's laboratory, or of Galton's, while pursuing abilities. Its focus is neither physics nor biology but the exploration of the limits of the concept of intelligence by adopting a logical categorisation of mental activity from a precise theory of the transmission of information. This particular biometric tradition is very much in evidence in Spearman's work, although it is not a central theme for him. That theoretical confluence seems to have vanished in the literature as the use of tests increased to the point of creating a specialist branch of psychology. The divisions that Cronbach observed and drew attention to, however, did not begin to narrow until a conscious effort was made once again to apply cognitive theory which derived from laboratory environments, to the measurement of individual differences. Such an effort emerged once more in the 1970s, and is catalogued in the texts by Resnick (1976), Friedman, Das, and O'Connor (1981), Sternberg (1985a) and, cross-culturally, by Irvine and Berry (1983).

Eysenck (Chapter 3) sees the divisions in the quest for a structure of intellect somewhat differently. He takes a fundamentalist position that evaluates the contributions made by different attempts to practise psychological measurement. For him, the Binet–Simon and Wechsler testing approach of definition by item analysis has been empiricism without guidance from the facts of experimental research. The quest for intellect structure, he insists, requires biochemical and neurological referents for the definition of information transfer. His model for intelligence (Eysenck, 1982) is unique in its emphasis not on the apparent complexity of thought, but on the ease with which some of these normative marks of complexity, such as IQ scores, can be defined by "simple" measures of the speed and regularity of transmission of information through the cortex. The stimuli are always identical and they can remain unchanged because they are "simple": a compelling argument. The chronometric approach currently favoured by Jensen (Chapter 4) is also perceived by Eysenck as contributing to a rethinking of the parameters by which the abilities of mankind shall and, as he would argue, must be measured if the science of individual differences is to remain credible. The difference between IQ measures and laboratory-based measures of brain waves (A. E. Hendrickson, 1982; D. E. Hendrickson, 1982), inspection times (Brand & Deary, 1982), and reaction times (Jensen, 1982) is palpable, but there is still one very critical link among them all. Every one of the studies that uses both types of measures employs the correlation coefficient to express the degree of relationship between them. Spearman's technology for anchoring mental measurement to the world of physics has transferred without questioning its hidden persuasion on the formulation of any new theory itself. The new wave of measurement is engaged in validating, or revalidating, the construct of intelligence. The trait is the same, the correlational debt to Spearman is the same, the measures are stipulated to be different: and perhaps they are.

Components as constructs. Perhaps Eysenck goes only part of the way to a cure for an imperfect approach to construct validity that uses only one type of measure. A theory that forswore the whole correlational approach, whose contributions and limitations are elegantly described by Royce (Chapter 5), would serve us if not better, then differently. In the 1970s, Sternberg (1977) produced such a theory and criticised the whole factor-analytic approach, whose foundation is the correlation coefficient, because it had not significantly advanced our knowledge of intellect. He confirms his emphasis in Chapter 2. Sternberg's paradigm had nothing to do with psychometric factors of any kind, and instead concentrated on defining the information content of reasoning in terms of *stages of processing*, each one of which could be defined, and its latency used as a measure of the process. The same term, *stages of processing*, is used in piagetian discourse, although it refers not to the immediate cognitive focus of a few seconds but to the total period, years or months, spent by the organism in growing from one state of consciousness to the next. Sternberg is still concerned with the nature of human intelligence, but he emphasises not energy, not biology and not, except indirectly, neurology as much as the constants in information-processing tasks that transfer across items in tests.

   There are hints, too, that *dynamic* images are informing the theories that are currently being constructed. Consider the definition of a *component* by Sternberg (1982, p. 233). "The component may translate a sensory input into a conceptual representation, transform one conceptual representation into another, or translate a conceptual representation into a motor output." Translations and transformations are dynamic mental concepts; and these are seldom seen in the factor-analytic literature outside Guilford's (1959; 1967) elaborate metaphor for the structure of intellect that never became scientifically viable. How unique is Sternberg's approach, and what are its points of contact with rival formulations?

First, Sternberg's use of the word *component* for all kinds of postulated processes is just as stipulative, and even arbitrary, as the "factors" they mean to replace. Nevertheless, the dependent variable is not the sum of scores on correct items. Instead, Sternberg's components are latency based, and in that they share with Eysenck's and Jensen's measures a common concern for speed of information transmission as an index of intelligence. Sternberg himself identifies *duration*, *difficulty*, and *probability of execution* as the markers for components. This can be compared with the transatlantic Furneaux–Eysenck–White (White 1982) emphasis on *speed, accuracy,* and *persistence in relation to problem parameters* such as difficulty and discriminating power. There is precious little between them in the long run. What about the short run? The information-processing approach to the abilities of mankind will dominate the next decade of research. Two recent textbooks (Sternberg, 1985b; Kail & Pellegrino, 1985) attest to its current popularity. The feasibility of large-scale research of this kind has already been demonstrated by Fairbank, Tirre, and Anderson (1984). The technology exists in networks of microcomputers. Spearman, though, would recognise that Sternberg, Eysenck, and Fairbank are still calculating correlations based on mean values of latencies instead of test scores. The mathematical bounds of the coefficient have not been breached. The dependent variable is still a deviation score from an average. As in all such research, the score itself is stipulated by the scientist to mean what he says it means, unless there is hard evidence from a multimethod and multitrait approach to back his assertion (Irvine, 1983d).

These three paradigms, *traditional testing, piagetian interviews,* and *information processing in quasi-experimental settings,* are the epistemological roots of enquiry into the abilities of mankind. Although their fruits, dependent variables that are the outcome of test or task items, seem distinct in some ways, they share affinities of scientific emphasis. The foundations of our taxonomy allow a rough sort of the cross-cultural material for building purposes. It is possible to take any study from exotic contexts that deals with cognitive measurement and classify it under one of these headings. There are certainly subemphases within each universe of discourse. For example, the item response field described by Poortinga and van der Flier (Chapter 6) comes under the heading of traditional testing, but in time will emerge as a paradigm in its own right. Similarly, one can distinguish the pioneering work of Segall, Campbell, and Herskovits (1966) on illusion susceptibility from the research by Poortinga (1971) on choice reaction time, from that of Scribner (1974) on free recall and of Berry (1969) on binocular resolution of conflicting and ambiguous stimuli. Each of these topics has a long history in mainstream psychology, and we return to them later, in the section on experimental routes to cognitive process. As part of the cognitive information-processing domain, however, they gain coherence and stability within the focussed context of cross-cultural enquiry into cognition.

Interpretation of empirical types

Ferguson's law of cultural differentiation is a universal, but it imposes strict limits on the interpretation of test data types. Berry (1972), as a reductio ad absurdum, applied the extreme form of the law, which already had shape in the Nissen et al. (1935) pronouncement, in his paper on radical cultural relativism. This extreme form prohibits the use of test scores from different membership groups to compare intellective task performance. The logical extension of Berry's argument would invalidate all cross-cultural comparisons using tests. Irvine (1966) preferred a less extreme position in the shape of a classification of the essential problems of the use of tests that served to validate constructs. He saw the first requirement as showing how any group average score could be used as a valid statistic for inferences about performance:

If one were using the same test to predict success on a common criterion. . . . the test score could be held to have finite and common meaning. This *predictive* meaning should be held separate from *descriptive* or environmental meaning. Predictive meaning allows value judgments when the criterion itself is recognised as a value judgment. Test scores taken by themselves, and group averages based on such scores are not sufficient proof of the superiority or inferiority of one group or another unless one is certain that the sources of variance, and more important the proportions of each definable source of variance within the test situation are the same for both groups and that, as a consequence, the test scores for the two groups have the same psychological meaning. (pp. 27–28)

Although this is also a difficult restriction to satisfy, it does not preclude comparisons between cultures. It does, though, put the onus of proof of comparability upon the test user for each and every experiment. The assumption of test score congruence is not accepted in the Irvine–Berry theory of mental measurement. Test scores are X scores until proved otherwise.

Variables and inferences

Unless there are ways to satisfy the restrictions placed on mean comparisons, an unfalsifiable veto is placed upon all test use. Subsequently, Irvine (1965, 1966, 1979) specified the sources of variance that accompanied test use across cultures and has suggested ways of regulating these (1966, 1973). He has proposed (Irvine, 1983b) a system for proving a test or test series by considering the claims made for the validity of a test score in a context of known data types. This context serves to classify the kinds of independent variables most commonly used to construct ability theory. Table 1.2 provides a convenient listing with some examples. At the same time, these variables

Table 1.2. *Types of independent variables and their inference*

Variable	Description	Inference level
Treatment	Practice, coaching, incentives	Low
Dispositional	Mental or physical handicap	Low
	Age	Low?
	Gender	High
Environmental	Streaming or allocation	Low
	School type, status	Low
	Social status	High
	Family size, birth order	High
	Ecological press	High
Domain	Test or factor score in other culture	High
Ethnographic	Known structural characteristics of society under scrutiny	High
	Ethnic origin of experimenter	Low?
	Anthropological veto	Low?

have also taken on causal properties, but they do not all have the same potential for ascribing cause to their relationship with test score variation between groups. Some examples will help to illustrate this argument.

Table 1.2 assumes that test scores are almost always outcomes of what subjects do to items, or stimuli. We began by stating that there were three main classes of outcome variable in measurement: psychometric, piagetian, and information-processing. The first row of Table 1.2 illustrates that test scores from any of these traditional modes of enquiry may also be used as dependent variables in situations where the cause of enhanced or restricted performance can be inferred without much doubt. These situations are most easily recognised as *treatments*, as in practice or coaching experiments, and are observable when motivational effects are linked with different testing conditions. Variables affecting test performance in quasi-experimental contexts are usually, but not always, *low-inference* variables. The evaluative label "low-inference" is not exclusive to laboratory manipulations. For example, studies using nothing but test scores have used the extremes of test distributions, say, of introversion–extraversion questionnaires, as internalised treatments to which direct cause is often attributed. Factor scores have also done duty as if they were low-inference variables, but not without protest. The *domain* category states that cross-cultural use of test or factor scores as quasi-independent variables is a high-risk event if cause is laid at the door of a trait measured by the test. This important category is treated in more detail at the end of this section.

Most scores are derived from one application of one test, so that the post hoc examination of variables that are assumed to influence performance is the norm. These variables may become either *low-* or *high-inference* variables because of their global or proxy characteristics. Typical data types that can be evaluated in this way are variables reflecting streaming in schools; schools themselves; urban or rural residence; number of years of schooling; parental occupation and educational levels; ecological demand characteristics. These are all *environmental* variables. Many are so general in their catchment of subjects that they are high inference, rather than low inference independent variables. By attributing cause to them, one is not much better off than when one started.

These may be distinguished from other data types that are not environmental, but *dispositional*. These include gender groups, broad comparison groups where little genetic similarity is evident; groups where genetic identity or peculiarity may be assumed, such as identical twins; and groups identified by the age of onset of some predisposing physical characteristic such as gynaecomastia, menarche, and even myopia. Other, usually high-inference variables of an even more complex, *ethnographic* nature include ethnic identity, or tribal groupings, and language characteristics. The ethnographic category can be extended to a second function, embracing the ethnic identity of the experimenter as an inadvertent but nonetheless powerful modifier of the research and its findings. Finally, the third type of ethnographic variable is the presence or absence in the literature of an anthropological veto. Usually available as a detailed case study, it is an extremely powerful modifier of claims by psychologists to have discovered the presence or absence of some mental characteristic. It, too, belongs in the category of manipulations to existing data. One of the best examples of the veto is seen in the work of Greenfield and Judith Irvine discussed in the section on cross-cultural piagetianism.

The point of this scheme is its potential for systematic analysis of quasi-causal evidence about tests, and the knowledge that each class of variable contributes different kinds of information about test scores. So far we have distinguished *one* evaluative dimension, high–low inference that has causal implications, and *four* quasi-independent variable types: treatments, dispositional, environmental, and ethnographic.

Finally, the last kind of information about tests comes from the correlations of tests or tasks among themselves, whether as predictive or descriptive variables. Construct validation without domain research is almost unheard of in individual differences theory construction. An illustration from testing will suffice to define the data type, but piagetian tasks (Dasen, 1984), measures of reaction times (Vernon, 1983), and illusion susceptibility (Taylor, 1974) have all been the subject of *domain* research.

When tests are subjected to correlation among themselves and factor analysed, the factors may be used as a means of classifying tests into broad families. The consistent appearance of the same test factors within subjects over many different experimenters, samples, and occasions is taken as evidence for the validity of the constructs used by theorists to explain performance. Early theories differed in the number of such test families that were claimed, and in the ultimate degree of dependence one family shared with any other. In general there were two camps: general factor theorists following Spearman, and multiple factor theorists who cathected to the thinking of Thurstone. Much evidence from cross-cultural test studies is of this kind, as the review by Irvine (1979) shows. Plentiful as it may be, factor analysis is not to be taken as the only evidence from tests that can be considered, or indeed should be considered. The use of a factor score as a trait-referenced classification of subjects into groups is only as good as the construct validity of the score for these subjects. To attribute cause to the trait that is supposed to be manipulating performance is a very high inference in most cross-cultural work.

Each kind of study, whether it is psychometric, piagetian, or information-processing, can concern itself with treatments, domain, environmental, dispositional, or ethnographic variables. By multiplying the three dependent variable types by the five independent variables, one can generate fifteen possible combinations. A study that employed all fifteen would be an impressive contribution to our understanding of mental life. These types can and do inform theory construction in quite different ways. Moreover, each type is capable of yielding low- or high-inference results: but the *weight* that can be attached to each type of finding does not simply depend on this classification, as we now demonstrate.

Causal explanations. The taxonomy, fully revealed in Figure 1.3, requires one other dimension for evaluation of the evidence for test score use in the mapping of the abilities of mankind. This is the determination of the *type of causal explanation* given by the researcher for any apparent difference between groups. Irvine (1979) showed that four classes of explanation have consistently been produced to account for observed differences in test performance involving groups. The first is *intra-hominem*, and associates observed differences with the structural properties of the brain, its biochemistry or neurology. The next is *extra-hominem*, and attributes performance differences to ecological press and the demands of survival in a particular environment: for example, Arctic nomadic lifestyles versus pastoral subtropical subsistence farming. Yet a third is termed *inter-hominem*, being a class of explanation that explains differences in terms of what people teach each other: language skills, educational curricula, values, and behavioural norms. A fourth explanation category is an interactive one. This is perhaps most clearly demonstrated in Vernon's (1957, p. 108) dictum that reminds theorists of the interdependence of the constructs of intelligence and attainment. "We should reject the view that Intelligence B 'causes' or 'makes possible' attainments; it would be equally true to say that it is the result of attainments." That remark is the epitome of interactive forms of explanation for test performance differences. The final category is an afterthought, but is valid. This is called *ad hominem*, and is called upon whenever any explanation appeals to "common sense." Anthropological vetoes on "abnor-

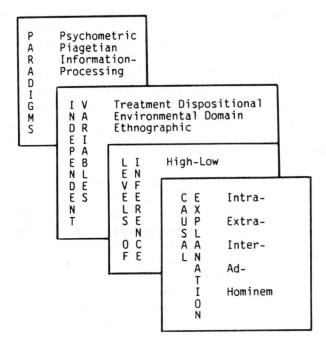

Figure 1.3. Taxonomy of empirical data types in cross-cultural cognitive research.

mal" results reported by psychologists are often like this. *Ad hominem* explanations are not scientific, but they can usefully lead to revaluations of existing research. They can be of great heuristic value, as shown in the debate between Judith Irvine and Greenfield in the section on the ethnographic variable.

The taxonomy for systematic analysis of studies about the abilities of mankind can now be seen to have four dimensions. One is epistemological, recognising that its three classes, psychometrics, piagetianism, and information processing, are separate and complementary ways of looking at the world of mental abilities. They are different universes of discourse. The second dimension is empirical, in that it describes the type of variable used to infer propositions about abilities. The other two classifications are concerned with causal inference from data types. Some studies require high or long inferences, others permit direct, low, or short inferences about what causes any alteration in the dependent measure. All inferences from data are part of a persistent form of explanation for causes, of which five types have been specified. The taxonomy is specified in Figure 1.3. As the figure shows, it is possible to generate many ideal types. In fact, far fewer types are customarily used for research purposes. This is a consequence of the frequent covariation of the two variable types, empirical and inferential.

Moreover, the choice of any one empirical type may predispose the experimenter to one explanatory emphasis, although it need not logically do so. Nevertheless, validation of any ability construct might yet require evidence from all three epistemologies and all five types of empirical design, leading logically to one class of explanation. The current need for inferential and explanatory categories for cross-cultural studies is probably an outcome of the failure to use sufficient data types for any ability construct to yield only one interpretation. Butterfield (1981) has already intimated strategies for cognitive process validation. Combined with this taxonomy, it allows for systematic theory construction and evaluation, within and across cultures.

In the context of the law of cultural differentiation, the taxonomy can now be employed as a prescriptive, or strategic, metatheory. Its use allows a form of definition of abilities, as a key to understanding the precise significance of some classic series of cross-cultural studies in the pursuit of the abilities of mankind. Now we move on to illustrate the power of the taxonomy in categorising the evidence for the nature and development of abilities in mankind. As far as possible, studies in any one series, or theme, have been selected to exemplify as many dimensions in the taxonomy as possible, so that the different types of evidence are seen together. The main epistemologies are well represented, and the decision to select a series in the first place is based on its contribution to the interpretation of findings presented in the subsequent parts of this volume.

Evaluating evidence for the abilities of mankind

Psychometric testing

As so much of this volume is concerned with psychometric test results from other cultures, we begin here with an account of the distinguishing features of this method of ability testing. The empirical database from cross-cultural research into human abilities is extensive. It is also marked by cautious inference, and a preoccupation with methods. These qualities are not always applicable to *enclave research*. Enclave research takes tests at their face value, focusses on a specific subgroup within a culture, and compares test performance in that group with majority or other subgroup norms. This is best identified in the American concentration on the performance of minority groups that live in the United States. A good survey of the issues and preoccupations of this research is available in Samuda (1975). Little resemblance is apparent when the typical cross-cultural study involving tests is compared with American research. The main concern of every test user who has begun testing exotic groups has been to ensure that the external test item receives adequate representation in the consciousness of the subject so that the processes that are assumed to be the universal components of mental life can operate upon it. The test score is seldom, if ever, taken to mean what the test manual declares it to mean without extensive trials and checks.

Early adaptations of tests. This distinction between cross-cultural and enclave use of tests was made early. There are four classic studies of testing
large numbers of subjects using *performance* tests. By this we mean that
the subjects manipulate apparatus to a prescribed solution. These are the
reports by Macdonald (1945), by Biesheuvel (1952, 1954), by Bhatia (1955),
and by Ord (1971). Although these could be classified as domain and criterion
studies, in which the occasional tribal or caste grouping was looked at as a
post hoc curiosity, the main emphasis is the experimenters' concern with
validating the *methods* of test presentation. The rationale was essentially
one that sought similarity in correlations among similar types of tests within
each culture as proof of the assumption that the tests were doing what they
were supposed to be doing. If they failed to show these structural similarities,
the test presentation methods were altered until they did. Most of the time
this meant that tests were borrowed, instructions translated, successful trials
observed, and then the tests proper given and scored. The interesting result
is how often the results vindicated this *contextual* approach to testing. Only
now, in theory construction, has the word *context* appeared as a construct
(Sternberg, 1985a).

Hence, pioneering field studies were first and foremost *treatment* approaches, as defined by the taxonomy. Instructions and procedures were
varied until a criterion was met. These variations underlined the frailty of
the assumption of external stimulus identity ensuring transcultural stimulus
equivalence for each subject. The scientists who carried out methodological
investigations also looked closely at the results of test intercorrelations,
because these were the outcomes of the changes they had made to adapt
tests to the cultural setting. They produced a finding that was to endure.

In a nutshell, Spearman's law of positive correlation emerged from the
interactions of illiterate subjects with the apparatus put before them. The
work of Macdonald, Biesheuvel, Bhatia, and Ord spanned Africa, India, and
New Guinea. Tests were positively correlated, not always producing the one
factor, but showing the factors that emerged from the matrices of correlations
to be general rather than specific, and related to each other to some extent.
The logical inference is that ecological press interacting with brain architecture ensures that operations on similar, although not necessarily identical,
tasks are demonstrated in consistent test clusters or families, which are
called "factors." Additionally, these early domain studies all had applied
referents. The tests that were constructed showed that they predicted success in schools and employment where a transfer of western technology had
already occurred. School organisation is not, after all, independent of the
culture that exports it; nor are the tools of primary or secondary industry.
These early attempts to export test technology seemed to reproduce the
Spearman law. Ferguson's law prescribed that adaptations of tests always
were necessary. It is as apparent as that, but not a simple matter.

Irvine's (1979) review of psychometric factor studies across cultures shows that extensive factor-analytic research was carried out on test results from the earliest days. These are all, by definition, *domain* studies. As schooling was made available to large numbers of children in the late 1950s and early 1960s in third world countries, the usual increase in numbers of subjects tested occurred with the use of *group paper-and-pencil* tests. It became possible to produce a meta-analysis of the cross-cultural test literature, and the following conclusions about this approach to human ability definition emerge from the data.

First, with rare exceptions, the analyses satisfied criteria of technical soundness. Parsimonious factor extraction was the norm, 3–4 being most often extracted; the average number of subjects per study was 100 + ; the average length of schooling, 4–6 years. Next, the factors could be grouped under six familiar dimensions: *reasoning*; *verbal abilities and skills*; *spatial and perceptual processes*; *numerical operations*; *memory functions*; and *physical/temperamental quickness*. Moreover, examination of each of the 91 studies showed that the factors identified were correlated wih each other. A general tendency for all tasks to be positively correlated was present, just as in the performance tests given to illiterates.

Explanation of consistent results. Irvine then attempted to account for the generality of the findings from the data of psychologists who had operated in all types of cultures, schools, languages, climates, and habitats. He extended his earlier description (Irvine, 1965) of the variance sources available in test scores from one exotic culture to account for universals of the six broad dimensions of abilities across all the literature, and the trend to positive correlation within each study. He suggested that if enough studies were available from enough psychologists operating in different contexts, then the families of tests that remained constant in spite of the widest possible range of cultural and experimenter idiosyncrasy had to be attributable to *intra-hominem* characteristics. The limitations of the human brain as a system for processing information were mapped or projected onto the basic dimensions, however crudely.

This *intra-hominem* interpretation, it should be clearly understood, is not a genetic one, except in the sense that Piaget might use the term. There is a fixed action pattern in the processing of information, in that the encoding, storage, and operational sequences followed by individuals from diverse cultures are common to mankind, as a general rule. This does not invalidate special adaptations and emphases of process for individual or group ends. In fact, Ferguson's law specifies that emphases within the general progression of mental events must emerge in response to cultural demands. But it recognises that the limits imposed by the structure and functions of the cortex are general. The law of cultural differentiation operates within these parameters. Test factors are indicators of where these functions are most likely to be found.

Quasi-experimental findings. So much for methodological domain studies. Now we turn to *treatment, environmental,* and *dispositional* variables used as quasi-experimental contrasts or controls. Perhaps the treatment studies are the most critical because they introduce the key notion of a direct effect on test performance. Throughout the long debate about ability theory, there has been one generally accepted asumption. If a test or task operationalises an ability, the measure provided by the test must remain at a "crude level of stability," as specified by Ferguson (1954, 1956) in his two major essays on transfer and the abilities of man. Such store is set by this requirement that energy on a vast scale will be mobilised to investigate claims of improvement on retesting or coaching before first exposure. Generally, it has been part of testing method to satisfy the requirement that the first test score from any test is not altered significantly by prior practice or subsequent retesting. If it were, the measure would no longer be regarded as an *ability* but as a *skill* capable of improvement with practice.

Perhaps the distinction between skill and ability is somewhat arbitrary, as underlined by Ferguson's definition of an ability as a skill learned to the point of stability. Cross-cultural research on coaching and practice, especially on tests that are supposed to test general capacity wherever they are administered, is particularly important. Much has been made of the importance of figural tests, popularly but erroneously referred to as nonverbal, as stable, nonmodifiable estimates of general intelligence. They have had to endure a great weight of inference, particularly in the comparisons of group performance so often made by those who have tested different ethnic groups.

Practice effects on general ability tests. The experience of those researchers who administered figural tests in Africa (McFie, 1961; Lloyd & Pidgeon, 1961; Silvey, 1963; Irvine, 1969b, 1979, 1983b) in repeated measure or differential treatment experiments, was that the first test score was always lower than the second. In addition, groups who were coached on the test items, or who were allowed more time, or both, always scored higher than those who did not.

Perhaps the best illustration of the need to test the assumption that a standard test yields a score that will not increase if it is given again in a standard way, is M. Verster's (1973, 1976) studies of repeated administrations of a general adaptability test battery to mineworkers over a period of 12 months. Even at intervals long enough to allow forgetting (3 months to 12 months) the initial score improved significantly with second and subsequent testings, asymptote occurring at the fourth session. An average 10-point increase on a first test mean of 60 was produced by retesting, and another 10 points had been added by the third session. Lloyd and Pidgeon's (1961) paper also showed that the rate of increase varied when different ethnic groups were involved, Africans increasing most, Indians next, and Europeans least. The recent report (Marmorale & Brown, 1982) of differential improvement rates for Hispanics, blacks, and whites on *WISC* scale scores adjusted for age increase, underlines the need for repeated measure studies of test behaviour.

An increase in performance would not matter too much if the correlation of the test before or after a practice or coaching session remained constant with other tests. However, Irvine and Carroll (1980) report that different treatment of experimental groups given *Raven's Progressive Matrices* not only altered means but also changed the correlations of that test with other tests that were given under uniform conditions. For those who stress the invariant properties of this test as a *g* measure, this finding is a challenge. Evidence for environmental variation producing both correlational change and mean performance is abundant in Berry's (1976) study of the intercorrelations of acuity and figural tests in different habitats. The correlation of visual acuity tasks, which are measures of perceptual threshold, with *Raven's Progressive Matrices* and *Embedded Figures Tests* (*EFTs*) is always positive. In groups with low levels of schooling, this correlation can be as great as the intercorrelation of *Matrices* and *EFTs* when these tests experience no abnormal "bottoming effects." In the Edinburgh and the Inverkeillor contrast groups, the acuity measures are not correlated with the figural tests significantly, although a positive trend is confirmed. We shall refer to this series more fully when discussing information-processing results, but the correlations *and* mean performances both alter with the habitat "treatments." Such covariance defines the effects of the law of cultural differentiation.

Dispositional variables. The easiest dispositional variable to use in test score comparison is the sex of the subject. Unlike age groups, which tend to be inexact when births are not registered by law, sex is an attribute that seldom undergoes any significant change. From the repeated assertion of female superiority in verbal performance and male superiority in figural tasks presented visually, western psychology has posited a male–female differential hypothesis. Genetic, hormonal, hemispherical, and social explanations of these observed differences have ensued. The first three of these are *intrahominem*, the other *extra* or *inter*, depending on the type of study encountered. No single class of explanation has survived for long. The evidence from cross-cultural studies of sex differences is great, and has been the subject of a special study by Born (1984). Her painstaking meta-analysis reveals not only cultural inconsistencies in the direction of sex differences in performance, but the extreme difficulty in reaching conclusions when the strict rules of sampling are applied to the large number of results available. That study will no doubt be heard of again because it alters most of what western psychologists believe to be consistent. In particular, it reveals that conclusions about the cause of sex differences in performance are premature.

Work that is well known to us (MacArthur, Irvine, & Brimble, 1964; Irvine, 1966, 1983b; Berry, 1971; Drenth, van der Flier, & Omari, 1983; Bali,

Drenth, van der Flier, & Young, 1984) shows that test scores vary *unpredictably* with habitats when sex is used for group membership. Berry reports no significant differences in figural test performance between sexes in Eskimo settlements, but indicates male advantage in West African subsistence ecology. In school ecologies in Africa, wherever females are minorities and the teachers are male, differences in verbal attainment have favoured males, quite the reverse of western practice. Figural test scores, for Irvine's ($N =$ 1,615) large sample in Zimbabwe (Irvine, 1969a) correlate $+.09$ with male–female category, a neglible relationship. Verbal tests of English attainment were male-oriented, with an average correlation of $+.25$ over 6 measures, ranging from $+.11$ to $+.37$. There were no negative correlations in the 13 tests administered, and hence no test in which females were superior. Only in one paper-and-pencil test, involving serial shape induction (an analogue of bead stringing: *Morrisby's Compound Series*) during a pilot study, did females outperform males in the Central African work. In seeking a cause, one might note that males, unlike females, were not present in bead embroidery classes.

Moreover, the companion study by MacArthur et al. (1964), in Zambian schools, secondary as well as primary, shows essentially the same results. There is a tendency for male students to outperform females, whatever the test. Figural test advantages are minimal, and in standard score terms are less than verbal score differences. Finally, the manual for the *AAT (Academic Aptitude Test)*, Human Sciences Research Council (1974), contains norms for black male and female students who had completed five years of secondary schooling and were eligible for university entry. Over 1,200 subjects, from all language groups, in the ratio of 2 males to 1 female were assessed on ten tests of academic aptitude. In all but one test, vernacular reading comprehension, males outperformed females. The highest differences were in English and African vocabulary, the next in two- and three-dimensional manipulation of figure drawings. One is almost tempted to conclude that girls, in such contexts, behave like deprived minorities, showing a general educational deficit, such as is often reported among acculturating groups (see McShane & Berry, Chapter 15). That may suffice as a local explanation, yet it does not fit all the African data.

The more recent work of a new generation of test users in East Africa is revealed in the studies by Bali, Drenth, and their associates. Essentially work that parallels the Central African school surveys of the 1960s just discussed, results from primary and secondary school cohorts in Kenya and Tanzania are reported, using a large number of subjects, tests, environmental, and dispositional variables. Sex differences in performance are again evident, with male advantage generally present in *primary* schools in both countries. Again, the differences are small, large sample sizes occasionally investing them with statistical significance. In Tanzanian *secondary* schools the results, from identical tests and questionnaires showing remarkable normative similarity, are reversed, with female superiority on almost every cognitive test, and no clear pattern of figural differences apparent. To complicate matters even further, younger students performed better than older ones, and the correlation between being older and being male was $+.43$. If one controls for either of these "variables," the correlation of age or sex with ability is lessened. The choice of which one of these gross categories (sex or age) to control for is not enviable, nor does the decision emerge from any theoretical position.

The effect of "environmental" variables. Apart from sex or age differences, which are dispositional, variables of an environmental nature have had an enduring place in the debate about the major influences on test performance. The most commonly advanced have been those concerned with the support for learning provided within the home of the subject. In that context, one can distinguish educational and material differentiation, broadly captured by indices of socioeconomic status, from psychological differences implicit in size of family, birth order, gender ratios, and the like.

In western empiricism, higher educational and material support is correlated with higher test performance *between* families, while smaller family size and primogeniture also have been said to foster the acquisition and retention of mental, and particularly language, skills *within* the family unit. The striking finding in the nationwide surveys from East and Central Africa cited here is the *lack* of relationship between material and psychological indices from family background and test results. Whereas the claim by Jencks (1972) that almost half the variance in American test scores can be predicted from indices of family status and material support, the Central and East African series of studies just referred to, and conducted 20 years apart, shows the predicted variance hovering between 1% and 4%. Even this tiny proportion of variance does not operate consistently for achievement or ability measures.

Family structure results, supposedly surfacing psychological environment differences *within* each family, are not consistent in the recent Kenyan and Tanzanian studies of Drenth and his colleagues, where, for family size, positive correlations in one country contrast with negative correlations in the other. A minimal trend to negative correlation is evident in Irvine's (1966, 1969a) work. These African correlations, it will be recognised, are based on mean family sizes of 7 children, and a range of 1 to 16, far beyond the norms of western families. Increase in range produces no effect on correlations, as it might be expected to do if confluence theory were exportable across cultures, and deficit worsened with extended family units. The absolute size of these correlations is no greater than those for correlations of attainment and ability test scores with occupational and material status, and no more consistent.

Our conclusion from sex difference studies in the measurement of abilities in nonwestern cultures is that there is no adequate form of explanation to account for the diversity of the results witnessed. That conclusion can be extended just as easily to *all* nonschool environmental variables, such as social class, religious and language groups, mother–child interactions, and the like. All show effects; but variable effects in cultures prevent the accurate prediction of which classification will produce what effect in any context.

Specific learning environments. We perceive these results as demonstrating the law of cultural differentiation, in that African contexts do not support the assumption of identical effects on test score variance for each and every culture. There is, however, one universal effect in the cross-cultural literature. Schooling exercises a pervasive effect on test performance. Chapter 12 by Kendall and his colleagues is conclusive, and Chapter 15 by McShane and Berry on Amerindian test performance is further proof. Not only does *amount* of schooling relate to test performance, but different *types of school* enhance or depress it. On the whole, in severe subsistence ecologies, boarding schools offering a totally supportive environment influence test performance most positively.

Extreme contrasts. There is a limit, in the apparent willingness to consider these contrasts as quasi-experimental, to the credibility of a science that accepts scores on tests as valid indicators of the mental competence of groups. We have tried to show, from the empirical evidence, what these limits may be when domain and group variable studies are involved. We are unable, however to make any positive comment on attempts to compare test scores across cultures and generations at one and the same time. For example, the comparison of *Wechsler* IQs of Japanese in 1936 versus Americans in 1970 (Lynn, 1982; Flynn, 1982), even if it is numerically feasible, lacks any epistemological rationale for its execution (Irvine, 1983a, 1983b). No doubt readers will also draw their own conclusions about the variable that distinguishes groups by the amount of "white blood" calculated to flow through the veins of respondents, carefully presented for us by McShane and Berry in Chapter 15. There are, though, worthwhile things that can be done from domain studies as starting points in the quest for intellect structure, and our taxonomy helps to classify them cohesively. Test studies do not preclude cross-cultural comparisons, but test users must henceforth be quite specific about what may be sought in comparisons and inferred from them.

Summary. The evidence for the abilities of mankind from test scores is derived mainly from domain studies and from the use of groups as quasi-experimental variables in order to attribute cause to the effects of various influences on performance. Domain studies reveal a remarkable similarity in the constructs that psychologists use to account for individual differences. No cross-cultural evidence exists to deny the validity of these broad divisions of capability that have been accessed by tests. Nevertheless, the use of categories to ascribe causes to variance is the weakest aspect of method and of inference from data. Test and environmental sources of variance are not stable across cultures, however well they parcel out within any one culture. The evidence from 20 years of sustained research into the study of test behaviour across cultures is conclusive. The abilities of mankind may be captured in western tests, but they are not fully expressed in them, nor are the causes of their growth and expression apparent in the use of groups to account for some of the variation in test scores. By far the largest source of variation that can be attributed to performance within groups is between subjects. The most critical between-group source is the amount of exposure to western education, a finding that is so widespread that it needs no separate reference. The sources already quoted all attest to that universal. There can therefore be no weaker scientific practice than the use of a single test score to make inferences about the structure or cause of abilities, when that score is summed over subjects who are preclassified into groups and the resulting averages submitted to a test of significance. Perhaps, though, other paradigms of measurement offer more than test scores. That, as we shall discover, is another empirical question.

Cross-cultural piagetianism

An important landmark for psychological assessment across cultures is any finding that is so radically different from anything ever encountered in the West as to cause a departure from an already entrenched theoretical position. After only 15 years of experience with the use of piagetian[4] tasks (PGTs) across cultures, reviewers believed that such a finding had emerged from cross-cultural studies of conservation among children from various cultures. Dasen and Heron (1981, p. 296) declared there is ''a rather odd but consistent finding, that in some populations a proportion of the children and adults do not seem to reach the last sub-stage of the concrete operational stage, which constitutes an important limitation to the universalist position.'' This conclusion from a review of several studies purporting to show the same finding, is another example, as application of the taxonomy shows, of a high inference from group comparisons. And it is discussed in full later in this section. How this degree of inference came to be tolerated is an interesting question that can be answered only when the methods employed by cross-cultural proponents of the piagetian paradigm are seen in perspective. And that understanding informs the specific emphasis of this section on the progression through one critical piagetian cognitive stage, conservation, in children and adults.

Transferring the piagetian paradigm. The relative acceptability of findings of less than universal progress through the stages of mental development, based on observed performance on piagetian developmental tasks, seems to us to be because of specific aspects of piagetian method across cultures, which are detailed now. More general aspects were described earlier, in the

[4] See note 3.

section on piagetian data. A comparison with the problems of developing psychometric tests sharpens the issues. Although the difficulties of test construction and interpretation in traditional psychometrics were quickly realised, much effort over many years was expended on finding solutions to problems of administering a great variety of tests (Irvine & Carroll, 1980; Irvine, 1986). It had been going on for decades. The piagetian enterprise, on the other hand, seemed initially to create fewer technical problems. At least, few were reported. The transfer of piagetian interview technology to other cultures was free from the internal questings and strife of psychometricians. A standard approach was developed by several fieldworkers (Greenfield, 1966; Bovet, 1968; DeLemos, 1969; Dasen, 1972b); and attempts by these and other scientists to ensure comprehension of task meaning and purpose through indigenous interpreters and research assistants produced no controversy until Judith Irvine (1978) produced a firm anthropological veto that we take heed of in due course.[5] Generally, there were fewer standardised items from the small number of subtests to apply, and these survived almost without change from their Genevan templates. Experimenters were assessing different groups from different cultures not so much to refute the null hypothesis, but more, with scrupulous heed to the rules of evidence, to confirm it. They did not expect to find the universal mental stage progression to be denied: nor did Piaget, who had given a personal blessing to the cross-cultural enterprise (Piaget, 1966). For the next fifteen years accounts of work in numerous exotic contexts issued from the journals.

The most comprehensive description of that era (Dasen & Heron, 1981) was also to become the most controversial. Part of that controversy can be traced to the lack of attempts to validate the construct of conservation by systematic domain studies. We examine it by applying the taxonomy to some of the work that has produced the controversy. These are not confined to *domain* but involve *ethnographic* and *training* studies. Each helps to evaluate the evidence from cross-cultural piagetian work in different ways, leading to a verdict that might not have been possible without the taxonomy. Domain studies are concerned with the technical aspects of item reliability and validity; ethnographic studies produce revisions of existing data; and training studies raise the issue of the confidence that can be placed in one administration of a task or test as a measure of a level of competence or capability. The accretion of different kinds of evidence lends weight to the final verdict.

Conservation across cultures. The controversy over piagetian studies of cognitive development concerns the previously quoted conclusion by Dasen and Heron that certain societies have almost 50% of their mature adult population unable to conserve quantity, weight, or volume, judged by their performance on "standard" piagetian tasks. The consistent appearance of this hiatus in cognitive development was visualised as a growth curve that flat-

---

[5] Judith Irvine is not related to, nor has she ever worked with or corresponded with the senior author, or for that matter the co-author, of this chapter.

tened out at 50% at a certain age, and remained like that however old the subjects were in the community. The construct used by Dasen and Heron to account for this phenomenon is *asymptote*. Their own work in Zambia, Australia, New Guinea, and Canada claims to show this failure of the organism to progress. Here one witnesses the same trend as is shown in psychometric test scores. The exotic groups show depressed performance compared with the samples to whom the tests, tasks, and interviews were indigenous, or home-grown. Far from a simple delay or underachievement, however, is the finding of *asymptote*. This would mean that half the people in the group were cut off from a whole array of mental tools and strategies that in western groups were in common use by the age of 8 or 9.

Retardation in test or task achievement is one thing, admitting various kinds of explanations; and leaving open the possibility of amelioration by treatment or training. Truncation of a universal progression through normal mental development is quite a different challenge to the whole body of piagetian theory. The taxonomy we constructed for data analysis shows that piagetian theory is based on the assumption of universal progression. Absolute measures are implied by the items. There is no mean score, no product of moments, but a mark on a universal continuum. To have this continuum denied would limit the universalist position, as Heron and Dasen point out. One could carry the argument one step further, however, and ask if it might undermine the very edifice of genetic epistemology. If mental progression is halted in any culture, it would be analogous to finding a subspecies of mankind in which people could progress as far as walking but were incapable of ever running, let alone jumping, however hard they tried or trained. To determine an explanation for the failure of people to reach a stage for purely environmental reasons would be difficult, although Harlow's monkeys who never became adequate mothers might well provoke a remote comparison, if necessary.

The difficulties, at the present time, of accepting the validity of the construct of *asymptote* to explain the findings from cross-cultural applications of PGTs are many. One problem is inconsistency within the domain of piagetian tasks administered to Euramerican groups. Not only are they inconsistent in their results across cultures, but even within our own laboratories the notion of *horizontal décalages* has to be invoked to explain anomalies in the observed difficulties of tasks given to subjects reputed to be at one and the same stage of mental development. No such explanation is needed in tests with a large number of items. The items themselves are held to be unreliable if their difficulties change from group to group: and they are replaced. The need for the notion of perturbation in order to maintain the validity of the theory of fixed progression should have alerted researchers to the possibility of a simpler explanation for the phenomenon. One of the most obvious explanations for *horizontal décalages* is the high risk of unreliability in a small number of cognitive tasks given to homogeneous age groups of heterogeneous ability. The lack of consideration of such plausible, and at the same time sceptical, rival hypotheses for divergence from the Euramerican age norms has marked much piagetian work across cultures. Recent scepticism (J. Irvine, 1978; Cole & Scribner, 1982; Chung, 1983), has invited a rescrutiny of some of the most revered tenets of the cross-cultural piagetian canon. How this fits into our taxonomy for data evaluation concerns us now.

The time and effort involved in individual interviews are great. Consequently, the strategy common to cross-cultural piagetian research has been to administer the conventional PGTs to small (typically $N = 10$) groups of subjects homogeneous by age. When the experimenters have been expatriates, interpreters have had to be used almost invariably, with, as we shall see, at least one notable exception (J. Irvine, 1978). To get around the language problem, mimetic strategies were also used (Heron & Simonsson, 1969; Heron, 1971; Heron & Dowel, 1973), but with no proof of reliability and no successful construct validation. Invariably, the intuition of the expatriate experimenter, enlightened by an interpreter, is offered as proof that the tasks, transposed from the parent to offspring cultures, have survived the winter of the new medium. With a question raised about what would constitute proof of cultural differences in cognitive operations in a context of small samples and few tasks, the credibility of such a proof is pushed to its limits by the taxonomy we have suggested, because of the inherent tendency to large standard errors in any database of that nature. We do know, however, that when frequency differences have been observed between cultural groups, Berry's ecological theory has been invoked by Dasen (1972a). An ecological, or *inter-hominem*, explanation has generally accompanied observation of differences, although asymptote could, if persistent, demand more than this.

As we suggested, explanations of differences are necessary only if the data are valid and reliable enough to warrant explanation. At the moment, the whole corpus of piagetian research across cultures requires revaluation following doubts cast on the database itself by a growing body of evidence. This evidence is not, as the taxonomy reveals, all of the same type, or origin. It includes reanalyses of the Dasen and Heron data, carried out by Irvine (1983a), that amount to *domain* studies; an *ethnographic* variable is introduced by Judith Irvine's failure to replicate Greenfield's attributed "magic action" study in the very village where it originated (J. Irvine, 1978; Greenfield, 1979); and conclusions from low-inference *training* studies (see Chapter 11 by Keats & Keats) in mono and bilinguals (Keats & Keats, 1974; Keats, Keats, & Wan Rafaei, 1976; Keats, Keats, & Liu, 1982). Finally, the power of the anthropological veto is visible in the discrepancy between the results of indigenous psychologists and expatriates (Chung, 1983; Dasen, 1983; Irvine, 1986); and in *anthropological* studies of indigenous legal (Gluckman, 1944) and metaphoric discourse that provide clear evidence of formal operational thought in contexts where piagetian studies have indicated lag or asymptote in conservation. A brief summary of each of these objections to taking the current piagetian cross-cultural data base at its face value is provided now, without necessarily referring again in detail to the sources just cited. The names of the authors suffice.

Domain studies: reliability and validity. The lack of reliability and construct validity studies for piagetian data on conservation are the concerns raised by Irvine (1983a). Focussing specifically on the work on asymptote, owing much of its credibility to Dasen and Heron's own empiricism, he finds that the single data points for each age group tested by Dasen in Australia, Canada, and West Africa, and by Heron and his associates in Zambia and Papua, New Guinea, reach significance so seldom as to suggest that further analyses are not warranted. Greenfield's (1966) data is similarly treated. Irvine concludes that the asymptote of 50% of the adult and child samples who were classified as conservers is well within the confidence limits of chance responses to one or both of two questions given in succession. Asymptote is concluded to be an experimenter-induced finding requiring no theoretical explanation.

The ethnographic variable. A similar conclusion, but from an anthropological perspective, is drawn by Judith Irvine about the classical study of so-called magic action carried out by Greenfield (1966) among the Wolof of West Africa. Greenfield performed conservation experiments with water levels in beakers and bottles, sometimes in sight of, and sometimes screened from, her subjects. When subjects answered that the changing water levels were indicative of altered *amounts* of water, they either were silent thereafter, or supplied the reason "You poured it" when questioned further. Greenfield interpreted this response – although she had limited knowledge of the language and culture – as the subjects' attributing *cause* to her, a white expatriate, through magical powers. The magic of the experimenter changed the amount of water in the beakers. In spite of Miner's (1956, p. 507) well-publicised warning against perceiving exotic groups as being magic-fixated, this explanation went unchallenged until Judith Irvine returned to the site of Greenfield's first study, taking the role of a language student and living alone in the village without the aid of an interpreter or assistant. Eventually, her credentials, language skills, and social network secure, she conducted water-level experiments in the context of learning the difference between the Wolof words *same, equal to, more than.* Initial laconic responses of "You poured it" were identical to those offered to Greenfield.

Hereafter, marked differences in the interpretation of the meaning of the same response characterise the debate between Judith Irvine and Greenfield. Short answers, or curtness, is explained by Irvine as typical of Wolof attitudes to talk (p. 307). However, the villagers offered more explanations when she paused, or said she was confused. In extending this courtesy to a visitor, they showed that they had conserved admirably, and that "You poured it" was a shorthand way of indicating that a transformation had occurred without altering the amount of water. Judith Irvine then argues that Greenfield's explanations are nothing more than expatriate attributions based on insufficient knowledge (for further examples, see Miner, 1956).

The effect of the ethnographic study on Greenfield was salutory. Her response, or defence, is that Judith Irvine got the results she did by altering the original experimental context, and thereby invalidating the clinical interview. However, Greenfield (1979, p. 252) then reveals that the veto forced a return to her original data. After rescrutiny, she explains that the published 55% "asymptote" figure applies only to a problem dividing one quantity of water among six beakers, whereas 85% of the villagers responded correctly to a problem involving, like Judith Irvine's experiment, only two beakers. Greenfield's decision to use the standard test as a pretest, and to confer conservation status only on those who replied correctly to both the two- and six-beaker questions is unexplained. We now know, however, that the tables in Greenfield's (1966) chapter are the result of joint probabilties of .85 and .55 for the two tasks. This was not made explicit in the original work. But we now have proof that asymptote for the standard two-beaker task is not applicable to either Greenfield's or Irvine's subjects. Asymptote, in Greenfield's study, is an artifact of two item difficulties, one of which, operating at the chance level for the sample size, contradicts the other. As we suggested in the taxonomy, the anthropological veto is a powerful part of the ethnographic variable in cross-cultural research. When it is produced, data become reanalysed and reassessed.

Both Judith Irvine and S. H. Irvine questioned the validity of the construct of asymptote from different viewpoints. The one shows that the statistical probabilities favour acceptance of the null hypothesis of observed responses being no more than the sum of chance or, in Greenfield's empirical work, joint probabilities. The other strongly emphasises the social and linguistic conventions that prescribe the meaning of a structured interview. These conventions alter the meaning of a stimulus, as Judith Irvine (1978, p. 309) so trenchantly puts it, saying that "formal experimental equivalence of operations is no guarantee that different cultural groups will interpret the experimental stimuli in the same way or that they will be motivated by the same concerns." She then goes on to make a point we have seen applied to the psychometric tradition, not by anthropologists but by psychologists themselves, that "the results of cross-cultural experiments are therefore suspect, since the performances elicited in these tests are not comparable manifestations of subjects' cognitive abilities."

Low-inference variables: Training. So far, domain and ethnographic criticisms have fostered a revaluation of conservation research across cultures. Training studies, giving rise to low inferences about cause and effect, are particularly difficult to accommodate within a framework for assessment that requires accuracy from a single application of only two or three items to a subject. Placement on a universal, absolute scale of development is the aim. Psychometric tests can determine a zone of confidence for an individual score; but this requires a large number of items administered to a large number of subjects. No such technology exists for piagetian tasks, and journal reports of asymptote and lag have been derived from first-time measures of small numbers of items. Nevertheless, treatment variables, such as training, are low-inference, and differences in performance can be attributed directly to their effects.

It is important to distinguish three concurrent approaches to training. First, training in rule application (Dasen, Lavallee, & Retschitzki, 1979; Dasen, Ngini, & Lavallée, 1979); next, exposure to successive sets of similar but culturally consonant items (practice and social context effects) as reported by Chung, (1983); finally, exposure to the same items after some intervening treatment, as reported in the Keats studies (see Chapter 11), but specifically transfer from one language to another (practice and language transformation effects). All of these interventions lead to the same conclusion. There are, as in psychometric testing, differential and pronounced gains in the subjects traceable to context or treatment differences.

The explanation of robust practice effects has produced a further construct in piagetian literature, the distinction between observed performance on a specific task, and the assumption that this observation serves as a marker for latent level of competence or, for want of a better word, ability. The debate is not a new one for psychometric test users. An important general debate about the stresses in piagetian theory induced by the gap between the task and its interpretation is found in Bovet (1981) and the commentary by Bryant (1981). Dasen, Ngini, and Lavallée (1979) assert that the asymptote in developmental curves may be an artifact of the *competence–performance* distinction. They go on to say, though, that lag is a real difference in competence remediable by training. The problem is that the initial baseline judgment is either one of competence or it is not; one cannot have it both ways. If asymptote is refuted by the effect of practice, so too must lag, because both are phenomena that depend on the accuracy of the first measurement. The studies by Keats and Keats (see Chapter 11) show, moreover, improvement across language structures, not invariance. Chung's work shows improvement in culture-consonant tasks compared with standard piagetian measures, not invariance. And Dasen's own work leads to the same conclusion. Mental stages in the subject, as assessed by standard piagetian tasks in other cultures, are attributes of the experimenter that require constant proof of validity. As in testing, the evidence against the assumption that one application of a test or task will accurately define the performance of subjects from exotic contexts is strong.

Variation with origin of experimenter. As a different type of ethnographic variable, the ethnic origin of the experimenter may mediate the type of research and its design. It may also influence the results and their interpretation, particularly in cross-cultural research. Irvine (1986) draws attention to an unrecognised feature of cross-cultural piagetian research stemming from Africa, where a number of western-trained indigenous psychologists have carried out field studies in piagetian mode. In Andor's (1983) extensive annotated bibliography, 20 post-1965 piagetian studies were identified where results about the relative ages of acquisition of piagetian stages could be listed. Half had been conducted by expatriates, and half by indigenous psychologists. Of the expatriate studies, only one (Lloyd, 1971) claimed normal age progression for African children. The other nine all reported either lag or asymptote. Of the ten African psychologists' studies, most of them unpublished doctoral theses, seven reported normal age progression, while only three reported lag. There are no prizes for correctly guessing the result of a chi-square performed, with Yates's correction, let it be said, on these frequencies regarded as random samples from a universe of such studies. Wry humour apart, there is a problem in a science that produces such results. It means one of two things. One might conclude that expatriate studies are all seriously flawed. Judith Irvine takes that position, arguing that only an insider can hope to administer piagetian tasks so that subjects can perform operations on them successfully. Alternatively, one might conclude that the attribution of mental progression is a judgment that is constructed from prior expectancies in the experimenter. Both sets of results, indigenous as well as expatriate, could then equally be regarded as ethnocentric. It is not a pleasant alternative to contemplate. The phenomenon is accounted for in the taxonomy: It is also a dramatic expression of the law of cultural differentiation within the experimenters themselves.

The issue is further complicated by Chung's (1983) rebuttal of asymptote and lag by introducing indigenous piagetian tasks that show perfect conservation in Malay children. To us, her work resembles the efforts made by Bhatia (1956) to adapt psychometric tests to the Indian subcontinent. Memory-span tests were realised not by digits but by Hindi monosyllables, and improved performance resulted. Dasen's (1983) critique of her work asserts that neither her tasks nor her procedures are standard. By such denials, he reinforces the criticism often advanced by Cole (1975) that the tasks as we know them are inadequate realisations for the construction of developmental theory, because the *ad hominem* evidence for logical thought is apparent in the daily interactions of the members of the community being studied. Without agreement on instrumentation, the possibility that Chung's work and Dasen's critique are part of the continuum of ethnographic variation postulated in the taxonomy has to remain an unwelcome hypothesis, in spite of the impeccable work and unquestionable integrity of the authors quoted in this section.

Indigenous formal operations: Ethnographic approaches. Anthropological vetoes are not unusual. As forms of *ad hominem* explanation, the afterthought in our taxonomy, they are often dismissed by psychologists in the name of science: But there is growing evidence that psychologists are taking them seriously. When Gluckman (1944) published his essay on the logic of African science, he used as an example his observations of the Barotse. He resisted any attempt to characterise the tribe as a whole, or its members in particular, as unintelligent, pointing to a sophisticated flood-plain agriculture, a highly structured social organisation, and, above all, a great logical sophistication in argument and advocacy in matters of communal dispute. Legal argument seems to require sophisticated mental operations, much of them formal, or logical, by adult standards. For the near neighbours of the Barotse, the Shona, Holleman (1952) produced an account of Shona customary law that left no doubt about the wit, logic, and retention of its protagonists. Recently, Irvine (Berry & Irvine, 1986) analysed Shona proverbs about intelligence and wisdom contained in Hamutyeni and Plangger (1974), concluding that the Shona clearly distinguished between an organismic attentional capacity, as a prerequisite to learning, and the repeated experiences that constituted the stuff of learning. Although this is an important point pursued later, in the section on the psychology of ethnic assessment, the proverbs address the question of the cognitive operations required to understand them. An outsider's view of the proverbs provides the key. For non-native speakers, three-quarters of the Shona proverbs are not understandable in literal translation. They require transformation to an oblique, metaphoric sense before they can be understood. The proverbs are full of recognisable oratorical figures of speech. They seemed to us to constitute a definition, in the sense of a key to understanding, of indigenous cognitive functioning. Its preliterate oral context, requiring formal operational thought, is such that no standard intelligence or piagetian test item could adequately encompass it. Without the understanding gained by study of the Shona proverbs it would be easy, and also erroneous, to underestimate the capacity for information processing that traditional wisdom implies. This type of anthropological veto is no less powerful than the replication attempted by Judith Irvine in Greenfield's original research environment. Both forms of the veto have the same function. They force a revaluation of existing empirical evidence.

Conclusion. The verdict on piagetian research provided by domain, training, and ethnographic studies is no more helpful than that on conventional testing. The theory of progression through qualitatively different stages of thinking is not invalidated, but the conclusion that it is faintly realised in the cadre of items at present in use across cultures is inescapable. The low-inference studies of practice and transfer inhibit the interpretation of one-time assessment. The work on traditional attitudes to talk places restrictions on the interpretation of brevity or silence. The discrepancy between indigenous and expatriate result frequencies for the same items in approximal contexts introduces doubts about experimenter construction of what might be identical responses. And reports of indigenous reasoning in oral contexts, before the emergence of an orthography, almost certainly point to the existence of what we would normally consider to be fully operational adult processing of abstract concepts. Piagetian epistemology is neither qualified nor modified by the conflicting evidence of its empiricism across cultures. It points to the exercise of the law of cultural differentiation in the percepts of the subjects in their responses to "identical" stimuli; and also, it should be said, to the responses of the psychologists who conducted the experiments.

Experimental routes to cognitive processes

The bedrock of strong effects

If tests are concerned with individual scores in relation to group means, and PGTs with progress along a maturing continuum of thinking, experimental approaches are primarily directed to detailed and sustained investigation of those robust effects in human cognition that are visible in all mankind. The most publicised, and one of the most influential, series of experiments ever to emerge from the cross-cultural literature is that initiated by Segall, Campbell, and Herskovits (1963, 1966) on the *degree of illusion susceptibility* of persons grouped not by a classification that arose out of biological, social, religious, or economic attributes, but by environmental artifact that is engineered by social change. Segall and his colleagues had access to decades of research that showed subjects, assessed by standard methods, susceptible to illusions of line length. Building on that certainty, they set out to demonstrate the effect of the presence or absence of linear environments on the habits of perception responsible for illusion susceptibility. How many right angles constituted the immediate visual environment was the criterion. These "carpentered worlds" were of mankind's own creation, and as such are important examples of the information-processing habits of humans being changed by the use of skills to create habitats that in turn demand further modification of percepts – the second condition of the law of cultural differentiation. For a decade afterwards, material relevant to this work occupied the journals. A neat summary of its heuristic impetus to the nature–nurture controversy that ensued about the cause of cultural differences, is given in Stewart (1973).

Similarly, the work of Scribner (1974) was anchored in the enduring effect of *clustering in free recall*. Because this is another strong effect, any group of subjects she worked with were very likely to cluster everyday household objects in memory to aid recall of a large number of them. Her particular aim was to observe the role of literacy on the networks of memory available to her subjects. The Kpelle were chosen because literacy and illiteracy existed side by side in the same communities and age groups.

Finally, Berry's (1969) paper on the effects of different habitats (Arctic deserts and African bush) in *the attribution of meaning to ambiguous line drawings* assumed that meaning would always be supplied to resolve ambiguity. Precisely what meaning, he correctly extrapolated from Bagby's

(1957) work, would be a function of ecological press. In these three "experimental" studies of information processing, no doubt existed about the phenomenon under investigation, and individual differences were not the issue. In each, the method was well proven and needed little modification. The interpretation of findings was a function of the new data, but had theoretical constraints from a large body of previously published work.

Our taxonomic approach shows that the work in this area relied on the presence of groups of subjects who, as groups, differ in their habituated, or learned, internal control mechanisms. Cultural influences of different kinds are thought to be responsible for these different responses to stimuli. For Segall, it was the carpentered environment, or lack of it that varied; for Berry, it was long-term memory, formed in the work environment that structured an ambiguous response; for Scribner, literacy or the lack of it on the way that memory was activated. These three aspects – perceptual process, the portability of meaning in the construction of ambiguity, and the tools of memory – are central to problem solving, in particular test performance. The use of groups, when these groups represent variability on a known dimension, in combination with a "hard" phenomenon, such as illusion susceptibility, clustering in free recall, or binocular resolution, is common to all. This kind of evidence for cultural differentiation is much more difficult to ignore than test averages or small group proportions solving piagetian tasks.

Implications for stimulus identity. The studies just discussed nevertheless provide some sharp contrasts that are instructive. In the work on illusions by Segall, and on ambiguous line drawings by Berry, stimulus identity was preserved consistently in the line drawings. Only the subjects differed in their perception of them. These two examples bow to the apparent logical necessity for stimulus identity, because alteration would prevent direct intergroup comparison. Different cultural groups were chosen by the experimenters as carrying in their heads dispositions to different habits of thought that would yield different responses. Causal attribution to group phenomena seemed a much shorter inference when the null hypothesis was rejected. Yet, as the subsequent nature–nurture debate about susceptibility to visual illusions was to demonstrate, any explanation that attributed *all* the variation between groups to the immediate environment was insufficient to account for the fact that retinal variations between ethnic groups were involved. An interactive conclusion is the only possible one that accounts for all the evidence.

Nevertheless, different environments exert strong effects on the perception of identical stimuli. Although the abandonment of identical stimuli presents scientific problems, there are experiments in which retaining identical stimuli can effectively nullify the strongest of cognitive effects. Scribner's work on free recall was predicated not on preserving the same objects used in Euramerican experiments, but in deliberately altering them. The universal clustering effect could be inadvertently destroyed by objects that did not form associative groupings. Objects that would cluster in Euramerican experience would not necessarily do so in the Kpelle village. Observation in the community allowed Scribner to choose those that were culture consonant. They then became nonrandom elements in concept formation for Kpelle subjects. Scribner's success in revealing clustering confirmed her judgment about what were valid objects for the Kpelle consciousness. Had her subjects failed to cluster objects, she would not then have known if the failure was due to the lack of cognitive strategies in the subjects, or to the lack of clustering potential in the objects. That, of course, is the dilemma faced by psychometric test or piagetian task users: how to account for inadequate performance.

Ethnographic variables as tests of hypotheses. Scribner's work, and the risks accompanying stimulus choice, began to test the limits of group comparisons. This presupposition is nevertheless as systematically misleading as it is intuitively compelling, because it confuses identity with equality or equivalence. One further example shows the danger of confusing stimulus identity with functional equivalence. Mitchell's (1956) early adaptation of the *Bogardus Social Distance Scale* for studies in tribal affinity in Zambia is not quoted in the psychological literature because it "belongs" in social anthropology. Nevertheless, Mitchell found that the construct "social distance" applied to the urban settlements in the mining towns of northwestern Zambia. A scale of six items correctly classified known ethnographic differences in location, language, and social organisation among the tribal groups represented in his samples. The original *Bogardus Social Distance Scale,* standardised for American urban use, could not be retained, nor were the orders of "equivalent" items the same in scale reproduction. Indices of .91 to .95 for the Zambian version are reported. Although it predicted social distance among Zambian tribes according to known external criteria, it would then have been imprudent to compare Zambians and Americans on their respective degrees of ethnocentrism by averaging scale scores and conducting analyses of variance. Neither Scribner nor Mitchell would have contemplated such a sequel for their data. Instead, their scientific task was completed by an exercise in construct validation that allowed the phenomenon to be investigated in a new cultural context. This approach has to be contrasted with the confusion that results from the comparison of test scores, and of frequencies attaining developmental status in exotic groups according to PGTs or their analogues. The maintenance of identical stimuli in these situations does not always remove a source of variation. In fact, Berry's perceptual research shows that one more source is added. Changing the stimuli may remove that same unwanted variation, but it issues new challenges for group comparisons.

These different studies by Segall, Berry, Scribner, and Mitchell are all, however, concerned with how groups in different cultures lend meaning to a stimulus that is not in itself devoid of meaning. If we were to examine performance on patterned and random *arrays* of data that was itself as meaningless as possible, what might the result be? For an answer to that question, we take up a slightly different approach.

The road to individual differences

The relevance of work on cognitive information processing across cultures is apparent from Chapter 3 by Eysenck and Chapter 4 by Jensen. These emphasise ways of measuring individual differences in abilities that depend on meaningless sounds, or on responses to apparently simple cognitive tests. As Jensen (1985), using American IQ tests and choice reaction time tasks, has extended his work to contrast the performance of blacks and whites, the cross-cultural archive has some important points to make about such initiatives, in particular the effects required from simple or meaningless stimuli to satisfy the assumption of stimulus equivalence. By this we mean the representation of an external stimulus internally so that it allows those mental operations normally associated with the class of stimuli to proceed.

Four case studies are listed below, illustrating the difficulties associated with the assumption of stimulus equivalence across cultures even allowing for stimulus identity. These deal with different kinds of stimuli: dots (Cole, Gay, & Glick, 1968); lights of different colours and sounds of different quality (Poortinga, 1971); size constancy (Winter, 1967; Humphriss & Wortley, 1971; and Reuning & Wortley, 1973); and a taxonomic classification of stimuli, including choice reaction time tasks, scored for speed and accuracy (Verster, 1983). These important, and sparsely cited sources are relevant to current Euramerican attempts to measure individual differences across and within cultures by latencies to complete items, and by brain waves (particularly evoked potentials) measured in the first quarter of a second after stimulus presentation.

Culture and the meaning of neutral stimuli. Cole et al. (1968) were early in the field with work on what they called "information processing" before the term was widely used. They contrasted the accuracy of perceiving random and ordered arrays of dots in adult Kpelle and American subjects. They found that cross-cultural performance was quite similar when a small number of dots was presented randomly, but American subjects were more accurate when large numbers of dots were presented randomly and in patterns. In fact, the Kpelle performance in patterned-dot tasks was on a par with their random dot recall frequencies. Patterning appeared to convey no appreciable gestalt advantage over randomness in recall. Cole concludes that "we are dealing with a non-trivial cultural difference" (p. 101), but that to pin down the cause was impossible. The research is also important for evidence of different levels of difficulty of the "same" stimuli for the two groups.

This finding of different difficulty indices for "identical" items in different cultures was apparent in Poortinga's (1971) lengthy report, which is also discussed by Jensen in Chapter 4. As information-processing approaches to cognition try to relate performance to what is known about the limits of human capacity, stimulus equivalence is critical. One must ask subjects to process information on tasks whose demands on that capacity can be estimated, if not modelled. In choice reaction time tasks, which some have shown to be correlated with IQs, the time to respond to a question about the presence or absence of a signal depends on the number of possible alternatives that have to be considered before a decision can be made. In fact, we know that the time to recognise one from a set of equally probable alternatives increases linearly with set size.

Hick's law and "bias" across cultures. One could take this general rule, known as "Hick's law," as a fresh starting point for enquiry about how people in different cultures process information. Poortinga (1971) did that, long before the current vogue in individual differences, in yet one more pioneering, but largely unrecognised, study of auditory and visual choice reaction times in Africans, black and white. He determined times for reacting to various types of neutral stimuli for female and male subjects within each ethnic group. He found that reaction time increased with set size irrespective of ethnic group, thereby establishing the usefulness of Hick's law as a construct, just as piagetian studies revealed progression through the stages. Intercorrelations derived from mental alertness and various ability tests were all positive but inconsistent across cultures; in fact, the failure to reproduce consistent correlations among the measures, including reaction times, for each subgroup, led Poortinga to begin enquiries into "bias" that have endured to the present, as his Chapter 6 with van der Flier reveals.

Bias identification in neutral stimuli. As in other epistemologies, comparisons reveal poorer performance in the exotic group. In Poortinga's work, African choice reaction times were observably slower, but sex differences in latency within ethnic groups and overall were not significant. Previously we drew attention to Cole's suggestion that the difference in Kpelle accuracy was nontrivial but pointed to anomalies in the difficulty values of the items between groups. Nevertheless, Cole was prepared to regard the performances as valid indicators of some unspecified cultural difference. Poortinga, on the other hand, was unable to interpret *time* differentials because he was not satisfied that the speed results he obtained were exactly equivalent for the black and white samples. He submitted the latency data to rigorous tests of the assumption of "bias-free" stimuli – and almost certainly was the first to do this with latency data – and found that the interactions between groups and stimuli types did not support the comparison of group averages thereafter, whether for lights or sounds.

That account shows that even the "simplest" stimuli prepare inferential traps for the unwary. The taxonomy we have provided carries with it no prohibition on inference from data, but this series of experiments shows that cognitive information-processing (CIP) models are not excused from justifying the comparison in the first place. Poortinga uncovered the complexity of everyday visual and auditory signals by applying to latencies what he already knew about techniques for estimating group differences in item difficulty. No current work has done this, so that his chapter on item-bias methods is all the more timely. The results of his empirical work in the 1970s, and his reflections in this volume, call into question any assumptions of easy routes to interethnic assessment through seemingly everyday and so-called simple or neutral or elementary information-processing tasks.

Speed and accuracy. The most complete study of cross-cultural information processing under current computerised conditions is obtained in Verster's work on speed and accuracy performance in black and white South Africans. Like the other casework in this section, a theoretical model was first postulated, which ordered the tasks along a continuum of cognitive complexity. The tasks were devised to test its robustness, and the groups were identified to extend the range of cultural (blacks vs. whites) and dispositional (white males were compared with white females) variation. No black female group was available for testing.

Verster found good fits for his models of performance in conditions of speed and accuracy. He also uncovered the same scientific evidence for restricting inferences from black–white average performance that is found in Poortinga's work. He was not always certain that the scores of different groups were comparable, especially when the patterns of intercorrelation of speed and accuracy scores were compared, and when construct validity studies involving other cognitive measures were attempted.

Particularly revealing was the failure to discover any systematic *increase* in correlation between latency and IQ as the complexity of the items increased. This qualifies Jensen's claims for the possible universality of such a trend. The presence of a small positive correlation between choice reaction times and IQ scores needed inferential restraint for black subjects. In this group time to comprehend the instructions for the tasks showed as great a correlation with choice reaction times as the IQ scores. Moreover, the correlation between *IQ* and *time to process the instructions for 58 subtests* was an ethnic variable. The value for black males $(-.50, N = 173)$ was significantly greater than for white males $(-.34, N = 100)$ and white females $(-.17, N = 100)$. It is appropriate to partial out the effect of this variable on the relation of IQ to choice reaction time tasks. When this is done for three choice reaction time tasks, the correlations with black IQ scores are, respectively: $-.11$, $-.17$ and $-.19$. In the white groups these are, for females: $-.30^*$, $-.43^*$ and $-.44^*$; and for males $-.21^*$, $-.35^*$ and $-.38^*$. The asterisked values are all beyond the 95% confidence limits of the black correlations. None of the correlations within groups is significantly different from any other. All we can do here is to note the differences, and conclude that the risks of interpreting a reaction time as a measure of "intelligence" for blacks, whether in domain, practice, or treatment conditions, without clear evidence for construct definition, are manifold.

Eysenck's and Sternberg's concern for the differentiation of speed and accuracy scores has current, and past, cross-cultural backing. As most differences have been associated with accuracy scoring, the inability of Verster to fit similar equations for the description of accuracy scores for the two comparison groups should be remembered by those who wish to compare scores of this type. Moreover, how one would go about discussing correlational differences from the black male versus white female results, even at an operational level, is not known at this time, because both ethnicity and dispositional characteristics separate the two groups in the definition of the domain differences.

Operationalising experimental measures. Although this recent work has reached a level of technological expertise that earlier work was unable to match, one more lesson might be learned from secure cognitive studies among groups whose cultural characteristics allow us to predict dimensions and degrees of cognitive performance. Other researchers began with progressions from simple to complex tasks and related these to test scores, or to dispositional and environmental variables, before computers became portable. Twenty-five years ago Reuning and Wortley (1960) in the only cognitive study ever planned and executed among the Kalahari Bushmen – and likely to remain so – pursued this approach some 10 years before it became popular in America. Measures of increasing cognitive demand were constructed, different modes of assessment were employed, and detailed structural analyses performed. Reuning summarises his major work here, in Chapter 18, but it has rested in obscurity for too long. Perhaps the most salient finding from Reuning's work is the tendency to positive correlation between all intellective tasks. One of the most portentous is the high positive correlation, with tests normally included in IQ batteries, of *Hand Steadiness* as measured by the time elapsing before error on serpentine rod, groove, and graded-hole tasks, and on the *Seashore Pitch Test* of 50 items of pure tones. Both of these extra-domain tasks yielded correlations in the range of .5 to .7 with versions of *Kohs Blocks, Detecting Squares,* and other analytical measures. In this respect, individual differences measurements involving simple tasks that were not IQ subtests had surfaced well ahead of Hunt's work in the 1970s, and Jensen's in the 1980s, and in a most exotic group.

These encouraging similarities are, nevertheless, not unqualified. The point of contrast is conflicting evidence from ecologies that are similar in their cognitive demands. The Reuning and Wortley work is an attempt at comprehensive measurement of cognitive skills in a nomadic and hunting culture under threat of extinction because of encroachment from rival patterns of land use. When the results are considered in general and in detail, there are some apparent departures from what one might have predicted, had, for example, the Berry hunting–gathering perceptual style been attributed to the Bushmen, survivors from an ancient and closed hunting and gathering culture. Reuning reports not only that the Bushmen find conventional embedded figures tasks "impossible," but that important sex differences, again not predictable from findings in Arctic desert groups, are apparent in figural test performance. The null hypothesis – no sex differences – was advanced by Berry as a proposition deriving from equal exposure to ecological press among nomadics of different gender. To prove a null hypothesis is always a difficult aspect of theory construction at the best of times. It is not upheld for sex differences among the Bushmen even in this most likely of ecological contexts.

A second ambiguous note might seem to be struck by the failure of the size constancy experiments carried out by Reuning, and by Wortley in other Bushmen groups, to confirm the predicted direction of association of individual differences in size constancy with a field-independent cognitive style. Once again the law of cultural differentiation operates. There are going to be differences between cultural groups that are obvious, but apparently not reconcilable with current theory. In seeking to reconcile discordant findings, one realises that there are only generic similarities among the instruments employed by Berry and Reuning, and one might be tempted to dismiss exact comparison because the stimuli are not identical. On the other hand, we have said that identical stimuli are not necessary to establish the validity of a construct. Reuning reports that *Embedded Figures Tests* proved "impossible" for the Bushmen to carry out, but there can be no doubt that they behaved, as hunters, in extremely foresightful and analytical fashion in other tasks that have not necessarily been associated with research into styles. The conclusion must be, as in the piagetian studies, that the operationalisation of the tests of cognitive function was unevenly realised. The difficulty of interpreting the results of any one test or class of tests or tasks in contrasting cultures, even in CIP research, is a function of the very law of cultural differentiation that these differences demonstrate.

Conclusions. Each of these studies has some precepts for modern assessment of individual differences. They are identified as first seeking robust and well-researched dimensions of cognitive operations. Then a performance model, or hypothesis for such a model, is framed. Tasks are defined to account for human variation within and across cultures. The first step is to fit the model. The subsequent cross-cultural studies serve to test the working limits of the model itself. They are not concerned with between-culture variance in initial proving of the assumptions that determine the construction and use of the task. If variation between gender or cultural groups persists, one has to decide if that is important enough to modify theories that account for performance, or if it can be assigned to some rather more trivial concern, such as experimental artifact. These artifacts usually occur in the means and methods of assessment, as this chapter makes very plain. That admission is seldom gratifying to the self-concept of practising scientists, with the result that group differences are more often than not taken as evidence for or against a theoretical position. The taxonomy helps to remind us that both the group identities and the tasks used to define the differences can be, and all too often are, high-inference classifications, whatever the mode of assessment. As a genre, CIP research is not exempt from the universal problem of construct definition within groups, because its proponents assert that the tasks are either more simple, or more loaded with the essence of intelligence, or both. Very few do this, in fact. Why they should be thought to do so is the last question that we attempt to answer.

The psychology of ethnic assessment

Much of what has been written so far will be well understood by cross-cultural psychologists who have carried out fieldwork. They have realised the limitations of work in comparative human assessment, whatever the paradigm. Their caution has been vindicated by the Dutch school of item analysis that Poortinga describes in Chapter 6 and that he helped to establish in his 1971 monograph on latencies. A similar restraint has not transferred to normative Euramerican studies of ethnic differences that have received widespread publicity. In fact, debate still continues about the assessment of blacks and Orientals, Hispanics and Amerindians, just as it has since Woodworth and Knight wrote in the 1940s. Controversy exists about whether one ethnic group performs better than any other, or, more subtle but still based on the same assumptions, whether within any one group, abilities are sufficiently differentiated to show superior performance in one set of cognitive abilities compared with any other – for example whether males have "overdeveloped" spatial skills compared to their verbal proficiency. Even more difficult to conceptualise are debates about scores derived from one generation to the next, accompanied by fears of a national decline in general ability or some specialised skill currently in demand. In the reviews offered in Part III of this volume, many such comparisons are mentioned, almost always on the basis of tests, but occasionally on the results from cognitive tasks, such as reaction times. To lend credibility to all of the studies that have purported to identify and evaluate ethnic differences might do science itself a disservice, but some have received notice in prestigious journals and are perhaps worthy of comment. We consider that comment reserved, for this debate has to be of a particularly circumscribed kind, after the specific delimitation of its worth described by Thoday (1969) in a paper that characterised it as unscientific. There has been no rebuttal of Thoday's position, which is that anyone who infers either genetic or environmental explanations for test performance is expressing an attitude, because measurements of performance do not permit logical inferences about the genetic or environmental causes of subspecies differences. Nevertheless, they do not preclude the formation of a belief system about the nature of intelligence.

Accepting Thoday's basic notion, that better science has to be a prerequisite of informed discussion, our comments take shape in describing the psychology of ethnic comparisons from the position that we have already developed, a taxonomy of data collection, and an evaluation of the cross-cultural work in three paradigms since 1960. We have some emphases to make, because a new dimension emerges from Part II of this book, which contains the current summation of approaches defining the field of modern individual differences. The discussion, in order to contribute to that perspective, now proceeds from an analysis of the concept of intelligence, through its operation in current instruments, to an evaluation of the enterprise. The metaphysics of ethnic assessment is defined in such a fashion.

The logic of constructs. Several years ago Irvine (1969a, 1969b) applied some of the ideas of Hare (1954) to the logic of the words *intelligence, ability,* and *skill.* He pointed out that to understand the theory of knowledge behind the use of such words was the first step towards their scientific appraisal as constructs. Irvine perceived them as belonging to the *logical* category of value words, such as *good* and *bad*; and that in order to understand what limitations were imposed upon people, even scientists, when they used them as constructs, one had to distinguish two ideas. One was the element of choice. Given the choice, people prefer intelligent, able, and skillful people to those who are not when work, a social phenomenon, is to be done. The other aspect of evaluative constructs is the need for consistency in choice when one commends instances of a certain class of action. One could not use the word *intelligent* logically if one adopted different criteria for commendation every time one made a choice that ostensively defined the word. Criteria across classes of activity are prescriptively different by use and wont. The ostensive behaviours for success in farming are not the same as those needed to judge hunters. Within categories, though, the commendations themselves must demonstrate consistency of choice. If one were inconsistent within categories, the notion of intelligence or skill would cease to have meaning because it could not be taught to a newcomer. Neither could it be taught if the same behaviours were commended irrespective of the kind of work to be done.

Even if its logical properties have not been fully used as a key to its understanding, the word *intelligence* itself has had many attempts at definition. Miles (1957) summarised their logical types admirably, but with little effect on measurement or theory. It does seem likely, however, that two persistent meanings of *intelligence* can be constructed. There is much evidence to show that different cultures agree on one definition of intelligence as a *dispositional quality* of alertness or "pricking up the ears" that, for example, the Shona of Zimbabwe (Hannan, 1974) carry into the word *ungwaru*, meaning "intelligent, sharp, prudent." This word itself derives from the ideophone *ngwa* – a basic attentional capacity in animals that is a universal. It may not be far away from Spearman's Victorian notion of mental energy, but the Shona express it in a sharply empirical but nonmechanistic way. That does not mean that the constructs are different, only that the law of cultural differentiation has prescribed the form of their description. *Ngwa* and *g* are interchangeable in their meaning, as necessary but not directly measurable constructs.

A second element in the definition of skills is by definition culturally differentiated, and is again captured by the Shona in the word *uchenjeri* meaning observed habits learned by experience, or *practical wisdom*. The differences in attentional capacity or alertness are recognised in all cultures: but the products or skills from which the existence of *g* or *ngwa* must be inferred are the interaction of that capacity with experiences formulated according to the needs and values of individual societies. Industrialists will learn skills different from those of farmers and hunters: and these in time will become habituated to what Ferguson calls "a crude level of stability." This meaning of intelligence has been called by Hebb (1949) "Intelligence B," the totality of learned strategies and skills that all tests have depended upon until now, at least when a sample of that experience is captured in a test score. The science of the Shona and of trained psychologists depends on two basic constructs: *g* or *ngwa*, and *practical wisdom* or *uchenjeri*. Psychologists must, however, make some use of these beyond the commonsense, ad hominem acceptance of their descriptive power, if a science is to first exist and then survive. Such attempts characterise the psychology of individual differences within and between ethnic groups.

Operational definition. In their epistemological heritage, there is nothing unique about the society of psychologists in their quest for measures of intelligence. They, too, recognise a fundamental alertness or attentional status that is the origin of all cognition in man; and they know that this structural legacy finds expression in the accumulated experience of a lifetime of learning, reinforcement, and extinction, the forces of habit that make skills fluent. The peculiarity of psychologists is their enduring belief that this alertness can largely be captured within and between *all* societies in instruments that have been developed in only *one* of them. There may be nothing very wrong with that notion as far as scientific measurement is concerned. Any tall building will do to derive the equation for falling bodies; a thermometer made in Switzerland will measure temperature in Fiji. But gravity and temperature are not in the same logical league as *good*, *bad*, or *intelligent* as value words. It is clear that gravity and temperature have nothing to learn from anyone before they can be measured. From what we know of value words, and the way that intelligence is measured, the application of identical scales of intelligence worldwide may be systematically misleading. From what crosscultural psychology has already demonstrated in its short life, such a practice could be analogous to asking industrialists to show how clever they are by tracking and hunting in frozen deserts. In extreme contrasts of context, the need to have developed fluent repertoires of learned skills that are locally congruent would censor the expression of *g* or *ngwa*. By such arguments the myth of the applicability of a single test context as a means of estimating the nature and amount of *ngwa* in mankind has to be seen as part of a metaphysical belief system that is a key to the understanding of the psychology of measuring ethnic differences.

If defence of this assertion is required, it will be found in every chapter in Part II that gives an account of measurement in Europe, Africa, Asia, or Australia. Constant reference is made to results on the *Wechsler Scales of Intelligence* (*WISC* and *WAIS*), or local adaptations of them, or some other measure such as *Raven's Progressive Matrices*, asserted to be *g* loaded. Much more often than one might hope, the scores from these and similar tests have been assumed to measure the same evaluative construct in any culture. These test forms seem to have been endowed with powers of forecasting intelligence that most Shona diviners (*ngangas*) would not dare to take unto themselves for fear of being accused of being a witch (*muroi*). The occupational psychology of this enterprise is easily described. Psychologists typically cite norms for the local population, and comparisons are made with the original IQ test standardisation. These sets of scores are then used as the basis for beliefs about relative gains or declines in intelligence, or specialised skills, within nations and across them.

The current ethos. The most compelling recent example of precisely this kind of work pattern is found in a long series about the "increase in IQ" in America and Japan, the cumulative references to which can be found in Flynn (1984). Briefly, on the basis of use of the *Wechsler Scales* in America and Japan, there was a long-drawn-out argument about the apparent score increases within cultures and between generations, within generations and across cultures, and, most extravagant of all, between generations across cultures. Even *Nature* found the controversy worthy of space for about seven years.

The difficulty of according credibility to such comparisons should now be obvious. Apart from the arguments advanced from the logic of constructs, time and again the empirical evidence confirms that cross-cultural transposition of items and tests is no guarantee of construct equivalence. Moreover, as Irvine (1983c) points out, transgeneration studies have no rationale to account for the use of identical items when confronted by social change within any one western culture. Berry's specification of the law of cultural differentiation requires that skills be construed as dynamic, adaptive functions. Changes in ecology may deliberately foster or make redundant elaborate algorithms for problem solution. Thus the tests of one culture, or of previous generations, are rendered invalid as indices of hypothetical constructs, but remain as cultural artifacts like discarded pottery.

For example, the decimalisation of the British currency made centuries of pedagogy devoted to fostering fluency in counting in different bases redundant within a generation. Before decimal currency, there were *4* farthings in a penny, *12* pence in a shilling, and *20* shillings in the pound. Such a system required division by three different bases to express money in pounds, shillings, and pence. Shopping, with no computerised tills, required attention and considerable practical wisdom that is assumed in the construction of Burt's (1917) tests of arithmetic, which are severe in their demands. Today's children do not have the overlearned skills that would allow them to be compared to those at school in 1917. One other illustration comes from this lack of computational strategies, induced by the use of calculators, in today's schoolchildren outside third world countries. It seems almost axiomatic that third world schoolchildren will soon be showing "superior" paper-and-pencil computational skills compared with Euramericans. The scientific value of the experiment that demonstrates this is dubious, and one could go on to amass good scientific reasons for eschewing such trivial comparisons, yet they persist.

Any of several reasons could be advanced for increases or decreases in performance between generations, many of them indefensible scientifically. Yet Flynn (1984, p. 200), in his response to Irvine's (1983c, 1983d) scientific critique of the practice of international and intergenerational comparisons of IQ scores, *believes* "in the reality of such gains despite the points raised." Flynn specifically makes it a matter of belief, whereas Irvine, and others, do not. They argue that the techniques for checking on the assumption of equivalence are already in place: and where circumstances prevent these checks, then no inference about intelligence or ability from test scores is possible. They ask for the kinds of checks on the equivalence of data sets in enclave research that has informed cross-cultural psychometrics, as a precondition of debate about any set of test scores, including IQs.

The fundamentalist canon. The most important mechanism of defence for belief by psychologists that IQ scores from different groups can be compared is *rationalisation*. This takes the form of interpreting the evidence for positive correlation among cognitive tasks, the Spearman law. The consistency with which this happens across cultures produces three assertions: first, the attentional capacity that is the universal force of mental life manifests itself in positive correlation, however faintly; and second, *ngwa* and *g* are particularly visible in the high intercorrelations of IQ tests and subtests. The second argument comes from a belief that one can distill the essence of this energy or *ngwa* from the correlations of IQ tests or tasks with each other. The third assertion is that the first attempt to reduce the matrix of IQ subtest correlations by the mathematical technique of factor analysis best represents that *ngwa*. This is variously called the "first principal factor," or, as Jensen and others would have us believe, *g* or general intelligence.

How much support is there for these assumptions? The most recent evidence from the analysis of correlations among tests has been provided by Carroll (1983). Carroll draws two conclusions from his reanalysis by standard procedures of the mass of data available within and across cultures. First, the evidence calls not for one general factor, but six or seven. He labels these *fluid intelligence, crystallised intelligence, visual perception, auditory perception, speed, idea production,* and *memory capacity.* All are generalisable families of skills at crude levels of stability. Next, he dismisses any notion that a principal factor, as the first attempt to reduce a matrix to its component variance, can everywhere be a measure of *g* or *ngwa.* The first attempt to reduce a matrix to its determinants is nothing more than a mathematically contrived summary of whatever variance happens to be contained in any set of measures; and like all summaries, it may be incomplete, and it may be distorted.

These conclusions are very important because their widespread acceptance by most theorists today limits claims that are made for the measurement of *g* or indeed any other construct defined wholly by a correlation matrix. Now we come to the second line of rationalisation that counts as a defence of the present practice of intergroup comparisons. This is captured in the assertion that although all intellectual activities presuppose *g*, some tasks are simpler or purer than others and actually measure *g* itself. These are held to be ultra-valid measures of intelligence. Moreover, some, including reaction time measures and clicks in the ear, obviously do not involve problem solving, as traditional IQ tests most assuredly do. These tasks, applied across ethnic groups, would allow psychologists to make inferences about intelligence levels in ways that traditional IQ tests might prohibit, provided that they can be said to demonstrate substantial common variance with these test scores.

"Simple" and "meaningless" measures of intelligence. This position is carefully documented by Jensen. His work on measures of intelligence and choice reaction times makes two primary assumptions. First, that analysis of IQ accuracy and speed scores yields one general factor that is a mathematical expression of *g*, and that reaction times are simpler forms of the same *g*. A secondary assumption is that these measures are invariant in their properties in different ethnic groups, permitting judgments about the relative levels of *g* or *ngwa* in such groups. The evidence from those who have carried out research in nonwestern groups has already been documented in the section on information-processing models, but critiques of Jensen's work on choice reaction times are available. In particular, Carroll (1980) showed conclusively that choice reaction time tasks are far from simple in their cognitive demands; next, Rabbitt (1985) finds much to take exception to, in method and inference, while Poortinga (1985), particularly objects to claims by Jensen (see Chapter 4) that his African studies support Jensen's claims to have measured *g* equitably in whites and blacks by using choice reaction time measures. Finally, the latest large-scale domain study of simple and choice reaction times (Fairbank et al., 1984) in male samples, shows that the magnitude of Jensen's reported correlations with IQ scores can not be replicated. They are, as they have always been, below .3.

The conclusion is plain. Theory does not support, even in the most meaningless of tasks, the assumption of stimulus equivalence that is a necessary precondition of such research. Next, present work on the structure of correlation matrices denies Jensen the assurance he seeks from the first general factor that this is an invariant expression of *g* whatever the context. Finally, choice reaction times are neither pure nor simple measures of general intelligence. The fact that they correlate slightly with such measures does not mean that they measure intelligence, or that the variance they have in common with IQ scores is a function of it.

Unconscious manifestations of g. Work originating in Eysenck's laboratory, and published by A. E. Hendrickson (1982) and D. E. Hendrickson (1982) reports correlations between IQ and averaged auditory evoked potentials (AEPs) of .7. Eysenck himself speaks to these findings in Chapter 3. He would be the first to agree that the empirical findings require replication in a context in which Hendrickson herself has not clinically determined the final shape of the evoked potential wave (a point made by Irvine 1983b). There have been no claims to be able to reproduce this very large correlation using computerised wave-forms. Next, the very meaninglessness of the original stimulus, a click, should not hide the fact that the dependent variable (AEP) is claimed to be as meaningful as the IQ measure itself. If this is so, then the stimulus has undergone a remarkable *unconscious* internal reformulation by the subject that encapsulates all the *conscious* mental effort expended on solving IQ problems.

Because it is not under conscious control, such a reformulation cannot then be said to be culture or value free, any more than the unconscious efforts of the Kpelle to capture the orderliness of dots in arrays could be said to be culture free; or the meaning attributed to ambiguous line drawings could be said to be nonspecific; or the meaning attached to sounds and lights could be said to be identical over all African groups. The problem of interpreting the Hendrikson findings is that they are too close to IQ measures to be regarded as any more fundamental, or closer, to the nucleus of *g* than conventional measures. They appear to have variance in common with them, but why they do is uncertain, especially as the theory of pulse-train transmission of information (put forward by Hendrikson, and apparently congenial to Eysenck [see Chapter 3]) is challenged by one that sees mobilisation of energy as the critical factor (Jervis, Nichols, Johnson, Allen, & Hudson, 1983; Jervis, Allen, Johnson, Nichols, & Hudson, 1984) in producing the wave form of the AEP. If that position is vindicated, mental energy and *ngwa* will suffice as constructs, but its mobilisation cannot be seen to be a "simple" matter of physiology and hence of genetics. There is no *hence* in the argument at all, because the mobilisation of mental energy in any context is a function of the perceived cues of that context, or the meaning that the brain supplies to the stimulus. Whenever meaning is involved, experience, or *uchenjeri*, has to account for human variation, as well as the inherited neurological fitness of the system.

The motivation of theory. The psychology of the persistence of a fundamentalist position may be determined from the high emotionality that colours
much of the writings of those associated with it. It has to be seen as a
sectarian belief system, a caste of mind, somewhat authoritarian in its stance,
with a basic defence mechanism first of *rationalisation*. Then, under severe
attack, the defence mechanism is *denial* that critics have made relevant or
even positive contributions to the study of intelligence or ability. It is also
highly selective in the attention it gives to proponents and opponents. In
fact, it resembles closely those who oppose the fundamentalist position as
strongly as it does those who support it.

A scientific position

This chapter proposes something quite different. It will be accepted by neither of the entrenched schools of ability measurement, fundamentalists or
radical environmentalists. Within a prescriptive frame of reference, we recognise the strengths and the weaknesses of psychometric, piagetian, and
information-processing approaches to measurement. By itself, each paradigm is insecure as a foundation for a scientific universe of discourse. Our
taxonomy emphasises how many different categories of data are essential
for the analysis of individual differences, and by implication, how many are
uncharted. Most of the time, argument about human abilities proceeds as if
the data types were veridical and identical in their potential for causal attribution. The contribution of cross-cultural psychology to the study of the
abilities of mankind lies in refusing, for sound empirical and logical reasons,
to accept any database that has not first undergone all the construct validity
checks that are possible to carry out on it. If data is collected in such a way
as to preclude or inhibit the prior exercise of item-bias statistics, or confirmatory factor analysis, or full examination of the type of analysis of variance in quasi-experimental studies, then no inference from it is logically
possible when group test performance is brought into the task of theory
construction.

Much published material on the abilities of mankind has a long way to go
before it can be valuable for theory construction. The pages that follow
ostensively define the limits of the inferences that can be made from the
world-wide export of western families of cognitive measures. Uncritical test
use may portend little more than an expedient borrowing of western technology and ideas about the way that mental life ought to be constructed.
The tenacity of indigenous cognition, about which so little is known, and
even less is understood, suggests that our ideas may be temporary. This
much, however, is clear: The basic ability dimensions of mankind are capable of description from the material to hand. There are, nevertheless,
persistent cultural differences in performance in Euramerican tests and tasks
that are empirical legacies from decades of work. The cultural differences
that encompass these results are real, but they are imprecisely captured for

the construction of a universal psychology of individual differences by the use of western artifacts.

The law of cultural differentiation, in its moderate form, is supported by the application of the logic of value constructs to the meanings of intelligence. Because the content of intelligent acts is transferred from one generation to the next in cultural context, the measurement of any inferred disposition by performance in any one form of task is likely to be invalidated by a series of intervening variables, any one of which may have causal properties. The conclusion is plain: The maintenance of Euramerican measures of intellect in standard form has restricted, more often than not, the development of valid measures of cognitive functions in exotic contexts.

The pages that follow increase our understanding of the constructs we might need in order to measure human abilities in cultural context. Given these constructs and others, psychologists may yet determine those cognitive differences that enrich our understanding of the human condition. But they should, perhaps, never again measure abilities in quite the same way as the collection of work in this volume describes. If the errors of the past are repeated, not only will this attempt at revaluation have failed, but differential psychology may forfeit its claim to be a cognitive science.

References

Andor, L. E. (1983). *Psychological and sociological studies of the black people of Africa, south of the Sahara*. Johannesburg: National Institute for Personnel Research.

Bagby, J. (1957). A cross-cultural study of perceptual predominance in binocular rivalry. *Journal of Abnormal and Social Psychology, 54*, 311–334.

Bali, S. K., Drenth, P. J. D., van der Flier, H., & Young, W. C. (1984). *Contribution of aptitude tests to the prediction of school performance in Kenya: A longitudinal study*. Lisse: Swets & Zeitlinger.

Berry, J. W. (1966). Temne and Eskimo perceptual skills. *International Journal of Psychology, 1*, 207–229.

Berry, J. W. (1969). Ecology and socialisation as factors in figural assimilation and the resolution of binocular rivalry. *International Journal of Psychology, 4*, 271–280.

Berry, J. W. (1971). Ecological and cultural factors in spatial perceptual development. *Canadian Journal of Behavioural Science, 3*, 324–336.

Berry, J. W. (1972). Radical cultural relativism and the concept of intelligence. In L. J. Cronbach & P. J. D. Drenth (Eds.), *Mental tests and cultural adaptation*. The Hague: Mouton.

Berry, J. W. (1976). *Human ecology and cognitive style*. New York: Sage-Halsted.

Berry, J. W. (1980). Ecological analyses for cross-cultural psychology. In N. Warren (Ed.), *Studies in cross-cultural psychology* (Vol. 2). New York: Academic Press.

Berry, J. W. (1984). Cultural relativism comes in from the cold. *The Behavioral and Brain Sciences, 7*, 288.

Berry, J. W. (1987). The comparative study of cognitive abilities. In S. H. Irvine & S. E. Newstead (Eds.), *Intelligence and cognition: Contemporary frames of reference*. Dordrecht: Nijhoff.

Berry, J. W., & Irvine, S. H. (1986). Bricolage: Savages do it daily. In R. J. Sternberg & R. K. Wagner (Eds.), *Practical intelligence: Origins of competence in the everyday world*. Cambridge University Press.

Bhatia, C. M. (1955). *Performance tests of intelligence under Indian conditions*. London: Oxford University Press.

Biesheuvel, S. (1943). *African intelligence*. Johannesburg: South African Institute of Race Relations.

Biesheuvel, S. (1952). Personnel selection tests for Africans. *South African Journal of Science, 49*, 3–12.

Biesheuvel, S. (1954). The measurement of occupational aptitudes in a multiracial society. *Occupational Psychology, 28*, 189–196.

Born, M. (1984). *Cross-cultural comparison of sex-related differences in intelligence tests: A meta-analysis*. Unpublished doctoral dissertation, Free University, Amsterdam.

Bovet, M. C. (1968). Etudes interculturelles de développement intellectuel et processus d'apprentissage. *Revue Suisse de Psychologie Pure et Appliquée, 27*, 190–199.

Bovet, M. C. (1981). Cognitive mechanisms and training. In M. P. Friedman, J. P. Das, & N. O'Connor (Eds.), *Intelligence and learning*. New York: Plenum.

Brand, C. R., & Deary, I. J. (1982). Intelligence and "inspection time." In H. J. Eysenck (Ed.), *A model for intelligence*. New York: Springer-Verlag.

Brislin, R. (1974). The Ponzo illusion: Additional cues; age, orientation and culture. *Journal of Cross-Cultural Psychology, 5*, 139–161.

Brislin, R. (1983). Cross-cultural psychology. *Annual Review of Psychology, 34*, 363–400.

Bryant, P. E. (1974). *Perception and understanding in young children*. London: Methuen.

Bryant, P. E. (1981). Training and logic: Comment on Magali Bovet's paper. In M. P. Friedman, J. P. Das, & N. O'Connor (Eds.), *Intelligence and learning*. New York: Plenum.

Burt, C. (1917). *The distribution and relations of educational abilities*. London: Report of the London County Council.

Butterfield, E. C. (1981). Testing process theories of intelligence. In M. P. Friedman, J. P. Das, & N. O'Connor (Eds.), *Intelligence and learning*. New York: Plenum.

Carroll, J. B. (1976). Psychometric tests as cognitive tasks: A new "Structure of Intellect." In L. B. Resnick (Ed.), *The nature of intelligence*. Hillsdale, NJ: Erlbaum.

Carroll, J. B. (1980). *Individual difference relations in psychometric and experimental cognitive tasks* (Report No. 163). Thurstone Psychometric Laboratory, University of North Carolina, Chapel Hill.

Carroll, J. B. (1983). Studying individual differences in cognitive abilities: Implications for cross-cultural studies. In S. H. Irvine & J. W. Berry (Eds.), *Human assessment and cultural factors*. New York: Plenum.

Cattell, R. B. (1971). *Abilities: Their structure, growth, and action*. Boston: Houghton Mifflin.

Chung, M. R. (1983). An examination of cognitive performance by children from contrasting social and educational backgrounds. In J. B. Deregowski, S. Dziurawiec, & R. W. Annis (Eds). *Expiscations in cross-cultural psychology*. Lisse: Swets & Zeitlinger.

Cole, M. (1975). An ethnographic psychology of cognition. In R. Brislin, S. Bochner, & W. Lonner (Eds.), *Cross-cultural perspectives on learning*. Beverly Hills, CA: Sage.

Cole, M., Gay, J., & Glick, J. (1968). A cross-cultural investigation of information processing. *International Journal of Psychology, 3*, 93–102.

Cole, M., & Scribner, S. (1975). *Culture and thought*. New York: Wiley.

Cole, M., & Scribner, S. (1982). On the status of developmental theories in cross-cultural psychology. In L. L. Adler (Ed.), *Cross-cultural research at issue*. New York: Academic Press.

Cronbach, L. J. (1957). The two disciplines of scientific psychology. *American Psychologist, 12*, 671–684.

Dasen, P. R. (1972a). Cross-cultural Piagetian research: A summary. *Journal of Cross-Cultural Psychology, 3*, 23–29.

Dasen, P. R. (1972b). The development of conservation in Aboriginal children. *International Journal of Psychology, 7*, 75–85.

Dasen, P. R. (1983). Commentary. In J. B. Deregowski, S. Dziurawiec, & R. Annis (Eds.), *Expiscations in cross-cultural psychology*. Lisse: Swets & Zeitlinger.

Dasen, P. R. (1984). The cross-cultural study of intelligence: Piaget and the Baoulé. *International Journal of Psychology, 19*, 107–134.

Dasen, P. R., & Heron, A. (1981). Cross-cultural tests of Piaget's theory. In H. C. Triandis & A. Heron (Eds.), *Handbook of cross-cultural psychology* (Vol. 4, Chap. 7). Boston: Allyn & Bacon.

Dasen, P. R., Lavallée, M., & Retschitzki, J. (1979). Training conservation of quantity (liquids) in West African (Baoulé) children. *International Journal of Psychology, 14,* 69–82.

Dasen, P. R., Ngini, L., & Lavallée, M. (1979). Cross-cultural training studies of concrete operations. In L. Eckensberger, W. Lonner, & Y. Poortinga (Eds.), *Cross-cultural contributions to psychology.* Lisse: Swets & Zeitlinger.

De Lemos, M. M. (1969). The development of conservation in Aboriginal children. *International Journal of Psychology, 4,* 255–269.

Drenth, P. J. D., van der Flier, H., & Omari, I. M. (1983). Educational selection in Tanzania. *Evaluation in Education, 7,* 95–209.

Eysenck, H. J. (Ed.) (1982). *A model for intelligence.* New York: Springer-Verlag.

Fairbank, B., Tirre, W., & Anderson, M. (1984). Measures of thirty cognitive tasks. In S. E. Newstead, S. H. Irvine, & P. L. Dann (Eds.), *Human assessment: Cognition and motivation.* Dordrecht: Nijhoff.

Ferguson, G. A. (1954). On learning and human ability. *Canadian Journal of Psychology, 8,* 95–112.

Ferguson, G. A. (1956). On transfer and the abilities of man. *Canadian Journal of Psychology, 10,* 121–131.

Fick, M. L. (1939). *The educability of the South African native* (Research Series, No. 8). Pretoria: South African Council for Educational and Social Research.

Flynn, J. R. (1982). Lynn, the Japanese, and environmentalism. *Bulletin of the British Psychological Society, 35,* 409–413.

Flynn, J. R. (1984). Japanese IQ. *Bulletin of the British Psychological Society, 37,* 200.

Friedman, M., Das, J. P., & O'Connor, N. (1981). *Intelligence and learning.* New York: Plenum.

Gluckman, M. (1944). The logic of African science and witchcraft. *Rhodes–Livingstone Institute Journal, 1,* 61–71.

Greenfield, P. M. (1966). On culture and conservation. In J. S. Bruner, R. R. Olver, & P. M. Greenfield (Eds.), *Studies in cognitive growth* (pp. 225–256). New York: Wiley.

Greenfield, P. M. (1979). Response to "Wolof 'magical thinking': Culture and conservation revisited," by Judith T. Irvine. *Journal of Cross-Cultural Psychology, 10,* 251–256.

Guilford, J. P. (1959). Three faces of intellect. *American Psychologist, 14,* 469–479.

Guilford, J. P. (1967). *The nature of human intelligence.* New York: McGraw-Hill.

Hambleton, R. K., & Swaminathan, H. (1985). *Item response theory.* Boston: Kluwer Nijhoff.

Hamutyeni, M. A., & Plangger, A. B. (1974). *Tsumo-shumo: Shona proverbial lore and wisdom.* Harare, Zimbabwe: Mambo Press.

Hannan, M. (1974). *Standard Shona dictionary.* Harare: Zimbabwe Literature Bureau.

Hare, R. M. (1954). *The language of morals.* London: Oxford University Press.

Hebb, D. O. (1949). *The organisation of behaviour.* New York: Wiley.

Hendrickson, A. E. (1982). The biological basis of intelligence. Part 1: Theory. In H. J. Eysenck (Ed.), *A model for intelligence.* New York: Springer-Verlag.

Hendrickson, D. E. (1982). The biological basis of intelligence. Part 2: Measurement. In H. J. Eysenck (Ed.), *A model for intelligence.* New York: Springer-Verlag.

Heron, A. (1971). Concrete operations, *g* and achievement in Zambian children. *Journal of Cross-Cultural Psychology, 2,* 325–336.

Heron, A., & Dowel, W. (1973). Weight conservation and matrix-solving ability in Papuan children. *Journal of Cross-Cultural Psychology, 4,* 207–219.

Heron, A., & Simonsson, M. (1969). Weight conservation in Zambian Children: A non-verbal approach. *International Journal of Psychology, 4,* 281–292.

Holleman, J. F. (1952). *Shona customary law.* Cape Town: Oxford University Press.

Hui, C. H., & Triandis, H. (1985). Measurement in cross-cultural psychology. *Journal of Cross-Cultural Psychology, 16,* 131–152.

Human Sciences Research Council. (1974). *Manual for the academic aptitude test (Form V) (AAT). Pretoria:* Human Sciences Research Council.

Humphriss, D., & Wortley, W. (1971). Two studies in visual acuity. *Psychologia Africana, 14,* 1–19.

Irvine, Judith. (1978). Wolof "magical thinking": Culture and conservation revisited. *Journal of Cross-Cultural Psychology, 9,* 300–310.

Irvine, S. H. (1965). Adapting tests to the cultural setting: A comment. *Occupational Psychology, 39,* 12–23.

Irvine, S. H. (1966). Towards a rationale for testing abilities and attainments in Africa. *British Journal of Educational Psychology, 36,* 24–32.

Irvine, S. H. (1969a). The factor analysis of African abilities and attainments: Constructs across cultures. *Psychological Bulletin, 71,* 20–32.

Irvine, S. H. (1969b). Figural tests of reasoning in Africa: Studies in the use of Raven's Progressive Matrices across cultures. *International Journal of Psychology, 4,* 217–228.

Irvine, S. H. (1970). Affect and construct: A cross-cultural check on theories of intelligence. *Journal of Social Psychology, 80,* 23–30.

Irvine, S. H. (1973). Tests as inadvertent sources of discrimination in personnel decisions. In P. Watson (Ed.), *Psychology and race.* London: Penguin.

Irvine, S. H. (1979). The place of factor analysis in cross-cultural methodology and its contribution to cognitive theory. In L. H. Eckensberger, W. H. Lonner, & Y. H. Poortinga (Eds.), *Cross-cultural contributions to psychology.* Lisse: Swets & Zeitlinger.

Irvine, S. H. (1983a). Cross-cultural conservation studies at the asymptote: Striking out against the curve? In S. & C. Modgil & G. Brown (Eds.), *Jean Piaget, an interdisciplinary critique.* London: Routledge.

Irvine, S. H. (1983b). Testing in Africa and America: The search for routes. In S. H. Irvine & J. W. Berry (Eds.), *Human assessment and cultural factors.* New York: Plenum.

Irvine, S. H. (1983c). Where intelligence tests fail. *Nature, 302,* 371.

Irvine, S. H. (1983d). Lynn, the Japanese and environmentalism: A response. *Bulletin of the British Psychological Society, 36,* 55–56.

Irvine, S. H. (1983e). Has Eysenck removed the bottleneck in IQ? (Essay review of H. J. Eysenck [Ed.], *A model for intelligence.* New York: Springer-Verlag, 1982). *New Scientist, 99,* 121–122.

Irvine, S. H. (1984). The contexts of triarchic theory. *The Behavioral and Brain Sciences, 7,* 293–294.

Irvine, S. H. (1986). Cross-cultural assessment: From practice to theory. In W. Lonner & J. W. Berry (Eds.), *Methods in cross-cultural psychology.* New York: Sage.

Irvine, S. H., & Berry, J. W. (Eds.). (1983). *Human assessment and cultural factors.* New York: Plenum.

Irvine, S. H., & Carroll, W. K. (1980). Testing and assessment across cultures. In H. C. Triandis & J. W. Berry (Eds.), *Handbook of cross-cultural psychology* (Vol. 2, chap. 5). Boston: Allyn & Bacon.

Jencks, C. (1972). *Inequality: A reassessment of the effect of family and schooling in America.* New York: Basic.

Jensen, A. R. (1982). Reaction time and psychometric *g.* In H. J. Eysenck (Ed.), *A model for intelligence.* New York: Springer-Verlag.

Jensen, A. R. (1985). The nature of the black–white difference on various psychometric tests: Spearman's Hypothesis. *The Behavioral and Brain Sciences, 8,* 193–219.

Jervis, B., Allen, E., Johnson, T., Nichols, M., & Hudson, N. (1984). The application of pattern recognition techniques to the contingent negative variation for the differentiation of subject categories. *IEEE Transactions on Biomedical Engineering, BME-31,* 342–349.

Jervis, B., Nichols, M., Johnson, T., Allen, E., & Hudson, N. (1983). A fundamental investigation of the composition of auditory evoked potentials. *IEEE Transactions on Biomedical Engineering, BME-30,* 43–50.

Kail, R., & Pellegrino, J. W. (1985). *Human intelligence: Perspectives and prospects.* New York: Freeman.

Keats, D. M., & Keats, J. A. (1974). The effect of language on concept acquisition in bilingual children. *Journal of Cross-Cultural Psychology, 5,* 80–99.

Keats, D. M., Keats, J. A., & Liu, F. (1982). The language and thinking relationship in bilingual Chinese children. *The Australian Journal of Chinese Affairs, 7,* 125–135.

Keats, D. M., Keats, J. A., & Wan Rafei, A. R. (1976). Concept acquisition in bilingual Malaysian children. *Journal of Cross-Cultural Psychology, 7,* 87–99.

Klingelhofer, E. (1967). Performance of Tanzania secondary school pupils on the Raven Standard Progressive Matrices Test. *Journal of Social Psychology, 72,* 205–215.

Knight, R. (1946). *Intelligence and intelligence tests.* London: Methuen.

Lloyd, B. B. (1971). The intellectual development of Yoruba children: A re-examination. *Journal of Cross-Cultural Psychology, 2,* 29–38.

Lloyd, F., & Pidgeon, D. A. (1961). An investigation into the effects of coaching on nonverbal test material with European, Indian and African children. *British Journal of Educational Psychology, 31,* 145–151.

Loney, S. L. (1890). *The elements of statics and dynamics.* London: Macmillan.

Loram, C. T. (1917). *The education of the South African native.* London: Longmans.

Lynn, R. (1982). IQ in Japan and the United States shows a growing disparity. *Nature, 297,* 222–223.

MacArthur, R. S., Irvine, S. H., & Brimble, A. R. (1964). *The Northern Rhodesia mental abilities survey.* Lusaka, Zambia: Rhodes–Livingstone Institute for Social Research.

Macdonald, A. (1945). *Selection of African personnel.* Report of the Personnel and Technical Research Unit, Middle East Force. London: Ministry of Defence Archives.

McFie, J. (1961). The effect of education on African performance on a group of intellectual tests. *British Journal of Educational Psychology, 31,* 232–240.

Malpass, R. (1977). Theory and method in cross-cultural psychology. *American Psychologist, 32,* 1069–1079.

Marmorale, A. M., & Brown, F. (1982). Constancy of WISC IQs of Puerto Rican, white and black children. In L. L. Adler (Ed.), *Cross-cultural research at issue.* New York: Academic Press.

Miles, R. T. (1957). Contributions to intelligence testing and the theory of intelligence. 1. On defining intelligence. *British Journal of Educational Psychology, 27,* 153–165.

Miner, H. (1956). Body ritual among the Nacirema. *American Anthropologist, 58,* 503–507.

Mitchell, J. C. (1956). *The Kalela Dance.* Manchester: Manchester University Press.

Nissen, H. W., Machover, S., & Kinder, B. F. (1935). A study of performance tests given to a group of native African children. *British Journal of Psychology, 25,* 308–355.

Oliver, R. A. C. (1932). The comparison of the abilities of races with special reference to East Africa. *East African Medical Journal, 9,* 160–204.

Oliver, R. A. C. (1933). The adaptation of intelligence tests to tropical Africa, Parts 1 & 2. *Overseas Education, 4,* 186–191; *5,* 8–13.

Oliver, R. A. C. (1934). Mental tests in the study of the African. *Africa, 7,* 40–46.

Ord, I. G. (1971). *Mental tests for preliterates.* London: Ginn.

Ord, I. G. (1972). Tests for educational and occupational selection in developing countries. *Occupational Psychology, 46,* Pt. 3 (Whole Number).

Piaget, J. (1926). *The language and thought of the child* (Marjorie Worden Trans.). New York: Harcourt Brace.

Piaget, J. (1950). *The psychology of intelligence* (M. Piercy & D. E. Berlyne, Trans.) London: Routledge & Kegan Paul.

Piaget, J. (1966). The need and significance of cross-cultural studies in genetic psychology. *International Journal of Psychology, 1,* 3–13.

Poortinga, Y. H. (1971). Cross-cultural comparison of maximum performance tests: Some methodological aspects and some experiments with simple auditory stimuli. *Psychologia Africana, Monograph Supplement No. 6,* 1–100.

Poortinga, Y. H. (1985). Empirical evidence of bias in choice-reaction time experiments. *The Behavioral and Brain Sciences, 8,* 236–237.

Rabbitt, P. M. A. (1985). Oh *g* Dr. Jensen! or, *g*-ing up cognitive psychology. *The Behavioral and Brain Sciences, 8,* 238–239.

Resnick, L. B. (Ed.). (1976). *The nature of intelligence*. Hillsdale, NJ: Erlbaum.

Reuning, H., & Wortley, W. (1973). Psychological studies of the Bushmen. *Psychologia Africana, Monograph Supplement No. 7*, 1–113.

Samuda, R. J. (1975). *Psychological testing of American minorities*. New York: Harper & Row.

Scribner, S. (1974). Developmental aspects of free recall. *Cognitive Psychology, 6*, 475–494.

Segall, M. H., Campbell, D. T., & Herskovits, M. J. (1963). Cultural differences in the perception of geometric illusions. *Science, 139*, 769–771.

Segall, M. H., Campbell, D. T., & Herskovits, M. J. (1966). *The influence of culture on visual perception*. Indianapolis: Bobbs-Merrill.

Silvey, J. (1963). Aptitude testing and educational selection in Africa. *Rhodes–Livingstone Institute Journal, 34*, 9–22.

Spearman, C. (1904). "General Intelligence," objectively determined and measured. *American Journal of Psychology, 15*, 201–293.

Spearman, C. (1927). *The abilities of man*. London: Macmillan.

Stephenson, W. (1981). Sir Cyril Burt [Letter to the editor]. *Bulletin of the British Psychological Society, 34*, 284.

Sternberg, R. J. (1977). *Intelligence, information processing, and analogical reasoning: The componential analysis of human abilities*. Hillsdale, NJ: Erlbaum.

Sternberg, R. J. (1985a). *Beyond IQ: A triarchic theory of human intelligence*. Cambridge University Press.

Sternberg, R. J. (Ed.). (1985b). *Human abilities: An information-processing approach*. New York: Freeman.

Sternberg, R. J., & Gardner, M. K. (1982). A componential interpretation of the general factor in human intelligence. In H. J. Eysenck (Ed.), *A model for intelligence*. New York: Springer-Verlag.

Stewart, V. M. (1973). Tests of the "carpentered world" hypothesis by race and environment in America and Zambia. *International Journal of Psychology, 8*, 83–94.

Taylor, T. R. (1974). A factor analysis of 21 illusions: The implications for theory. *Psychologia Africana, 15*, 137–148.

Thoday, J. M. (1969). Limits to genetic comparison of populations. *Journal of Biosocial Science Supplement, 1*, 3–14.

Thomson, G. H. (1951). *The factorial analysis of human ability* (5th ed.). London: University of London Press.

Thurstone, L. L. (1938). Primary mental abilities. *Psychometric Monographs, No. 1*.

Vernon, P. A. (1983). Speed of information processing and general intelligence. *Intelligence, 7*, 53–70.

Vernon, P. E. (Ed.). (1957). *Secondary school selection: A British Psychological Society enquiry*. London: Methuen.

Verster, J. M. (1983). The structure, organisation and correlates of cognitive speed and accuracy. In S. H. Irvine & J. W. Berry (Eds.), *Human assessment and cultural factors*. New York: Plenum.

Verster, M. A. (1973). *The effects of mining experience and multiple test exposure on performance on the Classification Test Battery*. Johannesburg: National Institute for Personnel Research.

Verster, M. A. (1976). *The effects of mining experience and multiple test exposure on test performance of Black mineworkers*. Unpublished master's dissertation, University of South Africa, Pretoria.

White, P. O. (1982). Some major components in general intelligence. In H. J. Eysenck (Ed.), *A model for intelligence*. New York: Springer-Verlag.

Winter, W. (1967). Size constancy, relative size estimation and background: A cross-cultural study. *Psychologia Africana, 12*, 42–58.

Woodworth, R. S. (1940). *Psychology*, London: Methuen.

2   A triarchic view of intelligence in cross-cultural perspective

Robert J. Sternberg

The time is 8:00 A.M. The place is Guayana Ciudad, Venezuela. An important inter-American meeting on intelligence and its improvement is scheduled to begin. Close to 100 people should be in the room. In fact, only a handful are there. The handful is not a random sample of the scholars invited to attend the meeting. To the contrary, it constitutes the North American contingent at the meeting. None of the South or Central Americans have arrived. After about a half-hour, the others start to trickle in slowly, but it is not until almost two hours have passed that the meetings truly get under way. By the end of the series of meetings, no one arrives at the scheduled time when a given meeting is to begin. Learning has taken place: The North Americans have learned not to arrive on time. More generally, they have learned something about adaptive behavior in Venezuela. And more importantly for them, they have learned that in Venezuela, it is often, in some sense, unintelligent to arrive at a time when a meeting is scheduled to begin, unless one wishes to kill time.

The North American investigators are surprised: The adult Kpelle tribesmen seem unable to sort nouns taxonomically. Rather, they sort them functionally, the way children would in the western world. Moreover, the tribesmen resist hints that should lead them to sort taxonomically. Evidence, perhaps, for the intellectual superiority of North Americans and Europeans over the African tribesmen? It would appear so. But then, in desperation, one of the investigators asks the Kpelle to sort the way stupid people would. The Kpelle then have no trouble at all sorting taxonomically (Cole, Gay, Glick, & Sharp, 1971). The lesson: The Kpelle lacked not "intelligence" but *the Western notion of intelligence* that would have led them to sort taxonomically.

Of course, it would be nice and simple if there were an "African" view of intelligence, a "South American" view, and a "North American" view. But no such luck: People from two tribes, the Baganda and the Batoro, are asked to fill out a semantic differential form regarding their conceptions of adjectives describing intelligence. The Baganda associate intelligence with mental order, whereas the Batoro associate it with mental turmoil – diametrically opposed points of view (Wober, 1974). The lesson: There is no one African view of intelligence, any more than there is any one North

60

American view. Perhaps there is no one African intelligence, or North American intelligence, for that matter.

The vignettes described above are merely illustrative of the quicksand pit that readily engages one upon attempting to study intelligence cross-culturally. The simplicities one can so easily accept in a single culture defy acceptance when one seeks to study and understand intelligence cross-culturally. More importantly, such study inevitably raises the theorist's awareness of the limitations of theories of intelligence that, proposed in a single sociocultural context, are immediately and unselfconsciously assumed to be applicable to everyone, everywhere. For the most part, they are not.

Just what is the relation of intelligence to culture, and the range of views regarding it? The remainder of this chapter will address this question. First, I will sketch some of the range of the alternative positions that have been taken. Second, I will present a framework for characterising these and other positions, attempting to specify just what it might be that could vary cross-culturally, if anything. Third, I will describe my own triarchic theory of human intelligence and show how this theory relates both to the other positions discussed in the first section, and to the framework presented in the second section. Finally, I will summarise the main conclusions to be drawn from the chapter.

The range of positions relating intelligence to culture

Positions on the relation of intelligence to culture have varied considerably. At one extreme are individuals who have claimed that intelligence can be an entirely different concept as a function of culture. At the other extreme are individuals who have claimed that intelligence is exactly the same thing, regardless of culture.

At one extreme, Berry (1974) has taken a position he refers to as "radical cultural relativism." This "position requires that indigenous notions of cognitive competence be the sole basis for the generation of cross-culturally valid descriptions and assessments of cognitive capacity" (p. 225). According to this view, then, intelligence must be defined in a way appropriate to the contexts in which the people of each particular culture reside. From an anthropological perspective, such a viewpoint might be characterised as fully "emic." From another (see Chapter 1), it may be a *reductio ad absurdum* forbidding any comparisons of performance across cultures.

The members of the Laboratory of Comparative Human Cognition (1982) have asserted that the radical cultural relativist position does not take into account the fact that cultures interact. According to their view, it is possible to make a kind of "conditional comparison," in which the investigator sees how different cultures have organised experience to deal with a single domain of activity. This comparison is possible, however, only if the investigator is in a position to assert that performance of the task or tasks under investigation is a universal kind of achievement, and if the investigator has a developmental theory of performance in the task domain. This position thus asserts that certain conditional kinds of comparisons are possible in the domain of intelligence.

Still less "radical" is the position of Charlesworth (1979a, 1979b), whose "ethological" approach to studying intelligence has focussed upon "intelligent behavior as it occurs in everyday, rather than test, situations – and how these situations may be related to changes in it over ontogenesis" (Charlesworth, 1979a, p. 212). Charlesworth distinguishes between intelligence of the kind that has been studied by psychometricians and intelligence of the kind that is of particular survival or adaptive value. He believes it necessary to concentrate on the latter kind of intelligence, especially because "test psychologists generally view test performance as a way of indexing the individual's adaptive potential, but take virtually no cognizance of the environmental conditions which tap this potential and influence its expression over ontogenesis" (p. 212).

Less radical is the position of contextualists such as Keating (1984) and Baltes, Dittmann-Kohli, and Dixon (1982), who have combined contextual positions with more or less standard kinds of psychological research and experimentation. For example, Baltes has conducted fairly standard psychometric research (Baltes & Willis, 1979, 1982), but has combined this research with a contextual position on it. Of course, not all contextualists are as optimistic as Baltes regarding the reconcilability of contextual and psychometric kinds of theorizing (see Labouvie-Vief & Chandler, 1978).

Irvine (1979; see also Irvine, 1983a) has elaborated this kind of position by specifying more exactly how factor analysis can be used in the cross-cultural analysis of intelligence. In particular, he has suggested that differences in factor structures across cultures can be understood in terms of three classes of explanation. According to Irvine, *intra-hominem* explanations trace differences in factor structures to individual or group differences in people's ways of understanding and ordering experience. Information is not processed differently from one culture to another, but the interpretation placed upon that information may differ considerably from one culture to another. *Extra-hominem* explanations attribute differences in factor structures to the influences of environmental context. On this view, the environment shapes cognition, and may structure it differently for different peoples. *Inter-hominem* explanations focus on differences in social interactions and communication as the source of factorial differences. Thus, the emphasis is on neither the individual nor the environment, but rather on the interactions between individuals and, potentially, between individuals and their environments.

Theorists such as Baltes and Irvine might be viewed as "centrists" on the continuum ranging from extreme relativists to extreme nonrelativists. Moving away from the middle, we have a theory such as Gardner's (1983) theory of multiple intelligences, according to which separate and distinct intelligences – such as linguistic intelligence, logical-mathematical intelligence, spatial intelligence, and interpersonal intelligence – are the same in every culture, although their manifestations may differ. On this view, then, the structure of intelligence is always the same, but not necessarily its ostensive definition in any one context.

Finally, at the extreme of nonrelativism, are theorists such as Jensen (1982) and Eysenck (1982), who hold that intelligence is the same thing from one culture to another, regardless of what differences there may be in customs and patterns of functioning. Eysenck, for example, would relate intelligence to *accuracy* of neuronal conduction, whereas Jensen would relate it to *speed* of neuronal conduction. Intelligence, on these views, is a fully internalised construct, and could not be expected to differ in nature from one culture to another, because the basic neuronal makeup of individuals does not differ, however much their cultural norms may vary. From an anthropological perspective, one might argue that this position is fully "etic."

In sum, then, this capsule documentation of the range of positions shows a complete range from radical cultural relativism, acccording to which the nature of intelligence may vary drastically and even completely from one culture to another, to positions of radical cultural constancy, according to which intelligence is exactly the same thing from one culture to the next. It could be useful to have some framework into which the various positions can be placed, and such a framework is suggested and described in the next section.

A framework for characterising theories of intelligence as applied cross-culturally

The alternative positions described in the preceding discussion could be viewed as falling in a continuum regarding their claims of relativity versus constancy in the nature of intelligence across cultures. However, such a continuum would not fully express the subtlety of the differences, as well as similarities, among positions. Although perhaps no schematic framework can fully capture these subtleties, the framework proposed here is an attempt to make at least one step in this direction. An interesting alternative, but related framework, is proposed by Irvine (1984).

Figure 2.1 shows five different conceptions of how intelligence might be conceived of cross-culturally. Of the different conceptions – Ia, Ib, II, III, and IV – the first two are variants of each other, so that there are really just four basic models. The models differ in two key respects: whether or not there are cross-cultural differences in the instruments used to measure intelligence, and whether or not there are cross-cultural differences in the mental organisation, or dimensionalisation by which performance on these instruments is accomplished.

What, exactly, is an instrument and a dimension underlying performance on the instrument? From the standpoint of the present abstract framework,

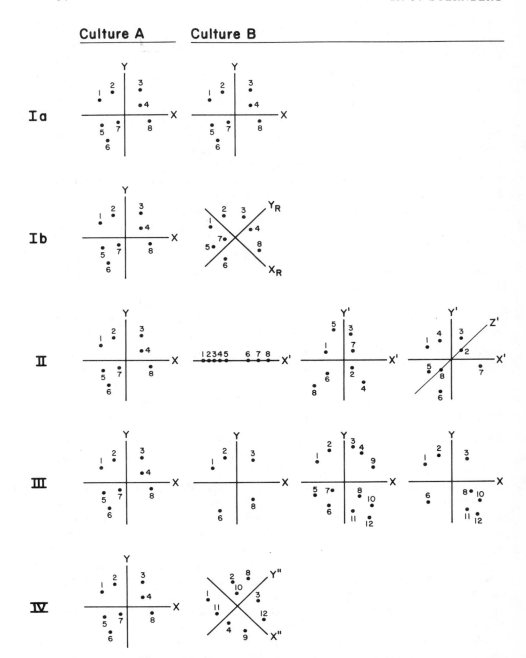

Figure 2.1 Four alternative models of the relationship between culture and intelligence. In Model Ia, intelligence is viewed as identical in Cultures A and B. In Model Ib, the locations of abilities in psychological space are the same, but the axes for interpreting these abilities are different. Thus, it is the interpretation of the psycho-

this question is left open, because it does not matter. For a psychometrically oriented psychologist, the instrument is likely to be an ability test, and the dimension is likely to be a factor (e.g., Irvine, 1979). For a Piagetian, the instrument is likely to be a piagetian task used to assess developmental level of a schema or possibly a developmental period (depending upon the orientation being pursued), and the dimension to be the actual schema or period (e.g., Dasen, 1977). For a cognitive psychologist, the instrument is likely to be a cognitive task, and the dimension, a cognitive ability, such as memory (e.g., Cole & Scribner, 1977). For a cultural relativist who emphasises the ecology of person–environment interactions, the instrument is likely to be a measure of cognitive style, and the dimension, the style itself (e.g., Berry, 1974, 1976). For a contextualist emphasising what Irvine (1979) referred to as *extra-hominem* variables (rather than *intra-hominem* variables, as in the four cases above), the instrument is likely to be a measure of environmental context, and the dimension is likely to be the kind of context being measured or otherwise assessed. For a Vygotskian, whose emphasis is likely to be on what Irvine refers to as *inter-hominem* variables, the instrument is likely to be a measure of interpersonal interaction, and the dimension one of the kinds of interaction possible (e.g., Vygotsky, 1962, 1978). The fundamental point to be made is that the basic framework can be applied to a large number of different cross-cultural orientations, regardless of the theory or theories upon which they are based.

The four basic models simply represent the four possible combinations of difference and no difference on the two binary attributes of *instrument* and *dimension*. Consider an abstract characterisation of each of these four basic models, as well as two examples of each, one psychometrically oriented and the other cognitively oriented.

Models Ia and Ib

In Model Ia, both the instruments and the dimensions into which these instruments are organised are the same across cultures. In Ib, the instruments are the same and the dimensions are rotational variants of the dimensions in Ia. If one assumes a "Euclidean psychological space," these dimensions

Caption to Figure 2.1 (*cont.*)
logical space of intelligence, rather than the space itself, that varies across cultures. In Model II, the same abilities are involved in Cultures A and B, but the locations of these abilities, and hence their interrelations, are different in the two cultures. The differences in locations may be affected by a change in the dimensionality of the space, or merely by different placements of points in the same number of dimensions. The new dimensions will almost inevitably have different interpretations than the old ones. In Model III, the number and interpretation of dimensions is the same in Cultures A and B, but different abilities enter into intelligence. The abilities in Culture B may be a subset, overlapping set, or superset of those in Culture A. In Model IV, both the abilities and the dimensions along which these abilities fall differ between Cultures A and B. In terms of testing, Models I and II allow the same tests between cultures (with adjustments for cultural variations), whereas Models III and IV do not.

are intermappable with the ones in Ia, and what may be taken to represent a genuine difference between cultures instead represents a different way of organising information on the part of the investigator rather than the investigatees! If one assumes any other metric for psychological space, however, Ib represents a genuine psychological difference in the subjects being studied.

Consider, for example, Model I from a psychometric orientation, such as that of Spearman (1927) or Thurstone (1938). Model Ia would refer to an identity across cultures in the tests and factors used to assess and understand intelligence, respectively. Model Ib would refer to an identity in tests but a set of factors that differ in orientation of axes across cultures. For instance, the same set of tests can yield a solution emphasising a general factor if left unrotated (along the lines of Spearman's theory), but a solution emphasising primary mental abilities if rotated to simple structure (along the lines of Thurstone's theory). From the present point of view, the differences in orientations of axes for the same set of tests represent a difference in emphasis rather than in psychological makeup (see Sternberg, 1977, 1984, 1985). Although there might be disagreements as to which are more basic – the general factor or the group factors (a disagreement into which Spearman and Thurstone actually got themselves) – such disagreements seem to be empirically irresoluble, and possibly less than meaningful psychologically as well.

Consider, next, Model I from a cognitive orientation, such as that of Cole et al. (1971). In this model, one can carry over the tasks used to assess cognitive abilities in one's own culture (although in translated form, of course, with suitable cultural adjustments). Moreover, it would be argued that the basic structure of the cognitive abilities being studied is the same – that members of other cultures perceive or remember things the same ways that members of one's own culture do. In Conceptualisation Ia, one would choose to focus on the complete identity of tests and structures. In Model Ib, one might choose to focus on different aspects of the system, such as levels of processing in memory rather than separate functional memory stores, despite the fact that one could view separate memory stores as generating multiple levels of processing, both within and between memory stores.

The theoretical positions of Jensen (1982) and Eysenck (1982), discussed in the preceding section, represent Model I types of positions. The argument is that the nature of intelligence is precisely the same cross-culturally, and that this nature can be assessed identically without regard to culture. For Jensen, the assessment would consist of a measure of choice reaction time using his choice-box apparatus. For Eysenck, the assessment would consist of a rather complex measure of evoked potentials obtained in a resting state on the part of the examinee (see Hendrickson, 1982). Theorists such as Jensen and Eysenck would not hesitate to acknowledge differences in the ways in which intelligence is manifested in different cultures, but they would view any observed differences as ones at a surface-structural level, rather than as ones at a more fundamental deep-structural level.

Model II

Model II represents a difference in dimensionality but no difference in instruments. The measures used to assess intelligence are the same across cultures, but the outcomes obtained from using these measures are structurally different as a function of the culture being investigated. It is thus not possible directly to compare scores on the measures across cultures, because the scores mean different things as a function of the cultures in which they are administered.

Consider, for example, what Model II would look like from a psychometric perspective. The basic tests would be more or less the same across cultures, but the factor structures would be different. As a result, whereas direct comparisons of factor scores are possible under Model I, such comparisons are not possible under Model II. The factors may differ either in number (more or less intellectual differentiation in one culture than in another) or in identities for a given number of factors. In the latter case, the difference across cultures is not in intellectual differentiation but in the way a given amount of differentiation is expressed mentally.

Model II would look similar from a cognitive point of view. Here, the cognitive tasks used would be essentially the same across cultures, but the results obtained by them would not be. One might find, for example, that the way in which information is organised in long-term memory differs from one culture to another (see, e.g., Wagner, 1978). Or one might find that susceptibility to perceptual illusions is so different between members of two cultures that one would be inclined to view the members of the two cultures as perceiving the objects in different ways, one of which leads to the illusion and the other of which does not (see, e.g., Segall, Campbell, & Herskovits, 1966). Such a conclusion would result not from small quantitative differences in amount of illusory perception, but from substantial qualitative differences, for example, in whether the illusion is even perceived in the first place.

Model III

Whereas in Model II, the instruments of measurement are the same but the dimensions are not, in Model III, the dimensions of intellect are the same, but the instruments of measurement are not. On this view, measurement processes must be emic, that is, derived from within the context of the culture being studied, rather than from outside it. A test such as *Raven's Progressive Matrices*, however appropriate it may be within the context of North American or European culture, might be viewed as inappropriate for measuring general intelligence in certain African cultures, where testing paradigms using abstract geometric forms may be much more nonentrenched than in North American or European cultures.

From a psychometric point of view, Model III would employ different testing instruments as a function of the culture being studied, but the factor structure obtained from the instruments would be the same (within measurement error), regardless of the culture. For example, one might measure reasoning skills by asking individuals to classify objects indigenous to their environment, or by asking them to seriate familiar objects. Such tests might measure the same skills as would *Raven's Progressive Matrices* in another culture.

From a cognitive point of view, different tasks might be used to assess the same skills. For example, Wagner (1978) had some individuals remember patterns of Oriental rugs, and others remember pictures of everyday objects, such as a rooster and a fish. There was no evidence of a difference in memory structure, but the evidence of a lack of difference depended precisely upon using tests that were appropriate in their content for the individuals being studied. Using the same tests might have resulted in the false appearance of differences that were artifactual.

Model IV

In Model IV, both the instruments of measurement and the ensuing dimensions of intelligence are different as a function of the culture under investigation. This position obviously embraces the radical culture relativist position, but also less extreme positions: For example, there may be substantial overlap in instruments and dimensions, even though they are nonidentical across cultures.

From a psychometric point of view, Model IV would result in the need to construct separate ability tests that are culturally appropriate. The result of testing would be a different factor space in each culture.

From a cognitive point of view as well, different instruments would be needed in each culture, with resultant different models of cognitive functioning across cultures.

The triarchic theory of intelligence

My newly proposed triarchic theory of intelligence (Sternberg, 1984, 1985) is a Model IV theory with respect to the relation between intelligence and culture, yet is by no means a radical culturally relativistic position. The reason it is not is that, according to the theory, there exist some aspects of intelligence that *are* universal and hence assignable to Model III. The reason the theory as a whole falls under Model IV, however, is that there exist other aspects of intelligence that *are not* universal, so that if one considers intelligence as a whole, both its nature and the ways in which it is appropriately measured do differ, at least potentially, from one culture to another.

A definition of intelligence

The triarchic theory of human intelligence consists of three closely inter-related subtheories: a contextual subtheory, a componential subtheory, and an experiential subtheory. These subtheories are motivated by a definition of intelligence, according to which *intelligence is the mental activity underlying purposive adaptation to, shaping of, and selection of real-world environments relevant to one's life*. The ways in which the theory elaborates upon the definition are considered below.

The contextual subtheory

The contextual subtheory deals with the definition as it relates to the external world of the individual, and we consider this relation first. We shall consider each aspect of the definition in turn.

Life-relevant real-world environments. The definition of intelligence limits intelligence to mental activity underlying environments relevant to one's life. I believe this delimitation is important, for several reasons.

A first reason is that it includes the range of environments one encounters in one's life, rather than merely some subset of them. Consider, for example, traditional intelligence tests. They seem to predict fairly well, at least in North America, if one's goal is prediction of school grades; but they do not predict very well at all if one's goal is prediction of job performance. Especially within the restricted range of IQs of persons within a given occupation, the predictive power of IQ tests is severely limited. According to the present definition, intelligence tests must be faulted for predicting at lower levels the performance one will exhibit on one's job. Indeed, most of the years of one's life are spent on the job, not in school.

Some might like to redefine intelligence in terms of the more academic skills needed in school; the present definition does not allow this, and hence moves a step away from the temptation to define or theorise about intelligence on the basis of the tests used to measure it. Factorial theories, of course, do just that: They start with the tests, and then generate theories that account for test performance. From the present point of view, factorial theories are inadequate, taken by themselves, because the tests on which they are based are themselves inadequate in predicting intellectual performance beyond the school years. Some people, of course, have attributed the lower predictive validity of the tests beyond the school years to the lower reliability of the criteria, or the lesser role of intelligence in later life (e.g., Jensen, 1980). The difference in criterion reliability cannot account for all of the difference in predictive validity, however, and I believe that the "residual" approach – declaring that portion of the criterion which is not predicted to be a residual from intelligence – not so subtly begs the question of just what practical elements of intelligence are not measured by IQ tests.

Essentially, it seeks to redefine the relevant criterion, rather than to reconceptualise the kind of test that would adequately measure the given criterion.

A second reason for the importance of limiting the definition of intelligence to life-relevant environments is that intelligence should not be conceptualised or measured in terms of life-irrelevant abilities. To illustrate this point, consider how the current definition differs in point of view from the point of view taken by Gardner's (1983) theory of multiple intelligences. One of Gardner's intelligences is musical intelligence. Now suppose that an individual is born and dies in a culture that forbids musical expression, perhaps for religious reasons. The question is: Can musical ability be considered an intelligence, or a part of intelligence, in that culture? The triarchic theory would say no. Certainly, musical ability *qua* musical ability still exists within the individuals of the culture, although the ability is not likely to be well developed. In other words, there still exists a cognitive competence that could, in another culture, be drawn upon and exploited. But musical ability *qua* intelligence does not exist in this culture. It would make no sense at all, for example, to include a music portion on an intelligence test, because musical ability has no adaptive value within that culture.

From the opposite point of view, there may exist within that culture abilities that are relevant to adaptation there but that are not relevant in our culture. Consider, for example, the fine motor skill that goes into threading a needle and similar activities. In today's world, at least in most of the United States, one can survive quite well without this ability. One would not want to include a needle-threading subtest of an intelligence test. But in other parts of the world, the fine motor ability required to thread a needle might be essential to survival: Indeed, in earlier times, this ability would have counted for much more in the United States. The ability might be measured on a specific ability test, but not on an intelligence test.

The point to be made, quite simply, is that intelligence is not the same thing as mental ability or abilities. Rather, it encompasses only that set of mental abilities that are relevant in the context of people's lives at a given time and place. These mental abilities may change over time and place, as the contexts of people's lives change. When such changes take place, the tests that are relevant for assessing intelligence will change as well. Our failure to recognise this fact results in our creation of tests that are much better predictors for some kinds of situations than for others. Our traditional solution to this dilemma has been to decide on the relevance of intelligence to the situation on the basis of the relevance of the test to that situation, rather than to start over and conceptualise how we might need to change the test.

Mental activity in relation to behaviour. Defining intelligence in terms of mental activity and its relations to behaviour represents a moderate position between two more radical positions, one defining intelligence solely in terms of latent capacities, and the other defining it solely in terms of observable behaviour. From the present point of view, it is necessary to understand the link between mental process and behaviour, not simply the mental process or behaviour itself.

There would seem to be two clear advantages to defining intelligence in terms of mental activity and its relationships to behaviour, other than in terms of static latent capacities or of observable behaviour. Consider each of these advantages.

First, mental activity is directly inferrable through techniques widely available to cognitive psychologists. By using any of a number of experimental techniques, most of which are variants of either the subtraction method or the additive-factors method (see S. Sternberg, 1969; Sternberg, 1977), it is possible to obtain a reasonably sound idea, at least to a first approximation, of the mental activity giving rise to observed behaviour. Alternatively, results of computer simulation can be compared to human data, and inferences about information processing made in this way. Or one might use protocol analysis, again as an approximation to the mental processes underlying observed behaviour. Probably the optimal strategy is to use a combination of methods, seeking convergence of their results. Whereas mental activity is directly inferrable, latent capacities are not, nor is it clear exactly what is meant by a latent mental capacity, as has been shown by the multiple conceptions psychometricians have had of the psychological meaning of factors (see Sternberg, 1977). In speaking of mental processes, it is possible to say that they (a) consume specifiable amounts of real time, (b) have a computable probability of being executed erroneously, (c) combine into certain strategies for task performance, (d) act upon specifiable mental representations, (e) can be trained, at least to some extent, and (f) can be used to understand individual differences in specifiable aspects of task performance. None of these statements can be made about latent mental capacities, because it is not at all clear what they are. Note that I am not saying that such capacities do not exist: I believe they do. But I believe that they form a less useful basis for defining intelligence than do mental processes. Moreover, speaking of latent mental capacities can convey misconceptions, for example, that intelligence tests directly measure such capacities independent of the use of these capacities. Those who score high on an intelligence test but who perform poorly in school are then often viewed as those who underutilise their mental capacities. This view may be true, in some sense. But it is important to realise that the test itself measured use of mental capacities, whereas schooling measures use of these capacities in a different context. Both test and school performance also measure other aspects of mental functioning as well, besides intelligence. The important point to be made, however, is that although school achievement is often used as a criterion and intelligence test scores as a predictor, both test scores and school grades are criteria relative to intelligence defined in terms of mental processes. Tests are in no sense sacred above other criteria. Looked at in this way, the school psychologist's goal becomes not one of understanding underachievement or overachievement, but one of understanding utilisation of intelligence in different kinds of tasks and situational contexts.

The cross-cultural psychologist taking this view is also less likely to be fooled into believing that there is anything sacrosanct about intelligence test scores. Transporting an intelligence test from one culture to another with only translation distinguishing the test given to members of one culture from that given to members of another culture is no more viable than directly translated lessons in school. All measures of intelligence are only proxies. Our using some as predictors and some as criteria is a matter of our own professional and societal goals, not a function of their intrinsic psychological status. The fact that a test is a predictor and school or job performance, a criterion, does not imply that either the one or the other is a better measure of the psychological construct of intelligence. Slipping in the assumption that the test is the better measure of intelligence obfuscates rather than elucidates the psychological relationship between intelligence and measures of it. Which is a better measure of intelligence is an empirical question answerable only by converging operations assessing the validity of each kind of measure as indexing a person's levels and patterns of intellectual performance.

Second, mental processes, and the relationships of mental processes to behaviour, are psychological phenomena, whereas behaviour in its own right is not, except as it reflects and manifests these mental processes. Obviously, behaviour is virtually always used as the basis for inferring mental processes. But from the standpoint of the theory of intelligence, the behaviour is of interest as a proxy or index of mental processing, not in its own right. There are any number of instances in which behaviour considered outside the context of the mental processes that gave rise to it can be extremely deceptive. If one defines intelligence in terms of behaviour rather than in terms of its relations to the mental processes underlying it, one can be in serious trouble. For example, individuals may score well on a test because they have been given the answers in advance. Or individuals may score poorly because they are sick or do not have suitable writing implements. Individuals may succeed in life because of circumstances of birth, attractive physical appearance, or other forms of luck, without the mental wherewithal that others would need to achieve the same level of success. If one were to define intelligence in terms of the behaviours exhibited, one would be in trouble indeed. Intelligence would end up being a psychological function of such things as wealth and physical appearance. Although there may indeed be a statistical association between these characteristics and intelligence, one would hope that such associations would be moderated by third (psychological) variables, rather than being direct causal relations!

Of course, it would be possible to make wrong inferences about mental processes because of the behaviours exhibited by individuals under certain circumstances. Individuals who succeed in life because their fathers buy their way to success or coach them at every step might seem to be good mental processors. But in such cases, the observable behaviour is probably not a good indicant of the mental processes underlying the behaviour. The problem in inferring a person's intelligence would be one of incorrect inferences about mental processes from behaviour, not the failure of mental processes themselves to be accurate gauges of intelligence.

The importance of distinguishing between mental processing and behaviour is especially important in cross-cultural psychological research on intelligence. Consider the finding of Cole et al. (1971) noted earlier with respect to the Kpelle's sorting performance. If one were to judge the Kpelle by their behaviour, they would look unintelligent in western terms. But this would be because of different contextual standards for behaviour. In this and many other instances, the difference in behaviour does not reflect a different capability for mental processing, but rather reflects a different preferred style of mental processing. Behaviours viewed as intelligent in one culture may be viewed as unintelligent in another culture, and vice versa. Indeed, if one looks at behaviour, intelligence will properly appear to be culturally specific. But the processes underlying the behaviour are not. A full understanding of intelligence can only derive from understanding how behaviour is linked to underlying mental processes.

The behaviourist position is not one limited to self-proclaimed behaviourists. Many psychologists take this position without being aware of it. Indeed, cross-cultural investigations that carry over measures from one culture to another without appropriate modifications are very much behaviourists. They are assuming that the relation between mental processing and behaviour as elicited by the test stimuli will be the same in both cultures, an assumption at least as likely to be wrong as to be right. I am not advocating a return to pure mentalism, which would leave the organism "buried in thought." Rather, I am arguing for the utmost attention to thought and its relations to behaviour, with the recognition that a given mental process can generate multiple alternative behaviours, and that a given observable behaviour can be generated by multiple alternative mental processes as well as other variables. Obvious as this all may sound, it seems to be heeded better in theory than in practice.

Adaptation. The view of intelligence as adaptation to one's environment has been a time-honoured one for many years (see, e.g., "Intelligence and its measurement," 1921; Wechsler, 1958). From the standpoint of the theorist of intelligence, the problem is that what constitutes adaptive behaviour in one culture does not necessarily constitute adaptive behaviour in another. Basically, survival skills differ from one culture to another. An elegant demonstration of the relation between cognitive task scores and survival skills derives from the work of Berry (1971), who found that individuals from low-food-accumulating societies tend to be superior on spatial ability tests and measures of cognitive differentiation to individuals from high-food-accumulating societies. People in the former societies typically depend on hunting and fishing for their food, and hence need to develop their spatial skills as fully as possible. Although this trend is not clearly general across all cultures (Berry & Annis, 1974), it suggests the cultural specificity of typical conceptions of ability. One could say, of course, that these results argue not for a difference in the nature of intelligence between the two kinds of societies (e.g., Eskimo, which is low-food-accumulating, and Temne, which is high-food-accumulating), but rather for a difference in levels of intelligence. The argument to be developed here is that both positions have some merit: If one looks at intelligence from a contextual point of view, what is required for adaptation clearly differs across cultures, and hence the cognitive needs differ across cultures; from a componential or strictly cognitive point of view, members of the two cultures do differ in levels of cognitive skill that lead to intelligent action. But then, spatial skill is not equally relevant for intelligence in the two different cultures. Again, the locus of intelligence is not strictly in the mental processes or in the behaviour, but in the interface between the two.

The contextualist interpretation above suggests that different cultures tend to develop different cognitive skills among their members. Is there any more direct evidence for this hypothesis? It appears there is. It has been found, for example, that African infants show superior early sensorimotor development relative to western infants (Werner, 1972). For example, Geber (1956, 1960) found that Baganda neonates are superior to western ones in sensorimotor skills; this finding has been replicated and extended by Ainsworth (1967) and by Kilbride, Robbins, and Kilbride (1970). In the Kilbride et al. study, 75% of the sample scored at least one standard deviation above the average on the *Bayley* scales. Although the immediacy of this superiority at birth suggests at least some genetic component to the difference, there appears also to be an environmental component that may derive from high levels of stimulation and low levels of stress among Baganda mothers during pregnancy, and from high levels of activity and stimulation for the infants upon birth (Munroe & Munroe, 1975; see also Segall, 1979).

Schooling appears to make a large difference in the pattern of developed abilities. Goodnow and Bethon (1966), for example, found that unschooled 11-year-old Chinese boys performed as well as American children of average IQ on all tasks except those requiring mental transformations (in the case of this study, combinatorial reasoning). Schooling appears to develop this skill in a possibly unique way, leaving those without schooling behind in this skill.

To understand the interaction between adaptation and cultural context, one must go beyond strictly cognitive indices and observe the way other, noncognitive aspects of a culture operate. An interesting analysis of this kind has been performed by Sinha (1983) for Indian populations. Consider just a subset of the factors that Sinha suggests may penalise Indians exposed to standard western tests of intelligence.

1. *Response set.* Western culture emphasises decisiveness and making up

one's mind. If westerners were to be given the choice "I'm not sure" or "I can't decide," they would know that neither answer would generate points, at least for most cognitive item types. But Indians are much more drawn to such responses than are others. For example, Kakar, cited in Sinha (1983), found that Indian subjects respond with uncertain answers (on a rating scale) five times as often as Japanese. Obviously, indecisiveness will not benefit one on a standard intelligence test. There may be times in anyone's life, however, when an indecisive response may be more adaptive than an incorrect or hastily conceived decision.

2. *Courtesy*. Indians will often show a "courtesy effect" (Doob, 1968; Sinha, 1977), giving an interviewer or tester the responses that the subject thinks are desired. In the United States, retarded children often show this same tendency (Zigler, 1971) (which is perhaps a sad commentary on the role of courtesy in U.S. culture).

3. *Cultural gap*. In some rural areas, subjects may be suspicious or evasive, and inhibited in responding. This tendency, like the tendency toward courtesy, directs attention away from the cognitive demands of the task and toward task-irrelevant thought and action likely to reduce a subject's score.

4. *Communication failures*. The examiner may simply not understand or misunderstand the response the examinee is trying to convey. Most often, failure in communication puts the examinee at a disadvantage, because it is natural for examiners to attribute blame for the breakdown in communication to a lack of cognitive skill in the examinees rather than in themselves. One has only to look at the way North Americans treat foreigners whose first language is not English to see where the attribution of blame is directed. People in the United States, in particular, are wont to believe that foreigners are stupid because of their inability to communicate effectively (in English, of course). The Americans can rarely speak the language of the visitor or, if they do, speak it more poorly than the visitor speaks the English language.

Sinha's work, as well as that of many others, makes clear that there is a substantial gap between intelligence as it is manifested in one's culture and intelligence as it is manifested in a testing situation. A theoretical account of this gap is given by Berry (1983), who distinguishes among four levels of context: ecological context (the natural habitat of an individual); experiential context (the pattern of recurrent experiences that provides a basis for learning); performance context (the limited set of circumstances under which "natural" behaviour is observed); and experimental context (the environmental circumstances under which test scores are generated). Adaptive intelligence is naturally exhibited in the ecological and experiential contexts. The gap between these contexts and the experimental one will be differentially large for individuals with differing backgrounds; and it will be greatest for those for whom the experimental context is most foreign, predictably, those whose cultures differ most from those of the experimenters coming into a given culture to do research. Yet, test scores take little or no account of the differential gap for different groups of people.

One need not go to exotic cultures to witness the effects of context upon adaptive (or maladaptive) patterns of behaviour. Heath (1983) performed a compelling ethnography of three different subcultures in the United States. She found that middle-class parents tend to give elaborate descriptions that provide reasons for certain events and behaviours; lower-class parents tend to give imperatives, often without providing as well the reasons for the imperatives. There is a reciprocality in these two patterns of parent–child interaction with respect to questioning of children as well. In middle-class environments, parents frequently ask children questions and expect the children to develop the capacity for explanation. In lower-class environments, such questioning is more rare and is often discouraged. For the child in the lower-class home, it would be an example of misbehaviour to question the parent and would be considered maladaptive by the parent. Describing one lower-class environment, "Trackton," Heath noted that

Children do not expect adults to ask them questions, for, in Trackton, children are not seen as information-givers or question-answerers. This is especially true of questions for which adults already have an answer. Since adults do not consider children appropriate conversational partners to the exclusion of other people who are around, they do not construct questions especially for children, nor do they use questions to give the young an opportunity to show off their knowledge about the world. (Heath, 1983, p. 103)

This pattern of interaction is in marked contrast to that of a lower-middle-class environment, such as the community of "Roadville," where young mothers begin to use questions and interpretive statements within the first month of a new-born's life. In this environment, questions are frequently asked to which the questioner knows the answer, but the goal is to develop understanding and communicational skills in the child.

The overall point to be made is simple: To understand intelligence within a given culture or subculture, one must understand it in terms of the adaptive requirements of that culture or subculture, and such understanding requires a grasp of how thought is linked to behaviour in that particular environment.

Shaping and selection. In the preceding section, I emphasised how environments shape people. But people also shape environments. Obviously, no one has complete control over the environments in which he or she lives; but most people have some control. Environments differ greatly in the amount of control they allow: A democracy is likely to offer more control to the individual than a totalitarian regime, or a prison camp.

Environmental shaping and selection are used in conjunction with adaptation to maximise individuals' fits to their contexts. Often, shaping and selection are used when adaptation fails. For example, many cultures are experiencing a "brain drain" as their most able members leave for more technologically advanced societies. Clearly, the advantage of the individual may differ from that of the group, which is disadvantaged further and further as its most able members leave for destinations outside the cultural setting.

A notable example of environmental shaping and selection in people's lives is the choice of a marital partner, in cultures – the majority – that allow relatively free marital choice. From one point of view, marital choice may seem far removed from the domain of intelligence and it is certainly far removed from the domain of conventional intelligence tests. Yet the effects of the choice of a marital partner on one's life are likely to be profound, affecting everything from the course of one's daily living to the children one has, and possibly one's level of attainment in one's career as well (both for men and for women). In terms of consequentiality and number of factors involved, marital choice would seem to be a better "intelligence test" than would simple analogy or number series problems. Career choice would seem to be a decision of equal complexity and consequentiality, and yet it, too, is not used. Choices to buy new cars, appliances, and homes would be less consequential, but also life-relevant. Why are choices such as these not studied in the literature on intelligence?

Our reluctance to judge someone's intelligence by the important real-world choices he or she makes is influenced by a number of beliefs that apply as well to other consequential decisions involving shaping and selection of environments. Some of these are (a) the effects of life circumstances upon our choices (we meet only a limited number of possible mates, or have only a limited selection of careers available to us); (b) the influence of noncognitive variables upon these choices (such as passion, the desire to be financially secure, one's motivation to pursue a certain kind of life rather than another); (c) the large number of unknown factors that cannot be experimentally controlled in real-life decision making, and so on.

All of these and other factors are perhaps good reasons for eschewing significant life decisions as measures of intelligence. Yet it is important to note that test scores are prey to many of the same "impurities," in varying degrees. Life circumstances (the kind of home environment one experiences, the kind of schooling one has had, the number of similar tests one has taken) influence one's ability to perform well on tests. Noncognitive variables such as test anxiety, motivation to do well, acceptance of the testing situation as it is presented, one's mood when taking the test, and so on, also influence test scores. And test situations are nowhere as well controlled as they may appear to be. For example, alertness, experience with stressful situations, and suitability of a given test for one's particular pattern of cognitive skills all subtly influence test scores, just as they influence life decisions.

The point to be made is that psychologists are, perhaps, suckers for the illusion of control. A test-taking situation seems to give the experimenter a level of control beyond that obtained in everyday life. In some sense, perhaps, this control is genuine. In another sense, it is not. The test-taking situation reduces ecological validity while at the same time introducing a host of irrelevancies that are easily hidden by the numbers so readily assigned to the scores on an "objective" test. We might gain more by studying real-world decisions, or at least simulations of them, and by studying the contextual variables that affect them, than by studying artificial behaviours and the variables that affect them. Much of what we gain in a test-taking situation is illusory, but much of what we lose is not.

The componential subtheory

Contextual views of intelligence tend to be vague. They usually state, in their strong form, that context can affect the nature of intelligence, or in their weak form, that context can affect people's levels of intelligence, without saying much about exactly what is affected.

The componential subtheory of the triarchic theory of intelligence states just what the mental mechanisms are that affect and are affected by context. One can no more understand intelligence solely in terms of its contexts than one can understand it wholly outside its contexts. The componential subtheory specifies the mental world that interfaces with environmental contexts.

The basic "mental unit" of analysis in this subtheory is the information-processing component, which is an elementary information process that transforms sensory inputs into conceptual representations, transforms conceptual representations, or transforms conceptual representations into motor outputs. Components can be classified, for convenience, into three kinds.

Metacomponents are higher order processes that plan, monitor, and evaluate one's problem-solving activity. In particular, they (a) formulate the nature of the problem, (b) select lower order components to solve the problem, (c) select one or more mental representations upon which the components are to operate, (d) select a strategy for combining lower order components, (e) decide how to allocate mental resources, and (f) monitor one's problem solving. *Performance components* are lower order processes that execute the instructions of the metacomponents. They encode, combine, compare, and respond to stimuli. *Knowledge-acquisition components* learn what it is the metacomponents and performance components need to know to act effectively. They are the source of the knowledge that guides metacomponential and performance-componential functioning. For more detailed analyses of the nature and functioning of these various kinds of components, see Sternberg (1983, 1985).

It is possible to understand performance on information-processing tasks in terms of the mental components that underlie such processing. For many years, I thought, as did others, that understanding the nature and identities of these components would, in itself, provide the key to a full understanding of intelligence (see, e.g., Sternberg, 1979; Hunt, 1980). I no longer believe this to be the case. Consider why.

Consider two tasks commonly used in intelligence tests: analogies and reading comprehension. There are many indications that these tasks, and others like them, are highly "saturated" with *g*, or general intelligence. Moreover, task analysis has given us considerable insight into how analogies are solved (e.g., Sternberg, 1977) and how reading comprehension is effected (e.g., Frederiksen, 1982). But do these tasks, as contrived in typical experiments and psychometric tests, measure intelligence in all cultures, or do they measure intelligence to the same extent? It seems doubtful.

First, consider verbal analogies as well as reading comprehension. Clearly, the measures will be of little use in an illiterate or semiliterate culture, or among people within literate cultures who are themselves not literate. Even within a highly literate culture, just what these tests measure will depend in large part upon the vocabulary level of each individual taking each test: The tests may be fine measures of reasoning skill for those with large vocabularies, but poor measures for those with poor vocabularies, who do not even understand the words upon which their reasoning is supposed to be based. Moreover, the relevance of the verbal medium to people's lives will differ considerably both within and across cultures, making tests relying exclusively upon this medium suspect as measures of intelligence.

Second, consider abstract analogies. It was originally thought that use of geometric forms would create a culture-fair test because of the absence of the verbal medium (Cattell & Cattell, 1963). But geometric forms are themselves susceptible to cross- and within-cultural bias. Some individuals will be well primed to work with geometric shapes, others will not. A culture that does not know plane geometry will be at a decided disadvantage on these "culture-fair" tests.

Finally, consider the very medium of testing. As noted in an earlier section of this chapter, the medium of the test itself creates biases, independent of the particular items contained in the test.

It is necessary to distinguish between the mental processes the test seeks to measure and the vehicle by which these processes are measured. Here, I would claim that there is a cross-cultural universal. The processes of analogical reasoning – encoding stimuli from the environment, inferring relations between stimuli, mapping higher order relations between relations, applying relations, and so on – are probably relevant to intelligence in any culture, as are the processes of comprehension (whether oral or written). I do not believe that the mental processes of intelligence differ from one culture to another. Hence, I would claim that whereas contexts are culture-specific, components are culture-general. But the important thing to realise is that the components of intelligence cannot be measured independently of some context, as the above analysis shows. If there were any pure way of getting at these processes, then perhaps we could have a culture-fair test. But there is no such pure way: Competencies can be assessed only through performance, and performance is mediated by all the "nuisance" variables that experimental psychologists and psychometricians detest. Unfortunately, many psychologists have been unable or unwilling to distinguish between the mental processes as they exist, in some sense, in people's heads, and the mental processes as they are measured by any available or potentially available instruments. The two are not the same. As a result, one

must be very wary of psychologists who claim to have a universal measure of intelligence, however respectable or culture-fair it may appear on
its surface.

Consider two of the more recently touted "culture-fair" tests, ones more
subtle in their biases than the tests of abstract reasoning that they have now
replaced.

One such test is the measure of choice reaction time, as used by Jensen
(1982). Is the test culture-fair? Most certainly not. It requires value placed
upon speeded performance, acceptance of the individual testing situation,
freedom from the distraction that the testing situation could cause many
people, acceptance of the importance of doing well on such a seemingly
trivial task, and fast motor responses. It is difficult to see how anyone would
want to claim that this seemingly "pure" measure of cognitive functioning
is culturally unbiased.

A more subtle bias enters into psychophysiological testing situations, such
as those advocated by Eysenck (1982) and Hendrickson (1982) as ultimates
in fair intelligence testing. In such situations, an individual sits at rest, with
electrodes pasted on his or her head. Evoked-potential recordings are taken
while the individual is at rest, and psychometric measurements are derived
from the averaged evoked potentials that are alleged to measure intellectual
ability. Certainly, this test would seem to be as "culture-fair" as one could
get. But to qualify as "a test of pure g" Eysenck would like us to assume
that the averaged evoked potential measures some inherent, innate property
of the nervous system, such as accuracy of neuronal conduction. But such
theorising is highly speculative, as Irvine and Berry show in Chapter 1, and
as Eysenck himself would admit. Although reductionist explanations of the
high correlation of Hendrickson's measure with *Wechsler* and other psychometric test scores – assuming such correlations are nonartifactual – ultimately must rest on psychophysiological explanation, as must all correlations involving tests, the proximal cause of the correlations may be less
interesting. It may be that higher scorers on the *Wechsler* react differently,
cognitively, to the testing situation, and thus think in certain ways rather
than in others during test. Or it may be that the higher scorers on the intelligence tests are more aroused by, and hence more attentive to, the testing
situation. In other words, the difference between better and poorer scorers
on the evoked-potentials measure may be a cognitive one that is as susceptible to cultural influence and bias as is any other cognitive measurement.
Until there is evidence for the cross-cultural validity of the test – which, to
my knowledge, is in doubt (Verster, 1983) – I would be most reluctant to
accept this measure as having any more cross-cultural validity than any other
single seemingly attractive measure.

In conclusion, the components of intelligence are cross-culturally universal, but their manifestations are not. The inferences that need to be made,
the problems that need to be recognised, the kinds of stimuli that need to
be encoded, and the kinds of knowledge to be learned can differ radically

from one culture to another. Hence, even if the components of mental functioning are cross-culturally relevant, their measurement must be tailored to the contexts in which the components are used. Moreover, the importances of various components may differ across cultures, so that even if one could get culturally appropriate measurement, there is no guarantee that a given cognitive skill will be as important to intelligence in one culture as it will be in another.

The experiential subtheory

It might seem that if one understood the components of intelligence, and the contexts in which they occur, one would have a complete understanding of intelligence, having encompassed both the inside and the outside of the organism. This is not the case, however. Consider a cognitive task given to the members of two cultures: Suppose, for the sake of argument, that the task is ecologically relevant in both environments, and that members of both cultures use the same mental processes in performing the task. Can one then be assured that the task is culture-fair? Unfortunately, the answer is no: One must take into account as well the differential experience of the members of the two cultures with the particular task and tasks like it.

The experiential subtheory states that tasks are particularly relevant to the measurement of intelligence when they measure cognitive performance either when a task or situation is relatively novel, or when that task or situation is in the process of becoming automatised (i.e., transiting from controlled to automatic information processing – see Schneider & Shiffrin, 1977). For a task to be culture-fair, it must be equally entrenched, or non-entrenched, for members of all cultures. It seems unlikely that there exists any task that satisfies this constraint, pointing out the near impossibility, from a triarchic point of view, of etic comparisons of intelligence. Consider, for example, a memorisation task. Memory plays at least some role in intellectual development in all cultures. Contextual relevance can be achieved by using stimuli to be remembered that are equally appropriate for each culture to be tested. But appropriateness involves both equal relative familiarity for the members of the two cultures and equal relevance of memorisation of items of the types used for the members of the two cultures. These equivalencies are not mere window dressing, as noted in some detail by the Laboratory of Comparative Human Cognition (1982; see also Rogoff, 1982). The difficulties of these equations can scarcely be underestimated. Thus, whereas the criteria of novelty and automatisation are alleged to be cross-culturally universal, exactly what is novel and what is automatic will differ across, and even within, cultures.

Conclusions

I have emphasised, in this chapter, the considerable difficulty of achieving measurement of intelligence that is cross-culturally fair. But it is important to keep distinct the measurement of intelligence and the theory that generates that measurement. I believe there are cross-cultural universals, not in the domain of measurement but in the domain of theory.

I have argued that the components of intelligence are cross-culturally universal, although their weights in contributing to intelligence may vary. Moreover, I have argued that the role of experience is universal: Components are most representative of a person's intelligence when they are measured either in a region of relative novelty with respect to a task or situation, or in a region of automatisation. My view of intelligence, therefore, is by no means a wholly relativistic one: There are universal constancies in the nature of intelligence.

Not all of intelligence is universal, however. The contexts of intelligence are culture-specific, although cultures may differ in the amounts of context they share with each other. From the standpoint of the measurement of intelligence, then, the problem occurs when one makes the crucial link between thought and behaviour, which is the locus of intelligence as it operates in the real world. Intelligence always operates in some context, no matter how impoverished, and for a task or situation to measure intelligence, that task or situation must be contextually relevant to people's lives, directly measuring or predicting adaptation to, shaping of, or selection of environments. There is no ultimate solution to the problem of culture-fair measurement. If it were possible to purify measures sufficiently so that they were devoid of context, then it might be possible to equate components of task performance and the level of novelty of the tasks and situations. But such measures would not be measures of intelligence precisely because of their contextual impoverishment. If we create measures that are contextually rich, we will necessarily give up exact equation on experiential and possibly componential grounds. In a sense, we are caught between Scylla and Charybdis, as the "stimulus identity" discussion by Irvine and Berry in Chapter 1 confirms.

The situation is only totally bleak if our goal is to be able to compare the intelligence of people across cultures according to some universal standard. Such comparisons are difficult to make. Indeed, the exact problems arise for comparisons across ages or generations within cultures, as Irvine (1983b) has pointedly shown. In such cases, too, it is impossible simultaneously to equate all three aspects of the triarchic theory. Suppose, instead, our goal is fully to understand intellectual functioning within culture, and to compare only those particular aspects of intelligence that do, in fact, intersect between pairs of cultures. These aspects will differ from one pair of cultures to another, both in nature and number of comparable aspects. Obviously, we will then be a far cry from the goal of a full comparison, but we will have set up a realistic goal instead. It will no longer be possible to attain any full comparison, and hence to rank-order cultures according to the intelligence of their inhabitants, but it will be possible to specify just what aspects of intelligence are specific to a given culture (in terms of contextual requirements) and what aspects are shared with at least one other culture. I do not think we will do at all badly if we accept this new goal instead of some of our more ambitious, but unrealistic, old ones.

References

Ainsworth, M. D. S. (1967). *Infancy in Uganda*. Baltimore: Johns Hopkins University Press.

Baltes, P. B., Dittman-Kohli, F., & Dixon, R. A. (1982). *Intellectual development during adulthood: General propositions toward theory and a dual-process conception*. Unpublished manuscript, Max Planck Institute for Human Development and Education, Berlin.

Baltes, P. B., & Willis, S. L. (1979). Toward psychological theories of aging and development. In J. E. Birren & K. W. Schaie (Eds.), *Handbook of the psychology of aging*. New York: Van Nostrand Reinhold.

Baltes, P. B., & Willis, S. L. (1982). Plasticity and enhancement of intellectual functioning in old age: Penn State's Adult Development and Enrichment Project (ADEPT). In F. Craik & S. Trehub (Eds.), *Aging and cognitive processes*. New York: Plenum.

Berry, J. W. (1971). Ecological and cultural factors in spatial perceptual development. *Canadian Journal of Behavioural Science, 3,* 324–336.

Berry, J. W. (1974). Radical cultural relativism and the concept of intelligence. In J. W. Berry & P. R. Dasen (Eds.), *Culture and cognition: Readings in cross-cultural psychology*. London: Methuen.

Berry, J. W. (1976). *Human ecology and cognitive style: Comparative studies in cultural and psychological adaptation*. New York: Sage-Halsted.

Berry, J. W. (1983). Textured contexts: Systems and situations in cross-cultural psychology. In S. H. Irvine & J. W. Berry (Eds.), *Human assessment and cultural factors*. New York: Plenum.

Berry, J. W., & Annis, R. C. (1974). Ecology, culture and psychological differentiation. *International Journal of Psychology, 9,* 173–193.

Cattell, R. B., & Cattell, A. K. (1963). *Test of g: Culture fair, Scale 3*. Champaign, IL.: Institute for Personality and Ability Testing.

Charlesworth, W. R. (1979a). An ethological approach to studying intelligence. *Human Development, 22,* 212–216.

Charlesworth, W. R. (1979b). Ethology: Understanding the other half of intelligence. In M. von Cranach, K. Koppa, W. Lepenies, & D. Ploog (Eds.), *Human ethology: Claims and limits of a new discipline*. Cambridge University Press.

Cole, M., Gay, J., Glick, J., & Sharp, D. W. (1971). *The cultural context of learning and thinking*. New York: Basic.

Cole, M., & Scribner, S. (1977). Cross-cultural studies of memory and cognition. In R. V. Kail, Jr., & J. W. Kagan (Eds.), *Perspectives on the development of memory and cognition*. Hillsdale, NJ: Erlbaum.

Dasen, P. R. (1977). *Piagetian psychology: Cross-cultural contributions*. New York: Gardner Press.

Doob, L. (1968). Just a few of the presumptions and perplexities confronting social psychological research in developing countries. *Journal of Social Issues, 24,* 71–81.

Eysenck, H. J. (Ed.) (1982). *A model for intelligence*. New York: Springer-Verlag.

Frederiksen, J. R. (1982). A componential theory of reading skills and their interactions. In R. J. Sternberg (Ed.), *Advances in the psychology of human intelligence* (Vol. 1). Hillsdale, NJ: Erlbaum.

Gardner, H. (1983). *Frames of mind: The theory of multiple intelligences*. New York: Basic.

Geber, M. (1956). Le développement psychomoteur de l'enfant africain. *Courrier, 6,* 17–28.

Geber, M. (1960). Problèmes posés par le développement du jeune enfant africain en fonction de son milieu social. *Travail Humain, 23,* 97–111.

Goodnow, J. J., & Bethon, G. (1966). Piaget's tasks: The effects of schooling and intelligence. *Child Development, 37,* 573–582.

Heath, S. B. (1983). *Ways with words.* Cambridge University Press.

Hendrickson, A. E. (1982). The biological basis of intelligence. Part 1: Theory. In H. J. Eysenck (Ed.), *A model for intelligence.* New York: Springer-Verlag.

Hunt, E. B. (1980). Intelligence as an information-processing concept. *British Journal of Psychology, 71,* 449–474.

"Intelligence and its measurement: A symposium." (1921). *Journal of Educational Psychology, 12,* 123–147, 195–216, 271–275.

Irvine, S. H. (1979). The place of factor analysis in cross-cultural methodology and its contribution to cognitive theory. In L. Eckensberger, W. Lonner, & Y. Poortinga (Eds.), *Cross-cultural contributions to psychology.* Lisse: Swets & Zeitlinger.

Irvine, S. H. (1983a). Testing in Africa and America: The search for routes. In S. H. Irvine & J. W. Berry (Eds.), *Human assessment and cultural factors.* New York: Plenum.

Irvine, S. H. (1983b). Where intelligence tests fail. *Nature, 302,* 371.

Irvine, S. H. (1984). The contexts of triarchic theory. *Behavioral and Brain Sciences, 7,* 293–294.

Jensen, A. R. (1980). *Bias in mental testing.* New York: Free Press.

Jensen, A. R. (1982). The chronometry of intelligence. In R. J. Sternberg (Ed.), *Advances in the psychology of human intelligence* (Vol. 1). Hillsdale, NJ: Erlbaum.

Keating, D. (1984). The emperor's new clothes: The "new look" in intelligence research. In R. J. Sternberg (Ed.), *Advances in the psychology of human intelligence* (Vol. 2). Hillsdale, NJ: Erlbaum.

Kilbride, J. E., Robbins, M. C., & Kilbride, P. L. (1970). The comparative motor development of Baganda, American White, and American Black infants. *American Anthropologist, 72,* 1422–1429.

Laboratory of Comparative Human Cognition. (1982). Culture and intelligence. In R. J. Sternberg (Ed.), *Handbook of human intelligence.* Cambridge University Press.

Labouvie-Vief, G., & Chandler, M. (1978). Cognitive development and life-span developmental theories. Idealistic vs. contextual perspectives. In P. B. Baltes (Ed.), *Life-span development and behavior* (Vol. 1). New York: Academic Press.

Munroe, R. L., & Munroe, R. H. (1975). *Cross-cultural human development.* Monterey, Calif.: Brooks/Cole.

Rogoff, B. (1982). Integrating context and cognitive development. In M. E. Lamb & A. L. Brown (Eds.), *Advances in developmental psychology* (Vol. 2). Hillsdale, NJ: Erlbaum.

Schneider, W., & Shiffrin, R. (1977). Controlled and automated human information processing: I. Detection, search, and attention. *Psychological Review, 84,* 1–66.

Segall, M. H. (1979). *Cross-cultural psychology.* Monterey, Calif.: Brooks/Cole.

Segall, M. H., Campbell, D. T., & Herskovits, M. J. (1966). *The influence of culture on visual perception.* New York: Bobbs-Merrill.

Sinha, D. (1977). Orientation and attitude of social psychologists in a developing country: The Indian case. *International Review of Applied Psychology, 26,* 1–10.

Sinha, D. (1983). Human assessment in the Indian context. In S. H. Irvine & J. W. Berry (Eds.), *Human assessment and cultural factors.* New York: Plenum.

Spearman, C. (1927). *The abilities of man.* New York: Macmillan.

Sternberg, R. J. (1977). *Intelligence, information processing, and analogical reasoning: The componential analysis of human abilities.* Hillsdale, NJ: Erlbaum.

Sternberg, R. J. (1979). The nature of mental abilities. *American Psychologist, 34,* 214–230.

Sternberg, R. J. (1983). Components of human intelligence. *Cognition, 15,* 1–48.

Sternberg, R. J. (1984). Toward a triarchic theory of human intelligence. *Behavioral and Brain Sciences, 7,* 269–315.

Sternberg, R. J. (1985). *Beyond IQ: A triarchic theory of human intelligence.* Cambridge University Press.

Sternberg, S. (1969). Memory scanning: Mental processes revealed by reaction time experiments. *American Scientist, 57,* 421–457.

Thurstone, L. L. (1938). *Primary mental abilities.* Chicago: University of Chicago Press.

Verster, J. M. (1983). The structure, organization and correlates of cognitive speed and accuracy. In S. H. Irvine and J. W. Berry (Eds.), *Human assessment and cultural factors.* New York: Plenum.

Vygotsky, L. S. (1962). *Thought and language.* Cambridge, Mass.: MIT Press.

Vygotsky, L. S. (1978). *Mind in society: The development of higher psychological processes.* Cambridge, Mass.: Harvard University Press.

Wagner, D. A. (1978). Memories of Morocco: The influence of age, schooling and environment on memory. *Cognitive Psychology, 10,* 1–28.

Wechsler, D. (1958). *The measurement and appraisal of adult intelligence* (4th ed.). Baltimore, MD.: Williams & Wilkins.

Werner, E. E. (1972). Infants around the world: Cross-cultural studies of psychomotor development from birth to two years. *Journal of Cross-Cultural Psychology, 3,* 111–134.

Wober, M. (1974). Towards an understanding of Kiganda concept of intelligence. In J. W. Berry & P. R. Dasen (Eds.), *Culture and cognition: Readings in cross-cultural psychology.* London: Methuen.

Zigler, E. (1971). The retarded child as a whole person. In H. E. Adams & W. K. Boardman (Eds.), *Advances in experimental clinical psychology* (Vol. 1). New York: Pergamon.

Biometric fundamentalism

3 The biological basis of intelligence

H. J. Eysenck

The difficulties attending cross-cultural comparisons in intelligence are well known, and are emphasised throughout this book. In large part, these differences derive from a choice between two different paradigms of intelligence, namely those of Sir Francis Galton and those of Alfred Binet, a choice made early in the history of intelligence testing on the basis of inadequate analysis and empirical study, and one giving rise to many of the difficulties encountered in this field. This fateful choice preferred the approach of Binet to that of Galton, and a brief discussion of these two paradigms may provide a useful introduction to this chapter's topic.

The differences between the approaches of Binet and Galton are manifold, but centre in the main around three major points. The first concerns the concept of intelligence itself. For Galton, intelligence was a unitary ability, underlying all intellectual cognitive tasks, differences in which accounted for the differential abilities of people to solve problems, learn complex material, and carry out many different cognitive tasks of everyday life. Binet, on the other hand, believed in the existence of a large number of separate abilities, including some, such as suggestibility, which we would not normally count as part of intelligence. According to him, intelligence would just be the average for a given person of all these independent and separate abilities, and hence not a unitary factor at all. This debate has continued over the years, with psychologists like Spearman, Burt, and Vernon postulating the existence of a general factor of intelligence, while others, such as Guilford (Guilford & Hoepfner, 1971), postulate a large number of independent abilities, reaching, to date, the astonishing sum of 120 in the case of Guilford. Thurstone (1938) at first interpreted his own results as indicating the existence of a number of primary factors, but no general factor; later on (Thurstone & Thurstone, 1941), he changed his mind and postulated the existence of both a general factor and a number of primary abilities, very much as suggested by Eysenck (1939). This recognition of the existence of a powerful factor of intelligence, as well as a number of less important special abilities, is probably nowadays the most orthodox interpretation of a large body of psychometric evidence (Eysenck, 1979; Vernon, 1979). In this sense, we may say that both Galton and Binet made an important contribution to the final compromise, which recognises Galton's general factor of intelligence, and also Binet's special abilities. The overall victory, however, must go to Galton, because it must be recognised that general intelligence is not, as Binet thought, an artificial conglomerate and a statistical artifact, but emerges very clearly as an essential postulate from the psychometric evidence. It is not only that the correlations between all types of different cognitive tests show a "positive manifold," but also that the matrices of intercorrelations, under suitable conditions, approximate to Rank 1. It is difficult to reconcile these findings with any theory which does not include the general factor of intelligence (Eysenck, 1979; Vernon, 1979).

The second great difference between Galton and Binet relates to the importance of genetic factors, which for Galton were dominant, whereas Binet, as an educational psychologist, was much more interested in educational factors and their power to determine individual differences in ability and achievement. The evidence on this point is now so enormous that it would be idle here to recapitulate it; discussions by Eysenck (1979) and Vernon (1979) indicate that the evidence is conclusive insofar as it implicates a strong genetic determinant in causing differences between people, although the precise estimates of heritability differ from something like 50% to something like 80%.

However, it should be remembered that these differences in estimates are not unexpected. In the first place, the term *heritability* has several different meanings. If we look at the proportion of the phenotypic variance accounted for in terms of the additive genetic variance, we are dealing with *narrow* heritability; these estimates are always less than estimates of *broad* heritability, which includes nonadditive factors such as assortative mating, dominance, and epistasis. In addition, uncorrected estimates of heritability, whether broad or narrow, include measurement error as part of the environmental variance; corrections for attenuation eliminate these errors from the total variance, and hence increase the size of the heritability estimates. Unless it is made clear which of these types of heritability we are discussing, differences may be far from real. In one and the same investigation, the narrow heritability, uncorrected, may be 50%; the broad heritability, uncorrected, may be 65%; and the broad heritability, corrected, may be 80%! This point should always be in mind in looking at the evidence.

In the second place, estimates of heritability are population estimates and hence are bound to differ from one population to another, and from one period to another. When we add to this the inevitable sampling errors, which in twin studies are quite large, it will be seen that identical estimates from different studies would not be expected; we would predict to find what we actually find, namely, a range of values which, in fact, are closer together than one might have expected. All in all, there is now no doubt about the vital importance of genetic factors in creating differences in intelligence, as measured by IQ tests.

This qualification, which is important, touches on the third difference between Binet and Galton, namely, the actual measurement of intelligence.

Galton suggested physiological measures, and simple tests of sensory capacity and motor reactivity, such as reaction times. Binet, on the other hand, preferred tests involving problem solving, learning, memory, and evidence of past learning such as vocabulary and other types of verbal achievement. Until quite recently, the measurement of intelligence tests has followed almost completely Binet's example, and typical test items in modern IQ tests do not differ substantively from those already appearing in the *Binet–Simon Scales* as they were contructed in the early years of this century, and later adapted to American conditions by Terman and to English conditions by Burt. The suggestion will be made in this chapter that this choice led to many of the difficulties of IQ testing; it invited many of the criticisms which have in fact been made of it, and, in particular, it made difficult if not impossible the cross-cultural study of intelligence. The reasons for this choice, and the differential meaning of the types of test proposed by Galton and Binet, cannot be understood without reference to the different meanings of the term *intelligence* which are customarily accepted nowadays.

It is now usual to discriminate between *Intelligence A*, *Intelligence B*, and *Intelligence C* – terms which are not self-explanatory but which have acquired very definite meanings through the writings of Vernon (1979) and others. Intelligence A refers to the physiological biological substrata which enable human beings to solve problems, learn cognitive contents, remember and reproduce learned material, and, quite generally, deal with cognitive content of various types. This is essentially the intelligence which Galton was concerned with, and which he attempted to measure by means of reaction times and the various other tests he proposed.

Intelligence B, on the other hand, is, as it were, Intelligence A in action, that is, the application of intelligence to the practical problems of everyday life. As such, Intelligence B obviously includes Intelligence A as an important determinant, but there are others as well, such as personality, temperament, education, cultural factors, socioeconomic status, and many more. High Intelligence A may be negatived by impulsivity or other personality traits, or by high degrees of anxiety and other temperamental variables. It may also be prevented from functioning properly by inadequate education, low socioeconomic status, or cultural factors of the kind discussed in a number of chapters of this book. Clearly, Intelligence B is much more *inclusive* than Intelligence A, and for scientific purposes it may be considered to be overinclusive as a concept.

Intelligence C refers to attempts to measure intelligence, embodied in the usual type of IQ test. IQ tests are inevitably geared more to Intelligence B than to Intelligence A, because of the determining influence of Binet. Hence, they have been found excellent predictors of educational success and achievement in school and university, success in the army and various occupations requiring cognitive ability, and quite generally in activities requiring high Intelligence A (Eysenck, 1979). However, from the point of view of scientific measurement, which requires unidimensional scales, the

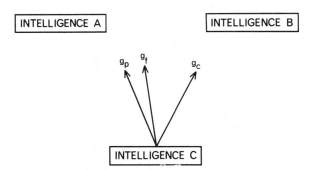

Figure 3.1. Intelligence A, Intelligence B, and Intelligence C:
their relation to crystallised intelligence, fluid intelligence,
and physiological intelligence.

mixture of genetic and environmental factors and the multifarious determinants, apart from Intelligence A, which are measured by typical IQ tests,
make these tests less valuable than they might otherwise be.

Figure 3.1 shows in a diagrammatic form the relationship between Intelligence A, Intelligence B, and Intelligence C. The three arrows refer to three
different types of measures of intelligence, namely, measures of crystallised
ability (g_c) tests of fluid ability (g_f), and physiological tests of intelligence
(g_p). These tests measure different combinations of Intelligence A and Intelligence B, with tests of crystallised ability being closest to Intelligence B,
and physiological tests of intelligence being closest to Intelligence A.

It is sometimes suggested that this diversity of conceptualisations of intelligence preclude it from being a useful scientific concept, but this is not
correct. There is no doubt that heat is a useful scientific concept, but it is
possible to discriminate here also between heat A, heat B, and heat C. Heat
A would be the physical basis of differences in temperature, namely, the
speed of movement of molecules and atoms. Heat B would be the subjective
feeling of heat, as experienced by individuals; this is obviously determined
to a large extent by heat A, but other factors also influence it, such as the
chill factor (the movement of air), the humidity of the air, intake of food,
and alcohol, exercise, and many other similar factors. A well-known experiment illustrates the difference between heat A and heat B. In this experiment, individuals put their right hand in a bowl of cold water, their left
hand in a bowl of hot water, and after a little while, put both hands into the
same bowl containing lukewarm water. This will feel hot to the right hand
and cold to the left hand, indicating that whereas heat A is identical, heat
B is experienced very differently.

Heat C is temperature as measured, and the measurement may be carried
out in many different ways. There is the mercury-in-glass thermometer, depending on the change in volume of the mercury with increase in heat, the
constant-volume gas thermometer, depending on the reactance of the welded

junction of two fine wires; resistance thermometers, depending on the relations between resistance and temperature; thermocouples, depending on the setting up of currents by two dissimilar metals with their junctions at different temperatures, and so on. Nor do these different measurements of temperature always agree on the actual temperature of the given body. Thus, when a mercury-in-glass thermometer reads 300°C, the platinum-resistance thermometer at the same place and at the same time will read 291°C! There is no meaning attached to the question of which of these two values is "correct," and it is clear that the notion that a temperature scale has "equal intervals" is a myth.

It will now be clear that Galton was concerned with Intelligence A, Binet, with Intelligence B, and that although the two are closely related – as shown, for instance, by the high contribution of genetic factors to Intelligence C – they are not identical. In comparing two groups of individuals, differentiated in terms of cultural, educational, or socioeconomic factors, we would expect Intelligence B to exaggerate any differences there might be in Intelligence A, for the simple reason that Intelligence A would take into account only genetic differences between the two groups, whereas Intelligence B would add to these educational, cultural, and other differences, thus increasing the total measure of the difference. An example of this is given by Eysenck (1982a), who compared a group of high socioeconomic status children with a group of low socioeconomic status children. On the *Wechsler Tests (WISC)* of IQ, the difference between these two groups was 20% higher than it was on a simple physiological test of intelligence, of the kind to be discussed presently. It would be possible for quite large differences in Intelligence B between different groups to disappear when intelligence was measured by tests more appropriate to the investigation of Intelligence A; hence, as will be discussed later in this chapter, it may be that measurements of Intelligence A are more appropriate than ordinary IQ tests for the investigation of cross-cultural differences.

It has been argued by Jensen (1982) that reaction time measurement, as suggested by Galton, does, indeed, provide a good measure of Intelligence A. He and many others have shown that there are substantial correlations between IQ, on the one hand, and simple and choice reaction times on the other. The correlations increase with the complexity of the task; thus, simple reaction times give the lowest correlation, choice reaction times with eight or more choices give the highest. In addition, it has been found that the slope of the regression line drawn through the points defining reaction times to different numbers of choices gives a good correlation with intelligence, with high-IQ subjects showing less steep slopes than low-IQ subjects. In other words, the increase in complexity as the number of choices grows, increases the reaction times of bright subjects less than it does the reaction times of dull subjects.

The last point emphasised by Jensen is that the *variability* of reaction time measured for a given person gives the highest correlation with IQ of all the reaction time measures, in the sense that the greater the variability, the duller the subject is likely to be. The point is an important one because it may help to decide between alternative theories of intelligence, and we will return to it later in the chapter.

In addition to simple and choice reaction time measures, and the other measures we have mentioned, there are tests of inspection time, and various reaction time paradigms involving short-term and long-term memory (Brand & Deary, 1982; Jensen, 1982a, 1982b) which also give positive results; we will not here go into these and others discussed by Eysenck (1982a, 1982b); suffice it to say that these tests depart significantly from Binet's suggestions for IQ tests in that they show no learning, do not involve problem solving, and are not dependent in any sense on previous learning. That they nevertheless correlate very highly with typical IQ tests must throw serious doubt on the theories concerning the reasons why the latter measure intelligence to a significant extent.

In Galton's time, of course, there was no way of measuring the physiological activity of the brain, but since then the discovery of the electroencephalogram (EEG) has presented us with an obvious approach to the problem of psychophysiological recording of events, possibly related to the IQ. Cattell (1971), Eysenck and Barrett (1983), and Gasser, Von Lucadou-Muller, Verleger, and Bacher (1983) have reviewed much of the evidence, which indicates that on the whole there is little correlation between ordinary EEG activity and intelligence, except perhaps in young and retarded children. Ellingson (1966) and Vogel and Broverman (1964, 1966) have put forward views, the one rather negative, the other somewhat more positive, with respect to the possible usefulness of EEG recordings for the measurement of intelligence. We would agree with Callaway (1975), who believes it would be more nearly correct to say that the EEG-intelligence correlations reported thus far are unpromising rather than that they are invalid, and that these repetitive waves, like aspects of the ongoing EEG, are not the best windows on the mind. This is presumably because such repetitive waves in the EEG tell us more about what the EEG is *not* doing than about what the mind is doing. Wavelike activities often signal a failure to operate, and if the brain is usually busy on a variety of jobs, the EEG is a jumble of signals appropriate to the jumble of underlying processes, and hence not likely to reflect disposition of such qualities as intelligence.

Gasser et al. (1983) suggest that the discrepant results of previous analyses may have been due to their reliance on parameters derived from a visual rather than a computerised analysis of the EEG. In their own work, broadband spectral parameters were mainly used, and when all the EEG parameters were standardised for age, quite high correlations were found between EEG and IQ, but only in certain frequency bands. Replications of this work are required before we can accept that certain results, at least, from the analysis of the ordinary EEG are highly correlated with IQ, but the findings

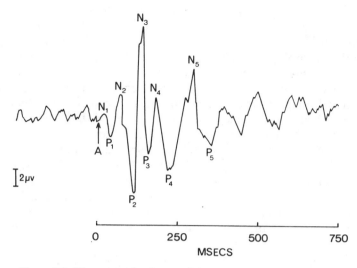

Figure 3.2. Diagrammatic picture of the average evoked potential.

are distinctly promising and may lead to a revaluation of the present unfavourable attitude to EEG measurement.

More successful than the analysis of ordinary EEG variations has been the study of events-related potentials, such as the contingent negative variation (CNV), and more importantly, the averaged evoked potential (AEP). The former of these variables has been less frequently used, and does not show much promise, but the AEP, after a slow initial start, has now achieved a quite unique status in the attempts to provide measures of Intelligence A, on a psychophysiological basis.

The nature of AEPs (Regan, 1972; Shagass, 1972; and Basar, 1980) is shown in diagrammatic form in Figure 3.2. The resting IQ is shown to the left of the arrow, which indicates the imposition of some kind of sensory stimulus that may be auditory, visual, or somato-sensory. The series of waves, negative and then positive in each case, is the averaged evoked potential, gradually dying out after something like 750–1,000 milliseconds. The AEP has a poor signal-to-noise ratio, partly because it is superimposed on the ordinary rhythm of the EEG, and hence a number of time-locked evocations have to be averaged in order to give a recognisable and measurable wave; in our own work, 90 such waves are averaged to obtain the recorded AEP.

The shape of the resulting wave form of the AEP differs from person to person, and is dependent on a number of factors, such as the nature of the stimulus, electrode location, electrode placement, intensity of the stimulus, and state of the subject. Hence, results are often difficult to replicate unless very close attention is paid to the precise parameters involved – a precaution seldom taken by psychologists attempting to replicate other psychologists' work! If different investigators use different electrode placements, bipolar versus unipolar recordings, different types of stimuli, different intensities of stimuli, different interstimulus intervals, different instructions, different wave form analyses, and other parameter differences which may be related to attentional and similar psychological factors, and then correlate these with different types of IQ tests, some of them measures of fluid, some of them measures of crystallised ability, some more likely measures of educational learning, then clearly confusion is likely to reign supreme and we will be lucky if we can disentangle the most promising types of arrangement likely to give positive results. As one might have expected from these considerations, early investigations of the relationship between IQ and AEP showed a bewildering conglomeration of positive, negative, and inconclusive results, producing sometimes quite acrimonious arguments between different workers.

Callaway (1975) surveys this early evidence in detail, and makes clear that there is much evidence of *some* relationship between IQ and evoked potential. The trend has been to try an approach rather similar to that of Binet, who related intelligence to the concept of mental age, that is, development of cognitive capacity from early to late childhood. Applying this approach to the AEP, it was suggested that those aspects of the AEP which change from early to late childhood might be measures of mental age, and possibly of IQ. With increasing age, there is a reduction in the *variability* of the AEP, a reduction also in latency, and an increase in amplitude. In other words, in the older child there is an increase in the frequency and height of waves, and the waves resemble each other more closely than they do at an earlier age. On theoretical grounds, these parameters might therefore be explored to some advantage, and the evidence has certainly suggested that there is a negative relationship between IQ and variability of AEP, similarly, a negative correlation between IQ and latency, and a positive correlation between IQ and amplitude of AEP waves. It should be noted that these different measures are not independent. Thus, high variability almost inevitably means *long* latencies and *small* amplitudes; this is because if, over a large number of repetitions of the experiment, variability is great, then the peak of one measurement will not coincide with the peak of another, and the trough of one will not coincide with the trough of another. This will inevitably *reduce* the amplitudes, and *increase* the latency, of AEP measures. If there is little variability, then peaks will coincide with each other, as will troughs, and amplitudes will be *greater*, and latencies will be *less*. The variability may be the most important parameter to be investigated, with amplitude and latency secondary variables, easier to measure directly, but dependent for their very existence on differences in variability.

The pioneer in this work was Ertl, who continued with various collaborators to publish in this field for a period of about 12 years, starting with his early paper (Chalke & Ertl, 1965) and continuing with a whole series of other papers (Ertl, 1971, 1973). This group tried many frequency-domain measures in their attempts to improve correlations – including Fourier analysis, complex demodulation, analogue spectro-analysis, and the like – but the time-domain measure has remained their preference. Using it, quite large samples have been tested and have produced correlations with standard IQ tests in the neighbourhood of .3 in a fairly consistent fashion. Not all investigators have found such correlations (Rhodes, Dustman, & Beck, 1969; Davis, 1971; Dustman & Beck, 1972; Engel & Henderson, 1973; Dustman, Schenkenberg, & Beck, 1975), and these negative findings have had a powerful effect on many research workers, but they have to be seen in the context of the particular design of Ertl's experiments, which were quite different from those of the people who tried to replicate them. These differences have been fully discussed by Eysenck and Barrett (1983); suffice it to say that in spite of these failures, there have been sufficient replications of Ertl's work giving positive results to assert that correlations between AEP latency and IQ, accounting for some 10% of the variance, are obtainable when suitable attention is paid to parameter values. Callaway (1975) and Shucard and Horn (1972) discuss the evidence in detail, as do Eysenck and Barrett (1983). Most of these successful studies have used visual stimuli, and it is odd that the evidence on auditory latency should be rather ambiguous. Work in our laboratories (Hendrickson, 1972) found, as one might have expected, that auditory stimuli are rather more likely to give high correlations with IQ than visual stimuli (Eysenck, 1973). She found that both latency (negatively) and amplitude (positively) were correlated with intelligence, with the average size of the correlations ranging from .30 to .50 for latency, from .30 to .45 for amplitude when we are considering verbal ability, and from .10 to .25 when we are considering spatial ability.

The reason for expecting verbal stimuli to give higher correlations with IQ than visual ones is simply that variability is likely to be higher for visual stimuli because the eye is in constant movement, and hence visual stimuli will excite different neurons each time, thus resulting in response variability. Auditory stimuli are much more likely to excite the same neurons, and hence to result in a lesser degree of variability. Increases in variability of this kind would act as other variants, reducing correlations with IQ.

There is good evidence to show that evoked potentials, with special reference to their amplitude and latency, have a strong degree of genetic determination. The evidence, much of it coming from our own laboratories, is discussed by Eysenck and Barrett (1983), and this aspect of the work will not be gone into here. Neither will we discuss the rather doubtful status of AEP *asymmetry* with respect to the measurement of intelligence. Asymmetrical AEPs can be produced by somato-sensory stimulation, which results in a contralateral parietal AEP that has more complex early components than does the ipsi-lateral parietal AEP. Similarly, one-sided stimulation of other modalities produces asymmetrical AEPs. Cognitive operations can also be used in this context, propositional (left-hemisphere) cognitive operations tending to suppress the EEG from the left hemisphere and to reduce AEPs to the relevant stimuli, with appositional (right-hemisphere) tasks suppressing right-hemisphere EEGs and task-irrelevant AEPs. There is some suggestion that greater asymmetry can be found in bright children, and in bright adults; Callaway (1975) has summarised these studies, but his own later work has given negative results. Much more work will have to be done in relation to this parameter to convince psychologists that it has positive contributions to make.

From the practical point of view most of this older work is of little interest; correlations with IQ are too small to suggest that these tests can throw much light on the nature of intelligence. From the theoretical point of view, their interest is also not very high, because much of the early work was entirely pragmatic and hence incapable of throwing light on the theoretical issues involved. In more recent times, both these conditions have changed drastically. There have been attempts to suggest theoretical considerations which might determine the variables to be measured, and these new types of measurement have been exceptionally successful, giving correlations with IQ tests in excess of .80.

We will here look briefly at two of the paradigms suggested, and the evidence brought forward to support them; a much more detailed survey will be found in Eysenck and Barrett (1983). The first paradigm to be considered is that by Hendrickson (1972, 1982) and Hendrickson and Hendrickson (1980). They actually suggest a psychophysiological and biochemical model, which is too complex and too far removed from the main purpose of this chapter to be considered in detail. Here we will rather take up the major proposition which links this work with the measurement of AEPs in such a way as to make possible an improved measurement of intelligence. The essential feature of this suggestion is that individuals differ in the fidelity with which messages and information are transmitted through the cortex: Some individuals have only few and occasional errors occurring in this transmission, while others have many and frequent errors. Error-free transmission is the basis of high intelligence, on this conception, thus leaving low-IQ individuals in the position of having their ability to learn, solve problems, and generally behave in an intelligent fashion curtailed by the frequency of transmission errors; these errors are supposed to occur most frequently at the synapse. We will not here argue about the plausibility of this hypothesis, nor will we consider its relationship to the underlying biochemical and psychophysiological theory of the Hendricksons; to do so would take us too far afield. We will rather now look at the deductions that can be made from this general hypothesis onto the actual measurement of AEPs, and thus indirectly on the measurement of intelligence.

The Hendricksons' suggestion is that individuals with neuronal circuitry that can maintain the encoded integrity of stimuli will form accessible memories faster, and will enable problems to be encoded and solved more quickly, than those individuals whose circuitry is more "noisy." In addition, for individuals of low neuronal integrity, the maintenance of long sequences of pulse trains, which in the Hendricksons' model transmit information, will be practically impossible; the total information content can never be stored in a meaningful way, thus preventing accessible memories from being formed. Hence one would observe differences within individuals' knowledge bases.

How would such errorless or errorful transmission be distinguished in terms of the AEP? The first point to be made, of course, is that error-free transmission would show less *variability* in the evoked potentials on different occasions, while error-full transmission should show a much higher degree of variability. On this hypothesis, variability itself would be the preferred measure of IQ, and this can be accomplished if we have the detailed evoked potential records for all the data points on which the average evoked potential is based. In our work, we have used recordings over 250 milliseconds with data points every 2 milliseconds; the AEP is based on 90 evocations. Hence, the variability is measured by taking the variance over 90 measures for each of the 125 data points, and then averaging these: This gives a direct measure of response variability.

Another measure is the "string" measure, named because in the early stages of development, attempts to measure the complexity of the trace were implemented by laying out a string along the contour of the AEP trace, then pulling it straight and measuring its total length. The name has remained, although, of course, more sophisticated computerised methods are now in use (Eysenck, 1982a). The reason for using a measure of complexity was simply that apparently those individuals with noisy channels would produce AEPs of a smoother appearance than those from individuals with less noisy channels, whose AEPs should be much more complex. Figure 3.3 will illustrate the actual difference between AEPs from bright and dull children, taken from our own work; the smooth appearance of the curves on the right, and the much more complex appearance of the curves on the left, will illustrate that these hypotheses are in fact borne out by the records of bright and dull children.

Given that the theory is along the right lines, it may be suggested that here we have a rational measure which can be objectively quantified and correlated with intelligence, and which can thus be used to verify or disprove the hypothesis on which it is based. Hendrickson (1982) carried out the requisite study on a group of 219 children, of average intelligence and with a standard deviation of 14, chosen from British schools on a random basis. These children were administered the *Wechsler Test (WAIS)* of IQ, as well as being tested on the AEP, with the two psychophysiological measures (variability and complexity) combined to form a single measure. The correlation between IQ and AEP was .83, a surprisingly high correlation which is, in fact, higher than the correlation normally found between the *Wechsler* and the *Binet*, or indeed between any two typical IQ tests! This is a highly

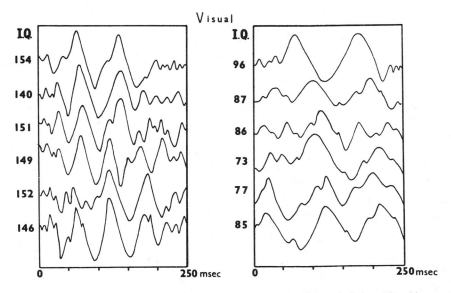

Figure 3.3. Evoked potential wave forms for six high and six low IQ subjects.

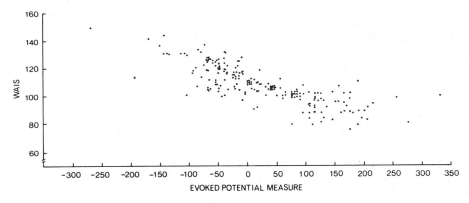

Figure 3.4. Scatter diagram of scores of 219 children on the *WISC* and the evoked potential measure.

unexpected finding, and one which, if replicated, would seem to be incompatible with the usual theoretical considerations applied to ordinary *Binet*-type IQ tests. Figure 3.4 shows the scatter diagram of the IQ–AEP correlation.

The first replication of the study has been reported by Blinkhorn & Hendrickson (1982), who correlated the complexity ("string") measure with performance on *Raven's Advanced Progressive Matrices* and a variety of verbal ability tests. As a sample, the authors used a student population, with a very restricted range of ability. The correlation between the matrices test and the string measure, corrected for range, was .84, the uncorrected correlation being .45. The correlation is reasonably similar to the one reported above, and also to a reanalysis by the Hendricksons of some published data of Ertl's, which showed a correlation of .77 between *WISC* IQ scores and with string scores from evoked potential; only extreme IQ scores were recorded in the Ertl study.

Of other replications, discussed by Eysenck and Barrett (1983), the most relevant is one by Haier, Robinson, Braden, and Williams (1983), reporting an investigation into the relationship between various AEP wave form amplitude measures, the string measure, and *Raven's Advanced Progressive Matrices*. These authors used several different intensities of visual stimuli, finding that the intensity of stimulus is important in determining the size of the relationship between both the string and amplitude measures and the scores on the IQ tests. The correlations reported for the string measure indicated values around .223 for low-intensity stimulation, up to .45 for high intensities. For the amplitude measures, these values ran from .35 to .63 respectively. Considering that the range of ability of their subjects was rather restricted, the correlations, if corrected, would be rather similar to those originally reported by Hendrickson. It does seem there is good empirical evidence to show that the measures suggested by the Hendricksons can give high correlations with IQ, and that these correlations are replicable. This is important information, although, of course, it cannot be assumed that because these predictions from the theory are verified, the theory itself is correct. This qualification is particularly important with respect to the biochemical and psychophysiological theory underlying the work of the Hendricksons; the empirical findings are too far removed from the basic theory to serve as sufficient verification for an acceptance of the theory, which has been criticised on various grounds by experts in the biochemical and psychophysiological fields. Whether these criticisms are or are not cogent is beyond our capacity to decide; the important point to remember is that the theory of error-free transmission as a basis for high intellectual achievement has found considerable support in the data. Further testing and replication seem urgently desirable in view of the apparent success of the methods used.

Of alternative paradigms to the Hendrickson one, we will here only mention the Schafer paradigm, which is related to a number of studies showing the influence of selective attention, (Hillyard, Hink, Schwent, & Picton, 1973; Picton & Hillyard, 1974), expectancy (Squires, Wickens, Squires, & Donchin, 1976; Schafer, Amochaev, & Russell, 1981), and information-processing work load (Schafer, 1978; Israel, Wickens, Chesney & Donchin, 1980) on the amplitude of AEPs, which have all demonstrated a cognitive modulation of EEG activity. This modulation is manifested as a tendency for unexpected or "attendant" stimuli to produce AEPs of larger overall amplitude than those generated using stimuli whose nature and timing are known to the individual. Schafer has extended the scope of this empirical phenomenon, hypothesising that individual differences in the modulation of amplitude (cognitive neural adaptability) will relate to individual differences in intelligence. The physiological basis mediating this relationship is hypothesised to be neural energy as defined by the number of neurons firing in response to stimulus. Functionally, an efficient brain will use fewer neurons to process a foreknown stimulus, whereas for a novel, unexpected stimulus, the brain will commit large numbers of neurons. This commitment of neural energy is observed in the AEP as amplitude differences between AEPs elicited from various stimulus presentation conditions.

Schafer used self-stimulation – that is, a condition in which the subject delivered clicks and flashes to himself by means of pressing a hand-held microswitch, with some attempt to deliver the stimuli randomly in time – as indicative of foreknown stimulus presentation, and contrasted this with machine stimulation where recorded stimulus events generated in the first condition were replayed to the subject, who, of course, had no memory of the precise sequence. There were also various control conditions, but the main point in the Schafer (1982) study is that quite high correlations were found by him in the expected direction; when corrected for restriction of range, the final correlation obtained was one of .82, with a higher IQ being accompanied by greater amplitude differences between the expected and unexpected stimulus amplitude measures. This implies greater flexibility between the intentional response to expected stimuli, that is, the higher IQ subjects habituate to a greater extent (as indexed by amplitude) to regular, expected stimuli than do the lower IQ subjects. Eysenck and Barrett (1983) have criticised some aspects of this study and have suggested that different methods of analysis would have given much more relevant results as far as Schafer's hypothesis was concerned, but these criticisms should not blind us to the fact that again a very high correlation has been found between AEP measures of one kind or another, and IQ. It must be admitted that the underlying paradigm is rather different from that of the Hendricksons, but it is possible to reframe the Schafer paradigm in terms of the Hendricksons' notion of error-free transmission, and consequently to reduce it to the latter. There are still other paradigms within the electrophysiological field, such as that of Robinson (1982a, 1982b), discussed in some detail by Eysenck and Barrett (1983). However, Robinson's theory is highly technical and has less empirical support than the paradigms of the Hendricksons or Schafer, and hence the reader must be referred to the original papers or to the Eysenck and Barrett (1983) discussion for details. There is an urgent need for a replication of all these studies and for a reconciliation in the sense that the same experimenter should employ all these different paradigms on the same sample of subjects, selected in such a way that the mean and standard deviation of the sample would be similar to, or identical with, that of the general population, a selection process hitherto attempted only by the Hendricksons. Such a study would considerably aid in formulating theories to bring together the different paradigms, and would also help in finally deciding on the acceptability of all this body of evidence.

We must now turn to an attempt to formulate a more general theory concerning the nature of intelligence, as derived from the work here reviewed of reaction time and evoked potential measurement. We may begin with an attempt to create such a theory, based on reaction times only, by Jensen (1982a, 1982b), which with some modifications will also serve very well for our purposes. As he points out, the conscious brain acts as a one-channel or *limited-capacity* information-processing system which can deal simultaneously with only very limited amounts of information. This limited capacity also restricts the number of operations that can be performed simultaneously on the information that enters the system from external stimuli, or from retrieval of information stored in short-term or long-term memory. As he points out, speediness of mental operations is advantageous in that more operations per unit of time can be executed without overloading the system.

Second, there is *rapid decay* of stimulus traces and information, so that there is an advantage to speediness of any operation that must be performed on the information while it is still available. The third relevant point is that to compensate for limited capacity and rapid decay of incoming information, the individual resorts to *rehearsal and storage* of the information into intermediate or long-term memory, which has relatively unlimited capacity. However, clearly the process of storing information in long-term memory itself takes time and therefore uses up channel capacity, so that there is a trade-off between the storage and the processing of incoming information. The more complex the information and the operations required on it, the more time will be required, and consequently the greater will be the advantage of speediness in all the elemental processes involved. Loss of information – because of overload interference and decay of traces inadequately encoded or rehearsed for storage or retrieval for long-term memory – results in "breakdown" and failure to grasp all the essential relationships among the elements of a complex problem needed for its solution. "Speediness of information processing, therefore, should be increasingly related to success in dealing with cognitive tasks to the extent that the information load strains the individual's limited channel capacity" (Jensen, 1982b, p. 122).

Jensen stresses *speed* as the essential component of cognitive ability or intelligence. I would prefer to look at it rather from the point of view of *error-free* information processing, regarding speed as a secondary and dependent variable, differences in which are causally produced by differences in the number of errors made in transmission. As a model, consider that information processing is always conducted on a multiple basis, that is, it is never carried through as a single process but is repeated a number of times, so that redundancy can avoid errors in transmission. We may conceive of a comparator, which looks at the incoming messages, and decides upon action on the basis of a judgment that the incoming messages are sufficiently similar to rule out errors in transmission. Where there are no errors in transmission, a small sample of incoming messages will suffice to trigger off action. However, where there are many errors, the sample will have to be much larger, and hence action will be delayed until certainty of accuracy can be approached if not reached. Thus the speed of reaction is dependent on error-free transmission, and the greater the number of errors, the longer will be the latency. Therefore speed is not an independent variable in itself.

It would be possible to go farther and elaborate a more detailed theory of intelligence on this basis, integrating it with concepts of heuristic research taken from work on artificial intelligence. However, this would again take us beyond the confines of this chapter, and I will instead discuss the relevance of these findings to the question of cross-cultural comparisons of intelligence. It will be clear that by returning to the Galton paradigm, we can avoid the difficulties of the Binet paradigm, and reduce or totally abolish the influence of educational, cultural, socioeconomic, and other factors which are, strictly speaking, irrelevant to the measurement of Intelligence A. Although it may not be impossible to reduce the influence of these disturbing factors along the lines discussed in other chapters of this book, it would seem more reasonable to try a direct approach and use methods of evoked potential measurement for comparisons between different cultural groups, in the hope of thus bypassing difficulties produced by Binet-type tests.

Obviously, this can be only a hope and not a certainty. We need much more experience with these methods, as well as direct experimental evidence relating to their culture-free nature, before accepting them as valid evidence for cross-cultural comparative studies. Callaway (1975) has reported some disturbing evidence suggesting that there may be racial differences which directly influence AEP comparisons, although his account merely raises the possibility and does not invalidate the cross-cultural use of such tests. The urgent need, clearly, is for direct research along these lines, but it is absolutely essential that such research be based on adequate preparation and knowledge, not only of cross-cultural research but also of psychophysiological studies. Technical details are vitally important in the carrying out and evaluation of research along these lines; unless a high level of technical competence is available, such studies are contra-indicated as being more likely to confuse than to elucidate important relationships. If properly conducted, and if the results available now stand up to replication and further study, then it would seem that we have in these methods a powerful tool for advancing our understanding of the complex relationships, which other authors have attempted to dissect in this book. There are no simple and easy ways of reaching conclusions, and any results that may be found with the use of AEPs should always be seen in the context of alternative approaches and other paradigms. However, although the hope that the new methods may be pure measures of Intelligence A is not likely to be realised in full, it would seem likely that they are more "culture-fair" than any existing tests, an approach to pure measures of intelligence coming closer to this aim than do ordinary IQ tests, even of the "fluid intelligence" type. If this be true, then their use would be of obvious interest, even though they do not reach the level of perfection which might ultimately be desirable.

References

Basar, E. (1980). *EEG-brain dynamics*. New York: Elsevier.

Blinkhorn, S. F., & Hendrickson, D. E. (1982). Averaged evoked responses and psychometric intelligence. *Nature, 295*, 596–597.

Brand, C. R., & Deary, I. J. (1982). Intelligence and "inspection time." In H. J. Eysenck (Ed.), *A model for intelligence* (pp. 133–148). New York: Springer-Verlag.

Callaway, E. (1975). *Brain electrical potentials and individual psychological differences*. London: Grune & Stratton.

Cattell, R. B. (1971). *Abilities: Their structure, growth and action*. Boston: Houghton Mifflin.

Chalke, F., & Ertl, J. (1965). Evoked potentials and intelligence. *Life Sciences, 4*, 1319–1322.

Davis, F. B. (1971). The measurement of mental ability through evoked potential recording. *Educational Record Research Bulletin*, No. 1.

Dustman, R. E., & Beck, E. C. (1972). Relationship of intelligence to visually evoked responses. *Electroencephalographic and Clinical Neurophysiology, 33*, 254–262.

Dustman, R. E., Schenkenberg, T., & Beck, E. C. (1975). The development of the evoked response as a diagnostic and evaluative procedure. In R. Karrer (Ed.), *Developmental psycho-physiology in mental retardation and learning disability*. Springfield, Ill: C. C. Thomas.

Ellingson, R. J. (1966). Relationship between EEG and test intelligence: A commentary. *Psychological Bulletin, 65*, 91–98.

Engel, R., & Henderson, N. B. (1973). Visual evoked responses and I.Q. scores at school age. *Developmental and Medical Child Neurology, 15*, 136–145.

Ertl, J. (1971). Fourier analysis of evoked potentials and human intelligence. *Nature, 230*, 525–526.

Ertl, J. (1973). I. Q., evoked responses and Fourier analysis. *Nature, 241*, 209–210.

Ertl, J., & Schafer, E. (1969). Brain response correlates of psychometric intelligence. *Nature, 223*, 421–422.

Eysenck, H. J. (1939). Primary mental abilities. *British Journal of Educational Psychology, 9*, 270–275.

Eysenck, H. J. (1979). *The structure and measurement of intelligence*. New York: Springer-Verlag.

Eysenck, H. J. (1982a). *A model for intelligence*. New York: Springer-Verlag.

Eysenck, H. J. (1982b). The psychophysiology of intelligence. In C. D. Spielberger & J. N. Butcher (Eds.) *Advances in personality assessment* (Vol. 1). Hillsdale, NJ: Erlbaum.

Eysenck, H. J. (Ed.) (1973). *The measurement of intelligence*. Lancaster, U.K.: MTP.

Eysenck, H. J., & Barrett, P. (1983). Psychophysiology and the measurement of intelligence. In C. R. Reynolds & V. Sillson (Eds.), *Methodological and statistical advances in the study of individual differences*. New York: Plenum.

Gasser, T., Von Lucadou-Muller, I., Verleger, R., & Bacher, P. (1983). Correlating EEG and IQ: A new look at an old problem using computerised EEG parameters. *Electroencephalography and Clinical Neurology, 55*, 493–504.

Guilford, J. P., & Hoepfner, R. (1971). *The analysis of intelligence*. New York: McGraw-Hill.

Haier, R. J., Robinson, D. L., Braden, W., & Williams, D. (1983). Electrical potentials of the cerebral cortex and psychometric intelligence. *Personality and Individual Differences, 4*, 591–599.

Hendrickson, A. E. (1982). The biological basis of intelligence. 1: Theory. In H. J. Eysenck (Ed.), *A model for intelligence*. New York: Springer-Verlag.

Hendrickson, D. E. (1972). *An examination of individual differences in the cortical evoked response*. Unpublished doctoral dissertation, University of London.

Hendrickson, D. E. (1982). The biological basis of intelligence. Part II: Measurement. In H. J. Eysenck (Ed.), *A model for intelligence*. New York: Springer-Verlag.

Hendrickson, D. E., & Hendrickson, A. E. (1980). The biological basis of individual differences in intelligence. *Personality and Individual Differences, 1*, 3–33.

Hillyard, S. A., Hink, R. F., Schwent, V. L., & Picton, T. W. (1973). Electrical signs of selective attention in the human brain. *Science, 182*, 177–180.

Israel, J. B., Wickens, C. D., Chesney, G. L., & Donchin, E. (1980). The event-related brain potential as an index of display monitoring workload. *Human Factors, 22*, 211–224.

Jensen, A. R. (1982a). The chronometry of intelligence. In R. J. Sternberg (Ed.), *Advances in the psychology of human intelligence*. Hillsdale, NJ: Erlbaum.

Jensen, A. R. (1982b). Reaction time and psychometric *g*. In H. J. Eysenck (Ed.), *A model for intelligence*. New York: Springer-Verlag.

Picton, T. W., & Hillyard, S. A. (1974). Human auditory evoked potentials: Effects of attention. *Electroencephalography and Clinical Neurophysiology, 36*, 191–199.

Regan, D. (1972). *Evoked potentials in psychology, sensory physiology and clinical medicine*. New York: Wiley-Interscience.

Rhodes, L., Dustman, R., & Beck, E. (1969). The visual evoked response: A comparison of bright and dull children. *Electroencephalography and Clinical Neurophysiology, 27*, 364–372.

Robinson, D. L. (1982a). Properties of the diffuse thalamocortical system and human personality: A direct test of Pavlovian/Eysenckian theory. *Personality and Individual Differences, 3*, 1–16.

Robinson, D. L. (1982b). Properties of the diffuse thalamocortical system, human intelligence and differentiated vs integrated modes of learning. *Personality and Individual Differences, 3*, 393–405.

Schafer, E. W. P. (1978). Brain responses while viewing television reflect program interest. *International Journal of Neuroscience, 8*, 71–77.

Schafer, E. W. P. (1982). Neural adaptability: A biological determinant of behavioural intelligence. *International Journal of Neuroscience, 17*, 183–191.

Schafer, E. W. P., Amochaev, A., & Russell, M. J. (1981). Knowledge of stimulus timing attenuates human evoked cortical potentials. *Electroencephalography and Clinical Neurophysiology, 52*, 9–17.

Shagass, C. (1972). *Evoked brain potentials in psychiatry*. New York: Plenum.

Shucard, D., & Horn, J. (1972). Evoked cortical potentials and measurement of human abilities. *Journal of Comparative and Physiological Psychology, 78*, 59–68.

Squires, K. C., Wickens, C., Squires, N. K., & Donchin, E. (1976). The effect of stimulus sequence on the waveform of the cortical event related potential. *Science, 193*, 1142–1146.

Thurstone, L. L. (1938). *Primary mental abilities*. Chicago: University of Chicago Press.

Thurstone, L. L. & Thurstone, T. G. (1941). *Factorial studies of intelligence*. Chicago: University of Chicago Press.

Vernon, P. E. (1979). *Intelligence: Heredity and environment*. San Francisco: Freeman.

Vogel, W., & Broverman, D. M. (1964). Relationship between EEG and test intelligence: A critical review. *Psychological Bulletin, 62*, 132–144.

Vogel, W., & Broverman, D. M. (1966). A reply to "relationship between EEG and test intelligence: A commentary." *Psychological Bulletin, 65*, 99–109.

4   Speed of information processing and population differences

Arthur R. Jensen

The purpose of this chapter is to propound the potential contribution of mental chronometry to the study of abilities in cross-cultural psychology. It informs researchers in this field of some of the techniques which have already proved useful in the study of individual differences within culturally homogeneous groups.

I use the term *cross-cultural* to refer to populations which differ in their symbolic systems, beliefs, values, and customs, without making any assumptions concerning the degree to which such cultural differences play a causal role in the variety of ability differences observed between particular populations. That is a question for empirical research. I would reject the assumption, which seems implicit in much cross-cultural research, that all behavioural differences between culturally different groups are attributable to, and wholly explainable in terms of, their cultural differences per se. The scientifically most defensible working hypothesis, I believe, is that the study of *all* human differences, in mental as well as physical characteristics, should be approached from a genetic–environment interactionist position. The culture of a population and its genetic structure are most plausibly a two-way process, each shaping the other in complex ways. It is difficult to imagine how cultural differences can be properly studied except within the broad framework of behaviour-genetic analysis, if our purpose is to go beyond the merely descriptive. Description of cultural environments and objective assessment of behaviour, however, remain crucial aspects of cross-cultural research. Chronometric techniques lend themselves to the assessment of virtually all variables that fall under the heading of "mental abilities." The choice of variables and techniques would depend upon the investigator's purpose.

To keep this chapter within the assigned limits, I shall focus on only the theoretical purposes of cross-cultural mental testing. The problems in this sphere are much more difficult than those involved in the practical use of tests, as in educational and personnel selection. The question of validity generalisation, when tests devised in one culture are applied in another, is a nontheoretical, empirical matter, if all we are concerned with is achieving practical predictive validity. The practical usefulness of a given test across different cultural groups can be evaluated by the standard psychometric methods, or a test may need to be markedly revamped in order to have practical validity in a different culture. Conceptually, the methods of applied psychometrics in test construction and validation remain fundamentally the same in different cultures, although many of the tests found to be most useful for similar purposes in different cultures may show very little superficial resemblance in form or content.

We face the really difficult, and largely unsolved but theoretically more interesting, problems when we focus on *construct validity* in cross-cultural testing. Essentially, this is the question of whether the *same ability* is measured in two (or more) different cultural groups, by whatever means are most appropriate in the particular culture. An even more difficult, but subsidiary, question is whether the same ability can be measured on directly *comparable scales* in different cultural groups. If so, it would mean that the scaled differences between individuals from two *different* populations are equivalent to the same-sized differences between individuals *within* either population. Both conditions are necessary if cross-cultural comparisons of abilities are to attain construct validity, rather than just practical predictive validity for a particular criterion. Confidence that the same ability is being measured in different populations is more easily achieved than confidence in the comparability of scales across populations. The latter condition is dependent on the former, but not vice versa.

One theoretical purpose of cross-cultural research, from the standpoint of differential psychology, is to discover those aspects of human behaviour, or the theoretical constructs "underlying" certain forms of behaviour, which are *invariant* across different cultures. By "invariant," in this context, I mean *structural invariance*, that is, invariant patterns of relationships among parameters in a limited behavioural domain, although the parameters' absolute scale values may vary between individuals or between populations. Human anatomy, for example, is replete with structural invariance across different racial groups, although numerous features statistically show *dimensional variation*. The concepts indicated by these two terms – *structural invariance* and *dimensional variation* – are also applicable to cross-cultural psychology, particularly in the study of mental abilities. Just as these properties are found in gross anatomy, they probably also apply to the fine structures of the brain. Hence, it is plausible to hypothesise that structural invariance and dimensional variation in the neural basis of behaviour are manifested also at the behavioural level. However, analysis of the brain–behaviour relationship is generally beyond the powers of unaided observation and must depend upon a number of technical developments to secure the necessary data.

The data derived from ordinary psychometric tests are often criticised, when used in cross-cultural research, on the ground that such tests reflect only the end *products* rather than the *processes* of problem solving, and that any given product or level of performance can arise in many different ways. This, in fact, is a common criticism of traditional IQ tests, even as they are used within a culturally homogeneous population. Obviously, ordinary test scores per se are too gross and far removed from the various cognitive processes that resulted in the scores to permit conclusions about structural invariance in cross-cultural studies. But analysis of item characteristics, such as the rank order of item difficulty, may reveal a considerable degree of invariance across populations. If many diverse test items maintain the same rank order of difficulty in two populations, it is presumptive evidence that the same process or processes involved in item responses are operating in both populations. If mean (or median) latencies (i.e., response times) of individual item responses also show the same rank order in both populations, and if item latencies are correlated with item difficulties in both populations, the presumption is greatly strengthened that the same cognitive processes are operating in both populations. These are examples of two types of evidence for structural invariance.

Two populations which are invariant for relative item difficulties, however, still might differ in the average efficiency of the hypothesised processes involved in item responses, which would be manifested as consistent differences in item difficulty between the two populations and, of course, in their overall test scores. It should be clear that at this level of analysis we are dealing entirely with descriptive phenotypic variables, which do not warrant inferences concerning the causes of the apparent information processing differences between populations. Special behaviour–genetic designs, such as cross-cultural adoptions and separated monozygotic twins, would be required for evidence of the relative influences of genetic and cultural factors (and their interaction) on the test performance in question.

Experimental studies in which certain abilities are trained up to asymptotic levels of performance may also be used to examine the claim that two given groups differ in some particular task performance entirely because of cultural difference in the amount of prior experience with the task. Asymptotic training is unfeasible for the kinds of complex items typically used in psychometric tests, and besides, asymptotic performance, if ever achieved by most persons, would result in near-perfect test scores by everyone, thereby precluding the possibility of measuring individual or group differences by means of psychometric test scores. This problem can be overcome by the measurement of response latencies to very simple items, performance on which is nevertheless significantly correlated with scores on complex psychometric tests. The items can be so simple that there is zero variance when performance is scored in terms of number of right or wrong responses. The only source of variance remaining is in the response latencies to each item, and these may be trained up to asymptotic levels in a fairly short time, possibly revealing stable individual or group differences in asymptotic performance – differences which may be correlated with differences on complex psychometric tests. Simple addition of pairs of integers is one example of a task which permits chronometric analysis at asymptotic levels of performance (Groen & Parkman, 1972).

Opposing hypotheses

Much of the cross-cultural research on abilities is influenced, explicitly or implicitly, by one or the other of two fundamentally different notions concerning the nature of human abilities. I shall refer to them as the *specificity-learning hypothesis* and the *structural-process hypothesis*, or, for short, the *learning* and *process hypotheses*.

The *learning hypothesis* holds that there is really only a single basic mental ability with which all humans are genetically endowed, namely, learning ability. (Whether individuals or populations are thought to be equally or unequally endowed is a separate issue; it is not intrinsic to either the learning or process hypothesis.) The apparent variety of abilities observed in performance and revealed by factor analysis of diverse tests is viewed as entirely a product of learning. According to this view, the structure of abilities discerned by factor analysis reflects only the structure of the environment in which learning occurs, rather than anything intrinsic to the learner. Original human nature, psychologically, consists of a homogeneous learning ability which gradually acquires whatever structure (i.e., interrelated skills and information) that is shaped by living in a given physical and cultural environment. Whatever invariance in cognitive structures there is across culturally different groups is the result of certain common cultural experiences and the many universal features of the physical environment. The specific-learning hypothesis thus implies virtually unlimited possibilities for the variety of abilities and their factor structure, just as a lump of clay can be moulded into innumerably different shapes in the hands of different sculptors. If abilities are entirely the result of context-specific learning, evidence of cross-cultural invariance in the structure of abilities must be viewed as due either to happenstance or to common cultural elements, rather than to common species-specific neural structures that have emerged in the course of human evolution. If various cognitive structures are not intrinsic to the human organism but are arbitrarily fashioned by the demands of a particular culture, we can take a completely relativistic view of mental abilities. "Intelligence," for example, would not be seen as a particular universal characteristic of humans, but only as whatever learned behaviours are most esteemed in any given culture. It has been suggested by some psychologists that intelligence, for Australian Aborigines, would be defined in terms of such specific adaptive skills as seeking sources of water in arid terrain, or tracking wallaby and felling them with a boomerang. As assessed by these criteria, Shakespeare and Newton might well be found mentally deficient. If we believe that context-specific learning is the whole basis of cognitive development, there would be little motivation in looking for invariance in cognitive structures across different cultural groups. Cross-cultural research would need only to describe similarities and differences in cultural environments. The only fundamental question of psychological interest, then, would be whether various populations differ in the primal learning ability itself.

The *structural-process hypothesis* agrees with the learning hypothesis only with respect to the *informational content* of learning. Of course, that is necessarily context-specific. It is like distinguishing between the specific words and syntax of different languages and the deep grammatical structures common to all languages. The main difference between the two hypotheses is this: The process hypothesis views learning as just one aspect of a number of cognitive processes which are built in or intrinsic to the organism. These distinct processes are a part of humans' "original nature," to use an old-fashioned term which is regaining currency. Just as the physical organism is not a homogeneous blob of protoplasm waiting to be shaped by the environment, so, too, mental abilities are not shaped out of a homogeneous capacity for learning. Rather, the evolution of the brain has resulted in a system of differentiated structures for information processing. In this view, individual differences and group differences can arise not only from differences in learning ability or differences in experience, but also from differences in the speed or efficiency of various component processes, such as stimulus encoding, short-term memory capacity, retrieval of information from long-term memory, and so forth. The process hypothesis invites investigation of the degree of invariance of processes (and their interrelationships) across populations from widely differing cultures. Does the set of processes that underpins an Ability factor (in the psychometric-factor analytic sense) in a given culture show up in the same configuration in a different culture? If the configuration of processes is invariant across cultures, we can then examine possible differences between populations in the efficiency of a given process or system of interrelated processes. How much of the variance in psychometric factors, such as the General Intelligence factor, or g, and in Verbal and Spatial factors, can be accounted for in terms of the efficiency or speed of the elementary cognitive processes that are the operational basis of these broad ability factors? Chronometric analysis of abilities lends itself to answering such questions. However, chronometric methods have been scarcely used by cross-cultural researchers, who have generally relied either on traditional psychometric methods or on experiments with specially devised tests or laboratory tasks which do not incorporate chronometric techniques.

General intelligence

Of all the factors identified by the factor analysis of various tests of mental abilities, the General Intelligence factor, which Spearman labelled g, has been the most prominent and the most important, theoretically and practically. It appears in virtually every battery of diverse tests when they are administered to samples that fairly represent the range of talent in the general population. The g factor shows more substantial correlations with other variables of importance in the real world than does any other single variable known to psychology. Its practical predictive power has been amply demonstrated, for example, in education and in personnel selection in business, industry, and the military (Jensen, 1984a). Two centuries ago, Adam Smith argued that the wealth of nations depends on the abilities and knowledge of their people. The g factor is central in this proposition. The perception of its importance for the economic welfare of a nation is seen in the recent establishment of a ministry of intelligence by the government of Venezuela, its mission being to raise the people's level of educability. This action suggests an awareness that educational achievement and its hoped-for effects on economic development and quality of life depend on something more than just the availability of schooling. The benefits of education depend heavily on characteristics of the pupils themselves, the prime national resource being reflected by the distribution of g in the pupil population. Other developing countries may well follow the lead of Venezuela in this concern.

The practical implications of cross-cultural investigations of g theory seem obvious. The prospect has probably been deterred by the close historical connection of g with traditional culture-loaded psychometric tests developed for use in western industrialised nations. Nevertheless, it remains a question of prime importance, theoretically and practically, whether the g construct is an identifiable characteristic of all *Homo sapiens* in *every* culture (Jensen, 1986, 1987a). The hypothesis that g is an intrinsic human trait is countered by the plausible claim that g is a cultural artifact: g reflects the all-positive correlations among diverse psychometric tests and this pattern of correlations reflects only the particular abilities, skills, and achievements that are most valued in modern industrialised societies and are inculcated by their educational and other cultural institutions. This hypothesis of g-as-artifact has gained popularity in present-day psychology. The hypothesis directly challenges the theory which originated with Francis Galton, that of intelligence as a general mental ability, a product of human evolution as a fitness character in the Darwinian sense. It should also be a challenge to cross-cultural researchers to test this theory. To prove that one and the same g can be identified in the populations of widely differing cultures would be a remarkable achievement. Whether proved or disproved, the knowledge gained in the attempt would profoundly advance our understanding of the nature of human abilities. For example, where do various abilities stand on the continuum between cultural specificity and species universality? Such research could obviously not be accomplished if we were limited to our ordinary psychometric tests. Chronometric data derived from various specific tasks devised so as to be equally appropriate within different cultures, however, may provide the needed common metric for cross-cultural analysis.

Time as a psychological variable

Every mental act, even the simplest imaginable, takes a finite amount of time, and the time taken is surprisingly long as compared to the amount of time taken by the sense organs and sensorimotor neural conduction per se. There are highly reliable time differences for various simple tasks which, subjectively, all seem of equally trivial difficulty. For example, it takes people significantly longer to add 5 + 3 than to add 5 + 2, and it takes university students, on average, more than 100 milliseconds (msec) longer to name a *glove* than to name a *chair*, and about 200 msec longer to name an *anvil* than to name an *anchor* (Oldfield & Wingfield, 1965). Such differences between the average speeds for naming various familiar objects are highly consistent across persons. (The differences in naming latencies are attributable not to word length or number of syllables but to the accessibility of the names in long-term memory, which is closely related to their frequency of use.) Moreover, there are highly reliable individual differences, even among young university graduates, in the average speed with which highly familiar objects can be named.

It is of considerable theoretical interest that virtually every type of measure of mental speed that has ever been used in experimental psychology has shown a correlation (in the expected direction) with psychometric intelligence in those studies which have included both chronometric variables and psychometric tests. This holds, however, only for chronometric tasks that are quite simple, in the sense of evoking response latencies not much greater than 1,000 msec. We are dealing here with extremely short time intervals that require great precision of measurement. They should not be trivialised by the fact that the differences between such brief time intervals are well below the threshold of our subjective awareness. One of the great advantages of mental chronometry is that it permits highly reliable measurement of sources of variance in performance, both between different tasks and between persons, that could not be discerned by any other means. Items requiring only the simplest forms of information processing would reveal absolutely no reliable variance whatsoever if performance on them were scored in the gross fashion of typical psychometric tests. Yet they are capable of yielding highly reliable measures of individual differences in terms of average response latencies.[1] For example, subjects are allowed 2 seconds

---

[1] Early studies of reaction time (RT) showed quite a low reliability of RT measurements for individuals. This was mainly because too few trials were given. The internal consistency reliability of RT, measured within a single test session, increases with the number of trials, closely in accord with the Spearman–Brown prophecy formula, and any desired degree of reliability, less than 1, can be obtained by increasing the number of trials. Test–retest reliability, when test sessions are one or more days apart, is generally lower than the internal consistency reliability, and differs according to the complexity of the RT tasks. Median RT (over trials), being less affected by outliers, is more reliable than mean RT. With 50 or more trials, median RT approaches the reliability of conventional psychometric tests. Internal consistency and test–retest reliability data on simple RT and choice RT (for varying numbers of choices) are reported by Jensen (1982b; 1987b; 1987c).

to read a brief statement on a video screen, such as "*A* after *B*," and then must respond with either *true* or *false* as quickly as possible upon the presentation of the letters *AB* (or *BA*). There are highly reliable individual differences in response latency, averaging about 500 to 600 msec in university students, and the latencies are substantially correlated with scores on untimed paper-and-pencil IQ tests (Paul, 1985). Chronometric paradigms do not depend on such crude indices of item performance as *can* versus *can't* or *right* versus *wrong*, but depend only on the time required to produce the correct response. An essential task requirement is that the correct response should be easily within the capability of all subjects for whom the test is intended. This is a crucial advantage in the study of the most fundamental components of information processing, measured by *elementary cognitive tasks* (ECTs), because these components are presumably possessed by all subjects and, of course, must be fully evoked by the ECT in order for their latencies to be measured at all.

Our chief interest in response latencies to various ECTs is that individual differences in the latencies, which can be measured with satisfactory reliability, are found to be correlated with various mental test scores and especially with psychometric *g*, the paramount factor in all IQ tests. A question of crucial theoretical importance is why reaction time (RT) to very simple tasks is correlated with performance on IQ tests comprising relatively complex items of knowledge, reasoning, and problem solving. The correlation seems counterintuitive to many psychologists. We naturally think of intelligence as being qualitatively different from, and of a higher order of mentality than, any such simple processes as could be reflected by reactions taking less than 1 second. Hence, we tend to appeal to superficial explanations, almost as if to ward off the possibility that mental speed is intrinsic to intelligence.

One such commonsense suggestion, for example, is that psychometric tests often have time limits or are "speeded," and therefore a Speed of Work factor enters into both the psychometric test and the RT task, making for the correlation between them. But there are several difficulties with this idea of a general Work-speed factor being responsible. Timed or speeded tests show no higher correlations with various RT tasks than do tests given with no time limit, in which subjects are urged to attempt every item and are encouraged to take all the time they need to finish the test (Vernon, 1983, 1985). The speed with which subjects perform on tests of intelligence is not correlated with their intelligence scores on the same or on other tests; thus work speed in the test situation is not a correlate of IQ as is RT to ECTs. Also, not all aspects of response latency in ECTs are correlated with IQ or with each other. We have found for some ECTs, for example, that when total response time is divided into RT (or *decision* time) and movement time (MT), the RT is more highly correlated with scores on an untimed intelligence test (*Raven's Progressive Matrices*) than with MT. Another line of evidence comes from looking at RTs on tasks that vary in complexity, such as *simple* and *choice* RT (SRT and CRT). In SRT, the subject responds to the occurrence of a single stimulus. In CRT, the subject makes different responses to the occurrence of two (or more) different stimuli. SRT reflects individual differences in sensory lag and motor skill common to *both* tasks, as well as differences in general effort, attention, and overall speediness of responding. Subtracting SRT from CRT gets rid of the time taken up by the noninformational aspects of task performance; the *difference* between CRT and SRT, therefore, reflects essentially the time required for processing one additional bit of information. There are reliable individual differences in the time increment of CRT minus SRT, and these differences are also correlated with IQ. All these findings are inconsistent with the idea of a general speediness factor in all types of performance, as the cause of correlations between RT and IQ. It is also noteworthy that measurements derived from the amplitude of the average evoked potential (see Chapter 3 by Eysenck), which is an involuntary cortical reaction to a "click," obtained while the subject is relaxed in a reclining chair, is correlated both with response latencies in ECTs and with psychometric *g* (Jensen, Schafer, & Crinella, 1981). In other words, response latencies that are correlated with various intelligence test scores are also correlated with a measurement of brain activity that bears absolutely no resemblance to the notion of work speed.

Another seemingly plausible explanation of the correlation between RT and IQ is in terms of speed–accuracy trade-off. Even some of the simplest ECTs can have a very low error rate (such as missing the response button or hitting the wrong button), amounting to as much as 4% or 5% of all trials. It has been shown in RT experiments that when subjects are specially instructed to maximise their speed, they do, in fact, make more errors in responding, and when instructed to maximise accuracy, they react less quickly. So it is quite conceivable that the more intelligent subjects may decide that the optimal strategy for performing an ECT is to sacrifice accuracy for speed. Brighter subjects would thereby show a higher error rate but faster RT than less intelligent subjects. The trouble with this plausible conjecture is that it turns out to be completely false. Brighter subjects, in fact, show both *faster* RT and a *lower* error rate. That is, individual differences in quickness and accuracy of response are *positively* correlated. We have never found an exception to this rule in any of our own RT studies or in any studies reported in the literature.

The evidence forces us to distinguish clearly and dissociate *speed of information processing* from speediness in the ordinary sense of working fast or hurrying to get things done in limited time, or deftness and quickness in overt behaviour (Jensen, 1984b). Individual differences in speed of information processing are probably not observable at the level of people's overt behaviour and can be detected only by means of chronometric techniques. Confusing speed of information processing with quickness of speech and other casually observable gross behaviours is a decided hindrance to understanding the relationship between mental processing speed and IQ or psychometric *g*.

The limited-capacity trace-decay theory of mental speed and psychometric performance

The most basic concept in understanding the correlation between mental speed and psychometric intelligence is the severe limitation of so-called working memory, or "short-term memory." STM has a quite limited capacity for processing incoming information or information retrieved from long-term memory (LTM). Without continuous rehearsal, the limited information in STM rapidly decays beyond retrieval, and must be replaced by future input. Manipulating information held in STM usurps some of its capacity for processing incoming information. Every mental operation takes up a certain amount of time, and if common processes are involved in two or more different operations, these must be performed successively to avoid interference with successful execution of the operations. Overloading the capacity of the system causes shunting or inhibition of the information input or a momentary breakdown in internal operations. All these effects have been demonstrated experimentally in numerous studies and are now generally acknowledged as well-established phenomena in experimental cognitive psychology (e.g., Posner, 1966, 1978, 1982).

How do these limitations of working memory figure in the observed correlation between mental speed in various ECTs and performance on untimed psychometric tests? A faster speed of mental processing, such as encoding stimuli, chunking, transformation, and storage of incoming information and retrieval of information from LTM, permits the system to overcome its limited capacity, by allowing critical operations to occur before the *decay* of information (or its memory trace) in STM. If the trace decays before solution is achieved, repetition of the information input is required until the correct response can occur. The memory span for recalling digits backward, for example, is smaller than the span for digits forward, because the operation of reversing the digits takes a certain amount of time, during which the information in STM decays. Hence, subjects who can recall 7 digits forward can usually recall only 5 digits backward. Beyond some optimal point, which varies across individuals, the average being 7 digits, the greater the number of digits presented, the smaller the number of digits recalled in correct order, because of overload and decay of memory traces. Forward and backward digit span are correlated with psychometric *g*, and are often included in IQ tests such as the *Stanford–Binet* and the *Wechsler* scales. Backward digit span, because of its greater processing demands, consistently shows a higher *g* loading than forward digit span.

Similarly, the correct responses to all mental test items depend on various elementary cognitive processes, the more complex items making the greater processing demands in terms of information storage, operations performed, information retrieved from LTM, and so forth. The more complex the information and the operations required on it, the more time that is required, and consequently the greater the advantage of speed in all the elementary processes involved. Loss of information due to overload interference and decay of traces that were inadequately coded or rehearsed for storage or retrieval results in "breakdown" in grasping all the essential relationships required for arriving at the correct answer. Speed of information processing, therefore, should be increasingly related to success in dealing with cognitive tasks to the extent that this informational load strains the individual's limited working memory. The most discriminating test items are those that "threaten" the processing system at the threshold of breakdown, beyond which erroneous responses occur. In a series of graded complexity, this breakdown would occur at different points for various individuals. If individual differences in the speed of the elementary components of information processing could be measured in tasks that are so simple as to rule out breakdown failure, it should be possible to predict the individual differences in the point of breakdown for more complex tasks, such as *Raven's Progressive Matrices* items or other items typically found in IQ tests. This is the hypothesised basis for the observed correlations between RT variables and scores on complex *g*-loaded tests.

This hypothesis is consistent with the following observed phenomena: (1) The mean response latencies to correctly answered *Raven* items (in a group of subjects) are highly correlated with the item difficulties (i.e., percentage of subjects failing an item); (2) simple true–false test items which are so easy as to elicit 100% correct answers among university students when the items are given as an untimed paper-and-pencil test, however, show highly reliable differences in average response latencies among the items when they are administered to university students as a reaction time test. The mean RTs to the items, as obtained in the university sample, are highly correlated with the *item difficulties* obtained in a group of primary school children, aged 7 to 9 years, to whom the simple true–false items were administered as an untimed paper-and-pencil test. In other words, there is a close relationship between the complexity of processing required by the items, as indicated by the items' average RTs among university students and the average item difficulties when the items are used as a typical psychometric test among primary school children. It should be noted that the items of this test (the *Semantic Verification Test* described later in this chapter) were so simple for university students that the response latencies were generally less than 1 second.

Processes and factors

The study of individual differences in mental abilities is largely based on the analysis of correlations. When more than two variables are involved, the

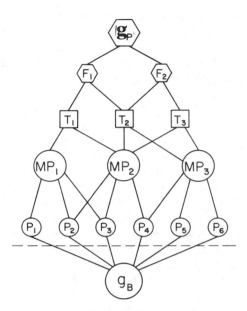

Figure 4.1. Simplified representation of relationships among processing and psychometric
variables.

most commonly used methods of correlational analysis are partial correlation, multiple correlation, canonical correlation, and factor analysis of various types. All of these methods have been used to advantage in studying
the relationships among various chronometric tasks designed to measure
certain elementary cognitive processes and psychometric tests.

At present, there is no generally agreed-upon model for representing the
relationships between these two domains. I believe that some form of hierarchical model, however, best serves as a basis for theoretical speculation
and the generation of important questions for research. One of the principal
aims of theory and research in this field is to understand how and why very
simple chronometric variables are related to broad factors of mental ability
measured by highly complex tasks. The literature, as yet, provides no complete or compelling account. But a tentative model may help to summarise
prevailing questions and focus further empirical enquiry. The simple hierarchical model shown in Figure 4.1 is one possible representation of the
most prominent variables and constructs of present concern.

The horizontal dashed line in Figure 4.1 separates the behaviourally or
psychologically measurable variables (above the line) from those that are
measurable only physiologically, such as evoked brain potentials, or are
inferred physiological processes, such as cortical conductivity (Klein &
Krech, 1952), synaptic errors (Hendrickson, 1982), neural oscillation (Jen-

sen, 1982b), and the like. The physiological level is represented as one general factor, g_B (B for "biological"), but in our present state of knowledge this level could just as well be represented as several distinct physiological processes or as correlated processes, because they share one common process, that is, g_B. The nature of this physiologic underpinning of human abilities is a major focus of Eysenck's (1982) theorising about the findings of correlations between features of the average evoked potential and psychometric g, or g_P, which is depicted in the hexagon at the top of the hierarchy in Figure 4.1. All of the solid lines in the figure represent correlations.

The various elementary cognitive processes (P) are correlated through sharing common physiological processes. Different parts of the brain or different neural assemblies are presumably specialised for various aspects of information processing. These processes are described as follows: stimulus apprehension; iconic memory; stimulus encoding; short-term memory (STM); rehearsal of encoded STM traces; memory scanning; retrieval of information from long-term memory (LTM); transfer; discrimination; generalisation; transformation of encoded information; mapping of relations; visualisation and mental rotation of figures in two- or three-dimensional space; and response execution. The *processes* (P) in this model – which are depicted here as all being closely connected with some biological substrate – can be measured by means of chronometric tasks, either directly or through derived scores, by subtraction of response latencies of simple tasks from those of more complex tasks, in order to measure the additional processes involved in the latter, or by the use of partial correlations, or by factor analysis of a combination of various tasks intended to tap different processes. The methodology of RT studies has been explicated in detail elsewhere (Jensen, 1985a).

Different sets of elementary processes (P) can be utilized by a given *metaprocess* (MP). The metaprocesses are further removed from the biologic substrate and are probably mainly products of learning and practice. Their connection to the biologic substrate is via the elementary processes which enter into the metaprocesses. Metaprocesses consist of strategies for selecting, combining, and using elementary processes, problem recognition, rule application, planning, allocation of resources, organisation of information, and monitoring one's own performance. Different metaprocesses are intercorrelated because they share certain processes in common and also because the experiential factors which inculcate metaprocesses are correlated in the educational and cultural environment. It is probably at the level of metaprocesses that cultural differences have their primary impact.

The processes and metaprocesses enter into performance on complex *psychometric tests* (T). Even a single complex test item may depend upon a number of Ps and MPs for correct performance. Various tests are intercorrelated because they share certain common Ps and MPs and also because they may share common information stored in long-term memory. Note that at each level in this hierarchy, something new is added in terms of environmental inputs. The cumulation of these acquired elements is at its maximum at the level of single items in psychometric tests. Item variance is largely *specificity*, a technical term in factor analysis, referring to a source of variance which is peculiar to a particular item (or a particular test) and is not shared in common with other variables. Specificity may arise from individuals' idiosyncratic experiences, making for unique and uncorrelated bits of information, or from complex and unique interactions among the *P* and *MP* demands and the informational content of a particular test item. In fact, all primary psychological measurements are infested with task-specific variance. Chronometric measurements of elementary processes are no exception. Specificity, which is the bane of individual differences research, can be reduced only by using composite scores or factor scores (which are a particular weighted composite of the component scores) derived from a number of varied tasks or tests, thereby "averaging out" the specificity of the individual tasks.

The top part of the hierarchy in Figure 4.1, including T, F, and g_P, comprises the realm of traditional psychometrics, including various test scores and hierarchical factors extracted by factor analysis. Here, for the sake of simplicity, are represented only two first-order factors (F and F_2) and one second-order factor, psychometric g, or g_P. The most general factor, of course, may emerge as a third-order or other higher-order factor. Each successively higher factor level excludes some source of variance. The primary factors, for example, exclude the test-specific variance, and the second-order factors exclude the variance that is peculiar to each primary factor, and so on. The most general factor, g_P, is the variance common to all the sources below it in the hierarchy.

Some homogeneous tests, such as *Raven's Progressive Matrices*, contain relatively little specificity and are therefore quite good measures of g_P. Other tests, such as the *Wechsler* scales, although containing quite heterogeneous items and subtests with considerable specificity, yield composite scores from which, in effect, the specificity is averaged out, providing a good measure of g_P.

Superficially very different tests, such as *Verbal Analogies, Digit Span*, and *Block Designs* are intercorrelated presumably not because of common content or correlated educational experiences, but because they have a number of elementary processes and metaprocesses in common. Because the more superficial differences between tests contribute mainly to their specificities, they are not reflected in g_P. Hence, it has been found that g factor scores are more highly correlated with chronometric measures of elementary processes than are any particular types of tests. Vernon (1983), for example, found that all of the correlations between the *Wechsler Adult Intelligence Scale* (*WAIS*) and a number of reaction time measures (from several elementary cognitive tasks) were due to the general factor of the *WAIS*. When the g factor was partialled out, none of the *WAIS* subtest scores correlated in the least with the RT measures. Thus, although g_P and P_1, P_2, and so on, appear widely separated in the schematic hierarchy, they actually seem to have greater variance overlap, as shown by the correlation, than do some of the more proximal variables. This picture may also help to elucidate the otherwise surprising finding that, although g_P is derived from factor analysis of psychometric tests which bear virtually no superficial resemblance in format, content, or method of administration to the RT techniques used in elementary cognitive tasks, g_P shows almost as large correlations with ECTs as with the psychometric tests from which g_P is derived.

One of the crucial theoretical questions, with reference to Figure 4.1, regarding which there is presently little consensus, is whether more of the variance in psychometric g (g_P) is attributable to the processes (P) or to the metaprocesses (MP). The learned information content in the psychometric tests (T) can already be virtually ruled out as an important source of g variance, because tests that differ extremely in their information content, such as vocabulary and matrices, are nevertheless highly saturated with one and the same g. The multiple correlation of several simple ECTs (which would tend to limit the role of complex metaprocesses) with g_P has been so substantial in some studies as to suggest that perhaps 50% or more of the g_P variance is accounted for by individual differences in elementary cognitive processes (e.g., Vernon, 1983). If task specificity were further minimised in such studies by using at least three or four different techniques for measuring each of the elementary processes which have already been shown to yield substantial correlations, it seems likely that even as much as 70% of the g variance would be associated with the processing variables. Also, the existing studies have not taken sufficient account of the reliability of these processing measures. Proper corrections for attenuation might appreciably raise the correlations between ECTs and g_P. Split-half or other internal consistency estimates of the reliability of ECTs usually overestimate the test–retest reliability, and it is the test–retest reliability which should be used in correcting correlations for attenuation when the correlated measurements were obtained in different test sessions, such as on different days or even at different times of the same day, say, before and after lunch. Some ECT measurements are so highly sensitive to an individual's fluctuating physiological state from morning till night and from day to day as to have quite low test–retest reliability as compared with most psychometric tests. Theoretical interest, of course, focusses on the *true-score* multiple correlation between g_P and the elementary cognitive processes. A conceivable goal of this research would be to determine the relative proportions of variance in g accounted for by each of a number of clearly identifiable processes and metaprocesses.

The model as presented here is admittedly a reductionist one, in the sense that g variance accounted for at the level of processes is subtracted from that accounted for at the level of metaprocesses. That is, the sources of individual differences in g_P are sought working from the bottom toward the top in Figure 4.1. This approach is arguable, of course. But it seems more plausible that elementary processes such as speed of stimulus apprehension and speed of encoding could affect performance on complex g-loaded tasks such as matrices or vocabulary than that the high-level reasoning skills and specific knowledge tapped by the psychometric tests would affect, say, choice RT to a pair of lights or speed of recognising whether two letters have the same or different names (e.g., *Aa* or *Ab*).

It also seems reasonable, at least in theory, to argue that the broad heritability of g_P sets the lower limit to the proportion of variance in g_P that is attributable to the biological substrate of intelligence (g_B in Fig. 4.1). Estimates of the broad heritability of highly g-loaded tests fall mostly in the range from about .4 to .8, with a central tendency close to .7 when corrected for attenuation. Broad heritability is defined as the proportion of variance in a trait that is attributable to all of the genetic factors that condition the development of the phenotype; it is the squared correlation between genotypes and phenotypes in the population. (For a fairly comprehensive review, see Scarr, 1982.) In what is perhaps the first published study of the heritability of reaction times in a number of ECTs and their correlations with several psychometric factors, based on twins reared apart, McGue, Bouchard, Lykken, and Feuer (1985) conclude, "The results reported here support the existence of a general speed component underlying performance on most experimental cognitive tasks which is strongly related to psychometric measures of g, and for which there are substantial genetic effects." But even if most of the g variance is ultimately traceable to inherited physiological mechanisms, it would not diminish the importance of deciphering the intervening processes and metaprocesses through which these mechanisms find expression at the behavioural level in people's performance on psychometric tests and in all the "real life" manifestations of intelligence. It is a task for behaviour–genetic research to discover the extent to which education and experience influence individual differences at each level of the hierarchy. It is also important to discover the amenability of processes and metaprocesses to specific training and the extent to which the effects of such training are reflected at the various psychometric levels of the hierarchy.

Factor analysis can also be applied to ECTs. This has not yet been attempted on a large enough scale to gain a clear picture of the factorial structure of a wide variety of ECTs. In several multivariate studies (e.g., Keating & Bobbitt, 1978; Vernon, 1983; McGue et al., 1985; Vernon & Jensen, 1985) that I have seen, however, one feature is quite clear: There is always a large General Speed factor along with other relatively smaller factors associated with particular processes, such as Stimulus-encoding Speed and Memory-scanning Rate. Thus the P's in Figure 4.1 are seen as all being highly intercorrelated because of a General Speed factor, yet they are differentiated by some variance unique to each of the processes. It is a reasonable hypothesis that the differentiated structure of abilities revealed by the factor analysis of psychometric tests is derived in part from the unique variance in different processes, which enter into performance on various psychometric tests in different combinations and degrees. Aside from a general Speed-of-Processing factor, for example, different processes are called upon in a vocabulary test (and in the acquisition of word knowledge) than in a test of arithmetic reasoning (and in the acquisition of quantitative skills).

How do seemingly small individual differences in the rate of information processing, as revealed, for example, by the difference between choice RT and simple RT, eventuate in large individual differences in performance on psychometric tests and in scholastic achievement? As indicated previously, because of limited channel capacity for information processing, and rapid decay of information held in working memory, speed of processing is most advantageous when the operations required for successful solution of a test problem are sufficiently complex to strain the subject's working memory. Thus, some part of the correlation between mental speed as measured by ECTs and the general ability measured by psychometric tests is attributable to conditions intrinsic to the *complexity* of the test item, quite apart from any information *content* required by the item. "Culture-free," "culture-fair," or "culture-reduced" types of tests depend mainly on the *complexity* of the mental operations demanded by the items rather than on their *content*, that is, the specific acquired knowledge or skills called for by a particular item. The research on ECTs proves, if nothing else, that it is possible to measure psychometric *g* by means which depend scarcely at all on individual differences in *content*.

But what about those test items which depend on knowledge content, such as the Vocabulary and General Information subtests of the *Wechsler* scales? These tests are highly *g* loaded and are correlated with RT parameters of ECTs. A reasonable explanation of the correlation is that persons with faster rates of information processing acquire more information per unit of time from their experiences than do persons with slower processing rates. Even small individual differences in processing rate, when multiplied by considerable lengths of time, can eventually result in surprisingly large differences in amount of acquired knowledge and skill. A car that on average takes 22.0 msec to travel a foot and a car that takes 22.7 msec will be a mile apart after only an hour's travel. Similarly, we have found that groups with average differences in information-processing rates of only five to ten bits of information per second (i.e., when bits/sec is measured by the reciprocal of the difference between simple and choice RT) differ by one standard deviation or more in tests of scholastic aptitude and achievement (e.g., Jensen, 1982b, Table 1).

It is now well established that time is a critical factor in scholastic achievement or in any type of cognitive learning which progresses from simple to more complex in a cumulative fashion, thereby continually making demands on the learner's working memory. A large part of the function of working memory in the educative process is the encoding and storage of new information into long-term memory and the retrieval of information from LTM, as well as performing a number of other operations on retrieved information, such as transformation, mapping, and transfer, in accord with task requirements (Anderson, 1983). Individual differences in the total time needed for learning scholastic material to a given criterion are correlated with IQ, or g. Time-to-learn (TTL) ratios, comparing the slowest to the fastest learners are typically of the order of 2:1 to 7:1 in most studies, depending on the range of talent in the sample and the complexity of the material to be learned (Gettinger, 1984). The ratios of low- to high-IQ groups in rates of information processing, as measured in terms of differences between simple and choice RT, fall within a somewhat narrower range, about 1:2 to 1:4. In comparing average or above-average groups with the mildly retarded (IQs 60 to 80), one does not find average subjects whose median choice RT (CRT) is as slow as the mean of retarded subjects, but there are a few retarded persons whose median CRT is faster than the mean CRT of the average group. The relationship between CRT and mental retardation could be stated as follows: Fast CRT is necessary but not sufficient for average or above-average intelligence, whereas slow CRT is sufficient but not necessary for mental retardation.

The speed–complexity "paradox"

The magnitude of correlation between individual differences in a reaction time task, or ECT, and psychometric g is related to task complexity. The relationship is not linear, however, but rather appears as an inverted-U function. That is, the correlation increases, going from very simple tasks to more complex tasks; but beyond some optimal level of complexity the correlation gradually decreases. Response latencies to highly complex items such as those in *Raven's Progressive Matrices*, which often require a minute or more to solve, show close to zero correlation with g. It may seem paradoxical that the *Raven*, which is highly g loaded when given as an untimed test, is not at all correlated with g in terms of the subject's mean response latencies to the correctly answered items. We have found that the range of task complexity (as indicated by mean latencies) for which the latencies show significant correlations with g is quite narrow: tasks with mean latencies between 300 and 1,000 msec, for university students. The limits of this optimal range of RTs probably differs according to the average level of ability of the group in which the RT × g correlation is computed, the optimal latencies being longer for less able groups and for children. In a series of 14 RT tasks of varying complexity, with mean response latencies ranging between about 400 and 1,400 msec (for university students), we have found the maximum correlation (about − .50) with g (*Raven's Advanced Progressive Matrices*) for those tasks with mean latencies close to 700 msec.

This finding suggests the hypothesis that a task becomes too complex for the optimal correlation with g when the solution time exceeds the decay time of the information in working memory. At that point, different complex strategies are invoked for rehearsing information in short-term memory and for getting information into LTM, or for searching LTM for relevant information for problem solution. In other words, when the mental operations required for successful performance of a problem cannot be performed, either simultaneously or sequentially, within the time constraints of working memory imposed by rapid decay of memory traces, other, more complex metaprocesses come into play, and the total response latency then is not as pure a reflection of the efficiency of the elementary cognitive processes. A highly complex problem is, in effect, divided into a number of subproblems for solution and, depending on the subject's strategy, time is allocated differently to the various subproblems. Personality variables and individual differences in other noncognitive factors, such as involuntary rest pauses, enter into the subject's performance, severely attenuating sheer response latency as a measure of *g*. It appears as if the metaprocesses or strategies are more susceptible to idiosyncratic interactions between subjects and tasks than are the elementary processes. This interactive strategy variance is, in effect, "averaged out" when response latencies to individual items are averaged over subjects, revealing a high correlation between *average* item latencies and the difficulty levels (i.e., percent failing) of the items when administered as an untimed psychometric test. One of my graduate students, Steven Paul (1985), has recently obtained data showing clearly that the mean latencies of simple test items that have short latencies in the range of optimal correlations with *g* in university students are highly correlated with the mean item difficulty levels (percent failing) in school children of ages 7 to 9 years, who took the items in the form of an untimed paper-and-pencil test. These are extremely simple items for university students, with average latencies mostly below 1,000 msec, and they reflect the efficiency of hardly more than elementary cognitive processes. This suggests to me that the elementary processes may be more consistently related to *g* than are the higher executive functions, or metaprocesses.

There remains a crucial question that has not yet been definitively answered by any research that I can find in the literature. Is the correlation of various ECTs with psychometric *g* attributable entirely to the common factor (Mental Speed) among the ECTs? Or do the different processes (encoding, retrieval, etc.) involved in various ECTs also contribute to their correlation with *g*? In terms of multiple regression, we know that successively adding ECTs to the regression equation for predicting *g* increases R^2, that is, the proportion of variance in *g* accounted for by the ECTs (e.g., Keating & Bobbitt, 1978). But this is an ambiguous finding, as it stands. Does the R^2 increase because independent processes are being successively added to the regression equation? Or does the R^2 increase merely because, by adding more ECTs, we are increasing the reliability of the Common Speed factor, and could just as well produce the same increments in R^2 by adding in repeated testings on one and the same ECT? This question can be answered only by obtaining highly accurate estimates of the test–retest reliability of each of the ECT variables and correcting all of the zero-order correlations for attenuation before calculating R^2. Then, if the common factor among the ECTs is solely responsible for their correlation with psychometric g, a step-wise multiple regression (entering the most highly predictive ECT first) should not show significant increments in R^2 by the addition of successive ECTs after the first one in the regression equation. This procedure has not yet been done.

A variety of elementary cognitive tasks

In the past few years, considerable research findings have accrued to a number of ECTs. The substantive and methodological aspects of much of this research have been reviewed in detail elsewhere (Carroll, 1980; Berger, 1982; Jensen, 1982a, 1982b, 1985a; Vernon, 1985). My purpose here is to provide very brief descriptions of the chronometric paradigms which have already shown dependable correlations with psychometric g, and to indicate in summary fashion the most salient findings and unresolved research questions associated with each paradigm.

The stimuli and task requirements of most of these chronometric paradigms are so universally available to experience, and are so simple and relatively free of intellectual and cultural content, that it seems they could be easily adapted to cross-cultural testing.

All of these paradigms, being chronometric, have the methodological and quantitative advantage of measurement on a ratio scale, being absolute measurements of real time, expressed in decimal fractions of a second, which are standard units in the universally adopted Système Internationale for all physical and scientific measurements. However, it is most important to note that the absolute time values obtained in any chronometric study, however reliable they may be, are a function not only of subject factors but also of apparatus characteristics. Seemingly slight variations in apparatus or procedures can result in quite marked differences in the absolute values of RT measurements (Jensen, 1985a). If a given paradigm is to be used in cross-cultural comparisons, it is essential that either the identical apparatus (i.e., the stimulus response console with which the subject interacts) or highly standardised replicas, as uniform in every respect as the technology of manufacture will permit, be used for all groups. *Relationships* among chronometric variables and between chronometric and psychometric variables remain quite stable across considerable variations in apparatus and testing procedure, but the *absolute values* of the chronometric variables are remarkably sensitive to even slight variations in these features.

Inspection time

The research on IT has been reviewed by Brand and Deary (1982), Brand (1984), and Nettelbeck (1987). IT measures speed of apprehension of visual or auditory stimuli. Brand (1984) describes IT as "a ready ability to apprehend the most simple perceptual realities that constitutes one major psychological and ontogenetic basis for the development in intelligence." The basic idea originated about a century ago with Galton, who argued that "the only information that reaches us concerning outward events appears to pass through the avenue of our senses; and the more perceptive the senses are of difference, the larger is the field upon which our judgment and intelligence can act" (Galton, 1883, p. 19).

In the simplest form of visual IT, two vertical parallel lines, differing about 30% in length, are exposed in a tachistoscope, followed, after a brief interval, by a masking stimulus. The subject reports whether the longer line appeared on the right or the left of the shorter line. (Their positions are randomised across trials.) There is no time constraint on the subject's verbal response per se. The interstimulus interval (i.e., time between exposure of the vertical lines and exposure of the mask) is varied systematically until that interval is found at which the subject responds correctly on 95% of the trials. This interval, measured in milliseconds, is the subject's IT. Individual differences in IT range widely, between about 20 and 700 msec (see Brand & Deary, 1982, Table 1).

Correlations between IT and IQ also range widely, depending mainly on the level and range of IQs in the sample. There is no simple way to summarise the IT × IQ correlations in the literature. But two generalisations seem warranted at present: (1) Almost all the IT × IQ correlations are in the expected direction, that is, slower IT is associated with lower IQ; (2) the overall results are highly significant, rendering the null hypothesis definitely untenable; (3) correlations are much higher in samples that fall in the lower half of the IQ distribution (i.e., IQs < 100) than in the upper half. IQ 85 seems to be the critical threshold; samples that include roughly equal numbers of subjects who are above and below IQ 85 show the most impressive IQ × IT correlation, and the inclusion of mentally retarded subjects with IQ below 70 increases the correlation. In samples of above-average IQ, correlations are typically around $-.25$. In samples covering the full range of IQ, correlations are typically above $-.50$. Brand (1984) suggests there is a linear relation between IT and IQ up to about IQ 110, but little relation beyond that point. Vernon (1983) found zero correlation between IT and IQ in a group of 100 university students with a mean *WAIS* IQ of 122 and in which the lowest IQ was 110; and in a factor analysis including nine RT variables with loadings ranging from $+.51$ to $+.91$ on the first principal factor, IT had a nonsignificant loading of $-.17$. Brand (1984) suggests an explanation of this apparently nonlinear relation of IT to intelligence throughout the full range of IQ with an analogy:

The relation between mental intake speed and intelligence may resemble the relation between income and patterns of investment and expenditure. Across the lower ranges of income there are fairly predictable relations between a person's income and his possessions; but, as the higher ranges of income are reached, big individual differences arise in the disposal of income – into luxuries, education, health care, addictions, and so on.

There are considerably more complex elaborations of the basic IT paradigm, however, which have shown quite impressive correlations (about .6 to .7) with IQ and scholastic aptitude scores in university students, despite the fact that the IT tasks involved no intellectual content (Livson & Krech, 1956; Raz, Willerman, Ingmundson, & Hanlon, 1983). In the study by Raz et al. (1983), an auditory recognition test (identifying a target tone followed by a masking tone as either "high" or "low") showed mean differences of more than two standard deviations (SDs) between a group of university students with total *Scholastic Aptitude Test* scores above 1,200 and a group with total scores below 800 (a mean difference of between 1 and 3 SDs).

Simple and choice reaction time

Simple reaction time (SRT) shows slight correlations with g, usually not much above $-.10$. Choice reaction time (CRT) involves some uncertainty as to which one of n possible response alternatives will be called for when one of n stimulus alternatives occurs. CRT almost invariably shows higher correlations with IQ or g than does SRT, the correlation increasing (up to a point) as the number of alternatives, and hence the amount of uncertainty, increases. RT increases as a linear function of the logarithm of the number of alternatives, a relationship now known as Hick's law. In information theory, the unit of information, known as a *bit* (for binary digit), is defined as the amount of information needed to reduce uncertainty by one-half. Accordingly, amount of uncertainty (and conversely, the quantity of information required to reduce it one-half) can be defined as the logarithm to the base 2 of the number (n) of alternatives, or choices. Thus a $bit = \log_2 n$.

These relationships, which I shall henceforth refer to simply as "the Hick paradigm," have been implemented for the study of individual differences in RT by means of the apparatus shown in Figure 4.2, called the reaction time–movement time, or RT–MT, apparatus. The number of light/button combinations used for any given RT task can be varied by the use of overlays, which may expose any number from 1 to 8 lights/buttons. A trial begins with the subject holding down the "home" button with the index finger of his preferred hand. A preparatory stimulus ("beep") sounds; after a random interval of 1 to 4 seconds, one light (the "reaction stimulus") goes on. The subject's task is to turn off the light as quickly as possible by touching the sensitive microswitch push-button adjacent to the light. Trials are spaced 5 to 10 seconds apart. Typically, 15 or 20 trials are given at any one level of difficulty. The most commonly used levels of difficulty are 1, 2, 4, and 8 choice alternatives (n) which correspond to 0, 1, 2, and 3 bits of information.

Two basic time measurements (in msec) are recorded on each trial: RT, or the interval between the onset of the light and the subject's release of the home button; and movement time (MT), the interval between release of the

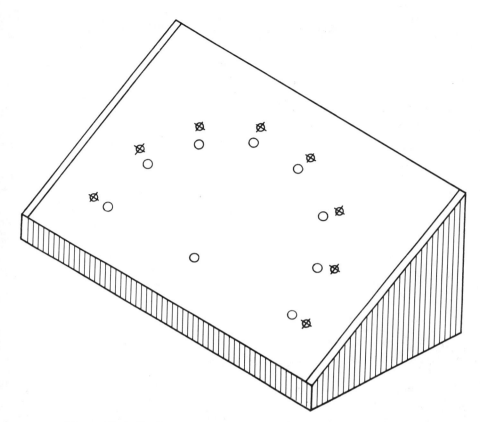

Figure 4.2. Subject's console of the RT–MT apparatus. Push-buttons are indicated by circles; green jewelled lights, by crossed circles. The "home" button is in the lower centre, 6 inches from each response button.

home button and touching the button which turns off the light. Older RT procedures did not distinguish between RT and MT; the two were confounded in a single measurement. The mixing of RT and MT in a single measure, however, attenuates its correlation with any other variable, such as *g*, if RT and MT (as here defined) are differentially correlated with the other variable. RT and MT evidently measure different processes. Their intercorrelation *within* subjects is zero; *between* subjects, the *r* is about +.30. Therefore, adding individual differences in MT to individual differences in RT is almost equivalent to adding random error to RT. It is likely that the failure of many older studies to show significant correlations between response latency and intelligence is the result of not separating RT from MT.

Results of research with this procedure have been comprehensively reviewed elsewhere (Jensen, 1982a, 1982b, 1987b). Typical features of RT and MT are shown in Figure 4.3. So far, MT has been of lesser interest than

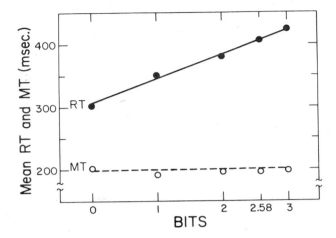

Figure 4.3. Mean RT and MT as a function of bits in 160 school-children in grades four to six. The correlation (r) between mean RT and bits is +.996.

RT. Usually, RT shows larger and more consistent correlations with IQ and mental age. Also, RT is always highly related to differences in task complexity, such as number of choices, whereas MT is relatively constant across variations in task complexity. The three most important individual difference RT parameters derivable from this paradigm are the RT intercept, slope of RT (as a function of bits), and intraindividual variability, labelled SDRT (the average standard deviation of RT over all trials at each level of bits). The *intercept* is complexly determined, reflecting sensory and motor lag, peripheral nerve conduction, apprehension and encoding of the stimulus, and preparation and initiation of the response. The *slope* reflects central processes: discrimination, comparison, choice, and response selection. The reciprocal of the slope can be interpreted as *rate* of information processing, in number of bits per millisecond. Intercept, slope, and SDRT are all correlated with *g*. Slope shows the lowest correlations, unless they are corrected for attenuation – a dubious procedure when test–retest reliability is quite low, as is usually true for the slope parameter. SDRT has shown the consistently highest correlations, despite its having lower reliability than the intercept, which is by far the most stable of the three parameters.

The simple "lawfulness" or regularity of the phenomena found in this paradigm, as seen in Figure 4.3, is always striking and consistent in every study and even for individual subjects. For example, the correlation between mean RT and bits is .996; it averages close to .97 for individual subjects. SDRT is equally regular, except that it is an exponential rather than linear function of bits, as seen in Figure 4.4. However, when SDRT is plotted as a function of number of response alternatives (*n*), the relationship is just as

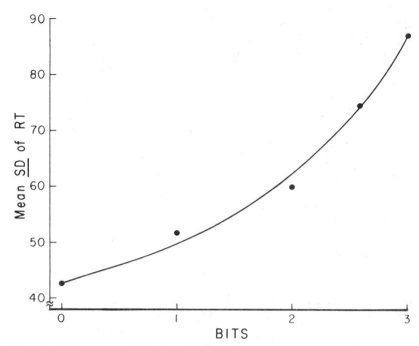

Figure 4.4. Mean intraindividual variability (measured by the standard deviation of RTs in milliseconds on 30 trials) as a function of bits, for 160 schoolchildren in grades four to six. When this RT parameter is plotted as a function of number of alternatives (n), rather than bits (i.e., $\log_2 n$), it is almost perfectly linear, showing a correlation (r) of $+.996$ between n and SD of RT.

perfectly linear as the regression of mean RT on bits. Linearity is confirmed by correlations of $+.996$ in both cases.

There is one other set of relationships, not heretofore mentioned in the literature, which is no less striking and in need of theoretical explanation. This is the simplex pattern of intercorrelations among the RTs at each level of difficulty (i.e., $n = 1, 2, 4, 6,$ or 8 lights/buttons). These correlations, based on the same data shown in Figures 4.3 and 4.4, are given in the area above the diagonal of the matrix in Table 4.1. All the correlations have been corrected for attenuation (based on Spearman–Brown boosted split-half reliabilities). The pattern of these correlations is an almost perfect simplex, that is, the correlations systematically decrease with each step that they are removed (in either direction) from the principal diagonal of the matrix. Interestingly, the identical pattern can be generated from a simple common-elements model of correlation. By this model, the correlation between RTs for $n = 1$ and $n = 2$ is $r_{1,2} = \sqrt{1/2}$. Similarly, $r_{1,4} = \sqrt{1/4}$, $r_{1,6} = \sqrt{1/6}$, and $r_{6,8} = \sqrt{6/8}$, and so on. The matrix of correlations below the diagonal in Table 4.1 was generated by this model. These generated correlations are correlated .997 with the corresponding empirical correlations (above the

Table 4.1. *Observed correlations (above diagonal) between RTs for different numbers of alternatives* (n), *and theoretical correlations predicted by a common-elements model (below diagonal)*

n	1	2	4	6	8
1		.90	.80	.76	.72
2	.71 (.90)[a]		.90	.80	.77
4	.50 (.79)	.71 (.90)		.96	.90
6	.41 (.74)	.58 (.83)	.82 (.96)		.99
8	.35 (.71)	.50 (.79)	.71 (.90)	.87 (.98)	

[a] Correlations in parentheses are a linear transformation (transformed $r' = .5305 + .5185r$) of the theoretical correlations predicted by the overlap model. The correlation between the observed and predicted correlations is $+.997$.

diagonal). The fact that the generated correlations are of overall lesser magnitude than the observed correlations is of no theoretical consequence, because each set of correlations is merely a linear transformation of the other set. For example, a linear transformation of the model-generated correlations (shown in parentheses in Table 4.1) makes them highly similar to the obtained correlations in absolute magnitudes. The correlation of .997 between the model-generated and empirically observed correlations, of course, remains unchanged by any linear transformation of the correlations. These regularities in RT data derived with the Hick paradigm look more like the data of physics than of psychology, and they invite theoretical efforts to construct a model of the brain mechanisms that could cause such lawful phenomena (Jensen, 1982b).

I emphasise these striking regularities in the Hick paradigm here, however, because of their importance for cross-cultural research. The linear relations of RT to bits, the linear relation of SDRT to *n*, the simplex pattern of intercorrelations of RTs at different levels of *n* – if all of these regularities appear in data obtained in two (or more) different cultural groups, it seems a safe presumption that the Hick paradigm measures individual differences in the very same processes that are responsible for these regularities in both groups. Differences between the groups in mean RT, or in any other parameters of the RT paradigm, could hardly be explained in terms of the task's measuring different processes or ability factors in the different cultures.

Short-term memory scan

This paradigm, introduced by S. Sternberg (1966), measures the time required to retrieve an item of information from short-term memory (STM). A set of digits (termed the *positive set*), varying in length from 1 to 5 or 7 digits, is presented for a sufficient time for the subject to memorise the series. After a 2-sec blank interval, a single probe digit is presented. On a random half of the trials, the probe is a member of the positive set and on half of the trials it is not. The subject's task is to respond as quickly as possible *Yes* or *No* as to whether the probe was or was not a member of the positive set. Response is made by pressing buttons labelled *Yes* and *No*. RTs consistently show two features: (1) They are longer for *No* than for *Yes* responses, and (2) they are a positive linear function of the *number* of digits in the positive set. Individual differences in the intercept and slope of this function have been found in several studies to be correlated with *g* (for reviews, see Jensen, 1982a, 1982b, 1987c). No one has yet explained why RT is a linear function of $\log_2 n$ in the Hick paradigm, but is a linear function of *n* in the Sternberg paradigm. There is an obvious need for a theoretical model that could explain this difference.

The slope of the linear function relating RT to the number of items that must be scanned in STM may be regarded as the speed of STM scanning in msec/item. Cavanagh (1972) has shown a Pearson correlation of $+.9975$ between this measure of mean STM scanning speed (msec/item) and the reciprocal of the mean memory span (for group data) for different types of items (digits, colours, letters, geometric shapes, words, random forms, and nonsense syllables). This striking discovery is highly consistent with the theory of trace decay in working memory as the basis for the relationship between RT and psychometric test performance, described earlier in this chapter. The greater the complexity or information load of the items that must be processed, the slower is the STM scan rate and the shorter is the memory span for the items. Memory span is limited by the number of items that can be reported before the STM trace decays. Memory span is correlated with *g* and has long been included among the items of individual IQ tests, most notably the *Binet* and *Wechsler* scales.

The Sternberg paradigm, in connection with Cavanagh's discovery, would lend itself nicely to the search for cross-cultural invariance of cognitive processes. A wide variety of stimulus items selected for their high familiarity in different cultures could be used to plot the Cavanagh function relating speed of processing to memory span in age-matched subject samples from the different cultures, in order to determine if the items selected from different cultures fall on a common regression line and in the same rank order in the subject samples from each culture.

Long-term memory retrieval paradigms

The purpose of these paradigms is to measure the time it takes to retrieve highly overlearned items of information from LTM. This is achieved by comparing RT on a simple discriminative task which involves an LTM component with RT on a task that makes virtually identical sensory-discrimination and response demands but does not require access to LTM. The simplest of such procedures, originated by Posner (1978, chap. 2), measures the time to access the names of highly overlearned single letters of the alphabet. Pairs of letters, printed in either upper or lower case, in which the letters in each pair are either the *same* or *different* in letter *name*, are presented, and the subject responds by pressing buttons labelled *Same* (*S*) and *Different* (*D*) in terms of whether the letters have the same or different names. For example, *Aa* (*S*) *AA* (*S*), *Ab* (*D*), *AB* (*D*). This task condition is known as *name identity*, or NI. The comparison task is *physical identity*, or PI. Here the very same letter pairs are presented, but the subject responds *Same* or *Different* on the basis of whether the letters are physically the same or different, thus: *Aa* (*D*), *AA* (*S*), etc. Average RT is longer for NI than for PI, and the difference, NI − PI, is a measure of the time required to access letter names in LTM. The difference, NI − PI, amounts to about 75 msec in university students, which is the same as their difference in RTs between 0 and 3 bits of information in the Hick paradigm. NI − PI is modestly correlated (about − .25) with IQ, and appears to be correlated with a verbal ability factor in addition to *g*. The NI task, however, involves so very little LTM search, at least in the case of university students, as to not disciminate individual differences in intelligence with as much precision as can be achieved with more complex processing tasks.

To increase the complexity and LTM search demands of the basic NI − PI paradigm, whole words have been substituted for single letters. Corresponding to the NI condition is the *Synonyms–Antonyms* (*SA*) *Test*, in which pairs of short, high-frequency (*AA* in the *Lorge–Thorndike* word count) words are presented. The paired words are of either similar or opposite meaning, and the subject responds on push-buttons labelled *Same* or *Different*, for example, *big–large* (*S*), *hot–cold* (*D*). The comparison test, corresponding to PI, is called the *Same–Different* (*SD*) *Test*. It consists of pairs of words (comparable in length and frequency to those used in the NI condition) which are either identical or unrelated. The subject responds *Same* or *Different* on the basis of physical identity, for example, *cow–cow* (*S*), *hot–table* (*D*). The mean RTs for *SA* − *SD* also measure time for retrieving information from LTM. This difference is about 300 msec for university students. This paradigm has shown quite substantial correlations with IQ (Vernon, 1983; Vernon & Jensen, 1984). An essential requirement for this procedure is that the stimulus words should all be highly familiar to all subjects. It should be a test not of knowledge but of speed of access to well-learned, highly available information stored in LTM. This requirement can be tested by first giving the items as a paper-and-pencil test to all subjects. In the version of the *Synonyms–Antonyms* test used in our studies, the error rate for university students is zero; it is only 10% for average 8- and 9-year-old schoolchildren. This test could be used in cross-cultural research, with the appropriate words or other symbols which have similar or opposite meanings in a given culture. Choice of words could be matched in terms of frequency within each language or culture.

Another speed of LTM retrieval task is *category matching*. It is easier (by about 90 msec) than the *Synonyms–Antonyms* task, for university students. The subject is presented successively 40 pairs of words, in which the first word is the name of one of five categories (animals, clothing, fruits, furniture, sports) and the second word of the pair is either a member of the named category or of one of the other four categories. The subject responds (by push-button) whether the second word is or is not a member of the named category. RT on this task is correlated about + .70 with RT on the *Synonyms–Antonyms* test, and with IQ (Vernon, 1985).

Semantic Verification Test (SVT)

This test, originally suggested by Baddeley (1968), measures the amount of time it takes for a person to decide whether a physical stimulus does or does not correspond to a brief "sentence" describing it (see also Clark & Chase, 1972). We have devised two chronometric forms of the SVT, differing in complexity. The simpler form involves only two capital letters, *A* and *B*. A "sentence" such as one of the following is presented visually for 3 seconds:

> *A* before *B*
> *A* after *B*
> *A* not before *B*
> *A* not after *B*

After a 1-sec blank interval, a pair of letters appears, for example, *AB*, and the subject responds on push-buttons labelled *True* or *False* according to whether the letter positions correspond to the descriptive statement. RT is the interval between onset of the letters and the subject's releasing the home button in order to touch the *T* or *F* button. The task is subject-paced, each trial initiated by the subject's depressing the home button. RT and MT are recorded on each trial.

The more complex form of the SVT uses three letters (*A, B, C*) and other descriptors besides *before* and *after: first, last, between.* "Sentences" in positive and negative forms are composed of every possible permutation of these descriptors, and the reaction stimuli consist of all permutations of *ABC*, half of them true and half of them false with respect to the given statements. Using *ABC*, instead of only *AB*, markedly increases the processing demands of the task, mainly because the "sentences" in the simple *AB* condition *always* permit the subject to form a mental image of the order of the letters that will appear as the reaction stimulus, whereas the "sentences" in the complex *ABC* condition allow more "degrees of freedom" for the reaction stimulus; the order of the three letters cannot be invariably or completely anticipated.

Before being given the chronometric form of the SVT, subjects are given the items as a true–false paper-and-pencil test to provide familiarity and practice on this paradigm and to ensure that all subjects are capable of errorless performance under nonspeeded conditions. RT on the SVT is correlated about − .50 with *Raven's Advanced* scores in university students. When corrected for attenuation and restriction of IQ range, in the university sample, this correlation comes close to − .80. The various sentences of the complex form of the SVT show large, reliable differences in mean RT, ranging from about 300 to 1,300 msec. MT, in contrast, is constant across all sentence conditions and shows negligible and nonsignificant correlation with the *Raven* (Paul, 1985).

Dual tasks

These tasks (also termed *competition tasks*) are a means for measuring storage/processing trade-off in working memory. The more of the capacity of working memory that is used for STM storage of information, the less there is available for other forms of processing information. A dual task thereby puts a greater strain on the storage and processing capacity of working memory. As a consequence, dual tasks show higher correlations with *g* than either of the component tasks given singly. In a classic set of experiments, Baddeley and Hitch (1974) showed that when persons were given a short string of digits to memorise, followed by a simple reasoning task, and then had to recall the previously memorised digits, their performance increasingly deteriorated as the number of digits to be remembered approached the subject's memory span. Following this lead, Stankov (1983) has made the important discovery that performances on a variety of ECTs are more highly intercorrelated, and are therefore more heavily *g* loaded, when they are presented in the dual task paradigm than when presented as single tasks. Also, Stankov distinguishes between the *active* and *passive* aspects of working memory, corresponding to the *processing* and *storage* of information. Stankov claims evidence that the active component of working memory is more highly correlated with fluid *g* than is the passive component and that "operations performed on information in working memory are more indicative of fluid intelligence than is the ability to hold this information in working memory" (Stankov, 1983, p. 51). This observation is very similar to Jensen's (1974) distinction between Level I and Level II abilities as *encoding and retention* of stimulus input (Level I) and *mental manipulation* of encoded material (Level II).

An obvious advantage of dual tasks in cross-cultural research is that, because dual tasks are more highly *g* loaded, the increments in RT produced by dual versus single tasks, when the component tasks are identical, are a content-free measure of mental efficiency.

In our laboratory we have used two dual tasks which yield four RT measures. They are composed of the Sternberg (1966) *Digit Scan test* and the *Same–Different* (SD) word pairs and *Synonyms–Antonyms* (SA) word pairs described previously. A single trial of each dual task can be summarised as follows:

Dual Task 2 (DT2)
Digit Series (2 sec)
Same–Different words – RT
Probe Digit – RT
Dual Task 3 (DT3)
Digit Series (2 sec)
Synonym–Antonym – RT
Probe Digit – RT

The subject is presented with a string of 1 to 7 digits (for 2 seconds), which he is told to rehearse for later recall. When the digits leave the screen, they are replaced by a pair of words to which the subject responds *Same* or *Different* on the push-button console, and RT is recorded. After responding, the subject presses the home button again, which triggers the appearance of a single probe digit; the subject then responds *Yes* or *No* as to whether the probe was a member of the string of digits that appeared before the words, and RT is recorded. In the three studies in which these dual tasks have been used, they have shown significant correlations with *g*, and the correlations are generally higher than for the same tasks given singly (Vernon, 1983, 1985; Vernon & Jensen, 1984).

Chronometric studies of population differences

Black and white (i.e., negroid and caucasoid) populations, in any part of the world, whenever they have been given psychometric tests, have been found to differ statistically, on average, at least one standard deviation (σ) in every kind of test that has a large *g* loading when it is factor analysed among any large and diverse collection of mental tests. In fact, Spearman (1927, p. 379) conjectured that the magnitude of the black–white difference on various tests is directly related to the tests' *g* loadings. This hypothesis is borne out by a number of factor-analytic studies and has so far been contradicted by none (Jensen, 1980a, pp. 535–539, 732–735; 1985b; 1985c; Naglieri & Jensen, 1987). Understanding the nature of this difference at a more basic level of analysis than the factor analysis of psychometric tests is a long-standing desideratum of differential psychology. Chronometric techniques would seem to afford one potentially fruitful approach toward this aim.

Several studies have used one or more of the chronometric techniques previously described in comparing black and white groups in Africa and America. No entirely consistent pattern of results emerges, and there is not yet enough data derived from sufficiently similar chronometric techniques or sufficiently large, representative, and comparable samples across studies to warrant any worthy general conclusions. In each study, however, statistically significant effects have been found, which suggests that further studies in this vein, more systematically designed and theory guided, and with proper replication, using standardised techniques and procedures, should lead to consistent, theoretically interpretable results. The few scattered studies reported thus far are reviewed here briefly. All differences between sample means are reported here in standard deviation (σ) units, where σ is the square root of the N-weighted mean of the variances of the two samples.

Bligh (1967), as reported in Poortinga (1971), compared 26 white European and 26 black African subjects on simple RT, using auditory ("click") and visual (flash of light) stimuli. Bligh used the peculiar procedure of having the subjects keep their eyes closed during presentation of the stimuli. Poortinga (1971, p. 70) suggests that the more heavily pigmented eyelids of the black subjects might have affected the results, causing the group difference in visual RT to be greater than that for auditory RT. The black–white differences for visual RT and auditory RT were .90σ and .57σ, respectively.

Poortinga (1971) measured simple and choice visual RT and auditory RT in 40 white and 40 black African university students between the ages of 18 and 24 years. Poortinga claims that "there seems to be no reason why the [black] African sample cannot be considered to be representative of all African students in South Africa" (p. 24). On three psychometric tests, the black–white differences were (from Poortinga, 1971, Table 24, p. 72): *Mental Alertness* (2.31σ); *Raven's Advanced Progressive Matrices* (2.16σ); *Blox* (spatial) (1.52σ). Poortinga also used a click and a flash as reaction stimuli, but his procedure was different from Bligh's. For *simple RT*, clicks and flashes were presented in alternative order and the subject responded to each stimulus as fast as possible by pressing a button. For *choice RT*, the click and flash occurred in random order, and the subject responded to each stimulus by pressing one of two designated buttons. On one-fifth of the choice RT trials, the click and flash were presented simultaneously and the subject was instructed to press the click or the flash button according to which stimulus seemed to occur first. The black–white differences, all of them nonsignificant, were as follows (from Poortinga, 1971, Table 17, p. 66);

	Auditory	Visual
Simple RT	.13σ	.02σ
Choice RT	$-$.03σ	.00σ

Poortinga also gave a more complex 4-choice RT task in visual and auditory modes to the same groups. The visual stimuli were four coloured lights (green, yellow, blue, red); each appeared in the same aperture. The auditory stimuli were four highly distinct sounds (Wundt hammer, buzzer, hooter, bell). Subjects responded on four push-buttons, using the index and middle fingers of each hand. Finally, an 8-choice task was given, consisting of the four auditory and four visual stimuli presented in a random order. Because stimulus–response compatibility (i.e., the physical proximity or spatial correspondence of the response buttons to the alternate stimuli) was quite low in this arrangement, there was a pronounced practice effect, amounting to about 10 to 15 msec, over the course of 100 trials. Hence, the task involves some degree of learning as well as reaction time per se. Internal consistency reliabilities were high (.71–.90), however, and permit correction of the mean group differences for attenuation. The black–white differences (with disattenuated differences in parentheses) are as follows (from Poortinga, 1971, Tables 7 and 10, pp. 47 and 50). All of the differences are significant beyond the .05 level.

	Auditory	Visual
4-choice RT	1.36σ (1.70σ)	1.53σ (2.06σ)
8-choice RT	1.30σ (1.71σ)	1.26σ (1.69σ)

Thus it appears, from Poortinga's study, that the black–white difference is nonexistent or negligibly small for quite simple visual and auditory RT tasks involving no more than 0 or 1 bit of information (i.e., simple RT and 2-choice RT). But when the RT task is more complex, involving 4-choice and 8-choice RT (or 2 and 3 bits), quite marked differences appear, averaging about 1.4σ (1.8σ corrected for attenuation), a difference about two-thirds as large as the groups' difference on *Raven's Advanced Progressive Matrices*, a highly *g*-loaded test.

The correlations between Poortinga's various RT tasks and the *Raven's*, however, are inconsistent, as shown below (from Poortinga, 1971, Tables 25 and 26, pp. 73–74):

		Black	White
Simple RT	Click	− .05	+ .06
	Flash	− .08	+ .18
2-choice RT	Click	+ .17	+ .09
	Flash	+ .28	+ .08
4-choice RT	Auditory	− .07	− .45*
	Visual	− .05	− .16
8-choice RT	Auditory	− .05	− .38*
	Visual	− .02	− .17

(*$p < .01$)

These mostly nonsignificant correlations, and their lack of consistency between the two samples, bring into question whether these RT tasks (or the *Raven*) are measuring any significant component of *g* in both racial samples. They pose an insoluble problem for interpretation, given only the results of Poortinga's study. Do Poortinga's RT results show any consistency with other RT studies? To some extent, yes.

Noble (1969) tested representative samples of white and black grade-school children (106 in each group) in rural Georgia, matched for age and sex, on a 4-choice RT test. As in Poortinga's study, there was a low degree of stimulus–response compatibility in Noble's RT task, so that part of the subject's task consisted of learning the multiple-choice connections between the four reaction stimuli (coloured lights) and the correct motor responses (pushing toggle switches). RTs therefore showed gradual, negatively accelerated improvement with practice over the course of 160 trials, but the practice curves trend toward significantly ($p < .01$) different asymptotes for blacks and whites. The results, when plotted in terms of response speed

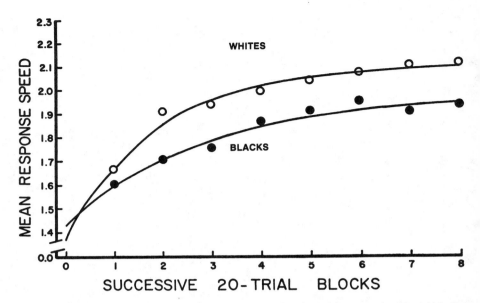

Figure 4.5. Mean response speed (reciprocal of RT in sec) in successive 20-trial blocks on a 4-choice reaction time test. Each curve is based on 106 children, with groups matched for age, sex, and pretest practice condition (from Noble, 1969).

(i.e., the reciprocal of RT in sec), are shown in Figure 4.5. Thus Noble's study is consistent with Poortinga's in showing a significant black–white difference in 4-choice RT under conditions of low S–R compatibility.

A study by Borkowski and Krause (1983) compared 20 black and 29 white children (grades two and three, ages 8 and 9 years) on simple and 2-choice RTs by means of a Gerbrand's reaction timer. The stimuli were red and green lights presented in the same aperture. This apparatus does not permit distinguishing between RT and MT. The black–white differences on the *WISC* IQ (based on Information and Vocabulary subscales) and the *Raven's Progressive Matrices* are .78σ and 1.55σ, respectively. These may serve as a basis for comparison with the black–white differences in RT which are shown below. As Borkowski and Krause have provided the split-half reliabilities of these RT measures, it is possible to correct the σ differences for attenuation, by dividing the σ difference by the square root of the reliability coefficient. The corrected values are shown in parentheses.

Simple RT:	.62σ (.67σ)	$p < .05$
2-choice RT:	.22σ (.28σ)	n.s.
Choice − simple:	−.35σ (−.61σ)	n.s.

Strangely, the only significant difference is on simple RT. The black–white difference's being larger on simple than on choice RT is at odds with the other studies reviewed here and has no obvious explanation. The black–

white difference of .62σ on SRT is considerably larger than the mean difference of .20σ between second and third graders, who differ 1.25 years in average chronological age. In this study, the correlations between RT and *Raven* scores were as follows (disattenuated values in parentheses):

	Black	White
Simple RT	− .58 (− .62)	+ .43 (+ .46)
Choice RT	− .60 (− .77)	(not given)

The apparent, inexplicable inconsistencies in these correlations may be attributable to sampling error. The *positive* correlation between SRT and psychometric *g* (*Raven* score) in the white sample is the only positive correlation between RT and psychometric *g* that I have come across in the entire RT literature. The correlations between intraindividual variability (*SD* of an individual's RTs over trials) in simple RT and *Raven* scores are striking: − .40 for black children and − .70 for white children. But the negative correlation in the white sample implies that there must be a negative correlation between RT and intraindividual variability in RT, which is opposite to every other correlation between these variables reported in the literature. These results of Borkowski and Krause should be shown to be replicable in another, larger study before anyone could reasonably attempt a theoretical interpretation of these peculiar findings. A detailed critique of this study appears elsewhere (Jensen, 1985a).

Studies of black–white differences in our laboratory have permitted distinguishing between RT and MT by using the RT–MT apparatus described earlier (see Fig. 4.2). In the first study, 99 black and 119 white first-year male students, ages 18 to 19, in a vocational college were given 30 trials at each of three levels of complexity on the RT–MT apparatus, 1, 4, and 8 light/buttons, corresponding to 0, 2, and 3 bits of information. The results are shown in Figure 4.6. On RT, the groups do not differ significantly in intercepts (a difference of only 3 msec at 0 bits), but the difference in slopes is significant ($t = 3.13, p < .01$). The black–white difference increases by approximately 10 msec per bit. The black–white difference of .63σ in mean median MT is significant ($t = 4.44, p < .001$). Also, intraindividual (i.e., between trials) variability (σ_i) of RT was significantly ($t = 3.50, p < .001$) greater for blacks than for whites, a difference of .54σ. A limitation of this study is that the groups are not representative of the white population or especially of the black population. Both groups have a restricted range in psychometric *g* (as indicated by the *Scholastic Aptitude* scores used for selecting vocational college applicants), with no very low or very high IQs. The white group is just slightly above the population average IQ for whites whereas the black group is about a standard deviation above the mean IQ of the general population of blacks. Under these conditions, the black sample's RT means should be expected to regress further away from the white group's RT means as the task complexity (i.e., number of bits of information) increases, as seen in Figure 4.6. These results may be interpreted as being

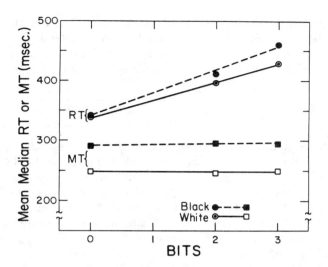

Figure 4.6. Mean median RT and MT of black (N = 99) and
white (N = 119) vocational students, ages 18–19, tested on the
RT–MT apparatus, shown in Figure 4.2.

consistent with those of Poortinga (and Noble) in showing a significant
black–white difference on 8-choice RT, but not on simple RT. (The difference on 4-choice RT is nonsignificant, two-tailed t = 1.71, p < .10.) However, more problematic is the fact that these black–white differences in the
RT–MT paradigm did not replicate in our laboratory in another study with
similar samples.

Vernon and Jensen (1984) tested 50 black and 56 white male vocational
college students on eight different speed-of-information-processing paradigms, including the RT–MT apparatus (Fig. 4.2). The groups were selected
from a subject pool similar to that of the previous sample, but in this study
the black and white groups differed about two-thirds of a standard deviation
in scholastic aptitude. Both groups, however, were above the average of
their respective populations. None of the parameters of the RT–MT paradigm showed significant correlations with the general factor of the *Armed
Services Vocational Aptitude Battery (ASVAB)* or significant differences
between the black and white groups. There is no plausible explanation, other
than sampling error, for the complete failure of the second study to replicate
the results of the previous study with the RT–MT apparatus, as the very
same apparatus and procedures were used in both studies, with the exception
that only half as many trials (15) were given in the second study instead of
all 30 trials given in the first study. Examination of the data with respect to
this procedural difference shows it as unable to explain the different outcomes. Statistical details of both studies are provided in Jensen (1987b).

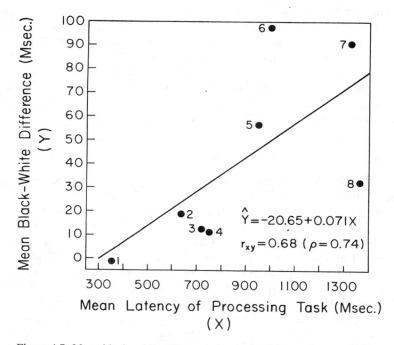

Figure 4.7. Mean black–white difference (msec) in RT to various processing tasks as a function of task complexity as indicated by mean of response latency on each task in the combined groups (from Vernon & Jensen, 1985).

The other, more complex, processing tasks used in the second study, however, showed highly significant effects. The entire battery of eight tasks yielded a shrunken multiple correlation with psychometric g factor scores of .47 in the combined groups, and the black–white mean difference on the general factor of the processing tests was $.21\sigma$ as compared with a mean difference of $.69\sigma$ on the *ASVAB*, a battery of ten paper-and-pencil tests heavily dependent on scholastic achievement. The processing tasks were RT–MT, *Digit Scan, Same–Different Words, Synonyms–Antonyms,* and *Dual Tasks* comprising Digits, Words, and Synonyms, as described in the previous section. The correlation of each task with the *ASVAB* g factor scores was quite closely related to the complexity of the task's processing demands, as indicated by the mean latency of response. A Pearson correlation of $+.98$ (rank–order correlation $= +.93$) was found between task complexity (i.e., mean RT) and the task's correlation with g. The black–white difference in mean RT on the various tasks is also related to task complexity, with a Pearson r of $+.68$ (rank–order correlation $= +.74$), as shown in Figure 4.7. These results are highly consistent with the general impression emerging from all these studies that the locus of the black–white difference exists only at the more complex levels of information processing. It is noteworthy that the two largest black–white differences occurred on the *Dual Tasks*, the largest RT difference (.40σ) occurring on Task No. 6, the *Dual Task* involving *Digit Scan* and *Same–Different Words*. The black–white differences on these two tasks when they were presented singly were considerably smaller (.11σ and .27σ, respectively), suggesting that the black–white difference resides more in the active, or processing, aspect of working memory than in the passive, or storage, aspect.

Summary

This chapter has summarised how recently developed analytical techniques of "mental chronometry" can advance our understanding of the nature of the abilities that underlie individual differences and cultural group differences in performance on conventional tests of scholastic aptitude and achievement. Scores on such tests are believed to reflect some unknown amalgam of more elementary abilities. But test scores on such global measures of ability as IQ and scholastic achievement afford virtually no possibility of making the kind of analytical assessments called for by modern theories of ability, which attempt to understand aptitude and achievement in terms of information processing. Individual differences in proficiency of information processing can result from differences in any one or a number of different processes that cannot be separately assessed by the kinds of complex tasks that ordinarily compose the items of conventional psychometric tests of intelligence and scholastic aptitude.

Because general ability, or intelligence, as measured by conventional tests, is now viewed by most researchers in the field of human abilities as a composite effect of a number of distinct cognitive processes, research is aimed towards investigating whether individual differences in each of these processes can be reliably measured by means of chronometric techniques. These techniques are based on the measurement of a person's reaction time (RT) to simple tasks, which are specially devised to engage only particular processes. Most such elementary tasks devised to measure the most fundamental cognitive processes are so simple that they are within the capability of every person who is without marked sensory or motor handicaps. Therefore, individual differences do not consist of whether some individuals can and some cannot perform the tasks, as is the case with ordinary test items. Individual differences in these tasks can be measured only in terms of the *speed* with which the underlying processes occur, as represented by reaction times under varying task conditions.

The three main classes of basic processes reflected in performance on most conventional aptitude tests are:

1. *Apprehension*, *discrimination*, and *encoding* of stimuli. *Apprehension*, or speed of awareness, of a stimulus varies according to the degree of uncertainty of the nature of the stimulus or of the exact time or location of

its occurrence. *Discrimination* consists of responding to a stimulus that is distinguished from others by some particular attribute, when the stimulus occurs simultaneously with one or more other stimuli. *Encoding* is the attachment of a particular meaning, label, interpretation, or classification to the stimulus, such as responding (vocally or subvocally) with the appropriate utterance when, say, the symbol *A* occurs, or the numeral *5* or the word *cat*, or the colour *red*.

2. *Short-term memory capacity*, or "working memory." This component of the information-processing system is reflected in the amount of information that can be held or manipulated simultaneously (or within a brief time period) in full awareness. Associated processes are the *speed of search and retrieval* of an item of information held in short-term memory.

3. The *store of acquired knowledge, strategies* for dealing with specific types of problems, and other *learned complex skills stored in long-term memory*. Associated processes are the *speed of search and retrieval* of task-relevant information in long-term memory. Learned cognitive strategies also include the "*executive*" *processes*, which govern the deployment of the most appropriate routines for problem solving, monitoring one's own performance, and planning a course of action.

All of these types of information processes are involved in such complex tests as defining words in a vocabulary test, reading comprehension, and solving arithmetic problems. And they are involved in learning new skills. Individual differences and population differences in proficiency of performance in these complex tasks can be analysed and described in terms of the more elemental cognitive processes that underlie such complex abilities. Because the chronometric variables derived from a variety of elementary cognitive tasks reflect mainly cognitive *processes* rather than cognitive *content*, they would seem an especially valuable technique in the investigation of mental ability differences between populations that vary racially and culturally.

References

Anderson, J. R. (1983). Retrieval of information from long-term memory. *Science, 220,* 25–30.

Baddeley, A. D. (1968). A 3 min reasoning test based on grammatical transformation. *Psychonomic Science, 10,* 341–342.

Baddeley, A. D., & Hitch, G. (1974). Working memory. In G. Bower (Ed.), *The psychology of learning and motivation* (Vol. 8). New York: Academic Press.

Berger, M. (1982). The "scientific approach" to intelligence: An overview of its history with special reference to mental speed. In H. J. Eysenck (Ed.), *A model for intelligence.* New York: Springer-Verlag.

Bligh, M. N. (1967). *A comparative study of visual and auditory responsiveness in two ethnic groups.* Unpublished master's thesis, University of Witwatersrand, Johannesburg.

Borkowksi, J. G., & Krause, A. (1983). Racial differences in intelligence: The importance of the executive system. *Intelligence, 7,* 379–395.

Brand, C. R. (1984). Intelligence and inspection time: An ontogenetic relationship? In C. J. Turner (Ed.), *The biology of human intelligence.* London: Eugenics Society.

Brand, C. R., & Deary, I. J. (1982). Intelligence and "inspection time." In H. J. Eysenck (Ed.), *A model for intelligence*. New York: Springer-Verlag.

Carroll, J. B. (1980). *Individual difference relations of psychometric and experimental cognitive tasks*. Chapel Hill: L. L. Thurstone Psychometric Laboratory, University of North Carolina.

Cavanagh, J. P. (1972). Relation between the immediate memory span and the memory search rate. *Psychological Review, 79*, 525–530.

Clark, H. H., & Chase, W. G. (1972). On the process of comparing sentences against pictures. *Cognitive Psychology, 3*, 472–517.

Eysenck, H. J. (1982). The psychophysiology of intelligence. In C. D. Spielberger & J. N. Butcher (Eds.), *Advances in personality assessment* (Vol. 1). Hillsdale, NJ: Erlbaum.

Galton, F. (1883). *Inquiries into human faculty and its development*. London: Macmillan.

Gettinger, M. (1984). Individual differences in time needed for learning: A review of the literature. *Educational Psychologist, 19*, 15–29.

Groen, G. J., & Parkman, J. M. (1972). A chronometric analysis of simple addition. *Psychological Review, 79*, 329–343.

Hendrickson, A. E. (1982). The biological basis of intelligence. Part I: Theory. In H. J. Eysenck (Ed.), *A model for intelligence*. New York: Springer-Verlag.

Jensen, A. R. (1974). Interaction of Level I and Level II abilities with race and socioeconomic status. *Journal of Educational Psychology, 66*, 99–111.

Jensen, A. R. (1980a). *Bias in mental testing*. New York: Free Press.

Jensen, A. R. (1980b). Chronometric analysis of intelligence. *Journal of Social and Biological Structures, 3*, 103–122.

Jensen, A. R. (1982a). The chronometry of intelligence. In R. J. Sternberg (Ed.), *Advances in the psychology of human intelligence* (Vol. 1). Hillsdale, NJ: Erlbaum.

Jensen, A. R. (1982b). Reaction time and psychometric g. In H. J. Eysenck (Ed.), *A model for intelligence*. New York: Springer-Verlag.

Jensen, A. R. (1984a). Test validity: g versus the specificity doctrine. *Journal of Social and Biological Structures, 7*, 93–118.

Jensen, A. R. (1984b). Mental speed and levels of analysis. *The Behavioral and Brain Sciences, 7*, 295–296.

Jensen, A. R. (1985a). Methodological and statistical techniques for the chronometric study of mental abilities. In C. R. Reynolds & V. L. Willson (Eds.), *Methodological and statistical advances in the study of individual differences*. New York: Plenum.

Jensen, A. R. (1985b). The nature of the black–white difference on various psychometric tests: Spearman's hypothesis. *Behavioral and Brain Sciences, 8*, 193–219.

Jensen, A. R. (1985c). The black–white difference in g: A phenomenon in search of a theory. *Behavioral and Brain Sciences, 8*, 246–263.

Jensen, A. R. (1985d). Race differences and Type II errors: A comment on Borkowski and Krause. *Intelligence, 9*, 33–39.

Jensen, A. R. (1986). g: Artifact or reality? *Journal of Vocational Behavior 29*, 301–331.

Jensen, A. R. (1987a). The g beyond factor analysis. In J. C. Conoley, J. A. Glover, & R. R. Ronning (Eds.), *The influence of cognitive psychology on testing and measurement*. Hillsdale, NJ: Erlbaum.

Jensen, A. R. (1987b). Individual differences in the Hick reaction time paradigm. In P. A. Vernon (Ed.), *Intelligence and speed of information processing*. Norwood, NJ: Ablex.

Jensen, A. R. (1987c). Process differences and individual differences in some cognitive tasks. *Intelligence, 11*, 107–136.

Jensen, A. R., Schafer, E. W. P., & Crinella, F. M. (1981). Reaction time, evoked brain potentials, and psychometric g in the severely retarded. *Intelligence, 5*, 179–197.

Keating, D. P., & Bobbitt, B. (1978). Individual and developmental differences in cognitive processing components of mental ability. *Child Development, 49*, 155–169.

Klein, G. S., & Krech, D. (1952). Cortical conductivity in the brain-injured. *Journal of Personality, 21*, 118–148.

Livson, N., & Krech, D. (1956). Dynamic systems, perceptual differentiation, and intelligence. *Journal of Personality, 25,* 46–58.

McGue, M., Bouchard, T. J., Jr., Lykken, D. T., & Feuer, D. (1984). Information processing abilities in twins reared apart. *Intelligence, 8,* 239–258.

Naglieri, J., & Jensen, A. R. (1987). Comparison of black–white differences on the WISC-R and the K-ABC: Spearman's hypothesis. *Intelligence, 11,* 21–43.

Nettelbeck, T. (1987). Inspection time and intelligence, In P. A. Vernon (Ed.), *Intelligence and speed of information processing.* Norwood, NJ: Ablex.

Noble, C. E. (1969). Race, reality, and experimental psychology. *Perspectives in Biology and Medicine, 13,* 10–30.

Oldfield, R. C., & Wingfield, A. (1965). Response latencies in naming objects. *Quarterly Journal of Experimental Psychology, 17,* 273–281.

Paul, S. (1985). *Speed of information processing: The Semantic Verification Test and general mental ability.* Unpublished doctoral dissertation, University of California, Berkeley.

Poortinga, Y. H. (1971). Cross-cultural comparison of maximum performance tests: Some methodological aspects and some experiments with simple auditory and visual stimuli. *Psychologica Africana* (Monograph Supplement No. 6).

Posner, M. I. (1966). Components of skilled performance. *Science, 152,* 1712–1718.

Posner, M. I. (1978). *Chronometric explorations of mind.* Hillsdale, NJ: Erlbaum.

Posner, M. I. (1982). Cumulative development of attentional theory. *American Psychologist, 37,* 168–179.

Raz, N., Willerman, L., Ingmundson, P., & Hanlon, M. (1983). Aptitude-related differences in auditory recognition masking. *Intelligence, 7,* 71–90.

Scarr, S. (1982). Genetics and intelligence. In R. Sternberg (Ed.), *Handbook of human intelligence.* Cambridge University Press.

Spearman, C. E. (1927). *The abilities of man.* New York: Macmillan.

Stankov, L. (1983). The role of competition in human abilities revealed through auditory tests. *Multivariate Behavioral Research* (Monograph No. 83–1).

Sternberg, S. (1966). High-speed scanning in human memory. *Science, 153,* 652–654.

Vernon, P. A. (1983). Speed of information processing and general intelligence. *Intelligence, 7,* 53–70.

Vernon, P. A. (1985). Relationships between speed-of-processing, personality, and intelligence. In C. Bagley & G. Verma (Eds.), *Personality, cognition, and values: A cross-cultural perspective of childhood and adolescence.* Calgary, Alberta: University of Calgary Press.

Vernon, P. A., & Jensen, A. R. (1984). Individual and group differences in intelligence and speed of information processing. *Personality and Individual Differences, 5,* 411–423.

Vernon, P. A., & Kantor, L. (1986). Reaction time correlations with intelligence test scores obtained under either timed or untimed conditions. *Intelligence, 10,* 315–330.

Structural psychometrics

5 The factor model as a theoretical basis for individual differences

Joseph R. Royce

Introduction

Nobody really understands the nature of human intelligence, but the impact of factor theory has made it clear that a simple IQ, as manifested in the *Stanford–Binet*, the *Wechsler*, or some other single index, is blatantly inadequate. The primary purpose of the factorial approach is to determine the basic parameters that are common to the interrelated variables of a given domain.[1] Obviously then, it is a matter of simplification, an application of

---

[1] In mathematical form, factor analysis begins with the basic factor equation, which states that any behaviour, indicated as a standard score, zji, where

$$z = \frac{\text{Raw score} - \text{mean}}{\sigma}$$

is equal to the product of the loading (a_jm) of the measurement j on Factor 1, times the amount of this factor possessed by individual i (F_{1i}), plus the product involving the loading of the variable on Factor 2 $(a_{j2}F_{2i})$, plus the product involving the loading of the variable on Factor 3, etc., until all the common factor variance is accounted for. In simplified terms, this has been expressed as follows:

$$Z_{ji} = a_{j1}F_{1i} + a_{j2}F_{2i} + a_{j3}F_{3i} + \ldots a_{jm}F_{mi} \tag{1}$$

If we now restate this in the more compact matrix (i.e., any rectangular arrangement of numbers) formalism, we get

$$Z = AF \tag{2}$$

where Z is a matrix of standardised test scores, A is a matrix of factor loadings, and F is a matrix of factor scores. However, because the focus of our attention is on the underlying factors rather than the original observations, we solve for F and get

$$F = A^{-1}Z \tag{3}$$

However, since this involves an impractical form of F because there is no inverse for A, we turn to a variation of F (see Harman, 1976, p. 45), as follows:

$$F = A'R^{-1}Z \tag{4}$$

where A' refers to the transpose of the matrix of factor loadings, R^{-1} is the inverse of the correlation matrix R, and F is a computable version of the factor matrix.

This exposition has been simplified by restricting the analysis to orthogonal (i.e., right angled or uncorrelated) factors – that is, by omitting all correlational, specific factors, and error terms.

The reader who is interested in the mathematical basis of factor analysis is referred to such introductory texts as Fruchter (1954) or Gorsuch (1974), and to such books as Thurstone (1947), Horst (1963, 1965), Mulaik (1972), or Harman (1976) for more advanced treatments. For more mathematics per se, see any of a number of texts on matrix algebra, such as Albert (1941), Bodewig (1959), Hadley (1961), and Paige and Swift (1961).

147

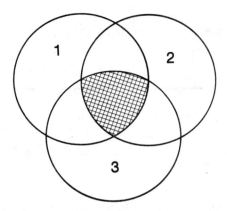

Figure 5.1. A schematic representation of a
cluster of three variables and one underlying
common factor.

the principle of parsimony to complex data whose interrelationships are
difficult to comprehend. More specifically, in the case of individual differences in intelligence, a limited number of abilities or factors are isolated as
the determiners of intellect.

The methodology of factor analysis

What does a psychologist do when he carries out a factor analysis? Stripped
down to its nontechnical essentials, a factor analyst's procedure is as follows:
(1) He administers a battery of tests to a sample of the population. (2) He
correlates each variable in the test battery with every other variable in the
test battery; that is, he computes a correlation matrix (R). (3) He goes
through a series of procedures known as factoring the matrix. The purpose
of this step is to determine how many factors will account for the data (i.e.,
he determines the rank of the matrix). (4) Because the reference frame in
step 3 is arbitrary, it is necessary to rotate it to a new position. Although
different criteria are available for guiding the rotation of the reference frame,
the most fruitful solutions have involved rotation to simple structure. ($N.B.$:
The structure of the test vectors in n-space is not affected by rotation of the
reference axes.) (5) After rotation he interprets the results. That is, he tries
to name or describe each of the factors.

The major factor theories of intelligence

The basic idea in factor analysis is that a factor is a latent unknown which
is shared by variables that form a cluster. For example, we can represent
a three-variable cluster sharing a common factor by Figure 5.1. In this figure

Table 5.1. *The major factor theories of intelligence*

Theory	Primary characteristic	Primary contributors
Single factor	One universal factor	Spearman
Bifactor	Universal plus several group factors	Spearman, Holzinger
Principal factor	Universal bipolar plus several group bipolar factors	Hotelling, Kelley
Multiple group factors	Many group factors, either correlated or uncorrelated	Thurstone (correlated) Guilford (uncorrelated
Hierarchical	Combines factors at several levels, such as one universal factor, two or more general factors, plus many correlated group factors	Burt, Cattell, Eysenck, Guilford, Royce and Diamond, Thurstone, Vernon

the correlated variables are shown as overlapping circles 1, 2, and 3, and the cross-hatched area in the centre is the area they share. Furthermore, the logic of factor analysis says that these three variables are intercorrelated because of the underlying common factor.

Although logically a factor can be common to any number of variables that constitute a test battery, the following four classes of common factors have been identified:

> *Universal factor* – a factor that is common to all the variables of a given domain.
> *General factor* – a factor that is common to most but not all of the variables of a given domain.
> *Group factor* – a factor that is common to a small subset (at least three but not as many as a general factor) of the variables of a given domain.
> *Bipolar factor* – any common factor identified by both positive and negative factor loadings.

As a result of combining these four kinds of common factors in different ways, a variety of theories of intelligence have emerged. Those that have had the greatest influence on research are summarised in Table 5.1.

The first factor theory of intelligence to be put forward was Spearman's (1904) single-factor theory. This theory postulated a single universal common factor (g), plus a factor specific to each test. Because it involved specifics in addition to g, it was originally called a two-factor theory. But this was an unfortunate misnomer because factor analysis is only concerned with identifying common factors; hence, I have referred to it as a single-factor theory. This was a reasonable theory at the turn of the century because of the dominance of such general intelligence approaches as the *Stanford–Binet* and *Wechsler* intelligence tests.

However, as the factor-analytic evidence accumulated over the ensuing decades, it became increasingly apparent that a viable factor theory of intelligence would have to take account of group factors in addition to Spearman's universal g factor. The first to recognize this was Spearman himself, along with his major supporter, Karl Holzinger. Their bifactor theory (see Holzinger & Harman, 1941) locates the first universal factor at the centre of the total battery of test vectors and the remaining group factors at the centre of each cluster of correlated test vectors.[2] Because they were committed a priori to the existence of g, they always interpreted the first general factor as such, and subsequent group factors in accordance with how the variables clustered. Holzinger took the view that one should rotate the reference frame to a position consistent with one's theoretical preference. Hotelling (1933) and Kelley (1928), on the other hand, functioning before the procedure of rotating the reference frame was known, simply tried to interpret the unrotated factors. This procedure forced them to adopt the concept of *bipolar* factors because in most test batteries the unrotated factor matrix includes factors that are identified at the negative pole as well as the positive pole. Hence, their principal-factor theory includes the identification of a large number of such bipolar group factors in addition to either a unipolar or a bipolar universal factor.

Before Thurstone factor analysis was a nonmathematical method which was based primarily on the intuitions of such early investigators as Spearman (1904), Garnett (1919), and Thomson (1939). However, in the mid-1930s, Thurstone (1935) realised that factor analysis could best be viewed as an application of matrix algebra. The story of this important development is told by Thurstone (1947, pp. vi–vii) himself.

I decided to investigate the relation between multiple-factor analysis and Spearman's tetrad differences. When I wrote the tetrad equation to begin this inquiry, I discovered that the tetrad was merely the expansion of a second-order minor, and the relation was then obvious. One might speculate as to whether multiple-factor analysis would have developed earlier if this interpretation had been stated earlier. If the second-order minors must vanish in order to establish a single common factor, then must the third-order minors vanish in order to establish two common factors, and so on? To have put the matter in this way would have led to the matrix formulation of the problem much earlier, as well as to the immediate development of multiple-factor analysis. Instead of dealing with the proportional columns and rows of a hierarchy and the vanishing tetrads, we now deal with the same relations in terms of the properties of unit rank, namely, proportional columns and rows and vanishing second-order minors. This formulation generalizes to the properties of higher rank. As far as I am aware this formulation of the factor problem has been generally accepted.

[2] A test is represented as a vector, and the degree of correlation between tests is indicated by the angle between the test vectors. Factors are represented as reference vectors. Before rotation, reference vectors are orthogonal. The number of reference vectors depends on the number of factors (mathematically, the rank of the matrix) identified in the analysis. For example, a two-factor solution will be a plane, and a three-factor solution will be a cube. Although visual representations are limited to three axes, matrix algebra can accommodate matrices of any size because matrix algebra is not limited by what is geometrically representable. However, all the visualiser has to do with solutions involving four or more factors, is to think of the three-dimensional case and then extrapolate to the required number of dimensions. Furthermore, any two dimensions can be plotted in a plane regardless of the total number of dimensions involved.

From these beginnings Thurstone integrated the relevant portions of correlational theory and matrix algebra into the first comprehensive, matrix algebra–oriented volume on factor analysis, *The Vectors of Mind* (1935). This was followed by his magnum opus, *Multiple Factor Analysis* (1947). Thurstone's mathematisation of factor analysis was so revolutionary that all subsequent factor-analytic research and textbooks have been cast in terms of matrix algebra. In short, the matrix formulation of factor theory has provided this approach with its conceptual foundations. However, this formulation, like any mathematical formalism, is substantively empty. This means that psychologists must supply the content appropriate to the domain in which factor analysis is applied.

Thus, although this work led Thurstone to a multiple-factor theory of intelligence, there was insufficient time available to him to develop a full-blown, substantive theory. In fact, he identified less than a dozen first-order factors of intellect, such as Number, Spatial Relations, Induction, Perceptual Speed, Verbal Comprehension, Word Fluency, Associative Memory, Speed of Closure, and Flexibility of Closure. Thurstone regarded such group factors as primary mental abilities – primary because they emerged repeatedly, despite differences in investigator, subjects, and identifying variables, in short, because they are invariant. It remained for an army of Thurstone adherents to identify an additional three or four dozen group factors of intelligence (e.g., see French, 1951; French, Ekstrom, & Price, 1963). However, it was Guilford (1967) who provided us with the most complete version of the multiple-factor theory in the form of his structure-of-intellect model. This model is an orthogonal, three-dimensional taxonomy of 120 elements or factors. The three major axes of this periodic table of intellectual processes are Contents, Products, and Operations. Each element of this cube is a hypothesised factor, around 100 of which have been empirically confirmed. Such factors occur at the intersection of the $4 \times 5 \times 6$ matrix reproduced as Figure 5.2.

Finally, we come to what is the most current and the most comprehensive synthesis of the several factor theories, the hierarchical model. The prototype for this theory is indicated in Figure 5.3. The basic idea is that there are correlated factors at several levels. The higher the level, the more general the factor. Thus, there is a universal factor (g_u) at the apex, 4 general factors (g_1, g_2, g_3, and g_4) at the next level, and 16 group factors (e.g., gr_{11}, gr_{21}, gr_{31}, and gr_{41}) at the lowest level.

The earliest versions of this theory were put forward by British psychologists, among them Burt (1941) and Vernon (1961). However, these early hierarchies were rather crude, as they involved the a priori postulation of g, and several unrotated, bipolar, group factors, with varying identifying variables, depending on the composition of the test battery.

It was not until after Thurstone pointed out the importance of identifying invariant factors via rotation to simple structure that less arbitrary hierarchical models emerged. A first step in this direction was Thurstone's sug-

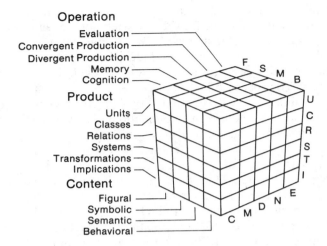

Figure 5.2. Structure-of-intellect model, with three parameters. Other parameters may be added (from Guilford, 1967).

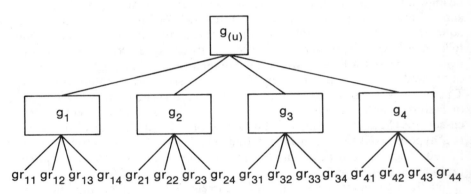

Figure 5.3. A prototypical representation of the hierarchical theory of intelligence.

gestion that Spearman's universal g factor could emerge as a second-order factor. This involved factoring the correlated primaries at the first order. Although there was a general reluctance to factor factors at first, about a dozen higher order factors of intelligence have been identified during the past three decades. Cattell and Horn, for example, have identified two general factors – Fluid Intelligence and Crystallised Intelligence – in their hierarchical "investment theory": Fluid intelligence refers to a general neurological nonexperiential general ability which has not been channelled in particular directions whereas crystallised intelligence refers to an experientially determined general ability which has been selectively channelled (Cattell, 1971, pp. 117–121). And in his most recent revision, Guilford (1981) has postulated some three dozen higher order general factors in his structure-of-intellect model. However, the most comprehensive hierarchical model currently available is the one recently put forward by Royce and Diamond (Diamond & Royce, 1980; Royce & Powell, 1983). This model (indicated as Fig. 5.4), which constitutes a synthesis of all the invariant factors identified to date, involves a hierarchy with four levels. But *cognitive type* lies at the apex rather than Spearman's *g*. Royce and Diamond point out that the universal claim involved in Spearman's *g* has never been met – that is, no factor has been shown to be common to all tests in the intellectual domain. Thus, the Royce–Diamond position is that Spearman's *g* is a very general, but not a universal, common factor. On the other hand, each of us can be characterised by an intellectual profile or a cognitive type. Hence, this construct appears at the apex of the cognitive or intellectual hierarchy. Three general factors are also postulated at Level III. The constructs at Level III are postulated rather than empirically arrived at for the simple reason that the evidence for them is currently inadequate. However the evidence for the 6 second-order factors and 23 first-order factors is highly convincing.

Although it is highly probable that additional factors will eventually have to be added, the overall structure will probably remain roughly the same. Progress will be slow because the demands for demonstrating factorial invariance are extremely difficult to meet. The imaginativeness subdomain of the symbolising subhierarchy, however, is the most obvious area where we can anticipate the addition of more factors. As the problems involved in measuring symbolising performance are resolved, we can anticipate an increase in the number of factor investigations in this area and the eventual identification of invariant factors. When the inventory of invariant first-order factors grows sufficiently large, we can also expect to see changes in overall organisation at the higher levels of the hierarchy.

The heredity–environment issue

A major aspect of individual differences theory involves an elaboration of hereditary and environmental sources of variation. Thus, we must find a way to link heredity and environment to factors. One approach is to decompose the A matrix, that is, the factor loadings (see equations 1 to 4 in footnote 1), into hereditary, environmental, interaction, and correlated components as follows:

$$A = H + E + I + C \tag{5}$$

substituting in equation 4, we get

$$F = H'R^{-1}Z + E'R^{-1}Z + I'R^{-1}Z + C'R^{-1}A \tag{6}$$

Because of our interest in this book on the effect of culture on intelligence, we are particularly interested in the second term (E), the environmental sources of variation. Unfortunately, however, relatively little research has

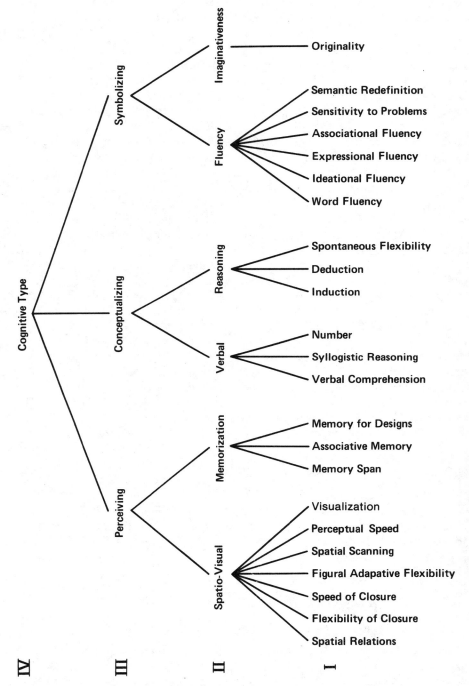

Figure 5.4. The hierarchical structure of the cognitive system (modified from Diamond & Royce, 1980).

been conducted on the effects of the environment on factors of intelligence. Nevertheless, this issue is elaborated in the next section under the rubric of the "factor-learning model." Unfortunately, there has been no research on heredity–environment interaction effects (I, the 3rd term), and heredity–environment correlation effects (C, the 4th term). There has, however, been an abundance of research on genetic effects (H, the 1st term). But I will not go into this, except to refer the reader elsewhere (e.g., Royce, 1979, and Royce & Powell, 1983), and to quote the conclusion to be drawn from this research: "The generally held view is that intelligence is the most heritable of the various facets of personality. In fact, it has been estimated that 60% to 80% of the observed variation in general intelligence . . . is due to genetic variation" (Royce, 1979, p. 614). And, summarising the factor findings,

there is direct evidence for a significant hereditary effect for seven (i.e., Thurstone's Primary Mental Abilities) of the thirty-two factors of the cognitive hierarchy, and indirect evidence for three additional cognitive factors (i.e., a total of around 31% of the cognitive system). The combination of high replicability and high magnitude [heritability] estimates indicates that a hereditary effect is particularly strong for three factors – verbal comprehension, spatial relations, and word fluency. However, the evidence is only moderately strong in the case of the memorization, perceptual speed, inductive reasoning, and number factors, and the evidence is weakest in the case of the associative memory, associational fluency, and ideational fluency dimensions. (Royce, 1979, p. 619)

Environmental effects, cultural effects, and the factor-learning model

Environmental effects refer to any aspect of the environment that can result in psychological change. In the case of animals the environment is composed of the physical surround and other animals; but in the case of humans, the environment includes culture as well. Whereas the physical environment is the most important determinant of the behaviour of animals, it is the cultural environment that is crucial in the case of humans. In fact, it has been held that personality is largely formed as a result of cultural conditioning; by a life-long process of enculturation, starting at birth and with special force during the earliest years and during "critical periods" such as adolescence.

One of the most convincing demonstrations of the validity of this claim is the massive study reported by the University of Chicago Committee on Human Development. The purpose of this study (Eells, Davis, Havighurst, Herrick, & Tyler, 1951) was to determine the relationship between social class and intelligence. It involved an analysis of the performance of 5,000 students from high and low social status backgrounds on more than 650 items of several widely used group intelligence tests. The major findings were that linguistic or academic test items resulted in large differences favouring the high social status groups, whereas test items of a perceptual or "practical" nature showed either smaller differences or favoured the low social status groups. "Variations in opportunity for familiarity with specific cultural

Table 5.2. *Mean group scores in verbal and nonverbal tests*

	Scale	
	Verbal	Nonverbal
White	53.2	54.1
Negro	45.4	43.4
Indian	47.8	53.0
Puerto Rican	44.9	45.8
Mexican-American	46.5	50.1
Oriental	51.6	56.6

Source: Coleman et al., 1966.

words, objects, or processes required for answering the test items" (Eells et al., 1951, p. 68) was indicated as the best explanation for these findings.

Although the Eells et al. (1951) research involved subjects from the same culture and did not employ factor analysis, it constitutes convincing evidence of the effect of cultural differences on intelligence. The basic premise of research on individual differences is that the genes determine the range of behaviour and that culture fixes the level of performance within that biologically determined range. Unfortunately there is a confounding of genetic and cultural causation which is typical of research in this area. The ethnic differences reported by Coleman et al. (1966) exemplify this situation (see Table 5.2). In this table we see that North American whites score the highest, blacks the lowest, with Indians, Puerto Ricans, Mexican-Americans, and Orientals ranging between these two extremes. Although there is no doubt concerning the existence of such average test performance differences, there is complete disagreement concerning the details of causation.

The guiding premise in cross-cultural psychological research is that human behaviour is a function of an unknown set of universal dispositional variables, and that cultural differences in behaviour can be explained in terms of these dispositions. Although several methods are available for identifying such universals, factor analysis was developed explicitly for the purpose of identifying invariant constructs.

However, whatever method is used must meet a range of difficult demands which are indigenous to cross-cultural research. These include such technical difficulties as developing culture-fair or culture-reduced tests, developing an adequate criterion for what constitutes cross-cultural universality, the fact that cross-cultural research is currently atheoretical because of the lack of viable cross-cultural theory, and achieving equivalence of meaning and content of stimulus inputs and response outputs from different cultures. Despite these difficulties factor analysis has been applied cross-culturally, but with limited success. And in spite of the fact that more factor studies have been conducted in the cognitive domain than any other, the most convincing example of such research that I'm aware of was conducted in the value domain. The research in question (Hofstede, 1979) involved administering a 150-item questionnaire to 116,000 *S*'s in 40 countries. The factor analysis, based on the countries (*N* = 40) rather than *S*'s (*N* = 116,000), identified 4 factors. The factor performance levels for each of the 40 countries is indicated in Table 5.3. If we focus on the Individualism factor, for example, we see that the United States scores the highest (91), that Colombia scores the lowest (13), and that Spain (51) is near the mean (50).

We can also detect similarities and differences in value profiles. The South American countries of Argentina, Brazil, Chile, Colombia, and Venezuela show a similar profile with a relatively high Power Distance Index (PDI) and a relatively low Individualism Index (IDV). An opposite profile with a relatively high IDV and a relatively low PDI is shown by Australia, Canada, Denmark, Great Britain, New Zealand, and the United States. And an unusual in-between profile is shared by Belgium, France, and Italy.

Unfortunately, the invariance of cognitive factors across cultures has only been demonstrated for fewer than a dozen factors, namely *g*, Memory, Fluency, Visualisation, Space, Verbal, Number, Perceptual Speed, and Reasoning. For example, Irvine's (1969, 1979) research demonstrates invariance for the *g*, Verbal, and Number factors across a wide range of African cultures, Guthrie (1963) finds that the Verbal, Numerical, Rote Memory, Visualisation, Fluency, and Speed factors occur in the Philippines as well as the United States, and Vandenberg's (1959, 1967) research demonstrates invariance for the Memory, Space, Verbal, Number, and Perceptual Speed factors across American, Chinese, and South American samples of subjects. And Werner (1979) presents evidence for invariance of the last five factors across five ethnic groups sampled in Hawaii. Furthermore, Werner reports differences in the level and pattern of performance on these cognitive factors (see Fig. 5.5). For example, in most cases the Caucasians and Japanese performed at the highest level, followed by the Filipinos, the Hawaiians, and the Portuguese. The most similar patterns were those of the Japanese, the Filipinos, and the Hawaiians.

Although it is difficult to demonstrate the reasons for these differences, Werner (1979, p. 170) offers the hypothesis that a major reason for the good standing of the Japanese is that "in the majority of the homes emphasis is placed on the value of education, on disciplined work habits, and on respect and esteem for intellectual pursuits." Iwawaki and Vernon (Chapter 14) also stress motivation as a major factor in Japanese intellectual achievement.

Guthrie (1963) also identified several "culturally transmitted" factors. These include an English Language Spelling factor and a Facility-with-Digits factor. Unfortunately, because of the highly inferential nature of the evidence, Guthrie (1963, p. 94) could not be any more specific than to say that these factors "appeared to be the product of the Philippine educational tradition."

Table 5.3. *Values of the four indices for the forty countries*

Country	PDI	UAI	IDV	MAS
Argentina	49	86	46	56
Australia	36	51	90	61
Austria	11	70	55	79
Belgium	65	94	75	54
Brazil	69	76	38	49
Canada	39	48	80	52
Chile	63	86	23	28
Colombia	67	80	13	64
Denmark	18	23	74	16
Finland	33	59	63	26
France	68	86	71	43
Great Britain	35	35	89	66
Germany F.R.	35	65	67	66
Greece	60	112	35	57
Hong Kong	68	29	25	57
India	77	40	48	56
Iran	58	59	41	43
Ireland	28	35	70	68
Israel	13	81	54	47
Italy	50	75	76	70
Japan	54	92	46	95
Mexico	81	82	30	69
Netherlands	38	53	80	14
Norway	31	50	69	8
New Zealand	22	49	79	58
Pakistan	55	70	14	50
Peru	64	87	16	42
Philippines	94	44	32	64
Portugal	63	104	27	31
South Africa	49	49	65	63
Singapore	74	8	20	48
Spain	57	86	51	42
Sweden	31	29	71	5
Switzerland	34	58	68	70
Taiwan	58	69	17	45
Thailand	64	64	20	34
Turkey	66	85	37	45
USA	40	46	91	62
Venezuela	81	76	12	73
Yugoslavia	76	88	27	21
Mean	52	64	50	50
Standard Deviation	20	24	25	20

Note: PDI: power distance index; IDV: individualism index; UAI: uncertainty avoidance index; MAS: masculinity index.
Source: Eckensberger et al., 1979.

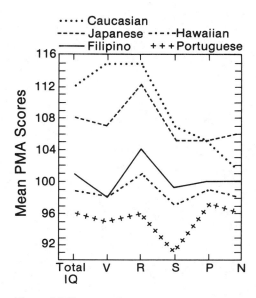

Figure 5.5. Patterns of PMA IQ and factor scores
by ethnic groups at age 10 (from Werner, 1979).

But the Guthrie report does have the virtue of highlighting learning as the process that is common to both environmental and cultural effects, where learning refers to any psychological changes in the subject due to experience. And the book by Hunt (1961) constitutes the best available summary of the relationships between learning, intelligence, and experience. He says, for example,

These studies [of the effects of infantile experience on later learning and problem solving] have shown that rats reared with ample opportunities for a variety of perceptual experience do learn mazes more readily than rats with minimal opportunities for a variety of such experience. Pet-reared rats with a background of highly varied experience have been found to perform with more facility on the Hebb-Williams test of intelligence than do cage-reared rats with a background of little variation in experience. Similarly Thompson and Heron have shown that in a wide variety of situations pet-reared dogs behave in a fashion much more intelligent than their litter mates who were cage-reared for the first eight months of their lives . . . In yet another example of the effects of infantile experience, this time on perception, Riesen has found that chimpanzees kept in darkness for the first months of their lives lack object-recognition and the various responses which depend upon such recognition. Moreover, even the anatomic development of the visual apparatus appears to be hampered by lack of visual stimulation. (Hunt, 1961, pp. 352–353)

The standard account of socialisation is that responses to specifiable stimuli are reinforced. However, if one looks at learning from a factor-analytic perspective it is the changes in the underlying factor components and their organisation that are important. Royce and Powell (1983) have looked at learning from the perspective of factor analysis and have developed a factor-learning model. The critical hypothesis in this approach is that different cultures or environments maximise different combinations of factor components. For example, the environmental forces of relatively "primitive" cultures are presumed to reinforce those cognitive components that are consistent with such activities as hunting, fishing, agriculture, and other basic survival behaviour. For empirical support for this position, see Berry (1976); furthermore, MacArthur (1973, p. 246) reports that "the Canadian Eskimo's hunting ecology and upbringing encouraging independence foster not only a spatial-field independence cluster of abilities, but also a distinctive cluster involving inductive reasoning from nonverbal stimuli; the Nsenga's agricultural ecology and upbringing encouraging conformity blur such differentiation." On the other hand, so-called developed cultures will require that their participants learn a great deal about numbers and words, in some cases to the extent of developing "experts" in some of the knowledge specialties such as the arts or the sciences. In short, differential reinforcement is probably the learning mechanism which can best account for the enculturation process. But, in the case of the factor-learning model the focus is on changes in the factors of intellect.

The essence of what is involved in the factor-learning model can be captured in an investigation conducted by Fleishman (Fleishman & Hempel, 1955). The major findings are shown in Figure 5.6. In this figure we see a progressive change in the contributions of various factors to total variance in a task involving the acquisition of a complex motor skill. In particular, Fleishman reports a systematic decrease in the contribution of cognitive factors, with an attendant systematic increase in the contribution of motor factors.

Factors as theoretical constructs

There has been disagreement concerning the theoretical nature of factors, ranging from regarding them either as convenient classificatory concepts (Anastasi, 1938) or, under certain experimental conditions, as artifactors (Roberts, 1959) at one extreme; and as reified concepts at the other extreme (Thurstone, 1947). Factors have been defined as dimensions, determinants, functional unities, parameters, and taxonomic categories. Although there is truth to all of these views, Royce (Royce, 1963; Royce, Kearsley, & Klare, 1978) has concluded that they can best be viewed as theoretical constructs.

His analysis begins with the noncontroversial view that a factor is a determinant which accounts for covariation in a specified domain of observation. However, he eventually takes the strong stance that factors are theoretical constructs because he confines his analysis to invariant factors – that is, factors which are empirically repeatable despite variations in initial factoring, populations sampled, measurements, and, in some cases, even spe-

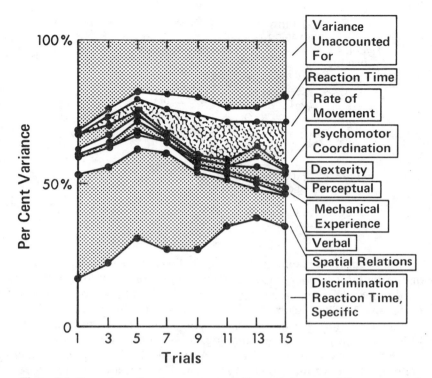

Figure 5.6. Percentage of variance represented by each factor at different stages of practice on a discrimination reaction time task (percentage of variance is represented by the area shaded in for each factor) (from Fleishman & Hempel, 1955).

cies and cultures. The point is that only invariant factors are capable of accounting for observed regularities, and thereby worthy of the designation as a theoretical construct.

Royce adopts the philosophy of science concept of a nomological network (Feigl & Scriven, 1956) as elaborated by Margenau (1950) as the point of departure. Margenau labels the nomological network the *C* or conceptual plane, which is epistemically connected to the empirical component or *P* plane. But Margenau makes the point that mature scientific theory cannot exist without the less operational concepts. He also makes it clear that advanced theory implies a very tight formal network, and that it is only because of its powerful deductive mathematics that physics can sometimes get by with minimal points of empirical contact. But most psychological constructs at least have multiple connections to the *P* plane. And the multiplicity of connections to empirical observables is also an obvious characteristic of factors because of the requirement that a minimum of three variables is required for factor identification. But what about the relationship between factors and other constructs in the nomological network? How do factors fit in?

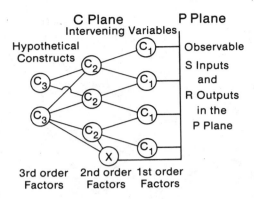

Figure 5.7. The location of factors in the nomological net (from Royce, 1963).

First-order factors emerge from an analysis of the correlation matrix, second-order factors emerge from the correlations of the first-order factors, and
third-order factors emerge from the correlations of the second-order factors.[3]
If we now link the logic of factor analysis with the concepts of Feigl and
Margenau, Figure 5.7 is the result. This shows how psychometric factors
fit into the Margenau–Feigl nomological network. Thus, first-order factors,
which lie closest to the data, are *intervening variables*, whereas higher order
factors, which are more distant from the *P* plane, are best regarded as *hypothetical constructs*. We can also say that Figure 5.7 depicts a continuum,
with the more descriptive factors at the *P* plane or right side of the diagram,
and the more explanatory factors deep within the nomological network on
the left side of the diagram.

In terms of the *S-O-R* paradigm, factors are identified inductively from
observations involving a standard stimulus input with a variable (covariation)
response output. In other words, factors are *O* variables which mediate between *S* inputs and *R* outputs. That is, factor analysis *per se* does not deal
with dependent or independent variables – it simply identifies mediating
variables that are embedded in complex causal chains.

The scientific role of factor analysis

Let us assume that science involves both empirico-inductive and hypothetico-deductive aspects, as described in Cattell's (1966) essay on the nature
of science.

---

[3] For a useful explanation of this concept, readers are referred to Horst (1965, chap. 21). The
situation is actually more complicated than this because higher order factors can also be
identified simultaneously with lower order factors. However, although this presentation is
oversimplified, it is the clearest way to convey the underlying logic for identifying underlying
higher order factors.

Table 5.4. *The empirico-inductive generation of hypotheses*

	Modification of Cattell's induction process	Morgan's logic	Royce's logic of factor analysis
Phase II	Plausible hypotheses ↑ Further reasoning to "explain the regularity"	Hypothesis selection	Factor identification
Phase I	Inductive reasoning to some regularity ↑ Experiment observation	Hypothesis generation	Pattern replicability

Source: Royce, 1976.

According to this approach, inductive reasoning based on empirical observations generates hypotheses from which one can logically derive deductions. These deductions can now be subjected to further observations and another induction–hypothesis–deduction cycle. This sequence forms a spiral, however, because science is a never-ending process in which answering questions begets further questions.

How does factor analysis fit into this picture? Although it is possible to employ factor analysis for the purpose of confirming what is already known, or to make deductions via the use of a criterion variable (e.g., see Eysenck, 1950), it is clear that its primary value is the exploratory one of identifying unknowns. The utilisation of massive correlation matrices of empirical variables covering a previously unexplored terrain, or a terrain where the relationships are blurred, particularly if the analyses involve an orderly and insightful progression of planned investigations, constitutes a powerful means for getting a handle on potentially useful theoretical constructs in complex domains where observables are confusedly interrelated.

Royce (1976) has suggested that there are two phases of scientific inference in the typical exploratory factor investigation. The first phase is focussed on the identification of replicable patterns of observables, and the second is concerned with the identification of latent unknowns. Further exposition of these two phases of scientific inference in factor analysis will be facilitated by reference to Table 5.4. In this table, I have juxtaposed the critical elements from three analyses: Cattell's (1966) analysis of scientific method; Morgan's (1973) analysis of the logic of discovery; and Royce's (1976) analysis of the logic of factor analysis. Reading from the bottom up the two phases are indicated in the left margin. The corresponding column terms for

Phase I are inductive reasoning, hypothesis generation, and pattern replicability. And the corresponding column terms for Phase II are plausible hypotheses, hypothesis selection, and factor identification. The main point is that factor analysis makes its contribution at the empirico-inductive end of Cattell's inductive–deductive spiral. This means that its major scientific role is the exploratory one of identifying theoretical constructs which have the potential of eventually becoming part of a nomological network that can "explain" the observables of a given scientific domain such as intelligence.

References

Albert, A. A. (1941). *Introduction to algebraic theories*. Chicago: University of Chicago Press.

Anastasi, A. (1938). Faculties vs. factors: A reply to Professor Thurstone. *Psychological Bulletin, 35*, 391–395.

Berry, J. W. (1976). *Human ecology and cognitive style*. Beverley Hills, CA: Sage-Halsted.

Bodewig, E. (1959). *Matrix calculus*. New York: Interscience Publishers.

Burt, C. (1941). *The factors of the mind*. New York: Macmillan.

Cattell, R. B. (1966). Psychological theory and scientific method. In R. B. Cattell (Ed.), *Handbook of multivariate experimental psychology*. Chicago: Rand McNally.

Cattell, R. B. (1971). *Abilities: Their structure, growth, and action*. Boston: Houghton Mifflin.

Coleman, J. S., Campbell, E. Q., Hobson, C. J., McPartland, J., Mood, A. M., & York, R. L. (1966). *Equality of educational opportunity*. Washington, DC: U.S. Office of Education.

Diamond, S., & Royce, J. R. (1980). Cognitive abilities are expressions of three "ways of knowing." *Multivariate Behavioral Research 15*, 31–58.

Eckensberger, L., Lonner, W., & Poortinga, Y. H. (Eds.). (1979). *Cross-cultural contributions to psychology*. Lisse: Swets & Zeitlinger.

Eells, K., Davis, A., Havighurst, R. J., Herrick, V. E., & Tyler, R. W. (1951). *Intelligence and cultural differences*. Chicago: University of Chicago Press.

Ekstrom, R. B., French, J. W., & Harman, H. H. (1976). *Manual for list of factor referenced objective tests*. Princeton, NJ: Educational Testing Service.

Eysenck, H. J. (1950). Criterion analysis: An application of the hypothetico-deductive method of factor analysis. *Psychological Review, 57*, 38–53.

Feigl, H., & Scriven, M. (Eds.) (1956). *The foundations of science and the concepts of psychology and psychoanalysis*. Minneapolis: University of Minnesota Press.

Fleishman, E. A., & Hempel, W. E., Jr. (1955). The relation between abilities and improvement with practice in a visual discrimination reaction task. *Journal of Experimental Psychology, 49*, 301–312.

French, J. W. (1951). *The description of aptitude and achievement tests in terms of rotated factors*. Chicago: University of Chicago Press.

French, J. W., Ekstrom, R. B., & Price, L. A. (1963). *List of reference tests for cognitive factors*. Manual for revised version. Princeton, NJ: Educational Testing Service.

Fruchter, B. (1954). *Introduction to factor analysis*. Princeton, NJ: Van Nostrand.

Garnett, J. C. M. (1919). On certain independent factors in mental measurement. *Proceedings of the Royal Society of London, 96A*, 91–111.

Gorsuch, R. L. (1974). *Factor analysis*. Philadelphia: Saunders.

Guilford, J. P. (1967). *The nature of human intelligence*. New York: McGraw-Hill.

Guilford, J. P. (1981). Higher-order structure-of-intellect model abilities. *Multivariate Behavioral Research, 16*, 411–435.

Guthrie, G. M. (1963). Structure of abilities in a non-Western culture. *Journal of Educational Psychology, 54*, 94–103.

Hadley, G. (1961). *Linear algebra*. Reading, MA: Addison-Wesley.

Harman, H. H. (1976). *Modern factor analysis* (3rd rev. ed.) Chicago: University of Chicago Press.

Hofstede, G. (1979). Value systems in forty countries: Interpretation, validation and consequences for theory. In L. Eckensberger, W. Lonner, and Y. H. Poortinga (Eds.), *Cross-cultural contributions to psychology*. Lisse: Swets & Zeitlinger.

Holzinger, K. J., & Harman, H. H. (1941). *Factor analysis*. Chicago: University of Chicago Press.

Horst, P. (1963). *Matrix algebra for social scientists*. New York: Holt, Rinehart & Winston.

Horst, P. (1965). *Factor analysis of data matrices*. New York: Holt, Rinehart & Winston.

Hotelling, H. (1933). Analysis of a complex of statistical variables into principal components. *Journal of Educational Psychology, 24*, 417–441.

Hunt, J. McV. (1961). *Intelligence and experience*. New York: Ronald Press.

Irvine, S. H. (1969). Factor analysis of African abilities and attainments: Constructs across cultures. *Psychological Bulletin, 71*, 20–32.

Irvine, S. H. (1979). The place of factor analysis in cross-cultural methodology and its contribution to cognitive theory. In L. Eckensberger, W. Lonner, & Y. H. Poortinga (Eds.), *Cross-cultural contributions to psychology*. Lisse: Swets & Zeitlinger.

Kelley, T. (1928). *Crossroads in the mind of man*. Stanford, CA: Stanford University Press.

MacArthur, R. S. (1973). Some ability patterns: Central Eskimos and Nsenga Africans. *International Journal of Psychology, 8*, 239–247.

Margenau, H. (1950). *The nature of physical reality*. New York: McGraw-Hill.

Morgan, C. G. (1973). On the algorithmic generation of hypotheses. *Scientia, 108*, 583–598.

Mulaik, S. A. (1972). *The foundations of factor analysis*. New York: McGraw-Hill.

Paige, L. W., & Swift, J. D. (1961). *Elements of linear algebra*. Boston: Ginn.

Roberts, A. O. H. (1959). Artifactor–analysis: Some theoretical background and practical considerations. *Journal of National Institute for Personnel Research* (Johannesburg), *7*, 168–188.

Royce, J. R. (1963). Factors as theoretical constructs. *American Psychologist, 18*, 522–528.

Royce, J. R. (1976). Psychology is multi: Methodological, variate, epistemic, world-view, systemic, paradigmatic, theoretic, and disciplinary. In W. J. Arnold (Ed.), *Nebraska symposium on the conceptual foundation of theory and methods in psychology*. Lincoln: University of Nebraska Press.

Royce, J. R. (1979). The factor-gene basis of individuality. In J. R. Royce & L. P. Mos (Eds.), *Theoretical advances in behavior genetics*. Alphen aan den Rijn: Sitjhoff & Noordhoff.

Royce, J. R., Kearsley, G., & Klare, W. (1978). The relationship between factors and psychological processes. In J. M. Scandura & C. J. Brainerd (Eds.), *Structural process theories of complex human behavior*. Leyden: Sitjhoff.

Royce, J. R., & Powell, A. (1983). *Theory of personality and individual differences: Factors, systems, and processes*. Englewood Cliffs, NJ: Prentice-Hall.

Spearman, C. (1904). The proof and measurement of association between two things. *American Journal of Psychology, 15*, 72–101.

Thomson, G. (1939). *The factorial analysis of human ability*. New York: Houghton Mifflin.

Thurstone, L. L. (1935). *The vectors of mind*. Chicago: University of Chicago Press.

Thurstone, L. L. (1947). *Multiple factor analysis*. Chicago: University of Chicago Press.

Vandenberg, S. G. (1959). The primary mental abilities of Chinese students: A comparative study of the stability of a factor structure. *Annals New York Academy of Sciences, 79*, 257–304.

Vandenberg, S. G. (1967). The primary mental abilities of South American students: A second comparative study of the generality of a cognitive factor structure. *Multivariate Behavioral Research, 2*, 175–198.

Vernon, P. E. (1961). *The structure of human abilities* (rev. ed.). London: Methuen.

Werner, E. E. (1979). Subcultural differences in ability, achievement, and personality factors among Oriental and Polynesian children on the Island of Kauai, Hawaii. In L. Eckensberger, W. Lonner, & Y. H. Poortinga (Eds.), *Cross-cultural contributions to psychology*. Lisse: Swets & Zeitlinger.

6   The meaning of item bias in ability tests

Ype H. Poortinga and Henk van der Flier

Introduction

Psychological tests are widely used in populations other than the one for which they were designed and originally standardised. If a test is transferred to another country, items are often modified or replaced to make the test more suitable for local subjects. In the case of a new population which forms part of the same society, only new norms tend to be established. If a test is used for comparative purposes, either within a culturally heterogeneous society or across countries, no changes in item content are made, but identity of the *metric* scale formed by the test score variables in the various groups is presupposed.

It can be argued that adaptation of a test does not involve any psychological or psychometric assumptions about the nature of intergroup differences and that problems of equivalence are avoided when no comparisons are made. This is correct only to a certain extent. In a properly conducted restandardisation study, items which do not differentiate between subjects are eliminated or replaced, new norms are established, and the validity of the test is investigated. However, it seems pointless to adapt an existing test (rather than to construct a new one on the basis of theoretical principles), unless it is assumed that the ability measured by the test is shared by the populations concerned.

When only new norms are established, it is implicitly taken for granted that the test content need not be altered; and that the test reflects the same "hypothetical construct" or empirical criterion in the new population. Differences in validity coefficients are seen more as a practical problem – new cut-off points have to be determined and different estimates of criterion scores have to be obtained – rather than as evidence that the test does not have the same meaning.

At the same time, the extensive literature on *test fairness* and *item bias* indicates that the comparison of subjects' scores has been recognised as a difficult and treacherous enterprise, at least in the domain of ability testing. Techniques to establish whether or not items are biased have become widely used to analyse the metric equivalence or comparability of test scores that have been obtained from subjects belonging to different populations. Various approaches have been developed during the last 15 years and are now available for serious researchers. We shall assume that the reader is familiar with at least some of the relevant techniques which have been summarised in various reviews (e.g., Jensen, 1980; Rudner, Getson, & Knight, 1980; Shepard, Camilli, & Averill, 1981; Berk, 1982).

So far, the objective of most studies in the item-bias tradition has been to identify biased items and to discard these in order to retain an unbiased assessment procedure. Such operations presuppose that an unbiased test is thought of as a realistic possibility, and that the standard by which the items are judged is adequate for the stated purpose. There is ample evidence from cross-cultural comparative research that for divergent groups the first assumption is precarious, especially in the case of ability tests. We shall argue that the choice of a standard is ambiguous and that for this reason also the second assumption is difficult to maintain.

By drawing a parallel between test adaptation and bias research we intend to focus attention on the similarities between the two research areas. These are not limited to the psychometric equivalence or inequivalence of items. Note too, that the population to which norms supposedly apply usually cannot be taken as a homogeneous set of subjects who only show quantitative differences in scores on the test concerned. Studies on *differential validity* and *moderator variables* have shown that the presence of identifiable subgroups within most populations cannot be ruled out. It requires little imagination to extend this line of reasoning to a level where a subgroup does not contain more than a single individual.

In this chapter we shall make some comments on item-bias research from a conceptual perspective. First of all, we shall analyse a few basic issues of test comparison in somewhat more detail. In a second section we shall postulate that the extent of bias is contingent upon the inferences or generalisations which are made on the basis of test scores, and that bias should not be seen as an inherent characteristic of an instrument. The viewpoint will be supported that "universality," "bias," and "population" should be defined in relative rather than absolute terms. In the last section of the chapter, we shall give two empirical illustrations of how the analysis of bias, at the group level and at individual level, can contribute to a better understanding of test results.

Some minimal assumptions

The use of an ability test in groups other than the one where it originated is based on certain assumptions about the identity of metric properties of the test score scale. Which assumptions have to be made depends on the intended usage of the test.

The logic of test transfer

A first question to be answered is whether abilities are concepts that are valid across cultures. One can take the position that cognitive functioning can only be understood as an adaptation to specific sociocultural and eco-logical conditions and consequently cannot be assessed in terms of universal concepts. Such a culturally specific, or emic, orientation, among others, has been suggested by Berry (1972), inspired by the ideas of anthropologists like Malinowski that behaviour can only be understood within the framework of the cultural system in which it occurs. The most obvious objection is that researchers could not communicate the meaning of psychological data if this were strictly true. In fact, when studies of authors who claim to favour a culturally specific explanation are analysed, it turns out that general psy-chological concepts are invoked which are not culture bound (Poortinga, 1982). We would like to submit that the interpretation of data in any cross-cultural study is given in terms of supposedly universal explanatory prin-ciples. Going a step further, we would argue that observed phenomena only acquire scientific meaning when they can be expressed in a presumably universal scientific language (Faucheux, 1976).

Most cross-cultural psychologists take as a starting point the notion of a "psychic unity of mankind." This is a term at a high level of abstraction with a rather fuzzy meaning. It is certainly not intended to imply that each ability is a universally valid hypothetical construct. Nevertheless, that is how it works out in practice. A cross-cultural psychologist who investigates whether group X has more of an ability A than group Y assumes that both groups share this ability. It may be noted that test results cannot provide absolute negative evidence about the universality of an ability. Extremely low or zero test scores tend to be taken as an indication that a particular test forms an inappropriate measurement procedure, rather than as evidence affecting the status of the theoretical notions on which the test is based.

In one respect our argument is oversimplified. There is a selection in the kinds of ability tests which are adapted for any specific group. For example, there are studies on the cognitive style of Bushmen and Pygmies, but none on their mechanical skills or geographical knowledge. On the other hand, it can be argued that the performance on a mechanical skills task reflects not so much an "ability" or similar traitlike notion, but rather the level of achievement in a particular culture-bound domain of knowledge. This point of view is compatible with Triandis's (1972, p. 38–39) opinion that if it is inappropriate to make cross-cultural comparisons for lack of equivalence in the data, a common dimension can be found at a higher level of abstraction. We conclude that manifestations of behaviour can be seen as characteristics of a certain cultural group, but that psychological theories and the concepts defined in these theories tend to be universal. This is a powerful rationale for the adaptation of tests in other cultures, provided that the item content is not too closely linked to the behaviour repertoire available to members of a specific culture.

The logic of computing new norms

When a positive answer has been given to the first, a second question can be asked, namely: Does a certain ability play an equally important role in the organisation of the behaviour of individuals belonging to different cultures? The problem posed is not restricted to cultural groups, but extends also to subject populations defined in other terms, such as age, sex, or socioeconomic status.

Even if the universality of psychological characteristics is accepted on theoretical grounds, so-called cultural factors could still have a differential effect on the organisation of behaviour – in the sense that a certain ability may be more important in one group than in another. Psychometrically this means that there exist intergroup differences in the relationships between abilities. These would be revealed by correlations between ability test scores that differed for each group. However, it can also be argued that the assumption about the universality of concepts implies that within a theoretical network the relationships between concepts should be identical and that unequal correlations can only reflect measurement artifacts (Poortinga, 1971). Even within culturally fairly uniform populations at least some evidence exists that discrepancies between factor structures of identifiable subgroups may be found. For example, Balzert (1968) showed that high- and low-scoring groups of subjects on an extraversion scale differed in respect of the factor structure which emerged from a battery of intelligence tests. In a more general sense we can refer to research on moderator variables as originally described by Saunders (1956) and to Ghiselli's work on differential validity (e.g., Ghiselli, 1972). The issues discussed here have consequences for the analysis of fairness and bias. It is an implication of most analyses of fairness that test–criterion validity coefficients should be equal across groups (cf. Jensen, 1980). One also finds that differences in item–test correlations are used as an index of item bias.

However, the rationale for imposing these conditions as requirements for psychometric equivalence falls away when structural differences, as reflected in correlation coefficients, do not necessarily indicate measurement artifacts. In that case it can be argued that only quantitative differences on a variable should be interpreted. This requires that explanations of differences in correlations and factor structures should be given in terms of concepts which can be quantitatively measured on a separate instrument. In Balzert's study the extraversion scale can be said to have served this purpose. Consequently, it can be argued that the tradition of test fairness analysis is based on the assumption that only quantitative differences in test scores can be valid.

Our answer to the second question has become rather ambivalent. On the one hand, we admit that differences in correlations can reflect valid differences in phychological functioning. On the other hand, we plead that such differences cannot be readily interpreted, unless they can be expressed on a separate quantitative scale, and supported with independent empirical evidence. It is obvious that the choice of a meaningful instrument to achieve this requires a sufficiently well-developed theory.

In summary, we argue that the relationships between abilities may be different across subject populations, but unless this difference can be measured quantitatively on some other observed variable, the attribution of the difference to either measurement artifacts or "real' differences in psychological functioning remains, at least to some extent, arbitrary. Therefore, it is a questionable practice to establish only new norms for a test which is going to be used in a different population without checks on its validity. Whether such an omission has serious consequences depends on the extent to which the new subject population differs from the original norm population. We shall come back to this point in the section on the notion of populations.

The logic of quantitative comparison

When to the second question a positive answer has been given there remains a third question, namely: Does a test for assessing an ability reflect that ability on a scale with the same origin and with equal units of measurement in different groups?

If one sees the first question as mainly epistemological, the second as partly theoretical and partly empirical, this third question should be almost exclusively empirical. What is needed to answer it is some standard in terms of which the scale of a score variable obtained in one group can be equated with the scale obtained elsewhere. Unfortunately such a standard is not easily identified for ability tests. The various kinds of analyses which have been proposed can only provide approximate answers.

There are analyses which are based on total test scores. Apart from correlational and factor-analytic approaches, which are mainly relevant for determining structural relationships, there are statistical techniques which provide information on quantitative aspects of scales. Most notable are regression functions, but they have at least two problems. Usually there is no obvious rationale for choosing a variable outside the test to serve as a standard for evaluating the test score scale. If regression functions are found to be different across groups, it is not clear which of two or (in the case of multiple regression) more variables are causing the differences. The second problem, which we only mention in passing, is that even if there is an equal test–criterion regression function in two populations, there is no unambiguous rule for making "fair" decisions on all individuals of both groups (Petersen & Novick, 1976).

There are also analyses for which the items in a test are considered as separate variables. In this chapter these are more central to our interest. Identity of statistical relationships between items across groups can be taken as a condition for absence of bias in an instrument. A significant item by culture interaction in an analysis of variance (ANOVA) or differences in the parameter values of an item on the latent trait scale in Item Response Theory are taken as evidence of bias. Item bias tends to be taken as an inherent characteristic of the instrument used for comparing individuals belonging to certain populations (e.g., Shepard, 1982). The absolute standard needed to evaluate the bias of each separate item is provided by the other items. Precisely which psychometric conditions are imposed depends to a large extent on the data model chosen by a researcher. In the studies based on the so-called classical model the major emphasis is on (transformations of) the item difficulty index (p_i). The most important requirement for an unbiased test is that an item does not show larger (or smaller) intergroup differences than the other items. Despite the fact that undesirable statistical properties may affect the outcome of various analyses (Lord, 1977; Petersen, 1980), the p_i index still is convenient and popular.

In the so-called latent trait models, unbiased items are supposed to have identical item characteristic curves in each of the groups concerned. The advantage of latent trait models is that the fit can be tested for each group separately. A disadvantage is the limited applicability. Either a highly restrictive model, such as the Rasch model, has to be specified, or a model with fewer constraints can be imposed, but in that case elaborate data sets in each population are needed. In recent years log-linear models have been developed for bias analysis which impose fewer restrictions than the latent trait models and evade the major statistical shortcomings of the p_i index (e.g., Mellenbergh, 1982).

By taking information based on other items of the same test as a standard to evaluate item bias, important constraints are imposed. First of all, implicitly an affirmative answer is given to the first two of the three questions we asked. Second, it has to be assumed that there are no bias effects common to all items, or to a large proportion of the items. Such a shared bias term will not be identified by means of statistical tests for item bias. For example, in an ANOVA design intergroup differences which are constant across items will not show up as a culture by item interaction, but as a main effect of cultural group. This latter component traditionally tends to be interpreted as reflecting a valid intergroup difference. Consequently, a definite positive answer cannot be given to our third question, unless on theoretical grounds the scale of the test score variable is declared to be identical across populations.

In *comparative* studies of groups with a divergent cultural background empirical evidence of item bias is almost invariably found if it is explicitly investigated (van der Flier, 1983). For more closely related groups the direct evidence is less clear-cut (Jensen, 1980), but it follows from what has been said so far that a failure to find item bias does not mean that the equivalence of scores can be taken for granted.

Comparison of test results across groups can easily lead to anomalous conclusions. We are inclined, therefore, to advocate a conservative strategy and to counsel against such comparison unless there is a reasonable certainty about the psychometric equivalence of the results. As equivalence seems difficult to attain in many cases, a positive answer to our third question is unlikely. However, the presence of bias in test results is not necessarily only a negative outcome which puts an end to all investigation. One can try to interpret observed bias to arrive at a better understanding of the cognitive processes that are assumed to underlie test performance.

Inferential contingencies and construct definition

So far we have treated bias as a psychometric problem, the analysis of which rests on deductive arguments. The psychological meaning of bias in a particular data set cannot be evaluated in mathematical terms. A theoretical framework is required. The interpretation that a researcher derives from test scores rests partly on inductive arguments which by their very nature are tentative. In the tradition of ability testing which we followed in the previous section, certain key concepts tend to be treated as absolute rather than approximative. In this section we shall argue for a more relative conceptualisation of bias.

One test – more generalisations

To make our point we shall first take a closer look at the inferences or generalisations which are made on the basis of test scores. Let us take again the example of a mechanical skills test. If the test is taken as a representative sample from a limited and well-described domain of manifest behaviours, the term *mechanical skills* is not much more than a summary label describing the item content. If properly sampled, the test items provide a valid assessment of a repertoire of behaviours available to a person. This interpretation is independent of any further information on the subjects. However, it is purely descriptive and not inferential. Any relationship with other variables which are not a sample from the same domain is to be seen as a coincidence.

If mechanical skill is treated as an ability which can manifest itself in widely divergent behaviours across cultures, such as building kayaks among Inuit and repairing cars in western countries, it is hardly possible to draw a representative sample from all relevant activities. Rather, items are chosen because they refer to some psychological characteristic which is essential for the ability as defined by the researcher. The test results are evaluated not in terms of manifest behaviours, but in terms of psychological functions which are supposed to determine those behaviours.

A framework which lends itself to the distinction just made is the *Generalisability Theory*, developed by Cronbach and his associates (Cronbach, Rajaratnam, & Gleser, 1963; Cronbach, Gleser, Nanda, & Rajaratnam, 1972). In this theory the interpretation of test scores is conceived as a generalisation to a universe of responses. A generalisation can be made to a very small or a very extensive domain or to a domain of any intermediate size. In this conception a lack of psychometric equivalence cannot be seen as an inherent characteristic of an instrument. Whether or not an item is biased primarily depends on what domain the test has to represent. If a test by some standard forms a random sample from some domain – in other words, if it has a perfect content validity – an analysis of item bias would be superfluous and even absurd. Evidence of item bias, such as an item by culture interaction in an ANOVA, could be observed, but this would point to a genuine nonhomogeneity of the domain across cultures. Unfortunately, total reliance on nonpsychometric considerations is rarely justified. Not only the topic an item is dealing with is of importance, but also formal aspects, such as the way in which a question is phrased and the response format.

For the study of bias it seems useful to differentiate among three kinds of domains: First, in item-bias analysis where the remaining items are used as a standard for assessment, there is, strictly speaking, no basis for generalisation beyond the test; next, bias in items, or, for that matter, tests, can also be evaluated in terms of some other measure of the domain of generalisation; finally, the evaluation of bias can refer to a hypothetical construct, such as a trait. When bias is treated as relative and depending on a specific domain, extension of results from a smaller domain of generalisation to a larger one is not allowed.

It is quite possible that ability tests and the criteria they predict, to a large extent share cultural "bias." Jensen (1980) has pointed out that tests in the United States specifically designed to give an advantage to certain minority groups do not correlate with the usual industrial and educational criteria. However, this hardly affects our argument, because both tests and criteria are embedded in the same (dominant) cultural context. In the final section of the chapter we shall give an example of how an analysis of item bias can help explain intergroup differences in test performance.

Population(s)

Not only can the absolute character of what is being measured by a test be challenged, but also the population concept. The term *population* can refer to any quantity of people, from a small group to the whole of the human race. In applied research an initial definition usually is given in terms of demographic variables. A differentiation between subgroups can be made on demographic grounds, but also on the basis of psychological variables.

We have already mentioned the so-called moderator variables. Another serious challenge against the notion of a population as a homogeneous set of subjects follows from the interactionistic approach in personality research (e.g., Endler & Magnusson, 1976). One can analyse the pattern of item scores within a given test to check for any individual subject, or for a subgroup of subjects, whether the observed pattern deviates from the average pattern found in the total sample, conditional upon the level of test performance. Approaches in this direction have in recent years been made by, for example, van der Flier (1977, 1982), who developed a statistic for detecting "deviant response patterns"; by Wright (1977), who applied tests for the "person fit" based on the Rasch model; and by Levine and Rubin (1979) and Drasgow

(1978), who used "appropriateness indices" based on the three-parameter logistic model. In such analyses group identity need not be specified in advance. When two cultural groups turn out to differ in average response pattern, there may still be subgroups with similar response patterns. Moreover, the condition of a nonsignificant deviation from a group's average pattern can also be applied to individual subjects, in order to investigate whether they can be reckoned to belong to that particular population; or, in more general terms, to find out with which of a set of populations a single score pattern shows the best fit. This approach to the analysis of bias we shall also illustrate in the next section.

Universality vs. specificity

One may wonder whether the concept of universality cannot be reformulated in less absolute terms, in a similar sense as the universe of generalisation and the population of generalisation. We have already indicated that to us universality is a formal property of theoretical concepts and that only explanatory concepts are admissable which refer to psychological characteristics supposedly invariant across cultures.

However, a distinction between theoretical concepts can be made according to the degree to which they lend themselves to empirical scrutiny of cross-cultural differences. A classification in terms of experimental rigour has been proposed (van de Vijver & Poortinga, 1982) with conceptual universals, weak universals, strong universals, and strict universals. Conceptual universals refer to theoretical concepts at a high level of abstraction, such as "psychic unity of mankind" or "intelligence." Weak universals are concepts for which empirical referents have been specified and construct validity demonstrated in each group where an investigation has been carried out. Negative findings on validity do not affect the universality of the theoretical concept, but indicate that it cannot be operationalised in an appropriate manner. Strong universals are measures in the same metric across cultures but without a specification of the origin of the measurement scale. This means that no absolute comparisons can be made across cultural groups, but that this can be done with intergroup differences of changes in performance level as a result of some treatment. For example, let the mean score on a test administered to two groups on two occasions be $\bar{a}_1$, and $\bar{a}_2$ for the one group and $\bar{b}_1$, and $\bar{b}_2$ for the other. If it is found that $\bar{a}_1 - \bar{a}_2 \neq \bar{b}_1 - \bar{b}_2$, an interpretable intergroup difference has been observed. For a concept to be scale equivalent it is necessary that an equal metric scale with a common origin exists. Only in this case it is possible to derive from a single variable that, for example, $\bar{a}_1 > \bar{b}_1$ reflects a valid difference. Dealing with universality in a more relative fashion does not relax but rather sharpens the metric requirements for intergroup comparison, thus underlining the futility of a search for unbiased ability scales at an empirical level.

In summary, universality and cultural specificity are the empirically unattainable end points of a continuum. Individuals form heterogeneous rather than homogeneous populations. Each measuring instrument which is used as an index of a psychological concept is affected by irrelevant context variables which are likely to differ from culture to culture. Consequently, it may generally be a better strategy to find out whether bias is the result of systematic intergroup differences rather than try to eliminate it.

Interpreting bias: Two examples

In this section we shall illustrate how bias analysis can help to *interpret* the test results obtained by (groups of) persons with a different cultural/educational background. The data come from a cooperative research project between the Free University of Amsterdam, the University of Nairobi/Kenyatta University College, the University of Dar es Salaam, and Makerere University in Kampala (Drenth, van der Flier, & Omari, 1983; Bali, Drenth, van der Flier, & Young, 1984). In this project the use of ability tests for educational purposes was investigated in Kenya, Tanzania, and Uganda. By making selection for further education dependent on more criteria than school achievement, it was expected that school curricula would become less exclusively directed towards the examinations. Also, it was felt that the ability tests might give children with good educational potentials but with a poor school background a better chance to qualify for higher education. A comparative analysis of the ability test results was envisaged, as there appeared to be sufficient similarities in the educational system of the three countries to make this interesting.

For the project large national samples of Standard 7 and Form 4 pupils were tested in the three countries. For a description of the samples we refer to the above-mentioned reports by Drenth and his co-workers. We shall restrict ourselves to the 4 unspeeded tests in the battery of 15 ability tests, namely, *Figure Exclusion, Word Exclusion, Symbol Exclusion* and *Word Analogies*. The first three tests are of the exclusion type. In rows of five geometrical figures, words, or groups of numbers or letters, four are similar in some respect. The task is to indicate the one that does not belong with the rest. In terms of the conceptual framework suggested by French, Ekstrom, & Price (1963), these tests can be classified as inductive reasoning tests. The *Word Analogies* test is also classified as an inductive reasoning test. The testees are presented with analogies in which the last word is missing. The missing word has to be chosen from five alternatives. Although some of the primary school samples took a Kiswahili version of the test series, the secondary school series was always given in English.

The means and standard deviations of the test scores for the Form 4 samples from Kenya, Tanzania, and Uganda are given in Table 6.1. The performance of the Tanzanian group is lower, when compared with Kenyan and Ugandan means in the four unspeeded tests. Although not reported here, lower Tanzanian performance was evident in all but 4 of the 15 tests ad-

Table 6.1. *Means (M) and standard deviations (S) of the results on four unspeeded ability tests*

	Kenya (N = 347)		Tanzania (N = 395)		Uganda (N = 400)	
	M	S	M	S	M	S
Figure exclusion						
Total score	20.30	5.58	19.04	4.98	20.20	4.61
Biased part	3.09	1.60	3.26	1.49	3.05	1.49
Unbiased part	17.20	4.46	15.79	4.14	17.15	3.69
Word exclusion						
Total score	21.99	4.97	17.66	4.76	22.37	4.34
Biased part	7.81	2.55	5.29	2.34	8.04	2.12
Unbiased part	14.18	3.13	12.37	3.11	14.33	2.95
Symbol exclusion						
Total score	20.28	5.65	16.69	5.26	19.07	5.68
Biased part	.81	.64	.76	.60	.80	.59
Unbiased part	19.47	5.30	15.93	5.03	18.27	5.43
Word analogies						
Total score	25.01	5.23	19.21	5.99	24.28	4.97
Biased part	10.64	2.52	7.25	2.68	10.20	2.40
Unbiased part	14.37	3.28	11.96	3.89	14.08	3.19

ministered to all three samples of Form 4 students, suggesting a general trend.

Item bias and construct validity

The question obviously arises how these differences may be explained. Two interpretations can be offered. The quality of education in Tanzania is not as high as in the other two countries; and the home language and the language of instruction at primary school for the Tanzanian pupils is Kiswahili rather than English. More English is spoken in the schools of Uganda and Kenya, where it is also the teaching language in primary education. It was hypothesised that the effect of differential familiarity with English is a significant factor which should manifest itself in item bias for tests with verbal item content.

An iterative item-bias detection method based on a log-linear model was applied to the data (van der Flier, Mellenbergh, Adèr, & Wijn, 1984). In this procedure the number of items classified as biased is increased with one after each iteration. After the first iteration the most strongly biased item in the test is eliminated, after the second iteration the two most strongly biased items, and so on. The test scores of the subjects are computed each time on the basis of the remaining items. Items which have been classified

Table 6.2. *Numbers of biased items in the four tests*

	Biased	Unbiased	Number of iterations
Figure exclusion	6	30	6
Word exclusion	13	27	13
Symbol exclusion	2	38	2
Word analogies	17	23	18

as biased at one stage can be reintroduced in later runs. The analysis ends after a specified number of iterations or when none of the remaining items exceeds a specified value of the appropriate likelihood ratio statistic. In a Monte Carlo study the procedure proved to be superior to a noniterative log-linear method and to two procedures based on the p_i-index, the delta method (Angoff & Ford, 1973), and the ANOVA arc sine method (Plake & Hoover, 1979). The main results of the item-bias analysis are presented in Table 6.2. The effects on the means and standard deviations are shown in Table 6.1.

The proportion of biased items in the two tests with verbal stimuli is considerably higher than in the two nonverbal tests. When the biased items are eliminated, the overlap in score distributions between the Tanzanian and the other two samples increases for the verbal tests, but decreases (slightly) for the nonverbal tests.[1] An orthogonal factor analysis followed by Varimax rotation on the entire battery was carried out for each of the three samples separately. In each analysis four factors were extracted, labelled as "inductive thinking" or "g," "divergent thinking" or "verbal fluency," "perceptual speed," and "memory." The patterns of loadings over all tests were so distinct that confusion of factors across groups could be ruled out. The squared factor loadings of the four tests of interest on the first two factors are presented in Table 6.3 in the column marked "Before."

The same factor analyses were repeated after the elimination of the biased items from the four tests. The squared factor loadings are presented in the column "After." The differences between the first and second columns are also given. The factor loadings of the nonverbal tests showed very few changes. For the two verbal tests the loadings on the first factor decreased in the Ugandan sample, while the loadings on the second factor decreased for the Kenyan and Tanzanian subjects, with the effect that the patterns of loadings became more similar. The most noticeable difference, namely, that the two verbal tests have the highest loading on the second factor in the Tanzanian sample and on the first factor in the other two groups, could

[1] This means that for the nonverbal tests the performance on the biased items was relatively better in the lower scoring group.

Table 6.3. *Squared factor loadings of the four unspeeded tests on two factors, before and after elimination of biased items, including differences*

	Factor 1			Factor 2		
	Before	After	Diff.	Before	After	Diff.
Figure exclusion						
Kenya	.58	.55	.03	−.01	−.02	−.01
Tanzania	.52	.52	.00	.00	.00	.00
Uganda	.32	.37	−.05	.00	.00	.00
Word exclusion						
Kenya	.32	.32	.00	.25	.11	.14
Tanzania	.13	.12	.01	.44	.36	.08
Uganda	.55	.37	.18	.08	.13	−.05
Symbol exclusion						
Kenya	.35	.32	.02	.01	.00	.01
Tanzania	.23	.24	−.01	.18	.18	.00
Uganda	.14	.16	−.02	.10	.10	.01
Word analogies						
Kenya	.36	.37	−.01	.22	.17	.05
Tanzania	.13	.17	−.04	.45	.32	.12
Uganda	.46	.31	.15	.06	.08	−.02

suggest that "verbal fluency" is more differentiated from "general" intelligence in the Tanzanian children.

It appears that item bias can explain in part the intergroup differences which were observed. Degree of familiarity with the English language was a fairly obvious determinant of bias. However, after the elimination of biased items most of the differences still remain. The question arises whether English as a medium of test instruction has played a role in the performance on *all* items. Looking at the factor structures this possibility cannot be ruled out as the verbal tests in the Tanzanian sample display a different pattern of loadings. The evidence we have presented here is definitely not strong enough to argue that the lower scores of the Tanzanian children are entirely due to the language of test administration. One would have expected a stronger impact on the factor loadings of the elimination of biased items. Also, the mean performance differences of verbal and nonverbal tests were too much alike to substantiate this interpretation. Nevertheless, the tests should not be used for a quantitative comparison of the performance of individual pupils with different nationalities. However, the evidence on construct validity provided by the factor analysis reveals no reason why the tests should not be used for educational advancement within the separate countries.

Deviance scores

So far we have treated each of the samples of secondary school pupils as homogeneous. It is also possible to look for lack of equivalence of an intrument between subjects within a group, making distinctions between them on the basis of their patterns of item responses.[2]

A different sample studied in the context of the same project was used for this purpose. It consisted of 571 Kenyan school pupils to whom a battery of 15 tests was given similar to the one at the end of the primary school (Standard 7). English was the medium of instruction from Standards 1 or 3 onwards, and the tests were also administered in English. The battery was similar to the one administered to the Form 4 subjects. The analysis has been restricted to four tests closely corresponding to those mentioned in the previous section except that the items were considerably less difficult.

The purpose of this analysis is to classify subjects on the basis of their item response patterns into subgroups and to investigate whether this classification can be related to certain background variables which can be seen as indices of westernisation. For each test, p_i-values of the items were calculated in two reference groups, namely the Kenyan sample itself and an English sample ($N = 447$) to which the same tests were administered. In both cases the p_i-values were separately determined for five score categories. For each subject (pattern of item scores), two deviance scores based on the corresponding sets of p_i-values were computed with a technique described by van der Flier (1982). The deviation between actual item scores and the expected item scores, given the total test score and the set of p_i-values, is not the same for all subjects. For example, the deviance score should be high for a subject who has only a few difficult items with low p_i-values correct. The theoretical distribution of the deviance scores for a set of items can be established. For each subject the value of a z-score corresponding to a probability within the theoretical distribution can be computed. These z-values have been used in this study.[3] As expected, there were substantial intercorrelations (.67–.71) between the deviance scores for the same test based on the English and the Kenyan sets of p_i-values. The correlations between the deviance scores on the four tests were positive but very low ($\leqslant .12$). On the basis of the difference between each pair of deviance scores, the patterns per test were divided into a more-western and a less-western category (median split). This provided a westernisation index.

It was expected that the pupils with a low westernisation score lack certain knowledge and skills required to solve the test items and that the tests consequently underestimate their reasoning ability. As an external criterion against which this hypothesis could be tested the sum score of the school

[2] Full details on the investigation reported here can be found in van der Flier (1980).
[3] In the case of an unfinished test the procedure allows the computation of the deviance score, eliminating the items which have not been completed.

Table 6.4. *Linear regression equations for subgroups with low and high westernisation indices*

Figure exclusion	high Western	: $y' = -15.519 + 1.110x$
	low Western	: $y' = -15.519 + 1.110x$
Word exclusion	high Western	: $y' = -24.805** + 1.054x$
	low Western	: $y' = -18.998** + 1.054x$
Symbol exclusion	high Western	: $y' = -21.635* + .913x$
	low Western	: $y' = -17.941* + .913x$
Word analogies	high Western	: $y' = -18.671** + .718x$
	low Western	: $y' = -12.746** + .718x$

Note: * $p \leq .05$; ** $p \leq .01$
Source: Reprinted from van der Flier, 1980.

examination results for *Mathematics* and *General Knowledge* was used, corrected for knowledge of English. The linear regression equations for the subgroups with low-western and high-western item score patterns are given in Table 6.4. For three of the four tests the intercept shows a significant difference.

The results indicate that pupils with a low westernisation index achieve better examination results than could be expected on the basis of their test scores. (However, the differences are small and their practical use has not been established.) The product–moment correlations were computed between certain background variables on which information was gathered by means of a questionnaire and the westernisation index on each test. The correlations with urbanisation, educational–occupational level, ethnicity (Asian vs. African), and school quality are all in the expected direction, although the values in Table 6.5 are not high.

In spite of the psychometric shortcomings of the background variables – the attitudinal modernity variable, especially, was of poor quality – the results can be seen as a clear indication that deviance scores can contribute significantly to the explanation of test performance differences within a population. Whether the contribution of deviance scores is not only statistically significant but also practically meaningful remains to be seen. The low intercorrelations between the deviance scores on the four tests point to the need for caution. Nevertheless, this example illustrates how test bias can be extended to identify meaningful differences between individuals, subgroups, and perhaps even populations.

Conclusion

Since its origin in simple comparisons of relative item difficulties in different groups of subjects, bias has had many meanings, and a corresponding number of techniques for assessing its influence on standardised tests. The

Table 6.5. *Correlations between background variables and the westernisation index for each of the four tests*

Background variables	Fig. excl.	Word excl.	Symb. excl.	Word anal.
1. Urbanisation level	.09	.15	.13	.04
2. Ethnic group	.10	.21	.11	.04
3. Education parents	.05	.09	.08	.02
4. Occupation father	.15	.19	.17	.03
5. Number of books	.14	.19	.14	.12
6. Attitudinal modernity	.01	.02	.02	.07
7. Examination success primary school	.13	.19	.10	.17
8. Teacher quality primary school	.15	.18	.10	.06

Note: correlations $\geq$ .08 are significant at the 5% level.

growth of interest in determining the degree of item bias in the interests of fairness (the primary ethical question) of test use has now led to the pursuit of bias in a more theoretical direction. In the past, biased or unsuitable items have been discarded, and then forgotten. With the improved methods of analysis that have emerged since the 1960s, the items identified as biased can be examined more closely. Moreover, the theoretical advances in test construction that require items to be cross-referenced to cognitive theory, now make the pursuit of biased items a positive contribution to the explanation of test score differences. The item is, after all, the nucleus of test construction. Bias research isolates those nuclei in which our assumptions and predictions of similarity have failed. From there, it seems a short step to computer simulations and real experiments on these failures as a further move forward.

References

Angoff, W. H., & Ford, S. F. (1973). Item-race interaction on a test of scholastic aptitude. *Journal of Educational Measurement, 10*, 95–106.

Bali, S. K., Drenth, P. J. D., van der Flier, H., & Young, W. C. E. (1984). *Contribution of aptitude tests to the prediction of school performance in Kenya: A longitudinal study.* Lisse: Swets & Zeitlinger.

Balzert, C. (1968). Untersuchungen über Zusammenhänge zwischen Extraversion/Introversion und der Faktorenstruktur der Intelligenz [Investigations on relationships between extraversion/introversion and the factor structure of intelligence]. *Zeitschrift für experimentelle und angewandte Psychologie, 15*, 195–238.

Berk, R. A. (Ed.). (1982). *Handbook of methods for detecting item bias.* Baltimore: Johns Hopkins University Press.

Berry, J. W. (1972). Radical cultural relativism and the concept of intelligence. In L. J. Cronbach and P. J. D. Drenth (Eds.), *Mental tests and cultural adaptation.* The Hague: Mouton.

Cronbach, L. J., Gleser, G. C., Nanda, H., & Rajaratnam, N. (1972). *The dependability of behavioral measurements.* New York: Wiley.

Cronbach, L. J., Rajaratnam, N. & Gleser, G. C. (1963). Theory of generalizability: A liberalization of reliability theory. *British Journal of Mathematical and Statistical Psychology, 16*, 137–163.

Drasgow, F. (1978). *Statistical indices of the appropriateness of aptitude test scores*. Unpublished doctoral dissertation, University of Illinois, Urbana-Champaign.

Drenth, P. J. D., van der Flier, H. & Omari, I. M. (1983). Educational selection in Tanzania. In H. J. Walberg and T. N. Postlethwaite (Eds.). *Evaluation in Education: An International Review Series, 7* (Whole No. 2). New York: Pergamon.

Endler, N. S. & Magnusson, D. (Eds.). (1976). *Interactional psychology and personality*. New York: Wiley.

Faucheux, C. (1976). Cross-cultural research in experimental social psychology. *European Journal of Social Psychology, 6*, 269–322.

French, J. W., Ekstrom, R. B., & Price, L. A. (1963). *Kit of reference tests for cognitive factors*. Princeton, NJ: Educational Testing Service.

Ghiselli, E. E. (1972). Comment on the use of moderator variables. *Journal of Applied Psychology, 56*, 270.

Jensen, A. R. (1980). *Bias in mental testing*. London: Methuen.

Levine, M. V., & Rubin, D. B. (1979). Measuring the appropriateness of multiple choice test scores. *Journal of Educational Statistics, 4*, 269–290.

Lord, F. M. (1977). A study of item bias, using item characteristic curve theory. In Y. H. Poortinga (Ed.), *Basic problems in cross-cultural psychology*. Lisse: Swets & Zeitlinger.

Mellenbergh, G. J. (1982). Contingency table models for assessing item bias. *Journal of Educational Statistics, 7*, 105–118.

Petersen, N. S. (1980). Bias in the selection rule – bias in the test. In L. J. T. van der Kamp, W. F. Langerak, & D. N. M. de Gruijter (Eds.), *Psychometrics for educational debates*. New York: Wiley.

Petersen, N. S., & Novick, M. R. (1976). An evaluation of some models for culture-fair selection. *Journal of Educational Measurement, 13*, 3–29.

Plake, B. S., & Hoover, H. D. (1979). An analytical method of identifying biased test items. *Journal of Experimental Education, 48*, 153–154.

Poortinga, Y. H. (1971). Cross-cultural comparison of maximum performance tests. *Psychologica Africana* Monograph Supplement, No. 6.

Poortinga, Y. H. (1982). Cross-culturele psychologie en minderhedenonderzoek [Cross-cultural psychology and minority research]. *De Psycholoog, 17*, 708–720.

Rudner, L. M., Getson, P. R., & Knight, D. L. (1980). Biased item detection techniques. *Journal of Educational Statistics, 5*, 213–233.

Saunders, D. R. (1956). Moderator variables in prediction. *Educational and Psychological Measurement, 16*, 209–222.

Shepard, L. A. (1982). Definitions of bias. In R. A. Berk (Ed.), *Handbook of methods for detecting item bias*. Baltimore: Johns Hopkins University Press.

Shepard, L., Camilli, G., & Averill, M. (1981). Comparison of six procedures for detecting test item bias using both internal and external ability criteria. *Journal of Educational Statistics, 6*, 317–375.

Triandis, H. C. (1972). *The analysis of subjective culture*. New York: Wiley.

van der Flier, H. (1977). Environmental factors and deviant response patterns. In Y. H. Poortinga (Ed.), *Basic problems in cross-cultural psychology*. Lisse: Swets & Zeitlinger.

van der Flier, H. (1980). *Vergelijkbaarheid van individuele testprestaties* [Comparability of individual test scores]. Lisse: Swets & Zeitlinger.

van der Flier, H. (1982). Deviant response patterns and comparability of test scores. *Journal of Cross-Cultural Psychology, 13*, 267–298.

van der Flier, H. (1983). Some applications of an iterative method to detect biased items. In J. B. Deregowski, S. Dziurawiec, & R. C. Annis (Eds.), *Expiscations in cross-cultural psychology*. Lisse: Swets & Zeitlinger.

van der Flier, H., Mellenbergh, G. J., Adèr, H. J., & Wijn, M. (1984). An iterative item bias detection method. *Journal of Educational Measurement, 21*, 131–145.

van de Vijver, F. J. R., & Poortinga, Y. H. (1982). Cross-cultural generalization and universality. *Journal of Cross-Cultural Psychology, 13*, 387–408.

Wright, B. D. (1977). Solving measurement problems with the Rasch model. *Journal of Educational Measurement, 14*, 97–116.

Part II

Cultural responses to ability measurement

Europe and North America

7   The British "cultural influence" on ability testing

Paul Kline

Jensen dedicated *Bias in Mental Testing* (Jensen 1980) to three pioneers of psychometry: Francis Galton, Alfred Binet, and Charles Spearman. The methods and constructs of these men, he writes, have dominated the field from its beginnings to the present day. Furthermore, although there is considerable agreement among psychometricians about the importance of this trinity there is no universal consensus about any others.

I therefore begin this chapter, which is concerned with the British influence on ability testing, with an examination of the work of Galton and Spearman. My treatment of these innovators consists of selecting out the essentials of their work and demonstrating how, even today, albeit in sometimes mutated form, its seminal nature can be discerned. Indeed, this is the approach I adopt with all the major figures in British psychometrics who have influenced the field. In a concluding section I attempt to summarise the British contribution. Thus, a scientific "cultural influence" on the quest for a structure of intellect is defined; and it represents the British response to problems of ability testing that were encountered from the very beginning and need resolution even today. From a scrutiny of the work of the early pioneers of psychometrics, their choice of subject matter and their general methodological approach – rather than the precise details of their results and statistical techniques – emerge as heritable characteristics. For, as is to be ex-

EDITOR'S NOTE: Paul Kline has produced a chapter that is unlike any other in this book, so much so that an earlier reviewer suggested we remove it from this section because it was out of place. At that point I realised that Kline had fulfilled his brief only too well; and that I owed students and critics an explanation. I asked him not to review British work on minorities and immigrants but to define "cultural influence" on testing in a different way, by pointing out what has been the development of one particular emphasis on how to conduct psychometric research that has spread far beyond the confines of Britain. His readable, almost inimitable style leaves a lasting impression. His implicit thesis, that there is more to cross-cultural testing than taking one's favourite tests into an exotic context, is one that readers will be familiar with. His explicitly demonstrated corollary, that if all one does is apply tests, one's native scientific culture passes on heritable characteristics to the data, is a valuable addition to the ethos of the volume. – S.I.

The author would like to thank Professor R. L. Reid for helpful comments on the first draft; Professor John Nisbet for some factual information; and S. H. Irvine for some additions and suggestions during the final stages of preparation of the manuscript.

187

pected in approximately 100 years of endeavour that has witnessed an enormous increase in scientific knowledge of all kinds, their work has been entirely superseded. However, their influence does live on, as we shall see, in terms of aims. Although, as will be argued later in this chapter, there is now an emphasis on linking psychometrics and cognitive psychology.

The work of Francis Galton

As can be seen from his life-span dates, Galton (1822–1911) was chronologically a Victorian scientist: and like many such, but unlike the majority today, he was able to devote himself to science, free from the necessities of having to earn a living.

Pearson has written a huge biography of Galton (Pearson, 1930) and more recently Forrest (1974) has examined his life. However, in a brief chapter of this sort such detail cannot be given. I shall begin by indicating the work which renders Galton so influential a figure in the development of a cultural context for British psychometrics.

The development of the anthropometric laboratory

This was set up in 1884 in London at the International Health Exhibition and moved to the Science Museum in South Kensington, where it remained until 1891. It was one of the first laboratories designed to measure human abilities objectively. Furthermore, as is clear from his 1865 paper "Hereditary Talent and Character," Galton believed that there was a general factor of human ability. In essence, therefore, the anthropometric laboratory at the Science Museum was offering tests with a rationale no different from that of the batteries designed by the most sophisticated modern psychometrists, the pursuit of an objective measure of g, or general intelligence.

As Hearnshaw (1964) and Jensen (1980) point out, Galton held that physical energy, sensory discrimination, and reaction time to both auditory and visual stimuli were indices of general intelligence. Hence many of the tests devised by Galton were of this kind. They provided measures of memory span, imagery, reaction time to sound, skin sensitivity, and weight discrimination. These tests were administered to thousands of subjects.

In spite of the massive scale of the enterprise, the results were disappointing. Generally the tests were not highly correlated with each other (as they should have been if they were all measures of g), nor did they relate well to real-life criteria of intelligence or ability. However, Jensen (1980) argues that these negative findings were due in part to the inefficiency of statistical analyses (many of them invented by Galton) at that time. Earlier I mentioned the search for a general factor of ability, intelligence, within a huge battery of tests. Begun and put into practice in Galton's anthropometric laboratory, the search for g formed the intellectual basis of Spearman's early work on the factoring of abilities (Spearman, 1904). Similarly, it underpins

R. B. Cattell's researches not only of the domain of ability but of the spheres of personality, motivation, and mood. Indeed, Cattell's work on objective personality tests (*T* data) can only be described as Galtonian, since Cattell argued that from any tests which revealed individual differences would emerge underlying explanatory factors. Some of Cattell's *T* tests are actually the same as those used by Galton (Cattell & Warburton, 1967).

Some may object that this is hardly surprising because Cattell is himself a veteran scholar, a descendant of Burt and Spearman. However, J. B. Carroll, sometime of Harvard, Educational Testing Service (ETS), and Chapel Hill, North Carolina (and thus by no means a London figure), is even now searching correlation matrices of ability variables for factors by utilising what are, in his view, the most powerful, simple structure, factor-analytic rotational procedures. His aim is to produce, inter alia, a definitive list of factors (Carroll, 1983). This was, as I have made clear, the essence of Galton's approach in his Kensington laboratory. Nor is Carroll's work an isolated idiosyncratic endeavour. Lists of replicated factors, of which the best known are those of French and his colleagues (Ekstrom, French, & Harman, 1976), are still being produced and the present writer employs precisely this approach in the field of personality (e.g., Kline & Barrett, 1983).

In brief, I contend that the exploratory use of factor analysis in the study of abilities and in psychometrics generally reflects (albeit indirectly) the influence of Galton's work in the anthropometric laboratory.

Hereditary Genius *(1869)*

In this book, Galton published the results of his enquiry into the abilities of the relatives of about 400 eminent men, an investigation aimed at determining whether intellectual ability was heritable or not. Hearnshaw (1964) has argued that this work reflects strongly the influence of Darwin: not only his evolutionary theory, but his cousinship to Galton himself. Not unnaturally this early work in biometrics will not stand careful scrutiny because the statistical designs and techniques had not been developed. Nevertheless, the approach – the comparison of eminence of the relatives of illustrious men with the distribution of eminence in the general population – is essentially biometric. Biometric analysis has been developed extensively in Britain through Pearson, Fisher, and, most recently, by the Birmingham school of Mather and Jinks (1971).

Biometric approaches are live issues in the modern study of abilities. Jensen's much publicised 1969 article in the *Harvard Educational Review*; the destruction of Burt's scientific reputation; the attempt by Kamin (1974) to demonstrate the minimal effects of genetic influences; and the biometrical analyses of Eaves (1976) and Fulker (1973) on a variety of psychometric variables, not to mention Cattell's recent work, *The Inheritance of Personality and Ability* (Cattell, 1982), which includes his own special contributions to biometric analysis – all bear witness to this. Modern biometric analysis uses the same assumptions as in this early work of Galton: Causes can be uncovered through multiple measurement. However, these have been clearly articulated and precise mathematical procedures have been developed. Significantly, two of the most important proponents of biometrics, Pearson and Fisher, both held the Galton Chair of Eugenics at University College London. Thus, although it may be true that biometrics would have developed without Galton, there can be little disputing his actual influence on British science.

As it happens, its traditional collegial links with biometrics have brought the psychometric study of abilities into disrepute – at least in the eyes of the general public. The profoundly egalitarian zeitgeist of today distrusts both racialism, which, albeit wrongly, is perceived to be explicit in the biometric approach to ability measurement, and also elitism, which is implicit in it. This, compounded with the fraudulence of Burt, one of the biometric movement's most famous figures, has, at least in Great Britain, eclipsed this particular enclave of psychometric culture.

Galton's statistical work

I do not intend to say much in this chapter about statistical analysis, other than factor analysis, which I see as developed by and for psychology. This is because statistics is a branch of mathematics which has proved useful in a variety of sciences. It is difficult to argue that Fisher in developing, for example, analysis of variance, had psychology particularly in mind. His work was developed for agricultural research and it was fortuitous that it turned out to be valuable in analysing many other kinds of data. Galton's work in statistics, on the other hand, deserves mention because it was developed to deal with psychological (in this case biometrical) problems and thus opened the eyes of the psychologists to the possibilities of correlational analysis in the solution of their research problems. In this sense, therefore, Galton's influence was profound.

Galton's permanent contributions, the development of percentiles and medians (e.g., 1874) and the first delineation of the correlation coefficient, are well known. Certainly Pearson (1920) attributes the invention of the correlation to Galton, and who should better know? The inventor of the correlation coefficient has much to answer for in respect of psychometrics (good or bad, according to one's taste); and Galton is again, as in biometrics and psychological testing, the originator.

There is a final point to be made about the work of Galton. The influence of the scientific context that he founded was directly spread into America by James McKeen Cattell (1860–1944) (who was not related to R. B. Cattell). James Cattell worked with Galton in London before returning to America. He later became head of the Psychology Department at Columbia University and one of the founders of the APA. Thus, Galton's influence in ability testing as a whole not only sprang from the preeminence of the London group whom he so inspired, but directly entered the United States in the person of Cattell.

The Contribution of Charles Spearman

I now turn to the second of the founding fathers of British psychometrics, Charles Spearman (1863–1945). Spearman was first an engineer and an officer in the army before entering psychology by studying with Wundt in Leipzig. Having completed his doctorate, he continued this work in Germany until his appointment to the University of London in 1907. There he founded what is usually known as the "London school" of psychology, being appointed Reader in Psychology at University College in 1907, and to a professorship in 1911, although he was not given the title of Professor of Psychology until 1928. This chair he held until 1931. On his retirement, Burt was appointed to the chair at University College, a decision that was to have a profound effect on the development of differential psychology in Britain.

Spearman's work on the structure and origins of human intelligence is so well known and documented that I intend to describe it only briefly. Its identification with a peculiarly British approach to psychometrics will be more extensively examined. In 1904, Spearman published in the *American Journal of Psychology* a paper that conceptually and methodologically has held psychometrics in thrall ever since: *General intelligence objectively determined and measured*. Its *conceptual* importance in the psychology of ability testing lies in its claims and evidence for a general factor of ability – *g*. Its *methodological* importance lies in the use of factor analysis to demonstrate the general factor.

In advancing Spearman's methodological claims, several points of clarification must be made. Any dispute as to the origins of factor analysis is a matter for historians of science. Certainly Pearson had outlined the principal axes method in 1901. However, Spearman's heuristic contribution was to develop a factor analytic *procedure* – to improve upon simple correlational analysis, and to demonstrate its power in the solution of psychological problems. From 1904 for those with the wit to see it, a multivariate statistical method of investigating human abilities was available. The great conceptual contribution was the elaboration of the notion of *g*, general ability. Spearman (1923) may have been wrong in his concept of *g* as a *single* general factor and certainly he was opposed by two of the major workers in the field in Great Britain, Burt (1940) and Thomson in Edinburgh (1951). Later work by Cattell (1982) and Carroll (1983) or indeed Sternberg (1977), who does not much favour psychometric tests and concepts, is concerned with the elaboration of precisely this concept of general ability. Thus, as is the case with the technique of factor analysis, so with the concept of *g* factorially defined, Spearman's original contribution is universally acknowledged. To miss the point entirely is to argue that his analyses were too simple, that his approach to the nature of *g* was primitive, or that it is clearly wrong in the light of modern cognitive psychology. A major part of the method and content of the psychometrics of ability springs from this 1904 paper.

In brief, then, the founder of the London school, by his use of factor analysis and his insistence on studying the cognitive nature of the factors, not leaving them as mere statistical artifacts, created psychometrics, at a stroke. However, his influence was greater than through his writings alone. As many a famous teacher, he produced disciples, among them the other members of the London school: Burt, Eysenck, Cattell, and Vernon. Before examining their individual contributions to the scientific approach most commonly associated with British ability theory, we can turn to an early example of the spread of the British "cultural influence" in psychometrics itself, originating in Spearman's laboratory. In the period between the world wars, the Commonwealth and the old Empire sent their most distinguished and talented scholars to Britain to be educated. The University of London was frequently their host, and Spearman, Burt, and Vernon had many, especially Indian, research students and assistants. More than twenty such theses were supervised by Burt, according to the list in Hearnshaw (1979).

Although it is not possible here to trace the careers of all these students, it is generally true to say that a British Ph.D. in psychology, until the mid-1960s at least, would ensure a good academic position for its holder and, by implication, produce a transfer of technology, if not of theory. One illustration will make the point, and show how the influence of the London school travelled far beyond our shores, from the Thames to the Ganges.

Professor M. V. Gopalaswamy was born in Madras on the last day of 1896. He went first to Madras University and then on to London, where he worked with Spearman as a research assistant. He graduated with a Ph.D. in 1923 and returned to India, aged 27, to become, in 1924, the first professor of psychology in the University of Mysore. Under the influence of his mentor, Spearman, he immediately built an experimental psychological laboratory, in order, according to Rao (1974), to free psychology from philosophy. Now this is a remarkable achievement, because elsewhere in India, what psychology there was, was merely a part of philosophy. In England in 1924, it must be remembered, there were then only two experimental psychology laboratories. From that time the Department of Psychology in Mysore flourished; and Spearman's influence is easy to discern in the large numbers of psychometric tests that have been constructed there for educational and clinical use. Because for many years Mysore was one of the few departments of experimental psychology in India, the influence of British ability theory on Indian psychology has been considerable. Mysore's laboratory is no special case, however, as Sinha (1983) shows in a comprehensive and critical review of human assessment in India. In this he takes Indian psychologists to task for their wholesale adoption of culture-alien tests and methods from British and American sources. Only now, he argues, are they freeing themselves from a "colonial" legacy of practice and theory. Be that as it may, we now turn to the second generation of British psychologists who inherited scientific characteristics from their forebears, just as the students from the Commonwealth themselves did.

The Contribution of Cyril Burt

Sir Cyril Burt (1883–1971) controlled the direction and emphasis of psychometrics in Britain almost unchallenged from 1935 until 1960, because of his editorial grip on two key journals, the *British Journal of Educational Psychology* and the *British Journal of Mathematical and Statistical Psychology*. Nothing was published that he did not approve of, or that he had not previously rewritten, or had written himself under his own or an assumed name. That fact is often forgotten in the debate over the importance of his fraudulent twin data in apportioning indices of heritability to IQ performance. Burt's deceptions harmed all of social science, but particularly affected work in the biometric pathway to construct definition begun by Galton. Hearnshaw's (1979) revealing biography has made evaluation of Burt's work very difficult. His editorial energies would themselves have established Burt's influence: but it extended beyond the journals. What precisely did it portend, and what are its consequences?

I do not intend to set out here Burt's background and education. All that has been fully and expertly documented by Hearnshaw in his biography. Instead, I shall single out those aspects of Burt's education which affected him as a psychometrician, and, by implication, ability theory in Britain during his undisputed reign. There can be no doubt that the major influences on Burt's psychometrics and his whole approach to the investigation of intelligence were Galton and Spearman. Burt, indeed, can be seen as a modern proponent of their ideas. Furthermore, as might be expected, it appears that their ideas were taken over early in Burt's career.

Burt first met Sir Francis Galton socially as a child. Burt's father was a country physician whose practice included the Galton family. Thus the young Burt met Galton as he accompanied his father on his rounds, and was heavily impressed. Burt claimed that his aim while in the chair at University College had been to develop that branch of psychology which Galton had originated. As we have seen, this was the integration of psychometrics and biometrics. Schooldays over, Burt went up to Oxford, to read classics, in 1902. There he worked with McDougall, the Wilde Reader in Mental Philosophy, on psychological topics. In his final year, 1905, he was sent to London to work in anthropometrics, as it was then called. In this project he met Galton again, and also Karl Pearson, the great statistician, holder of the Galton Chair of Eugenics at University College London. Finally he met Spearman, who had just published his paper on factor analysis. It seems that in this year there came together all the critical influences on Burt's work on psychometrics: biometrics, cognition, and mathematics. Although he was not a trained mathematician, Burt's mathematical powers were not inconsiderable, as anyone familiar with his comments (albeit under various pseudonyms) in the *British Journal of Mathematical and Statistical Psychology* would be forced to admit. *The Factors of the Mind* (Burt, 1940) bears eloquent witness to his eventual mastery. His emphasis on statistical analysis of data stems from his contact with these University College psychologists. Moreover, Burt's huge output of publications shows his considerable *intellectual* debt to Galton and Spearman. Thus his first paper in 1909, "Experimental tests of general intelligence," was followed by several similar, and these represent Spearman's influence. In 1912, Galton's influence can be seen with a paper in *Eugenics Review* on the inheritance of mental characteristics. From his earliest writings on the causes and effects of human mental performance, Burt was dedicated to a fundamentalist approach inherited from the role models of his youth.

Testing and the inheritance of mental characteristics

The influence of Burt on psychometrics and the measurement of ability can be summarised thus: He was one of the first to appreciate the significance and power of factor analysis in elucidating the structure of abilities. Through his own writing and researches he demonstrated how factor analysis could be applied to problems and he explicated and developed factor-analytic methods. Burt also standardised and developed a large number of ability tests, and helped to introduce individual intelligence testing into Great Britain. His book *Mental and Scholastic Tests* (Burt, 1921), which ran into a fourth edition in 1962, exemplifies his practical and technical skill in this respect. Perhaps above all he trained a large number of researchers who put these ideas into practice. Their contribution to psychometrics must be discussed. However, before this I shall briefly mention the aspect of Burt that is now best remembered – his fraudulent work, especially on the heritability of intelligence.

There can be no satisfactory explanation for Burt's fraudulent twin studies, and his campaign to claim priority over Spearman in the origination of factor analysis. His attempts at long-term deception have eclipsed from memory Burt's real achievements, his intellectual brilliance and his prodigious learning. In the short course, the discovery of fraud has caused nonspecialists in the study of human abilities (Gillie, 1976) to argue that there is now no scientific basis for the conclusion that intelligence is largely heritable. Kamin (1974), indeed, has argued that there is no evidence that a rational person could accept in favour of the genetic determination of intelligence. In the light of all the research that is not fraudulent (Eysenck, 1979), this is simply mistaken. In spite of the weight of such evidence, that the leading figure in British psychometrics has turned out to be a fraud has not endeared the psychometric subculture to the scientific community as a whole. To sum up, perhaps all Burt's empirical work should be treated with caution. Even so, the methodological influence on ability testing exerted by Burt is still considerable, especially as it survived in the allocation of children to types of secondary school in Britain from 1944 onwards. In fact, the next section deals with Burt's influences as a psychologist concerned with education policy and practice.

Burt as an educational psychologist

As Hearnshaw points out in his concise history of British psychology (1964), before World War II there was remarkably little psychological research carried out in British departments. Burt's University College department, where he followed Spearman to the Chair of Psychology in 1932, was an exception. Research poured out of it; and much of Burt's influence on psychometrics arose not so much from his own work at this period, but through his research students, and his editorial control of important journals.

Before examining what the influence of his students was and its results, another signal fact is important. Burt had always carried out research before his appointment to Spearman's chair, but it had been in the context of *education*: first as a practical educational psychologist employed by the London County Council, and later as a professor at the London Day Training College. This emphasis on education influenced British school selection practices; and it also resulted in much of the subsequent efforts of Burt's students being confined to the necessary but applied tasks of standardising tests, or of developing practical selection procedures. These pursuits are worthy, technically demanding, but unlikely to advance our understanding of human abilities in the context of routine test administration to large groups of subjects. Some of Burt's own students, of course, became influential psychometrists in their own right and these are discussed in the next section. Nevertheless, reading the long list of Burt's research students is disappointing. Few of them have contributed much to psychometrics.

Such, then, in my view, are the fruits of Burt's educational involvement: a failure to develop a British psychometric research school, despite the standing of the London group. Of course, there are other reasons for this failure: the emphasis in other departments, especially Cambridge under Bartlett, on experimental studies; the growing postwar egalitarian social ethos; and lack of research funds. Nevertheless, there were sufficient good researchers trained by Burt to have made a more general imprint on psychometrics: Raymond Cattell, Fred Schonell (perhaps not a psychometrist), F. W. Warburton, H. J. Eysenck, J. B. Parry, E. Anstey, A. Clarke, and Max Hamilton, to mention those graduating before 1951. Many of these have made important contributions, and in two cases have truly influenced the development of the field. But no British school of psychometry can now be said to exist.

The influence of Burt's students

Although no London school of psychometrics ever developed from the work of Burt, the influence of his best students has been pervasive, as will now be discussed. Because these are current figures, it is necessary for the purposes of this chapter to describe them only briefly, for their work will be part of the working knowledge of anybody concerned with psychometrics or the testing of ability. With no disrespect to any of Burt's students, two names stand out for prodigious energy, output, and ideas over long careers: Raymond B. Cattell and Hans J. Eysenck.

The world-view of Raymond Cattell

Cattell, after working briefly in England as head of the Leicestershire educational psychological service, went to America just before the war and established himself at the University of Illinois. From that base came a stream of publications, more than 500 in all branches of psychometrics – personality theory, ability theory, tests of all sorts, factor analysis, and biometric analysis. Huge and technically demanding books emerged regularly describing his work, giving it some coherence. In recent years his whole theory, measurement based, has been described: *Personality and Learning Theory* (Cattell, 1980). Cattell's views on factor analysis have been summarised in his book on that topic (Cattell, 1978), as has his extensive work on biometrics in *The Inheritance of Personality and Ability* (Cattell, 1982). These books, each one alone more than most psychologists produce in a lifetime, have been written by Cattell after retirement, in his seventies. To encapsulate so huge and complex a contribution to psychometrics and the testing of ability is no simple matter. After working with Cattell and collaborating on a book, *The Scientific Study of Personality and Motivation* (Cattell & Kline, 1977), I feel that I am in a position to state what Cattell, at least, thinks his most important work to be:

The emphasis on quantification and multivariate analysis, especially factor analysis, in the elucidation of the structure of ability and personality. This is in direct descent from Spearman and Burt. Cattell's work on factor analysis has been aimed not at statistics per se but at producing replicable clear solutions.

The biometric work aimed at answering questions concerning the determination and development of the traits isolated by factor analysis. This is in direct line from Galton.

The concentration on producing good tests to measure efficiently the factors isolated. This again is in the Galtonian tradition. Cattell's *Culture Fair Tests* of intelligence and his *Comprehensive Ability Battery* aimed at assessing the main ability factors are widely used tests. His objective (*T*) personality tests are indeed, in some cases, adaptations of Galton's tests (Cattell & Warburton, 1967).

The attempts to build a coherent theory of personality and ability. These works are again directly in the tradition of Spearman and Burt, who were both concerned with the nature of the factors they had isolated.

Thus these four main contributions, each fully described in the recent publications cited above, reveal that one of the main contributors to the study of abilities is carrying out the research ideas of Galton and Spearman in a modern and computationally sophisticated form.

The substantive contribution of Cattell to psychometrics, for example, his tests of ability, personality, motivation, and mood, is more open to debate concerning its value. However, his work on abilities, the triadic theory, the splitting of *g* into crystallised and fluid ability, and his delineation of the main factors (Cattell, 1971) as well as his work on the biometrics of intelligence, despite the statistical problems with the Multiple Abstract Variance Analysis (MAVA) method, may well stand the test of time.

The biological emphasis of Hans Eysenck

Eysenck's career at the Institute of Psychiatry began in the 1940s and has only just ended (1983), although he still works there, Professor Emeritus. Eysenck's work, described in nearly 1,000 publications (so rapid is his writing that no published number can perhaps ever be accurate), is again in the anthropometric London tradition of Galton, Spearman, and Burt. His work has gone far beyond the confines of factor analysis and psychometrics, although these have been used to discover and measure some of the concepts basic to his theorising – notably, of course, neuroticism, extraversion, and psychoticism. However, this work and his incorporation of learning theory and psychophysiology into a general theory of personality set out in *The Biological Basis of Personality* (Eysenck, 1967) and its application in the fields of behaviour therapy, sexuality, smoking, and political beliefs, even astrology, we must omit in this chapter as irrelevant. Nevertheless, Eysenck is indeed a true product of the London school of biometric and biosocial measurement.

Eysenck's contribution to the testing of ability can be summarised under three heads:

His insistence on the biometric analysis of intelligence scores. Eysenck (1979), in a book incidentally dedicated to Galton, shows how biometric analyses, elaborated by Mather and Jinks (1971), can be used and reveal high genetic determination for IQ in the West. Thus, in the face of current egalitarian ideas, Eysenck resolutely defends what he regards as the best supported position. Certainly the biometric analyses which he favours are difficult to counter.

His recent work (reported in Chapter 3) on EEG measures of intelligence. Eysenck supports the work of Elaine and Alan Hendrickson (1980). They used a "string" measure of EEG (evoked potential in response to a tone), essentially measuring variability, and found high correlations between these measures and IQ scores. Eysenck has argued that here is, in fact, a "pure" measure of intelligence, unconfounded by social class or educational experience, although this is a difficult assertion to maintain. These EEG measures reflect the information-processing efficiency of the brain. They measure, according to Eysenck, Intelligence A (Vernon, 1961) or Burt's innate ability, perhaps Cattell's fluid ability (Cattell, 1971). What is interesting is that correlations between these measures and the subtests of the *WAIS* and the *WAIS* subtest *g* loadings are almost unity. In other words, the higher a test loads on *g*, the higher it correlates with the EEG measure. If this work can be properly replicated and shown not to be too artifactual, then it is of theoretical importance and, of course, of practical significance, especially in the elucidation of racial, social class, and cultural differences. Eysenck's attempt to get at the underlying determinants of test factors is in the tradition of the London school, both Spearman (1923) with his notion of mental energy, and Burt (1940).

Speed, accuracy, and persistence. The third aspect of Eysenck's contribution to the measurement of ability is one that has really become the centrepiece of modern psychometrics: investigating underlying cognitive processes in order to understand the nature of factors. Eysenck (1953, 1973) was an early pioneer in this field, claiming that intelligence test scores contained three components: *speed, accuracy*, and *persistence*, accuracy being defined as error checking. The most fundamental aspect, in Eysenck's view (e.g., 1979), is cognitive speed, which fits well with his interest in the evoked potential. White (1973), a colleague of Eysenck, has developed a neat statistical model to relate these components, which can be separately measured, to IQ scores. This is potentially important work, which Eysenck has somewhat neglected for his more central interests. As was made clear in our discussion of Spearman and Burt, such investigation of the nature of the factors is indeed in the London tradition.

With around 1,500 publications between them, Eysenck and Cattell, both students of Burt, have clearly played a dominant part in psychometrics and in the study of ability. Of the other students of Burt whom I mentioned, all distinguished, I shall simply list their contributions: Schonell, expert in backward children and diagnostic and attainment tests; Parry, whose work in the armed forces did so much for officer selection; Anstey, who developed selection methods in the Civil Service; Clarke, who, like Schonell, has great expertise with backward children; Hamilton, who pioneered the use of factor analysis in depression and the psychiatric field; and Warburton, who did much to introduce Cattell's work on personality to Britain and was responsible for the beginnings of the British Intelligence Scale. All these, alas, are retired or dead (with the exception of Clarke), so that British psychometrics is in other hands. Before I examine psychometry in Britain today, for the London school is now dissipated, it is necessary to consider another locale for British psychometric skill – Edinburgh.

The work of Godfrey Thomson

Godfrey Thomson (1891–1955) was a contemporary of Burt and one of the great early experts on factor analysis, although he worked exclusively in the education of teachers as a professor of education at Newcastle and from

1925 as a professor at Moray House in Edinburgh. In the *Factorial Analysis of Human Ability* (1951), there is a remarkable exposition not only of factor analysis (from which, indeed the present writer first gained whatever glimmerings he has in this matter) but also of the nature of ability and the meaning of factors. He was opposed to what he regarded as Spearman's (1923) simplistic interpretation of *g*, regarding the common factor as resulting from the sampling of neural elements. However, his huge knowledge of factor analysis resulted in his training, through the B.Ed. course at Edinburgh, large numbers of future leaders in educational research who were competent in factor analysis and testing. Among these were the Nisbets at Glasgow and Aberdeen, Oliver at Manchester, Eaglesham at Durham. From Thomson's lectures in Edinburgh emerged educational psychologists and administrators who had a sound knowledge of ability testing and its theoretical background.

Despite his mathematical and theoretical power, Godfrey Thomson was nothing if not practical. One of his great feats was the development of the *Northumberland* and *Moray House Intelligence and Attainment* tests – carefully standardised tests of high reliability and validity which allocated many children to different types of secondary school as fairly as psychometrics could devise – and this is with far greater justice than selection methods that dispense with tests. All this was a supreme example of applied psychometrics, as, indeed, was the *Scottish Mental Abilities Survey*, a monument of measurement in an age without computers.

Nevertheless, despite his learning, his energy, and the excellence of his teaching, few of his students really made an impact on psychometrics. Hence, it has to be said that Thomson, like Burt, failed to establish a school of psychometrics. I think probably this was largely because he was in a college or department of education. Not unnaturally, his students wanted to apply their skills, rather than develop them, for their own sake. This was indubitably good for education. It was sad for the survival of ability theory as an important focus for teaching in British psychology.

Although Thomson did not leave behind a large band of influential psychometrists, as was the case with Burt, a number of overseas students, especially from the Indian subcontinent, were trained in his department. Some of these did practise psychometry, applied rather than theoretical, on their return. In this way, it could be argued, cross-cultural testing got off to a sound start. A good example of this is *Performance Tests of Intelligence*, the work of Bhatia (1955), who was director of the Bureau of Psychology in Allahabad. Although one must be careful of accepting avowed aims at their face value, this book contains an interesting preface by Godfrey Thomson, who argues that the object of the testing movement is that "the rising generation should be well educated, each in the way best fitted to his or her talents." So much for the claim that psychometrics is an elitist's tool. Furthermore, examination of Bhatia's results shows that (pp. 98–99) these tests were highly successful in offering opportunities to all social groups, literate and illiterate. The mean IQ differences between them were small and generally not significant. Almost all other tests, especially of attainment, would have shown very large differences in favour of the better-off groups.

The work of P. E. Vernon

Before we move on to the small remnant of current British psychometrists, one great figure, until recently working in Alberta, must be discussed. This is the late P. E. Vernon, a masterly expositor of the most complex issues, whose balanced and careful approach to vast bodies of evidence and contradictory data is a tribute to his dispassionate scholarship. Much of Vernon's writing on ability and intelligence (Vernon, 1950, 1961, 1979) is definitive. A major contribution in the practical field was his work on personnel selection; and his book with Parry – *Personnel Selection in the British Forces* (Vernon & Parry, 1949) – is a fine example of applied psychometrics. His cross-cultural work on ability testing, although on a small scale, is meticulous and careful (Vernon, 1969). I do not intend to say more about Vernon's work. It is well known and readers can observe its quality in Chapters 13 and 14. It is a major part of current psychometrics; and there must be few students of psychology, at any level, who are not required to read his books.

Vernon was trained at Cambridge and Harvard, so his psychometrics was learned relatively free from the personal influences I have outlined before. His academic career began in Glasgow (1938–1947). From there he took the Chair in Educational Psychology at the Institute of Education in London, which he left in 1968 to take a similar position in Calgary in Canada. His work, like Burt's and Thomson's, had more impact on education than on mainstream psychology.

Before turning to evaluation of modern psychometrics in Britain, one further illustration of the influence of psychologists at the University of London, and particularly Vernon in the Institute of Education, on work in cross-cultural assessment is available. Among many of Vernon's postwar students were C. A. Rogers, a New Zealander, and the late Russ MacArthur, from Edmonton, Alberta. Both of them completed original work in cross-cultural measurement. A landmark study of intelligence (*Measuring Intelligence in New Zealand*) was conducted in 1956 by Rogers, who shortly thereafter was appointed to a senior post in the University College of Rhodesia and Nyasaland. MacArthur produced with Elley an important study of "culture-reduced" tests (MacArthur & Elley, 1963) and went on to do extensive factor-analytic work in Inuit and African abilities. For his part, Rogers extended his range with a comprehensive study of race attitudes among Rhodesian whites, working with the American anthropologist Charles Frantz (Rogers & Frantz, 1962). Both Rogers and MacArthur worked with S. H. Irvine in Zambia and Zimbabwe from 1961 to 1964. Rogers was Irvine's local Ph.D. supervisor, and MacArthur, while on leave from Alberta, and largely at Rogers's request, worked with Irvine on the study of abilities in Zambia that parallelled Irvine's own work, begun a year previously in Zimbabwe. To complete the circle, by chance, Irvine, when asked by Alec Rodger, his London Ph.D. supervisor at Birkbeck College, who might be best qualified to examine his thesis, is said to have suggested either Burt or Vernon. Rodger thought Vernon more appropriate – and this may have been a very wise judgment.

The vignette shows, of course, that influence is far wider than personal contact; and this is particularly true of Vernon, who, in the twenty years postwar in Britain, helped to foster cross-cultural ability testing through his own successful Commonwealth students and through the next generation that they, in turn, trained. Not only were his books on general psychometrics influential because of their clarity, authority, and balanced judgment, but their ethos also was inherited by his own students, as the work of Rogers and MacArthur will demonstrate to anyone who cares to read it. Finally, Ord (1972) usefully reviews research on educational and occupational selection (during Vernon's tenure at the institute) in developing countries. He lists more than 450 references, and the trail more often than not comes back to London and Edinburgh. A meta-analysis might be misleading, because not all are of the same quality. Nevertheless, the fair-minded and dispassionate summing-up of empirical evidence that is associated with Vernon and Thomson features in a large number of them. Often, too, that evidence is correlational and factor-analytic, as Irvine's (1979) study shows.

Modern psychometrics in Great Britain

This is an invidious task and one that should ensure evil reviews from those left out. Nevertheless, first it must be said that in my view there are no psychometrists in Great Britain at present of the quality of Burt or Cattell, let alone Galton or Spearman. However, psychometrics is not entirely dead.

I shall attempt to be objective in my selection. An analysis of the major figures whom I have discussed hitherto reveals several common points.

Most have huge numbers of publications. These may include many monographs (*not* edited volumes), and 100 publications is a relatively small achievement in this field. Many of them were awarded the D.Sc. for their work, a degree that is relatively rare in psychology. Spearman, Burt, Thomson, Cattell, Eysenck, and Vernon, all fit this category. Spearman was a Fellow of the Royal Society and Burt, a Fellow of the British Academy. Today, only one British psychometrist meets even two of the criteria above. So criteria have to be lowered. Even in so doing, the haul is meagre. Nevertheless, some achievements may be listed.

The British Intelligence Scale

Perhaps the most tangible achievement, or attempt to continue the great empirical traditions of Spearman and Thomson, was a new test of intelligence and abilities sponsored by the British Psychological Society under the direction of Frank Warburton at Manchester in the early 1960s. It was based on the then current views of Guilford and Piaget and aimed to provide a series of scales measuring separate abilities, more than just an IQ score. On Warburton's untimely death the project was completed by Elliott (1983). It is certainly a large-scale research with large standardisation samples (more than 3,400 children) with a wide variety of scales. It is also technically adventurous in that Rasch scaling (Rasch, 1961) was used despite the problems of constructing adequate tests for fitting the item response model. Considerable though the research effort was, the provision of a test, albeit factored and Rasch scaled, is hardly innovative psychometrics. However, in the field of abilities it is the best there is in Great Britain. It is an example of large-scale applied research, as is fitting for a department of education.

More recently, Brand in Edinburgh (Brand, 1980) has concentrated upon using inspection time as a culture-free test of intelligence. However, this measure was developed not by Brand but by Nettlebeck and Lally (1976). Further, some of Brand's samples were small and of a constitution likely to produce overestimates of the size of correlation between inspection time and intelligence. Recently Nettlebeck (1982) demonstrated that this correlation of inspection time and *Raven's Progressive Matrices* in an undergraduate sample was only about .4.

Irvine, whose published work is listed fully in Chapter 1, has made a psychometric contribution to the cross-cultural study of ability. His careful analytic work in Zambia and Zimbabwe showed that western tests could be adapted to different samples, and that western factors such as g and $v.ed$ do have predictive abilities in the new culture. More importantly perhaps, there were other factors specific to that culture. The extensive fieldwork in the early 1960s produced a model of large-scale psychometric and educational research in developing countries. Irvine's later work with Berry is much more theoretical.

Irvine's African work inherited the postwar British influence. Trained at Aberdeen by Nisbet, who studied in Edinburgh with Thomson, Irvine registered for a doctorate with Alec Rodger at Birkbeck College; but his local supervisor in Harare was Cyril Rogers, whom Vernon himself supervised in the early fifties. Vernon and Thomson remain influential in Irvine's more recent work on the theory of abilities. Their flexible, group factor approach to intelligence has been extended to cultural contexts other than Britain.

I shall mention myself as being the sole Professor of Psychometrics in the country and as having also satisfied two of the criteria distinguishing the earlier figures whom we discussed. My contribution to the study of ability has not been considerable (my work has involved personality), although I am now researching into flexible thinking. However, I do claim to be among the last ossified remnants of the London and Edinburgh schools. Like Irvine, I was trained in Aberdeen, by Nisbet, but also by Warburton (a student of Burt) in Manchester. I have also worked with Cattell (Cattell & Kline, 1977).

Thus I have connections via Warburton and Nisbet with Thomson and Burt. In the University of Exeter, I have trained a number of psychometrists. I hope that the British psychometric tradition will continue with them.

Other aspects of British influence

In a chapter of this length, only an outline of one of all the many influences on an academic tradition can be delineated. I have tried to show that certain key British psychometrists by their writing and through their research students had a "cultural" impact on the testing of abilities. Now I am aware that by merely pointing out that certain psychologists wrote certain books and trained certain other psychologists, I have not demonstrated their impact; to do this it is necessary also to show that other contemporary work was less advanced or that there was no comparable research. However, I shall not carry out this second task, which would be too long. Rather, I shall simply assert that they were major figures and that their writings did, in fact, have a considerable influence on future development in ability testing. This is not to deny the influence of Thurstone or Guilford and, of course, Binet in the early years. Cattell (e.g., 1978) was clearly influenced by Thurstone while Eysenck, at least in the area of personality, owes much to Guilford (Eysenck, 1947). Naturally, these American workers had a considerable influence in their home country. Thus I am not claiming that British psychometrists were the only influences on ability testing. Far from it: merely that they were influential in areas that define a British scientific subcultural context for ability theory.

Although I have been keen to trace the personal influence of the great psychometricians, I am not suggesting that their influence is wielded only through such personal contact. After all, they were prolific writers. Nevertheless, it is clear that meeting great figures does have an effect, especially if they happen to be charismatic. Thomson made a lasting impression upon his pupils, as did Burt. To have worked with such men does far more for inculcating their views and ideas than simply to have read them. That is why the influence of their students, even when they were not themselves outstanding, is perhaps very great indeed. Later generations are influenced by them, as the next section dramatically, and perhaps ironically, reveals.

Quote *The Raven* evermore?

To mention *Raven's Progressive Matrices* in a section on contemporary British influence on psychometrics might be judged by the younger generation of readers to be at best an anachronism, or at worst the sign of some psychometric dementia. But it is neither. One of the most enduring of the operational definitions of intelligence coming from the London school was a test constructed by a student who worked with Penrose, and whose master's thesis was examined by Burt (or so Burt claimed) in the early 1930s.

Burt thereafter seemed to take a proprietary interest in the test, and later increasingly convinced himself that he had made a major contribution to its formation. Although that certainly was not so, Penrose and Raven hit upon the idea that the complexity of the test could be increased by beginning with a simple figure and then adding elements. As each element was added, so it had to be discovered by the subject. Hence, the "ranks of the matrices" were increased by the addition of perceptual, arithmetical, and seriation principles or rules, and the items became more difficult.

The test grew in influence; and in this volume it is second only to the *Wechsler* in citation. Its legendary reputation as a test-of-as-pure-*g*-as-one-might-hope-to-get is vigorously opposed by all except those who make the claim; and the claimants tend to be fundamentalists in the Galton mould. Others – and there are more than 2,000 studies on the test alone, not counting other work where the test is mentioned but not subjected to special scrutiny – have used it as a cross-cultural tool, not without careful adaptation and even restandardisation. History might well accord it pride of place in attempts to construct items from a priori principles or rules of item generation – in this case an analogy from matrix algebra – as we move forward to item-generative methods within computers.

Operationally, then, the London school lives on in *Raven's Progressive Matrices*, a figural (but by no means nonverbal if one observes subjects at work on it) test of reasoning defined as rule discovery. The items constructed by Penrose and Raven operationally define the permanent scientific test culture of British influence. The ability tests of Burt and Cattell have had no similar degree of acceptability.

Conclusions

Clearly, a British subculture in psychometrics once existed, but its influence is now merely operational. What theoretical force still exists stems from the "old guard," the Galton–Spearman–Burt tradition upheld by Eysenck, Cattell, and their students. The new fields of cognitive processing underlying abilities and item scaling are not well represented in Great Britain, although much of the experimental work behind it is credited to British cognitive psychologists such as Broadbent and Baddeley.

I think the causes of this are relatively clear. The Cambridge Chair in Psychology is prestigious and influential. Its holder, Bartlett, placed many of his students into new chairs as they were created after 1945; and as Hearnshaw (1964), a great admirer of Bartlett, points out, he was opposed to statistics and psychometrics. Little correlational analysis was taught at Cambridge: and condemnation through ignorance is easy. Further, psychometrics that involves the time of a large number of human beings is labour intensive and therefore expensive. On the other hand, small-scale experimental research involving a handful of naive students is not. Thus, Cattell turned down the chair at University College London because they could not provide him with sufficient facilities for research.

I do not think that the academic climate is likely to change in the near future. The delinquencies of Burt and the egalitarian zeitgeist do not bode well for ability testing. Indeed, it will be an achievement if it continues at all in modern psychology courses. The hope is that the combination of cognitive psychology and psychometrics as seen in the work of such diverse figures as Carroll, Jensen, and Sternberg can be developed and extended. This will sit well in the arms of mainstream British cognitive psychology: and as the ghost of Bartlett fades, so British psychometrics may rise again in a variety of cultural contexts.

References

Bhatia, C. M. (1955). *Performance tests of intelligence.* Bombay: Oxford University Press.

Brand, C. (1980). General intelligence and mental speed: Their relationship and development. In M. Friedman, J. P. Das, & N. O'Connor (Eds.), *Intelligence and learning.* New York: Plenum.

Burt, C. S. (1909). Experimental tests of general intelligence. *British Journal of Psychology, 3,* 94–177.

Burt, C. S. (1912). The inheritance of mental characteristics. *Eugenics Review, 4,* 168–200.

Burt, C. S. (1917). *The distribution and relations of educational abilities.* London: King & Son.

Burt, C. S. (1921). *Mental and scholastic tests.* London: King & Son.

Burt, C. S. (1940). *The factors of the mind.* London: University of London Press.

Carroll, J. B. (1982) *The measurement of intelligence.* In R. J. Sternberg (Ed.), *Handbook of human intelligence* (pp. 29–122). Cambridge University Press.

Carroll, J. B. (1983). Studying individual differences in cognitive abilities: Implications for cross-cultural studies. In S. H. Irvine & J. W. Berry, (Eds.), *Human assessment and cultural factors* (pp. 213–235). New York: Plenum.

Cattell, R. B. (1971). *Abilities: Their structure, growth and action.* Boston: Houghton Mifflin.

Cattell, R. B. (1978). *The scientific use of factor analysis.* New York: Plenum.

Cattell, R. B. (1980). *Personality and learning theory.* New York: Springer-Verlag.

Cattell, R. B. (1982). *The inheritance of personality and ability.* New York: Academic Press.

Cattell, R. B., & Kline, P. (1977). *The scientific analysis of personality and motivation.* New York: Academic Press.

Cattell, R. B., & Warburton, F. W. (1967). *Objective personality and motivation tests.* Champaign: University of Illinois Press.

Eaves, L. J. (1976). The effect of cultural transmission on continuous variation. *Heredity, 37,* 41–57.

Ekstrom, R. B., French, J. W., & Harman, H. H. (1976). *Manual for kit of factor-referenced cognitive tests.* Princeton, NJ: Educational Testing Service.

Elliot, C., Murray, D. J., & Pearson, L. S. (1983). *The British Ability Scales* (Manuals 1–4). Windsor, U.K.: National Foundation for Educational Research.

Eysenck, H. J. (1947). *Dimensions of personality.* London: Routledge & Kegan Paul.

Eysenck, H. J. (1953). *Uses and abuses of psychology.* Harmondsworth: Penguin.

Eysenck, H. J. (1967). *The biological basis of personality.* Springfield, IL: C. C. Thomas.

Eysenck, H. J. (Ed). (1973). *The measurement of intelligence.* Lancaster, U.K.: Medical and Technical Publishers.

Eysenck, H. J. (1979). *The structure and measurement of intelligence.* New York: Springer-Verlag.

Forrest, D. W. (1974). *Francis Galton: The life and work of a Victorian genius.* London: Elek.

Fulker, G. W. (1973). A biometrical genetic approach to intelligence and schizophrenia. *Social Biology, 20,* 266–275.

Galton, F. (1865). Hereditary talent and character. *Macmillan's Magazine.*

Galton, F. (1869). *Hereditary genius: An enquiry into its laws and consequences.* London: Macmillan.

Galton, F. (1874). A proposed statistical scale. *Nature, 9,* 342.

Garnett, J. C. M. (1919). On certain independent factors in mental measurement. *Proceedings of the Royal Society* (A), *96,* 102–105.

Gillie, O. (1976, October 24). Crucial data was faked by eminent psychologist. London. *Sunday Times.*

Hearnshaw, L. S. (1964). *A short history of British psychology: 1840–1940.* London: Methuen.

Hearnshaw, L. S. (1979). *Cyril Burt psychologist.* London: Hodder & Stoughton.

Hendrickson, D. E., & Hendrickson, A. E. (1980). The biological basis of individual differences in intelligence. *Personality and Individual Differences, 1,* 3–33.

Horn, J. L. (1976). Human abilities. *Annual Review of Psychology, 27,* 437–485.

Hunt, E. (1978). Mechanics of verbal ability. *Psychological Review, 85,* 109–130.

Irvine, S. H. (1969). Contributions of ability and attainment testing in Africa to a general theory of intellect. *Journal of Biosocial Science, 1,* 91–102.

Irvine, S. H. (1979). The place of factor analysis in cross-cultural methodology and its contribution to cognitive theory. In L. Eckensberger, W. Lonner, & Y. Poortinga (Eds.), *Cross-cultural contributions to psychology.* Lisse: Swets & Zeitlinger.

Irvine, S. H., & Berry, J. W. (1983). *Human assessment and cultural factors.* New York: Plenum.

Jenks, C. (1973). *Inequality: A reassessment of the effects of family and schooling in America.* London: Allen Lane.

Jensen, A. R. (1969). How much can we boost IQ and scholastic achievement? *Harvard Educational Review, 39,* 1–123.

Jensen, A. R. (1980). *Bias in mental testing.* London: Methuen.

Kamin, L. J. (1974). *The science and politics of IQ.* Harmondsworth: Penguin.

Kline, P. (1983). Cognitive processes and flexible thinking: A research proposal. *Personality Study and Group Behaviour, 3,* 21–34.

Kline, P., & Barrett, P. (1983). The factors in Personality Questionnaires among normal subjects. *Advances in Behaviour Research and Therapy, 5,* 141–202.

MacArthur, R. S., & Elley, W. B. (1963). The reduction of socio-economic bias in intelligence testing. *British Journal of Educational Psychology, 33,* 107–119.

Mather, J., & Jinks, K. L. (1971). *Biometrical genetics: The study of continuous variation.* London: Methuen.

Nettlebeck, T. (1982). Inspection time: An index for intelligence? *Quarterly Journal of Experimental Psychology, 34A,* 299–312.

Nettlebeck, T., & Lally, M. (1976). Inspection time and measured intelligence. *British Journal of Psychology, 67,* 17–22.

Ord, I. G. (1972). Testing for educational and occupational selection in developing countries – a review. *Occupational Psychology 46*(3), Monograph Issue.

Pearson, K. (1920). Notes on the history of correlation. *Biometrika, 13,* 25–45.

Pearson, K. (1930). *Life, letters, and labours of Francis Galton* (Vols. 1–4). Cambridge University Press.

Rao, C. K. V. (1974). A tribute to the memory of Dr. M. V. Gopalaswamy. In the *Souvenir for the Golden Jubilee of the Department of Psychology, University of Mysore* (pp. 6–12). University of Mysore Press.

Rasch, G. (1961). *Probabilistic models for some intelligence and attainment tests.* Copenhagen: Institute of Education.

Rogers, C. A. (1956). *Measuring Intelligence in New Zealand* (Monograph Series No. 2). Auckland: Auckland University College.

Rogers, C. A., & Frantz, C. (1962). *Racial themes in Southern Rhodesia.* New Haven, CT: Yale University Press.

Sinha, D. (1983). Human assessment in the Indian context. In S. H. Irvine & J. W. Berry (Eds.), *Human assessment and cultural factors.* New York: Plenum.

Spearman, C. (1904) "General Intelligence" objectively determined and measured. *American Journal of Psychology, 15,* 201–292.

Spearman, C. (1923). *The nature of 'intelligence' and the principles of cognition.* London: Macmillan.

Sternberg, R. J. (1977). *Intelligence, information processing and analogical reasoning: The componential analysis of human abilities.* Hillside, NJ: Erlbaum.

Sternberg, R. J. (1982) (Ed.). *Handbook of Human Intelligence.* Cambridge University Press.

Thomson, G. (1951). *Factorial analysis of human ability* (5th ed.). Boston: Houghton Mifflin.

Vernon, P. E. (1950). *The measurement of abilities.* London: University of London Press.

Vernon, P. E. (1961). *The structure of human abilities.* London: University of London Press.

Vernon, P. E. (1969). *Intelligence and cultural environment.* London: Methuen.

Vernon, P. E. (1979). *Intelligence: Heredity and environment.* San Francisco: Freeman.

Vernon, P. E., & Parry, J. B. (1949). *Personnel selection in the British forces.* London: University of London Press.

White, P. O. (1973). Individual differences in speed, accuracy and persistence: A mathematical model for problem solving. In H. J. Eysenck (Ed.), *The measurement of intelligence.* Lancaster, U.K.: Medical and Technical Publishers.

8 Cultural influences on patterns of abilities in North America

Philip Anthony Vernon, Douglas N. Jackson, and Samuel Messick

It has long been recognised – as several of the chapters in this volume attest – that cultural differences between groups may exert a profound influence on the differential development of distinct patterns of mental abilities. Ferguson (1954) states succinctly that "individuals reared in different cultures will develop different patterns of abilities" (p. 104). A similar appreciation of the role of culture in shaping mental development may be found in most of the work in which this issue has been addressed.

In this chapter, we discuss cultural influences on patterns of abilities within North America, or, more specifically, within the United States. As will be seen, a quite considerable body of research has sought to describe patterns of abilities typical of the members of different subgroups living in the United States and to attribute these differences to cultural characteristics specific to each of the various groups. This research is described in some detail below, although we will anticipate the conclusion we have drawn from it by suggesting now that much of it has been equivocal. Contrary to what appears to be a prevalent belief, it is not an *established fact* that members of different cultural or ethnic groups in the United States – for example, whites, blacks, Chinese, Jews, and Puerto Ricans – typically develop different patterns of abilities or different profiles of mean performance levels on such ability dimensions as verbal comprehension, spatial relations, and reasoning. Furthermore, when such patterns appear to emerge, their nature and meaning are by no means clear nor is their social and educational import. The emphasis has been added because we do not wish to imply that such differences do not exist: Our argument will be rather that studies of differential ability profiles have suffered from a number of inadequacies or indeterminacies which, at this point, render their results inconclusive.

Cultural group differences in ability patterns

As we are using the term, the "patterns-of-abilities hypothesis" has two components. First, it states that members of different cultural groups will typically develop different mental abilities or, more likely, that they will develop the same abilities but to different degrees. With respect to the former point of different mental abilities, this might be revealed in the form of group

208

differences in factor structures – for example, with some ability factors emerging in one group and not another, with broad factors differentiating into subfactors in one group and not another, or with specific factors integrating into broad factors in one group and not another. With respect to the latter point of the same abilities but to different degrees, this might be revealed in the form of profiles of mean group performance on separate abilities, the profiles displaying different peaks and valleys for the different group strengths and weaknesses. Second, the patterns-of-abilities hypothesis holds that a major contributing factor in the development of differential patterns of abilities between groups is the difference in the cultures to which the members of the groups have been exposed – especially with respect to learning experiences, opportunities, and value emphases. The discussion that follows refers primarily to cultural influences on group profiles of performance across the same but separate abilities.

The salience of group profiles

A study by Lesser, Fifer, and Clark (1965) provided one of the first demonstrations of apparent differences in the profiles of abilities of members of different ethnic or cultural groups within the United States. They administered a modified version of the *Hunter College Aptitude Scales for Gifted Children* to 320 first-grade pupils from four ethnic groups in New York City – Chinese, Jewish, black, and Puerto Rican – obtaining measures of verbal, reasoning, numerical, and spatial abilities. Scores on these tests were converted to normalised standardised scores, using the means and standard deviations of the combined samples. As is shown in Figure 8.1, distinct profiles appear when the groups' mean standardised scores are plotted. Also shown in Figure 8.1 is another set of distinct profiles obtained from eleventh-grade students (Project Access) in Los Angeles (Flaugher, 1971). The similarity between the two sets of profiles is particularly noteworthy in view of the differences in the age levels of the students, differences in the definition of the ethnic groups, and differences in the tests used to tap the four ability factors.

In the Lesser et al. (1965) study, children were further classified as lower or middle socioeconomic status (SES) within ethnic group. Interestingly, although the low SES children obtained lower average scores on each test, very much the same patterns of abilities were observed regardless of SES. The data have been interpreted as showing that members of these different ethnic groups typically develop distinct profiles of abilities which are largely independent of SES. Lesser et al. also suggest that "it is, perhaps, the differential reinforcement in each culture for performance in each of the mental-ability areas that accounts most plausibly for the emergence of patterns of mental ability specific to each ethnic group" (p. 73).

A follow-up study by Stodolsky and Lesser (1967) compared the ability profiles of low and middle SES Chinese, black, and Irish-Catholic children

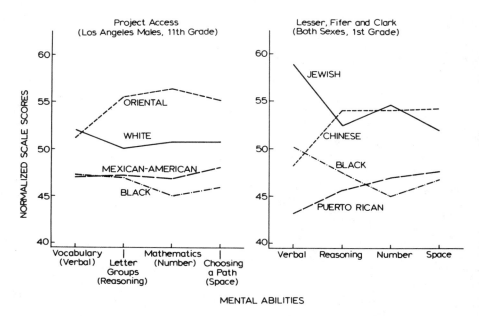

Figure 8.1. Patterns of abilities of different ethnic groups in the United States (from Lesser, Fifer, & Clark, 1965; Flaugher, 1971).

in Boston. The first two groups displayed remarkably similar patterns of abilities to those observed by Lesser et al., but the Irish Catholics showed no distinctive profile nor any similarity of profile for low and middle SES members. Stodolsky and Lesser also reanalysed the original Lesser et al. (1965) data to investigate the extent to which individuals within each of the four ethnic groups showed the same profiles of abilities as the groups to which they belonged. Overall, 57% of the pupils were correctly classified in the appropriate ethnic group, ranging from a low of 47% for Puerto Rican to a high of 79% for Jewish children. However, when social class as well as ethnic group was taken into account, only 43% of the children were correctly classified (Feldman, 1973; Lesser, 1973). When a random half of the pupils was used to establish the profiles and the other half to appraise the goodness of classification, 47% of the children were correctly classified into the appropriate ethnic group and 37% (three times chance expectation) into both ethnic and social class groups (Lesser, 1973).

To investigate the stability of these differential ability profiles, Lesser (1976) was able to relocate and retest 208 of the original 320 children (65%) when they reached sixth grade. When these children were in the first grade, 56% of them – more than twice the chance expectation of 25% – could be correctly classified in the appropriate ethnic group on the basis of their ability scores; in the sixth grade, 58% could be correctly classified. However, there was considerable variation by ethnic group in this apparent stability. From first grade to sixth grade, the percentage of correct classifications increased for both Chinese (66% to 75%) and Puerto Rican (40% to 71%) children, while the percentages decreased for both Jewish (70% to 52%) and black (45% to 33%) children. If ability profiles are reflective of cultural influences, these trends suggest an increasing entrenchment of cultural influence with age for Chinese and Puerto Rican groups in the United States and an increasing diffusion for Jewish and black groups.

One clue to the entrenchment of cultural influence in Chinese and Puerto Rican groups may reside in the role of the language used in the home combined with socioeconomic level. Laosa (1984) found that significant profile differences across verbal, reasoning, quantitative, memory, and motor abilities between two-and-a-half-year-old Chicano and non-Hispanic white children remained significant when socioeconomic level was controlled statistically. This finding is consistent with that of Lesser et al. (1965) and extends downward to 30 months of age the phenomenon of group ability profile invariance across socieconomic levels. In addition, the significant group profile differences remained essentially unchanged when language use in the home was controlled. However, when both language use and socioeconomic level were simultaneously held constant, the adjusted ethnic-group profiles were not significantly different.

Continuing this general line of research, Sitkei and Meyers (1969) compared low and middle SES white and black four-year-olds on tests tapping six factors of ability derived from Guilford's structure of intellect model (verbal comprehension, ideational fluency, perceptual speed, figural or spatial reasoning, auditory memory for letters and digits, and object-picture memory). Factor analysis indicated that the hypothesised factors were relatively stable in both white and black groups, so there were no group differences in factor structure. However, with respect to group profiles of ability scores, whites scored higher than blacks only on verbal comprehension and no distinct ethnic-group profiles of abilities were observed. Sitkei and Meyers suggest that the younger age of their sample, compared to that of Lesser et al. (1965), might be responsible for the lack of ethnic ability profiles: At 4 years of age, the children may not have been sufficiently exposed to their particular cultures to adopt the patterns apparently typical of older members of their group. However, Laosa (1984) demonstrates differences in ethnic profiles at an even younger age. Moreover, Willerman (1979) points out that other studies of the abilities of 4-year-olds have reported race differences and questions the sensitivity of the tests employed by Sitkei and Meyers.

In a study conducted in Canada, Marjoribanks (1972) tested 11-year-old boys from five ethnic groups – Canadian Indians, French-Canadians, Jews, southern Italians, and white Anglo-Saxon Protestants – on the *SRA Primary Mental Abilities Test*. The profiles of the groups' standardised scores on verbal, number, spatial, and reasoning abilities are shown in Figure 8.2, revealing, as in Lesser et al., distinct profiles for each cultural group. In addition, Marjoribanks' Jewish group follows a pattern quite similar to that

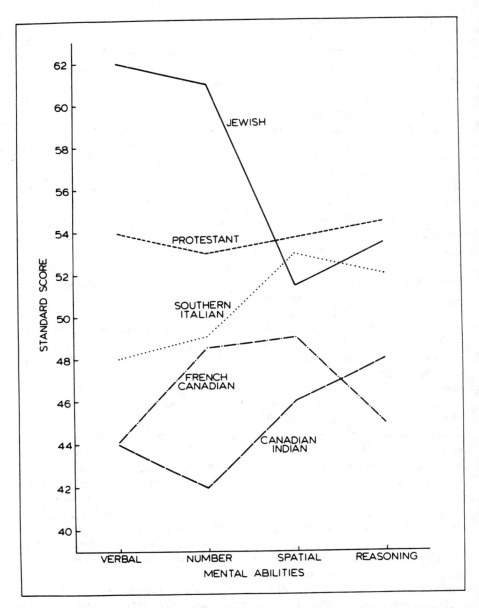

Figure 8.2. Patterns of abilities of five ethnic groups in Canada (from Marjoribanks, 1972).

of the Jews in the Lesser et al. (1965) study – that is, highest on verbal and number, relatively lower on reasoning and space. Marjoribanks also measured eight parental environmental variables (achievement, activeness, intellectuality, independence, English, ethnic language use, father and mother dominance). In general, these environmental variables were more highly related to the ability profiles than was ethnicity, although both made independent contributions.

Gross (1967) demonstrated ability differences *within* an ethnic group which could still plausibly be linked to cultural differences. Two groups of middle- or higher-SES American Jewish children, who lived in adjacent neighbourhoods in Brooklyn but who were of either Sephardic or Ashkenazi ancestry, were compared on the *Stanford-Binet*, the *Peabody Picture Vocabulary Test*, and the *Bender Visual Motor Gestalt Test*. On each test, the Ashkenazi children obtained significantly higher scores than the Sephardic, which Gross attributes to cultural differences in child-rearing practices related to instilling a respect for learning. One wonders to what extent similar ability differences might be observed within other groups which could have been but were not subdivided: for example, breaking out Japanese and Chinese from the conglomerate "Oriental" group reported in the Coleman et al. (1966) equal educational opportunity survey.

One of the largest studies of patterns of abilities in the United States was reported by Backman (1972). Her sample, drawn from 12th graders who had participated in Project TALENT, consisted of 1,236 Jewish whites, 1,051 non-Jewish whites, 488 blacks, and 150 Orientals. The students were administered a battery of 60 achievement and aptitude tests and were subsequently compared on six orthogonal factors representing verbal knowledge, English grammar and language use, mathematics, visual-spatial reasoning, perceptual speed and accuracy, and short-term memory. In addition to the four ethnic groups, Backman categorised the subjects into two SES levels (lower-middle and upper-middle) and by sex. A 4(ethnicity) × 2(SES) × 2(sex) ANOVA indicated that sex accounted for the largest part (69%) of the ability differences, followed by ethnicity (13%), and SES (2%). Presumably, the narrow range of SES in the sample was responsible for its minimal contribution.

Table 8.1 shows the weighted mean scores of the four ethnic groups on the six ability factors (scaled to have a mean of 50 and standard deviation of 10 in the complete high school Project TALENT sample), derived from Table I in Backman (1972, p. 5). Jewish whites obtained high mean scores on verbal knowledge and math and relatively low mean scores on visual reasoning and memory. Non-Jewish whites showed no distinct profile at all. Blacks obtained their highest scores on perceptual speed, memory, and English, but were relatively low and showed little variation on the other three factors. Orientals obtained high math scores, were relatively low on verbal knowledge and visual reasoning, and were intermediate on the other three factors. Comparing these ability profiles to those reported by Lesser et al.

Table 8.1. *Mean scores of four ethnic groups on six ability factors*

	Verbal knowledge	English	Math	Visual reasoning	Perceptual speed	Memory
Jewish white	58.23	50.37	60.88	47.08	51.40	47.39
Non-Jewish white	51.98	51.42	51.78	51.65	49.53	51.09
Black	43.57	50.11	44.86	42.21	51.45	52.29
Oriental	48.59	53.30	57.88	48.71	50.59	51.98

Note: Weighted means are derived from Table I in Backman (1972, p. 5).

(1965), there is some congruence between the Jewish groups in the two studies (both are higher on verbal and math and lower on spatial ability), but the profiles for Orientals and blacks show less resemblance. Nor is the similarity of Orientals and blacks in the Backman study to the corresponding groups in the Flaugher (1971) Project Access study much more compelling (see Fig. 8.1). Of course, the use of different tests from study to study denies a truly meaningful comparison, but insofar as the extracted factors underlying the test scores have been found to be roughly similar across these studies, one might have anticipated a closer correspondence in ethnic ability profiles than is evident.

Finally, Jensen (e.g., 1971, 1973, 1974) has reported several large-sample studies of profiles of abilities of different ethnic groups in the United States, primarily relating ability differences among groups to his Level I–Level II theory of intelligence. Level I denotes rote learning and memory and involves minimal mental transformation of the stimulus input prior to the output or response. It is usually measured by forward digit span or serial rote learning. Level II refers to a general class of abilities that involve the effective transformation or manipulation of stimuli. It is usually identified with general intelligence or the *g* factor common to tests of intelligence. Much of Jensen's work has focussed on white–black differences, and the results of several studies support the conclusion that these groups typically differ by about one standard deviation unit on Level II but differ minimally, if at all, on Level I (see P. A. Vernon [1981] for a review of the Level I–Level II literature). This is borne out in Backman's study (see Table 8.1), where non-Jewish whites and blacks show their largest differences on verbal knowledge and visual reasoning but virtually no difference on memory.

The 1973 Jensen study included samples not only of whites and blacks but also of Mexican-Americans, who obtained their lowest scores on verbally loaded tests of crystallised intelligence and relatively higher scores on nonverbal tests of fluid intelligence. Jensen points out that English was spoken exclusively in only 16% of the Mexican-American homes in his sample, suggesting that limited English proficiency is largely responsible for the lower Mexican-American scores on the verbal tests. Despite the fact that the Mexican-Americans were found to be more socioeconomically disadvantaged than either the whites or the blacks in this study, this proved to have little effect on their fluid intelligence scores. Blacks, on the other hand, obtained their lowest scores on the nonverbal tests. This pattern of results suggests that white–black differences in fluid intelligence cannot readily be attributed solely to SES differences.

Jensen and Inouye (1980) studied the Level I and Level II profiles of 2,898 whites, 2,361 blacks, and 426 Asian-Americans (Chinese and Japanese) in grades two to six. Whites and Asians both obtained high Level II scores, whereas blacks, as before, scored about one standard deviation unit lower. Interestingly, blacks *and Asians* both obtained significantly lower Level I scores than whites, resulting in a distinctive – but unexpected – profile of ability for the Asian group.

Indeed, Orientals in North America provide a unique case study of a group which historically suffered much discrimination and adversity and yet shows evidence of achievement exceeding that not only of other minority groups, but of the white majority as well. Recently, Philip E. Vernon (1982) has addressed the question of how Oriental immigrants, drawn largely from peasant stock and from cultural and linguistic traditions quite different from those of North America, have been so successful in an environment that was at least indifferent to their aspirations and sometimes hostile (see also Chapters 13 and 14). The fact of their achievements is supported by statistical data on occupational distribution and median wages, which in the case of persons of Chinese and of Japanese ancestry exceed levels achieved by whites.

In searching for clues for explaining the success of Oriental groups, Vernon reviews much of the literature. While recognising its limitations, for example, in often failing to provide data on socioeconomic status, Vernon notes with regard to Chinese a "remarkable degree of consistency" from samples drawn from such diverse places as Hawaii, Canada, and Hong Kong. Vernon summarises these results:

Right from the 1920s Chinese American children have been found somewhat lower than whites on verbal intelligence tests and on verbal types of school achievement (e.g., reading comprehension). But they have come out the equal of, or higher than, whites on nonverbal intelligence tests such as *Raven Matrices, Figure-Copying, Lorge-Thorndike*, or performance tests such as *Kohs Blocks* and *Draw-a-Man*. In the earlier studies the verbal deficiency was quite considerable, but the more recent ones indicate mean IQs on verbal group tests of about 97 (i.e., little below the white average), and 110 on nonverbal and spatial tests (much above average). Chinese boys generally do better than girls, especially on the nonverbal side. Chinese are also superior in mechanical arithmetic, though not in problem or applied mathematics. Both sexes are also surprisingly, though quite consistently, superior in spelling. (p. 28)

Studies of Japanese children point in a similar direction. For example, P. E. Vernon (1982, p. 74) cites an unpublished 1980 study by the Los Angeles school board comparing reading and mathematics percentile scores of Japanese school children in grades three and five with those of the total school population. Despite the inclusion of some children with limited English language skills, the Japanese children's mean percentile scores were much superior in reading as well as in mathematics. Cross-cultural studies also support the superior educational achievement of Japanese children reared in Japan, especially at the earlier grade levels.

Among the cultural influences considered by Vernon are the positive and negative effects of bilingualism, child socialisation, differential emphases on parental and familial obligations, and concomitant resulting modal personality patterns. Although there are some similarities in the child-rearing practices of Japanese and Chinese which might impact on their higher levels of achievement in North America, there are also substantial cultural differences, differences which might account for the perseverance, stoicism, and patience of the Chinese, and the aggressiveness, focussed competitiveness, innovation, and adaptability of the Japanese. Many of these characteristics are similar superficially to the Protestant work ethic described by Weber and employed to account for differences between whites and some minority groups, although the origins of the latter spring from quite different ideological traditions. Paradoxically, the conditions thought to interfere with intellectual development – poor living conditions, poverty, overcrowding, and discrimination and repression by the white majority – have not in the case of Orientals resulted in adverse consequences, at least in comparison with the white majority. Apparently, the presence of superior motivation to achieve academically and personality characteristics consistent with achievement may compensate for poor environmental conditions. Present data do not permit conclusions regarding the biological basis for certain personality differences between Orientals and Caucasians, but the observation that newborn Oriental infants are less irritable than are white infants is suggestive. Vernon (1982) also suggests that the consistency of the data bearing on Oriental–white comparisons raises the possibility of genetic differences, but acknowledges that the data are insufficient to draw definite conclusions.

Counterclaims and caveats

The studies cited above appear to provide strong support for the patterns-of-abilities hypothesis. However, Feldman (1973) and Jensen (1980) argue that the results are not as conclusive as has generally been supposed. They both point out that the profiles of ability of the different groups in these studies are entirely a function of the particular groups that happen to have been included in the analysis, as well as of the particular method by which raw scores have been transformed before plotting the group means. To illustrate the magnitude of the effect that just one of these conditions can produce, consider the group profiles in Figure 8.3. These represent the mean raw scores of three *hypothetical groups* on three different mental abilities. Each "test" that the groups were given is assumed to have had an equal

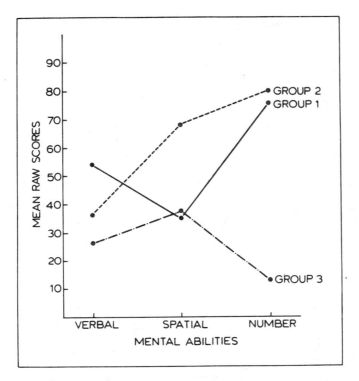

Figure 8.3. Mean *raw* scores of the three hypothetical groups on three measures of mental ability.

number of items, the same average level of difficulty, and the same reliability. Hence, to some extent meaningful comparisons can be made among the groups' profiles. Briefly, it can be seen that Group 1 receives its highest mean score on number, its lowest on spatial, and is intermediate on verbal ability. Group 2 is also highest on number, less high on spatial (though higher than the other two groups), and lowest on verbal. Group 3 obtains its highest mean score on spatial, its lowest on number, and is intermediate in verbal ability.

As stated, Figure 8.3 shows the mean *raw* scores of these imaginary groups. When the groups are combined and their raw scores converted to standardised (*Z*) scores, rather different profiles are revealed. In Figure 8.4, plotting the mean *Z* scores, we see that Group 1 now receives its highest score on verbal, is less high on number, and, as before, is lowest on spatial. The largest change is observed in Group 2, which is now markedly higher on spatial and less high on number; the raw scores showed the reverse pattern for these two tests. Only Group 3 retains the same profile of abilities for both raw and *Z* scores.

Finally, if only two groups are combined before their raw scores are trans-

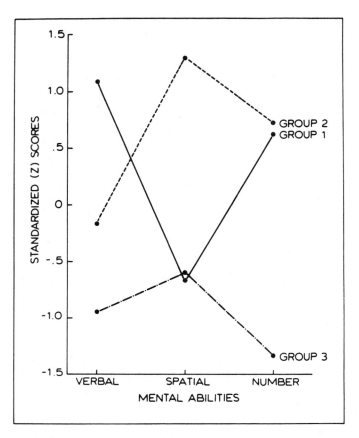

Figure 8.4. Mean Z scores of three hypothetical groups on three measures of mental ability.

formed to Z scores, their ability profiles will necessarily be exact mirror images of one another, as depicted in Figure 8.5 (unless, of course, both groups obtain identical scores). Here, too, it can be seen that the profile for Group 3 has changed: It is now highest on verbal and less high on spatial, the reverse of the pattern for these two abilities appearing in Figures 8.3 and 8.4. As Feldman (1973) summarised these effects, "the distinction to be made is between rank orderings for groups *within* an ability area and rank orderings *among* ability areas within a group. The former relationships do not change with data transformations, the latter do" (p. 14). Because the latter profiles of abilities within ethnic groups are changeable by arbitrary data transformations, there are serious questions about what the profiles are and what they mean. There is less contention over the fundamental point that the ability profiles appear to be different from one cultural group to another.

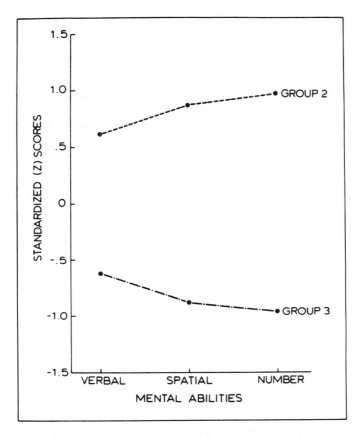

Figure 8.5. Mean *Z* scores of two hypothetical groups on three measures of mental ability.

When Feldman (1973) described the possibly artifactual nature of the profiles of abilities reported by Lesser et al. (1965), Lesser (1973) replied: "I have pointed out repeatedly that the particular patterns we identified are not absolute. They are relative patterns. . . . each ethnic group's pattern surely will change depending upon the different ethnic groups included in the samples. . . . The main point simply is that the mental-ability patterns for the ethnic groups studied are different" (p. 19).

Jensen (1980) and Reynolds and Jensen (1983), however, describe two additional factors which could contribute to the *appearance* of different profiles of ability within different groups even when the patterns do not really exist. First, if two or more groups differed only in their average level of general intelligence but in no other mental abilities, differences in the *g* loadings of a number of different tests would result in the appearance of distinct ability profiles for the groups in question. Second, even if all the tests had the same g loadings, any differences in their reliabilities would lead to group differences when these were expressed in standardised score units. Jensen (1980) concludes: "The interpretations of such ethnic group profiles in the forms in which they are presented in all the published studies that I have seen on this topic are virtually meaningless. Certainly they can tell us nothing about any given group's 'pattern of abilities' in any absolute sense" (p. 731). But as Jensen (1980) subsequently avers, "there can be no such thing as an ability profile in any absolute sense; any ability profile is merely the result of group comparisons" (p. 732). The issue, as Lesser (1973; Lesser et al., 1965) has consistently maintained, concerns the existence of *relative* group differences in ability profiles.

In his own work, Jensen (Reynolds & Jensen, 1983) compared the patterns of abilities of 270 black and 270 white children, drawn from the sample used in the standardisation of the *WISC-R*, and matched for age, sex, and full-scale *WISC-R IQ*. Despite equivalent IQs, a MANOVA revealed significant differences between the groups on a set of 15 variables (12 subtests, Verbal, Performance, and Full-Scale IQ). Univariate analyses showed whites scoring significantly higher than blacks on comprehension, object assembly, and mazes, while blacks scored significantly higher than whites on digit span and coding. Contrary to Lesser et al. (1965), blacks did not obtain significantly higher scores on verbal subtests, relative either to themselves or to the whites (see Figure 8.1, which shows that the blacks in Lesser et al. obtained their highest scores on verbal ability).

Reynolds and Jensen (1983) proceeded to factor analyse the scores of the combined white and black samples and to assign each subject factor scores on the orthogonal verbal, performance, and memory factors which were extracted. Comparisons between the groups revealed no difference on verbal ability, while whites obtained significantly higher performance factor scores and significantly lower memory factor scores than blacks. Reynolds and Jensen concluded that, in the population, white–black differences in ability are primarily attributable to differences in general intelligence but that *reliable differences between the groups do exist on some abilities other than* g. Jensen and Reynolds (1982) reached a similar conclusion when they compared the test performance of 1,868 whites and 305 blacks constituting the *WISC-R* standardisation sample. In this study, significant white–black differences were observed on g, verbal, performance, and memory factors (with blacks higher than whites on memory), although g accounted for more than seven times as much of the between-group difference as did the other three factors combined.

Jensen and Reynolds (1982) also compared the ethnic group profiles of ability with the patterns associated with groups of different SES. With full-scale IQ partialled out, whites obtained higher scores than blacks on tests tapping spatial-perceptual abilities and lower scores than blacks on short-term memory. In contrast, comparisons between groups differing in SES revealed quite different profiles: High SES groups obtained higher scores than low SES groups primarily on verbal ability subtests and lower scores than low SES groups on spatial-perceptual tests. The conclusion here, as in Lesser et al. (1965), is that whatever factors are responsible for *ethnic-group* differences in ability must be different from those responsible for *SES* differences in ability. Further, white-black differences cannot be solely attributed simply to SES differences between the races, although these are frequently cited as the major cause of ability differences between these racial groups.

Cultural impact on intellect

Cultural influences on patterns of abilities

What conclusions can be drawn from these studies of mean profiles of abilities associated with different ethnic groups in the United States? First, as has been suggested, the evidence regarding the existence of distinct ethnic-group ability profiles is at best sparse and at worst equivocal. The profiles that have been reported are variously stable across studies, although differences in the age levels of students, in the definition of the ethnic groups involved, and in the ability tests employed render such judgments highly questionable. Lesser's (1973) comment, cited above, that even though the patterns are not absolute they are still different, is both debatable in particular instances and potentially misleading overall. If a particular group consistently performed better on one type of ability test than it did on another – however standardised in relation to whatever other comparison groups – it might indeed be possible to investigate cultural factors predominant in that group which could plausibly be related to such a consistent pattern. But group ability profiles are dependent upon arbitrary data transformations introduced, resulting in groups sometimes appearing high on one ability and sometimes relatively lower on the same ability and higher on another. This makes the task of identifying causal factors virtually impossible. Because test scoring and other data transformations are truly arbitrary in the sense that they may be accomplished defensibly in a variety of ways, it does not help to agree upon a standard procedure to define the ability profiles to be related to cultural factors, because any ability profile so defined is still arbitrary. For example, if the standard procedure yields a pattern with verbal higher than spatial ability in a particular group while the "true" pattern has spatial higher than verbal, the cultural underpinnings of such standard profiles would be abstruse indeed.

Second, even if consistent nonarbitrary profiles were revealed when group means are compared, the finding that less than 50% of the individual members of ethnic groups follow the same patterns produces a serious setback to the identification of culture-specific variables responsible for the groups' profiles (Feldman, 1973) – although more refined subcultural groupings might be more effective in this regard. One might even question whether a variable can be considered "cultural" if it only manifests its influence on roughly half the members of the culture with which it is being identified. At least, such findings encourage recognition of the diversity that exists within cultures.

In the 1960s, a considerable amount of research was directed towards identifying environmental factors responsible for the lower intelligence test scores and scholastic achievement of disadvantaged and minority groups in the United States (e.g., Deutsch, 1967; Katz, 1967; Deutsch, Katz, & Jensen, 1968). In the majority of cases, this research was triggered by a fundamental belief that children from deprived backgrounds or disadvantaged home environments entered school with a serious handicap which impeded their ability to learn. Deutsch (1967) summarises this position when he writes: "The thesis here is that the lower-class child enters the school situation so poorly prepared to produce what the school demands that critical failures are almost inevitable" (p. 37). In a later chapter, he concludes: "The problem here is more than a simple disharmony between the implicit value system of the home and the explicit values of the school. Rather, there seems to be a complete absence of preparation for the school experience" (p. 102).

Perhaps as a result of their own educational deficiencies, lower SES parents tended to pay less attention to their children and to provide them with less reinforcement in their early attempts to acquire language and solve problems (Hess, Shipman, & Jackson, 1965; Katz, 1967; Jensen, 1968). They were also less likely to recognise intellectual behaviours in their children (Katz, 1967) and were unwilling or unable to provide the opportunities or experiences necessary for their children to develop the verbal, conceptual, and attentional skills prerequisite for scholastic success (Whiteman & Deutsch, 1968). Once in school, these children were faced with an essentially alien environment. They tended to perceive their teachers as rejecting or hostile (Katz, 1967) and to suffer from the belief that they had no control over their situation (Coleman et al., 1966). Disruptive behaviour in the classroom was the rule rather than the exception, resulting in the majority of classroom time being devoted to discipline and other nonacademic activities (Deutsch, 1967). This, in turn, contributed to the children's cumulative deprivation, progressively decreased learning, and reduced chance of scholastic achievement over time.

More recently, Laosa (1978, 1980, 1982) has extended this line of research, focussing specifically on the effect of the home environment on the cognitive development and scholastic achievement of Chicano children. In a series of studies, Laosa demonstrated a pronounced relationship between parents' years of schooling and the sorts of behaviours they manifested in interactions with their children. The pattern which emerged was for more educated parents to be more likely to behave in a fashion similar to that of a classroom teacher: employing more frequent praise or positive reinforcement, asking more questions, and being less likely simply to tell their children what to do or to do the task for them. Of particular interest was the finding that the frequency of these behaviours was essentially independent of the parents' occupational status. Comparisons between Anglo and Hispanic mothers showed the Anglos to demonstrate reinforcing and enquiry positive behaviours to a greater extent even when occupational status was controlled. When years of schooling were held constant, however, the ethnic-group differences in maternal teaching strategies diminished and became nonsignificant. Laosa suggested that if educational parity became a reality, many of the differences in the child-rearing patterns and subsequent scholastic achievement of Chicanos and Anglos might disappear.

As it stands, Laosa views the sociocultural differences between the home and school environments of many Chicano children as a self-perpetuating cycle, whereby children may exhibit behaviours that are functionally adaptive in the context of their homes and neighbourhoods but these same behaviours may be maladaptive for success in the school environment. Such children enter schools less well prepared for what they will encounter than do children from home environments socioculturally consonant with that of the school. They may also behave less adaptively to the social constraints of schooling and may benefit less from typical classroom instruction. As a consequence, they are more likely to leave school after a relatively few years. Subsequently, as adults, they may tend to interact with their own children in ways that are little affected by school experiences and that primarily perpetuate their own early home cultural context.

It seems likely that a similar cycle of sociocultural disjunction between home and school operates in other ethnic groups, specifically among low SES blacks. Recent statistics reported in *Time* magazine (May 1984) show that 55% of black children are born to unmarried, often teenage mothers. Fifty percent are raised in single-mother households in which the median annual income is less than $7,500. Among black teenagers, the birth rate has declined slightly over the past decade, but there is still a tendency for teenage mothers to have children who themselves become parents as teenagers. Under such circumstances, it is hardly surprising that the benefits of schooling fade into insignificance or, indeed, that they are given no consideration at all.

A strong argument can be made that conditions such as these have a profound effect on the intellectual development and scholastic achievement of children who are raised under them. It seems probable, however, that they would primarily affect the children's *general* cognitive development and would be less likely to result in the emergence of a distinct *pattern* of abilities. In addition, although these conditions may well be more prevalent among black families, they are not restricted to blacks. They may, in fact, be fairly typical of low SES, disadvantaged families regardless of race. If this is the case, other factors must be sought to explain those white–black differences in profiles of abilities that have been found because, as has been described, they bear little or no resemblance to the profiles associated with low versus high SES populations (Jensen & Reynolds, 1982). Furthermore, the low SES members of other ethnic groups – for example, Mexican-Americans and Orientals – also show different patterns and levels of intellectual development compared to blacks (Jensen, 1973; Jensen & Inouye, 1980).

Cultural influences on the organisation of abilities

Another possibility is that sociocultural factors influence not only general cognitive development but also the organisation and regulation of cognitive processes, and hence cognitive styles, and that both of these effects contaminate our attempts to understand the emergence of distinct group patterns of abilities. Cultural influences on cognitive styles have been extensively studied, especially in relation to socialisation practices and the adaptive requirements of the cultural setting, but for the most part only with respect to the style of field independence versus field dependence (Witkin, 1967; Witkin & Berry, 1975; Berry, 1976). In order to comprehend the nature of the cultural effects and how they might differentially impact different cultural groups, we must first briefly consider the major characteristics of this cognitive style. Field-independent persons are relatively analytical, self-referent, and impersonal in orientation, whereas field-dependent persons are relatively global, socially sensitive, and interpersonal in orientation; more generally, field independents are relatively high in their degree of psychological differentiation and field dependents are relatively low (Witkin & Goodenough, 1981). To highlight the positive features of both stylistic poles, this dimension has also been characterised as field independence versus field sensitivity (Ramirez & Castaneda, 1974). However, although the conceptual basis for the field-independence dimension is quite distinct from conceptualisations of intellectual ability factors, from a *measurement* standpoint they have substantial communality (Jackson, 1957; Gardner, Jackson, & Messick, 1960; P. E. Vernon, 1972; Messick, 1984).

Socialisation practices fostering field independence encompass, among other things, the achievement of separation from the mother and the development of a personal identity independent of the family and community, while practices fostering field dependence emphasise protectiveness, close ties between mother and child before adolescence, and respect for social convention (Witkin, Dyk, Faterson, Goodenough, & Karp, 1962; Dyk & Witkin, 1965). Because these sociocultural influences operate differentially in white, black, and Mexican-American groups in the United States, one might expect to find ethnic differences in cognitive style. For example, traditional Mexican-American socialisation has been described as developing strong identification with family, community, and ethnic group; establishing close personal ties to and respect for others; fostering achievement through cooperation; and, developing sensitivity to social stimuli and respect for convention (Ramirez & Castaneda, 1974). Moreover, the world-view of blacks, especially those with an African perspective, has been portrayed as universalistic, intuitive, and very person-oriented, with a value emphasis on affect, communalism, oral communication, expressive individualism, and social time perspective (Shade, 1982; Boykin, 1983). There is, in addition, accumulating evidence that both samples of blacks and samples of Mexican-Americans tend to be relatively more field dependent or field sensitive while samples of whites are relatively more field independent (Ramirez & Castaneda, 1974; Ramirez & Price-Williams, 1974; Shade, 1982).

Since particular socialisation practices frequently predominate in a given ethnic group, ethnicity per se often serves as a gross proxy for sociocultural factors that may at the same time display considerable within-group variation, as was previously noted in connection with parental environmental variables in Marjoribanks's (1972) study. As an instance, Dershowitz (1971) found that Orthodox Jewish boys, raised in families typically dominated by a mother who encouraged the child to form close personal ties with her while the father was only minimally involved in child rearing, scored more often in the direction of field dependence or field sensitivity than did a group of New York Jewish boys whose families had adopted values more characteristic of middle-class Anglo-Saxon Protestants. A group of Anglo-Saxon Protestant boys scored still more strongly in the direction of field independence.

Group differences in cognitive styles imply group differences in the organisation and regulation of cognitive processes. These in turn have marked implications for the differential development and organisation of abilities, especially as such development might be differentially facilitated or inhibited by the requirements of schooling. By and large, the context of schooling in the United States favours cognitive approaches that are analytical, sequential, and task- or object-oriented, with numerous impersonal behavioural requirements – as when pupils must "learn to sit increasingly long periods of time, to concentrate alone on impersonal learning stimuli, and to observe and value organized time-allotment schedules" (Cohen, 1969, p. 830). The prevalence of this analytic and impersonal context would seem to favour and strengthen the psychologically differentiated cognitive style of field independence. And if other individuals and groups with different cognitive styles find such conditions of learning less congenial to varying degrees, then this might lead to differential ability development and the emergence of group profiles that are correlated with ethnicity by virtue of ethnic predilections for modes of thinking, socialisation practices, and other sociocultural features.

Cultural influences on levels of abilities

Between 1952 and 1963, the mean *SAT-Verbal* and *SAT-Mathematics* scores for test takers seeking college admission in the United States remained essentially stable. The mean *SAT-V* score rose 2 points to 478 over this period. The mean *SAT-M* score rose 8 points to 502. In 1964, the mean scores on both tests began to decline. Until about 1970, the decline was relatively gradual. Thereafter, and particularly on *SAT-V*, the decline became more pronounced. It has continued until 1980, stabilising in 1981 and showing a modest reverse trend (i.e., a slight increase in mean scores) in 1982, 1983, and 1984 (Report of the Advisory Panel on the Scholastic Aptitude Test Score Decline, 1977; Wainer, 1984). This reversal reflects, at least in part, not only a gradual decrease in the mean black–white score difference beginning about 1976, but an increasing residual score trend (relative to the general decline) over the same period for such lower-scoring groups as black, Mexican-American, Puerto Rican, and possibly American Indian students (Jones, 1984; Wainer, 1984).

From 1963 to 1977, the mean *SAT-V* score dropped 49 points (to 429) and the mean *SAT-M* score dropped 32 points (to 470). The Advisory Panel on the Scholastic Aptitude Test Score Decline (1977) noted at the outset of its report that this cannot be attributed to changes in the tests themselves. Not only is there no evidence that later editions of the SAT were inherently more difficult, the Panel found that the 1972 and 1973 tests were actually some 8 to 12 points "easier" than the one used in 1963. Thus, the mean score declines reported above are underestimates of the true decline.

What factors can be identified which may be responsible for this decline? Although it is true that students who take the *SAT* are not representative of American youth as a whole, they do constitute a significant proportion. In 1960, some 564,000 high school juniors and seniors took the *SAT*, or about 30% of the 1,864,000 high school graduates of that year. By 1970, the number of *SAT* takers had tripled, then representing about 60% of all high school graduates. A decline of the magnitude that has been reported is clearly a serious matter, and when it affects such a large percentage of the young-adult population, identification of its causes – in addition to changes in the composition of the test-taking population – deserves equally serious attention.

The Advisory Panel (1977) suggested that at least two factors, or sets of factors, need to be considered. During the first six or seven years of the decline, between 1963 and 1970, there were large increases in the proportionate numbers of the *SAT*-taking population of students from low SES backgrounds, members of minority ethnic groups, and females. The first two of these groups have consistently obtained below-average scores on the *SAT*; females, on average, have scored below the mean on *SAT-M* but not on *SAT-V*. During the same period, another compositional change in the *SAT*-taking population reflected an increased proportion of students who went on to less selective colleges and universities, to two-year colleges, or to technical-vocational colleges. On average, *SAT* takers who went on to more selective four-year colleges scored 60 to 85 points higher than those who entered two-year colleges. The latter constituted about 8% of the *SAT*-taking population in 1960 and had risen to about 15% in 1972.

The Advisory Panel estimated that between two-thirds and three-fourths of the *SAT* score decline between 1963 and 1970 can be attributed to these compositional changes in the test-taking population. By 1970, however, the relative proportions in the *SAT*-taking population of the various groups mentioned above had become fairly stable. Yet not only did the decline in scores fail to stop, it became more pronounced. In addition, the Panel noted that the decline was now pervasive: It occurred among students with high and low high-school grades, in private and in public schools, from high and low SES backgrounds, among whites and blacks, and in students planning to go to more selective and less selective universities and colleges. At the same time, the pattern of the decline was not restricted to the *SAT*. A similar drop-off in scores – particularly since 1970 – has been found among high school students on the college entrance examination administered by the American College Testing Program, on the *Iowa Tests of Educational Development*, and on the *Minnesota Scholastic Aptitude Test*. Among college graduates, verbal and quantitative scores on the *Graduate Record Examinations* have also declined since 1967.

For the purposes of this chapter, it is important to emphasise that the second stage of the *SAT* score decline – from 1970 to at least 1980 – appears across the entire *SAT*-taking population, granted the relative muting or even turnaround of that decline in recent years, especially for the ethnic groups mentioned earlier (see Jones, 1984; Wainer, 1984). We are moving, then, from a consideration of cultural factors and profiles of abilities which may be specific to one or another ethnic group in the United States to a consideration of cultural factors which appear to have affected the scholastic achievement of a significant percentage of the nation's youth as a whole. Addressing this issue, the Advisory Panel was careful to point out that many of their suggestions are conjectural and a similar caution can be interjected here. Nevertheless, the Panel identified a number of trends which are likely contributors to the decline, and these will now be briefly described.

First, there has been a marked change in the types and number of courses that high school students are required to take. Particularly in English, enrollment in "basic" courses such as English composition has declined and enrollment in "electives" has increased. More important, until quite recently there has been considerably less emphasis on reading and writing. Students are less exposed to literature which might enhance their vocabularies and are seldom required to express their ideas in careful, clear, and correct writing. The effect of these factors may be reflected by the relatively larger decline in *SAT-V* scores than in *SAT-M* scores. There has not been a similar increase in electives in high school mathematics curricula, and enrollment in high school math courses has not declined to the same extent as it has in English courses.

Even more pervasive are changes over the past 15 years in the standards which high school (and younger) students have been expected to meet. Homework assignments have been approximately halved, absenteeism has increased dramatically, and promotion through the grades is no longer as dependent as it once was on demonstrating an acceptable level of competence. In 1977, the Panel noted that current 11th-grade textbooks were at a 9th- to 10th-grade level in terms of difficulty and readability; they contrasted this with the 11th- to 12th- or higher grade-level of readability of *SAT-V* passages and questions. It also noted that 16-year-olds would have spent between 10,000 and 15,000 hours watching television – more time than they would have spent in school – and suggested that this must be considered an important factor: At the very least, it detracts from the time that might have been devoted to homework or reading.

The period between the late 1960s and the mid-1970s was also one of considerable national unrest and disillusionment, particularly among students of high school and college age. America's presence in the Vietnam war, the revelation of corruption in the highest levels of government, riots, and political assassinations had a profound effect on the nation's youth, who frequently directed their protest at educational institutions and towards the process of education. Coupled with this, and perhaps partly as a result of it, students' motivation to succeed in scholastic pursuits seems to have diminished. This may be related to the declining standards of the schools, mentioned above, but it is surely also a manifestation of a more general disillusionment with society and traditional American values. Violence, crime, alcoholism, and drug usage have increased alarmingly in America's schools. It seems likely that an underlying discontent and frustration with American society and the rejection of what are perceived to be outdated if not irrelevant values are in part responsible both for the growth of these delinquent behaviours and the parallel decline in scholastic ambition and achievement. On the other side, the recent relative score increases for blacks and Hispanics may stem from the long-term effects of social and compensatory programmes, from the increasing entrenchment of desegregation, and from attitudinal or motivational changes resulting from the broader participation of minorities in American society (Jones, 1984).

Overview

We recognise that this chapter has probably raised more questions than it has answered, but that is not necessarily undesirable. Cultural influences on patterns of abilities in the United States are clearly immensely complex and, if they are to be more fully understood, will require considerably more research than is currently available. We have, it is hoped, illustrated that the evidence regarding distinct profiles of abilities specific to different ethnic groups in America is sparse and uneven and, at present, too equivocal to allow drawing valid conclusions about cultural factors which may be responsible for them. At the same time, it is evident that members of different ethnic groups in the United States achieve different *average levels* of abilities, but here, too, further research is needed to untangle the separate and interacting influences of race, SES, and group-specific mores and values.

Finally, as if the picture were not already sufficiently complicated, changes in the culture and society of America as a whole are undoubtedly to some extent responsible for declining levels of ability and achievement. With respect to this issue, a number of the more obvious changes in educational curricula and practice and the trauma associated with national events during the 1970s were described. But as plausible as the effect of these phenomena may be, it remains to be established empirically that they are the main or even minor causes of the decreased levels of performance. Our conclusion, then, is that it would be premature to offer a definitive statement regarding cultural influences on patterns of abilities in the United States. Much work must still be done to unravel facts from fiction, causes from effects, and truth from conjecture.

References

Backman, M. E. (1972). Patterns of mental abilities: Ethnic, socioeconomic, and sex differences. *American Educational Research Journal, 9*, 1–12.

Berry, J. W. (1976). *Human ecology and cognitive style: Comparative studies in cultural and psychological adaptation*. New York: Sage-Halsted.

Boykin, A. W. (1983). The academic performance of Afro-American children. In J. T. Spence (Ed.), *Achievement and achievement motives: Psychological and sociological approaches*. New York: Freeman.

Cohen, R. A. (1969). Conceptual styles, cultural conflict, and nonverbal tests of intelligence. *American Anthropologist, 71*, 828–856.

Coleman, J. S., Campbell, E. Q., Hobson, C. J., McPartland, J., Mood, A. M., Weinfeld, F. D., & York, R. L. (1966). *Equality of educational opportunity*. U.S. Department of Health, Education, and Welfare. Washington, DC: Government Printing Office.

Dershowitz, A. (1971). Jewish subcultural patterns and psychological differentiation. *International Journal of Psychology, 6*, 223–231.

Deutsch, M. (1967). The disadvantaged child and the learning process. In M. Deutsch (Ed.), *The disadvantaged child: Selected papers of Martin Deutsch and Associates*. New York: Basic.

Deutsch, M., Katz, I., & Jensen, A. R. (Eds.). (1968). *Social class, race, and psychological development*. New York: Holt, Rinehart & Winston.

Dyk, R. B., & Witkin, H. A. (1965). Family experiences related to the development of differentiation in children. *Child Development, 36*, 21–55.

Feldman, D. (1973). Problems in the analysis of patterns of abilities. *Child Development, 44*, 12–18.

Ferguson, G. A. (1954). On learning and human ability. *Canadian Journal of Psychology, 8*, 95–112.

Flaugher, R. L. (1971). *Project Access research report No. 2: Patterns of test performance by high school students of four ethnic identities* (RB 71–25 & RDR 70–71, No. 9). Princeton, NJ: Educational Testing Service.

Gardner, R. W., Jackson, D. N., & Messick, S. J. (1960). Personality organization in cognitive controls and intellectual abilities. New York: International Universities Press. (*Psychological Issues, 2[4]*, Monograph 8.)

Gross, M. (1967). *Learning readiness in two Jewish groups*. New York: Center for Urban Education.

Hess, R. D., Shipman, V., & Jackson, D. (1965). Early experience and the socialization of cognitive modes in children. *Child Development, 36*, 869–886.

Jackson, D. N. (1957). Intellectual ability and mode of perception. *Journal of Consulting Psychology, 21*, 458.

Jensen, A. R. (1968). Patterns of mental ability and socioeconomic status. *Proceedings of the National Academy of Science, 60,* 1330–1337.

Jensen, A. R. (1971). Do schools cheat minority children? *Educational Research, 14,* 3–28.

Jensen, A. R. (1973). Level I and Level II abilities in three ethnic groups. *American Educational Research Journal, 4,* 263–276.

Jensen, A. R. (1974). Interaction of Level I and Level II abilities with race and socioeconomic status. *Journal of Educational Psychology, 66,* 99–111.

Jensen, A. R. (1980). *Bias in mental testing.* New York: Free Press.

Jensen, A. R., & Inouye, A. R. (1980). Level I and Level II abilities in Asian, white, and black children. *Intelligence, 4,* 41–49.

Jensen, A. R., & Reynolds, C. R. (1982). Race, social class and ability patterns on the WISC-R. *Personality and Individual Differences, 3,* 423–438.

Jones, L. V. (1984). White–black differences: The narrowing gap. *American Psychologist, 39,* 1207–1213.

Katz, I. (1967). Some motivational determinants of racial differences in intellectual achievement. *International Journal of Psychology, 2,* 1–12.

Laosa, L. M. (1978). Maternal teaching strategies in Chicano families of varied educational and socioeconomic levels. *Child Development, 49,* 1129–1135.

Laosa, L. M. (1980). Maternal teaching strategies in Chicano and Anglo-American families: The influence of culture and education on maternal behavior. *Child Development, 51,* 759–765.

Laosa, L. M. (1982). School, occupation, culture, and family: The impact of parental schooling on the parent–child relationship. *Journal of Educational Psychology, 74,* 791–827.

Laosa, L. M. (1984). Ethnic, socioeconomic, and home language influences upon early performance on measures of ability. *Journal of Educational Psychology, 76,* 1178–1198.

Lesser, G. S. (1973). Problems in the analysis of patterns of abilities: A reply. *Child Development, 44,* 19–20.

Lesser, G. S. (1976). Cultural differences in learning and thinking styles. In S. Messick (Ed.), *Individuality in learning: Implications of cognitive styles and creativity for human development.* San Francisco: Jossey-Bass.

Lesser, G. S., Fifer, F., & Clark, H. (1965). Mental abilities of children from different social-class and cultural groups. *Monographs of the Society for Research in Child Development, 30* (Whole No. 4).

Marjoribanks, K. (1972). Environment, social class and mental abilities. *Journal of Educational Psychology, 63,* 103–109.

Messick, S. (1984). The nature of cognitive styles: Problems and promise in educational practice. *Educational Psychologist, 19,* 59–74.

Ramirez, M., & Castaneda, A. (1974). *Cultural democracy: Biocognitive development and education.* New York: Academic Press.

Ramirez, M., & Price-Williams, D. R. (1974). Cognitive styles of children of three ethnic groups in the United States. *Journal of Cross-Cultural Psychology, 5,* 212–219.

Report of the Advisory Panel on the Scholastic Aptitude Test Score Decline. (1977). College Entrance Examination Board.

Reynolds, C. R., & Jensen, A. R. (1983). WISC-R subscale patterns of abilities of blacks and whites matched on full scale IQ. *Journal of Educational Psychology, 75,* 207–214.

Shade, B. J. (1982). Afro-American cognitive style: A variable in school success? *Review of Educational Research, 52,* 219–244.

Sitkei, E. G., & Meyers, C. E. (1969). Comparative structure of intellect in middle- and lower-class four-year-olds of two ethnic groups. *Developmental Psychology, 1,* 592–604.

Stodolsky, S. S., & Lesser, G. S. (1967). Learning patterns in the disadvantaged. *Harvard Educational Review, 37,* 546–593.

Time magazine. (1984, May 14). A threat to the future.

Vernon, P. A. (1981). Level I and Level II: A review. *Educational Psychologist, 16,* 45–64.

Vernon, P. E. (1972). The distinctiveness of field independence. *Journal of Personality, 40,* 366–391.

Vernon, P. E. (1982). *The abilities and achievements of Orientals in North America.* New York: Academic Press.

Wainer, H. (1984). An exploratory analysis of performance on the SAT. *Journal of Educational Measurement, 21,* 81–91.

Whiteman, M., & Deutsch, M. (1968). Social disadvantage as related to intellective and language development. In M. Deutsch, I. Katz, & A. R. Jensen (Eds.), *Social class, race, and psychological development.* New York: Holt, Rinehart & Winston.

Willerman, L. (1979). *The psychology of individual and group differences.* New York: Freeman.

Witkin, H. A. (1967). A cognitive style approach to cross-cultural research. *International Journal of Psychology, 2,* 233–250.

Witkin, H. A., & Berry, J. W. (1975). Psychological differentiation in cross-cultural perspective. *Journal of Cross-Cultural Psychology, 6,* 4–87.

Witkin, H. A., Dyk, R. B., Faterson, H. F., Goodenough, D. R., & Karp, S. A. (1962). *Psychological differentiation.* New York: Wiley.

Witkin, H. A., & Goodenough, D. R. (1981). *Cognitive styles: Essence and origins – Field dependence and field independence.* New York: International University Press.

Cigdem Kagitcibasi and Isik Savasir

Introduction

This chapter reviews research in human abilities assessment in the Eastern Mediterranean region and attempts to evaluate this research in terms of its general contribution to a basic understanding of the structure and relations of human abilities. It covers a sample of studies conducted mostly within the last 10 to 15 years, although some go back to the 1950s. The chapter reviews work mainly from Israel, Turkey, Greece, and Yugoslavia and is necessarily selective rather than comprehensive in its coverage. It nevertheless presents a general picture of psychological research on human abilities in a particular cultural context. Issues of theoretical significance in cross-cultural assessment are discussed whenever relevant to the work under consideration.

A number of problems were encountered in preparing this chapter, which required certain decisions about delimiting its scope. First, it turned out to be necessary to focus on certain topics in the vast area of human abilities, at the exclusion of others. Thus, for example, research on memory, language, and physiological correlates has not been covered. Second, a comprehensive review of all relevant research in all the countries in the area was not possible. Language and communication difficulties were the main reason. Although a thorough search of research reports and articles was conducted through major abstracts and indices, much work published in local languages could not be covered. Third, the very nature of research and the academic community in this part of the world proved to be problematic for this kind of review. Specifically, lack of communication or collaboration among the countries in the region and their researchers and the scattered nature of individual studies have made for a diffuse picture. This situation has rendered generalisation and systematisation difficult, notwithstanding the limited amount of total research conducted in the region.

As a result, coverage of Israeli and Turkish research is quite thorough, whereas the work in Greece and Yugoslavia is less well represented. This is due to better response from Israel to our enquiries and our familiarity with the Turkish research, as well as relatively greater amount of research activity in these two countries. Work in some other countries in or around the region is barely touched upon.

232

Sociocultural context

The Eastern Mediterranean region is characterised by a great deal of ethnic, religious, cultural, and historical diversity as well as heterogeneity in terms of socioeconomic development, rural–urban lifestyles, and modernisation. Such variation presents a challenge to research in human assessment, which has nevertheless disclosed some commonalities in abilities.

Cross-cultural psychologists doing research in different sociocultural contexts are mainly interested in the effects of these contexts on behaviour. So, "culture" is often conceptualised as an independent or treatment variable, albeit a quasi-experimental one (Campbell & Stanley, 1963; Sechrest, 1977), as random assignment of subjects to the different treatment conditions is not feasible. Yet, even though culture is so basic to any cross-cultural psychological work, the cross-cultural psychologist is generally far less sophisticated and knowledgeable about the cultural context than the anthropologist. There has been a growing concern with this recently as well as a call for greater sensitivity to, and improved knowledge, specification, and "unpackaging" of, "culture" (Whiting, 1976; Berry, 1979, 1980a; Greenbaum & Kugelmass, 1980; Segall, 1983; Kagitcibasi, 1984).

Similarly, a thorough understanding of the material discussed in this chapter would be greatly informed by familiarity with the Eastern Mediterranean–Middle Eastern area. Within the confines of this chapter and given the constraints of our subject matter, it is impossible to dwell upon even the most apparent characteristics of this highly complex cultural region – the site of some of the oldest historical traditions and civilisations – of great heterogeneity and complexity. In spite of religious, national, political–ideological, linguistic, and other variety, however, some significant commonalities can be detected through careful study and may, in fact, justify a comparative discussion, in a single chapter, of research within the different countries. Anthropological research has shown that in different parts of the region common experiences occur, especially in family dynamics, gender roles, child socialisation, close-knit familial, kinship, and communal networks, and social interaction patterns; and in values about honour and shame, ingroup–outgroup distinctions, feuds and solidarities. From myriad social science literature on the area, a few anthologies and special journal issues (mostly edited volumes) might be singled out, focussing on these topics, for the interested reader: Peristiany (1965, 1976a, 1976b), Sweet (1974), Black-Michaud (1975), Van Nieuwenhuijze (1977), Eickelman (1981), Kagitcibasi (1982), Bates & Rassam (1983).

Specification of these experiences and systematically relating them to observed behaviour, however, are often lacking in human assessment in the region. Thus, social class, urban–rural, ethnic, and gender differences are commonly studied, although which aspects of these environmental and dispositional variables (Irvine, 1983) predict what kinds of behaviours and why is not thoroughly examined. In other words, linkages with background variables are often established without identification of the processes underlying these linkages. Better collaboration between psychologists and anthropologists and closer attention to cultural and environmental variables would seem to be called for (Whiting, 1976; Ciborowski, 1979) as, for example, seen in the detailed cognitive anthropology of Cole, Gay, Glick, and Sharp with the Kpelle of Africa (1971) as well as in other research detailing environmental factors (e.g., Dasen, 1974; Berry, 1976; Super, 1981).

Theoretical–methodological issues

Even a cursory glance at research on human abilities in the Eastern Mediterranean shows that research has not been organised in any concerted or programmatic effort to refine or develop test theory. Rather, it has been conducted in scattered individual studies. On the whole, it has focussed on standardisation and application of tests originating in the West rather than on construction of tests in the cultural setting. Factor-analytic studies to establish construct similarity across cultures or groups are not widespread; there has been more work relating test performance to environmental variables and to gender than to other test scores and to criterion variables through concurrent and predictive validation of tests.

Thus, theory development in the region has lagged behind empirical applications, which have benefitted from advances in the technology of test administration, standardisation, and the like. Accordingly, less questioning and concern is apparent in the region regarding theoretical and methodological issues which have prevailed in the literature of cross-cultural psychology for more than a decade (as reflected, for example, in a number of conference proceedings, such as Cronbach & Drenth, 1972, Poortinga, 1977; Eckensberger, Lonner, & Poortinga, 1979; Irvine & Berry, 1983; Kagitcibasi, 1987).

There is much interest in the region, for example, about the effects of environmental factors on abilities. However not as much interest is apparent in methodological refinements necessary for the establishment of these effects. Thus, the judgments about ethnic, SES, gender, or rural–urban differences on abilities have been based mainly on group differences on subscales of a single test or series of verbal or performance tests. Although this work has provided valuable descriptive information about the effects of sociocultural, gender, and ethnic variables, differences in scores may not indicate true differences in the structure of abilities. This is because often the equivalence (Brislin, Lonner, & Thorndike, 1973; Berry, 1980b; Poortinga, 1983) of the measures used is not assured.

Similarity of factorial structures of a test in different cultural–ethnic groups and in different environments can be taken as a good indicator of test equivalence for these groups. When patterns of correlations are similar between groups, it becomes more feasible to compare their mean scores, and vice versa (Irvine & Sanders, 1972; Irvine, 1979, 1983). Factor analysis can provide information about the similarity of the pattern of intercorrelations among different groups. Despite these obvious advantages, the potential of the factor-analytic technique has not been fully exploited in research in the Eastern Mediterranean.

This lack of theoretical–methodological involvement may be due to many reasons, ranging from lack of access to adequate computer technology to an exclusive interest in applied empiricism. It also probably reflects a non-critical attitude towards the use of tests created in the West, as a part of a larger picture – that of the "traditional acquiescence" of the nonwestern psychologist (Kagitcibasi, 1984). Nevertheless, in the field of human abilities assessment more critical evaluation may be emerging than in other areas of psychology, probably because of the greater accumulation of research and application in this area.

Research areas

Orientations and instruments

The substantive areas of human abilities assessment in the region have embodied two major orientations, psychometric and cognitive. The former orientation has been manifest in testing at different age periods (infants, children, and adults); in the study of the effects of institutionalisation in infancy and childhood; in the examination of ethnic, cultural, SES, urban–rural, and sex differences; and in attempts at establishing general components of abilities. The latter orientation has marked studies of cognitive processes and cognitive style. Some recent work with applied emphasis has attempted to combine the two orientations.

Within the psychometric approach considerable research effort was initially placed on investigating the appropriateness of tests developed in the West, mostly in the United States. In this kind of research, typically a test of general, verbal, or performance abilities, is selected, translated, or adapted for the home country and its suitability is tested for a given sample. The appropriateness of the adapted test is judged usually by the examination of the distribution of the scores (closeness to normal distribution), by order of item difficulty and concordance with original norms, and, less frequently, by reliability and validity studies of the given sample. Examples of such research include the *Cattell Culture Free Test* (Togrol, 1974; Tanaltay, 1980; Camalan, 1981); the *Stanford-Binet* (Semin, 1972a, 1972b); the *Wechsler Intelligence Test for Children* (Haritos-Fatouros, 1972, 1973; Ozturk, 1974; Savasir & Sahin, 1978; Alexopoulos, 1979); the *Goodenough-Harris Drawing Test* (Georgas & Papadopoulou, 1968; Georgas & Georgas, 1972; Ucman, 1972); *Raven's Progressive Matrices* (Georgas & Georgas, 1972); the *Porteus Maze Test* (Togrol & Ozugurlu, 1974); the *Lorge–Thorndike Intelligence Test* (Miron, 1977); the *Beery Visual-Motor Integration Test* (Georgas & Georgas, 1972); the *WAIS* (Epir & Iskit, 1972); the *KIT Experimental In-*

telligence Test (Buvet, 1970); the *Analytic Intelligence Test* of Richard Meili (Semin, 1976); the *D48* (Kagitcibasi, 1972); the *Bayley Infant Scales of Mental and Motor Development* (Ozelli, 1978); the *Illinois Test of Psycholinguistic Abilities* (Paraskevopoulos, 1973, 1975, reported by Haritos-Fatouros, 1984); and the *Goldstein–Scheerer Block Design Test* (Maniou-Vakali, 1977).

In a number of the above studies considerable effort has also been put into the standardisation of widely used tests. In most standardisation studies verbal items are adapted or newly developed for the local culture and new norms are obtained. A major difficulty faced by researchers in the region is the choice of the normative sample. In countries where vast differences exist in styles of living and the complexity of the environment, especially with urban–rural or ethnic variations, having one normative sample to represent all of the diverse groups has obvious disadvantages in terms of test validity. On the other hand, having several different norms for the same test also poses difficulties. The problem of appropriateness of items sampled cannot be solved by having different norms for disadvantaged groups.

This is a serious problem in the region given the great diversity of socioeconomic development levels, modernisation, education, mass-media exposure, and the like. In fact, the diversity of experience may be greater in this part of the world than in some other areas, including western societies. For example, intrafamily status of women and values related to children have been found to change more with social change and development, and along the rural–urban dimension in this region than in Southeast Asia and the United States (Kagitcibasi, 1986). These are segments of culture which may have direct relevance to behaviours studied in human abilities assessment. Again, better delineation of such background variables is called for.

Different approaches have been used in different studies and countries in trying to deal with this issue; they range from attempts to represent different development levels and ethnic variation within one standardisation sample to the use of different norms for different populations. Thus, a representative urban sample was chosen for the standardisation of *WISC-R* for the Turkish culture (Savasir & Sahin, 1983) and a representative national sample was used in Greece (Alexopoulos, 1979); different ethnic groups were included in the normative sample of Israeli *WISC* (Ortar, 1968) and *WPPSI* (Lieblich, Ninio, & Kugelmass, 1972). The second revision of *Binet–Simon Scales* in Yugoslavia contains two sets of norms for children living in urban and rural areas (Ivic, Milinkovic, Rosandic, & Smiljanic, 1976), and in the standardisation of two nonverbal tests of intelligence (*Non-Verbal Series of Intelligence Tests* and Bujas's modification of *Raven's Progressive Matrices*) different norms were provided for boys and girls of cities, towns, and villages (Dragicevic & Momirovic, 1976); three sets of norms were given for village, *gecekondu* (shantytown), and city for the *Turkish Peabody Picture Vocabulary Test* (Katz, Onen, Demir, Uzlukaya, & Uludag, 1974); and three of the verbal subtests of *WAIS* were standardised on a representative sample of Athenians in Greece (Georgas, Vassiliou, & Katakis, 1971).

Finally, there are a few studies developing new tests for the given culture (Vassaf, 1975; Smiljanic, 1976; Stevanovic, Dragicevic, Bukvic, & Stajnberger, 1976; USYM, 1979). The major motivation for such research effort seems to be the need for instruments to aid in intellectual assessment in clinical settings and investigation of differences in structure of abilities in children from different backgrounds and SES levels.

Themes and issues

In the review that follows, research on the effects of environmental variables and gender on test scores is covered and the emerging commonalities among the countries are pointed out. Standard testing of infants and children is discussed extensively, in accordance with the research emphasis on these age groups. Factor-analytic studies of abilities and their implications are also included.

Effects of sociocultural variables on human abilities are examined with both standard testing and in studies of cognitive processes. "Cognitive style" seems to be a focal concept linking different socialisation practices with perceptual and cognitive processes. Accordingly, studies on cognitive style are reviewed.

A recently emerging line of research is concerned with intervention programmes. Several questions about the differences in abilities among groups can be answered by the results of these interventions. For example, intervention programmes may show that some ability differences reflected on test scores are in fact trivial (in the sense that they can be easily corrected), whereas some others are more persistent and require a longer training in specific skills or content areas. The intervention studies have another advantage of allowing for detailed observations of the qualitative aspects of cognitive functioning, such as cognitive strategies used in the solutions. These are also reviewed.

Infant testing

In much of the work on cognitive development of infants, standard infant tests are used, such as *Bayley Infant Scales of Motor and Mental Development, Brazelton Neonatal Assessment Scale, Brunet–Lézine Infant Test,* and the like. Less criticism is directed towards the use of common instruments in the cross-cultural comparative studies of infants than in the assessment of older children (2 years onward). Werner (1972, p. 12), in her review of infant psychomotor development, notes "a good deal could be said in favor of using the same test(s) in various cultures and attempting to tease out the causes of such differences as are found." *Bayley Infant Scales of Motor and Mental Development* were administered to samples of Turkish rural and urban children in age groups of 3, 6, 9, and 13 months (Ozelli, 1978). The rural sample was chosen from one of the more impoverished rural regions of Turkey. No significant differences between urban and rural samples were found. The mean Turkish raw scores of the mental and motor scales were comparable to mean American raw scores.

Kohen-Raz (1968), using the *Bayley Scales,* studied the development of infants from 1 to 27 months in different environments in Israel. Higher scores were obtained in comparison to the United States sample for motor behaviour at 1–4 months and for mental development at 8–15 months. Early differences in favour of Israeli infants were also reported by Horowitz et al. (1977). Up to one week, the new-borns scored higher than Americans and Uruguayan infants on orientation, consolability after crying, and self-quieting behaviour measured on *Brazelton Neonatal Assessment Scale.* No differences were found on general activity, motor maturity, and response to startle. In a longitudinal study (Smilansky, Shephatia, & Frankel, 1976) Israeli children of western and Moroccan origin were followed from 3 months to 30 months with the *Brunet–Lézine Infant Test* and at 3 to 4 years with the *Stanford–Binet.* The Moroccan-origin infants were found to be superior in overall development until the age of 18 months, but the situation was reversed from this age onward.

Werner (1972), in reviewing some 50 cross-cultural studies of the psychomotor development of infants in Africa, Asia, Oceania, Latin America, Europe, and the United States, concluded that there was a distinct acceleration of psychomotor development among samples of infants reared in traditional, preindustrial communities in Africa and Latin America. The Smilansky et al. (1976) findings are in accord with this generalisation, while no such precocity is seen in infants from rural Turkey.

The *Denver Development Screening Test* (Frankenburg & Dodds, 1967) was standardised on an urban sample of Turkish children ages ranging from 2 weeks to 4–6 years (Yalaz & Epir, 1982). Except for the somewhat later development of raising of the chin in Turkish infants, there were no consistent differences in the rate of development as compared to American norms (S. Epir, personal communication, 1983). Sex differences were minor. Social class differences, however, were consistently in favour of the more advantaged children in all areas of functioning from about 10 months onward. These differences became more marked with age, particularly in language and fine motor skills (Epir & Yalaz, 1984). The authors question the validity of the scale for lower SES groups and suggest development of two sets of norms.

Decline in the developmental quotients of children beginning around the age of 10 to 12 months and continuing throughout early childhood has been commonly shown in nonwestern cultures and lower SES groups of western cultures. The reasons underlying the common finding of shifts in early infant development have not been pursued in depth in the studies carried out in the region. For example, no concerted effort has been made to relate shifts in infants' performance to specific aspects of early child-rearing or mother–child interactions or characteristics of the tests used. Super (1981), for example, offers environmental explanations for the "precocity" of sub-Saharan infants in terms of both specific early learning experiences and the characteristics of the *Bayley Scales*: Mothers want their babies to sit and walk early and therefore provide them with much training in these skills, thus the early high scores on the *Bayley Scales*. However, as there is no training in learning skills, such as stair climbing, for example, the precocity ends at the point the scales require such skills. There may be other contributing environmental factors as well, such as the birth of a younger sibling in high fertility contexts, followed by cessation of breast feeding and the shifting of maternal attention to the new-born. Clearly more careful examination of similar contextual variables, and their possible interaction with test items, is needed for a better understanding of the relevant psychological processes involved in infant testing in the Eastern Mediterranean.

Ethnic and cultural differences

The use of standard tests to compare and contrast different cultural, ethnic, and socioeconomic groups is highly problematic. Both conceptual and methodological difficulties abound in such comparisons, some basic ones being appropriateness of the sample of behaviours chosen to be measured for each group and differential motivational factors and general orientations affecting the test situation underlying competence–performance discrepancy. Quite a few studies, nevertheless, have addressed themselves to mapping out such differences among diverse sociocultural groups in Eastern Mediterranean countries. Studies of this kind can be beneficial when treated as descriptive data to lay the groundwork for hypothesis formation and more thorough examination of the different psychological processes at work. Greenbaum and Kugelmass (1980), who have extensively reviewed the research conducted with standardised tests in Israel, note that such research deals mainly with the pattern of intellectual abilities in different cultural groups. The process of immigration, diverse ethnic group composition, and the presence of unique social institutions such as kibbutzim provide Israeli psychologists with opportunities to study the effects of different cultures on abilities. In general, two kinds of comparisons have been made in the comparative studies of different ethnic groups: (1) comparisons between Jewish populations of eastern (traditional) and western origin; (2) comparisons between Arab and Jewish groups.

Ortar (1953) compared western, native eastern, and immigrant eastern children using various intelligence tests, including the *Hebrew Standardisation of WISC*. Overall comparisons yielded results indicating higher performance of western Jews. However, no differences were found in verbal abstraction – a factor formerly thought to be the major contributor of low performance of eastern children (Frankenstein, 1953). Although no great differences were observed in verbal tests, compared with the American norms, Israeli children scored 11 IQ points below average level in all performance tests.

In another study, Ortar (1958) reported significant differences in intelligence levels (*WISC*) of immigrant and Israeli-born children of the same ethnic origin in favour of the latter. The inappropriateness of the *WISC* performance IQ for comparisons and the distinct effects of cultural factors on achievement in performance scales were again noted.

Among primary school graduates immigrant children from Oriental countries scored lowest on achievement tests of arithmetic, language skills, and the like. However, differences in comparison to western Israelis decreased in the second generation. Furthermore, significant correlations were found between fathers' country of origin, education of the fathers, and the children's achievement scores. When the fathers' education was held even roughly constant, ethnic group differences decreased markedly (Ortar, 1967). In a later research Reeb (1976) also found ethnic differences to decrease when SES was controlled among young adults. On the basis of experience with the standardisation of *WISC*, an adaptation of *Lorge–Thorndike Scales,* together with research findings indicating low discriminatory power of performance scales in Israel, Ortar (1972) claims that verbal scales are more appropriate and valid as measures of general intelligence especially for the disadvantaged groups. Language, along with numbers, is seen as the one parameter common to all cultures as a means of communication. This conclusion is quite different from the commonly held convention, based on empirical work in the West, about the greater sensitivity of verbal scales to social class differences.

Ortar's view is supported by research in other Eastern Mediterranean countries. Adaptation of *WISC* to a Greek sample of 9- , 10- , and 14-year-olds shows a consistent difference between verbal and performance IQs in favour of verbal IQ (Haritos-Fatouros, 1972). *Performance Object Assembly* scales, in particular, were found to be less reliable than verbal scales. Savasir and Sahin (1982) found similar trends in the standardisation of *WISC-R* for urban Turkish children. Independent scoring of children was made according to American and Turkish norms. On the average, American norms assigned 12 points less to Turkish children in performance IQ. This difference is strikingly similar to the one reported by Ortar (1953). A similar verbal-performance discrepancy was found even with a sample of university students in Turkey (Epir & Iskit, 1972). Furthermore, although verbal IQ was correlated with general academic achievement, the correlation between achievement level and performance IQ was insignificant. Reliability coefficients of performance tests were also much lower than verbal subtests, the lowest being the *Picture Arrangement* test.

Recently, there has been a renewed interest in studying pattern differences in Israel using *Wechsler* tests. Dershowitz and Frankel (1975) administered the Israeli edition of *WISC* (Ortar, 1968), scored according to Wechsler (1949) norms. Comparisons were made separately for children at below average, average, and high intelligence levels. In each group, three of the performance tests (*Picture Completion, Block Design,* and *Object Assembly*) were found to be below the mean of all subtests for its own group. Lieblich et al. (1972) examined preschool urban children of different ethnic origin and SES using Israeli standardisation of *WPPSI*. Higher scores were earned by western-origin Israelis as compared to children from eastern families. Contrary to the findings of studies using *WISC,* no verbal-performance discrepancy was found. It is to be noted, however, that no comparisons were made with the original norms of *WPPSI*. Similar results using *WPPSI* were reported by Gross (1978) among higher SES preschoolers. No verbal-performance differences were found, but children of European origin scored higher than those of African origin. In another study (Kugelmass, Lieblich, & Bossik, 1974) using the *WPPSI,* systematic relative superiority of verbal over performance IQ was found among Arab village children. These results were further supported by data later collected from a representative sample of Arab children using *WISC-R* (Lieblich & Kugelmass, 1981). The discrepancy of verbal and performance mean IQs were maximal when the child was entering school and remained significant through 11 years of age.

Review of research on effects of ethnic and cultural background on test performance suggests some possible conclusions. First, differential effect of ethnic origin on overall test performance decreases when SES is taken into consideration. Second, there appears to be a general trend in Eastern Mediterranean countries towards better use of verbal than of nonverbal skills. Verbal-performance discrepancy seems to be even more pronounced in the disadvantaged groups, although studies on immigrant populations indicate that the differences tend to diminish in subsequent generations.

Certain clues towards an explanation of the latter conclusion might be found in the differential traditional-cultural emphases on verbal and nonverbal skills. In this region, compared with the West, there is much less emphasis put on using blocks, Lego-type toys, mazes, and, in general, construction or building types of toys or paper-and-pencil materials involving geometric designs, shapes, symbols, and so on, in child-oriented activities consciously aimed at the child's cognitive development. Especially in the disadvantaged areas children have very limited experience with manipulating objects, parts of objects, abstract forms, and shapes to form wholes. If they have any toys at all, they are usually of a "make-believe" type, such as dolls or trucks. In contrast, children are exposed from early ages to verbal skills, as they are constantly in the company of adults in shared spaces rather than being isolated in private rooms. Furthermore, verbal skills are often encouraged and valued in small traditional communities in public performances, riddle competitions, jokes, and the like, forming altogether a rich verbal tradition, as also noted by Greenbaum and Kugelmass (1980, p. 111). Finally, even children in the disadvantaged areas are exposed to the mass media, which may have further equalising effect on verbal skills.

Environmental variables and gender

Lower performance of low SES groups are repeatedly reported in studies carried out in western societies; similar trends are also noted in the Eastern Mediterranean. Especially relevant in this region are also the differences between rural and urban populations. Vast differences exist in lifestyles between cities and villages, especially in the developing countries of the region. Gender differences have also been studied, but results obtained do not parallel those from western countries. There appears to be an interaction between SES, urban–rural residence, and the sex of the subject, such that in more traditional and less-developed settings where sexual roles are more clearly defined and differentially valued, greater sex differences are noted in the performance of a variety of tasks. As mentioned before, especially in sex roles and women's status dramatic differences obtain between urban–rural areas and SES levels, more marked than in many other parts of the world. This is commonly seen in the region across national and religious boundaries (Denich, 1974; Peristiany, 1965, 1976a, 1976b; Kagitcibasi, 1982, 1986) and appears to be characteristic of the total area.

In Yugoslavia, sex differences were noted on the *Second Belgrade Revision of Binet–Simon Scales*. The performance of boys both from the city and from the country was superior to that of girls for almost all age levels. Analysis of each test for sex differences indicated that 12 tests were easier for boys and 2 for girls in the urban centre; in the rural sample 10 tests were easier for boys and none was for girls (Smiljanic, 1980). Also, earlier, sex differences were found in two nonverbal tests of intelligence, boys being superior to girls (Dragicevic & Momirovic, 1976).

Consistent urban–rural differences are noted by Yugoslav investigators in standardisation studies of several intelligence scales (Ivic, Milinkovic, Rosandic, & Smiljanic, 1976; Dragicevic & Momirovic, 1976), which led them to develop separate norms. Effects of SES on *Binet–Simon Scale* were also found to be significant for ages 4 to 9, while no differences were observed at age 10, probably due to the equalising effects of education (Rosandic & Bukvic, 1970).

Similar trends emerge in Turkey, also. Kagitcibasi (1979) in a study of fifth graders from five different environments found overall socioeconomic development to explain 40% of the variance in *Goodenough Draw-a-Man Test* performance, using a multiple regression design. A dramatic linear progression was obtained from most remote rural villages to urban middle-class groups. An earlier normative study of *Goodenough–Harris Drawing Test* (Ucman, 1972) also found significant SES differences. Sex differences were also obtained in the latter study, favouring girls. A third study utilising pictorial materials (Katz, et al., 1974) obtained urban (shantytown)–rural differences in children constituting the standardisation sample for the *Peabody Picture Vocabulary Test*. No sex differences were found. Similarly, no sex differences were obtained in an urban centre on the performance of the *Bender-Gestalt Visual Motor Test* (Yalin, 1974). However, in a rural sample sex differences emerged favouring boys on the same test, while for both sexes higher error scores were obtained compared with the urban sample (Yasar, Aldemir, & Yalin, 1974). This specific finding appears to reflect the urban–rural variation in women's status just mentioned, and the corresponding different environmental demands on male and female children in these contexts.

Comparison of children in high, middle, and lower SES groups in the Turkish *WISC-R* standardisation sample showed consistent differences in verbal, performance, and full-scale IQs favouring higher SES groups for all age levels, 6 through 13. After age 13, differences diminished for children in school (Savasir & Sahin, 1982). SES differences were also noted in studies using *Cattell 2A* and *Benton Visual Retention Test* with adults (Gokhan, Binyildiz, Gurses, & Arman, 1975; Karaboncuk & Palabiyikoglu, 1975). Finally, in a large-scale study conducted with *National University Entrance Examinations* in Turkey, composed of a general ability scale and achievement scales, sociocultural variables accounted for 30% of the variance in a multiple regression design (USYM, 1978).

Similarly, in Greece significant SES and urban–rural differences are found (Georgas & Georgas, 1972; Haritos-Fatouros, 1972, 1973, 1984; Alexopoulos, 1979). Significant correlations between SES and scores on a Vocabulary Test, the *Goodenough-Harris Drawing Test*, the *Visual-Motor Integration Test*, and *Raven's Progressive Matrices* were reported in a sample of 227 children, ages 6–12 (Georgas & Georgas, 1972). Sex differences were also observed; however, no information on interaction of sex with SES is provided. Boys scored higher than girls on Vocabulary, the *Visual-Motor Integration Test*, and *Raven's Progressive Matrices*. Girls scored higher on *Draw-a-Woman Test* (similar to Ucman's [1972] finding in Turkey). Sex differences favouring males on all *WISC* subtests were also noted by Haritos-Fatouros (1972) for children and by Georgas et al. (1971) on three verbal subtests of *WAIS* on an Athenian sample of adults. The results are attributed to the advantageous position of males in society (Georgas et al., 1971; Haritos-Fatouros, 1984).

SES differences are also commonly found in Israel (Lieblich et al., 1972; Lieblich, Kugelmass, & Erlich, 1975; Reeb, 1976). No SES differences are obtained by Weller and Levi (1981), however, using the *Lorge-Thorndike Intelligence Test* with a sample of eighth graders. Higher age level of the schooled subjects possibly reflects the equalising effect of education.

Ortar (1967) noted sex differences in favour of boys with the greatest difference for eastern children. No sex differences were observed, however, in a kibbutz setting, where children perceive their sex roles as similar and equal (Gross, 1978). Shanan and Sagiv (1982) studied sex differences in intellectual performance of a middle-aged group. Although the overall comparisons yielded results favouring men, a strong differential effect of social status was also noted.

In general, these results suggest that on both verbal and nonverbal tests rural and lower SES subjects score lower than urban and higher SES subjects, differences being more pronounced with nonverbal tests. Advanced school attendance appears to make up for the disadvantage of lower SES in urban contexts, although not necessarily at lower grades and rural areas (Kagitcibasi, 1979). Sex differences are more pronounced in rural and low SES groups. The general western finding regarding the relative superiority of females on verbal tasks and of males on spatial-mechanical tasks does not hold for the Eastern Mediterranean any more than it does in Africa (see Chapter 1). In groups with clear-cut sex roles and differential sex-role status, as found in traditional rural, low SES contexts, boys outperform girls on both types of tasks. On the other hand, in relatively equalitarian environments sex differences diminish.

Components of abilities

In the assessment of abilities it is often more meaningful to compare general dimensions rather than specific content, using diverse instruments (Irvine, 1983). Through factor analysis and similar statistical techniques a number of variables can be reduced to fewer theoretical constructs or dimensions on the basis of associations among them, providing parsimony and facilitating inferences and interpretations. However, there are also difficulties in comparing the results of studies using these techniques, such as large variations in composition and size of the samples, and the number of tasks or tests used.

A factor-analytic study of *WISC-R* was conducted in Turkey (Sahin, 1983). In the *WISC-R* standardisation sample the principal components factor analysis yielded a single general factor accounting for 66.4% of the total variance; all subtests had high loadings on this factor. On the basis of separate factor analyses by age groups, however, a different pattern was obtained. In all age groups studied (6–15) two factors consistently emerged which are labelled Verbal Comprehension and Perceptual Organisation. The existence of a third factor, labelled Distractibility, was observed between age groups 11–15. The Verbal Comprehension factor is found to be stronger in all age groups included in the analyses (accounting for not less than 50% of the total variance).

In factor-analytic studies conducted on the *WISC-R* standardisation sample in the United States, two factors were identified (Kaufman, 1975). Compared to the U.S. findings, the results obtained from the Turkish sample suggest that differentiation of abilities is somewhat delayed and/or solution strategies used are more global and rely more heavily upon verbal skills.

The results of factor analysis fit in with the previously reported finding of relative difficulty of performance tests for Turkish subjects, as well as similar findings from Greece and Israel, especially among disadvantaged groups. A similar study was carried out with *WISC* in a Greek sample of children ages 9 through 16 (Haritos-Fatouros, 1972, 1973). Four oblique factors were obtained by Tyron–Bailey cluster analysis. The first was a general factor accounting for 68% of the total variance, very similar to the one obtained in the Turkish sample, that is, a robust Verbal factor. The second factor was labelled a Spatial factor with high loadings on some of the performance and verbal subtests. The third and fourth factors accounted for little variance and were labelled Freedom from Distractibility and Numerical Facility, respectively.

Configurations of intercorrelations for the Jewish and Arab samples were studied by Guttman–Lingoes nonmetric smallest space analysis using *WPPSI* subtest scores in Israel (Kugelmass et al., 1974). Performance and verbal tests appeared to be located in two different space zones for the two samples to suggest the existence of two factors. Some difference in the Arab and Jewish configurations was observed, interpreted as greater reliance of Arab children on verbal means. The results of factor-analytic studies lend further support to findings regarding relative superiority of verbal subtests in the region, discussed in the previous section. Guttman and Guttman (1963) examined intercorrelations of achievement scores of Israeli-born children from different ethnic groups (family origins of Iraq, Iran, Europe, and North Africa). The same simplex pattern of intercorrelations was observed in each group despite variations in the mean scores. The simplex pattern was interpreted as reflecting the cross-cultural invariance of structure of abilities. In a later study, Guttman and Shonan (1979) used a similar analysis to study the pattern of abilities in families. The structure of intercorrelations among scores of tests was found to be the same for fathers, mothers, and children.

Factor-analytic studies in Yugoslavia seem to be geared to the delineation of factors when large numbers of tests are used. In a study investigating numerical abilities, factor analysis of 21 numerical, 3 verbal, and 3 figural tests yielded 3 numerical factors labelled Numerical Ease, Numerical Reasoning, and Numerical Transformation for 13-year-olds (Kovacevic, 1973). Likewise, Bukvic and Kovacevic (1976) applied 26 verbal tests to 13- to 14-year-olds. In addition to the formerly obtained general verbal factor, two additional verbal factors were identified in the Serbo-Croatian linguistic area. Bukvic, Stojanovski, and Kostarova (1979) compared the same verbal tests in different regions of Yugoslavia where different languages are spoken, and found the Macedonian sample to yield a more complex factorial structure.

Finally, a factor-analytic study was performed on musical ability and its association with general intelligence (Mirkovic, 1983). A stable and significant but small degree of correlation between basic musical abilities and verbal aspects of general intelligence was found for musically unselected populations in younger ages. In the older groups (secondary school) differentiations of abilities were observed, musical appreciation–type tests forming a separate factor. For the selected sample of music school pupils, a separate musical factor relatively independent of intelligence was obtained.

As mentioned, although factor analysis is used in some research, it is not a widely used technique in the Eastern Mediterranean except in Yugoslavia, where theoretically and practically meaningful dimensions have been delineated in different abilities. In general, the technique is used in standardisation efforts, for comparison between the ability structures of the local culture and the original culture from which the test has been adapted. A basic similarity of the intellectual abilities among cultures can be advocated on the basis of the results of the factor-analytic studies; similarities of factorial structures are also evident within the region.

Cognitive processes

A general course of study in human abilities has aimed at specifying basic cognitive structures and processes, and the most important theoretical framework in this area has been Piaget's formulations of cognitive development. Psychologists working in the piagetian framework have asked the basic questions of "how the child gets to know about his world, how he develops basic scientific concepts and how reasoning obeys certain structural properties which can be described by models drawn from logic and mathematics" (Dasen, 1972, p. 23). Universality of development stages and their structural properties and within-stage sequencing have been subjects of major research interest. In the Eastern Mediterranean *conservation of quantity, weight* and *volume, seriation, class inclusion,* and *multiple classification* are the most frequently studied topics. The emphasis on concrete operations, and specifically on conservation, parallels that of research in the rest of the world (Dasen, 1972, 1977).

Conservation studies with urban middle-class children in the region obtained acquisition ages similar to the western norms. Thus, a study examining the development of conservation of quantity, weight, and volume in middle-class Turkish children using both liquid and clay as materials (Ataman & Bayraktar, 1971) showed that the type of material did not affect the acquisition age, which was similar to the age levels found in western cultures. Conservation of quantity and weight was acquired about the same age level and volume later. A similar study was conducted with Yugoslavian children in Belgrade, ages ranging from 5 to 9 (Ivic, 1976). No conservation was observed at age 6, conservation of quantity with discontinuous quantities was obtained at ages 7–8, and conservation of quantity with continuous quantities and of weight, at ages 8–9 years. Again age of acquisition was similar to that of other western countries. Similarly, school children in Teheran (Mohseni, cited in Piaget, 1974), in Shiraz, Iran (Bat-Hace & Hosseini, 1971), and in Beirut (Za'rour, 1971) developed conservation of quantity, weight, and volume at approximately the same time as Europeans.

When compared with middle or higher SES children living in cities, rural children in the region generally show delayed acquisition of conservation concepts, much like the lower SES children in western countries. Mohseni (cited in Piaget, 1974) reported a systematic time lag of 2 to 3 years among illiterate rural children in Iran. Similarly, a study conducted in a mountain village near Ankara using the same research strategy and materials as reported by Ataman and Bayraktar (1971) yielded results indicating that village children were 1 to 2 years delayed in acquiring conservation of quantity, weight, and volume (Canborgil, 1973). Again, quantity and weight were acquired at the same age. However, conservation tasks were found to be easier when water was used as material. In this village, children are expected to carry water in buckets from the village fountain and thus have more experience with quantity and weight of water.

A number of studies examined cognitive processes among children who have moved from underdeveloped rural areas to urban centres. Conflicting results have been obtained regarding gains through changing lifestyles. The results are not comparable as there is much uncontrolled variation both in the use of materials and the ages of subjects as well as in the age at migration, length of stay, and the level of living in the urban context, and so on. Thus, a study showing the positive impact of migration (Peluffo, 1967) found that only 30% of children ages 11–12 living in an underdeveloped region of Sardinia could conserve volume, whereas 40% of the 9-year-olds who had immigrated from southern Italy to Geneva showed volume conservation.

On the other hand, Heron and Dowel (1974) found no such positive impact. They investigated conservation of number, quantity, weight, and volume as well as seriation, class inclusion, and multiple classification in recently immigrated Yugoslav children in Australia, ranging in age from 9 to 12½. These children originally came from lower class urban and rural families. Only 55% succeeded in conserving weight, indicating that they were 2 years behind Genevan norms. The same sample was reexamined 2 years later (Heron, Gardner, & Grieve, 1977). The performance of the Yugoslav retest group was 2 to 4 years retarded on conservation of both weight and volume in comparison with Genevan norms, at the level of Australian children who were 2 years younger.

Aspects of concrete operational behaviour other than conservation are also investigated. In the above-mentioned study by Heron and Dowel (1974) the majority of the Yugoslav children displayed operational performance on seriation and class inclusion, but the overall percentage of operational responses was much lower for multiple classification. The relationship between conservation performance and other aspects of concrete operational behaviour was also examined. One-third of the nonconservers of weight were able to give operational solutions on multiple classification tasks. On the basis of these results the authors question the unity of the concrete operational stage and suggest that this stage should be construed as a set of structures without necessary interdependence.

The connection between the development-of-logic and the formation-of-number concepts was examined in a study by Yugoslav investigators (Ivic, Cvijovic, & Dimcovic, 1976). Children of 6 to 9 years old from a high SES district of Belgrade were given problems of quantity, transitivity, class inclusion, serial ordering, length, and serial correspondence. Individual problems of logical thinking proved to be of various degrees of difficulty, the most difficult being serial correspondence and class inclusion. No consistent relationship was found between the development of logical thinking and elementary mathematical knowledge across ages. Although the authors suggest that mathematical problems could be solved by perceptual and intuitive means, these results seem to support Heron and Dowel's (1974) conclusions.

Greek migrant children in Australia were tested for conservation of number and length both in English and in Greek (Kelly, Tenezakiz, & Huntsman, 1973). Of the children who had passed the language pretest and failed to conserve in English, 25% did show conservation when tested in Greek and again failed to conserve in a post-test in English. This finding is interpreted as not supporting Piaget's view on the interrelationship of language and cognition. This interpretation should be taken with caution, however, because equivalence of concepts in a new language and the mother tongue may not be assured by passing a language test. A series of studies were conducted in Turkey by Bayraktar (1979, 1980, 1982, 1983), which have implications both for Piaget's formulations on children's concept of space and also for assessment devices using children's drawings. She showed that there are contextual effects on children's drawings (ages 4 to 9), and that children have strong biases even in drawing simple lines (e.g., perpendicular error). Thus, it is argued that inspection of finished products (drawings of children) may not lead to valid and reliable inferences.

In summary, research on cognitive processes in the Eastern Mediterranean appears in accord with experimental evidence available from other cultures. Urban children acquire conservation and other concrete operational tasks at about the same age levels as children from western cultures. The research results also appear to support the notion of horizontal décalage, that is, that the sequence of quantity, weight, and volume is not invariant (no differences were found at the age of acquisition of quantity and weight in Yugoslavia and Turkey) and that not all tasks of the concrete operational stage are acquired at the same age levels. Cultural factors affect the acquisition of concrete operational tasks, rural and lower SES children showing lower performance. The type of material used appears to affect acquisition of conservation, if there is a culture-specific experience with it. Research results on the effects of migration are inconclusive, mainly because of methodological problems. Better comparative research on this issue is greatly needed, as such work promises to develop an insight into environmental impact on cognitive processes and the possibility of changes (reversibility, acceleration, etc.) in the latter.

Cognitive style

Cognitive style, psychological differentiation, and, more specifically, field dependence–independence are basic concepts in studying the individual's manner of dealing with perceptual and intellectual tasks. As evidenced by a great deal of work on this topic (e.g., Witkin, 1967; Witkin et al., 1974; Berry, 1976, 1979, 1980a; Witkin & Goodenough, 1977; Witkin, Goodenough, & Oltman, 1977), generally a field-dependent cognitive style is associated with ecological settings, close-knit familial and communal systems, and cultural norms and institutions which make for restrictive socialisation, prescribing conformity to family and social authority, whereas field-independent cognitive style is considered to be a result of socialisation practices with emphasis on individual freedom and self-reliance.

Commonly the *Embedded Figures Test* (*EFT*) and the *Rod and Frame Test* (*RFT*) are used to measure field dependency. Some of the subtests of *Wechsler* scales (*Picture Completion, Block Design* and *Picture Arrangement*) and *Draw-a-Man Test* are also found to be sensitive to cognitive styles. In general, high correlations are obtained between the two main measurements of field dependency in research conducted in the United States (Witkin, Oltman, Raskin, & Karp, 1971). However, the correlations are less consistent in studies carried out in Africa and nonwestern societies (Wober, 1967; Okonji, 1969) as well as in Israel (Handel, 1973), where the empirical equivalence of the two measures (*RFT* and *EFT*) has been questioned because they were found to share only 13% of their variance.

A number of studies in Israel attempted to compare traditional subgroups with relatively more westernised and assimilated cultural groups. Preale et al. (1970) compared young Israeli adults of Middle Eastern and western origin. The Middle Eastern family, as more tradition-oriented and having an authoritarian patriarchal structure, was hypothesised to produce more field dependence. When intelligence was controlled, Ss of western ethnic origin achieved a higher level of perceptual articulation than Ss of Middle Eastern origin. Amir (1975) contrasted a group from Iran, a group of Arabs from Israel and neighbouring countries, and two Israeli groups of Jews originating in western and Middle Eastern countries. When intelligence was controlled, the western Israeli group had higher scores than the Arabs, Iranians, and the Middle Eastern Israeli groups; no differences were found between the Muslim and Jewish Middle Eastern groups. Similar differences between western and Middle Eastern groups were found in another study in which children were assessed (Weller & Sharan, 1971). The Witkin et al. (1974) work in Italy, Holland, and Mexico provided further support for a social conformity explanation of field dependency.

High correlations have been reported between scores on measures of field dependency and success on various cognitive tasks, including piagetian-type conservation problems (Witkin et al., 1974; Witkin & Goodenough, 1977;

Witkin et al., 1977) resulting in the claim for a pervasive influence of field dependence–independence throughout cognitive behaviour. Tasks that would require an analytic approach, differentiation, and reconstruction of parts for solution would correlate highly with field independence, but no correlations would be expected with tasks that do not involve such an approach. Field independence has also been construed, however, as a multifactorial measure of nonverbal ability. Horn (1976, p. 450) asserts that "because *EFT* appears to have little reliable variance independent of *GV* (general visualization) it seems wise to drop the theory 'field independence' when the measure is *EFT*, and to direct research along the lines of identifying and distinguishing correlates and determinants of GV."

Bukvic (1980) also supports an ability conception of field dependency on the basis of a factor-analytic study in Yugoslavia. A battery of figural and verbal tests, including the *Embedded Figures Test*, was administered to a group of children, and two main factors were extracted, namely, Verbal and Figural. The *EFT* loaded on the Figural factor. However, both factors also correlated with parts of a General Intelligence factor. Eski (1980), working with 11-year-old Turkish children, found a *General Ability Test* (*GAT*) to predict academic success significantly on a multiple regression analysis, while *EFT* had no significant contribution. However, she argues that the academic achievement was composed of scores on learning a new language, thus no analytic approach was needed. Finally, in another study with Turkish children (Okman, 1979) a high correlation was obtained between *EFT* and the nonverbal intelligence test *D48*. Inconsistencies in these findings need to be explained by more research and theoretical progress in the area. In general, research findings indicate that boys score higher than girls in measures of field independence, although both Okman (1979) and Eski (1980) report no sex differences. It should be noted, however, that in both studies samples of high SES children were selected.

Field independence, whether conceived of as a cognitive style or as a dimension of general ability, appears to be associated with important environmental variables. Although some work in the Eastern Mediterranean has been done with cognitive style, its theoretical potential has hardly been exploited in this respect, and there appears to be much room for work in this area.

Problem-oriented applied focus

Given the pressing social problems in the developing countries of the Eastern Mediterranean, psychologists often feel the need and the responsibility to study these problems and to search for solutions. Although this need has always been there, its realisation and channelisation into applied intervention research is a more recent phenomenon (Kagitcibasi, 1983). Work on the effects of institutionalisation in infancy and childhood is an example of a social problem area that has interested the psychologists in the region; intervention research is another one, which has solution of the problem as its goal.

Effects of institutionalisation

An early work on effects of institutionalisation was by Dennis, who compared the development of Lebanese children in a Beirut foundling home (creche) to home-reared infants from low SES families in Beirut. Developmental quotients of creche infants dropped from 100 (at 2 months) to 63 (between 3 and 12 months) as measured on the *Cattell Infant Intelligence Test,* while home-reared infants continued having a mean DQ of 101 (Dennis & Najarian, 1963). Furthermore, whereas orphanage children adopted into private homes at very young ages (0–2) compensated for early deprivation to reach a normal intelligence level, those adopted later never completely recovered from early deterioration (Dennis, 1973). The importance of the length of exposure to the dire orphanage conditions and the possibility of a critical period in early cognitive development are implied by these findings.

Dennis (1963) also studied psychomotor development of infants in three different institutions in Teheran, one private and two public. Gross retardation of motor functions, such as sitting alone or walking, was found in children cared for at public orphanages where few opportunities for handling of infants were provided. No such retardation was observed at the private orphanage with more favourable environmental stimulation.

Kohen-Raz (1968) compared psychomotor and mental development of kibbutz, institutionalised, and home-reared infants in Israel. The institutionalised infants were again found to be significantly retarded in comparison to kibbutz and private home infants. Their mean mental ability scores dropped from 99 at age 2 months to 60 indexed on the *Bayley Scales of Infant Development.* They were also retarded on motor functioning, but the differences were not as drastic as those indicated by the mental ability scales.

The more behaviour-specific response of smiling among institutionalised, kibbutz, and middle-class home-reared infants and lower-class infants in day-care was investigated by Gewirtz and Gewirtz (1969). The institutionalised and lower-class infants in day-care had lower frequencies of smiling as compared to kibbutz and home-reared infants. Institutionalised infants reached the peak of smiling at 5 months, whereas middle-class and kibbutz children did so at 4 months. Varying amounts of social contact is thought to be responsible for the observed differences.

Several studies from Israel searched for what specifically contributes to the general retardation of institutionalised infants or differences among social classes. Observational studies of the infant, interactions of others with the infant, and the setting showed wide variations in the amount and quality of stimulation the infant is exposed to. Landau (1976, 1977) and Greenbaum and Landau (1972, 1977, 1979) provide information about infant environment and the development of the related response systems. Such research is fruitful in providing information on specific factors affecting cognitive development and lays the groundwork for initiating intervention projects.

Detrimental effects of institutionalisation are also demonstrated on children at older ages. A sample of Turkish children aged 8–11 who were institutionalised around 3 years of age were compared to home-reared children of the same SES and age levels (Yanbasti, 1974). The mean scores of institutionalised children on *Thurstone's Primary Mental Abilities Test* administered at ages 8, 9, and 10 were considerably lower than those of home-reared children. No differences were found at age 11. In a similar study (Biyikli, 1982) institutionalised boys at ages 7, 9, and 11 were compared to boys from low SES homes. Significant differences favouring home-reared children were found on the verbal, performance, and full-scale IQs of *Turkish WISC-R* for all age levels. Institutionalised boys were also found retarded on the Turkish version of the *AAMD Adaptive Behaviour Scale* (Epir, 1976).

Problem-oriented research of the kind described above does not enjoy wide recognition in cross-cultural psychology, as evidenced, for example, by scarce coverage in conference proceedings referred to previously. (The main problem-oriented applied emphasis is found in clinical/abnormal psychology, and in organisational/industrial psychology). Similarly, applied research involving "action research" or intervention is not commonly undertaken in cross-cultural work (although an early emphasis is found in Cronbach and Drenth [1972], it has not been kept up). Aside from the practical difficulties involved in doing such research, this situation is due at least partially to the common assumption of the superiority of "pure" over "applied" science, an assumption also inherited from the West. This view is untenable even in the West, where applied research has made significant contributions to scientific progress; in the context of underdevelopment, it has to be rejected outright, given the crying needs and the great potential of applied research for contributing both to development and to universal social science (Sinha, 1973; Kagitcibasi, 1984). In particular, much can be learned from research on institutionalisation, for example, about the specific effects of environmental variables for different aspects of human development.

As indicated, there is a growing realisation of this need in the nonwestern world in general and also in the Eastern Mediterranean, although the total research involvement is still very limited. From insights developed about the detrimental effects of institutional and disadvantaged environments the logical next step is intervention research, designed to alleviate the unfavourable environmental influences.

Intervention research

Most educational intervention and cognitive enrichment programmes have been carried out within the formal educational institutions (schools) or in special programmes, directed exclusively to the child, whereas some have gone beyond the institutional setting to involve the family and even the community.

An example of the former type of intervention research at later ages is a study in Yugoslavia involving a 4-year follow-up of high school students (as a part of a 20-year project). An experimental group was provided with a programme which stressed a creative approach to problem solving, while the control group received the regular curriculum. Pre- and post-test evaluations were done with batteries of verbal and nonverbal intelligence tests, creativity tests, and tests for measuring learning abilities which were subsequently factor analysed. Stable differences of long duration, especially on factors representing fluid and crystallised intelligence and on a number of more specific factors of verbal abilities, were found (Kvascev, 1981).

A rural intervention study was conducted in Turkey in a village nearby Ankara but not exposed to modernisation (Ozturk, 1974). Two groups of children (ages 4½–6) were pretested by *WPPSI* and one group was provided with an opportunity of playing with toys, paper and coloured pencil, chalk, and so on, for an average of 15 hours a week under the supervision of a nurse for 8 months. Post-testing 2 years after training showed 10–12 points increase in IQ (*WISC*) for the trained group while no differences were observed for the controls.

Effects of integration of underprivileged and lower-class children with more privileged children in schools have been studied extensively in Israel. Azri and Amir (1977), for example, contrasted educational and intellectual achievements of underprivileged children in homogeneous and integrated classrooms. Differences in favour of Ss in integrated classes were found in mathematics and nonverbal intelligence but not for verbal achievements. The latter result is probably related to the relatively higher verbal skills of disadvantaged children to start out with, as discussed before. When the effects of both integration and classroom innovation were studied (Eshel & Klein, 1978), lower-class children were found to perform best in settings characterised by both integration and classroom innovation and lowest in homogeneous settings.

Other intervention work in Israel with socially disadvantaged "high risk" immigrant adolescents, focussing on group adaptation (Feuerstein et al., 1976), and with mentally retarded socioculturally deprived adolescents, using a special "Instrumental Enrichment" programme (Feuerstein et al, 1979), produced better cognitive functioning, compared with control groups. Israel stands out in the Eastern Mediterranean, and probably in the world, together with the United States, in concern with educational research and experimentation, especially regarding disadvantaged groups (Weiss, 1971; see Peleg & Adler, 1977, for a comprehensive review of work in Israel).

However, early intervention work, especially in the United States, has often not produced lasting effects, as reversals take place when enrichment programmes end (see Kagitcibasi, 1983, for a review). Some of the "failures" of early intervention programmes that are reported in the literature appear to be due, at least partially, to the common practice, in research and application, of abstracting the child from his environment and treating him in isolation from his "natural" setting. There is much evidence of the importance of supporting the immediate social environment of the child, and especially helping the mother (Weikart, 1970; Gordon, 1975; Levenstein, 1976; Smilansky, 1979; Lombard, 1981). In general, in preschool intervention programmes initial IQ gains are achieved with exposure to the "directive cognitive" approach (Smilansky, 1979). However, if this cognitive development is not supported by the induction of corresponding growth of the child's self-confidence, autonomy, and initiative, it would not be self-sustaining after the completion of the programme. This would be especially the case if there were no fostering of the child's immediate social environment, mainly the mother, which could have provided the child with continued support. Thus, it is possible that some of the disappointing results of intervention programmes in producing lasting IQ gains or cognitive development may be due, ironically, to the exclusive concern of these programmes with cognitive growth (Kagitcibasi, 1983).

Comprehensive enrichment work involving the family-community is less common in the region, as it is more difficult to undertake. Two examples of such intervention research are ongoing work in Israel and Turkey.

The Home Instruction Programme for Pre-school Youngsters (*HIPPY*) (Lombard, 1981) is a widely known programme which started out as an experimental research project in 1969 and now involves work with 16,000 families throughout Israel. This intervention programme uses the mother as educator of her child, so that while the child is exposed to early cognitive enrichment, the mother's status and self-confidence are also raised, qualities which, in turn, help sustain an enriching environment for the child.

An intervention study, which was independently developed in Turkey (Kagitcibasi, 1983), has also incorporated the *HIPPY* programme. In addition to mother training, this longitudinal research studies the differential effects of custodial and educational day-care and home environments on the overall development of children through ages 3–9. Extensive abilities assessment is undertaken, including both psychometric and cognitive approaches, as well as time-sampled observations in homes and institutions. Paraprofessionals are used for individual home instruction as well as for group meetings of the mothers for mutual support and learning. In this way, community involvement/change is accomplished as well as changes in women's roles and self-concepts. Thus, the child is not abstracted from his or her environment but instead the environment itself is changed, for lasting mutual growth. Furthermore, not only cognitive development but overall development of the child is under focus, including the development of autonomy, self-concept, social development, and the like.

This experimental study and the *HIPPY* project are notable for a comprehensive holistic approach to child development that goes beyond the individual and extends into the family, community, and "culture," in general. They also represent a rare case of cross-national research collaboration in the Eastern Mediterranean.

Last word

This review of research on human abilities in the Eastern Mediterranean has pointed both to promising paths and to possible blind alleys; it has provided us with insights into some of the basic commonalities of behaviour as well as persistent variations; and it has made us more aware of the great cultural diversity and complexity of this region. It becomes apparent from such a review that there is a great potential in the area for theoretical development that is also ecologically and culturally relevant, given the research involvement of substantial numbers of local psychologists in the field of human abilities assessment. With greater theoretical–methodological sophistication, substantive contributions to universal social science can be made in this part of the world, rather than merely adopting contributions made somewhere else.

References

Alexopoulos, D. J. (1979). *Revision and standardization of the WISC-R for Greek children aged 13 to 15 years*. Unpublished doctoral dissertation, University College, Cardiff.

Amir, Y. (1975). Perceptual articulation in three Middle-Eastern cultures. *Journal of Cross-Cultural Psychology, 6*, 406–417.

Ataman, I., & Bayraktar, R. (1971). Cesitli yas gruplarindaki cocuklarda miktar, agirlik ve hacim korunumu (conservation) ilkesinin incelenmesi [A study of quantity, weight and volume conservation in several age groups of children]. *Hacettepe Sosyal ve Beseri Bilimer Dergisi, 3*, 127–133.

Azri, Y., & Amir, Y. (1977). Intellectual and academic achievements of underprivileged children in homogeneous and heterogeneous classrooms. *Child Development, 48*, 726–729.

Bat-Hace, M., & Hosseini, A. A. (1971). Conservation of quantity attained by Iranian elementary children in Shiraz, Iran. *Psychological Reports, 29*, 1283–1288.

Bates, D. G., & Rassam, A. (1983). *Peoples and cultures of the Middle East*. Englewood Cliffs, NJ: Prentice-Hall.

Bayraktar, R. (1979). *Children's copying errors of simple geometric figures*. Unpublished doctoral dissertation, Sussex University.

Bayraktar, R. (1980). Contextual cues and the perpendicular bias. In N. H. Freeman, *Strategies of representation in young children* (pp. 163–165, 174) New York: Academic Press.

Bayraktar, R. (1982). Zemin olarak kullanilan kagidin sekli basit geometrik sekilleri cizme yetenegini etkiliyor mu? [Does the shape of the background paper affect skill in drawing geometric shapes?]. *Psikoloji Dergisi*, 8–16.

Bayraktar, R. (1983). Dikaci hatasi ve dikeylik etkisinin kulturler arasi duzeyde dogrulanmasi [Cross-cultural validation of right angle and perpendicular effect]. *Hacettepe Edebiyat Fakultesi Dergisi*.

Berry, J. W. (1976). *Human ecology and cognitive style*. New York: Wiley.

Berry, J. W. (1979). Culture and cognitive style. In A. J. Marsella, R. G. Tharp, & T. J. Ciborowski (Eds.), *Perspectives on cross-cultural psychology* (pp. 117–135). New York: Academic Press.

Berry, J. W. (1980a). Ecological analyses for cross-cultural psychology. In N. Warren (Ed.), *Studies in cross-cultural psychology* (Vol. 2, pp. 157–189). New York: Academic Press.

Berry, J. W. (1980b). Introduction to methodology. In H. C. Triandis & J. W. Berry (Eds.), *Handbook of cross-cultural psychology* (Vol. 2). Boston: Allyn & Bacon.

Biyikli, L. (1982). *Yetistirme yurduna yuvadan gelen 7–11 yas cocuklarinin zihinsel ve psikososyal gelisimlerinin incelenmesi* [A study of cognitive and psychosocial development of 7–11-year-olds with orphanage background]. Unpublished habilitation thesis, Ankara.

Black-Michaud, J. (1975). *Cohesive force: Feud in the Mediterranean and the Middle East.* New York: St. Martin's.

Brislin, R. W., Lonner, W. J., & Thorndike, R. M. (Eds.). (1973). *Cross-cultural research methods.* New York: Wiley.

Bukvic, A. (1980). Models of the theory of the dependent-independent field in verbal abilities. *Psikoloska Istrazivanja 2,* 86–87. Institut za Psikologiju, Belgrade.

Bukvic, A., & Kovacevic, P. (1976). Factor and logical approach in psychological analysis of verbal ability tests [English summary]. *Psikologija, 3–4,* 112.

Bukvic, A., Stojanovski, Z., & Kostarova, L. (1979). Two factor analyses of verbal ability tests adapted to Macedonian language [English summary]. *Psikologija, 1,* 18–19.

Buvet, F. (1970). Kit exp. zeka testinin 8 yasindaki yuz Turk cocuguna tatbiki [Application of Kit exp. intelligence test to 100 Turkish children]. *Istanbul Universitesi Tecrubi Psikoloji Calismalari,* 57–61.

Camalan, M. (1981). Cattell kultur etkilerinden arinmis zeka olcegi 7–12 yas gruplari arasinda standardizasyonu, cozum strateji analizlari [The standardisation and analysis of strategies of the Cattell culture-free test with 7–12-year-olds]. Unpublished thesis, Psikoloji Kursusu, Ankara Universitesi.

Campbell, D. T., & Stanley, J. C. (1963). *Experimental and quasi-experimental designs for research.* Chicago: Rand McNally.

Canborgil, F. (1973). *Koy ortamindaki cocuklarda miktar, agirlik ve hacim korunumunun gelismesi ve anne tutumu ile iliskisi.* [The development of quantity, weight and volume conservation in rural children and its relation to mothers' attitudes]. Unpublished master's thesis, Hacettepe Universitesi, Psikoloji Bolumu, Ankara.

Ciborowski, T. J. (1979). Cross-cultural aspects of cognitive functioning: Culture and knowledge. In A. J. Marsella, R. G. Tharp, & T. J. Ciborowski (Eds.), *Perspectives on Cross-cultural Psychology.* (pp. 101–116). New York: Academic Press.

Cole, M., Gay, J., Glick, J., & Sharp, D. W. (1971). *The cultural context of learning and thinking.* New York: Basic.

Cronbach, L. J. C., & Drenth, P. J. D. (Eds.). (1972). *Mental tests and cultural adaptation.* The Hague: Mouton.

Dasen, P. R. (1972). Cross cultural Piagetian research: A summary. *Journal of Cross-Cultural Psychology, 3,* 23–39.

Dasen, P. R. (1974). The influence of ecology, culture and European contact on cognitive development in Australian Aborigines. In J. W. Berry & P. R. Dasen (Eds.), *Culture and cognition: Readings in cross-cultural psychology* (pp. 381–408), London: Methuen.

Dasen, P. R. (1977). Are cognitive processes universal? A contribution to cross-cultural piagetian psychology. In N. Warren (Ed.), *Studies in cross-cultural psychology* (Vol. 1, pp. 155–201). New York: Academic Press.

Denich, B. (1974). Sex and power in the Balkans. In M. Z. Rosaldo & L. Lamphere (Eds.), *Women, culture and society* (pp. 243–262). Stanford, CA: Stanford University Press.

Dennis, W. (1963). Environmental influences upon motor development. In W. Dennis (Ed.), *Readings in child psychology* (2nd ed., pp. 83–94). Englewood Cliffs, NJ: Prentice-Hall.

Dennis, W. (1973). *Children of the creche.* East Norwalk, CN: Appleton-Century-Crofts.

Dennis, W., & Najarian, P. (1963). Development under environmental handicap. In W. Dennis (Ed.), *Readings in child psychology* (2nd ed., pp. 315–331). Englewood Cliffs, NJ: Prentice-Hall.

Dershowitz, Z., & Frankel, Y. (1975). Jewish culture and WISC and WAIS test patterns. *Journal of Consulting and Clinical Psychology, 43,* 126–134.

Dragicevic, E., & Momirovic, K. (1976). The standardization of nsi and rbm on the territory of the Socialist Republic of Serbia. *Psikoloska Istrazivanja* (p. 399). Belgrade: Institut za Psikilogiju.

Eckensberger, L., Lonner, W., & Poortinga, Y. H. (Eds.), (1979). *Cross-cultural contributions to psychology*. Lisse: Swets & Zeitlinger.

Eickelman, D. F. (1981). *The Middle East: An anthropological approach*. Englewood Cliffs, NJ: Prentice-Hall.

Epir, S. (1976). *Ilkckul cocuklari icin AAMD uyumsal davranis skalasi (1974 revizyonu) Turkce adaptasyon* [Turkish adaptation of AAMD adaptive behaviour scale (1974 revision) for primary school children]. Milli Egitim Bakanligi, Talim ve Terbiye Dairesi, Ankara.

Epir, S., & Iskit, U. (1972). Wechsler yetiskinler zeka olcegi Turkce cevirisinin on analizi ve universite danismanlik merkezlerindeki uygulama potensiyeli. [Preliminary analysis of the Turkish translation of the Wechsler Adult Intelligence Scale and its applicability in university consulting centres]. *Hacettepe Sosyal ve Beseri Bilimler Dergisi, 4*, 198–205.

Epir, S., & Yalaz, K. (1984). Urban Turkish children's performance on the Denver Developmental Screening Test. *Developmental Medicine and Child Neurology, 26*, 632–643.

Eshel, J., & Klein, Z. (1978). The effects of integration of open education on mathematics achievement in the early primary grades in Israel. *American Educational Research Journal, 15*(2), 319–323.

Eski, R. (1980). *Genel yetenek, psikilojik ayrisiklik ve akademik basari arasindaki iliskiler* [Relations among general ability, psychological differentiation, and academic achievement]. Unpublished doctoral dissertation, Hacettepe Universitesi, mezuniyet sonrasi egitimi fakultesi, Ankara.

Feuerstein, R., et al. (1976). The effects of group care on the psychosocial habilitation of immigrant adolescents in Israel, with special reference to high risk children. *International Review of Applied Psychology, 25*(3), 189–201.

Feuerstein, R., et al. (1979). Cognitive modifiability in retarded adolescents: Effects of instrumental enrichment. *American Journal of Mental Deficiency, 83*(6), 539–550.

Frankenburg, W. K., & Dodds, J. B. (1967). The Denver Developmental Screening Test. *Journal of Pediatrics, 71*, 181–191.

Frankenstein, C. (Ed.). (1953). *Between past and future: Essays and studies on aspects of immigrant absorption in Israel*. Henrietta Szold Institute, Jerusalem.

Georgas, J. G., & Georgas, C. (1972). A children's intelligence test for Greece: Psychometric properties, intracultural effects, cross-cultural comparisons. In L. J. Cronbach and P. J. D. Drenth (Eds.), *Mental tests and cultural adaptation* (pp. 217–223). The Hague: Mouton.

Georgas, J. G., & Papadopoulou, E. (1968). The Harris-Goodenough and the Developmental Form Sequence with five-year-old Greek children. *Perceptual-Motor Skills, 26*, 352–354.

Georgas, J. G., Vassiliou, V., & Katakis, H. (1971). The verbal intelligence of Athenians. *Journal of Social Psychology, 83*, 165–173.

Gewirtz, H. B., & Gewirtz, J. L. (1969). Caretaking settings, background events and behaviour differences in four Israeli child-rearing environments: Some preliminary trends. In B. M. Foss (Ed.), *Determinants of infant behaviour* (Vol. 4., pp. 229–252). London: Methuen.

Gokhan, H., Binyildiz, P., Gurses, C., and Arman, A. (1975). 9–12 yas grubundaki Istanbul cocularinda antropometrik olculer, fiziksel yetenek ve zeka testleri uzerine on arastirma [A preliminary study of anthropomorphic measures, physical ability and intelligence tests with 9–12-year-olds from Istanbul]. *Istanbul Universitesi Tip Fakultesi Mecmuasi, 38*, 342–352.

Gordon, I. (1975). Research report of parent-oriented home-based early childhood education program. College of Education, University of Florida, Gainesville.

Greenbaum, C. W., & Kugelmass, S. (1980). Human development and socialization in cross-cultural perspective: Issues arising from research in Israel. In N. Warren (Ed.), *Studies in cross-cultural psychology* (pp. 95–155). New York: Academic Press.

Greenbaum, C. W., & Landau, R. (1972). Some social responses of infants and mothers in three Israeli child-rearing environments. In F. Monks, W. Hartup, & J. de Wit (Eds.), *Determinants of behavioral development*. New York: Academic Press.

Greenbaum, C. W., & Landau, R. (1977). Mothers' speech and the early development of vocal behavior: Findings from a cross-cultural study in Israel. In P. H. Leideman, S. R. Tulkin, & A. Rosenfeld (Eds.), *Culture and infancy variations in human experience* (pp. 245–270). New York: Academic Press.

Greenbaum, C. W., & Landau, R. (1979). The infant exposure to talk by familiar people: Mothers, fathers and siblings in different environments. In M. Lewis & L. Rosenblum (Eds.), *The child and its family*. New York: Plenum.

Gross, A. D. (1978). Sex-role standards and reading achievement: A study of an Israeli kibbutz system. *Reading Teacher, 32,* 149–156.

Gross, M. B. (1978). Cultural concomitants of preschoolers' preparation for learning. *Psychological Reports, 43,* 807–813.

Guttman, L., & Guttman, R. (1963). Cross-cultural stability of an intercorrelation pattern of abilities: A possible test of a biological basis. *Human Biology, 35,* 53–60.

Guttman, R., & Shonan, I. (1979). Intrafamilial invariance and parent-offspring resemblance in spatial abilities. *Behavior Genetics, 9,* 367–378.

Handel, A. (1973). Cognitive styles among adolescents in Israel. *International Journal of Psychology, 8,* 255–267.

Haritos-Fatouros, M. (1972). The influence of maturation and education on the development of mental abilities. In L. S. Cronbach & P. J. D. Drenth (Eds.), *Mental tests and cultural adaptation* (pp. 401–411). The Hague: Mouton.

Haritos-Fatouros, M. (1973). A study of the Wechsler Intelligence Scale for Children applied to Greek schoolchildren. *Scientific Annals* (School of Philosophy, Aristotelian University of Thessaloniki), *12,* 145–160.

Haritos-Fatouros, M. (1984). Research studies on testing in Greece: A review. *International Review of Applied Psychology, 33,* 351–370.

Heron, A., & Dowel, W. (1974). The questionable unity of the concrete operations stage. *International Journal of Psychology, 9,* 1–9.

Heron, A., Gardner, L., & Grieve, N. (1977). Concrete operational development in Yugoslav immigrant children. In Y. H. Poortinga (Ed.), *Basic problems in cross-cultural psychology*. Selected papers from the Third International Conference of the International Association for Cross-Cultural Psychology. Lisse: Swets & Zeitlinger.

Horn, J. L. (1976). Human abilities: A review of research and theory in the early 1970s. *Annual Review of Psychology, 27,* 437–485.

Horowitz, P. D., Ashton, J., Culp, R., Geddis, E., Levin, S., & Reichman, B. (1977). The effects of obstetrical medication on the behavior of Israeli newborn infants and some comparisons with Uruguayan and American infants. *Child Development, 48,* 1607–1623.

Irvine, S. H. (1979). The place of factor analysis in cross-cultural methodology and its contribution to cognitive theory. In L. Eckensberger, W. Lonner, & Y. H. Poortinga (Eds.), *Cross-cultural contributions to psychology*. Lisse: Swets & Zeitlinger.

Irvine, S. H. (1983). Testing in Africa and America: The search for routes. In S. H. Irvine & J. W. Berry, (Eds.), *Human assessment and cultural factors*. New York: Plenum.

Irvine, S. H., & Berry, J. W. (Eds.). (1983). *Human assessment and cultural factors*. New York: Plenum.

Irvine, S. H., & Sanders, J. T. (1972). Logic, language and method in construct identification across cultures. In L. H. Cronbach & P. J. D. Drenth (Eds.), *Mental tests and cultural adaptation* (pp. 427–446). The Hague: Mouton.

Ivic, I. (1976). The development of conservation concepts. *Psiholoska Istrazivanja*. Belgrade: Institut za Psikologiju.

Ivic, I., Cvijovic, B., & Dimcovic, N. (1976). Development of operational thinking and learning of elementary mathematics. *Psiholoska Istrazivanja*. Belgrade: Institut za Psikologiju.

Ivic, I., Milinkovic, M., Rosandic, R., & Smiljanic, V. (1976). The revision of Binet-Simon's Scale for measuring intelligence and the development of intelligence of children in Serbia. *Psiholoska Istrazivanja* (p. 397). Belgrade: Institut za Psikologiju.

Kagitcibasi, C. (1972). Applications of D48 Test in Turkey. In L. J. Cronbach & P. J. D. Drenth (Eds.), *Mental tests and cultural adaptation* (pp. 223–233). The Hague: Mouton.

Kagitcibasi, C. (1979). The effects of socioeconomic development on Draw-a-Man scores in Turkey. *Journal of Social Psychology, 108,* 3–8.

Kagitcibasi, C. (1983). Early childhood education and preschool intervention: Experiences in the world and in Turkey. In *Preventing school failure: The relationship between preschool and primary education* (pp. 108–116). Ottawa: IDRC.

Kagitcibasi, C. (1984). Socialization in traditional society: A challenge to psychology. *International Journal of Psychology, 19,* 145–157.

Kagitcibasi, C. (1986). Status of women in Turkey: Cross-cultural perspectives. *International Journal of Middle East Studies, 18,* 485–499.

Kagitcibasi, C. (Ed.). (1982). *Sex roles family and community in Turkey.* Bloomington, IN: Indiana University Press.

Kagitcibasi, C. (Ed.). (1987). *Growth and progression in cross-cultural psychology.* Selected papers from the Eighth International Conference of the IACCP. Lisse: Swets & Zeitlinger.

Karaboncuk, F., & Palabiyikoglu, R. (1975). Benton Gorsel bellek Testinin Gulhane askeri tip akademisi askeri personeline uygulanmasi [The application of the Benton Perceptual Memory Test to the personnel of Gulhane Military Medical Academy]. *XI. Ulusal Psikiyatri, ve Norolojik Bilimler Kongresi,* Izmir.

Katz, J., Onen, F., Demir, N., Uzlukaya, A., Uludag, P. (1974). Turkish Peabody Picture Vocabulary Test. *Hacettepe Bulletin of Social Sciences and Humanities, 6,* 129–142.

Kaufman, A. S. (1975). Factor analysis of the WISC-R at 11 age levels between 6½ and 16½ years. *Journal of Consulting and Clinical Psychology, 43,* 135–147.

Kelly, M., Tenezakiz, M., & Huntsman, R. (1973). Some unusual conservation behaviour in children exposed to two cultures. *British Journal of Educational Psychology, 43,* 181–182.

Kohen-Raz, R. (1968). Mental and motor development of kibbutz, institutionalized and home-reared infants in Israel. *Child Development, 39,* 489–504.

Kohen-Raz, R. (1976). Scaleogram analysis of some developmental sequences of infant behavior as measured by the Bayley Infant Scale of Mental Development. *Genetic Psychology Monographs, 76,* 3–21.

Kovacevic, P. (1973). Numerical abilities as a component of intellectual activity [English summary]. *Psihologija, 1–2,* 123.

Kugelmass, S., Lieblich, A., & Bossik, D. (1974). Patterns of intellectual ability in Jewish and Arab children in Israel. *Journal of Cross-Cultural Psychology, 5,* 184–198.

Kvascev, R. (1981). *Possibilities and limitations of intelligence development.* Belgrade: Nolit.

Landau, R. (1976). The extent to which the mother represents the social stimulation to which the infant is exposed: Findings from a cross-cultural study. *Developmental Psychology, 12,* 399–406.

Landau, R. (1977). Spontaneous and elicited smiles of infants in four Israeli environments. *Developmental Psychology, 13,* 389–400.

Levenstein, P. (1976). The mother–child home program. In M. C. Day & R. K. Parker (Eds.), *The pre-school in action.* Boston: Allyn & Bacon.

Lieblich, A., & Kugelmass, S. (1981). Patterns of intellectual ability of Arab schoolchildren in Israel. *Intelligence, 5,* 311–320.

Lieblich, A., Kugelmass, S., & Erlich, C. (1975). Patterns of intellectual ability in Jewish and Arab children in Israel II: Urban matched samples. *Journal of Cross-Cultural Psychology, 6,* 218–226.

Lieblich, A., Ninio, A., and Kugelmass, S. (1972). Effects of ethnic origin and parental SES and WPPS performance of preschool children in Israel. *Journal of Cross-Cultural Psychology, 4,* 159–163.

Lombard, A. (1981). *Success begins at home.* Lexington, MA: Heath.

Maniou-Vakali, M. (1977). New findings on the Goldstein–Scheerer Block Design Test for diagnostic and therapeutic purposes. *Scientific Annals* (School of Philosophy, Aristotelian University of Thessaloniki), *16,* 169–200.

Mirkovic, K. (1983). *The psychology of musical abilities* [English summary]. Belgrade.

Miron, M. (1977). A validation study of a transferred group intelligence test. *International Journal of Psychology, 12*, 193–205.

Okman, G. (1979). *Bilissel stili belirleyen etkenler: ergenler uzerinde bir inceleme* [Factors determining cognitive style: A study with adults]. Unpublished thesis, Bogazici Universitesi, Istanbul.

Okonji, M. O. (1969). The differential effects of rural and urban upbringing on the development of cognitive styles. *International Journal of Psychology, 4*, 293–305.

Ortar, G. (1953). A comparative analysis of the structure of intelligence in various ethnic groups. In C. Frankenstein (Ed.), *Between past and future*. Henrietta Szold Foundation for Child and Youth Welfare, Jerusalem.

Ortar, G. (1958) *A contribution to the research of intelligence levels in immigrant and Israeli-born children from oriental communities*. Unpublished doctoral dissertation, The Hebrew University, Jerusalem.

Ortar, G. (1967). Educational achievements of primary school graduates in Israel as related to their socio-cultural background. *Comparative Education, 4*, 23–24.

Ortar, G. (1968). *Wechsler Test for Children* [in Hebrew]. Jerusalem: Ministry of Education and Culture.

Ortar, G. (1972). Some principles for adaptation of psychological tests. In L. J. Cronbach & P. J. D. Drenth (Eds.), *Mental tests and cultural adaptation*. The Hague: Mouton.

Ozelli, L. (1978). A pilot study with the Bayley Infant Scales of Mental and Motor Development: A Turkish sample. *Turkish Journal of Pediatrics, 20*, 35–43.

Ozturk, F. (1969). *Okul oncesi koy cocuklarinda zeka bolumu calismalari* [Studies on IQ in rural preschool children]. Unpublished thesis, Hacettepe Universitesi, Psikiyatri Bolumu, Ankara.

Ozturk, F. (1974). Cevresel uyaranlar ve ilgi degisikliklerinin cocuk zeka gelisimi uzerine etkileri [The effects of environmental stimulation and changes in interests on children's intellectual development]. *IX. Milli Psikiyatri ve Norolojik Bilimler Kongresi, Istanbul*.

Peleg, R., & Adler, C. (1977). Compensatory education in Israel: Conceptions, attitudes and trends. *American Psychologist, 32*, 945–958.

Peluffo, N. (1967). Culture and cognitive problems. *International Journal of Psychology, 2*, 187–198.

Peristiany, J. G. (Ed.). (1965). *Honour and shame: The values of Mediterranean society*. London: Weidenfeld & Nicolson.

Peristiany, J. G. (Ed.). (1976a). *Mediterranean family structures*. Cambridge Studies in Social Anthropology, 13. Cambridge University Press.

Peristiany, J. G. (Ed.). (1976b). *Kinship and modernization in Mediterranean society*. Rome: Centre for Mediterranean Studies and the American Universities Field Staff.

Piaget, J. (1974). Need and significance of cross-cultural studies in genetic psychology. In J. W. Berry & P. R. Dasen (Eds.), *Culture and cognition: Readings in cross-cultural psychology* (pp. 299–309). London: Methuen.

Poortinga, Y. H. (Ed.). (1977). *Basic problems in cross-cultural psychology*. Lisse: Swets & Zeitlinger.

Poortinga, Y. J. (1983). Psychometric approaches to intergroup comparison: The problem of equivalence. In S. H. Irvine & J. W. Berry (Eds.), *Human assessment and cultural factors* (pp. 237–257). New York: Plenum.

Preale, I., Amir, Y., & Sharon, S. (1970). Perceptual articulation and task effectiveness in several Israeli sub-cultures. *Journal of Personality and Social Psychology, 15*, 190–195.

Reeb, M. (1976). Differential test validity for ethnic groups in the Israeli army and the effects of educational level. *Journal of Applied Psychology, 61*, 253–261.

Rosandic, R., & Bukvic, A. (1970). Effects of socio-cultural background upon success in solving tests of the Binet-Simon Scale [English summary]. *Psihologija, 2*, 221.

Sahin, N. (1983). The factorial structure of the WISC-R in Turkish standardization (unpublished paper).

Savasir, I., & Sahin, N. (1978). WISC uyarlama calismalari, on rapor I [Adaptations of WISC preliminary report]. *Psikoloji Dergisi, 1,* 33–38.

Savasir, I., & Sahin, N. (1982). *Wechsler cocuklar icin zeka olceginin Turk kulturune uyarlanmasi ve standardizasyonu* [Standardisation and adaptation to Turkish culture of the Wechsler Intelligence Scale for Children]. Paper presented at the Second National Congress of Psychology, Ankara.

Savasir, I., & Sahin, N. (1983, October). *Turkish standardization of the WISC-R.* Paper presented at the 4th Mediterranean Congress of Social Psychiatry, Ankara.

Sechrest, L. (1977). On the dearth of theory in cross-cultural psychology: There is madness in our method. In Y. H. Poortinga (Ed.), *Basic problems in cross-cultural psychology.* Lisse: Swets & Zeitlinger.

Segall, M. H. (1983). On the search for the independent variable in cross-cultural psychology. In S. H. Irvine and J. W. Berry (Eds.), *Human assessment and cultural factors* (pp. 127–137). New York: Plenum.

Semin, R. (1972a). *Mekanin degerlendirilmesi Binet–Stanford testlerinin Istanbul cocuklarina standartlanmasi* [Education, intelligence and the standardization of Stanford–Binet tests on children from Istanbul]. I.u. Edebiyat Fakultesi Yayinlari, Istanbul.

Semin, R. (1972b). Why certain tasks from mental tests must be adapted whereas operational tasks need not. In L. J. Cronbach & P. J. D. Drenth (Eds.), *Mental tests and cultural adaptation* (pp. 129–135). The Hague: Mouton.

Semin, R. (1976). Richard Meili'nin analitic zeka testinin Istanbul cocuklarina uygulanmasi [Adaptation of Richard Meili's Analytical Intelligence Test on children from Istanbul]. *Istanbul Universitesi Tecrubi Pedagoji ve Cocuk Psikolojisi Bulteni, 3,* 41–87.

Shanan, J., & Sagiv, R. (1982). Sex differences in intellectual performance during middle age. *Human Development, 25,* 24–33.

Sinha, D. (1973). Psychology and the problems of developing countries. *International Review of Applied Psychology, 22,* 5–27.

Smilansky, M. (1979). Priorities in education: Preschool, evidence and conclusions (Staff Working Paper No. 323). Washington, DC: World Bank.

Smilansky, S., Shephatia, L., & Frenkel, E. (1976). Mental development of infants from two ethnic groups (Research Report No. 195). Henrietta Szold Institute, Jerusalem.

Smiljanic, V. (1976). A test for the prediction of scholastic achievement. *Psiholoska Istrazivanja* (p. 394). Belgrade: Institut za Psikologiju.

Smiljanic, V. (1980). Sex and performance on intelligence tests. *Psiholoska Istrazivanja 2.* Belgrade: Institut za Psikologiju.

Stevanovic, B., Dragicevic, C., Bukvic, A., Stajnberger, I. (1980). The composition of verbal series. *Psiholoska Istrazivanja.* Belgrade: Institut za Psikologiju.

Super, C. M. (1981). Behavioral development in infancy. In R. H. Munroe, R. L. Munroe, & B. B. Whiting (Eds.), *Handbook of cross-cultural human development* (pp. 181–270). New York: Garland STPM Press.

Sweet, L. E. (Ed.). (1974). Visiting patterns and social dynamics in eastern Mediterranean communities [Special issue]. *Anthropological Quarterly, 47,* 1.

Tanaltay, A. R. (1980). Cattell kultur etkilerinden arinmis zeka olceginin 12–22 yas guruplari arasinda standardizasyonu [Standardisation of Cattell Culture-Free Test for 12–22 age groups]. Unpublished thesis, Ankara Universitesi.

Togrol, B. (1974). R. B. Cattell. Zeka testinin 2A ve 2B formlari ile Porteus Labirenti Zeka Testinin 1,300 Turk cocugunu uygulanmasi [Application of Cattell Intelligence Test Forms 2A and 2B and Porteus Maze Test to 1,300 Turkish children]. *Istanbul Universitesi Psikoloji Calismalari, 11,* 1–32.

Togrol, B., & Ozugurlu, K. (1974). Kulturden arinmis zeka testleri verilerinin istatistik degerlendirilmesi [Statistical evaluation of culture-free intelligence test results]. *IX. milli psikiyatri ve norolojik bilimler kongresi,* Istanbul.

Ucman, P. (1972). A normative study of the Goodenough-Harris Drawing Test on a Turkish sample. In L. S. Cronbach & P. J. D. Drenth (Eds.), *Mental tests and cultural adaptation.* (pp. 365–371). The Hague: Mouton.

USYM. (1978). 1977 universitelerarasi secme sinavina katilan adaylarin sosyal ekonoik ve egitimsel nitelikleri uzerine bir inceleme [A study of socioeconomic and educational characteristics of university entrance examination candidates]. Ankara.

USYM. (1979). Universitelerarasi secme sinavi ge cerlik arastirmasi [University entrance examination validity study]. Ankara.

Van Nieuwenhuijze, C. A. O. (Ed.) (1977). *Commoners, climbers and notables.* Leiden: Brill.

Vassaf, G. (1975). Ulkemizde zeka olcumunde yeni bir arac: temel zihin yetenekleri testi [A new local intelligence test: Basic Cognitive Abilities Test]. *XI. Ulusal Psikiyatri ve Norolojik Bilimler Kongresi,* Izmir.

Wechsler, D. (1949). *Manual for the Wechsler Intelligence Scale for Children.* New York: Psychological Corporation.

Weikart, D. P. (1970). *Longitudinal results of the Ypsilanti Perry Preschool Project* (Final report to the U.S. Office of Education). Washington, DC.

Weiss, S. (1971). *Education – the disadvantaged, Israeli style.* Westchester, PA: Westchester State College.

Weller, L., & Levi, S. (1981). Social class, IQ, self-concept and teachers' evaluations in Israel. *Adolescence, 16,* 569–576.

Weller, L., & Sharan, S. (1971). Articulation of the body among first-grade Israeli children. *Child Development, 42,* 1553–1559.

Werner, E. E. (1972). Infant psychomotor development. *Journal of Cross-Cultural Psychology, 3,* 113–134.

Whiting, B. (1976). The problem of the packaged variable. In K. F. Riegel & J. A. Meacham (Eds.), The developing individual in a changing world (Vol. 1, pp. 303–309). Chicago: Aldine.

Witkin, H. A. (1967). A cognitive-style approach to cross-cultural research. *International Journal of Psychology, 2,* 233–250.

Witkin, H. A., & Goodenough, D. R. (1977). *Field dependence revisited* (ETS RB 77–16). Princeton, NJ: Educational Testing Service.

Witkin, H. A., Goodenough, D. R., & Oltman, P. K. (1977). *Psychological differentiation:* Current status (ETS RB 77–17). Princeton, NJ: Educational Testing Service.

Witkin, H. A., Oltman, P. K., Raskin, E., & Karp, S. A. (1971). *A manual for the Embedded Figures Tests.* Palo Alto, CA: Consulting Psychologists Press.

Witkin, H. A., Price-Williams, D., Bertini, M., Christiansen, B., Oltman, P. K., Ramirez, M., & Van Meel, J. (1974). Social conformity and psychological differentiation. *International Journal of Psychology, 9,* 11–29.

Wober, M. (1967). Adapting Witkin's field independence theory to accommodate new information from Africa. *British Journal of Psychology, 58,* 29–38.

Yalaz, K., & Epir, S. (1982). *Denver gelisimsel tarama testi el kitabi – Turk cocuklarina uygulanmasi ve standardizasyonu* [Denver Developmental Screening Test handbook: Adaptation and standardization for Turkish children]. Ankara: Hacettepe Cocuk Sagligi Enstitusu vakfi.

Yalin, A. (1974). *Bender Gestalt Gorsel Motor Algilama Testinin bir sehir orneklemine uygulanmasi* [Application of Bender-Gestalt Visual-Motor Perception Test to an urban sample]. *X. Milli Psikiyatri ve Norolojik Bilimler Kongresi, Bilimsel Calismalari,* Ankara.

Yanbasti, G. (1974). Anne yoklugunun 8–11 yaslari arasinda zihinsel yetenekler ve okul basarisi uzerinde etkileri [The effects of mother abuse on mental abilities and school achievement among 8–11-year-olds]. *IX. Milli Psikiyatri ve Norolojik Bilimler Kongresi,* Istanbul.

Yasar, A., Aldemir, A., & Yalin, A. (1974). Bender Gestalt Gorsel Motor Algilama Testinin bir kirsal yorede 7–11 yas gruplarinda uygulanmasi [The application of the Bender-Gestalt Visual-Motor Perception Test to rural 7–11-year-olds]. *X. Milli Psikiyatri ve Norolojik Bilimler Kongresi Bilimsel Calismalari,* Ankara.

Za'rour, F. G. (1971). The conservation of number and liquid by Lebanese school children in Beirut. *Journal of Cross-Cultural Psychology, 2,* 165–172.

10 The Norwegian experience of test use: A selective review of Norwegian tests and measurements in cultural context

Knut A. Hagtvet and Johan O. Undheim

This chapter reviews the development of ability tests in Norway and psychometric-oriented Norwegian research in intelligence and language. The cultural contexts of this outline take three forms: discussion of validity assumptions underlying test development; relating ability measurement to sociocultural changes in Norway; and the attempt to interpret differences in ability performances across nations. As will become clear, the Norwegian experience of development in tests and measurements has been much influenced by human ability research in the United States. This mirrors the cultural stream of technological influence generally and the direction of research more specifically.

Test development

Norwegian involvement in ability testing may be traced back to the first decades of this century. In many cases test instruments have been used in their original versions, especially apparatus or performance tests, while tests based on language acquisition were used after translation. Thus, the evaluation of scores was based on a "cautious" pragmatic use of foreign norms, and mostly United States norms at that. However, there are also several cases of more elaborate adaptations of ability tests. We turn now to some illustrations of cultural response to tests as forms of technological importation.

In 1913, Looft (1913) used the *Binet* test in investigations of school children. Some years later Dahlstrom (cf. Sandven, 1943) translated these tests into Norwegian. However, the first Norwegian adaptation of the *Stanford–Binet* revision of 1916 was carried out by Lofthus (1931). The adaptation process of the Stanford revision of 1937 was initiated by Eng and carried through by Sandven and collaborators (Sandven, 1954).

During the 1960s, *Wechsler's Intelligence Scale for Children, (WISC)*, and the *Wechsler Adult Intelligence Scale (WAIS)*, were introduced to Norwegian psychologists and were used fairly extensively. In 1967, *WAIS* was standardised on 220 persons aged 55 to 74 (Beverfelt, Nordvik, & Nygård, 1967), and in 1980 it was supplemented by norms for age groups 18–25 (Engvik, Hjerkin, & Seim, 1980). In 1974 the revised edition of the children's test, *WISC-R,* was standardised on a nationwide sample of 800 children aged 6 to 15½ (Undheim, 1978b). A Norwegian edition of Wechsler's preschool test, *WPPSI,* has recently been published (Langset, 1984). Clearly, Norwegian attention to the Binet–Wechsler school of intelligence testing has been considerable, and also systematic, in its attempt to adopt standard measures.

The interest in group tests has been no less than in individual tests. The first translation of the American *Army Alpha Test* into Norwegian was carried out by Reymert (cf. Sandven, 1943). However, the work and application of group tests by Eng seem to have been the most systematic and thorough contribution in this period (cf. Sandven, 1943). *The Dearborn Group Test* was standardised in Norwegian for grades one to four by Pedersen (1933) and later by Lofthus, Rasmussen, and Ribsskog (1937) for the first grade. A few years later Ribsskog (1941) carried through a standardisation of the *Kuhlman–Anderson Test* for the same grade level. *Raven's Progressive Matrices* has been used by Norwegian psychologists for many years, but without Norwegian norms. In 1978, however, this test was standardised on about 3,000 clients of the Work Psychology Unit in Oslo (Eckhoff, 1978).

In addition to these adaptations of international tests, one should mention a few examples of Norwegian measures – based, however, on tests of Thurstone or in the Thurstone tradition. Mønnesland (1948) published a group test for adolescents and adults based on a sample of 1,200. New norms were published in 1978 based on about 4,000 clients of the Work Psychology Unit in Oslo (Sarfi & Smørvik, 1978). Finally, at the beginning of the 1950s, Sandven and collaborators standardised three intellectual maturity group tests covering the span from 6 to 15 years of age (Sandven, 1962; see also Rand, 1979) based on large samples.

Within the language ability domain the well-known *Illinois Test of Psycholinguistic Abilities* (*ITPA*) was standardised by Gjessing and collaborators (Gjessing, Nygaard, & Solheim, 1975; Nygaard, 1975; Solheim, 1975) based on a nationwide sample of 1,700 children from six age groups in the age span between 4 and 11 years. Quite recently the *Reynell Developmental Language Scale* (*RDLS*), frequently used in Great Britain and Commonwealth countries, has been adapted to Norwegian by B. Hagtvet and Lillestølen (1985). The standardisation was based on a random sample of 700 children covering eight age groups from 1½ to 6 years of age from a large county in southeastern Norway, including urban, suburban, and rural areas. As an example of Norwegian language measures, one should mention the test battery of *Auditory Language Perception* developed by Bø (1971, 1978a, 1978b) and standardised on 450 second graders (8–9 years old).

These ability tests represent some selective landmarks of the early and later stages of the test movement in Norway. A major drive in the development of such ability tests in Norway – as in most other countries – was their use in psychological counselling, particularly in the schools and in institutions for special education. Another and somewhat distinct impetus for the construction of tests has been the need for research instruments. A considerable number of *Thurstone–Guilford* ability measures have been constructed and adapted in the course of studying such topics as creativity (Foros, 1969), problem solving and intelligence. (Raaheim, 1974, 1986; Raaheim & Brun, 1985; Raaheim, Kaufman, & Kaufman, 1972; Undheim, 1972, 1976, 1978a, 1981a, 1981b, 1981c). A third impetus, the demand for instruments in the selection of personnel, has fostered development of several *Thurstone–Guilford* tests by the Psychology Unit of the Norwegian armed forces, and to a lesser extent within the Work Psychology Unit in Norway.

The assumption of universal validity

Because most of the ability tests used in Norway have been adapted from abroad, mainly from the United States, the assumption of "universal" validity of such measures within the western industrialised countries seems implicit. This assumption is probably based on the presence of certain common cultural factors, which represent necessary and sufficient conditions for interpretation of "western" test scores. Specifically, the conditions include compulsory primary education leading to almost 100% literacy based on a common core of content: and Norway satisfies this key requirement. Nevertheless, we now examine empirical evidence for the assumption that tests imported from other countries are valid in Norwegian contexts.

Intelligence tests

Criterion validities. Results from criterion-related validity studies generally support this assumption. Test correlations with school grades, teacher ratings, and achievement test scores in Norway are generally comparable to those found in other countries. Other kinds of concurrent validity data include ability test correlations with indices of socioeconomic level (see, e.g., Hofset, 1968; Undheim, 1972, 1978b; Vormeland, 1967). Also, a positive relationship between intelligence and upward social mobility has been demonstrated on data for male military recruits, paralleling similar findings elsewhere (Ramsøy, 1965). Studies relating measures of general intelligence to measures of achievement motivation, test anxiety (fear of failure), and learning disabilities give results in accordance with findings in other western countries (Gjesme, 1971, 1972, 1973; Gjessing & Nygaard, 1984; Nygård, 1977; Undheim, 1984).

Domain and construct validity. Simple structure factor analysis of the Norwegian *WAIS, WISC*, and *WISC-R* indicate a close correspondence to the structural relations of the performances as obtained in the original standardisation samples (Engvik, 1978; Engvik, Hjerkin, & Seim, 1980; Nordvik, 1963; Undheim, 1972, 1978b). Further support for construct validity of *WISC* and of factor-type group tests is found in more theory-oriented research in the vein of Guilford's structural model of intelligence (Undheim, 1972). Although further analyses led to a critical reevaluation of Guilford's model on account of chance factors in his factor-analytic techniques (Undheim, 1979; Undheim & Horn, 1977), there are no indications of dissimilarities in the structural relations across the two cultures. In more recent factor-analytic studies designed to check on the Cattell–Horn broad factor theory of fluid and crystallised intelligence, the structural relations of 25–30 ability measures match quite closely previous United States findings, at both the first-order level (primary factors) and the second-order level (broad factors) (Undheim, 1976, 1978a, 1981a). However, Undheim (1981b, 1981c) finally reinterprets both American and Norwegian data so as to restore Spearman's General Intelligence factor, proposing a neo-Spearman hierarchical model of intelligence.

Factor analyses of the two Norwegian group tests constructed by Sandven and Mønnesland (Sannum, 1976; Sarfi & Smørvik, 1978) seem to indicate that they represent no exception from the fate of most differential ability tests of this scope: They give a reliable total score of intelligence, a Verbal factor, and a Reasoning factor of some kind – and little more (see McNemar, 1964). By applying a variance components analysis model to the problem of dimensionality (Burt, 1966; Cronbach, Gleser, Nanda, & Rajaratnam, 1972; Eikeland, 1972) the relative strength of a general factor compared to the impact of differential factors was examined by Eikeland (1973) and Hagtvet (1974). Both studies supported the existence of a strong general factor with a correspondingly weaker contribution from differential constructs in the Sandven scale. This finding was stable across 12 samples of boys and girls in grades 6, 7, and 8 in the study by Eikeland (1973).

Data, then, generally support the *construct validity* of intelligence tests in Norway relative to other western countries. Particular attention should be drawn to the *Wechsler* tests when one is concerned with intra- and cross-cultural settings for intelligence measures. Even though use of the same instruments is not an essential condition for sociocultural comparison, it is often desirable. This should imply that comparability in terms of functional equivalence (Poortinga, 1975, 1983) is best satisfied in studies of the *Wechsler* scales. One would not, however, extrapolate from functional equivalence, implying structural similarity, to direct metric comparisons involving mean levels of performance between nations or generations where the necessary social supports for test interpretation were absent.

Language scales

Data backing up the assumption of "universal" validity for the transcultural use of language scales is scarce. The standardisation data of *ITPA* and of the *Reynell* scales (*RDLS*) has not been subjected to correlational analyses. Moreover, the *RDLS* scales show little evidence of domain study in their country of origin, Britain. However, there is some indication of Norwegian validity for the *RDLS* provided by Smith, Smørvik, Sommer, and von Tetzchner (1982, 1984), and Smith and von Tetzchner (1984). Using a prestandardised version of the *RDLS* on children 3 years old with birth weight under 2,000 g, the *Comprehension Scale* of *RDLS* was seen to be closely related to *Stanford–Binet* ($r = .71$) and also related to such other variables as socioeconomic status, birth weight, and subscales of sensorimotor skills, in much the same way as the *Binet* test. This close relationship of the *Comprehension Scale* with total scores on a standard intelligence test, also shown in the pattern of correlations with measures of *Stanford–Binet* and of *ITPA* two years later, corresponds quite well with the results reported by Silva, Bradshaw, and Spears (1978) studying English-speaking children in New Zealand.

A further analysis of the New Zealand data by K. Hagtvet and B. Hagtvet (1984) took into account available correlational information from 25 tests covering intelligence and language abilities (*ITPA, WPPSI,* and *FROSTIG* scales) at 5 years of age. The data analysis supported the operationalisation of all the 5-years measurements in terms of a general second-order cognitive factor dominated by two primary *ITPA* factors (Autonomic and Representational) and the Verbal *WPPSI* factor. The two *RDLS* subscales given at the age of 4 strongly predicted this second-order factor, the *Comprehension Scale* being slightly stronger than the *Expressive Scale.*

A fairly confusing picture seems to emerge from factor analyses of the *ITPA* psycholinguistic abilities battery in other countries, and this may partly be caused by methodological inadequacies (cf. Newcomer, Hare, Hammill, & McGettigan, 1975). There is no adequate Norwegian study. The small sample of children 4 to 12 years, analysed by Birkemo (1982) could not provide adequate controls for the effect of age in the analysis. Of more direct relevance to the question of universal validity are research studies critically examining the modality assumptions of the scale (Bø, 1968; Wold, 1975). The empirical evidence so far seems to make cross-cultural comparisons based on *ITPA* performance somewhat premature.

The problem of differential diagnosis in the language domain has also been the focus of carefully developed test construction work by Bø (1971, 1977, 1978a, 1978b). Based on a structural model of auditory language perception with features common to Osgood's model (Osgood, 1957), two test batteries with a total of eight subtests were developed. A series of exploratory and confirmatory factor analyses of each of the batteries has been carried out. In an overall evaluation of the results, Bø seems to favour an interpretation of four factors: a General Language Perception factor, a Decoding factor, a Figure-ground factor (distorted speech), and a combined Memory–Discrimination factor. A substantial amount of specific factor variance was recognised (Bø, 1977). However, it should be noted, as also suggested by Bø himself (1977), that the confirmatory factor solutions based on six hypothesised factors in addition to a General Language Perception factor appear to be a more parsimonious model. The group factors were reported to relate moderately to variables measuring information acquisition via language expression, general intelligence (*Kuhlman–Anderson*), teacher ratings of reading aloud, silent reading, and dictation.

Because the construct validity or comparability of the Norwegian *ITPA* is unclear and the diagnostic battery of Bø has not yet been subject to analysis for comparability, the *RDLS* seems to be the only language test for the time being that lends itself to a suggestive intercultural comparison.

Performance on ability measures in Nordic cultural settings

Assuming now the functional or near-functional equivalence of the adapted ability tests, the following short survey of studies that have replicated and extended international research on ability measurement in a cultural context further attests to cultural similarities. Also, the more intriguing question of cultural changes specific to Norway or to Scandinavia are raised. Finally, the problematic question of direct cross-cultural comparisons of performances is discussed.

Intra-cultural change: General and sex differences in performance

General changes toward higher ability scores in the course of postwar generations have been observed for adolescents and adults. This upward trend parallels similar findings in other western countries (Engvik, 1984; Engvik, Hjerkin, & Seim, 1980; Rist, 1982; Sarfi & Smørvik, 1978). Also, differences in ability scores between urban and rural children (Thrane, 1961) have become smaller and are, in fact, reduced to zero in the *WISC-R* standardisation data (Undheim, 1978b), as in the United States standardisation data (Kaufman & Doppelt, 1976). A unique Norwegian study of schooling and intelligence (Lund & Thrane, 1983) was based on a longitudinal sample of about 3,500 adolescents. This displays potent effects of schooling on ability scores, with the usual reservations regarding the possibility of confounding variables. Only a few well-designed longitudinal studies examining the influence of schooling during the teens have been carried out; but the study by Lund and Thrane corresponds well with the results of two Swedish studies (Härnquist, 1968; Husén, 1950).

Girls have often been reported to have higher total scores than boys on intellectual maturity tests that emphasise school-related knowledge acquisition; and this is so on the *Sandven Test* (Gjessing, 1958; Hofset, 1968; Holter, 1961; Vormeland, 1967). This trend bears correspondence to the often found sex difference favouring girls in most central school subjects, usually with the exception of mathematics (see, e.g., Holter, 1961; Thrane, 1961). In a recent nationwide sample of young teenagers, Hagtvet (1984) finds girls consistently superior to boys in both "formal" and "practical" aspects of language (English and Norwegian). Based on the same sample,

Jernquist's (1982) findings showed boys to be somewhat better in geometry and applied mathematics but not in arithmetic and algebra. On the *WISC-R* test no consistent sex differences were found in *Full Scale* IQ or on the *Verbal* and *Performance Scale* over the eight age groups (Undheim, 1978b). However, there was a small difference in favour of boys in the *Verbal Scale* in age groups above 9, corresponding to similar findings in the United States standardisation sample, the differences there being slightly larger.

One may note that Gjesme (1971, 1972, 1973) has proposed a more complex relationship between sex and school achievement. His hypothesis, cast within the vein of achievement motivation, suggests ̣that *moderate*-ability boys have their motive dispositions strongly aroused in school (motive to achieve success and motive to avoid failure), while the same happens in *high*-ability girls. Gjesme finds a pattern of correlations mostly in accordance with these predictions. K. Hagtvet (1986) has recently replicated Gjesme's interactional findings, but only when ability is defined in terms of a Verbal-crystallised factor and anxiety is defined in terms of affective components (K. Hagtvet, 1985). Nygård (1977) is debating causal relationships between measured IQ and motive strength. Even though he holds that this relationship may be of an interactional nature, he seems to defend the idea of motives *causing* differences in measured intelligence scores, taking an educationist point of view. He presents some data in general accordance with motivational implications. However, to determine empirically his ideas of causal relationships and cumulative effects of motive dispositions, a causal modelling approach seems to be called for.

As for sex differences in specific ability areas, boys have repeatedly been found superior in visual-spatial abilities in many countries. However, data support a trend towards disappearance of such differences in Norway and Sweden, in school-age children up to 15 years. Comparable data from other countries on adequate samples have not been found. Norwegian data on 1,500 children aged 13 to 14 on a test of *metal folding* (measuring the primary factor of Visualisation, Vz) collected around 1955 showed a difference of .3 standard deviation (SD) units in favour of boys (Thrane, 1961). Data collected 20 years later on 600 youngsters of the same age resulted in a difference of .1 SD (based on data reported in Sannum, 1976). A comparable Swedish finding was reported by Härnquist and Stahle (1977), who related the change to the policy of comprehensive schools and the introduction of new curricula stressing equality between boys and girls in various ways (including handicraft instruction). Of particular note, the Härnquist and Stahle (1977) report, being based on a large sample of 10,000 from each of two cohorts, was able to demonstrate both a positive correlation between score increases in a metal folding test and increases in comprehensive school coverage, with density–times–location as unit of analysis. Also, there was an interaction with sex: Girls' ability scores showed the higher correlation with variations in schooling indices.

It has been argued that folding tests to some extent may be solved analytically rather than visually, at least when one is somewhat familiar with the test. However, a similar change has probably taken place in the performance of *Figural Rotation Tests* (measuring the primary factor of Spatial Relations, *S*). The best evidence for such a change are results obtained in Swedish youngsters (Gustafsson, 1976; Gustafsson, Lindström, & Björk-Åkeson, 1981). Data collected on 400 Norwegian children aged 10 to 15 during 1971 to 1976 resulted in a difference of .25 SD in favour of boys (based on material supplementary to Undheim, 1976, 1978a, 1981a), whereas Sannum's data from 1976 on 600 13- to 14-year-olds indicate no difference between the sexes (data on 13- and 14-year-olds taken together, see Sannum, 1976, pp. 114–115). One should note, however, that the rotations test used by Sannum was not highly speeded. Recent research by J. Vavik (personal communication, September 28, 1983) indicates that sex differences on two-dimensional rotations now may be negligible, whereas the correct identification of solid objects in three dimensions and topological understanding of maps may still show some differences favouring boys. A possible explanation may be that textbooks now provide all children with much experience in interpreting *two-dimensional* illustrations of movement, although there undoubtedly are still considerable differences between the two sexes in the amount of play activity with construction kits and similar activities providing experience of relevance to *three-dimensional* cognitive tasks. However, one should point out that the fitting together of solid blocks as in the *Block Design Test* of *WISC-R* does not show any sex differences (Undheim, 1978b); and there were no consistent sex differences on any other of the *WISC-R* performance tests with visual-spatial content. The United States standardisation sample gave differences of about .1 SD to .2 SD on all performance subtests of the *WISC-R* except *Coding* (Kaufman, 1979, p. 117).

The frequently observed sex difference in perceptual speed tasks in favour of girls seems to have remained sizable. On the *WISC-R* sex differences are found on the *Coding Test* in all age groups $6\frac{1}{2}$ to $15\frac{1}{2}$, averaging .5 SD (Undheim, 1978). This corresponds well with findings on the original *WISC-R* (Kaufman, 1979, p. 117). The only other consistent sex difference on the Norwegian *WISC-R* was the boys' better performance on the *Information Test* from about the age of 9, averaging .5 SD. (The *Information sub-scale* was the main contributor to the boys' somewhat better *Verbal Scale* scores.) Because the difference in means was related to a difference in the distribution of higher scores, it has been suggested that the sex difference in the *Information Test* may be related to the self-concept of a knowledgeable person (in an academic sense) being more central in able boys than in able girls (Undheim, 1978c). Data on cognitive self-concept are about to be analysed in a study of Swedish youths carried out by Gustafsson and Undheim.

Ability and cultural changes specific to Norway

Although the above studies have related their findings to sociocultural settings and sociocultural changes common to the western world, such as the impact of more comprehensive schooling, the spread of television and mass media in general, upward social mobility, increase in the occupational activity of mothers, child-development movements regarding the importance of cognitive stimulation, and so on, there are some studies that have related their findings to cultural changes specific to Norway and Sweden, though-possibly generalisable to a larger subset of the western nations. A study by Sundet, Tambs, and Magnus (1981) analysed twin data and related findings to potential effects of the egalitarian ideology emphasised by Norwegian governments during the last three decades. The reasoning was as follows: If the explicitly formulated goal of removing social and economic differences between layers of the population has been reached to some extent, these changes may be expected to reduce environmental variance in ability measures due to social classes and the like. Thus, to the extent that the influence of other environmental sources of variation remain approximately constant, the relative magnitude of the genetic variance component in such scores should be expected to increase.

Sundet et al. (1981) analysed the potential effects of social changes on intelligence by means of heritability analysis of data from 40 MZ and 40 DZ twins divided into two samples: those who were born before 1940 and those born after 1940. Their conclusions were based on relative magnitudes of *between-* and *within-* family environmental variances. Between-family variances *decreased* over time whereas within-family variances *increased*. The authors took these findings as evidence supporting the hypothesis that social change affects IQ performance. However, some surprising trends in data may have violated assumptions built into the LISREL model, as the authors themselves indicated. Also, small sample size may have introduced sampling errors, besides being a potential reason for obtaining the tight fit of the reported models estimated by the LISREL method. The problem of small sample size combined with single chi-squared tests in LISREL analyses should have been discussed to provide the reader with a firmer basis for evaluating the conclusions drawn. Also, attributing such findings to the egalitarian ideology of successive governments is rather speculative without relating the findings to other potential contributors to social change. The paper by Sundet et al. should be looked upon as primarily a methodological and substantive introduction to the study of twins in the perspective of societal changes.

Cross-cultural performance-level differences

Even in the case of comparable functional validity of ability measures, as probably is the case among western industrialised nations, it is extremely difficult to establish all the types of validity necessary for comparing level of performance across countries. In verbal tests this problem is fairly evident – a direct translation of words for use in a vocabulary test may, of course, change item difficulties rather dramatically. Not only are the responses to verbal reasoning problems influenced by the exact wording in item presentation, but the ecological premises for the reasoning problem may be different in two cultures. Even in performance or apparatus tests, there is a difficulty in guaranteeing comparability. Consider, for example, the changes thought necessary in adapting *WISC-R* subtests for Norwegian subjects in the *Picture Completion* subtest. Pictures of a doorknob and of a telephone were redrawn to resemble Norwegian versions. The playing card picture was deleted because such cards are less widespread and, in fact, still evoke negative affect in some religious groups of Norway. In the *Picture Arrangement Scale,* those showing a series of events in a boxing match were actually deleted, because boxing as a sport is very controversial in Norway and rarely seen by Norwegian children. In fact, only five subtests of the *WISC-R* were kept identical to those of the original United States version – *Block Design, Object Assembly, Coding, Digit Span,* and *Mazes.* Furthermore, to determine whether those tests are "culture-fair" to Norwegian children independent of the children's scores would probably require an ecological analysis of child culture. Also, changes in the children's experience with test-similar material may happen all the time – play kits with block designs very similar to Wechsler's *Block Design* test have only recently been observed in Norwegian stores for educational toys.

However, even if one makes the assumption of comparability of tests across western countries for some selected tests, the question of sample comparability remains and looms large. Because none of the nationwide standardisation procedures have been based on truly random sampling, institutional and other differences among the countries undoubtedly influence the sample tested. Furthermore, there are very few attempts at even coming close to nationwide samples for testing purposes. In Norway the standardisation of the *WISC-R* represents the only scientifically constructed one in the area of ability measurement. The sample was based on a quota sampling of primary and secondary public schools, while the selection of individuals was a random sample of equal numbers of boys and girls in each age group (Undheim, 1978b). According to the description given in the original *WISC-R* handbook (Wechsler, 1974, p. 19), the United States sample was wholly based on quota sampling. No further data is given on how each test supervisor proceeded to fill his or her quota.

It is thus difficult to argue that data indicating a *general level* of performance should provide results that have any "face validity" for interpretive purposes other than suggesting some kind of selection effect caused by different sampling procedures. However, one may argue that a *pattern* of results may offer a better chance. This is akin to arguing that a pattern of results showing sex differences on a battery of tests may give some valuable information about performances of the two sexes even when sampling procedures do not ensure representativeness. Although one must acknowledge that selection effects may show some interaction with the profile of performance levels, in most cases a possible selection bias is mainly on general intelligence, and not necessarily on all the operational measures that define it.

With these cautioning notes in mind we may now turn to data on cross-cultural performance differences, largely limited to a comparison between mean scores in the United States and Norway on the *WISC-R*. Three of the five tests that were kept unchanged in the Norwegian edition showed *higher* mean values for Norwegian children in all age groups: *Block Design, Object Assembly,* and *Mazes*. Differences were considerable, about .5 SD units relative to the United States data, and significant in age groups 7½ to 13½ (p ≤ .05). Interestingly, however, the other two tests, *Digit Span* and *Coding,* showed the opposite trend; significantly higher mean values were found in the United States standardisation sample for all eight age groups, also in the order of .5 SD (or about equivalent to one developmental year). Furthermore, when due consideration is given to the very few changes and deletions made in the *Picture Completion* and *Picture Arrangement* tests, the performance differences were on par with those of the three other apparatus tests, showing a lead in the performances of Norwegian children, of approximately half a standard deviation.

Because four of the five tests showing results favouring Norwegian children have fairly large correlations with *WISC-R Full Scale* IQ, this may indicate a higher "general intelligence" in the sample of Norwegian children, whether due to sampling procedures or other factors. In any case, this leaves us subsequently to explain the lower performance on *Digit Span* and *Coding* subtests.

The inclusion of disadvantaged groups of nonwhites in the United States sample is an obvious biasing difference among the two samples. The presence of low-scoring minorities reduce the performance IQ by about .15 SD according to data presented by Kaufman and Doppelt (1976). Data on ethnic differences on each subtest of the *WISC-R* have not, to our knowledge, been published, but depending on the existence of somewhat distinct subtest score differences among whites and nonwhites in the United States sample, the inclusion of nonwhites may alone explain one-third to one-half of the differences in favour of the Norwegian children.

Normative changes in measured intelligence that reveal an increase in performance level since the postwar period should not represent an important contributor to the bridging of the remaining gap. Because the Norwegian edition of the *WISC-R* was standardised only 4 years later than that in the United States (1976, vs. 1972) the two groups are of the same generation. Data comparing *WISC* and *WISC-R* in the United States suggest an increase of about 5 to 7 IQ points on the *Full Scale* IQ (Kaufman, 1979, p. 127), amounting to a bit over one-third SD in about 25 years.

We have pointed out that unknown sampling differences are a likely explanation of performance discrepancies on general ability tests. If this were so, then the comparison of average performance would be tendentious, because the finding is a trivial one due to uncontrolled error. Nevertheless, if additional findings suggest alternative explanations to sampling, then these may be cautiously advanced as having heuristic value. We propose to examine differences in cultural contexts that can be specifically identified; and to propose these variables as reasons for performance differences.

The reader who has examined the McShane–Berry chapter on Native North American abilities (Chapter 15) might be tempted to extend Berry's general theory of ecological press to account for relatively high visual-spatial ability in all Nordic peoples, compared with American norms. The rationale would be a biological and habitual derivation of this facility in Arctic and sub-Arctic regions similar to those inhabited by the Inuit. Moreover, the same lack of sex differences in apparatus tests is evident. Against this there is no verbal-spatial difference within the Norwegian groups. But no one ever tested Norwegians in English and then compared their norms with United States performance, because this would be nonsensical! Finally, Berry himself has insisted that his model does not apply to "acculturated" groups; and Norwegians are certainly more like Euramericans than Inuit in their lifestyle. Intriguing as such speculations may be, we seek explanations that are closer to home and that are testable.

One possible reason for test score differences is a *treatment* variable such as school quality. Some evidence supports the view that there are wide school differences in North American society compared with Norwegian homogeneity in school provision, particularly at the primary level. The Norwegian system itself simply functions more efficiently in delivering the skills that lead to effective test performance. There are no direct indices of comparative school effectiveness, except the crude index of pupil–teacher ratios. The most recent source (*Statistical Digest,* 1983, p. 146) reveals that at the time of the *WISC-R* standardisations, the ratio in Norway was 17:1, against the United States ratio of 20:1. Other aspects of culture that have been measured and also evaluated as conducive to school efficiency include homogeneity of language use and of religious affiliations, small numbers of foreign residents, and a low immigration rate (Galtung & Gleditsch, 1975). These authors also cite cultural variables that show Norway to be well placed on a societal scale of "encouragement to learn." They cite low rates of aggressive violence, industrial disputes, unemployment, and divorce.[1] Finally, the number of book titles published, the circulation of newspapers, and the number of volumes in public libraries, all calculated per head of population, show Norway to be in an extremely advantageous position (*Statistical Digest,* 1983, pp. 146, 292) compared with most other countries, including the United States.

This kind of evidence by itself is no proof of any hypothesis. It offers only a key to understanding how a hypothesis of differential quality of life could be thought to account for test differences. There are two separate studies

[1] However, there is now a rapid rise in divorce rates. It took 23 years before 10% of those who married in 1955 were divorced, but only 8 years for those who married in 1965 (Bjøru & Sørensen, 1983).

pointing in the same direction, hinging on the fact that countries have different ages for primary school entry. Norwegian children do not enter school until they attain 7 years. They begin late compared to British (5 +) and American (6 +) children.

The important finding in comparison with American children is that American *WISC-R* norms are higher *only* in the 6½-year-olds, when Norwegian children sampled were *not* at school and the American sample was. As soon as the influence of schooling can be assumed for the Norwegian age groups at 7 and upward, the Norwegians show enhanced performance compared with the American samples.

For another comparative view, the notion of a cultural context conducive to learning has support from the *Reynell Development Language Scale* (*RDLS*) used for preschool groups. B. Hagtvet, (1982) shows consistent average performance differences in favour of Norwegian preschool groups in the *Comprehension* scale, which has strong correlations with the *Stanford–Binet*. These differences persist from 2 through 5 years, when children in both countries are not at school, and are nonsignificant at age 6, when only English children are at school.

The common finding in both of these studies is that when the Norwegian groups are seen to be on level terms with their United States or English counterparts, either in or out of school, their performance is superior. Furthermore, the pancultural influence of schooling on test performance is neatly demonstrated by an accident of policy. The differential age entries in the three countries compared – England, Norway, and the United States – show the effects of school attendance on "ability" tests. What, though, about those tests where Norwegian children show relatively less effective performance?

The above reasoning, whether in terms of sampling selection or educational effectiveness, surely emphasises a need to explain the opposite trend, the higher mean values of United States children on *Digit Span* and *Coding*. Specifically, the pattern of lower *Digit Span* scores relative to performance on other subscales was also found in five age groups on the *WAIS*, whereas *Digit Symbol* showed a more diverse pattern (Beverfelt, Nordvik, & Nygård, 1967; Engvik, Hjerkin, & Seim, 1980). Because nonwhites certainly do not exceed whites on any one subtest, the differences in favour of whites in the United States are even greater than the .5 SD difference indicated by the standardisation data.

In factor analyses of the *WISC-R* both in the United States and in Norway, *Coding* and *Digit Span* load on a factor called Freedom of Distractibility together with the *Arithmetic* subtest (see, e.g., Kaufman, 1979, p. 22). According to Lutey (1977) the factor may as well be interpreted "freedom from disruptive anxiety" because there is reason to believe that these tests are particularly influenced by a state of test anxiety. Applying this interpretation now to these group differences rather than to individual differences, one might observe that although direct and vicarious test-taking experience may reduce test anxiety, such experience is less a part of the educational system in Norway. Hence, Norwegian children may suffer somewhat higher anxiety in test-taking situations. One should bear in mind that familiarity with test content tends to reduce such anxiety, so that their functioning on the *Arithmetic* subtest should not be much affected. We do not have much confidence in this explanation, nevertheless, and suggest another rationale.

The *Coding Test* is more generally interpreted as one specific measure of the broad Cognitive Speed factor (*Gs*), which comprises such primary factors as Perceptual Speed and Number Facility (Undheim, 1978a). Task analysis indicates that it involves writing speed, rapid eye movements as well as the learning of digit-symbol relations (Levy, 1973). This may suggest that the *Coding Test* depends on a careful trade-off between speed and accuracy in the continuing course of carrying out an intellectually easy, repetitive task. Accordingly, it does not seem unreasonable to hypothesise that children in the United States are more practised in finding the optimal balance between speed and accuracy through habituation to multiple-choice formats and the like in school. Possibly also the United States intellectual "climate" is generally more rewarding of the quick-and-fast answer than most European countries. Habituation and social reinforcement probably lead to payoff on an intellectually easy test in terms of choice behaviour. Although a test such as *Block Design* also depends on speedy cognitive functioning – as evidenced by the fact that, at least in higher age groups, a time bonus is needed in order to obtain a good score – a high rate of speediness relative to "power" ability will surely be detrimental to overall performance, which penalizes guessing.

Whether or not a quick-and-fast answer is also beneficial to *Digit Span* score can only be decided by a closer scrutiny of the relative importance of "recency" in the memory tasks of the test. The authors want to call attention to two other possibilities, a *word-length* effect and *phonetic similarity* in pronouncing digits. Both are detrimental to fast performance. The first hypothesis is based on studies of Welsh children who show similar low scores on the *Digit Span* relative to the United States standardisation sample (William & Roberts, 1972). Experiments by Ellis and Hennelly (1980) have demonstrated that the difference between Welsh and English children may be attributable to differences in word length, the Welsh digits taking longer to pronounce. Observation suggests the possibility that the mean reading time of digits 1 to 9 will be slightly greater in Norwegian than in English. This remains to be demonstrated. Regarding the second hypothesis, it is possible that the pronounciation of Norwegian digits 1 to 9 have higher phonetic similarity and therefore lead to more acoustic confusion (see Conrad, 1964; Wickelgren, 1977, p. 220).

These differences in *Coding* and *Digit Span* may mark cultural emphases that enhance American performance, including strategy variables in speed and accuracy, and phonetic variables that slow Norwegian perception of digits and their execution in working memory. At the moment, plausible hypotheses exist for the observed score differences between American and Norwegian samples on tasks that traditionally show some independence of General Intelligence factors. The means to test them would involve specific experimental investigations with carefully chosen samples, and would undoubtedly involve repeated measures. Significantly, *Coding* (or digit-symbol substitution) and *Digit Span* are more often, nowadays, regarded as information-processing tasks than ability tests. In such tasks the effects of individual and group differences in *habits* of processing information are well documented.

Conclusions

The Norwegian experience of testing began with the adaptation of tests from donor cultures, namely, the United States and Britain. Gradually, however, research activity has shifted from pragmatic adaptation and standardisation to questioning the assumptions of test theory itself. In recent years, domain and experimental studies of test structures and motivational factors have become more commonplace. As theoretical clarification has become possible, the Norwegian work has given cautious support to the operational definition of cultural contexts that modify and define the meaning of test scores.

References

Beverfelt, E., Nordvik, H., & Nygård, Aa. (1967). *WAIS Håndbok, Wechsler Adult Intelligence Scale*. Oslo: Norsk Psykologforening.

Birkemo, A. (1982). En faktoranalytisk studie av Illinois Test of Psycholinguistic Abilities. *Skolepsykologi, 17*, 23–27.

Bjøru, K., & Sørensen, A. (1983). Fragment av norske kvinners livsløp. In K. Skrede & K. Tolnes (Eds.), *Studier i kvinners livsløp*. Oslo: Universitetsforlaget.

Bø, O. O. (1968). ITPA. Beskrivelse og vurdering. *Skolepsykologi, 5*, 93–113.

Bø, O. O. (1971). *Faktorer i språkpersepsjonen*. Unpublished doctoral dissertation, University of Oslo.

Bø, O. O. (1977). Faktorer i språkpersepsjonen (Report No. 5). Institute for Educational Research, University of Oslo.

Bø, O. O. (1978a). *Språkperseptuelle tester SP1 og SP2*. Oslo: Universitetsforlaget.

Bø, O. O. (1978b). General or specific meaning of figure ground perception. *Scandinavian Journal of Educational Research, 22*, 129–153.

Burt, C. (1966). The appropriate uses of factor analysis and analysis of variance. In R. B. Cattell (Ed.), *Handbook of multivariate experimental psychology* (pp. 267–287). Chicago: Rand McNally.

Conrad, R. (1964). Acoustic confusions in immediate memory. *British Journal of Psychology, 55*, 75–84.

Cronbach, L. J., Gleser, G. C., Nanda, N., & Rajaratnam, N. (1972). *The dependability of behavioral measurements: Theory of generalizability for scores and profiles*. New York: Wiley.

Eckhoff, R. (1978). *Ravens Standard Progressive Matrices. Rapport fra Normeringsarbeid*. Unpublished manuscript, Arbeidspsykologisk Institutt, Oslo.

Eikeland, H. M. (1972). *The structure of generalizability theory for hierarchically stratified tests.* Unpublished manuscript, Institute for Educational Research, University of Oslo.

Eikeland, H. M. (1973). *On the change in mental organization with age: An alternative approach.* Unpublished manuscript. Institute of Educational Research, University of Oslo.

Ellis, N. C., & Hennelly, R. A. (1980). A bilingual word-length effect: Implications for intelligence testing and the relative ease of mental calculation in Welsh and English. *British Journal of Psychology, 71,* 43–51.

Engvik, H. (1978). *Faktorstrukturen i WAIS.* Unpublished manuscript, Department of Psychology, University of Oslo.

Engvik, H. (1984). Amerikanske normer for norsk WAIS? *Tidsdkrift for Norsk Psykologforening, 21,* 413–417.

Engvik, H., Hjerkin, O., & Seim, S. (1980). *Håndbok WAIS. Norsk Utgave.* Oslo: Norsk Psykologforening.

Foros, P. B. (1969). *Fluency – omgrepet i skapande intelligens.* Unpublished master's thesis, Forskning fra Psykologisk Institutt, Universitetet i Trondheim.

Galtung, J., & Gleditsch, N. P. (1975). Norge i verdenssamfunnet. In N. R. Ramsøy & M. Vaa (Eds.), *Det Norske Samfunnet 2.* Oslo: Gyldendal.

Gjesme, T. (1971). Motive to achieve success and motive to avoid failure in relation to school performance for pupils of different ability levels. *Scandinavian Journal of Educational Research, 10,* 81–99.

Gjesme, T. (1972). Sex differences in the relationship between test anxiety and school performance. *Psychological Reports, 30,* 907–914.

Gjesme, T. (1973). Sex differences in the connection between need for achievement and school performances. *Journal of Applied Psychology, 56,* 270–272.

Gjessing, H. J. (1958). *En studie av lesemodenhet ved skolegangens begynnelse.* Oslo: Cappelen.

Gjessing, H. J., & Nygaard, H. D. (1984). Orientering om Bergensprosjektet. In I. A. Bjørgen (Ed.), *Lesning og lesevansker* (Rapport no. 5, pp. 146–196). Trondheim: NAVF – Senter for barneforskning.

Gjessing, H. J., Nygaard, H. D., & Solheim, R. (1975). *Illinois Test of Psycholinguistic Abilities (ITPA). Håndbok med instruksjoner og normer.* Revidert utgave. Oslo, Universitetsforlaget/Seksjon for Skolepsykologi.

Gustafsson, J. E. (1976). *Verbal and figural abilities in relation to instructional methods: Studies in aptitude–treatment interaction.* Gothenburg: Acta Universitatis Gothoburgensis.

Gustafsson, J. E., Lindström, B., & Björk-Åkeson, E. (1981). *A general model for the organization of cognitive abilities.* Unpublished manuscript, Department of Education, University of Gothenburg.

Hagtvet, B. E. (1982, July). Word explanations of Norwegian preschoolers assessed by the Reynell Developmental Language Scales. Paper presented at the 20th International Congress of Applied Psychology, Edinburgh.

Hagtvet, B. E., & Lillestølen, R. (1985). *Reynells språktest* [The Reynell Developmental Language Scale]. Håndbok. Oslo; Universitetsforlaget.

Hagtvet, K. A. (1974). *The effect of time limits on the variance structure of test scores.* Unpublished master's thesis, Institute for Educational Research, University of Oslo.

Hagtvet, K. A. (1984). *Utviklingstendenser i engelsk og norsk prestasjoner på ungdomskoletrinnet i tidsrommet 1973–1981.* Department of Psychometrics, University of Bergen.

Hagtvet, K. A. (1985). A three-dimensional test anxiety construct: Worry and emotionality as mediating factors between negative motivation and test behavior. In J. J. Sánchez-Sosa (Ed.), *Health and clinical psychology* (pp. 109–133). Amsterdam: North-Holland.

Hagtvet, K. A. (1986, April). *Interaction of anxiety and ability on academic achievement: A simultaneous consideration of parameters.* Paper presented at the International Symposium on Test Anxiety, annual meeting of the American Educational Research Association, San Francisco.

Hagtvet, K. A., & Hagtvet, B. E. (1984). *The predictive validity of the Reynell Developmental*

Language Scales. A causal modeling study. Unpublished manuscript, Department of Psychometrics, University of Bergen/The Norwegian Institute for Special Education.

Härnquist, K. (1968). Relative changes in intelligence from 13 to 18. *Scandinavian Journal of Psychology, 9,* 50–82.

Härnquist, K., & Stahle, G. (1977). *An ecological analysis of test score changes over time* (Report No. 64). Institute of Education, University of Gothenburg.

Hofset, A. (1968). *Evnerike barn i grunnskolen.* Oslo: Universitetsforlaget.

Holter, H. (1961). Kjønnsforskjeller i skole – og arbeidsprestasjoner. *Tidsskrift for samfunnsforskning, 2,* 147–161.

Husén, T. (1950). *Testresultatens prognosvärde.* Stockholm: Gebers.

Jernquist, S. (1982). *Utviklingstendenser i matematikkprestasjoner på ungdomstrinnet i tidsrommet 1973–1981.* Unpublished master's thesis, University of Oslo.

Kaufman, A. S. (1979) *Intelligence testing with the WISC-R.* New York: Wiley.

Kaufman, A. S., & Doppelt, J. E. (1976). Analysis of WISC-R standardization data in terms of stratification variables. *Child Development, 47,* 165–171.

Langset, M. (1984). *Håndbok for WPPSI. Norsk utgave.* Oslo: Norsk psykologforening.

Levy, P. (1973). On the relation between test theory and psychology. In P. Kline (Ed.), *New approaches in psychological measurement.* New York: Wiley.

Lofthus, J. (1931). *Intelligensmåling.* Oslo.

Lofthus, J., Rasmussen, A., & Ribsskog, B. (1937). *Evnemålinger i folkeskolens 1. klasse. Dearborn gruppeprøve.* Oslo.

Looft, C. (1913). Intelligensundersøkelser av skolebarn. *Medicinsk Revue,* 569–585.

Lund, T., & Thrane, V. C. (1983). Schooling and intelligence. A methodological and longitudinal study. *Scandinavian Journal of Psychology, 24,* 161–173.

Lutey, C. (1977). *Individual intelligence testing: A manual and sourcebook* (2nd and enlarged ed.). Greeley, CO: Carol L. Lutey Publications.

McNemar, Q. (1964). Lost: Our intelligence. Why? *American Psychologist, 19,* 871–882.

Mønnesland, K. (1948). *Intelligensprøver for voksne.* Oslo: Norli.

Newcomer, P., Hare, B., Hammill, D., & McGettigan, J. (1975). Construct validity of the Illinois Test of Psycholinguistic Abilities. *Journal of Learning Disabilities, 8,* 220–231.

Nordvik, H. (1963). *Strukturen i intelligensen hos eldre mennesker.* Unpublished master's thesis, Department of Psychology, University of Oslo.

Nygaard, H. D. (1975). Den norske utgaven av Illinois Test of Psycholinguistic Abilities (ITPA). *Skolepsykologi, 10,* 3–10.

Nygård, R. (1977). IQ og intelligens. Noen betraktninger omkring individuelle forskjeller med utgagnspunkt i en motivasjonsteori. In T. Nordin & B. Sjøvall (Eds.), *Individualism och samhørighet. En vänbok til Wilhelm Sjøstrand.* Lund: Doxa.

Osgood, C. E. (1957). Motivational dynamics of language behavior. In M. R. Jones (Ed.), *Nebraska Symposium on Motivation* (pp. 348–424). Lincoln: University of Nebraska Press.

Pedersen, M. (1933). *Intelligensprøving av barn.* Oslo.

Poortinga, Y. H. (1975). Limitations on intercultural comparison of psychological data. *Nederlands Tijdschrift voor de Psychologie, 30,* 23–29.

Poortinga, Y. H. (1983). Psychometric approaches to intergroup comparison: The problem of equivalence. In S. H. Irvine & J. W. Berry (Eds.), *Human assessment and cultural factors* (pp. 237–257). New York: Plenum.

Raaheim, K. (1974). *Problem solving and intelligence.* Oslo: Universitetsforlaget.

Raaheim, K. (1986). Intelligence and task novelty. In R. J. Sternberg (Ed.), *Advances in the psychology of human intelligence* (*Vol. 4*). Hillsdale, NJ: Erlbaum.

Raaheim, K., & Brun, W. (1985). Task novelty and intelligence. *Scandinavian Journal of Psychology, 26,* 35–41.

Raaheim, K., Kaufman, G., & Kaufman, A. (1972). *Attempts to predict intelligent behavior. I. The ability to categorize flexibility.* Department of Psychology, University of Bergen.

Ramsøy, N. R. (1965). On the flow of talent in society. *Acta Sociologica, 9,* 152–174.

Rand, P. (1979). Main features of Johs. Sandven's research activity. In H. Dahl, A. Lysne, & P. Rand (Eds.), *A spotlight on educational problems*. Oslo: Universitetsforlaget.

Ribsskog, B. (1941). *Evneprøver for 1. klasse i folkeskolen. Standardisert på grunnlag av Kuhlmann-Andersons gruppeprøver*. Oslo.

Rist, T. (1982). *Det intellektuelle prestasjonsnivået i befolkningen sett i lys av den samfunnsmessige utviklinga*. Unpublished master's thesis, Department of Psychology, University of Oslo.

Sandven, J. (1943). *Intelligensmåling ved gruppeprøver*. Oslo: Cappelen.

Sandven, J. (1954). *Norsk standard av Terman–Merrill Stanford–revisjon av Binet-prøvene*. Oslo: Cappelen.

Sandven, J. (1962). Det teoretiske og metodiske grunnlag for modenhetsprøving. *Scandinavian Journal of Educational Research* (Pedagogisk Forskning), *6*, 147–168.

Sannum, L. (1976). *En studie av Sandvens modenhetsprøve Serie I–III med vekt på faktoranalyse*. Unpublished master's thesis, University of Trondheim.

Sarfi, S., & Smørvik, F. (1978). *Kristian Mønneslands gruppe-prøve, serie III. Rapport fra renormeringsarbeid utført sommeren 1978 ved Arbeidspsykologisk kontor i Oslo*. Unpublished manuscript.

Silva, P. A., Bradshaw, J., & Spears, G. F. (1978). *A study of concurrent and predictive validity of the Reynell Developmental Language Scales*. Otago, New Zealand: NFER.

Smith, L., Smørvik, D., Sommer, F. F., & von Tetzchner, S. (1982). A longitudinal study of low birthweight children: Reproductive, perinatal and environmental precursors of developmental status at three years of age. *Seminar in Perinatology, 6*, 294–304.

Smith, L., Smørvik, D., Sommer, F. F., & von Tetzchner, S. (1984, April). Longitudinal follow-up of low birthweight children to five years. Paper presented at the International Conference on Infant Studies, New York.

Smith, L., & von Tetzchner, S. (1984). Communicative, sensimotor, and language skills of young Down's Syndrome children. Department of Psychology, University of Oslo.

Solheim, R. (1975). Illinois Test of Psycholinguistic Abilities. *Skolepsykologi, 10*, 12–21.

Statistical Digest. (1983). Paris: UNESCO.

Sundet, J. M., Tambs, K., & Magnus, P. (1981). Heritability analysis as a means of analyzing the effects of social changes on psychological variables. An empirical study of IQ-scores. *Psychiatry and Social Science, 1*, 241–248.

Thrane, V. C. (1961). *Avgangskarakterer i folkeskolen. Militærpsykologiske meddelelser*. Oslo: Forsvarets Psykologiske Avdeling.

Undheim, J. O. (1972). *A classificatory system of intellectual performance: The Structure-of-Intellect model* (Psychological Research Report No. 1). University of Trondheim, AVH, Department of Psychology.

Undheim, J. O. (1976). Ability structure in 10–11-year-old children and the theory of fluid and crystallized intelligence. *Journal of Educational Psychology, 68*, 411–423.

Undheim, J. O. (1978a). Broad ability factors in 12- to 13-year-old children. The theory of fluid and crystallized intelligence, and the differentiation hypothesis. *Journal of Educational Psychology, 70*, 433–443.

Undheim, J. O. (1978b). *WISC-R håndbok. Norsk utgave*. Oslo: Norsk Psykologforening.

Undheim, J. O. (1978c). Intelligens og kjønn. *Forskningsnytt fra NAVF, 23*, 5, 11–15.

Undheim, J. O. (1979). Capitalization on chance: The case of Guilford's memory abilities. *Scandinavian Journal of Psychology, 20*, 71–76.

Undheim, J. O. (1981a). On intelligence I. Broad ability factors in 15-year-old children and Cattell's theory of fluid and crystallized intelligence. *Scandinavian Journal of Psychology, 22*, 171–179.

Undheim, J. O. (1981b). On intelligence II: A neo-Spearman model to replace Cattell's broad ability theory of fluid and crystallized intelligence. *Scandinavian Journal of Psychology, 22*, 181–187.

Undheim, J. O. (1981c). On intelligence III. Examining developmental implications of Cattell's broad ability theory and of an alternative neo-Spearman model. *Scandinavian Journal of Psychology, 22,* 243–249.

Undheim, J. O. (1984). Diagnostisering av dysleksi – en første rapport fra Trondheimsprosjektet angående leseprosessen og spesielle lese – og skrivevansker. In I. A. Bjørgen (Ed.), *Lesning og lesevansker* (Rapport no. 5). Trondheim, Norway: NAVF-Senter for barneforskning.

Undheim, J. O., & Horn, J. L. (1977). Critical evaluation of Guilford's Structure-of-Intellect theory. *Intelligence, 1,* 65–81.

Vormeland, O. (1967). *Begynnerundervisningen i norsk og regning.* Oslo: Universitetsforlaget.

Wechsler, D. (1974). *WISC-R. Wechsler Intelligence Scale for Children* (rev. ed.). New York: The Psychological Corporation.

Wickelgren, W. A. (1977). *Learning and memory.* Englewood Cliffs, NJ: Prentice-Hall.

William, U., & Roberts, G. (1972). *The Welsh Children's Intelligence Scale.* Windsor, U. K.: NFER.

Wold, A. H. (1975). Illinois Test of Psycholinguistic Abilities. En kritisk diskusjon. *Skolepsykologi, 10,* 3–14.

Africa, Asia and Australia

11   Human assessment in Australia

Daphne M. Keats and John A. Keats

Introduction

The psychological assessment of human abilities in Australia has a very long history. An Australian had, by 1917, created a test for the assessment of cognitive abilities in Australian Aborigines. This was the famous *Porteus Maze Test* (Porteus, 1917). Its appearance then was remarkable, because for a long time only anthropologists had shown much interest in the abilities of Aborigines. There was, indeed, little interest of any kind in ethnic or cultural minorities, let alone their capabilities. It was even more remarkable that the first example of cross-cultural test development for a specific culture occurred in Australia so soon after the start of modern psychological testing signalled by Binet's work.

The prevailing view of *pre–World War II* Australians was, nevertheless, that they were a white people of British stock. Britain was home and many family members remained there. Family-kinship terms were often invoked when people referred to their British background. As American influence spread from World War II onwards, Australians moved closer culturally to those other "cousins." Thereafter, many British visiting or settling in Australia found it too American, whereas the few Americans who came there found it quaintly British. Americans barely knew its geographical location: Even today, many have little idea of its size or of its predominantly urban development, or that the language spoken is English. The cultural shift was in one direction only.

In the last 30 years far-reaching changes have affected the structure of Australian society. With the end of the "White Australia Policy" and a yearly intake of many thousands of immigrants, Australia has become a multicultural society. Now more than 100 languages are spoken and the immigrants are drawn from all continents. Over 25% of the population have parents born in non-English-speaking countries. The proportion of those under 16 years of age who have parents born in non-English-speaking countries is even greater. The larger number of these children of non-British overseas origin and the increase in the recorded Aboriginal population present a strong challenge to the traditional stereotypes of national identity as British. The problems associated with the assessment of the abilities of

283

these educational and cultural minorities are now becoming apparent. Both academically and politically, the presence of sizable minority groups influences the assessment of abilities generally in Australia.

The mainstream of abilities testing in Australia developed in order to serve the applied fields of educational diagnosis and classification, clinical assessment, and vocational selection. The major producer and distributor of tests is the Australian Council for Educational Research (ACER), which began its work in 1930. Apart from the psychological profession, the main users are the State Departments of Education. ACER distributes its own tests as well as those imported from overseas. It has developed a high level of expertise in the construction of tests, and researchers from ACER have been in the forefront of psychometric developments. Other Australians have also made substantial contributions to psychometric theory: An evaluation of these appears near the end of the chapter.

The 1980s brought a marked change in attitude towards abilities testing. As is often the case in Australia, the wave of reaction against intelligence testing came somewhat later than in the United States, but reflected it. By the time such movements reach Australia, there has been time for the basis for both the challenges and the responses to have become well known and much of the furore has gone from the debate. Nevertheless, the antitest movement has had an impact, driven by protagonists from the immigrant communities and the Australian Teachers Federation. The immigrant communities, where the native language is not English, are mainly concerned with the possibility that the language component in general ability tests may militate against the fair assessment of children of migrant origins. The teachers' groups, on the other hand, are concerned with the possibility of inherent biases reflecting hierarchical social stratification and differential opportunity related to sex and socioeconomic status.

A sense of identity?

The question mark must remain, for it is doubtful whether Australian society in the 1980s is any closer to a unique cultural identity than it was in the 1930s. Even if the pioneer traditions were derived from the British in the 1930s, they gave credence to the myths of an egalitarian society, individualistic and struggling against hostile environmental forces. The myths of "mateship" and "the pioneering spirit" had been reinforced by war experience and were well entrenched, especially in Australian males. Strong labour union traditions had been established; sex roles were clear and questioned by few; and egalitarianism was accepted as a prevailing value. For treatments of these issues, see, for example, Clark (1963) and Horne (1964). These myths, and others like them, were pervasive enough to bestow a sense of cultural identity which was discernible to Australians themselves, if not to others. Nowadays Australians are caricatured by "outsiders" for these very qualities. In the 1930s, however, Aboriginal Australians and newcomers alike found themselves under pressure to conform. The wave of postwar European migrants was confidently expected to blend into this same identity within a short time. It did not happen as easily as that.

At present, Australia is trying to come to terms with the effects of the immigration policies which have turned it into a "multicultural" society. Many of the "old" Australians, that is, those of British stock, have difficulty in coping with this concept. The newcomers, on their part, meet some resistance. Many find difficulties with the language and acculturation and cling to contrary norms. Today problems of assessment are not with the adult immigrants themselves but with the second generation: children who find themselves juggling the expectations of their family to do better than others so as to make the most of their chances on one hand, and the demands of peers and school on the other. Most do it very well. Possibly the greatest problems are faced by the teachers of classes in areas of high immigrant density where up to three-quarters of the class may not be native speakers of English and may have school backgrounds as varied as the languages they speak.

Assessment and selection for an egalitarian society

There is no doubt that the widespread use of standardised ability testing in Australia had its ideological base in the ideal of the egalitarian society. Special opportunities had to be created for the very bright, as well as the handicapped; unless a child was selected into the upper academic stream, he or she would have little chance of proceeding to university education. In the 1930s the first special classes were set up in New South Wales for gifted and retarded children. Entry to selective high schools was based on similar testing, as well as school performance. It was a paradox that children were tested to establish their potential and for streaming into schools and classes based on ability. Many bright children of the working classes thus gained their opportunity, as many prominent public figures now testify. The paradox rested in the fact that although a gifted child was thus given an opportunity despite unfavourable social background, the hierarchical streaming system in both primary and secondary schools created its own rigid social system.

The 1970s and 1980s have seen the gradual disappearance of special classes for bright children and a trend away from selective to community-based high schools. Special schools for the severely mentally retarded continue, but the present trend is away from mass assessment for the purpose of placement towards individual assessment with a view to integrating children with intellectual handicap – and severe physical handicap also – into the mainstream of classes (Doherty, 1982). Thus the demand for group general ability testing is now waning, while the need for more "valid" and more "reliable" methods of individual assessment is increasing. Although this description of events and trends is accurate for the state of New South Wales, it may be judged less so for some other states. However, the trend away from mass ability testing and towards individual assessment is general.

Tests: Derivative or Australian?

The group ability tests used in these assessments have mostly been produced by the ACER. The norming base is Australian, although the format and style of the tests and the psychometric techniques of item construction and validation are all strongly influenced by overseas models, especially the work of the Educational Testing Service (ETS) in the United States. The tests constructed in the late 1940s and 1950s remained in use for many years. The main criticism levelled at these tests is that they were kept in use far too long, although the demand persisted. However, some of the most frequently used tests have recently been updated and renormed. Recent developments of new group tests include the production of the *Non-Verbal Ability Tests* (*NAT*). As described by Rowe (1984), the *NAT* is a battery of 18 nonverbal group-administered tests in four groups – *perceptual ability, conceptual categorisation, attention,* and *memory*. The perceptual ability group includes tests of matching shape and direction. The conceptual categorisation group includes tests of picture completion, embedded figures, figure formation, mazes, sequencing, and picture arrangement. The attention group includes a simple attention task, a combined attention/conceptual test, and three attention/perceptual tests. The four memory tests include visual and auditory recognition and recall.

The derivative nature of much of assessment by *group* tests can be illustrated by the extensive use of the *Raven's Progressive Matrices Tests* (*RPM*). These tests were conceived by Raven in the early 1930s, and have remained unchanged, although not unchallenged, ever since. For example, in the 1970s almost all New South Wales high school students aged 15 years were tested by the Vocational Guidance Bureau using *RPM*, backed up by an ACER general ability test with numerical and verbal subtests. That the *RPM* has acceptance as a standard testing instrument in Australia is shown by the continuing demand for it and the very large volume of research in which it has been employed. However, current norms for Australia are based on data collected in 1949 and 1952–1953; and Australian norms for *Raven's Standard Progressive Matrices* were available for the first time in 1955. De Lemos (1984) shows that substantial anomalies exist between these norms and data from more recent studies and from the British 1979 norms. A restandardisation of the *Standard Progressive Matrices* is planned by ACER. That alone will ensure its survival for even longer.

Individual assessment is even more dependent on overseas tests, if that seems possible. The assessment batteries most used are *WAIS, WISC, WISC-R* and *WPPSI*, and the *Stanford–Binet*, and all the standard repertoire of North American and British psychological tests are available. Adaptations of content have been made to *WAIS* (Harwood & Naylor, 1972) and *WISC-*

R (Rowe, 1976), but these are minor changes in only a few items. The *British Abilities Scales* have not yet had much application in Australia, although they have attracted some interest. No Australian norms are available. The *Kaufman Test* (Kaufman & Kaufman, 1983) is also enjoying some use, but again no Australian norms are available. The only Australian individual tests to have been constructed in many years are the *Queensland Test* (McElwain & Kearney, 1970) and the *ACER Early School Series* (Rowe, 1981) for school beginners and lower primary grades.

The *Queensland Test* is of special interest in cultural context. It employs a performance mode and may be given using vernacular instructions and mime. It was designed for use with tribal Aborigines, Papua–New Guineans, non-English speakers, and the deaf. The item types were derived after extensive field trials from other nonverbal tests used in early work overseas: for example, the *Alexander Passalong Test,* a two-dimensional version of the *Kohs Block Designs,* and the *Beads Test.* Norms for tribal, fringe-dwelling, and urban-dwelling Aborigines have shown a high correlation between performance levels and degree of acculturation to the white society, hence sets of norms are presented separately for each of these three groups. The test appears to have potential when applied to subjects with hearing loss, expressive language difficulty, and limited facility in English, while retaining its robustness in nonliterate societies. Finally, for an account of its New Guinea origins, and complete description of its components, readers are referred to Ord (1971).

The *ACER Early School Series* comprises 10 tests, namely *Auditory Discrimination; Recognition of Initial Consonant Sounds; Number Test; Figure Formation Test; Prepositions; Pronouns; Verb Tense; Negation; Comprehension; Word Knowledge.* The contrast between this test with its emphasis on school-based learning and the *Queensland Test* with its nonverbal, non-school aspects is striking.

Assessment of educational and cultural minorities

It can be seen from these examples that Australian psychologists have at their disposal an extensive test repertoire for the assessment of abilities, but that few of the instruments in that repertoire are Australian in origin. How *appropriate,* then, are such assessment instruments to Australian children or adults, whether of British, European, Asian, or Aboriginal cultural origin? This question is probably easiest to answer for the group ability tests devised by ACER, which are based on Australian samples and Australian norms. Whatever drawbacks they have are related to the adequacy of the sampling frames used for the norming and the statistical techniques used for item selection. As the children of the immigrant population are well represented in the sampling frames, their performance does contribute to those norms. Also, the use of such tests is not recommended for children who lack familiarity with the language or who have been fewer than 4 years in Australia

(O'Neill, 1984). The more subtle problems relate to the role of cultural bias in the content of the items and the underlying theory or theories of intelligence upon which they are based.

These questions are central to the recent criticisms coming from teachers' groups. Much of such criticism has been ill-founded and misguided and has been trenchantly answered by O'Neill (1984). The questions have been addressed at a more sophisticated level in the writing of Klich and Davidson (Davidson & Klich, 1980; Davidson, 1984), and are discussed more fully in relation to Aboriginal cognition in Chapter 17. The general problem transfers also to other ethnic and cultural minorities in Australia. Davidson (1984) is critical of using norm-referenced ability testing with *any* educational minority group. He argues that performance estimates based on this type of testing have been shown to be so strongly influenced by situational factors, especially schooling, that it is not possible to compensate for the inherent cultural biases in either the language or the cultural content of the items. Davidson asserts that the same is true of nonverbal tests and, further, that experimenter attention to the test situation in order to improve motivation does not make any difference to the ability of the tests to show how the child is thinking. Such facts are concerned only with the answers, not with the method of reaching them. Many of these shortcomings could in theory be overcome by individual testing, but the presence of cultural bias in the content of tests such as the *WISC-R* and *Binet* tests can be easily demonstrated by modern item-bias techniques such as those surveyed by Poortinga and van der Flier in Chapter 6. Modifications made to the *WISC-R* and *Binet* by ACER have been confined to minor changes in the item content only.

Another approach to this problem has been to look for alternative models of intelligence. An example of this is the distinction between simultaneous and successive processing as developed by Das and Kirby (Das, Kirby, & Jarman, 1979). This idea has been used as a possible explanation for reports of Aborigines' superior memory for visually presented stimulus arrays (Kearins, 1976). However, Klich and Davidson (1983) showed that apparent deficits in non-Aboriginal children could be counteracted by drawing their attention to the critical features of the stimulus sets and the task demands; in effect, using a brief "orientation" or training procedure before commencing the task. The application of the simultaneous–successive processing distinction to school performances in reading (Gordon, 1982) and mathematics (Becker, 1984) has shown some promise of assisting children with problems in these areas. However, much more work must be done to validate this model and show its applicability in various situations.

The effects of small changes in procedure and instructions (which Irvine and Berry refer to in Chapter 1 as *treatment* variables) have been shown to be quite substantial for other Australian minorities. For example, Davis and Goodnow (1977) reduced differences between the performance of Greek-born and Australian-born children on a concept-learning task by changes in instructions. In a cross-cultural study of formal operational thinking comparing Australian, Malay, and Chinese high school students, Munnings (1980) found that emphasis on speed was detrimental to the performance of the Australians and Malays but not of the Chinese, whereas emphasis on *parsimony* – making as few mistakes as possible – was able to bring about the best performance in all groups. Such findings suggest that more attention needs to be paid to the cultural basis of what is regarded as good performance and the "right" way to approach cognitive tasks in cross-cultural assessment situations. These questions have been raised in the Australian context by Goodnow (1980). A beginning has been made with some cross-cultural work in Malaysia and Australia (Gill & Keats, 1980), and China and Australia (Keats, 1982), but more work needs to be done within Australia itself.

The role of language

The role played by language usage in cognitive performance has been the focus of much attention, especially as it might affect the assessment of children from non-English-speaking ethnic backgrounds. The interdependence of language and cognitive performance is stressed by those who judge the non-English-speaking child to be unduly disadvantaged in assessment and who at the same time wish to promote the use of ethnic languages (Smolicz & Lean, 1979).

The evidence for this position is not as strong as their claims might suggest. For example, Tenezakis (1979) carried out a study relating the acquisition of conservation concepts to language use in Australian-born Greek-speaking children. Following the procedures used by Sinclair-de Zwart (1967), she compared the frequency of the use of coordinated syntax and differentiated terms by conservers and nonconservers. Despite variations in the languages used at home and in the testing, all groups displayed equivalent performance on the conservation tasks, and there were no significant differences between conservers and nonconservers on the use of coordinated syntax or relational terms and no differences on the language comprehension measure used. Tenezakis concludes (p. 138):

This study showed that children, whether they are bilingual or monolingual, may be found to use well-organised patterns of expression and yet miss the point on the conservation problem. Also children may understand the principle of conservation even though absolute terms (and, indeed, grammatically incorrect forms as well) may be displayed more frequently in their speech than comparatives and correct grammatical forms. These results do not support the view that, within the age range considered, language leads thought. Rather, the results provide support for the Genevan hypothesis that language is structured by logic, rather than vice versa.

Keats and Keats (1974) came to a similar conclusion in a study of concept acquisition in bilingual German-English- and Polish-English-speaking children. Using a crossover design and a training procedure, they found that training in *one* of the children's two languages produced substantial improvement in the concept when testing was carried out in the *other* language immediately after training. Approximately equal long-term effects on delayed post-tests were found in both languages 1 to 2 months later. The stability of these effects was demonstrated in further studies in Malaysia with Chinese-English- and Malay-English-speaking children (Keats, Keats, & Wan Rafaei, 1976) and in China with two different Chinese dialects, and one dialect and another language, Uyghur (Keats, Keats, & Liu, 1982). The training effects overcame the initial performance differences among different language groups and between bilinguals and their monolingual controls. Performance on concept-formation tests was not found to be related to language usage measures. Despite robust results such as these the question of the precise role of language in cognitive performance is still debated. The work from the Keatses and their colleagues specifies that the effects of language deficit in English are largely confined to those aspects of the assessment procedures which are concerned with understanding the instructions and comprehending the expectations of the task, but where translations are available, as in the above studies, the effects are minimal.

A further illustration of this trend, using another measurement paradigm, can be seen in the findings of Evans and Poole (1975). They carried out not a *training*, but a *domain* factor-analytic study of the relative performance of an Australian-born and a migrant group of children on a broad-spectrum battery of 14 tests. These were reading and word knowledge; picture vocabulary; aural comprehension; visual-spatial tests; some mathematics tasks; and a group of tasks testing the ability to follow simple instructions. The children were all in fifth grade. Half came from schools with a high migrant density and half from schools with low density. The ethnic groups represented were Italian, Greek, Yugoslav, Turk, and some others, but no breakdowns by ethnic group were reported in the analysis.

The migrant children's poorer performance in language was evident in their functional use of language in listening, reading, following instructions, noting details, and grasping the general impact of a statement. Once a cognitive task was understood, the deficit was not great. For the migrant children Reading, Reasoning, and Mathematics factors were highly related, but for the Australian children the correlations between these variables were much lower, although they were also clustered. These results confirm the general cross-cultural trend. Performance becomes less differentiated when fluency in the official language is an intervening variable.

The practical problems of assessing the cognitive abilities of non-native English-speaking Australians lie in the difficulty of finding substitutes for instruments designed for use with native English speakers. Translation alone is not the answer. School psychologists and administrators of education systems most need these assessments for placement of children and for deciding what special programmes may be required. There are so many language groups that it is not a practical proposition to suggest that testing should be in the children's native languages. What would the norms of tests mean in Australia if they were devised for use within the child's native culture? How would one deal with a child from a culture where no such tests were available? At present the only feasible way to handle the problem is to use "nonverbal" measures and individual testing in which the child's functional use of English for understanding the instructions and task demands can be maximised by careful attention to this aspect of the testing procedures.

Relationships between cognitive performance and social variables

The contribution of motivational and socioeconomic factors to performance has been of greatest concern in regard to migrant children and Aborigines. In social contexts these two factors are seldom independent and in research have frequently been confounded with the effects of culture and ethnicity. Perhaps the most incisive study of these interactions has been carried out by Marjoribanks (1979), who uses the term *ethclass* for the combined category of ethnicity and social class. His work has revealed substantial differences in motivational levels between *ethclasses* and different patterns of expectations and school performance. However, the relationship between performance and motivation – either the child's or the parents' – was not found to be consistently positive and social class differences in most cases outweighed differences based on ethnic group.

The possibility of sex-based bias in Australian ability tests continues to be debated. On the *ACER Australian Scholastic Aptitude Test (ASAT)* a detailed analysis by Adams (1984) revealed no bias based on sex. Despite recent controversy, sex bias is not a significant factor in the standardised general ability tests constructed by ACER. Far more influential are social role and status factors which are reinforced by teachers' perceptions, by parental expectations, and by the boys and girls themselves. These subtle, and powerful, networks of social reinforcements persuade girls into some educational channels and boys into others.

Piagetian approaches

Australian psychologists have been active in Piagetian research since the 1950s. One of the first empirical reports of the transition from concrete to formal operational thinking was that of Keats (1955). In the following two decades Piagetian research centred on the cognitive abilities of Aborigines was carried out under Seagrim in Canberra by Dasen (1972), De Lemos (1969), and Somerville (1970). At Newcastle under the influence of Keats work by Halford (1969), Sheppard (1973), Collis (1972), Seggie (1971), and Jurd (1975) was carried out and is reported in Keats, Collis, and Halford (1978). In Queensland, Halford (1982) continues the tradition with considerable success. Cross-cultural studies, for example by Kelly (1977), Heron and Dowel (1973), and D. Keats and her students (Keats, 1979) have extended this work to other cultures in the Asian and Pacific region. Piagetian studies with Aboriginal groups are discussed in Chapter 17 by Klich.

These studies have been of both theoretical and practical significance. Keats, Collis, and Halford (1978) and Halford (1985) draw together and review some of the major theoretical progress. Integration of measurement theory and Piagetian theory was developed further by Keats (1983) and is dealt with separately in this chapter. Practical applications in education have been the concern of many writers, including Collis's (1978) work with mathematical concepts and Jurd's (1978) with concepts in history. Applications in mathematics led Collis to formulate a stage between the concrete and formal operational stages, which he termed the stage of "concrete generalisation." Collis and Biggs (1980) have also made a major applied contribution in their SOLO (Structure of the Observed Learning Outcome) Taxonomy. This is a method of analysing cognitive performance according to levels which can be applied to any subject matter. They applied it to aspects of mathematics and creative writing.

Another extension from Piagetian work has been the use of training to facilitate advances in thinking. Training has also been used as a methodological device to examine confounded variables such as language and culture. The effectiveness of training programmes has been demonstrated in the studies of the language and thought relationship (Keats & Keats, 1974, and elsewhere), in cross-cultural studies of operational thinking (Munnings, 1980; Keats, 1985), and in studies of the acquisition of the concept of correlation by Jurd (1978) and Thomson (1983). The latter study owed much to the training studies by Case (1983).

In all, the Piagetian researchers have brought much influence to bear upon the assessment of cognitive abilities. One of their strengths has been the integration of theoretical and applied advances. The cross-cultural material gives support to Piaget's general theory of development and has provided much needed evidence to refute myths of nonwestern inferiority in cognitive tasks. This body of work is derivative in that it was dependent in the first instance upon Piaget's pioneering thinking, but it has pursued a vigorous and independent line.

Australian contributions to psychometric theory

As noted by Keats (1967b) the shortage of research funds for empirical studies of human assessment in Australia has led to a number of theoretical contributions which are much less expensive. As would be expected, the construction of psychological tests by Porteus (1917) and Cunningham and McIntyre in the 1930s was assisted by the developed methodology from Europe and North America to a considerable extent; but even in those days some mathematical innovations were introduced by McIntyre using theoretical frequency distributions and later by Bradshaw in unpublished work on the concept of suppressor variables. For a review of such early developments, see Connell (1980).

World War II led to a massive increase in test construction for the services and this was carried over to educational research after the war. With the wealth of Australian data collected, Keats (1951; Keats & Lord, 1962) took up again the question of the application of theoretical frequency distributions to psychometric test data. He was able to develop a mathematical model, which led to what is now called the *beta-binomial* model, and generalised this to nonlinear cases. The way was paved for a number of original Australian contributions to psychometric theory which have current significance; for example, the first latent state theory of test performance was proposed by Brownless and Keats (1958).

The origins of the concept of homogeneous tests seem to have been lost in history. Certainly, workers in the United Kingdom and North America were using the concept in the 1950s, but Lumsden (1957) in Australia was also working towards a resolution of the problem of test homogeneity. The uniquely Australian contribution came from McDonald (1967) when he showed that the nonlinear factor-analytic methods he developed had an important significance, theoretically and practically, for solving the problem of defining test homogeneity. These two researchers have continued to develop this line of thinking (Lumsden, 1978; McDonald, 1981) and to show its relevance to current theory and practice.

The original work of Rasch (1960) was accepted by Australian and British psychometricians more readily than by North American psychometricians, for both its theoretical and its practical significance (Keats, 1967a). More generally, "latent trait" models have been more congenial to them than American "item response theory" models, which tend to obscure the chief significance of this work. The objective is to quantify individual differences on latent abilities rather than to emphasise the significance of item parameters. In this context the European approach is more acceptable to Australians and this fact reflects an independent approach to the subject matter. The work of Andrich and of Douglas reported in Spearritt (1982) and elsewhere, as well as work noted below, illustrates this point.

At the ACER conference reported in Spearritt (1982), Keats noted that the use by Rasch and others of the term *person parameter* was strictly statistical and referred to the theoretical quantity being estimated at the time. However, for subjects under 15 years of age, this quantity is a *variable increasing with age* and could hardly be thought of as a single quantity characteristic of the person. On the other hand, parameters of a cognitive growth model which varied from person to person but remained constant for a given person over time could be thought of as person parameters in a strict sense and should predict the person's change in performance over time.

The model suggested by Keats related ability (A) at a given age (t) to a latent adult level (C) and a rate of development parameter (D) according to a projective law, that is, $A = aCDt/(Dt + C)$ where a is a constant to allow for changes in units. It is more convenient to write this equation in terms of $c = 1/C$ and $d = 1/D$ whence $A = at/(ct + d)$. It may be noted that in terms of the new symbols, adult level becomes a/c in units of ability, and d/c in units of time corresponds to the age at which the person reaches half of the adult level. Part of the strength of this formulation lies in the fact that it is possible to relate the ratio IQ of *Binet–Stern* to the parameter values $c(i)$ and $d(i)$ for a particular individual (i) such that $100/IQ = [c(i) - $ Mean $c] t/$Mean $d + d(i)/$Mean d. Thus the model predicts that subjects with an estimated adult level greater than average – that is, $c(i) < $ Mean c – will have increasing ratio IQs until their performance becomes affected by the ceiling of the test, but that those with estimated adult levels less than average will have decreasing ratio IQs. Data reported by a number of writers confirm this prediction (Keats, 1983).

The cognitive development model may be extended to include an environmental factor e which remains the same for subjects within similar cognitive environments but differs from environment to environment. Longitudinal data collected by Braggett (1975) conform to this extended model and indicate that home and preschool together are one and a half times as cognitively stimulating as home environment alone (Keats, Fulham, & Braggett, 1985). The model is consistent with other findings from the study of both physical and psychological development. These analyses emphasise the need for longitudinal data collection if the effects of various cognitive environments are to be assessed.

Conclusion

The assessment of cognitive abilities continues to be one of the major foci of psychological and educational research in Australia. We have not attempted in this chapter to catalogue all the work being done. Our aim was rather to comment on it as a response from the Australian cultural context.

One theme which emerges is the problem of developing appropriate instruments for use in what is now a multicultural, multilingual society. It is recognised that language and the cultural content of the assessment instruments may have different biasing influences. This theme has attracted much critical and emotive writing, but as yet the precise nature of these biases has not been empirically demonstrated.

A second theme, implicit rather than explicit in our analysis, is the lag between the publication of sophisticated Australian contributions to measurement theory and methods and their appearance in the applications of the users. Practitioners have not, for example, demanded the creation of Australian-based instruments for individual assessment; and they continue to use American and British instruments with very little concern for their validity in the Australian environment. Significantly, the IQ measure used by Keats in developing the model described above was the *Binet Test*.

Human assessment in Australia is moving slowly towards the use of computers (Spearritt, 1982). Doubtless, after a decade or so, much of the research and application will be carried out using such devices; but many questions will need to be answered theoretically and empirically before this transition can be effected. Unfortunately, the resources required to carry out pure and applied research in this field are not readily available in Australia, and many of the issues are being ignored elsewhere. The question of the extent to which computerised tests measure the same variables and with the same reliability as pencil-and-paper tests with the same items has seldom been explored. Although it is true that computers can provide adaptive testing using the Rasch model or some variation of it, as well as random parallel tests, instant feedback, and response times, the usefulness of these additional options does not seem to have been thoroughly evaluated. However, awareness of the need for applied research as well as theoretical studies is becoming more general; and at the University of Newcastle some pure and applied studies on these very questions are proceeding.

References

ACER (1982). *Australian Scholastic Aptitude Test*. Melbourne: ACER.

ACER (1985). *Non-Verbal Ability Tests*. Australian Council for Educational Research (ACER). Melbourne.

Adams, R. (1984). Sex bias in ASAT? *ACER Research Monograph No. 24*. Melbourne: ACER.

Becker, L. (1984). *Learning disabilities in arithmetic: An information processing approach*. Unpublished master's thesis, University of Newcastle, Australia.

Braggett, E. J. (1975). *The effect of preschool kindergarten attendance on aspects of cognitive development*. Unpublished doctoral dissertation, University of Newcastle, Australia.

Brownless, V., & Keats, J. A. (1958). A re-test method of studying partial knowledge and other factors influencing item response. *Psychometrika, 23*(1), 67–73.

Case, R. (1983). *Intellectual development: A systematic reinterpretation*. New York: Academic Press.

Clark, M. (1963). *A short history of Australia*. London: Mentor Books, New English Library.

Collis, K. F. (1972). *A study of concrete and formal operations in school mathematics*. Unpublished doctoral dissertation, University of Newcastle, Australia.

Collis, K. F. (1978). Operational thinking in elementary mathematics. In J. A. Keats, K. F. Collis, & G. S. Halford, *Cognitive development: Research based on a neo-Piagetian approach*. Chichester, U.K.: Wiley.

Collis, K. F., & Biggs, J. (1980). *The SOLO Taxonomy*. Melbourne: ACER.

Connell, W. F. (1980). *The Australian Council for Educational Research, 1930–1980*. Melbourne: ACER.

Das, J., Kirby, J., & Jarman, R. (1979). *Simultaneous and successive processing*. New York: Academic Press.

Dasen, P. R. (1972). Cross-cultural Piagetian research. *Journal of Cross-Cultural Psychology, 3*, 23–29.

Davidson, G. R. (1984). Cognitive testing of educational minorities: A search for alternatives. *Australian Educational and Developmental Psychologist, 1*(2), 39–53.

Davidson, G. R., & Klich, L. Z. (1980). Cultural factors in the development of temporal and spatial ordering. *Child Development, 51*, 569–571.

Davis, M., & Goodnow, J. J. (1977). Problem-solving strategies: Use by Australian children with Australian and Greek parentage. *Journal of Cross-cultural Psychology, 8*(1), 33–47.

De Lemos, M. M. (1969). Conceptual development in Aboriginal children: Implications for Aboriginal education. In S. S. Dunn & C. M. Tatz (Eds.), *Aborigines and education* (pp. 244–263). Melbourne: Sun Books.

De Lemos, M. M. (1984). A note on the Australian norms for the Standard Progressive Matrices. *ACER Bulletin for Psychologists* (No. 36), 9–12.

Doherty, P. J. (1982). *Strategies and initiatives for special education in New South Wales.* A report of the Working Party on a Plan for Special Education in N.S.W.

Evans, G. T., & Poole, M. E. (1975). Relationships between verbal and non-verbal abilities for migrant children and Australian children of low socio-economic status: Similarities and contrasts. *Australian Journal of Education, 19*(3), 209–230.

Gill, R., & Keats, D. M. (1980). Elements of intellectual competence: Judgements by Australian and Malay university students. *Journal of Cross-Cultural Psychology, 11*(2), 233–243.

Goodnow, J. J. (1980). Concepts of intelligence and development. In N. Warren (Ed.), *Studies in cross-cultural psychology* (Vol. 2). London: Pergamon.

Gordon, C. J. (1982). *A comparative study of the role of word-based skills and processing strategies in the reading comprehension of primary school children.* Unpublished master's thesis, University of Newcastle, Australia.

Halford, G. S. (1969). *An investigation of concept learning: A study of conservation of quantity in children.* Unpublished doctoral dissertation, University of Newcastle, Australia.

Halford, G. S. (1982). *The development of thought.* Hillsdale, NJ: Erlbaum.

Halford, G. S. (1985). Cognitive development. In N. T. Feather (Ed.), *Australian psychology: A review of research.* Academy of Social Sciences, Australia.

Harwood, E., & Naylor, G. F. (1971). Changes in the constitution of the WAIS intelligence pattern with advancing age. *Australian Journal of Psychology, 23,* 297–303.

Heron, A., & Dowel, W. (1973). Weight conservation and matrix solving ability in Papuan children. *Journal of Cross-Cultural Psychology, 4,* 207–219.

Horne, D. R. (1964). *The lucky country: Australia in the sixties.* Ringwood, Victoria: Penguin.

Jurd, M. (1975). *Some aspects of the understanding of social science concepts in adolescents.* Report presented to the National Committee for Social Science Teaching, Canberra.

Jurd, M. (1978). Concrete and formal operational thinking in history. In J. A. Keats, K. F. Collis, & G. S. Halford, (Eds) *Cognitive development research based on a neo-Piagetian approach.* Chichester, U.K.: Wiley.

Kaufman, A. S., & Kaufman, N. L. (1983). The Kaufman assessment battery for children (K-ABC). Girder Pines, MN: American Guidance Service.

Kearins, J. (1976). Skills of desert Aboriginal children. In G. E. Kearney & D. W. McElwain (Eds.), *Aboriginal cognition.* Canberra: Australian Institute of Aboriginal Studies.

Keats, D. M. (1979). Cross-cultural studies in cognitive development and language in Malaysia and Australia. *Educational Research and Perspectives, 6,* 46–63.

Keats, D. M. (1982). Cultural bases of concepts of intelligence: A Chinese versus Australian comparison. Proceedings: Second Asian Workshop on Child and Adolescent Development, 67–75.

Keats, D. M. (1985). Control and manipulation of variables in cross-cultural studies of cognitive functioning in Asian contexts. In R. Diaz-Guerrero (Ed.), *Cross-cultural and national studies in social psychology. Proceedings of the XXIII International Congress of Psychology.* Amsterdam: North-Holland.

Keats, D. M., & Keats, J. A. (1974). The effect of language on concept acquisition in bilingual children. *Journal of Cross-Cultural Psychology, 5,* 80–99.

Keats, D. M., Keats, J. A., & Wan Rafaei (1976). Concept acquisition in Malaysian bilingual children. *Journal of Cross-Cultural Psychology, 7,* 87–99.

Keats, J. A. (1951). *A statistical theory of objective test scores.* Melbourne: ACER.

Keats, J. A. (1955). *Formal and concrete thought processes.* Unpublished doctoral dissertation, Princeton University; University Microfilms, Ann Arbor.

Keats, J. A. (1967a). Test theory. *Annual Review of Psychology, 18,* 217–238.

Keats, J. A. (1967b). Australian advances in mathematical psychology. *Australian Journal of Science, 29,* 450–455.

Keats, J. A. (1983). Ability measures and theories of cognitive development. In H. Wainer & S. Messick (Eds.), *Principals of psychological measurement.* Hillsdale, NJ: Erlbaum.

Keats, J. A., Collis, K. F., & Halford, G. S. (Eds.). (1978). *Cognitive development: Research based on a neo-Piagetian model.* Chichester, U.K.: Wiley.

Keats, J. A., Fulham, R., & Braggett, E. J. (1985). *A model of environmental effects on cognitive development: Theory and applications.* Paper delivered at the 50th Annual Conference of the Psychometric Society, Nashville, TN.

Keats, J. A., & Keats, D. M. (1974). The effect of language on concept acquisition in bilingual children. *Journal of Cross-Cultural Psychology, 5,* 80–99.

Keats, J. A., Keats, D. M., & Liu, F. (1982). The language and thinking relationship in bilingual Chinese children. *The Australian Journal of Chinese Affairs, 7,* 125–135.

Keats, J. A., & Lord, F. M. (1962). A theoretical distribution of mental test scores. *Psychometrika, 27,* 59–72.

Kelly, M. (1977). Papua New Guinea and Piaget: An eight-year study. In P. Dasen (Ed.), *Piagetian psychology: Cross-cultural contributions.* New York: Gardner Press.

Klich, L. Z., & Davidson, G. R. (1983). A cultural difference in visual memory: On le voit, on ne le voit plus. *International Journal of Psychology, 18,* 189–201.

Lumsden, J. (1957). A factorial approach to unidimensionality. *Australian Journal of Psychology, 9,*(2), 105–111.

Lumsden, J. (1978). Tests are perfectly reliable. *British Journal of Mathematical and Statistical Psychology, 31,* 19–26.

McDonald, R. P. (1967). *Nonlinear factor analysis* (Psychometric Monograph No. 15).

McDonald, R. P. (1981). The dimensionality of tests and items. *British Journal of Mathematical and Statistical Psychology, 34,* 100–117.

McElwain, D. W., & Kearney, G. (1970). *The Queensland Test.* Melbourne: ACER.

Marjoribanks, K. (1979). *Ethnic families and children's achievements.* Sydney: Allen & Unwin.

Munnings, A. (1980). *A cross-cultural investigation of strategies used in concept learning by Australian and Malaysian adolescents.* Unpublished honours thesis, Department of Psychology, University of Newcastle, Australia.

O'Neill, W. M. (1984). Recent criticisms of group ability testing in the schools. *Australian Psychologist, 19*(3), 271–274.

Ord, I. G. (1971). *Mental tests for pre-literates.* London: Ginn & Jacaranda.

Porteus, S. D. (1917). Mental tests with delinquent and Australian Aboriginal children. *Psychological Review, 24,* 34–42.

Rasch, G. (1960). *Probabilistic models of some intelligence and attainment tests.* Copenhagen: DIER.

Rowe, H. A. H. (1976). *The comparability of WISC and WISC-R* (Occasional Paper No. 10). Melbourne: ACER.

Rowe, H. A. H. (1981). *A.C.E.R. Early School Series.* Melbourne: ACER.

Rowe, H. A. H. (1984). Non-verbal measures of ability within the context of ability assessment. *Australian Educational and Developmental Psychologist, 1*(2), 53–59.

Seggie, J. L. (1971). *An investigation of formal operational thought.* Unpublished doctoral dissertation, University of Newcastle, Australia.

Sheppard, J. L. (1973). *A study of the development of operational thought.* Unpublished doctoral dissertation, University of Newcastle, Australia.

Sinclair-de Zwart, H. (1967). *Acquisition du langage et développement de la pensée.* Paris: Dunod.

Smolicz, J. L., & Lean, R. (1979). Parental attitudes to cultural and linguistic pluralism in Australia: A humanistic sociological approach. *Australian Journal of Education, 23*(3), 227–249.

Somerville, S. C. (1970). *The transition from concrete to formal thinking.* Unpublished doctoral dissertation, Australian National University.

Spearritt, D. S. (Ed.) (1982). *The improvement of measurement in education and psychology.* Melbourne: A.C.E.R.

Tenezakis, M. D. (1979). Language and cognitive development in bilingual and monolingual children. In P. R. de Lacey & M. E. Poole (Eds.), *Mosaic or melting pot: Cultural evolution in Australia* (pp. 88–105). San Diego, CA: Harcourt Brace Jovanovich.

Thomson, A. (1983). *The effect of training in the transition from concrete to formal operations: A study using the concept of correlation.* Unpublished master's thesis, University of Newcastle, Australia.

*I. M. Kendall, Mary Ann Verster, and
J. W. Von Mollendorf*

Introduction and scope of the review

Research into the abilities of black people in Southern Africa has been motivated primarily by pragmatic objectives, chiefly in the spheres of assessing educability at school and trainability in the work situation. Relatively few studies were undertaken with the intention of testing the universality of (western) theories of cognitive behaviour. Research in South Africa has been dominated, furthermore, by the psychometric paradigm, although some interest has also been shown in the more experimental approaches to the study of cognition. Despite these limitations, there is sufficient literature from which to draw some conclusions regarding the nature of the psychological constructs underlying African performance on cognitive tests.

This chapter is prefaced by an historical sketch of events and is organised into three broad content areas:

1. The criterion-related validities of tests.
2. The moderating influence of environmental, dispositional, and other nontest variables on level of test performance.
3. The structure and patterning of cognitive abilities.

Although our concern is with Southern Africa, the considerable body of research findings from the rest of the continent, south of the Sahara, cannot be ignored. The distinction between "black" and "white" Africa is a political and not a cultural one. South Africa is fundamentally a "third world" nation with the majority of its inhabitants being subject to the same acculturative forces that operate elsewhere on the continent. We therefore feel justified in referring, where appropriate, to the African literature as a whole, the more so because there is unfortunately no contribution to this book from Central, West, or East Africa.

The authors express their gratitude to Dr. J. M. Verster, Assistant Director of the National Institute for Personnel Research, and Dr. K. F. Mauer, Executive Director of the Institute for Psychological and Edumetric Research, for comments received on the draft version of this chapter and for their support and encouragement during its preparation.

The views expressed in this chapter are those of the authors and do not necessarily reflect those of the Australian Council for Educational Research, or of the Human Sciences Research Council or any other institution whose work is referred to in the text.

299

To review and integrate well over 2,000 publications in a complex and somewhat amorphous field is too vast an undertaking for a chapter of this nature. For copious leads into the sub-Saharan literature, the reader is referred to bibliographies compiled by Andor (1966), Hoorweg and Marais (1969), Irvine, Sanders, and Klingelhofer (1970), and, more recently, Andor (1983). Wober's (1975) book contains comprehensive overviews of research in various cognitive and other fields while surveys of the literature by Cryns (1962), Irvine (1963), Doob (1965), Ord (1972), McLaughlin (1976) and Hoorweg (1976), together with Wickert's (1967) book of readings on Francophone Africa, would help complete the picture.

The study of the abilities of black Africans in historical perspective

The colonial era: The first faltering steps

Commencing with Martin's (1915) and Rich's (1917) experiments in Zululand, approximately a dozen attempts were made in sub-Saharan Africa between the two world wars to administer intelligence tests which were then in vogue in Europe. The majority of these studies were conducted in South Africa with the sole aim of assessing the educability of black children. Fairly frequently, the results were regarded at the time as ample evidence of the black's inherent inferiority to the white, Fick (1939) being the extreme protagonist of this viewpoint. Several pioneers in the field, however, had already begun to question the wisdom of utilising test materials which were unfamiliar to Africans. Dent (1937), for instance, confined his investigations to performance tests and was also among the first to draw attention to the importance of satisfying conventional psychometric requirements before it could be claimed that a test was fulfilling its purpose. Oliver's (1932a) work in East Africa is particularly noteworthy, being probably the first attempt to *construct* rather than adapt a test for use under local conditions.

Taking a pragmatic view of the pioneering studies that had been conducted throughout the nonwestern world, Ord (1972) remarks that at best they had proved mildly productive, particularly regarding the mechanics of testing and suggestions as to which tests to avoid or to take further. The care with which standardised test instructions are today put across to uneducated African testees is just one of the lessons to have been learned from the mistakes of earlier researchers.

The culture-free movement: Culture viewed as a contaminating and unwanted variable

During the 1940s and 1950s a new approach to ability measurement – based on the belief that cultural influences on test performance could be held constant by including in the test content only those elements which were supposedly common to all cultures – was rapidly to find favour among investigators in Africa. Cattell's (1940) *Culture-Free Intelligence Test* was the first of such measures, examples from sub-Saharan Africa being the work of Verhaegen (1956) and Xydias (1956). Although not a "culture-free" measure by design, the test which found the widest application in Africa, particularly the French-speaking parts, is *Raven's (1938) Progressive Matrices* (see Irvine, 1969b and 1969c, for reviews of the earlier literature).

It was the conclusion of most authors, however, that marked cultural biases were still evident using these tests. The influence of formal schooling and other environmental variables was just as substantial as when using other types of tests, while coaching and test–retest effects were also found to be pronounced (Laroche, 1959; Lloyd & Pidgeon, 1961; Ombredane, Robaye, & Plumail, 1956; Silvey, 1963b). Thus the mere substitution of diagrams and symbols for words and numbers in the test content was soon shown to be too simplistic a solution to the culture-fairness problem.

Putting culture back into the research paradigm: Recognition of cultural factors as powerful moderator variables

The realisation that each culture fosters and reinforces certain modes of behaviour and suppresses or discourages others has seldom been questioned by African researchers over the past twenty years. What is clear to contemporary investigators is the unavoidable role which culture plays in determining the observed level of group performance on cognitive tests. The importance of investigating the degree of environmental influence on the development of African abilities had already been emphasised by Biesheuvel (1943) at a time when most of his contemporaries were still preoccupied with cross-cultural comparisons. In his landmark monograph *African Intelligence*, Biesheuvel urged that investigators take a closer look at the influence of factors such as culture, the home environment, formal education, and nutrition on African intelligence.

It was the pragmatic nature of most African research that forced the awareness of culture as a powerful moderator of cognitive test performance. Large-scale psychometric investigation of African abilities owes its impetus to the rapid industrial expansion which parts of Africa underwent after World War II. Industrialists required quick solutions to identifying the occupational suitability of "seemingly inexhaustible pools of near illiterate manpower" (Ord, 1972, p. 125). This was later followed by a further acceleration of interest in ability testing throughout the rest of Africa concomitant with the movement toward decolonisation (cf. Irvine [1965] in Zimbabwe; MacArthur, Irvine, & Brimble [1964] in Zambia; Morgaut [1960] in eleven Francophone countries; Schwarz [1961] in West Africa; Silvey [1963a] in Uganda). Testing procedures such as the *General Adaptability Battery* (*GAB*) for use on the South African gold mines (Biesheuvel, 1949; 1952a; 1952b) and the Belgian approach to measuring scholastic aptitude (reviewed by Dague, 1972) explicitly recognised the importance of culture in ability testing. The rationale behind the construction of the *GAB* is set out by Biesheuvel (1972) wherein it is stated that since Africans are undergoing cultural change, it is important to be able to measure their capacity to *adapt* to such change. Hence the emphasis in the *GAB* on the opportunity to learn during the test session and the Belgian emphasis on multiple retest sessions.

Focus on cognitive processes: Venturing beyond the confines of the psychometric tradition

The period since the mid-1960s has witnessed the appearance of various nonpsychometric approaches to the study of what hitherto had been referred to loosely as "African intelligence." This resulted in a number of studies which were often less pragmatic and more academic in their objectives.

Pioneered by Price-Williams (1961) in West Africa and Murray (1961) in South Africa, experimentation with Piagetian tasks has been by far the most dominant force in the recent African literature. By the early 1970s, this approach had virtually displaced the earlier focus on normative trends (Geber, 1958; Geber & Dean, 1957; Lloyd, 1971; Vouilloux, 1959, and many others) with reference to developmental scales such as the *Gesell, Merrill–Palmer*, or *Stanford–Binet*.[1] Following the Piagetian approach, African investigators concluded that any retardation in the emergence of specific skills and abilities among Africans is less a function of maturation and more a question of culturally determined factors. Many studies – and in particular those of Greenfield (1966), Miller and Meltzer (1978), Okonji (1971), Owoc (1973), and Pinard, Morin, and Lefebvre (1973) – have stressed the importance not only of formal education but also of good-quality schooling as a primary variable associated with the ability to perform well on Piagetian tasks. Another important conclusion drawn by several researchers was the particularly weak performance of many African children on tasks involving spatial relations (cf. Okonji, 1971; Omari, 1975; Otaala, 1971; Page, 1973; Poole, 1969).

Witkin's concept of psychological differentiation has been extensively applied to the study of cognition in Africa. The results of such studies (reviewed by Okonji, 1980) make a strong case for the implication of cultural and even ecological factors in the fostering of a cognitive style which has been variously termed "global," "field dependent," or "nonanalytic," and which is seen to be a limiting factor in the development of sound perceptual analytic ability. The familiar (western) finding that males appear to be less field dependent than females has been replicated in several African as well as other nonwestern studies, particularly when differentiation was operationalised in terms of *Embedded Figures Test* performance (see Van Leeuwen, 1978, for a review of the cross-cultural literature). Related to the study of field de-

---

[1] This was a broad field of study in which prominence had been given to the seeming psychomotor precocity of African infants and the alleged effects of abrupt weaning on later cognitive development. See Super (1972), Warren (1972), and Wober (1975) for reviews of this literature.

pendence and its correlates, albeit indirectly, are certain avenues of investigation into what Wober (1975) has termed "special difficulties." These mainly arise in the field of visual perception and have to do with the interpretation of depth in pictures (Abiola, 1967; Hudson, 1960; Kilbride, Robbins, & Freeman, 1968; Miller, 1973); the spatial orientation of objects (Deregowski, 1977; Serpell, 1971; Shapiro, 1960); and visual illusions (Berry, 1968; Jahoda, 1966; Segall, Campbell, & Herskovits, 1966; Stewart, 1973; Wober, 1970, 1972).

A further major theme in recent African studies has been centred on learning- and memory-based experiments, especially in concept formation (cf. Cole, Gay, Glick, & Sharp, 1971; Irwin, Schafer, & Feiden, 1974; Parker, 1977; Super, 1972). Education and urbanisation were found to be major correlates of experimental task performance, which reinforces the conclusions reached by other nonpsychometric and psychometric researchers alike.

Overview

From the foregoing highly select historical survey, it is apparent that research has been wide-ranging and has been pursued from many different methodological perspectives. Although the major concern has been a practical one, namely, the identification and optimum utilisation of Africa's human resources, there has been growing emphasis on the study of human abilities as a field of scientific enquiry in its own right. In the process, Africa has proved to be a popular "natural laboratory" for testing the universality of cognitive theories.

The concerns of South African researchers appear to differ little from those of their colleagues in the rest of Africa. Indeed, it is often difficult to discern which studies are conducted north and south of the Limpopo. South Africa's contributions are to be found in all the major fields of cognitive endeavour, from studies of child development in the Piagetian or Gesellian tradition to investigation of psychological differentiation and special perceptual difficulties. But its biggest contribution has been – and continues to be – in the psychometric and, more especially, in the pragmatic, problem-solving field. In this chapter an attempt is made to highlight the major investigations in these last-mentioned areas and to consider their implications for the meaning which should be attached to the scores obtained from cognitive ability tests.

The criterion-related validity of cognitive tests

Given the economic necessity in Africa of providing places within the educational system, jobs appropriate to the products of this system, and the manpower to run the industrial machinery of developing nations, it was natural that many psychologists should have focussed their attention on the predictive validities of cognitive tests. For many years, the National Institute for Personnel Research (NIPR) in Johannesburg has been recognised internationally as a leader in the field of African ability measurement. One of the major contributions of the NIPR was the development of the *General Adaptability Battery* in the 1950s for classifying technologically unsophisticated recruits to the South African gold mines into manual, operative, and supervisory grades. Many more NIPR tests for general industrial use were to follow (see Lätti & Verster's [1975] listing of tests and Crawford-Nutt [1977c], Kendall [1977], and Werbeloff & Taylor [1982] for more recent examples). The Institute for Psychological and Edumetric Research (IPER) in Pretoria was similarly engaged during the 1970s on a programme of constructing multiple aptitude test batteries for specific use with black school children at various age levels (Hoar, 1983; Swanepoel, 1971, 1975; Van Staden, 1976; Von Mollendorf, 1974). In the case of both the NIPR and IPER, ideas for test formats and item writing were often inspired by existing (overseas) tests, but the entire process of test construction, from item analysis through production of norm tables to validation studies, was with sole reference to black samples.

Work in the areas of educational and personnel selection of blacks in Southern Africa is typical of what Poortinga (1971) has termed "intracultural research," the accent being on understanding the behaviour of people within a particular culture. Criterion-related validity studies thus provide some clues as to the nature of the constructs underlying test performance, and for this reason it is considered appropriate to review the Southern African literature in this field.

Assessing scholastic and academic ability

Research at the IPER has demonstrated fairly strong relationships between academic performance on the one hand and the test performance of African primary and secondary school pupils on the other. Of particular interest is the finding that tests of number ability emerge as the single best predictor of examination results in general (cf. Swanepoel [1971] in the third and fourth grades; Thiele [1964] in the ninth grade; and Swanepoel [1975] in the tenth grade). English and vernacular language achievement tests have also been found to be predictive of scholastic success. Tests of general reasoning ability on the other hand – particularly of the figural or nonverbal variety – would appear to add very little to the predictive success already achieved by the arithmetic and language tests. The conclusion that general reasoning ability tests are less strongly associated with scholastic success is a reflection, perhaps, on the state of affairs whereby memory-based learning is rewarded in the current educational system. Landman (1978) did, however, provide evidence that general reasoning ability was strongly associated with ninth-grade examination results in mathematics while Von Mollendorf (1978) reported very good predictive validities for nearly all the tests in IPER's *Academic Aptitude Test Battery* against most school subjects.

NIPR investigations of the validity of tests as predictors of success at university or technical college have yielded several positive findings. Tests of number ability, for instance, correlate well with first-year engineering and B.Sc. examination results (Taylor, 1985; Visser, 1978) while well-developed spatial abilities appear to be critically important for success in engineering drawing and design courses (Taylor, 1985; Visser, 1981). It is also significant to observe that on virtually all the cognitive tests applied to a sample of black first-year university students, those students who enrolled for science and commerce degrees performed at a substantially higher level than those who enrolled for arts degrees (Visser, 1978).

Assessing industrial and commercial trainability

In South Africa, the strongest evidence in support of the criterion-related validity of tests comes from studies conducted on samples of illiterate and semiliterate trainees on the gold mines. The importance of these studies lies in the fact that fairly large samples of trainees were drawn and were evaluated on reliable and valid post-training criteria. These samples were fully representative of the range of ability level in the populations concerned in that no preselection was attempted on the basis of test scores. Thus high and low scorers alike were given the chance to respond to training. Grant (1970a), Blake (1972), and Kendall (1976), for instance, reported impressive multiple correlation coefficients between a set of carefully constructed criteria on the one hand and the *General Adaptability Battery* (*GAB*) and its replacement, the *Classification Test Battery* (*CTB*) on the other. The multiple R in respect of the four *GAB* subtests was found to be .50 against a composite criterion of practical and theoretical post-training examination results, while that in respect of the three *CTB* subtests was .65 (sample size = 149). The criteria comprised two manual labour tasks (teamwork construction of a "mat pack" and the laying of underground ventilation pipes and railway tracks), two machine-operating tasks (winch and locomotive driving), and supervisory duties. Earlier studies during the 1950s by Mkele (1952; 1953) and Sichel (1951) had proved equally positive.

The results of more recent research in other sectors of the South African economy are less impressive and more equivocal. Truncated predictor variance is a common problem in many of these studies, while the criterion measurement problem itself frequently bedevils the outcome of such investigations. Spagnoletti (1974) nevertheless reported a correlation of .45 between performance on a nonverbal reasoning test and a behaviourally anchored job performance rating scale in a sample of 95 trainee sewing machinists. A study of forestry workers by Verster (1977) yielded similarly positive findings in respect of another nonverbal test. Using the percentage marks awarded to novices after having attended an orientation course, Verster reported validity coefficients ranging from .37 to .52 in four geographically distinct regions of South Africa. The sample sizes in each instance were well over 150. On the other hand, a typical concurrent validity study produced no significant correlations between test performance and the productivity ratings of asbestos-cement moulders (Breger, 1971).

Similar results were found in validation studies concerning better-educated black samples. Werbeloff and Taylor (1982), for instance, report predictive validities in the region of .24 to .54 for verbal and nonverbal reasoning tests against training course examinations in a number of business equipment servicing fields. A study of 91 training instructors in the building industry (Christierson, 1977) yielded a multiple R of .50 between a composite training criterion on the one hand and three predictors on the other (a verbal reasoning, nonverbal reasoning, and computational test). A factor analysis of Christierson's tests and criteria suggested that the construct underlying performance on the verbal reasoning test was strongly associated with formal learning ability, a finding which supports the general literature in South Africa and the United States concerning Otis-type tests. Fourie's (1982) investigation of the concurrent validity of tests applied to black insurance salesmen produced nonsignificant findings in respect of the cognitive tests but significant findings as regards personality and interest measures.

The moderation of test performance by nontest variables

Psychometric methodology as it is practised, is recognised as having shortcomings for the development of our knowledge of individual differences in ability (Carroll, 1983; Irvine, 1983; Jenkins, 1981). A shift in emphasis from the macro level of analysis to an in-depth analysis of the fundaments of score meaning is thus to be welcomed. In this connection, a focus on one of the principal paradigms identified by Irvine (1983) for establishing test score meaning, namely the correlation of test scores with nontest variables, becomes an appropriate avenue of research to follow. The following review of African – and especially Southern African – research has been organised around three major classes of nontest variables: test-taking behaviours; environmental factors; and the supposedly "dispositional" variables of age and sex. For convenience, the environmental variable of formal education will be treated together with test-taking behaviours because, in African studies, they are very closely interrelated through the common operation of general learning experience.

Learning: Formal and informal learning and the acquisition of test-taking skills

It is virtually axiomatic that formal education has a marked effect on test performance in the African context. Strong positive relationships between test performance and the amount of schooling have been found in nearly every African study, regardless of whether it was conducted within the strictly psychometric or the more experimental cognitive research paradigms. In South African studies where correlation coefficients between the two variables have been reported, these have been observed to vary from .66 (Kendall [1977] in an educationally very heterogeneous sample of adults) to around .10 (Crawford-Nutt [1977b] in a more homogeneous group). The relationship between education and test performance remains a substantial one even after the effect of age has been partialled out or otherwise taken into account (e.g., Fahrmeier, 1975; Kendall, 1980; Ombredane, 1957; Xydias, 1956). In Africa, about the only ability tests which have not been found to correlate with formal education are those relating to dexterity and certain very elementary perceptual skills (cf. Xydias, Cottin, & Lambert [1963] in the Saharan region; De Wet [1967] in South Africa).

The implication of studies conducted in this area is that access to education at an early age is the single most powerful factor facilitating the development and unfolding of the cognitive potential of the mind. One may conclude, therefore, that the difference in test performance levels of individuals at different educational levels reflects true differences in ability. It is the exact mechanism accounting for this relationship that needs further exploration, however. In-depth analysis of the learning process and how it affects mental capacity within the limits of the testing situation and in the broader educational context, is called for. Test instructions, test-taking skills, repetition of the testing experience, practice on or exposure to the underlying ability being assessed by psychometric tests, become legitimate and important areas of enquiry.

The concept of "adaptability testing" (Biesheuvel, 1972) embodied the idea that the testing experience itself should represent a learning task. When the *General Adaptability Battery* was constructed (Biesheuvel, 1952a), provision was made for the incorporation of learning opportunities. There was a lengthy practice session during which new concepts necessary for the solution of test items were introduced and some practice on them was provided. The importance of this approach to testing is underscored by more recent work by Pons (1974) and Crawford-Nutt (1976). By making the instructions for *Raven's Progressive Matrices* into a session for teaching test requirements and familiarising subjects with test material, substantially improved mean test performances were recorded. The mean test scores of Crawford-Nutt's black school sample were not significantly different from those achieved by the British sample on which *Raven's* initial norms were established. If learning during a period of test instructions can have such a significant result, what is the nature of the learning which takes place during testing and how does this affect the measurement of the underlying ability in an adult population?

A series of investigations conducted within the South African gold-mining industry addresses this problem specifically. M. A. Verster (1974, 1978) found that the *Classification Test Battery* (*CTB*) performance of groups of black mineworkers subjected to different conditions of retesting, described a classic learning curve, approaching an asymptotic level around the fourth retest. The relative contributions of two sources of variance were investigated, namely: multiple test exposure and exposure to the technologically sophisticated and novel environment on the mines.

The effect of retesting was found to be highly significant and more powerful than the effect of experience. It was particularly noteworthy that the score increments between the first and second testing sessions were of the same magnitude irrespective of the intervening time period (3, 6, 9, or 12 months) between test exposures. Significantly, the effects of mining experience were in the expected direction and did reach significance after 9 and 12 months in the case of an illiterate subsample. Methodological limitations do not permit more than a cautious interpretation of this finding, but the possibility that some development of the underlying ability was taking place in adults in response to informal learning associated with environmental stimulation could not be excluded.

These findings raise some interesting questions. In any one test exposure, is one measuring at a point on the acquisition curve for the ability being measured? If so, what is the relative meaning of an initial measurement against a retest measurement taken at the height of the acquisition curve? This brings to mind the original work of Fleishman and Hempel (1956). If the factor structure of simple psychomotor tasks can change as a function of practice, is there a parallel situation when dealing with tasks of a more intellectual nature? Even if such changes are established, however, their meaning may be highly specific to the particular test task and may not generalise beyond it.

In the search for an explanation of the observed effects in Verster's study, a second series of investigations was mounted in which the analysis was taken to a more micro level. Specific hypotheses were formulated to account for the observed increments in test performance (J. M. Verster & Muller, 1975). The learning which contributed to test score increases was hypothesised to have resulted from exposure to five possible sources: *test items; test format; mental operations involved in the underlying construct; test procedure; and environmental stimulation*. It was proposed that these effects were components of a broad concept learning model and would be hierarchically interdependent, that is, the most direct effect would result from item learning and the least direct from environmental learning. This allowed for a systematic determination of the most powerful level of explanation for the increases. A rigorous experimental design (Table 12.1) was devised to test the hypotheses, with each learning condition operationalised psychometrically, and the effects of these conditions assessed on the same test, namely, a *Form Series Test* (*FST*) for two samples at different educational levels.

The results confirmed that learning from exposure to the first three sources had contributed significantly to test score improvements. No substantial learning could be attributed to familiarity with test procedures and general intellectual stimulation associated with work experience (J. M. Verster, Muller, & Kendall, 1977). It may well be that a period of three months is

Table 12.1. *Experimental design of study by J. M. Verster, Muller, and Kendall (1976, 1977)*

Learning condition	Test	Initial test Low Ed	Initial test High Ed	Test	Retest after three months Low Ed	Retest after three months High Ed
Item learning	FST_1	a	b	FST_1	k	l
Format learning	FST_2 (parallel to FST_1)	c	d	FST_1	m	n
Construct learning	*Object Series Test* (measuring same construct as FST_1 but using different format)	e	f	FST_1	o	p
Procedure learning	Form boards (unrelated in terms of construct, format, and items to FST_1)	g	h	FST_1	q	r
Environmental learning	No test. Work experience and training in Fanakalo (lingua franca on the mines)	i	j	FST_1	s	t

insufficient for any real benefit to be realised from the stimulating effects of a working environment and that an investigation over a longer period may well yield different results.

A particularly interesting finding in this study was that some construct learning, representing actual growth in ability, had been demonstrated. As the construct learning condition was operationalised psychometrically, however, it is uncertain to what extent this growth would generalise to applications beyond the specific test situation. Had it been possible to show in addition that the advantage of practice on the underlying construct was transferable to real-life behaviour in the work situation, then it would have been justified to question the differential validity of test scores obtained with different test exposures.

In developing the instruments for this study, attention was given to extending the range of item difficulty so that the results of retesting would not be limited by ceiling effects. This was particularly important for investigating the differential effects of the education variable on retest gains. The interpretation of results with respect to the educational variable (in particular the case of the higher educated samples) in M. A. Verster's study (1974, 1978) was limited by such ceiling effects. The advantage of the extended range was evident in that a U-shaped relationship was found between education and test score gains. Those at the extreme ranges on the educational variable showed the highest mean gains, while those in the middle range showed smaller mean gains.

Kendall's (1980) investigation of rural–urban differences in test performance levels of a group of adult black South Africans sheds further light on the nature of the relationship between formal schooling and psychometric test performance. Analyses of the sources of variance in test performance attributable to the educational, rural–urban, and age variables confirmed the overriding importance of the benefits of having attended school. Although it was not possible, within the confines of Kendall's research design, to advance firm conclusions concerning the precise reasons for the educational influence on test performance level, it cannot be doubted that education itself had played a powerful stimulating role, during childhood, on the development of the intellect. No other cultural learning experience is as concentrated and as fundamental as that which is provided, systematically, through the formal education system.

Influences supplementing the direct, causative role of education in fostering measured ability levels should also be considered, however. For instance, persons who have received some education are generally placed in jobs which are intellectually more demanding than are those in which their illiterate counterparts are placed. Consequently, the opportunity to continue exercising abilities developed through schooling is afforded the educated worker. Continued environmental support for previously acquired abilities could thus be an important source of variance contributing to the gross educational effect on test performance.

Another factor could simply be familiarity with materials and testing procedures which are typically associated with the classroom. These include facility in using a pencil; familiarity with booklets, letters, numbers, and elementary symbols; speed and accuracy of work; sitting still; paying attention to and obeying instructions; and the examination situation in general. Subjects who have attended school should be in a position to transfer the above skills and attitudes to the testing situation, which would place them at an immediate advantage over their illiterate companions who are given the same tests. It is informative to note that the educational influence on test scores in Kendall's study was far stronger for those tests which called for the manipulation of a pencil (to copy patterns) than for tests which required the subject to build a cube or tripod, sort washers, bolts, and nuts into compartments, or place plastic tiles on a board to continue a given series. The educational effect was particularly pronounced in respect of the only test in the battery which looked and read like a book and which required rapid perceptual scanning of symbols.

Other authors in the African literature (Doob, 1960; Ombredane, Bertelson, & Beniest-Noirot, 1958; Schwarz, 1963) have drawn attention to similar sources of psychological test sophistication and have added further considerations such as the testee's attitudes toward working against time, his attitude toward individual as opposed to joint problem solving, and even his aesthetic and culturally based preferences for solving "problems" in a manner which was never intended by the western psychologist and which would lose him points on an ability test. The question which should be asked, however, and which has rarely been pursued in Africa, is whether or not

the lack of sophistication in tackling ability tests transfers to criterion behaviour such as trainability or success on the job. Should it be found that
the industrial trainability of illiterate black workers, relative to that of workers who have received some schooling, is underestimated by psychological
tests of abilities, then a strong case for test bias could be made.

Cultural and environmental variables: The urban–rural factor

On the basis of Anastasi's (1958) review of comparative urban–rural studies
in North America, it could be expected that urban Africans should likewise
surpass the intellectual capabilities of their rural cousins. With one or two
notable exceptions, the African literature is indeed largely supportive of
western findings. The majority of these studies are with reference to children
and adolescents, it being concluded that city children appear to acquire
certain cognitive skills at an earlier stage than do rural children (Weisner,
1976). By way of a few examples from the literature, urban children, for
instance, were found to be more adept at learning to sort objects by function
(Evans & Segall, 1969); were more inclined to use multiple criteria for classifying objects (Schmidt & Nzimande, 1970); were better able to perceive
depth in drawings (Omari & MacGinitie, 1974); and showed greater proficiency with regard to number concept (Etuk, 1967; Setidisho, 1965; Super,
1972) and scientific concept attainment (Poole, 1968), than rural children.
Page (1965, 1973) and Greenfield (1966) have also demonstrated differences
favouring urban adolescents and young adults on a variety of piagetian tasks,
as did Okonji (1969) with reference to the *Embedded Figures* and *Rod and
Frame* tests. In contrast, very few studies have shown no differences whatsoever between urban and rural samples, the only examples of which we
are aware being Klingelhofer's (1971) investigation of Tanzanian schoolchildren's performance on *Raven's Progressive Matrices,* Omari's (1975)
study of the development of spatial concepts among schoolchildren (also in
Tanzania) and Orbell's (1975) investigation into abstract thinking among high
school students in Zimbabwe, in which various piagetian tasks and psychometric tests were administered.

In evaluating the above and similar studies, one is unfortunately faced
with the problem of rural–urban comparisons often having been confounded
with other cultural and environmental influences, notably the amount and
quality of formal education. Greenfield's experimental design, for instance,
was imperfectly crossed as far as the urbanisation and education variables
were concerned. Whereas her rural group was divided into schooled and
unschooled children, her urban group consisted only of children who were
attending school. In other African studies, schooling and urban–rural residence are sometimes totally confounded, yet the results are interpreted in
terms of rural–urban effects.

There are, however, at least three large-scale investigations which have
succeeded in differentiating between the effects of urbanisation and formal

education on cognitive test performance levels: Grant's (1969, 1972b) study of the abilities of adult male Vendas, Kendall's (1971, 1980) sequel in respect of adult male Pedis, and Miller and Meltzer's (1978) investigation of concept formation (in terms of piagetian developmental tasks) among Pedi-speaking children, all of which were conducted in Southern Africa. In all three cases, it was concluded that urban subjects did significantly better than rural subjects but that the effect due to urbanisation was greatly overshadowed by the independent effect attributable to formal education.

In the studies by Grant (1969) and Kendall (1971), clear trends in the level of psychometric test performance emerged as a function of increased acculturation. A continuum from rural illiterate, through urban illiterate and rural literate, to urban literate was discerned, with the least acculturated group achieving the lowest mean level of test performance and the most acculturated group the highest. Statistical tests of the significance between mean group performances on each cognitive test in the battery were conducted using t tests. Kendall (1980) reanalysed the Pedi data using more powerful multivariate and univariate analysis of variance procedures. A three-way analysis of variance design was adopted, to allow for the simultaneous investigation of the main effects of urbanisation, education, and age on psychometric test performance and to be able to detect any possible interactions between these variables. It was found that the main effects of the three variables were all highly significant. Moreover, these effects were independent of one another, as witnessed by the nonsignificant interactions between urbanisation, education, and age. This implies that urban domicile, for example, has the same effect on the test performance of both educated and uneducated subjects, irrespective of age. It was also concluded that the education factor appeared to be of greater importance in moderating the level of test performance than urbanisation; while urbanisation appeared to be somewhat more important than age. It should be cautioned, perhaps, that the rank ordering of the magnitude of the main effects for the three nontest variables investigated by Kendall would not necessarily be true for all African populations.

In itself, urbanisation is a gross variable which cannot offer an explanation for the psychological mechanism accounting for increments in test performance. One needs to look to a finer level of analysis, to break it down into meaningful constituent components, before one can understand its contribution to the meaning of test scores. Social scientists generally agree that urbanisation entails more than the mere movement of people from rural areas to the towns and cities (cf. Beales, 1951; Mayer, 1961). The quality of life in urban centres – including parent–child interaction, formal education, material possessions, dietary practices, and the like – could be a major contributing factor. However, such factors could well be confounded with effects which might be independently attributable to industrial work experience, contact with people from other cultures, and general "sophistication" which, in combination, could result in *attitudinal* and *stylistic* changes in problem-solving strategy. Grant (1969, p. 46), for instance, speculates that urbanisation, as a process, facilitates the loosening of bonds with tribal societies governed by custom and conformity. Curiosity would be encouraged in place of reliance on traditional answers (including magic) for most questions, which in turn would lead to a fuller intellectual life. In a similar vein, Weisner (1976) comments that "city residence seems to make children and adults less compliant, more 'savvy,' and perhaps more talkative in test situations, and hence more likely to display multiple classification criteria, to alter initial perceptual cues into more 'abstract' ones, and generally to act in ways likely to be successful in many experimental settings" (p. 230). On the question of compliance and conformity, protagonists of the psychological differentiation school of cognition have agreed that severe socialisation practices result in a global and undifferentiated style of cognitive functioning. Empirical evidence from Africa and other parts of the world would appear to support this contention (cf. Dawson, 1967; Wober, 1967).

In consideration of the above, "just what it is about the city that makes for test differences is hard to disentangle" (Weisner, 1976, p. 224). The fact that, in Kendall's (1971, 1980) investigation of rural–urban differences in psychometric test performance, the entire urban Pedi sample proved to be a migrant labour group, born and bred in the same geographical region as the rural sample, puts a different perspective on the urban–rural differences that were established. The most probable explanations could be in terms of the generalised effects of current industrial work experience, the nature of previous work experience, the urban experience itself, and possible self-selection of the sample in having chosen to migrate, if only temporarily, to a large metropolitan area.

Demographic analysis of the "urban" and rural Pedi samples by the sociologist in the multidisciplinary research team (Hall, 1971) strongly supports Kendall's assertions. The most obvious feature differentiating the samples was gainful employment at the time of the study (100% in the "urban" sample and only 20% in the rural sample). Moreover, subjects in the urban group reported having spent the greater part of their working lives in the urban-based manufacturing sector of the economy, whereas the rural subjects, when employed, had been engaged mainly as mineworkers or farmhands and had consequently not experienced city life to the same extent as their "urban" brethren. It is thus conceivable that exposure to an urban, industrial environment during one's *adulthood* could provide the opportunity to develop and to practise certain abilities that are important for survival in a western cultural milieu. Urban, industrial experience could also provide continued environmental support for abilities which were already developed at an earlier age. In the rural environment, western-type abilities of the kind measured by psychological tests and tasks could be of limited functional value. It would thus be logical to anticipate a certain amount of decay in the type of cognitive processes which underlie the performance of unemployed, rural persons on objective tests of abilities. Finally, if sample self-selection is indeed a contributing factor, it is informative to observe in Kendall's (1980) analysis that the particular tests which most sharply differentiated the urban from the rural group were found, after factor analyses of the data, to involve a quality conventionally regarded as being very similar to general nonverbal intelligence. Tests of a more spatial reasoning nature or those involving little more than sorting or perceptual scanning operations performed under pressure of time, were far less strongly associated with the urban–rural factor. It could be, therefore, that the urban (migrant) sample represented a truly more adaptable (in the purely western sense of the term) group of adult blacks than did the rural sample.

Cultural and environmental variables: Ethnicity

The question of ethnic affiliation as a source of test score variance has kindled the fires of the nature–nurture debate for many years. For all the attention it has received, however, this debate has contributed little to furthering our understanding of how test performance may be influenced by this variable. A reason for this may be that one is dealing not only with one variable but with complex interaction effects which must be unravelled through in-depth analyses before establishing any cause-and-effect relationships.

The reason for focussing on ethnicity as a factor which may contribute to test score variance stems from the observation of apparent job and test performance differences between ethnic groups employed on the South African gold mines. The results of early work were not conclusive (Gouws, 1950; Hudson, 1953; Naude, 1962). Mauer (1974) looked more systematically at the effects of education, age, and tribal grouping on the *Classification Test Battery* performance of a very large sample ($N = 12,505$) of black mineworkers. The analysis of variance indicated that the main effect of tribal grouping was significant but was far smaller than the main effects of education and age. A multiple classification analysis was also conducted, using the three subtests as dependent variables and recoding the data into a composite predictor of education, tribe, and experience, with age as a second predictor. The differences in test performance observed between the tribal groups were very small and thus of no practical significance. On the basis of this study, therefore, individual differences could not be attributed to the tribal variable alone.

Kendall's (1972) comparative investigation into the abilities of Pedi and Venda adult males, in which the factors of age, rural–urban domicile, and education were controlled for, elucidates the relationship further. The differences he noted in favour of the Pedi could be explained as a function of "low inference variables" (Irvine, 1983) such as work opportunity and experience, without having to imply a direct causal relationship between the "high inference variable" of ethnicity and test performance. The importance of looking not at broad, multidimensional variables, but rather at their fundamental, component parts, seems to be borne out by the results of this research.

In conclusion, whatever differences in tested ability levels may well be found between members of different ethnic groups, these are very likely to be reduced to negligible proportions once schooling, age, the urban–rural factor, and industrial experience are controlled for. Any remaining covariance in the relationship between test performance and ethnic affiliation is then likely to be mediated by a complex web of less obvious explanatory variables. It is possible that, as well as the factors already referred to, influences such as the following could be of importance: traditional ethnic preferences for employment in different sectors of the economy; degree of resistance to cultural change; degree of remoteness of the tribal homelands from urban centres; ecological characteristics of the homelands; dietary preferences; history of disease and malnutrition during childhood; and several others.

Other cultural and environmental factors

Studies by Nelson (1959) and Nelson and Dean (1959) suggest that permanent brain damage can result from kwashiorkor or protein malnutrition during infancy. Research by Gilbey (1964) on infants in South Africa and Fisher et al. (1972) on children in Zambia lends partial support to the deleterious longer-term effects of a history of malnutrition, while Howard (1966) advances some tentative findings that calorie intake could be a limiting factor in the development of intellectual abilities. More recently, Hoorweg and Stanfield (1976) have supplied firmer evidence with reference to a follow-up study of 60 Ugandan children who had been admitted to hospital for treatment of malnutrition between the ages of 8 to 27 months. On attaining adolescence, they were administered a comprehensive battery of ability tests. The results suggested a general impairment of intellectual abilities relative to the performance of a control group of subjects. Reasoning and spatial abilities were most affected by "chronic undernutrition" at admission during infancy; memory and rote learning were intermediately affected; and language ability least, if at all.

Socioeconomic status is yet another factor which, in the light of western studies, could have a bearing on the abilities of Africans. Heyneman (1976) points out, however, that the limited evidence from Africa for such a relationship is equivocal. Part of the problem is the definition of social class in African societies. Heyneman, for instance, used a "summary socio-economic scale" based on parental education and occupation, and the number of "modern" consumer items to be found in the subject's home. The correlation between this scale and scores on *Raven's Progressive Matrices* was found to be .13 in a sample of 2,293 Ugandan primary school leavers. Grant (1969) views socioeconomic status in the African context as part of the wider phenomenon of urbanisation. He points out that urban Africans have a steady income which, although limited, can help provide their children with a somewhat materially enriched environment. Rural Africans, on the other hand, cannot afford toys, furniture, household utensils, and other items which supposedly offer scope for the child's development of manipulative and spatial-perceptual skills.

Ecological demands and the resultant cultural adaptations to such demands have also received attention as possible moderators of test performance levels. Berry's (1966) comparison of West African (Temne) and Canadian Inuit performance on certain spatial-perceptual and visual discrimination tests suggested that the level of cognitive development within a given culture could be predicted from an analysis of certain ecological demands. The superiority of Inuit test performance over that of a group of rural Temne at "comparable levels of westernisation and education," was attributed to the survival value of spatial skills for the Inuit. Wober (1967), however, interprets Berry's findings as leaving the orthodox differentiation explanation of Temne socialisation practices in a strengthened position. To Wober's way of thinking, it was hardly surprising that Berry's Temne group fared so poorly on the test battery, because their socialisation practices, by both western and Inuit standards, are somewhat severe. It would appear that the evidence with respect to ecological influences on nonwestern test performance is inconclusive because cultural practices which may or may not be related to ecological demands, could easily be confounded with this variable.

Dispositional variables: The examples of gender and age

Investigation of sex differences in performance levels on cognitive tests and tasks has been a fairly popular topic in the African literature concerning children and adolescents. Adult studies, on the other hand, are a rarity. Without enquiring too closely into the methodological merits of the studies involved, it would appear that the overwhelming majority of the findings point to boys being decidedly ahead of girls on most abilities (cf. Bakare [1972] in Nigeria; Bowden [1969], Drenth, van der Flier, & Omari [1979], Klingelhofer [1967], Munroe & Munroe [1971], and Nerlove et al. [1971] in East Africa; Hendrikz [1975], Irvine [1966], and Orbell [1975] in Zimbabwe; Fourie [1967], Hoar [1983], and Swanepoel [1975] in South Africa). In only a handful of studies have substantial differences between the sexes not been found, including a study of first-year students at the University of Fort Hare in the Ciskei (Erwee, 1981) in which it was established that males outperformed females on only one psychometric test (English vocabulary) in a battery of language and general reasoning tests. Investigations in which sex differences are reported to be in favour of African girls are even rarer (cf. Otaala, 1970; Durojaiye, 1972).

The apparent superiority of males over females is particularly evident in the spatial-reasoning domain. Several authors have speculated that this could be attributed to girls in most African societies still leading very restricted lives which would inhibit exploration of their environments. Erwee (1981) advances the same explanation to account for greater male student proficiency in English vocabulary. It is probable, therefore, that sex differences in test performances are more a comment on cultural influences than on purely constitutional and biological factors.

Chronological age is one of the best established moderators of test performance levels in the western psychometric literature. African investigations generally confirm that ability level improves throughout childhood, levels off by late adolescence, and starts to decline by middle adulthood. Focussing specifically on studies involving adults, most researchers in South Africa have reported small but statistically significant negative correlations between age and psychometric test performance (e.g., Grant, 1969; and Kendall, 1971, in investigations of adult male illiterates and semiliterates).

In Kendall's (1980) investigation, the conclusion was reached that the relationship between age and test performance tends to be similar among educated and uneducated, rural and urban persons. The *nature* of the relationship varied from one test to another in the battery. Most relationships were generally linear and negative, the test showing the greatest decline in performance with advancing years being a paper-and-pencil measure of perceptual speed. On other tests, especially those believed to measure aspects of general nonverbal reasoning ability, persons in the age range 27 to 36 years performed at a level only marginally lower than persons in the 16 to 26 year range, but substantially higher than persons older than 37. Three of the tests in Kendall's battery yielded curvilinear relationships with age, with the task involving the rapid sorting of a variety of nuts, bolts, screws, rivets, and washers markedly so; and two object constructional tasks (*Cube* and *Tripod*) to a marginal degree. It was found that well over 75% of the men in the 27- to 36-year age group were gainfully employed at the time of testing. The tendency for this group to outperform both the younger and older members of the sample on certain tests might well be attributable to regular practice on the factory floor of the kind of skills which facilitate performance on the ability tests in question (skills such as the physical handling, assembling, or sorting of objects similar to those used in the sorting and constructional tasks in the test battery). Continued environmental support for previously acquired abilities, practice of fine psychomotor skills, and perhaps even some real growth in the underlying psychological construct as a function of work experience, could all be possible explanations for the age-test performance relationships found in Kendall's study.

The particularly poor performance of Kendall's 37 years and older group relative to the two younger age groupings could, as Anastasi (1982) has pointed out in reviewing western studies of ageing, be a comment on intergenerational differences. The *youngest* person in the 37 years and older Pedi sample would have been born during the early 1930s, with the average person being born even earlier. The process of large-scale urbanisation and industrialisation of South Africa's black population is of recent origin, which suggests that nearly everyone in the group would have grown up in a rural area, and if they had attended school at all, it would have been in the same area.

In the light of Kendall's findings and the explanations advanced tentatively to account for these findings, it could be that the age factor, in the same way as the sex factor, is itself mediated by cultural influences. On the other hand, a decline in general physiological efficiency with age cannot be ruled out as a significant dispositional moderator of test performance level.

Factor-analytic explorations of African performance on cognitive tests

Because the outcome of a factor analysis is dependent on the particular battery of tests which was administered, and because the choice of such a battery is dependent on the age and educational characteristics of the testees, different factor structures are expected in different populations. The African literature is therefore discussed under two headings: illiterate and semiliterate adults; and schoolchildren, adolescents, and literate adults. To conclude the review, mention is also made of the handful of psychometric studies which have attempted to look beneath the surface trait as represented by a test raw score, in order to answer questions relating to problem-solving strategy or style.

Illiterate and semiliterate adults

The earliest factorial studies (Biesheuvel, 1954; MacDonald, 1945; Murray, 1956) were conducted in the "British" tradition of drawing inferences about psychological constructs from unrotated factor matrices. MacDonald's (1945) landmark selection testing programme involved the administration of a battery of 13 cognitive and psychomotor tests to some 1,800 East African recruits to the British Army. A centroid factor analysis was performed, yielding a three-factor structure. MacDonald did not venture an interpretation of these factors, but Vernon (1950) found the data sufficiently interesting to warrant reanalysis. Three factors were again extracted, one of which was discarded as it failed to produce a logical grouping of tests. In accordance with the British approach to factor interpretation, Vernon identified the first factor as "general adaptability" because all the tests loaded on it. The second factor emerged in bipolar form, dividing the battery into the primarily cognitive tests on the one hand, and the psychomotor tests on the other.

Two South African researchers, Biesheuvel (1954) and Murray (1956) also provided evidence of a strong general intellectual component underlying black test performance. Murray in addition carried out several factor analyses of test data on black South African schoolchildren (Biesheuvel, 1949;

de Ridder, 1956) as well as on East African laboratory assistants. In all instances, only one factor was found to be significant according to various statistical rules of thumb. Murray's analyses led him to conclude that in so far as the African is concerned, "simplicity of factor structure is determined by a simplicity of mental structure" (p. 63), which he attributed, in part, to inferior education in the formative years.

Grant and Schepers (1969) took exception to Murray's pronouncement on the apparent simplicity of African mental structures. Proponents of the Thurstonian approach to factor analysis, these authors argued that Murray's conclusions were a direct consequence of his having adopted the equally "simplistic" British approach to factor interpretation. Grant and Schepers also criticised earlier factor-analytic studies in Africa on the grounds of inadequately assembled test batteries, which made it difficult for separate factors to emerge. Interpretations of the structure of African abilities in terms of the Thurstonian approach were first offered, independently, it would seem, by Irvine (1969a) and Grant and Schepers (1969). The latter authors chose to reanalyse Vernon's (1950) intercorrelation matrix, which in turn had been derived from MacDonald's (1945) data. It was concluded that MacDonald's tests defined two distinct factors to which Grant and Schepers assigned the labels "Eduction of Relations" and "Dexterity." It was argued on this basis that the general factor was little more than a procedural artifact and that by increasing the range and diversity of cognitive tasks in a given test battery, there is no reason why additional factors should not be uncovered in the structure of preliterate African intellect.

The apparent advantages of adopting a Thurstonian approach to the study of African abilities led to a series of exploratory investigations (Grant, 1970b and 1972a; Grant & Schepers, 1969; Schepers, 1974). With reference to recruits to the Witwatersrand gold mines whose educational achievement typically averaged no more than two years' schooling, evidence of at least five group factors underlying performance on visual sorting, assembling, series completion, and pattern arrangement/continuation tasks was claimed. These factors were labelled Eduction of Relations (later interpreted as Perceptual Analysis), Perceptual Speed, Conceptual Reasoning, Perception of Form Relations, and Space.

A large-scale study was conducted by Grant (1969; 1972b) to confirm the presence of these factors. A battery of 16 tests, chosen on the basis of their performance in the various pilot studies, was administered to large samples of illiterate and semiliterate Venda-speaking adults in a rural area and an urban area of the Transvaal. Although Grant concluded that he had been able to confirm the specified five factors, two salient features of his results cannot be ignored. First, the intercorrelations between most of his factors were generally high, which suggests that too many factors may have been extracted. Kaiser's (1985) criterion of factor significance had, in fact, indicated three, not five, factors for the sample as a whole. Vandenberg and Hakstian (1978) are sceptical of Grant's five-factor solution. Having calculated coefficients of congruence between the factors in each of the Venda subsamples (educated urban, uneducated urban, educated rural, and uneducated rural), these critics concluded that the factors could well have capitalised on error variance. Second, Grant interpreted the finding that most of his factors had emerged as *doublets* as indicating the need for an even broader battery of tests in future investigations. What was apparent, however, was that in most instances the doublets were made up of tests that might almost be considered alternate forms of one another (e.g., two sorting tests, two form boards, two series continuation tests, and two design-copying tests).

Kendall's (1971) study of an adult group of Pedi speakers was designed as a sequel to Grant's (1969) investigation of the Venda. Using a shortened battery of supposedly "pure" reference tests, evidence to support Grant's anticipated factor structure was indeed found, but once again, correlations between factors were very high and the factor solutions failed to meet Thurstone's requirements for simple structure. A reanalysis of the data was performed several years later (Kendall, 1980). In an attempt to make the sample a little more homogeneous, a few subjects were eliminated (those older than 59 years or who had received 9 or more years' schooling) while two tests were discarded altogether on the grounds of their marginal reliabilities. The influence of age on test performance was also partialled out before proceeding with factor analysis. These minor changes between the 1971 and 1980 analyses resulted in substantially different conclusions being drawn. In particular, hardly any support for Grant's anticipated factor-structure was found. Exploratory factor analysis suggested, instead, a broad General Reasoning component for both the illiterate and semiliterate subgroups supported by a Perceptual Speed factor in the case of urban and rural illiterates and a Spatial factor in the case of urban semiliterates. Interestingly enough, the factor solutions based on age-adjusted test performance yielded a clearer picture than the solutions based on the unadjusted raw scores.

Comparison of the Pedi (Kendall, 1980) findings with those of Warburton (1951) in Malaysia, the Australian Aboriginal and Papua–New Guinean studies cited by Ord (1970), and Grant's (1969) *two-factor* solutions for his Venda sample, suggests striking resemblances in factor structures, albeit at a purely impressionistic level. In all these instances very similar tests had been used on people of similar age and educational attainment. There is also no apparent contradiction between the results of the above studies and those of Biesheuvel (1954) and Murray (1956), provided it is recognised that the Thurstonian and the British approaches to interpreting factors emphasise different levels in the hierarchy of human abilities. The presence of a strong General Cognitive factor underlying illiterate and semiliterate African test performances cannot be denied, but at the same time there is usually sufficient residual variance to warrant exploration of more specialised factors. Grant may have erred, however, in insisting that his factors are the preliterate African equivalent of Thurstone's well-known primary factors in the intellect of adult, educated westerners. Along with many other western researchers, psychologists in Africa seem to have forgotten that their tests sample a very narrow range of cognitive operations. When it is considered that investigators throughout the world have concentrated on measuring only those abilities which western technological societies deem important, it is dangerous to conclude that they constitute universally valid yardsticks of intelligence per se. As Bakare (1972) and other black psychologists have pointed out, it would be "improper to use such tests to measure the 'intelligence' of people in Africa. . . . Such tests could measure their spatial ability, their perceptual speed, their visual-motor coordination and the like but certainly not their 'intelligence.'. . . It is equally illogical to put them into a factor analysis to find 'the factorial structure of African intelligence'" (Bakare, 1972, p. 362).

Had psychologists in Africa constructed a truly varied array of tests, capable of surfacing visual, auditory, *and* proprioceptive abilities and focussing in addition on those (unresearched) crystallised abilities which are of functional value in adapting to the demands of traditional societies, only then could it have been claimed that exploration of the "structure of intellect" of African peoples was under way. Some suggestions for this kind of work have been made in the literature, notably traditional games, riddles, sayings, handicrafts, and the like (Biesheuvel, 1952a; Hopkins & Wober, 1973; Irvine, 1970; Wober, 1975), homemade toys and models (Serpell, 1974), visual symbolism (Wober, 1975), music, singing, and dance choreography (Ombredane, 1954), auditory abilities in general (Biesheuvel, 1943), and proprioceptive skills (Wober, 1975). African psychologists could doubtless list a whole range of additional behaviours which westerners might find difficult to appreciate and to conceptualise in familiar "maximum performance" test terms. Exploration of these behavioural domains has never really got off the ground, some rare examples being Serpell's (1974) study of the skills involved in making model vehicles out of wire and a very early study of musical talent in East Africa by Oliver (1932b). This is unfortunate because there could have been considerable scientific merit in using indigenous materials to test the generality of western theories of the structure and patterning of human abilities across cultures. Research of this nature could also have created a broader, less ethnocentric base from which to investigate the universals of human behaviour. As remarked by Frijda and Jahoda (1966), it is now too late to mount such research given the difficulty in finding contemporary societies that have not been influenced by modern technological culture.

The results of factorial studies on the abilities of African schoolchildren and educated adults are less contentious because here one is dealing with people who are the products of a modern educational system. Because of the literacy and numeracy of such samples, the range of customary cognitive abilities amenable to measurement is considerably less restrictive than in the case of uneducated samples.

Schoolchildren, adolescents, and young (educated) adults

Fouché (1973; 1974) factor-analysed the test performance of very large samples of young schoolchildren, drawn from the four main cultural groupings in South Africa (blacks, whites, Asians, and coloureds). The battery comprised nine tests, but the analyses were conducted on the correlations between selected item pairs from each test. Seven factors were identified within each cultural group, the congruences between the factors across cultures being reported to be very high (Vandenberg & Hakstian, 1978). The factors were very similar to the original tests and were interpreted as Perception, Spatial Ability, General Reasoning, Number Ability, Gestalt, Coordination, and Memory. In view of the method of analysis, we are not convinced that these factors constitute a statement on the primary ability structure of school beginners. They are possibly more a comment on the high degree of internal consistency of the items within each test. The high degree of factor congruence across cultures is nevertheless noteworthy. Focussing more specifically on number ability in young schoolchildren, Dreyer (1974) concluded that the factorial composition of 25 piagetian tasks differed somewhat between blacks on the one hand and whites, Asians, and coloureds on the other. Whereas the sequence of stages in the acquisition of number concept appeared to be invariant across the four cultures, the underlying operations were found to be far more strongly intercorrelated in the black group than in the others. Only Conservation and Cardinal Number Compositions emerged as two well-developed constructs in the case of black pupils, compared with six clearly defined factors in the other three samples.

Among older pupils, a large number of factors has been identified in a variety of studies throughout sub-Saharan Africa (cf. Fourie, 1967; Irvine, 1969a; MacArthur, 1973; Vernon, 1967a; Von Mollendorf, 1974). In view of the different test batteries used in each study, objective comparison of factor structures across samples is not possible. Most investigations have yielded evidence of one or more General Reasoning factors, as well as clearly defined Numerical, Verbal and Spatial-Perceptual abilities, dependent on the composition of the test battery (see Irvine's [1979] review). Broadly comparable factors have also emerged in analyses of young adults (mainly university students, schoolteachers, and student nurses), with authors claiming support for the particular theoretical standpoint which guided their choice of test battery. Classically Thurstonian primary mental abilities were identified by Nsereko-Gyagenda (1973) in Uganda, for instance, while El-Abd (1970) favoured a more Guilfordian interpretation and Claeys (1972), working in Zaïre, produced evidence of Cattell-type crystallised and fluid general intellectual factors as well as a perceptual analytic component akin to Witkin's field dependence construct. In a Southern African study (Crawford-Nutt, 1977a), factors were identified as broad information-processing constructs such as long-term versus short-term memory store processes, in preference to more conventional factor labels following Cattell or Vernon. Focussing more specifically on tests considered to be potentially useful predictors of technical aptitude, Epstein (1983) produced evidence of well-defined Spatial Reasoning and Mechanical Insight constructs, alongside factors of a more general intellectual nature.

Of considerable methodological interest is Von Mollendorf's (1974) investigation of the influence of *repeated testing* on the factor structure of tests applied to black pupils in their eighth year of school. A clear three-factor solution, which satisfied Thurstone's criteria for simple structure, was obtained, the factors being identified as General Reasoning, Spatial Ability, and Verbal Ability. The factor structure became progressively clearer and more crystallised with each successive readministration of the battery. Coefficients of congruence between the third and final administrations were exceptionally high and were superior to those between the first and final administrations. Von Mollendorf's findings support McFie's (1961) earlier work in Uganda, which demonstrated a similar sharpening of factor definitions as a function of coaching and retesting.

The relative ease with which the factors identified in studies of literate blacks can be assigned familiar western labels is certainly evident and demonstrates that there is probably a broad degree of construct equivalence of psychometric tests across cultures. Factor analysis, however, has its limitations as a means of establishing construct equivalence, one of the reasons being that it cannot account for suspected *stylistic* differences in the approach of different samples to the same battery of tests. Factor analysis is a gross taxonomic tool and, apart from confirming hypotheses derived from a sound theoretical model, cannot in itself explain the nature of the underlying psychological constructs. The final section of this review gives examples from the African literature of research focussed on cognitive processes and problem-solving strategies.

Cognitive processes and test performance

In African studies, scant attention has been given to exploring the meaning of a test result at a level beyond the obtained raw score, its norm equivalent, its predictive validity, or its factor loading. Psychologists working in the former Belgian Congo made a start by analysing errors frequently made by testees on *Raven's Progressive Matrices* (Laroche, 1956; Ombredane & Robaye, 1953; Ombredane, Robaye, & Robaye, 1957). Their findings pointed to the prominence of stereotyped pattern-copying errors, which was also found to be an important reason for poor performance on the South African–developed *Form Series Test* (Grant, 1965; Kendall, 1977; Melamed, 1977a; 1977b). In Melamed's (1977b) study, it was noticed that just over half of the subjects, who were mainly illiterates, adopted the incorrect strategy of continuing a figural series by simply duplicating the two forms which were at the end of the series. Kendall (1977) and Melamed (1977a) also provided compelling evidence that testees could successfully adopt an essentially pattern-seeking strategy to solve conceptually complex series and still achieve a good score. When, however, a series problem became so complex that a more abstract, analytic approach to its solution was the only feasible strategy, considerable problems were encountered by most subjects, including those with a high school education. This finding implied a resistance on the part of the subjects to abandoning a previously appropriate strategy and gave credibility to Laroche's (1956) earlier conclusion that a test such as *Raven's Progressive Matrices*, when applied to an African sample, provides "not so much a measure of the ability of the subjects to reason by analogy as a measure of their mental rigidity or flexibility" (Laroche, 1956, p. 170, our translation). Whether the apparent lack of problem-solving flexibility on the part of many African children and adults is due to cultural influences or to basic flaws in the design of the tests themselves, remains an open question. The important point is that testees do not necessarily solve problems in a test in the manner originally intended by the test constructor. Grant's (1969) labelling of the factor referenced by the *Form Series Test* as Conceptual Reasoning *Ability* could be a misattribution; and is one more example of the limitations of factor analysis as a method of establishing the construct validity of tests.

It is perhaps time that researchers took a more penetrating look at the cognitive *processes* underlying test performance and stopped thinking only in terms of factors or *abilities*. Very little research of this nature has come out of Africa, the most recent and certainly the most significant being J. M. Verster's (1983) study of the relationship between speed and accuracy of cognitive processing and intelligence. His computerised testing investigation provided evidence of the hierarchial structure of four differentiated information-processing subsystems (psychomotor, sensory, perceptual, and conceptual) as well as some powerful evidence of the functional equivalence across cultures (educated black and white South Africans) and between the sexes of psychometrically reliable measures of these processes. Of particular interest to psychometricians was Verster's demonstration of the differential correlation of the various information-processing measures with three selected subtests in the South African version of the *Wechsler–Bellevue Adult Intelligence Scale (WAIS)*. For example, performance on the *Block Design* subtest was correlated with speed scores on the perceptual process tasks and with accuracy on the conceptual tasks whereas a verbal subtest, *Similarities,* correlated highest with accuracy on the conceptual tasks and *Digit Symbol Substitution* highest with speed of sensory encoding.

It is perhaps too early to assess the implications of the above-mentioned insights into cognitive behaviour for the meaning that should be attached to a test score. It is possible that further research in this field might well point to the universality of basic cognitive *processes* across cultures while conceding at the same time the possibility of variations in cognitive style between cultures and subcultures when it comes to measuring specific *abilities.*

Conclusions and some suggestions for further research

The usefulness of psychological tests as predictors of the industrial trainability of black Africans cannot be doubted. Impressive predictive validity coefficients have been recorded, particularly in studies conducted on illiterate and semiliterate recruits to the South African gold mines. As predictors of scholastic educability, on the other hand, psychometric tests have often not come up to expectations. In particular, the South African research suggests that a negligible contribution is made towards improved predictive efficiency when general reasoning tests, especially of the nonverbal variety, are used in conjunction with more achievement-type tests. As Silvey (1972) has pointed out with regard to his Ugandan studies, however, this could be more a reflection on the nature of school examinations in Africa, which are widely believed to be characterised by rote learning, than on any fundamental differences across cultures regarding the construct validity of general reasoning tests.

Criterion-related validity studies have demonstrated the fundamental relevance of the kinds of abilities measured by psychometric tests in so far as general adaptability to the classroom and the work situation are concerned. Some firmer evidence of the nature of the underlying constructs, or "abilities," has been forthcoming from the large body of research which has sought to explore the relationships between test performance on the one hand and a variety of environmental, dispositional, and other nontest variables on the other. The Southern African findings strongly support the conclusions reached in the rest of Africa. The picture which has emerged vividly portrays the influence which culture plays in fostering, stimulating, and supporting human abilities.

At a macro-level of analysis, the variables of formal education and urbanisation exert a particularly strong and seemingly independent influence on those abilities which have been measured by psychologists, an influence which would appear to override ethnicity as a factor. This is hardly surprising because education and urbanisation represent two of the most powerful agents of acculturation towards a modern, competitive, and achievement-oriented way of life. This would suggest that culture is an extremely "high inference" (Irvine, 1983) variable, far more so than ethnicity as such and, on a global scale, is probably more important than the traditional correlates of age, sex, and socioeconomic status.

The kinds of human abilities that are of functional value in the technology-based societies of Europe and North America, and that are highly valued by members of those societies, are precisely those abilities for which western psychologists have constructed measuring instruments. Rarely have psychologists even begun to attempt measurement of the human skills and abilities valued by members of traditional African societies. The disdain for exploring and measuring the kinds of abilities which traditional African cultures could well have fostered is summed up in a few words by Fontaine (1963), who remarked that one is not selecting blacks to make bows and build canoes! Given, then, that the tests that have been used on the African continent since the inception of "objective" scientific enquiry more than 70 years ago, are essentially western in flavour, it is hardly surprising that black Africans do not achieve the same levels of test performance as westerners.

In Africa, the psychological literature suggests a wide range of cultural and environmental factors which, in extreme combinations, would inhibit adaptability to a modern, technology-based lifestyle. From the moment of birth, traditional socialisation practices, with their frequent emphasis on conformity to custom, unconditional respect for one's elders and the authorities, and the limits to parental stimulation of the child's natural curiosity imposed by the high work-load of mothers in subsistence economies, put constraints on the development of western-type cognitive abilities. The problem is compounded by the ecological press of harsh environments where disease, drought, and famine are endemic and affect many millions of African children. These conditions impoverish (by western standards) the typical domestic environment of the rural African peasant, and also foster a diet which more often than not is rich in carbohydrates but protein-deficient. Education systems throughout Africa are often inadequate and the quality of teaching can vary markedly from school to school. The dropout rate is still extremely high and many products of the educational systems emerge as rote learners, handicapped in their ability to apply their knowledge to the solution of complex problems in the world of commerce and technology. The benefits of a thorough (western) education are accessible to the select few, the elite and emerging middle classes in Africa's wealthier nations. Industrialisation and urbanisation as major social forces have a recent history on the African continent, which means that hardly any blacks – including today's children – are completely free of past generational influences. For example, being born a female appears to be an added handicap. In South Africa, the apartheid system, which until recently had retarded the process of urbanisation of blacks, has restricted contacts with members of other ethnic groups. It has resulted in an inferior educational system for blacks and may have placed further environmental constraints on the development of abilities necessary for survival in the modern world. There would thus appear to be many cultural and environmental variables at play in moderating test performance levels; so many, in fact, that one wonders whether there is any point in even considering genetic factors as an additional source of variance between the average performance levels of westerners and Africans.

Apart from having demonstrated the crucial role of culture in giving shape to specific human abilities, African research has also challenged conventional notions of the relative degree of influence of such factors on test performance. For instance, in view of the considerable degree of learning which can take place in the testing situation itself, it should no longer be held that coaching and practice on tests constitute low inference variables. Neither should age and sex necessarily be regarded as primarily dispositional and constitutionally related factors. The finding that African males almost invariably outperform females on cognitive tests is probably an indication that males are acculturating more readily than females. The decline in test performance level with age is possibly also culture-linked, reflecting perhaps fairly large differences in level of acculturation between generations as well as lack of cultural and environmental support for western-type abilities among older people. It may also be concluded, from research on the African continent, that abilities cannot be conceived of as fixed potential which reaches an invariant state once adulthood is attained. The demonstration that changes in test performance may occur in response to environmental circumstances even after the prime period of growth and development must represent a challenge to the concept of fixed ability patterns. This conclusion is in line with recent trends in life-span developmental research, where significant intellectual plasticity has been evident in response to conditions of retesting and training, even late into adulthood (Willis, Baltes, & Cornelius, 1981). The value of using the cross-cultural paradigm in a search for human universals must be clearly apparent. One of the messages to come out of this research is that if test score meaning is so tentative and difficult to pin down, then psychometrics has serious limitations in contributing to our overall understanding of general mental processes.

The most profound implication by far of the African literature concerning the role of moderator variables is the culture-boundness of our cognitive measures. Explorations of the factorial validity of psychometric tests give added weight to the general conclusions which have emerged concerning the essentially western flavour of the constructs being measured. Far from producing evidence of an array of exotic, peculiarly "African," cognitive abilities, studies in Africa would appear to underline the robustness across cultures of the kind of information-processing parameters that have been identified in the western literature. It would seem that Africans and North Americans alike tend to draw on broadly similar mental processes when presented with similar problem-solving situations. This should not come as a surprise, because one is dealing only with those particular abilities that are fostered and supported by the demands of a modern, technology-based culture. It is understandable, too, that the greater the degree of acculturation in any one particular group of subjects, the easier it is to demonstrate the existence of cognitive abilities in that group's "structure of intellect" which are seemingly comparable to the abilities of fully westernised groups.

The kinds of factors typically identified in analyses of uneducated adult Africans have been found to be mainly perceptual analytic in essence, with a lack of clear differentiation between different forms of conceptual, abstract, and spatial reasoning processes. Speed of perception is also frequently identified in view of the availability of a number of perceptual sorting, scanning, and classifactory tests. Most factors appear to be quite highly correlated with one another to the extent that a broad second-order intellectual factor, often labelled "general adaptability," is strongly suspected. Given the availability of a far wider range of tests for use with literate subjects, a broader and seemingly more "complex" or differentiated picture emerges of the structure of intellect of African children and adults. Familiar labels such as "verbal ability," "spatial reasoning," "number ability," and so on, are readily assignable to factors which are identifiable, mathematically, in samples that are both numerate and literate.

Despite the superficial and indirect evidence in support of the congruence between ability constructs across cultures on a seemingly global scale, we are still far from a scientifically defensible understanding of the manner in which people from different cultures process the same information. It is all too easy to conclude that some evidence of the universality of human abilities has been obtained when one proceeds within the parameters of a common methodology and within the confines of a common acculturation process. Our procedures, which have been quite ethnocentric in their points of departure, have perhaps succeeded in demonstrating what Van de Vijver and Poortinga (1982) call "functionally equivalent or weak universals" of behaviour. These same procedures, however, have taught us very little about the capabilities of African people as distinct from people in other cultures. As a result of their preoccupation with constructing visual, maximum performance tests, psychologists have lost sight of the fuller range of human accomplishments of which the conventionally measurable abilities admired in the West form but a part. Accused by many of not even sampling the intelligent behaviours of westerners adequately, it would be rash to suppose that psychometric tests constitute valid measures of intelligence among non-westerners. The inability of most psychologists to look beyond the confines of their own culture has led to the kind of arrogance whereby judgments are made concerning the "simplicity" of African mental structures and "retarded" cognitive growth. Psychologists would do well to consider just how "simple" and "retarded" *westerners* would appear to black people conducting imaginary investigations of "intelligence" using African-designed techniques of evaluation. Given only a short period of exposure to the indigenous culture, it is unlikely that westerners would perform at the same level as illiterate villagers on measures of the ability to discern rhythms and counterrhythms in African music, the ability to construct arguments that cannot be countered with logic, and the ability to derive secondary meaning from various forms of visual symbolism. Put into a factor analysis, it would also not be surprising to find that western test performance might possibly be accounted for by only one general strategy to solve such problems with little evidence of specific aptitudes. Attempts to make the test materials a little "fairer" by westernising their content might help somewhat, but the surest solution to the "problem" would be to accelerate the process of Africanisation of westerners over successive generations of contact with an African culture. In short, psychologists around the world have invested an enormous amount of time and energy in demonstrating how people from other cultures are able to perform our (western) "tricks," with little thought having been given to researching performance on their own "tricks" (Wober, 1969).

The truth of the matter is, of course, that Africans have perforce to acquire classically western abilities if they are to survive in today's dominant culture, which is largely western in its inspiration. This fact accentuates the importance of continuing with present research concerns. There should be an acceleration of criterion-referenced validity studies accompanied, in multicultural societies such as South Africa, by urgent investigation of the culture fairness of tests. This is an issue of paramount concern in view of the increasing numbers of black South Africans who are now competing with members of other ethnic groups for technical, clerical, and managerial positions. Preliminary impressions are that certain tests, especially those in the spatial reasoning domain (Taylor, 1985) could be biased against blacks, but research in this area has barely begun. In addition to investigating this issue in a black–white context, this line of research should be extended to explore other sources of possible test bias on an *intracultural* basis, notably bias against females, elderly job applicants, illiterates, and persons from rural areas.

Fuller exploration of environmental, cultural, and dispositional correlates of test performance levels is strongly recommended, in an attempt to unravel the complex web of interrelationships between the variables at play. It having been established beyond doubt that education and urbanisation have a marked moderating influence on test performance, the time has perhaps arrived to mount in-depth investigations of the *mechanisms* which account for the relationships. One strategy would be to adopt factorial designs in which the sources of test or task score variance can be partitioned among the main effects of carefully selected cultural and environmental variables and their interactions, using samples which have been chosen in such a way as to account for rival explanations for the findings. For instance, studies of the rural–urban effect on test performance could be taken to a deeper level of analysis by varying length of residence in an urban area, the nature and amount of industrial experience, and degree of adherence to traditional cultural values while exercising control over age, education, sex, and other relevant factors. Simultaneously, in the quest for a deeper scientific understanding of human cognition, psychologists would do well to abandon their exclusive concerns with either the psychometric paradigm or more experimentally anchored approaches. The marriage of the psychometric and experimental traditions is still in its infancy in South Africa. There is a need to pursue the kind of work recently initiated by Verster (1983) which utilises experimental tasks demonstrating acceptable degrees of reliability and construct validity, and which focusses on information-processing parameters. Provided the tasks themselves are not heavily biased in favour of classically western styles of problem solving and systems of logic, a focus on information-processing parameters could well be a promising alternative to contemporary tests and tasks in researching the fundamental elements of human cognition.

Finally, the student of African intelligence should ponder the point that with one or two exceptions (cf. Durojaiye, 1971; Irvine, 1970; Wober, 1969) hardly any psychologist has taken the trouble to ask African subjects what *they* understand by the term *intelligence*. Is it a criterion which is consciously used when evaluating other people or is it of importance only in so far as adaptation to the individualistic, achievement-oriented world of the westerner is concerned? In the process, the western researcher must be fully prepared for such surprises as Wober's finding that *slowness* rather than quickness is associated in traditional Ugandan culture with the concept "cleverness." Explorations of the place of "intelligence" in the personal construct systems (see Irvine & Berry, Chapter 1) of Africans at varying degrees of acculturation or modernisation would go a long way towards determining the construct's degree of relevance to a scientific understanding of African behaviour.

References

Abiola, E. T. (1967). Nigerian children's pictorial representation of objects in their environment. *Teacher Education, 7,* 196–201.

Anastasi, A. (1958). *Differential psychology: Individual and group differences.* New York: Macmillan. 1958.

Anastasi, A. (1982). *Psychological testing.* New York: Macmillan.

Andor, L. E. (Compiler). (1966). *Aptitudes and abilities of the black man in Sub-Saharan Africa, 1784–1963: An annotated bibliography.* Johannesburg: National Institute for Personnel Research.

Andor, L. E. (Compiler). (1983). *Psychological and sociological studies of the black people of Africa, South of the Sahara, 1960–1975: An annotated select bibliography.* Johannesburg: National Institute for Personnel Research.

Bakare, C. G. M. (1972). Social-class differences in the performance of Nigerian children on the Draw-a-Man test. In L. J. Cronbach & P. J. D. Drenth (Eds.), *Mental tests and cultural adaptation* (pp. 355–363). The Hague: Mouton.

Beales, R. (1951). Urbanism, urbanization and acculturation. *American Anthropologist, 53,* 1–10.

Berry, J. W. (1966). Temne and Eskimo perceptual skills. *International Journal of Psychology, 1,* 207–229.

Berry, J. W. (1968). Ecology, perceptual development and the Muller–Lyer illusion. *British Journal of Psychology, 59,* 205–210.

Biesheuvel, S. (1943). *African intelligence.* Johannesburg: South African Institute of Race Relations.

Biesheuvel, S. (1949). Psychological tests and their application to Non-European peoples. In *The year book of education* (pp. 87–126). London: Evans.

Biesheuvel, S. (1952a). Personnel selection tests for Africans. *South African Journal of Science, 49,* 3–12.

Biesheuvel, S. (1952b). The study of African ability. Part I: The intellectual potentialities of the Africans. Part II: A survey of some research problems. *African Studies, 11,* 45–58, 105–117.

Biesheuvel, S. (1954). The measurement of occupational aptitudes in a multi-racial society. *Occupational Psychology, 28,* 189–196.

Biesheuvel, S. (1972). Adaptability: Its measurement and determinants. In L. J. Cronbach & P. J. D. Drenth (Eds.), *Mental tests and cultural adaptation* (pp. 47–62). The Hague: Mouton.

Blake, R. H. (1972). Industrial application of tests developed for illiterate and semiliterate people. In L. J. Cronbach & P. J. D. Drenth (Eds.), *Mental tests and cultural adaptation* (pp. 37–46). The Hague: Mouton.

Bowden, E. A. F. (1969). Perceptual abilities of African and European children educated together. *Journal of Social Psychology, 79,* 149–154.

Breger, R. A. (1971). *The Selection of Bantu for a skilled job – the moulding of asbestos–cement* (Confidential Report C/PERS 192). Johannesburg: National Institute for Personnel Research.

Carroll, J. B. (1983). Studying individual differences in cognitive abilities: Implications for cross-cultural studies. In S. H. Irvine & J. W. Berry (Eds.), *Human assessment and cultural factors* (pp. 231–235). New York: Plenum.

Cattell, R. B. (1940). A culture-free intelligence test. I. *Journal of Educational Psychology, 31,* 161–180.

Christierson, V. A. B. (1977). *Selection of trainees for a course in instructional techniques in the field of civil engineering – a validation study* (Contract Report C/PERS 252). Johannesburg: National Institute for Personnel Research.

Claeys, W. (1972). The factor structure of intelligence among teachers in the Congo. In L. J. Cronbach & P. J. D. Drenth (Eds.), *Mental tests and cultural adaptation* (pp. 381–389). The Hague: Mouton.

Cole, M., Gay, J., Glick, J. A., & Sharp, D. W. (1971). *The cultural context of learning and thinking: An exploration in experimental anthropology.* London: Methuen.

Crawford-Nutt, D. H. (1976). Are black scores on Raven's Progressive Matrices an artifact of method of test presentation? *Psychologia Africana, 16,* 201–206.

Crawford-Nutt, D. H. (1977a). *The assessment of mental ability among black teachers in Bophuthatswana* (Contract Report C/PERS 257). Johannesburg: National Institute for Personnel Research.

Crawford-Nutt, D. H. (1977b). The effect of educational level on the test scores of people in South Africa. *Psychologia Africana, 17,* 49–59.

Crawford-Nutt, D. H. (1977c). The SYMCO test as a test of ability. *Psychologia Africana, 17,* 79–98.

Cryns, A. G. J. (1962). African intelligence: A critical survey of cross-cultural intelligence research in Africa South of the Sahara. *Journal of Social Psychology, 57,* 283–301.

Dague, P. (1972). Development, application and interpretation of tests for use in French-speaking black Africa and Madagascar. In L. J. Cronbach & P. J. D. Drenth (Eds.), *Mental tests and cultural adaptation* (pp. 63–74). The Hague: Mouton.

Dawson, J. L. M. (1967). Culture and physiological influences upon spatial-perceptual processes in West Africa. *International Journal of Psychology, 2,* 115–128, 171–185.

Dent, G. R. (1937). Applicability of certain performance and other mental tests to Zulu children. In E. G. Malherbe (Ed.), *Educational adaptations in a changing society* (pp. 456–465). Johannesburg: Juta.

Deregowski, J. B. (1977). A study of orientation errors in response to Kohs-type figures. *International Journal of Psychology, 12,* 183–191.

De Ridder, J. C. (1956). *An investigation into educational and occupational differences in test performance on a battery of adaptability tests designed for Africans.* Unpublished doctoral dissertation, University of the Witwatersrand, Johannesburg.

De Wet, D. R. (1967). Simple skill tests applied to Africans. *Psychologia Africana, 11,* 189–205.

Doob, L. W. (1960). *Becoming more civilized.* New Haven, CT: Yale University Press.

Doob, L. W. (1965). Psychology. In R. A. Lystad (Ed.), *The African World* (pp. 373–415). London: Pall Mall Press.

Drenth, P. J. D., van der Flier, H., & Omari, I. M. (1979). The use of classroom tests, examinations and aptitude tests in a developing country. In L. Eckensberger, W. Lonner, & Y. H. Poortinga (Eds.), *Cross-cultural contributions to psychology*. Lisse: Swets & Zeitlinger.

Dreyer, H. J. (1974). The present status of number conceptualisation in the Zulu child. *Paidonomia* (No. 2), 9–24.

Durojaiye, M. O. A. (1971). Is the concept of African intelligence meaningful? *East Africa Journal, 8,* 4–12.

Durojaiye, M. O. A. (1972, August). *Conservation in six African cultures*. Paper presented at the 20th International Congress of Psychology, Tokyo.

El-Abd, H. A. (1970). The intellect of East African students. *Multivariate Behavioral Research, 5,* 423–433.

Epstein, B. I. (1983). *Factors related to mechanical aptitude in blacks*. Unpublished master's thesis, University of South Africa, Pretoria.

Erwee, R. (1981). Cognitive functioning, achievement motivation and vocational preferences of black university students. *Psychologia Africana, 20,* 29–51.

Etuk, E. E. S. (1967) *The development of number concepts: An examination of Piaget's theory with Yoruba-speaking Nigerian children*. Unpublished doctoral dissertation, Columbia University, New York.

Evans, J. L., & Segall, M. H. (1969). Learning to classify by color and by function: A study of concept–discovery by Ganda children. *Journal of Social Psychology, 77,* 35–53.

Fahrmeier, E. D. (1975). The effect of school attendance on intellectual development in Northern Nigeria. *Child Development, 46,* 281–285.

Fick, M. L. (1939). *The educability of the South African Native* (Research Series No. 8). Pretoria: South African Council for Educational and Social Research.

Fisher, M. M., et al. (1972). Malnutrition and reasoning ability in Zambian schoolchildren. *Transactions of the Royal Society of Tropical Medicine and Hygiene, 66,* 471–478.

Fleishman, E. A., & Hempel, W. E. (1956). Factorial analysis of complex psychomotor performance and related skills. *Journal of Applied Psychology, 40,* 96–104.

Fontaine, C. (1963). Notes sur une expérience d'application de tests au Mali [A note on experiences with testing in Mali]. *Revue de Psychologie Appliquée, 13,* 235–246.

Fouché, F. A. (1973). Ability structure invariance at five educational levels. *20th International Congress of Psychology, Abstract Guide* (p. 514).

Fouché, F. A. (1974). The development of psychological tests for different ethnic groups in South Africa. *Hiroshima Forum for Psychology, 1,* 35–43.

Fourie, A. B. (1967). *Ondersoek na die implikasie van gestandaardiseerde toetse vir st. VI Bantoeleerlinge* [A study on the implications of standardised tests for standard VI Bantu pupils]. Unpublished doctoral dissertation, University of Pretoria.

Fourie, J. C. (1982). *Validation of a test battery for the selection of black insurance salesmen* (Confidential Report C/PERS 324). Johannesburg: National Institute for Personnel Research.

Frijda, N., & Jahoda, G. (1966). On the scope and methods of cross-cultural research. *International Journal of Psychology, 1,* 109–127.

Geber, M. (1958). The psycho-motor development of African children in the first year, and the influence of maternal behaviour. *Journal of Social Psychology, 47,* 185–195.

Geber, M., & Dean, R. F. (1957). Gesell tests on African children. *Pediatrics, 20,* 1055–1066.

Gilbey, R. J. (1964). *Some effects of a history of kwashiorkor on the behaviour of young African children*. Unpublished master's thesis. University of Natal, Pietermaritzburg.

Gouws, D. J. (1950). The influence of tribal origin on the test performance of native mine labour. *Bulletin of the National Institute for Personnel Research, 2*(2), 77–90.

Grant, G. V. (1965). *The construction of a non-verbal test of reasoning ability for African industrial workers*. Unpublished master's thesis, University of the Witwatersrand, Johannesburg.

Grant, G. V. (1969). *The organization of mental abilities of an African ethnic group in cultural transition*. Unpublished doctoral dissertation, University of the Witwatersrand, Johannesburg.

Grant, G. V. (1970a). *The development and validation of a classification test battery constructed to replace the General Adaptability Battery* (Confidential Report C/PERS 181). Johannesburg: National Institute for Personnel Research.

Grant, G. V. (1970b). Spatial thinking: A dimension in African intellect. *Psychologia Africana, 13*, 222–239.

Grant, G. V. (1972a). Conceptual reasoning: Another dimension of African intellect. *Psychologia Africana, 14*, 170–185.

Grant, G. V., (1972b). The organization of intellectual abilities of an African ethnic group in cultural transition. In L. J. Cronbach & P. J. D. Drenth (Eds.), *Mental tests and cultural adaptation* (pp. 391–400). The Hague: Mouton.

Grant, G. V., & Schepers, J. M. (1969). An exploratory factor analysis of five new cognitive tests for African mineworkers. *Psychologia Africana, 12*, 181–192.

Greenfield, P. M. (1966). On culture and conservation. In J. S. Bruner et al. (Eds.), *Studies in cognitive growth* (pp. 225–256). New York: Wiley.

Hall, S. K. P. (1971). *Motivation among a rural and an urban employed group of adult Pedi males* (PERS 154). Johannesburg: National Institute for Personnel Research.

Hendrikz, E. A. (1975). Spatial reasoning and mathematical and scientific competence: A cross-cultural study. In J. W. Berry & W. J. Lonner (Eds.), *Applied cross-cultural psychology* (pp. 219–223). Lisse: Swets & Zeitlinger.

Heyneman, S. P. (1976). A brief note on the relationship between socioeconomic status and test performance among Ugandan primary school children. *Comparative Education Review, 20*, 42–47.

Hoar, R. M. N. (1983). The assessment of aptitude in black school beginners. *Humanitas – RSA, 9*, 175–180.

Hoorweg, J. (1976). Africa (South of the Sahara). In V. S. Sexton & H. Misiak (Eds.), *Psychology around the world* (pp. 8–28). Monterey, CA: Brooks/Cole.

Hoorweg, J., & Marais, H. E. (1969). *Psychology in Africa: A bibliography*. Leyden: Afrika – Studiecentrum.

Hoorweg, J., & Stanfield, J. P. (1976). The effects of protein energy malnutrition in early childhood on intellectual and motor abilities in later childhood and adolescence. *Developmental Medicine and Child Neurology, 18*, 330–350.

Hopkins, B., & Wober, M. (1973). Games and sports: Missing items in cross-cultural psychology. *International Journal of Psychology, 8*, 5–14.

Howard, J. K. (1966). Calorie intake and intelligence: A study among Bantu school children. *Central African Journal of Medicine, 12*, 63–64.

Hudson, W. (1953). *The occupational classification of Africans*. Unpublished doctoral dissertation, University of the Witwatersrand, Johannesburg.

Hudson, W. (1960). Pictorial depth perception in sub-cultural groups in Africa. *Journal of Social Psychology, 52*, 183–208.

Irvine, S. H. (1963). Ability testing in English-speaking Africa: An overview of predictive and comparative studies. *Rhodes–Livingstone Journal* (No. 34), 44–55.

Irvine, S. H. (1965). *Selection for secondary education in Southern Rhodesia*. Salisbury (Harare): University College of Rhodesia and Nyasaland (University of Zimbabwe).

Irvine, S. H. (1966). Towards a rationale for testing attainments and abilities in Africa. *British Journal of Educational Psychology, 36*, 24–32.

Irvine, S. H. (1969a). Factor analysis of African abilities and attainments: Constructs across cultures. *Psychological Bulletin, 71*, 20–32.

Irvine, S. H. (1969b). Figural tests of reasoning in Africa: Studies in the use of Raven's Matrices across cultures. *International Journal of Psychology, 4*, 217–228.

Irvine, S. H. (1969c). How fair is culture? Factorial studies of Raven's Progressive Matrices across cultures. In K. Ingenkamp (Ed.), *Developments in educational testing* (Vol. 1, pp. 372–390). London: University of London Press.

Irvine, S. H. (1970). Affect and construct – a cross-cultural check on theories of intelligence. *Journal of Social Psychology, 80,* 23–30.

Irvine, S. H. (1979). The place of factor analysis in cross-cultural methodology and its contribution to cognitive theory. In L. H. Eckensberger, W. J. Lonner, & Y. H. Poortinga (Eds.), *Cross-cultural contributions to psychology* (pp. 300–341). Lisse: Swets & Zeitlinger.

Irvine, S. H. (1983). Testing in Africa and America: The search for routes. In S. H. Irvine & J. W. Berry (Eds.), *Human assessment and cultural factors.* New York: Plenum.

Irvine, S. H., & Carroll, J. B. (1980). Testing and assessment across cultures: Issues in methodology and theory. In H. C. Triandis & J. W. Berry (Eds.), *Handbook of cross-cultural psychology: Methodology* (Vol. 2, pp. 181–244). Boston: Allyn & Bacon.

Irvine, S. H., Sanders, J. T., & Klingelhofer, E. L. (1970). *Human behaviour in Africa: Bibliography of psychological and related writings.* London: University of Western Ontario.

Irwin, M. H., Schafer, G. N., & Feiden, C. P. (1974). Emic and unfamiliar category sorting of Mano farmers and U.S. undergraduates. *Journal of Cross-Cultural Psychology, 5,* 407–423.

Jahoda, G. (1966). Geometric illusions and environment: A study in Ghana. *British Journal of Psychology, 57,* 193–199.

Jenkins, J. J. (1981). Can we have a fruitful cognitive psychology? *Nebraska Symposium on Motivation, 1980: Cognitive Processes. 28,* 211–238.

Kaiser, H. F. (1985). The varimax criterion for analytic rotation in factor analysis. *Psychometrika, 23,* 187–200.

Kendall, I. M. (1971). *The organization of mental abilities of a Pedi group in cultural transition* (PERS 156). Johannesburg: National Institute for Personnel Research.

Kendall, I. M. (1972). *A comparative study of the organization of mental abilities of two matched ethnic groups: The Venda and the Pedi* (PERS 171). Johannesburg: National Institute for Personnel Research.

Kendall, I. M. (1976). The predictive validity of a possible alternative to the Classification Test Battery. *Psychologia Africana, 16,* 131–146.

Kendall, I. M. (1977). Some observations concerning the reasoning styles of black South African workers: Perceptual versus conceptual considerations. *Psychologia Africana, 17,* 1–29.

Kendall, I. M. (1980). *A comparative study of the structure of intellect of rural and urban adult Pedi.* Unpublished master's thesis. Rand Afrikaans University, Johannesburg.

Kilbride, P. L., Robbins, M. C., & Freeman, R. B. (1968). Pictorial depth perception and education among Baganda school children. *Perceptual and Motor Skills, 26,* 1116–1118.

Klingelhofer, E. L. (1967). Performance of Tanzanian secondary school pupils on the Raven's Standard Progressive Matrices Test. *Journal of Social Psychology, 72,* 205–215.

Klingelhofer, E. L. (1971). A note on language, school and examiner effects on the performance of Tanzanian school children on Raven's Standard Progressive Matrices tests. *Journal of Social Psychology, 83,* 145–146.

Landman, J. L. (1978). *Die voorspelling van waarskynlike skoolprestasie met behulp van die aanlegtoetsbattery (ATB) vir swart leerlinge* [The prediction of expected scholastic performance with the aid of the Aptitude Test Battery (ATB) for black pupils]. Unpublished master's thesis, University of Pretoria.

Laroche, J. L. (1956). L'analyse des erreurs sur le Matrix 38 [Error analysis of Matrices 38]. *Bulletin du Centre d'Etudes de Recherches Psychotechniques, 6,* 161–172.

Laroche, J.-L. (1959). Effets de répétition du Matrix 38 sur les résultats d'enfants Katangais [Effects of retesting on Matrices 38 on the results of Katangan children]. *Bulletin du Centre d'Etudes de Recherches Psychotechniques, 8,* 85–99.

Lätti, V. I., & Verster, M. A. (1975). *NIPR tests for the assessment of blacks* (PERS 230). Johannesburg: National Institute for Personnel Research.

Lloyd, B. (1971). The intellectual development of Yoruba children: A re-examination. *Journal of Cross-Cultural Psychology, 2,* 29–38.

Lloyd, F., & Pidgeon, D. A. (1961). An investigation into the effects of coaching on non-verbal test material with European, Indian and African children. *British Journal of Educational Psychology, 31,* 145–151.

MacArthur, R. S. (1973). Some ability patterns: Central Eskimos and Nsenga Africans. *International Journal of Psychology, 8,* 239–247.

MacArthur, R. S., Irvine, S. H., & Brimble, A. R. (1964). *The Northern Rhodesian mental ability survey, 1963.* Lusaka: Institute of Social Research, University of Zambia.

MacDonald, A. (1945). *Selection of African personnel; final report on the work of Selection of Personnel, Technical and Research Unit, Middle East Force.* A.A.G. (Tech.) OZE (SP). GHQ. MEF. London: War Office Archives.

McFie, J. (1961). The effect of education on African performance on a group of intellectual tests. *British Journal of Educational Psychology, 31,* 232–240.

McLaughlin, S. D. (1976). Cognitive processes and school learning: A review of research on cognition in Africa. *African Studies Review, 19,* 75–93.

Martin, A. L. (1915). Experiments with Binet–Simon tests upon African children, chiefly Kaffirs. *Training School Bulletin, 12,* 122–123.

Mauer, K. F. (1974). Differences in Classification Test performance of Bantu mineworkers. *Psychologia Africana, 15,* 89–100.

Mayer, P. (1961). *Townsmen or tribesmen: Conservation and the process of urbanization in a South African city.* New York: Oxford University Press.

Melamed, L. (1977a). Computer models of response strategies used in answering the Form Series Test. *Psychologia Africana, 17,* 61–71.

Melamed, L. (1977b). Response strategies used in performing a test of cognitive reasoning. *Psychologia Africana, 17,* 111–116.

Miller, R. J. (1973). Cross-cultural research in the perception of pictorial materials. *Psychological Bulletin, 80,* 135–150.

Miller, R., & Meltzer, L. (1978). The effect of schooling and technology on the cognitive development of African children. *Genetic Psychology Monographs, 98,* 113–155.

Mkele, N. (1952). Preliminary report on the predictive efficiency of a screening battery for the selection of winch drivers. *Bulletin of the National Institute for Personnel Research, 4*(2), 151–159.

Mkele, N. (1953). Validation of aptitude tests for the selection of winch drivers on the Witwatersrand gold mines. *Journal of the National Institute for Personnel Research, 5*(2), 100–109.

Morgaut, M.-E. (1960). Un dialogue nouveau: L'Afrique et l'industrie [A new dialogue: Africa and industry]. *Bulletin du Centre d'Etudes des Problèmes Sociaux Indigènes,* (No. 1), 131–149.

Munroe, R. L., & Munroe, R. H. (1971). Effect of environmental experience on spatial ability in an East African society. *Journal of Social Psychology, 83,* 15–22.

Murray, C. O. (1956). *The structure of African intelligence: A factorial study of the abilities of Africans.* Unpublished master's thesis. University of Natal, Durban.

Murray, M. M. (1961). *The development of spatial concepts in African and European children.* Unpublished master's thesis, University of Natal, Pietermaritzburg.

Naude, W. T. van S. (1962). *The African mine labourer: A study of six tribes employed in the mining industry.* Unpublished doctoral dissertation, University of Stellenbosch.

Nelson, G. K. (1959). The electroencephalogram in kwashiorkor. *Electroencephalography and Clinical Neurophysiology, 11,* 73–84.

Nelson, G. K., & Dean, R. F. A. (1959). The electroencephalogram in African children: Effects of kwashiorkor and a note on the newborn. *Bulletin of the World Health Organization, 21,* 779–782.

Nerlove, S. B., et al. (1971). Effect of environmental experience on spatial ability: A replication. *Journal of Social Psychology, 84,* 3–10.

Nsereko-Gyagenda, T. (1973). *Intellectual abilities of Ugandan adolescents.* Kampala: National Institute of Education and Faculty of Education, Makerere University.

Okonji, M. O. (1969). The differential effects of rural and urban upbringing on the development of cognitive styles. *International Journal of Psychology, 4,* 293–305.

Okonji, M. O. (1971). Culture and children's understanding of geometry. *International Journal of Psychology, 6,* 121–128.

Okonji, M. O. (1980). Cognitive styles across cultures. In N. Warren (Ed.), *Studies in cross-cultural psychology* (Vol. 2, pp. 1–50). Academic Press.

Oliver, R. A. C. (1932a). *General intelligence tests for Africans (with manual of directions).* Nairobi: Government Printer.

Oliver, R. A. C. (1932b). The musical talent of natives in East Africa. *British Journal of Psychology, 2,* 333–343.

Omari, I. M. (1975). Developmental order of spatial concepts among schoolchildren in Tanzania. *Journal of Cross-Cultural Psychology, 6,* 444–456.

Omari, I. M., & MacGinitie, W. H. (1974). Some pictorial artifacts in studies of African children's pictorial depth perception. *Child Development, 45,* 535–539.

Ombredane, A. (1954). L'exploration de la mentalité des noirs congolais au moyen d'une épreuve projective, le Congo T.A.T. [Exploration of the mentality of Congolese blacks using a projective test, the Congo T.A.T.]. *Mémoires de l'Institut Royale Belge, 37*(5).

Ombredane, A. (1957). Etude du problème psychologique posé par les noirs congolais. [Study of the psychological problem posed by Congolese blacks]. *Revue de l'Université de Bruxelles, 9,* 183–197.

Ombredane, A., Bertelson, P., & Beniest-Noirot, E. (1958). Speed and accuracy of performance of an African native population and of Belgian children on a paper-and-pencil perceptual task. *Journal of Social Psychology, 47,* 327–337.

Ombredane, A., & Robaye, F. (1953). Le problème de l'épuration des résultats des tests d'intelligence étudié sur le Matrix-Couleur: Comparaison des techniques de reduplication et d'explication [The problem of treating intelligence test results on the Coloured Matrices: Comparison of the effects of repeated testing and explanation]. *Bulletin du Centre d'Etudes et Recherches Psychotechniques, 32,* 3–17.

Ombredane, A., Robaye, F., & Plumail, H. (1956). Résultats d'une application répétée du Matrix-Couleur à une population de noirs congolais [Results of the repeated administration of the Coloured Matrices to a group of Congolese blacks]. *Bulletin du Centre d'Etudes de Recherches Psychotechniques, 5,* 129–147.

Ombredane, A., Robaye, F., & Robaye, E. (1957). Analyse des résultats d'une application expérimentale du Matrix 38 à 485 noirs Baluba [Analysis of the results of an experimental administration of Matrices 38 to 485 Baluba blacks]. *Bulletin du Centre d'Etudes de Recherches Psychotechniques, 6,* 235–255.

Orbell, S. F. W. (1975). *An investigation into the capacity for abstract thinking among Shona pupils.* Unpublished doctoral dissertation, University of London.

Ord, I. G. (1970). *Mental tests for pre-literates.* London: Ginn.

Ord, I. G. (1972). Testing for educational and occupational selection in developing countries – a review. *Occupational Psychology, 46,* 123–166.

Otaala, B. (1970). The performance of Ugandan African children on some Piaget conservation tasks. *Uganda Journal, 30,* 171–179.

Otaala, B. (1971). *The development of operational thinking in primary schoolchildren: An examination of some aspects of Piaget's theory among the Iteso children of Uganda.* Unpublished doctoral dissertation, Columbia University, New York.

Owoc, P. J. (1973). On culture and conservation once again. *International Journal of Psychology, 8,* 249–254.

Page, H. W. (1965). *The African's concept of geometrical space: A rural-urban comparison.* Unpublished master's thesis. University of Natal, Durban.

Page, H. W. (1973). Concepts of length and distance in a study of Zulu youths. *Journal of Social Psychology, 90,* 9–16.

Parker, J. F. (1977). Free recall of abstract and concrete words by American and Ghanaian college students. *International Journal of Psychology, 12*, 243–252.

Pinard, A., Morin, C., & Lefebvre, M. (1973). Apprentissage de la conservation des quantités liquides chez les enfants rwandais et canadiens-français [Training on the conservation of liquid quantities among Rwandese and French-Canadian children]. *International Journal of Psychology, 8*, 15–23.

Pons, A. L. (1974). *Administration of tests outside the cultures of their origin.* Paper presented at the 26th Annual Congress of the South African Psychological Association, Johannesburg.

Poole, H. E. (1968). The effect of urbanization upon scientific concept attainment among Hausa children in Northern Nigeria. *British Journal of Educational Psychology, 38*, 57–63.

Poole, H. E. (1969). Restructuring the perceptual world of African children. *Teacher Education in New Countries, 10*(2), 165–172.

Poortinga, Y. H. (1971). Cross-cultural comparison of maximum performance tests: Some aspects and some experiments with simple auditory and visual stimuli. *Psychologia Africana* (Monograph Supplement No. 6).

Price-Williams, D. R. (1961). A study concerning concepts of conservation of quantities among primitive children. *Acta Psychologica, 18*, 297–305.

Raven, J. C. (1938). *Progressive Matrices.* London: H. K. Lewis.

Rich, S. G. (1917–1918). Binet–Simon tests on Zulus. *South African Journal of Science, 14*, 477–482.

Schepers, J. M. (1974). Critical issues which have to be resolved in the construction of tests for developing groups. *Humanitas – RSA, 2*, 395–406.

Schmidt, W. H. O., & Nzimande, A. (1970). Cultural differences in color/form preference and in classificatory behavior. *Human Development, 13*, 140–148.

Schwarz, P. A. (1961). *Aptitude tests for use in the developing nations.* Pittsburgh: American Institute for Research.

Schwarz, P. A. (1963). Adapting tests to the cultural setting. *Educational and Psychological Measurement, 23*, 673–686.

Segall, M. H., Campbell, D. T., & Herskovits, M. J. (1966). *The influence of culture on visual perception: An advanced study in psychology and anthropology.* Indianapolis, IN: Bobbs-Merrill.

Serpell, R. (1971). Discrimination of orientation of Zambian children. *Journal of Comparative and Physiological Psychology, 75*, 312–316.

Serpell, R. (1974). Aspects of intelligence in a developing country. *African Social Research* (No. 17), 576–596.

Setidisho, N. O. H. (1965). *An empirical study of mathematical ability in school children.* Unpublished doctoral dissertation, University of South Africa, Pretoria.

Shapiro, M. B. (1960). The rotation of drawings by illiterate Africans. *Journal of Abnormal and Social Psychology, 52*, 17–30.

Sichel, H. S. (1951). A validation of the boss boy selection procedure. *Bulletin of the National Institute for Personnel Research, 3*(2), 20–29.

Silvey, J. (1963a). Aptitude testing and education selection in Africa. *Rhodes-Livingstone Journal* (No. 34), 9–22.

Silvey, J. (1963b). Testing ability tests: Issues in the measurement of ability among African schoolboys. In East African Institute of Social Research, *Conference papers, January 1963, Section B.* Kampala: Institute of Social Research, University of East Africa.

Silvey, J. (1972). Long-range prediction of educability and its determinants in East Africa. In L. J. Cronbach & P. J. D. Drenth (Eds.), *Mental tests and cultural adaptation* (pp. 371–378). The Hague: Mouton.

Spagnoletti, M. P. (1974). *Development and initial validation of a selection test batttery for sewing machinists: Interim report* (Confidential Report C/PERS 226). Johannesburg: National Institute for Personnel Research.

Stewart, V. M. (1973). Tests of the "carpentered world" hypothesis by race and environment in America and Zambia. *International Journal of Psychology, 8*, 83–94.

Super, C. M. (1972). *Cognitive changes in Zambian children during later pre-school years* (H.D.R.U. Report No. 22). Lusaka: Human Development Research Unit, University of Zambia.

Super, C. M. (1976). Environmental effects on motor development: The case of African infant precocity. *Developmental Medicine and Child Neurology, 18,* 561–567.

Swanepoel, H. F. (1971). *'n Geldigheidondersoek na die Skolastiese Aanlegtoets vir standerd 1- en standerd 2-Bantoeleerlinge met spesiale verwysing na die Noord-Sotho taalgroep* [An investigation into the validity of the Scholastic Aptitude Test for standard 1 and standard 2 Bantu pupils with special reference to the North Sotho language group]. Unpublished master's thesis, Potchefstroom University for Christian Higher Education.

Swanepoel, H. F. (1975). *'n Psigometriese ondersoek na die geldigheid en gebruik van die Voorligtingstoets vir Junior Sekondêre Bantoeleerlinge in vorm 111* [A psychometric investigation of the validity and use of the Guidance Test for Junior Secondary Bantu Pupils in Form III]. Unpublished doctoral dissertation, Potchefstroom University for Higher Christian Education.

Taylor, J. M. (1985). *The prediction of academic success of black engineering technicians* (PERS 386). Johannesburg: National Institute for Personnel Research.

Taylor, T. R. (1977). The measurement of concept identification differences among literate blacks. *Psychologia Africana, 17,* 31–47.

Thiele, G. A. (1964). *Die opstel en voorlopige standaardisering van 'n battery skolastiese aanlegtoetse met die oog op die voorspelling van sukses in die Bantoe junior sekondêre skool* [The construction and preliminary standardisation of a battery of scholastic aptitude tests with a view to predicting achievement in Bantu junior secondary school]. Unpublished master's thesis, University of South Africa, Pretoria.

Vandenberg, S. G., & Hakstian, A. R. (1978). Cultural influences on cognition: A reanalysis of Vernon's data. *International Journal of Psychology, 13,* 251–279.

Van de Vijver, F. J. R., & Poortinga, Y. H. (1982). Cross-cultural generalization and universality. *Journal of Cross-Cultural Psychology, 13,* 387–408.

Van Leeuwen, M. S. (1978). A cross-cultural examination of psychological differentiation in males and females. *International Journal of Psychology, 13,* 87–122.

Van Staden, J. D. (1976). Keuring van begaafde standerd 5-Bantoeleerlinde vir versnelde bevordering [Selection of gifted standard 5 Bantu pupils for rapid promotion]. *Humanitas – RSA, 3,* 427–436.

Verhaegen, P. (1956). Utilité actuelle des tests pour l'étude psychologique des autochtones congolais [Practical usefulness of tests in the psychological study of Congolese natives]. *Revue de Psychologie Appliquée, 6,* 139–151.

Vernon, P. E. (1950). *The structure of human abilities.* London: Methuen.

Vernon, P. E. (1976). Abilities and educational attainment in an East African environment. *Journal of Special Education, 1,* 335–345.

Verster, J. M. (1983). The structure, organization, and correlates of cognitive speed and accuracy: A cross-cultural study using computerized tests. In S. H. Irvine & J. W. Berry (Eds.), *Human assessment and cultural factors.* New York: Plenum.

Verster, J. M., & Muller, M. W. (1975). *Further investigation of the effects of multiple exposure to the Classification Test Battery: Hypothesis and proposed research design* (Confidential Report C/PERS 231). Johannesburg: National Institute for Personnel Research.

Verster, J. M., Muller, M. W., & Kendall, I. M. (1976). *Further investigation of the effects of multiple exposure to the Classification Test Battery: The minor study* (Contract Report C/PERS 244). Johannesburg: National Institute for Personnel Research.

Verster, J. M., Muller, M. W., & Kendall, I. M. (1977). *Further investigation of the effects of multiple exposure to the Classification Test Battery: The major study* (Unpublished report). Johannesburg: National Institute for Personnel Research.

Verster, M. A. (1974). *The effects of mining experience and multiple test exposure on performance on the Classification Test Battery* (Confidential Report C/PERS 220). Johannesburg: National Institute for Personnel Research.

Verster, M. A. (1977). *Installation of testing procedures for the classification of workers in the forestry industry* (Confidential Report PERS 260). Johannesburg: National Institute for Personnel Research.

Verster, M. A. (1978). The effects of industrial work experience and repeated test exposure on the test performance of black industrial workers. *Psychologia Africana, 17,* 201–227.

Visser, B. L. (1978). *Development of a testing programme for black university students for purposes of selection and careers counselling* (PERS 281). Johannesburg: National Institute for Personnel Research.

Visser, S. (1981). *An evaluation of the effectiveness of various NIPR tests in predicting success in Engineering Analysis and Design: Interim report* (Confidential Report C/PERS 317). Johannesburg: National Institute for Personnel Research.

Von Mollendorf, J. W. (1974). *Die invloed van herhaalde toetsing op die faktorstruktuur van 'n battery vermoëtoetse toegepas op Bantoeskoliere* [The influence of repeated testing on the factor structure of a battery of ability tests applied to Bantu scholars]. Unpublished doctoral dissertation, University of South Africa, Pretoria.

Von Mollendorf, J. W. (1978). *Sielkundige meting en aspekte van skolastiese prestasie in die daarstelling van 'n voorligtingsprosedure vir swart skoliere in Vorm V* [Psychological measurement and aspects of scholastic performance in the establishment of a counselling procedure for black scholars in Form V]. Unpublished doctoral dissertation, Potchefstroom University for Higher Christian Education.

Vouilloux, D. (1959). Etude de la psychomotricité d'enfants africains au Cameroun. Test de Gesell et réflexes archaïques [Study of the psychomotor abilities of African children in the Cameroons. Gesell tests and hereditary reflexes]. *Journal de la Société des Africanistes, 29,* 11–18.

Warburton, F. W. (1951). The ability of the Gurkha recruit. *British Journal of Psychology, 42,* 123–133.

Warren, N. (1972). African infant precocity. *Psychological Bulletin, 78,* 353–367.

Weisner, T. S. (1976). Urban-rural differences in African children's performance on cognitive and memory tasks. *Ethos, 4,* 223–250.

Werbeloff, M., & Taylor, T. R. (1982). *Development and validation of the High Level Figure Classification Test* (PERS 338). Johannesburg: National Institute for Personnel Research.

Wickert, F. R. (1967). *Readings in African psychology from French language sources.* East Lansing: African Studies Center, Michigan State University.

Willis, S. L., Baltes, P. B., & Cornelius, S. W. (1981). Development and modifiability of adult intellectual performance: An examination of cognitive intervention in late adulthood. In M. P. Friedman, J. P. Das, & N. O'Connor (Eds.), *Intelligence and learning* (pp. 169–178). New York: Plenum.

Wober, M. (1967). Adapting Witkin's field independence theory to accommodate new information from Africa. *British Journal of Psychology, 58,* 29–38.

Wober, M. (1969). Distinguishing centri-cultural from cross-cultural tests and research. *Perceptual and Motor Skills, 28,* 488.

Wober, M. (1970). Confrontation of the H-V illusion and a test of 3-dimensional pictorial perception in Nigeria. *Perceptual and Motor Skills, 31,* 105–106.

Wober, M. (1972). Horizons, horizontals, and illusions about the vertical. *Perceptual and Motor Skills, 34,* 960.

Wober, M. (1975). *Psychology in Africa.* London: International African Institute.

Xydias, N. (1956). Aptitudes and training of Africans. In International African Institute, *Social implications of industrialization and urbanization in Africa South of the Sahara* (pp. 319–352). Paris: UNESCO.

Xydias, N., Cottin, H. J., & Lambert, G. (1963). Etude comparative des populations sahariennes: Tests et influence des facteurs sociologiques sur les performances [Comparative study of Saharan populations: The influence of sociological factors on test performance]. *Travail Humain, 26,* 57–89.

13   Individual differences among the peoples of China

J. W. C. Chan and Philip E. Vernon

Introduction

The term *intelligence*, as used in the vast majority of psychological publications, obviously refers to the higher mental processes of those reared in the western world (including Western Europe and North America). But the corresponding terms for cognitive abilities in Asian, African, or other less developed countries might very well differ considerably in content, and in the kind of behaviour regarded as "intelligent." It should be feasible for Chinese or Japanese or Indian psychologists to explore and isolate the major features of intellectual growth in their own peoples, and then devise intelligence tests to sample these features. Such tests might differ considerably from those used in the western world, not only in language and content but also in method of approach. For example, it might be found that multiple-choice items, or time-limited tests, were inappropriate in other cultures, although no attempt has yet been made to discover if this is so. Hence, this chapter will discuss the abilities of Chinese as measured by western-type tests, either of intelligence or other abilities, for example, Thurstone's factors.

One would expect differences in intellectual development between Asians and Caucasians because of their different cultures, child-rearing practices, and educational systems. But in China, additional factors hamper technological and educational progress: for example, the sheer size of the country with its population of 1 billion, four-fifths of whom are classified as rural dwellers. The average standard of living is very low, malnutrition is rife because of dependence on rice as the staple diet; overcrowded conditions of living in the cities are horrendous. Also, the use of a variety of dialects in different parts of the country must hinder communication and education. The effects of warfare, political instability, and totalitarianism, especially over the past 50 years, are incalculable. Thus, if it were possible to give any mental tests (suitably translated) to samples of Chinese adults or children, it is highly probable that the score distributions would fall much below those of western populations. In contrast, the Japanese have become so acculturated to western norms and technology that it is reasonable to apply western tests among them, with only minor adaptations.

340

The above reasons for objecting to the use of American or British tests in China have much less weight among Asians who have emigrated to more developed countries, where their children attend English-type schools, for example, those in the United States or Canada, Hong Kong or Singapore, or even in Taiwan, because this island is relatively advanced technologically. Although the Koreans are racially and culturally different, they, too, are in a transitional state, and those who have emigrated to America, Hawaii, or Canada show the same high level of ability and achievement as do Chinese- or Japanese-Americans. In all such regions there is considerable exposure to western products and customs; also the schools commonly teach the English language, although the everyday medium of communication is still one or other of the Chinese dialects. In Hong Kong, the most prestigious secondary schools actually teach in English, and all instruction in the University of Hong Kong is in English.

One could reasonably argue, then, that the test performances of Chinese immigrants and their children afford a better estimate of their mental powers than would any test given now to representative samples of the population of mainland China. Hence, this chapter discusses more psychological studies of Chinese abroad than of Chinese in their home country.

Another major obstacle to comparative studies of Chinese and other cultures or national groups is the great difficulty in securing representative samples in countries where schooling does not reach all members of the population. Indeed, even in North America in the early 1900s, compulsory education did not extend to all Oriental children. Probably most of the children who did attend school came from families where the parents were already somewhat acculturated and were anxious themselves to learn English. The same is true of Hong Kong today, where many of the children of illegal immigrants, and other disadvantaged groups, are probably not registered. When non-attenders are not tested, the average scores of those who do attend are naturally higher than the average should be for the total population.

In view of these difficulties of measurement and interpretation across cultures, the greatest caution must be observed in making any cross-cultural comparisons. A test adapted from abroad may give quite valid and useful indications of individual (or subgroup) differences within a particular culture, although they may be unsuitable for measuring similarities or differences between cultural groups.

The development of psychology in China

It is interesting that the earliest use of written tests or examinations in the world occurred in China, where from 206 B.C. to A.D. 1905 government officials and administrators were selected by such instruments. The aim was to eliminate wealth, social class, or political influence in the choice of rulers. However, these examinations were based almost entirely on knowledge of the Confucian classics, and by the beginning of the 20th century it was realised that bookish men, with good rote memory, were not necessarily best suited to deal with practical administrative problems.

According to C. C. Ching (1980), the first university courses in psychology (as distinct from philosophy) were given in Beijing (Peking) as early as 1917. The *Chinese Psychological Journal* was first published in 1922; but its appearances were irregular, and the major, internationally known journal *Acta Psychologica Sinica* started in 1956. The Chinese Psychological Society was founded in 1937 and grew to some 1,000 qualified members by 1965. However, in the 1930s psychological teaching was disrupted by Japanese aggressive attacks, and universities were closed in 1939. In those early days most of the leading Chinese psychologists studied in the United States, the best known being Z. Y. Kuo, a radical behaviourist. After World War II and civil war in China, psychology departments were reorganised, and flourished under Mao's regime until 1966. Now, however, they followed the Marxist interpretation of psychology and used textbooks by Pavlov and other Russian writers. Western psychology was strongly criticised, particularly any work on intelligence and its measurement. Publications were mainly in the areas of physiological, experimental, and educational psychology. But with the "Cultural Revolution" of 1966, all psychological work was banned by the Gang of Four, until their deposition in 1976. Their main target was the concept of universal laws of the mind. For example, the existence of Colour versus Form types was pilloried because it ignored the influence of "class" on mental development. Many leading psychologists did not survive this period, and both institutional and private libraries were largely destroyed. But since 1976 there has been a slow revival, much hampered by lack of funds and of books, and by less virulent but still influential ideological restrictions.

Several accounts of Chinese psychology during the Mao period and from 1976 on have been published by Hsiao (1977), Hsu (1978), Hsu, Ching, and Over (1980), Ching (1980), Gardner (1980), and – the most thorough – by L. B. Brown (1981), an Australian psychologist who spent much of 1978–1980 as a university teacher in China. Hsu describes the setting up of the Institute of Psychology in Beijing in 1956, under the Chinese National Academy. This was (and is now again) a specialist research centre with a staff of 80 to 90 researchers. Other important departments were set up at most universities, for example, in Shanghai and Hangchow. The main areas of interest at that time, according to Brown, were:

1. Perception, constancies, illusions, information theory.
2. Child psychology, age-related functions, concept development, verbal processes.
3. Reading, programmed instruction, and other educational topics.
4. Labour and engineering, pilot skills, lighting standards, design of control rooms.
5. Medical, psychotherapy for psychotics, use of hypnosis and breathing exercises, acupuncture.

6. Neurological, EEG in the orienting reflex, thinking and perception, and disturbances in schizophrenia.

Brown shows that in 1978, psychologists were much aware of gaps in their knowledge, and eager to learn. But they ascribed most of their difficulties to the Gang of Four. They still attend political discussion groups weekly, and are still more concerned with discussing what theories are "correct" than with carrying out and publishing complete researches. When they do publish, they habitually apologise for shortcomings, and invite criticisms which will help them to improve their work. For several years there were "forbidden areas," regarded as reactionary or bourgeois: for example, psychoanalysis, mental testing, socialisation of children, ideals and values, delinquency, and the like. Indeed, almost any brand of social psychology or sociology was considered as the purview of ideological discussion rather than scientific research. Also, in contrast to the American emphasis on individuality, self-realisation, and competitiveness, everything is considered in the context of social interrelatedness, and the subservience of the individual to the collective good.

Nowadays there is a gradual loosening of restrictions, and psychologists claim that no areas are forbidden. With the increase in teaching of English in schools, more foreign books are getting past the censor. Some testing is allowed, and, as well as the *Binet*, *Wechsler Scales* and *MMPI* have been adapted for Chinese use. The study of mental retardates and other exceptional children has always been encouraged, so long as it did not imply genetically determined levels of ability. Children highly gifted in science are being picked out with the help of tests, which are also used in the selection of aircraft pilots. In 1978, Chu-Chin Fan actually published an article on *The Advantages of Streaming* (translated in Brown's book). The author admitted that some 80% of children have difficulties in covering the secondary education curriculum, and advocated putting the more able in classes where they could learn at their own rate, so long as they were also given sound political training. However, this view is not generally accepted.

To conclude: There are very little empirical data and few publications relating to individual differences in intelligence and other abilities, attitudes, interests, motivation, personality, or achievement, which could be compared with psychological research abroad. Yet at the same time we should recognise that remarkable advances in many directions have been made over the past quarter of a century: the eradication of many diseases; the raised standards of living of the masses, the introduction of a common language, Pinyin, throughout China; the promotion of adult and child literacy; the reduction in crime; the use of discussion groups to work out social and personal problems; the incredible discipline to achieve one-child families; day-care; and the stimulation of the creative flair in young children while also socialising them. It is to be hoped that with the more open-door policy, Chinese psychologists will be able to play a larger part in such developments, without becoming dominated by either Marxist or western concepts and methods.

Taiwan

Originally part of China, the island of Formosa, or Taiwan, was occupied from 1895 to 1945 by the Japanese, who did much to modernise the economy. With the defeat of the Kuomintang in 1949, Chiang Kai-shek with his army, and many refugees, moved to Taiwan and took over the government. With American financial support the so-called Nationalist Chinese brought about spectacular technological growth. Large numbers of students were trained in the United States. However, some 80% of the population are of indigenous Taiwanese descent; they maintain much of their traditional culture, including the extended family system (Tseng & Hsu, 1969), whereas the Nationalists are more Americanised. There are two universities in Taipei with psychology departments. The research activities of psychologists seem to be concentrated on social attitutes, stereotypes, family patterns, and educational aspirations, as well as on student mental health problems and clinical studies. However, since 1982 a considerable expansion has been noticeable in the number, and range, of research studies.

Much of the published research has been carried out in Taiwan by psychologists from America, and by some from Australia. Rodd's (1959) investigation is of interest because it compares Nationalist and indigenous samples. Some 1,300 grade 11 students were given the *Cattell Culture-Fair Tests*, achievement tests in mathematics and science, and the *Allport-Vernon-Lindzey Study of Values*. Only minor differences were found between the two groups, and both scored a little higher than American norms in nonverbal intelligence and achievement. But obviously it is likely that the Taiwan students who had reached grade 11 would be quite highly selected. The value patterns were also very similar to those of American students.

As described in Iwawaki and Vernon's Chapter 14, Stigler, Lee, Lucker, and Stevenson (1982) found Taiwanese children in grades 1 and 5 to be significantly more advanced than U.S. children in arithmetic, and they were more nearly comparable to the Japanese. Stevenson et al. (1982), using reading tests which had been constructed to be of equivalent difficulty in Japan, Taiwan, and the United States, obtained very similar score distributions at grade 5 in all three countries. Apparently, then, the educational standards of Taiwanese and Nationalist children are much the same as those in such technologically developed countries as America and Japan.

Other studies by foreign visitors include Chiu's (1972) work on cognitive styles of Chinese and American children, and Chen's (1981) investigation of the eye-movement patterns of college students when looking at complex visual arrays of letters, numbers, or shapes.

Hong Kong

Hong Kong is a British crown colony, seized from China as a treaty port in 1841; it was largely administered by British civil servants until the Japanese occupation in 1941. After World War II, more Chinese were brought into government, and the future status of the colony has now been settled. In 1997 the sovereignty of Hong Kong will revert to China and Hong Kong will become a Special Administrative Region of China. About 99% of the population are Chinese, and Cantonese is the major spoken dialect, although English is used in government and in most business enterprises. The culture of Hong Kong is essentially traditional Chinese but is interwoven to various degrees with western ideas and practices.

The economy is based almost entirely on commerce and export, and is highly prosperous, thus attracting floods of immigrants from mainland China. Despite the steps taken to prevent illegal immigation, the population has risen to some 5 million; and this is accompanied by serious problems of overcrowding, public health, and the provision of housing and education. Nevertheless, 9 years of free and compulsory education (6 years of primary and 3 of the 5 years of secondary education) are provided for all legal residents, and the secondary schools can be government, aided, or private Chinese middle schools and Anglo-Chinese schools. The latter use English as the medium of instruction and are much sought after because they are regarded as the main avenue to business, administrative, and academic careers. There are two universities: the English-medium University of Hong Kong, and the Chinese University of Hong Kong.

At the University of Hong Kong, Dawson (1970) was largely concerned with what he calls bio-social research, that is, the adaptation of cultures to the biological demands of their environments, and the consequent development of social norms which influence the acquisition of skills, perceptual processes, and values. Thus Dawson, Young, and Choi (1973, 1974) have compared the cognitive styles, and susceptibility to visual illusions, of Chinese and other groups. The Chinese scored higher on field-independence tests than West African samples, although not so highly as the Inuit; and they were superior to whites in three-dimensional perception, and relatively less affected by the Muller-Lyer and other illusions. It was also found that students whose social attitudes were more modern than traditional tended to be more field independent. Further, Chinese students who were right dominant (right-handed and and right-eyed) were more field independent on the *Rod and Frame Test* than those of mixed dominance (right-handed and left-eyed) (Dawson & Wong, 1983). A variety of other topics have been investigated, ranging from the effects of sex hormones on spatial learning in rats, to problems of language usage, and attitudinal conflict among bilingual Hong Kong students.

Studies of educational psychology were initiated in the early 1960s by N. K. Henderson. Godman (1964) surveyed the abilities and attainments of primary 4 children with the *Raven's Progressive Matrices*, *Cattell's Culture-Fair Test*, and tests of English, Chinese, and arithmetic. Rowe (1966) compared the backgrounds of primary 3 children who were backward in school achievements with others who obtained high achievement scores. The backward children tended to come from poorer homes, where the parents were more traditional or were neglectful and lax in discipline. The children did less reading or working at jobs outside school hours; and they spent more time watching television. However there were no differences in the use of English language at home, nor in length of residence in Hong Kong.

Several investigations have compared the development of Hong Kong children on Piaget's stages with those found in American or other cultures. Goodnow (1962) gave tests of conservation and combinatorial reasoning to schoolchildren, and others who had not attended any school ("boat" children). Both groups were similar to Americans of the same age in conservation, but the unschooled were lower in reasoning, as also on the *Raven's Progressive Matrices* test. Jahoda, Deregowski, and Sinha (1974) studied the transition from what Piaget calls topological to Euclidean space perception in 4–12-year-old children. There was no clear trend as described by Piaget, but the Hong Kong school children, and also Scottish children in Scotland, obtained higher Euclidean scores than unschooled boat children, together with Indian and Zambian samples. Douglas and Wong (1977) gave some of Piaget's formal operations problems to secondary school samples of 13 and 15 years, and found that the Hong Kong students scored a little lower than Americans.

A large amount of research into abilities and achievements in Hong Kong schools has been carried out by J. Chan. He constructed a high-level intelligence test for sixth-form secondary students, including verbal, numerical, and nonverbal subtests. The *Raven's Progressive Matrices* (1938) was also given (Chan, 1974). The students seemed to have no difficulty in following instructions and answering items in English, and 95% scored 50 or over on the *Matrices*. However, the correlations of all four tests with scholastic grades were low, as is frequently found at this level in the United Kingdom.

In 1976, the *Raven's Progressive Matrices* test was given to 209 Chinese students attending Anglo-Chinese schools, and 213 European students attending private schools, both groups having a mean age of 15. The average scores were 53.3 and 50.2, respectively – a highly significant difference. The Chinese were particularly successful in the most difficult Section E of the test. This difference occurred in both sexes. Chan suggests that the eye movements involved in reading the Chinese language, and its use of complex ideographs, give the Chinese some advantage in the *Matrices* items. However, it is likely that Chinese students who gain entry to Anglo-Chinese schools are highly selected, and strongly motivated towards educational achievement, whereas non-Chinese, although of high socioeconomic status, are sometimes more mediocre in abilities.

The same test was used in primary Grades 4 to 6, with more than 1,000 children in each grade (Chan, 1982); mean ages were $9\frac{1}{2}$, $10\frac{1}{2}$, and $11\frac{1}{2}$. The percentile levels for all groups combined are shown in Table 13.1, along with the original J. C. Raven norms for British children, and the more up-to-date norms provided by J. Raven in 1979. The mean difference of 4 to 5 points

Table 13.1. *Raven's Progressive Matrices percentiles for primary 4 to 6 Hong Kong children, and British norms*

	Percentile						
	95	90	75	50	25	10	5
Hong Kong	52	51	48	43	38	29	23
J. C. Raven (1938)	47	45	39	33	23	15	—
J. Raven (1979)	50	47	43	39	32	26	20

between Chinese and present-day British children corresponds to an IQ of nearly 110 among the Chinese. This is a striking result, because it seems probable that both Raven's and Chan's samples were representative of their populations. A small sex difference was also noted, Chinese boys scoring 1 point on average higher than girls.

Similar results were obtained with more than 5,000 Hong Kong students aged 16 taking Heim's *AH4 Intelligence Test*. This contains a verbal and a nonverbal part. Compared with the scores of Canadian Grade 11 students, the Chinese were considerably lower on the verbal part but were higher on the nonverbal. Both groups would, of course, be quite highly selected. In another study (Chan, 1976a), parallel tests for language and number, at primary grade 6 level, were given either in English or in Chinese. The mean scores were: Language (English), 68.67; Language (Chinese), 85.85; Number (English), 87.48; Number (Chinese), 89.46. Naturally, children who speak Chinese at home, but who also study English at school, are more successful in their native language. But there is very little difference in the number tests, apart from a few items which involved a lot of reading.

An extensive investigation of parental attitudes and child-rearing was carried out among form 4 (i.e., grade 10) students, who answered *Ginsburg's Parent Image Differential Test* (Chan, 1981). It was found that favourable parent–child interactions, which avoided parental autocracy, restrictiveness, and demandingness, were correlated with good reading, science, and overall achievement. In Hong Kong, many fathers are apt to be unduly autocratic and restrictive toward their children, although this is less true of girls, who are trained to be submissive at home but are under less pressure to do well at school, than boys. The mothers naturally have a considerable influence in the socialisation, discipline, and education in the home. Students who described their mothers as not too restrictive also showed better achievements at school.

Parkay and Chan (1983) investigated children's perceptions of their classrooms in Hong Kong and in the United States (Texas). The Americans were generally satisfied with their reading and language classes as they are, although desirous of more opportunities for self-expression. The Hong Kong students were less satisfied, partly because of the strong emphasis by their parents on academic achievement. Thus they regarded school as a place for obtaining academic knowledge and skills which are highly valued in their culture; and they desired more cooperative, group-oriented instruction. Another cross-cultural enquiry by Chan and Worley (1984) elicited students' expectations of the benefits of reading and language classes. They found that the Hong Kong students stressed immediate goals such as "to improve comprehension," "to become more informed." But Americans stressed more long-term goals, including economic benefits, for example, "to communicate better," "to understand people, places and events around us," "to enrich life," "to get ready for higher education," "to get a good job."

Ripple, Jacquish, Lee, and Chan (1982) collected data on the development of divergent thinking in the United States, South Africa, and Hong Kong among children ranging from 9 to 12 years upward, and young, middle-aged, and elderly adults. They used Cunnington and Torrance's (1965) *Sound and Images Test*, in which the subjects hear a variety of auditory stimuli, for example, a thunderstorm, an electronically synthesised cymbal roll, and so forth. They write down their interpretations of each of these, or their associations, and are scored, in the usual way, for Fluency, Flexibility, and Originality.

Both Caucasian groups showed similar growth and decline curves, that is, rises from 9 to 25 years, a gradual drop till 60, and a greater drop after 60. But the Hong Kong scores increased only from 9 to 17, and then started to decline slowly. The U.S. and African means were much the same for Fluency and Flexibility, but the Africans were lower in Originality. The Hong Kong scores were lower at all ages, particularly on Originality. These results strongly suggest that American and South African cultures favour the rapid production, and variety, of imaginative ideas. But the Chinese emphasise the avoidance of mistakes, and they try to give the "correct" responses after careful deliberation.

Finally, Götz and Eysenck have published a new *Visual Aesthetic Sensitivity Test (VAST)*, asking for preferences among nonrepresentative or abstract shapes. These are scored by comparison with the judgments of artists as to which shapes are aesthetically superior. Chan, Eysenck, and Götz (1980) tabulated mean scores among English, Japanese, and Hong Kong children and adults of both sexes. English scores ranged around 30 to 36 (out of 42); Japanese averaged 33. Hong Kong groups ranged from 25 to 30. But the Hong Kong children were mostly younger than those in England and Japan. It is quite possible that western and eastern views of artistic merit differ; but the rank orders of item difficulty in the different samples showed considerable consistency, with correlations mostly between .87 and .70.

Singapore

Like Hong Kong, Singapore has a long history of British rule and commerce; but it became an independent republic in 1965. The make-up of the population is different. Originally, Singapore was part of Malaysia, but currently only 15% of the population are Malaysian. Chinese, with 76%, are the great majority, and there are 7% of Indians and 2% of other nationalities. Yet Singapore residents think of themselves not as members of a particular race but rather as a multicultural community. The great majority of all groups are bilingual, speaking English as well as their mother tongue. Singapore has an excellent educational system, and higher living standards than any other Asian country except Japan.

Very little psychological or educational research has been published, but Phua (1976) gave a varied battery of tests to 147 Chinese and 190 Malaysian boys, aged 14 years, with comparable social class, and exposure to English-type education. Several of the familiar Thurstone factors were found in both groups. But the mean scores often differed; thus on the *Raven's Progressive Matrices* the means were 47.8 and 41.9, which are equivalent to IQs of 101 and 90. The difference is similar to that which separates blacks from whites in the United States. Phua believes it is attributable to the much higher motivation for school learning among the Chinese.

Chinese immigrants and their descendants in the United States and Canada

There was very little contact between Chinese and Caucasian peoples until the late 19th century, although the first English-speaking traders arrived in 1784, and missionaries began to work in China from 1824 on. However, in the 1840s many natural disasters in China led to widespread starvation. At the same time, gold prospectors in California and British Columbia required large numbers of unskilled labourers, as did road and railway builders and the Hawaiian sugarcane planters. The imperial government was pressured into allowing recruitment of gangs of coolies, mainly from the southern province of Kwangtung, and including the Hakka tribe. Most of these men hoped to make their fortunes in North America in a few years, and then return and settle down with their families. Despite the extremely low wages, many of them did send home substantial sums; but more stayed on and were joined by further immigrants, until the Exclusion Act of 1882 prohibited more entries except for certain limited categories. By 1890, 124,000 had reached the United States or Hawaii. However, there were few wives or children, hence the total numbers did not rise again until after World War II, when discriminatory racial laws were abolished. By 1981 the totals reached some 800,000. Although the total numbers of Orientals never exceeded 1% of the North American population, they were mostly concentrated in West Coast cities such as San Francisco and Vancouver, and thus became highly visible minorities.

The white majority showed extreme prejudice and intolerance against the Oriental immigrants, who were hated and feared because they differed in so many ways from whites. They could seldom speak English, and they undercut whites by working for lower wages. A criticism which had somewhat more justification was that many Chinese were involved in secret societies, or tongs, which were responsible for drug and criminal offences. Egged on by the politicians and the press, the white majority made every effort to bar further Oriental immigration, to deny civil rights to those already there, and to prevent any economic advancement. But despite many violent attacks, the Chinese survived stoically, and by their patience and thrift continued to build up small businesses (e.g., restaurants and laundries) and gain other manual employment. In 1924 all immigration of Orientals to the United States was prohibited (similar legislation had been passed in Canada in 1923). As a result, the agitation died down, and the Chinese – living mostly in ghettos, or Chinatowns – were largely able to run their own affairs. Families made many sacrifices to give their sons a good education; and as the second generation could usually speak English and had absorbed much of the American culture, they eventually gained acceptance in middle-class business and professional occupations (see Lee, 1960; Lyman, 1970; Vernon, 1982). By now they constitute substantial minorities in many large eastern cities as well as in the west.

There was less trouble in Hawaii, in spite of much prejudice among white settlers; and acculturation took place more harmoniously. Actually, from 1900 on the total numbers of Chinese plus Japanese greatly exceeded those of whites, and there were several other large ethnic groups – Hawaiians, Filipinos, and the like – who were less able, and less law-abiding, than the Orientals. Thus the latter soon supplied many of the commercial and political leaders in the community (Lind, 1955).

Intelligence tests of Chinese in North America

The first study of the abilities of Chinese children in California was published by Pyle (1918). Some 500 students aged 10 to 18 years, including whites, blacks, and Chinese, of both sexes, were tested. On physical tests such as height and hand grip, Chinese were lower than whites, and the same was found for psychological tests involving comprehension of English, such as *Verbal Analogies* and *Digit-Symbol Substitution*. But on rote memory tasks, Chinese of both sexes were higher than whites. On all mental tests the Chinese scored higher than blacks.

A similar study (Graham, 1926) of performance on varied tests by 63 Chinese boys and 40 whites, aged 12, showed the Chinese to score much lower on verbal abilities such as the *National Intelligence Test*, *Reading Comprehension*, and *Franzen's Mentimeter Tests*. But they were superior on *Memory for Shapes*, *Kohs Blocks*, and *Paper Formboard*, and nearly equal on *Digit Memory* and *Mazes*.

The abilities of Chinese and other ethnic groups in Hawaii were investigated from the 1920s on. The extensive findings by Porteus and Babcock (1926) and Murdoch (1925) are summarised by Iwawaki and Vernon in Chapter 14. Chinese and Japanese children generally obtained quite similar scores, and both groups approximated to or surpassed whites on nonverbal or performance tests. In Vancouver, Canada, Sandiford and Kerr (1926) gave the *Pintner–Paterson Performance Tests* to 224 Chinese and 276 Japanese schoolchildren (grades 1–6). The median IQs were Chinese 107.4, and Japanese, 114.2; but the norms for this test battery were somewhat dubious. Still the authors concluded that children of Oriental immigrants were not inferior to whites in nonverbal abilities, especially in view of the fact that the children's parents were mostly of low socioeconomic status, and that the children spoke mainly Chinese or Japanese at home.

The relative deficiency on verbal tests persisted until the 1960s, when Stewart, Dole, and Harris (1967) found Oriental Hawaiian students in grades 10 and 12 scoring a little higher than whites on the *School and College Aptitude Verbal Test*, and significantly higher on the *Quantitative Test*.

About the same time, Lesser, Fifer, and Clark (1965) in New York gave tests of four Thurstone factors – *Verbal, Reasoning, Number*, and *Spatial* – to 80 grade 1 children in each of four ethnic groups: Chinese, Jewish, black, and Puerto Rican. All scores were normalised to a mean of 50. Jews were much superior on the Verbal factor, scoring 59, but a little below Chinese on Reasoning and Spatial. Chinese were still just below average on Verbal, with 48, but higher on all the other 3 factors, with scores of 54 (see also Backman, 1972). Much the same pattern emerged on the verbal and nonverbal tests given in Coleman et al.'s (1966) extensive investigation of white, Oriental, and other minority groups.

A more recent study in Vancouver, by Kline and Lee (1972), threw light on the reading abilities of 277 Chinese children in grades 1 to 3. They were given the *WISC Verbal* and *Performance Scales, Monroe's Oral Reading*, and other tests. As in Sandiford's (1926) sample, they were said to be below average in SES, and speaking Chinese at home; they were also attending Chinese-language classes besides English-language schools. Taking account of reading tests and school grades, 13% were found to have difficulties in reading Chinese, 9% in English, and 6% in both languages. The mean Verbal IQ of all those with problems in English was 90, and for the remainder, 102. But all groups were above average in Performance IQ, with a mean of 112. Moreover, the numbers with problems in English declined with age, and only 5% were found at the end of grade 3.

Vernon (1982) tabulated the scores on standard ability and achievement tests of 540 Chinese students in grades 3, 4, 7, and 9 in Calgary schools, and the same number of white controls. The most interesting results were obtained with the *Differential Aptitude Test Battery* in grade 9, where 82 Chinese boys obtained a mean deviation quotient of 100 on *Verbal Analogies* and *English Usage*, but averaged 110 on *Number Computation, Nonverbal Reasoning*, and *Spatial Ability*. Girls obtained somewhat lower scores on the nonverbal tests but, like the boys, were much above average in Number and Spelling.

Chinese also seem to do well in *Conservation* and other developmental tasks, as described by Piaget. Tuddenham (1970) adapted 10 of such tasks suitable for children in grades 1 to 4, and gave them to 200 whites, 43 blacks, and 23 Orientals (mostly Chinese) in Berkeley, California. Orientals performed better than whites on 7 of the 10 tasks, although the numbers are too small to be statistically significant.

Chinese-American and Chinese-Canadian college students

At college student level, Hsia (1980) quotes means on the *Scholastic Aptitude Test* for 10,000 Orientals and 503,000 whites, namely:

	SAT Verbal	Quantitative
Whites	474	505
Orientals	442	517

The Orientals (Chinese and Japanese not separated) are consistently a little below average on the verbal section, but above average on the quantitative section. Note, however, that the proportion of Oriental applicants was three times greater than that of whites, after allowance is made for their total population figures. Had the selection ratios been even, the Chinese would have scored appreciably higher.

According to Yee (1976), 25% of all Chinese-Americans completed university degrees, versus 13% for the total U.S. population. Similar statistics have been collected by McCarthy and Wolfle (1975) on Ph.D. degrees. Oriental graduate students in 1969–1972 obtained 3 times as many doctorates as whites, and nearly 10 times as many as blacks, after allowing for their population numbers. But the Orientals gained half their degrees in engineering, science, or mathematics, and relatively few in the social sciences, arts, or education.

Meredith (1965), at the University of Hawaii, and Watanabe (1973), at the University of California, mention that about twice as many Oriental as white students fail the English proficiency test and have to attend remedial English classes. Thus there is still some verbal difficulty, although they and their parents have been speaking English at home for two or more generations.

Vernon (1982) analysed the convocation lists of all degrees awarded during one year (1978) at the universities of Calgary (Alberta), British Columbia, and Hawaii. He classified the proportions of degrees in each faculty, or subject, achieved by Chinese, Japanese, and non-Oriental students. In Calgary, only 6% of all degrees were obtained by Chinese, but they captured 17% of all degrees in science, engineering, and business, and only 2% of all other arts, social science, and education degrees. In the University of British Columbia and in Honolulu there were much larger numbers of Oriental college students, especially of females; and they were more widely diversified in their choice of subjects. But the main concentration was still in business, science (mostly physical), and engineering at all degree levels from bachelor's to doctorate. Thus, in all three universities, Chinese preferred to avoid arts subjects and education, where they would be relatively weak on the verbal side, and concentrated on subjects where their spatial and mathematical talents would be useful.

The same situation is found when the numbers of ethnic group members in different professions are counted. Weyl (1969) classified the representation of 6 ethnic groups, including Chinese, in 12 commonly chosen professions, on the basis of the 1960 U.S. Census returns. The total proportion of Chinese in all professions approximated to the same figure as Jews, namely about two and a half times as many as would be expected on the basis of numbers in the U.S. population. The Chinese included five times as many teachers, scientists, engineers, and doctors. But they produced fewer than average in the law and the clergy, which are the most verbal professions. Japanese produced one and a half times as many professionals as expected, that is, considerably fewer than Chinese.

Factorial studies

Another approach to studying ability differences between different cultural groups is to give a large battery of tests to samples of both cultures, to intercorrelate the tests in each group separately, and then to apply factor analysis for isolating the major underlying components of the battery. If virtually the same factors appear in both samples, this indicates that the structure or organisation of abilities is closely similar, and that the tests are measuring the same things in both groups. But if some of the factors are different, or if several tests get quite different factor loadings, this indicates that different abilities are being measured. Vandenberg (1959) gave 35 tests in all, including 20 taken from the original *Thurstone Primary Mental Abilities* investigation. His subjects were 92 college students from Taiwan or China, who were working at several American universities. Five of the 13 factors extracted were very similar to the factors that Thurstone obtained among white students: Spatial, Number, Verbal, Perceptual Speed, and Rote Memory (the other factors were smaller ones, deriving mostly from Chinese-language tests). Vandenberg regards his results as showing that the same major abilities are present in different ethnic groups, in spite of differences in education, language, and cultural experiences. To us, it seems much more likely that the Chinese students, who must have become quite fluent in the English language, were also acculturated to American thought and therefore resembled American students in their responses to American tests.

Investigations by Backman (1972) and Flaugher and Rock (1972) of high school students, representing several ethnic groups, likewise yielded very much the same factors in whites, Jews, blacks, Orientals, and Hispanics. Here, of course, the students in all groups had been brought up in the same culture, using the same language and attending the same schools. There were, however, significant differences between the mean scores of the groups on most factors, the Orientals being high on Number and Spatial abilities, but close to average on Verbal ability.

An extensive series of researches among ethnic groups in Hawaii have been reported by DeFries, Vandenberg and McClearn (1974), Marsella and Golden (1980), and others. But most of the subjects were Caucasians or Japanese, or mixed Oriental, and no separate results are given for Chinese. Quite close resemblance on four major factors was found in most studies, although the loadings of the tests, and the content of additional factors, differed more widely.

Studies of personality, attitudes, and child-rearing practices

A great many studies of Chinese-Americans have been concerned with personality and attitude differences between them and whites. Others have made use of Chinese in Taiwan or Hong Kong. Some details of 45 such studies are given by Vernon (1982). For example, the *Thurstone Psychoneurotic Inventory*, the *Edwards Personal Preference Schedule*, and *Rotter's Locus of Control Test*, have frequently been used. Many of the tests have shown significant differences, either with children or with college students. No attempt will be made here to discuss these results, since personality questionnaires and attitude scales are very dubious instruments for crosscultural purposes. Responses to such tests are greatly influenced by the subjects' desire to appear socially respectable, or to "fake good," and other biases. In view of the emphasis among Chinese on social etiquette, their answers might be even more distorted. Moreover, questions dealing with personal values, or social and emotional problems, may often be interpreted differently by persons reared in different cultures. Indeed, it may sometimes be impossible to make exact translations from English to Chinese, or the reverse.

Much more satisfactory information can be obtained by observations of the actual behaviour of infants or children in natural daily-life situations. Freedman (1974) found that Chinese, together with Japanese and American Indian, babies were calmer and more passive, less excitable than whites. Kagan, Kearsley, and Zelazo (1978) compared Chinese and white children aged 3 to 29 months in a day-care centre. The Chinese were generally quieter, calmer, less given to fighting, and more docile to adult demands. But they were also more dependent on their mothers. Although it is obvious that such behavioural differences should be attributed largely to maternal handling and rearing, they are noticeable at birth before the mothers' care can have had any effect. Freedman believes that there is a basic temperamental difference between mongoloid and caucasoid peoples, which partly accounts for the remarkable conformity, patience, and willingness to work among indigenous or emigrant Chinese.

Conclusion

The superior educational, and especially nonverbal and mathematical, achievements of Chinese abroad is not readily explained by the conventional theories. Thus it is unlikely that Chinese-Americans are superior genetically, because the early Chinese immigrants are known to have been of poor peasant stock. Conceivably, though, there is some biological factor underlying the consistent capacity of Chinese to do better on visual-spatial and mathematics tests, and in the visual arts, than on verbal tests.

Nor can environment, in its usual sense, be regarded as contributing to Chinese achievement, because immigrants, at least until the 1930s, mostly lived under conditions of great poverty and racial discrimination. And they were further handicapped because their home language was totally different from that used in schools and everyday life in North America. Yet they overcame these adversities. (These topics are discussed more fully in Chapter 14).

We would conclude that apart from the possible temperamental differences just mentioned the major explanation of Chinese achievement must surely lie in their values and child-rearing practices, which they brought with them when they emigrated, and still persist in, despite their acculturation to most American norms. However, with increasingly frequent cross-racial marriages, Chinese-Americans will presumably become more and more Americanised.

Though there are quite large populations of Chinese immigrants in the major cities of England and Australia, their performance in the various educational and psychological tests is largely unknown, and hence comparisons with local citizens are not possible. It will be of great interest to carry out investigations into the individual differences of Chinese people in these two countries and to see whether findings are similar to those for Canada and the United States.

References

Backman, M. E. (1972). Patterns of mental abilities: Ethnic, socioeconomic, and sex differences. *American Educational Research Journal, 9*, 1–12.

Brown, L. B. (1981). *Psychology in contemporary China.* Oxford: Pergamon.

Chan, J. (1974). Intelligence and intelligence tests in Hong Kong. *New Horizons, 15*, 82–88.

Chan, J. (1976a). Problems of psychological testing in two languages in Hong Kong. In R. Lord (Ed.), *Studies in Bilingual Education* (pp. 110–113). University of Hong Kong Language Centre.

Chan, J. (1976b). Is Raven's Progressive Matrices test culture-free or culture-fair? *Proceedings of the Third IACCP Congress*, Tilburg, Netherlands.

Chan, J. (1981). Parenting styles and children's reading abilities. *Journal of Reading, 1*, 411–415.

Chan, J. (1982). Correlates of Raven and other scores of students in Hong Kong. *Proceedings of the International Association of Applied Psychology*, 20th Congress, Edinburgh.

Chan, J., Eysenck, H. J., & Götz, K. O. (1980). A new visual aesthetic sensitivity test. III. Cross-cultural comparison between Hong Kong children and adults, and English and Japanese samples. *Perceptual and Motor Skills, 50*, 1325–1326.

Chan, J., & Worley, S. (1984). The expectations of teachers, parents, and pupils in reading across cultures. *Proceedings of 10th Congress of the International Reading Association,* Hong Kong.

Chen, M. J. (1981). Directional scanning of visual displays. *Journal of Cross-Cultural Psychology, 12*, 252–271.

Ching, C. C. (1980). Psychology in the People's Republic of China. *American Psychologist, 35*, 1084–1089.

Chiu, L-H. (1972). A cross-cultural comparison of cognitive styles in Chinese and American children. *International Journal of Psychology, 7*, 235–242.

Coleman, J. S., et al. (1966). *Equality of educational opportunity.* Washington, DC: U.S. Office of Education.

Cunnington, B. F., & Torrance, E. P. (1965). *Sounds and images.* Lexington, MA: Ginn.

Dawson, J. L. M. (1970). Psychological research in Hong Kong. *International Journal of Psychology 5*, 63–70.

Dawson, J. L. M., & Wong, D. C. M. (1983). Hand-eye dominance, cognitive style, and reversing: Geometric illusion susceptibility. *Psychologia, 26*, 21–39.

Dawson, J. L. M., Young, B. M., & Choi, P. P. C. (1973). Developmental influences on geometric illusion susceptibility among Hong Kong Chinese children. *Journal of Cross-Cultural Psychology, 4*, 49–74.

Dawson, J. L. M., Young, B. M., & Choi, P. P. C (1974). Developmental influences in pictorial depth perception among Hong Kong Chinese children. *Journal of Cross-Cultural Psychology, 5*, 3–22.

DeFries, J. C., Vandenberg, S. G., & McClearn, G. E. (1974). Near identity of cognitive structure in two ethnic groups. *Science, 183*, 338–339.

Douglas, J. D., & Wong, A. C. (1977). Formal operations. Age and sex differences in Chinese and American children. *Child Development, 48*, 689–692.

Flaugher, R. L., & Rock, D. A. (1972). Patterns of ability factors among four ethnic groups (Research Memorandum No. 7). Princeton, NJ: Educational Testing Service.

Freedman, D. G. (1974). *Human infancy: An evolutionary perspective.* New York: Wiley.

Gardner, H. (1980, August). China's born-again psychology. *Psychology Today,* 45–50.

Godman, A. (1964). The attainments and abilities of Hong Kong Primary IV pupils: A first study. *Educational Research Publication No. 2,* Hong Kong University Press.

Goodnow, J. J. (1962). A test of milieu effects with some of Piaget's tasks. *Psychological Monographs, 76* (No. 555).

Graham, V. T. (1926). The intelligence of Chinese children in San Francisco. *Journal of Comparative Psychology, 6*, 43–71.

Hsia, J. (1980). Cognitive assessment of Asian Americans. *Symposium on Bilingual Research.* Los Alamitos, CA.

Hsiao, H. H. (1977). Psychology in China. *American Psychologist, 32*, 374–376.

Hsu, L. T. (1978). Some psychological investigations in the People's Republic of China. *Australian Psychologist, 13*, 359–367.

Hsu, L. T., Ching, C. C., & Over, R. (1980). Recent developments in psychology within the People's Republic of China. *International Journal of Psychology, 15*, 131–144.

Jahoda, G., Deregowski, J. B., & Sinha, D. (1974). Topological and Euclidean spatial features noted by children. *International Journal of Psychology, 9*, 159–172.

Kagan, J., Kearsley, R. B., & Zelazo, P. R. (1978). *Infancy: Its place in human development.* Cambridge, MA: Harvard University Press.

Kline, C. L., & Lee, N. (1972). A transcultural study of dyslexia. *Journal of Special Education, 6*, 9–26.

Lee, R. H. (1960). *The Chinese in the United States of America.* Hong Kong University Press.

Lesser, G. S., Fifer, G., & Clark, D. H. (1965). Mental abilities of children from different social-class and cultural groups. *Monographs of the Society for Research in Child Development, 30* (No. 102).

Lind, A. W. (1955). *Hawaii's people.* Honolulu: University of Hawaii Press.

Lyman, S. M. (1970). *The Asian in the West.* Reno, NV: Western Studies Center.

McCarthy, J. L., & Wolfle, D. (1975). Doctorates granted to women and minority group members. *Science, 189,* 856–859.

Marsella, A. J., & Golden, C. J. (1980). The structure of cognitive abilities in Americans of Japanese and of European ancestry. *Journal of Social Psychology, 112,* 19–30.

Meredith, G. M. (1965). Observations on the acculturation of Sansei Japanese Americans in Hawaii. *Psychologia, 8,* 41–49.

Murdoch, K. (1925). A study of differences found between races in intellect and in morality. *School and Society, 22,* 628–632, 659–664.

Parkay, F. W., & Chan, J. (1983). Students' perceptions of the classroom: A cross-cultural comparison of Hong Kong and Texas high school pupils. *Proceedings of the American Educational Research Association,* Montreal.

Phua, S. L. (1976). *Ability factors and familial psychosocial circumstances: Chinese and Malays of Singapore.* Unpublished doctoral dissertation, University of Alberta.

Porteus, S. D., & Babcock, H. (1926). *Temperament and race.* Boston: Badger.

Pyle, W. H. (1918). A study of the mental and physical characteristics of the Chinese. *School and Society, 8,* 264–269.

Raven, J. (1981). *The 1979 British standardization of the Standard Progressive Matrices.* London: H. K. Lewis.

Ripple, R. E., Jaquish, G. A., Lee, H. W., & Chan, J. (1982). Cross-cultural perspectives on the life-span development of divergent thinking abilities. *Proceedings of the 6th IACCP Congress,* Aberdeen.

Rodd, W. G. (1959). A cross-cultural study of Taiwan's schools. *Journal of Social Psychology, 50,* 3–36.

Rowe, E. (1966). Failure in school: Aspects of the problem in Hong Kong. *Educational Research Publication No. 3,* Hong Kong University Press.

Sandiford, P., & Kerr, R. (1926). Intelligence of Chinese and Japanese children. *Journal of Educational Psychology, 17,* 361–367.

Stevenson, H. W., Stigler, J. W., Lucker, G. W. et al. (1982). Reading disabilities: The case of Chinese, Japanese, and English. *Child Development, 53,* 1164–1181.

Stewart, L. H., Dole, A. A., & Harris, Y. Y. (1967). Cultural differences in abilities during high school. *American Educational Research Journal, 4,* 19–30.

Stigler, J. W., Lee, S., Lucker, G. W., & Stevenson, H. W. (1982). Curriculum and achievement in mathematics: A study of elementary school children in Japan, Taiwan, and the United States. *Journal of Educational Psychology, 74,* 315–322.

Tseng, W-S., & Hsu, J. (1969). Chinese culture, personality formation and mental illness. *International Journal of Social Psychiatry, 16,* 5–14.

Tuddenham, R. D. (1970). A 'Piagetian' test of cognitive development. In W. B. Dockrell (Ed.), *On Intelligence.* Toronto: OISE.

Vandenberg, S. G. (1959). The primary mental abilities of Chinese students: A comparative study of the stability of a factor structure. *Annals of the New York Academy of Science, 79,* 257–304.

Vernon, P. E. (1982). *The abilities and achievements of orientals in North America.* New York: Academic Press.

Watanabe, C. (1973). Self-expression and the Asian-American experience. *Personnel and Guidance Journal, 51,* 390–396.

Weyl, N. (1969). Some comparative performance indexes of American ethnic minorities. *Mankind Quarterly, 9,* 106–119.

Yee, A. H. (1976). Asian Americans in educational research. *Educational Researcher, 5*(2), 5–8.

14   Japanese abilities and achievements

Saburo Iwawaki and Philip E. Vernon

Ability testing in Japan

Since the 1905 version of the *Binet–Simon Intelligence Test* was introduced in Japan in 1908, many researches on IQ and other tests have been conducted by Japanese psychologists. Both translations of western tests, and tests constructed by Japanese psychologists on the basis of western models, have been used. After World War II, the Japanese Ministry of Education adopted the recommendations of the U.S. Educational Mission, and formulated a school record form which contained a column for the children's scores on standardised tests. Schoolteachers had to fill in IQs every 1 or 2 years. This promoted the production of new tests, and group tests were put on sale by Japanese publishers in the 1950s. Some university staff members of psychology or education departments were involved in constructing tests for Japanese children, often according to Thurstone's multifactor theory of intelligence. Their researches on these tests usually appeared in bulletins or technical reports of their own universities, which were not widely distributed.

After World War II, when Japan achieved remarkable economic growth, upper secondary and higher education made rapid progress. This growth enabled a large proportion of Japanese families to think of sending their children to higher education. Although educational opportunities in general have greatly expanded over the past three decades, Japanese adolescents have to face difficult examination barriers in order to gain entry to universities, especially the elite universities which are believed by the Japanese to constitute the means of entrance to distinguished careers in big business, government service, and the professions. Younger children also compete for acceptance by higher grade secondary schools so as to improve their chances of reaching one of the many well-known universities. Many attend coaching schools (*juku*) out of ordinary school hours in order to improve their achievements.

The examination system in Japan induces the public schools to teach materials which are useful for examinations. Since objective or multiple-choice examinations are usually used for selection to higher grade schools, they are more often applied in classrooms than essay-type examinations. Educational publishers have issued many such examinations, which have taken the place of examinations written and marked by teachers. These examinations are entirely different from standardised instruments designed to measure what students have learned up to a given time. Indeed standardised achievement tests are rarely used in schools, except for academic investigations. The selection system for national and local public universities has changed somewhat since 1979. A joint standard first-stage achievement test was introduced by the National Centre for University Entrance Examinations. This consists of multiple-choice tests of scholastic achievement in upper secondary school subjects. Each university then conducts its own second-stage entrance examination, which is more often essay-type.

In the 1960s, many books on intelligence, and articles in academic journals and university bulletins, were published in Japan. A useful survey of Japanese work on intelligence and achievement tests from 1908 to 1958 was published by Osaka (1961). The *Binet Test* was standardised in Japan in the 1930s. In the 1950s and 1960s the *Wechsler (WISC* and *WAIS) Scales* were adapted and standardised as diagnostic tests for Japanese children and adults. A Japanese version of the *Illinois Test of Psycholinguistic Abilities* (*ITPA*) was developed in the 1970s. These individual tests have been, and still are, widely used for counselling or clinical diagnosis at clinics, hospitals, and so on.

Scholastic achievements

In 1959, Uemoto and Haslerud collected cross-cultural data on mathematics achievement in the United States and Japan. Their subjects were 247 fifth and 264 ninth graders in Japan, and 216 fifth and 161 ninth graders in the United States. The mathematics test, which contained eight calculation items and four problem-solving items for each grade, was given in the first semester. The percentages of correct answers to each item were compared across cultures. On all items (except one in the fifth-grade test) the Japanese equalled or excelled the U.S. performance. Although the numbers of items were small, the results demonstrated that Japanese children are significantly better than Americans in arithmetical accuracy.

These findings received support from much more systematic studies of mathematics and science achievement by Husén (1967), and Comber and Keeves (1973). Japanese students have consistently achieved the highest scores in these multinational enquiries. Stigler, Lee, Lucker, and Stevenson (1982) carefully analysed mathematics curricula through elementary school textbooks in Japan, Taiwan, and the United States. The Japanese mathematics curriculum was found to contain more advanced and more complex concepts and skills, and to introduce these earlier, than the curricula in Taiwan and the United States. On the basis of this analysis, Stigler constructed a 70-item mathematical test. At both first- and fifth-grade levels, Taiwanese and Japanese boys and girls obtained significantly higher scores than a parallel sample of U.S. children. In the interpretation of their findings, Stigler et al. (1982) pointed out factors other than curriculum content, namely, (1) the amount of time devoted to teaching mathematics, (2) time spent on homework, and (3) the importance of children's achievements to parents. However, class size was not a factor. The average class in Taiwan and Japan was twice as large as in American schools. It is not difficult for Japanese children to understand the fundamental rules of arithmetic because their language uses a simple and clear system of decimal numerals. These numerals are linguistically constructed for convenience of memorisation; and Japanese children take only 2 months to memorise the multiplication tables (up to 9 × 9). However, this makes it more diffficult for Japanese to master numerals in western languages, for example, French.

According to Kuraishi et al. (1958), the arithmetical achievement of Japanese schoolchildren is strongly associated with verbal abilities, as measured by the *Kyoto NX Intelligence Test* verbal subscales, although not with non-verbal subscales. But beyond the seventh grade, the correlations with non-verbal scales were higher. Kuraishi also suggested that Japanese and English-speaking children differ in the way they conceive arithmetical operations such as adding, subtracting, and so forth. Once Japanese students learn to use the abacus, they become much quicker and more accurate in their calculations than western students.

Japanese language

Japanese children read and write words in two types of script: *kana* and *kanji*. *Kana* has two alternatives: *hirakana* and *katakana*. Hirakana, which is taught first, consists of a set of 46 symbols, which are phonetic signs. Katakana is introduced next; it consists of another set of symbols which are more frequently used for foreign words and names. Kanji is ideographic (like Chinese script), and has to be learned chiefly by rote. Before finishing compulsory schooling, children are taught 1,945 kanji words, which are considered to be necessary for the literate person. In everyday Japanese, many more kanji characters are generally used. Although a single kanji has its own meaning, it is quite common for a combination of two or more kanji to make another word. Saito, Inoue, and Nomura (1979) have described the complicated nature of information processing that applies to the *graphemic*, *phonemic*, and *semantic* aspects of kana and kanji. In information processing of kana, the phonemic properties play an important part, whereas in processing kanji, which are directly expressing a meaning, all three properties overlap.

Nomura (1981) stated that the conceptually oriented processing of kanji is more effective than the use of kana, in which graphemic processing always goes along with phonemic. By presenting kana and kanji symbols tachistoscopically to the right or left visual fields, Hatta (1978, 1981) demonstrated that kana are mainly processed in the left hemisphere, and kanji mainly in the right. He also stated that the level of information processing is related to cerebral lateralisation. The right hemisphere is superior at the lower level of kanji processing in physical-identity matching, but not at the higher level of lexical decision, whereas at the highest level of semantic congruence, the left hemisphere is superior.

Despite the complicated system of Japanese characters, it was claimed by Makita (1968) that the incidence of reading disabilities is lower in Japan than in western countries. However, his figures were based only on teachers' impressions. But he is probably justified in claiming that Japan has a very high literacy rate, possibly 99%, and that there are few dyslexics apart from the pathologically brain injured (Sakamoto & Makita, 1973).

Stevenson et al. (1982) constructed a reading test which they administered to schoolchildren in Taiwan, Japan, and the United States, four months after they had entered the fifth grade, together with a battery of 10 cognitive tests. The test was based on an examination of the curricula and textbooks in each country. It provided three scores: vocabulary, reading of sentences, and comprehension. The authors found that the incidence of reading backwardness was nearly the same in all three countries, and showed that, of the cognitive tests, general information and verbal memory were most closely related to the reading ability of Japanese children. Their results did not support the hypothesis that the incidence of reading disabilities across cultures was mainly due to orthographical differences. The reading of kanji in Japan has its difficulties, just as does reading phonetically in the United States.

More recently the methods of reading and writing single words were compared between 7-year-old Japanese and English children (Kimura & Bryant, 1983). Japanese were found to read kanji using visual strategies, and relying on a phonological strategy for kana; whereas English children read single words as visual wholes. The authors suggested that there was a similarity in the methods of reading in the two countries, but that Japanese children write kana in the same way as English children write words, on the basis of sound–symbol relationships.

By presenting different kinds of verbal statements tachistoscopically to 4-year-old Japanese children, Akiyama, Takei, and Saito (1982) found that they had more difficulty in verifying false negative statements than true negative statements; whereas English 4- to 5-year-old children showed no difference. However, among American college students, Akiyama, Brewer, and Shoben (1979) found the verification of true negative statements more difficult than false ones. This suggests that Japanese children acquire their language in a different way from Americans, because of the different linguistic characteristics of Japanese and English.

Need for achievement

In their review of achievement motivation in Japan, Maehr and Nicholls (1980) showed that it is very different from McClelland's concept in America.

It is not oriented towards individual success, but towards the family or the company in which adults work. It originates in the strong dependence of Japanese children on their mothers; and they remain close to them throughout their lives. "Japanese achievement motivation is often high and is associated with a high need for affiliation" (Morsbach, 1980, p. 322). Also, in Japan, there is no relation between independence training in the home and achievement motivation (Hayashi, Okamoto, & Habu, 1962), as there is in the United States.

In Morsbach's (1980) penetrating analysis of the main factors in Japanese social adjustment, he observes that achievement motivation is often connected with pressures for high educational achievement. In the early school years, Japanese teachers pay great attention to motivation, and stress collective obligations to the group (e.g., the family, the classroom, the school, and the community). Cummings (1980) regarded the high level of scholastic achievement in Japan as due to the high quality of the teachers, their concern over motivation, and the demanding curriculum. And Gensley (1975) attributed high achievements in mathematics and science to good schooling, the students' aspirations, and the parental pressures to do well.

Japanese children attend school six days a week, totalling 240 days a year; and their school hours are longer than in most other advanced societies (Cummings, 1980). Family trips are rare except in the summer holidays, or occasional school breaks. As just mentioned, the pressures of the entrance examination system are notorious, because education in Japan is virtually the only means to raising one's social status and achieving security in a highly status-conscious society. In secondary schools, club and other extracurricular activities have little support, especially among ambitious students.

As for quality of teachers, most teachers in Japan look on their jobs as lifetime careers. Thus, 35.4% of elementary school teachers were found to have had more than 25 years of service, and only 23.2% had fewer than 5 years. Most teachers are active also in government- or union-sponsored workshops, which introduce new teaching techniques; and many study groups for improving professional training are voluntarily organised by the teachers themselves.

Many western commentators are so impressed by Japanese educational and technological achievements that they fail to mention the considerable unrest, especially among teenagers and young adults, which accompanies this phenomenon. The suicide rates in these age groups were very high in the early 1970s in comparison with western countries, but have now much declined. Suicide was often attributed to the "examination hell," although this was only one of many causal factors (Ishii, 1977). With so much affluence the younger generation pays less attention to the traditional values and is becoming materialistic and self-seeking (Sato, 1982). Delinquency rates are rising, although they are still far lower than in the West. Disobedience in the family and at school is increasing and is often accompanied by physical violence against parents or teachers. Riots among college students and young adults were also notorious, but have now become quite infrequent. In any case, such signs of instability are still confined to a small minority of Japanese males.

Child rearing and cognitive development

Child-rearing practices are the key factors in cognitive development. Conroy, Hess, Azuma, and Kashiwagi (1980) interviewed 58 Japanese and 67 American mothers of young children (median age 3.8 years) who were matched for socioeconomic status (SES). Six situations likely to provoke parental intervention were presented, and the mothers were asked what they would say to control the child in each situation. Japanese mothers were found to use feeling-oriented appeals and persuasion more frequently than Americans, who made more use of their authority and of imperative or moderate demands. Using the same group of mothers, Hess et al. (1980) compared their expectations regarding child development. They were asked about the ages at which they expected their children to acquire each of 38 skills. Japanese mothers desired them to master skills indicative of emotional maturity, self-control, social courtesy, and compliance earlier than did Americans, whereas American mothers expected verbal assertiveness, independence, and social skills with peers earlier than did Japanese. They also found that SES related significantly to maternal expectations of early development of school-related skills in both countries. Expectations of early development of verbal assertiveness correlated with children's school aptitude and IQ (measured at age 6) to the extent of .39 in America, and .28 in Japan.

Kashiwagi and Azuma (1981) studied the relations between maternal variables (mothers' attitudes towards child rearing, teaching and communication styles, etc.) and cognitive performance (IQ and school aptitude) among preschoolers in Japan and the United States. In both countries there were significant differences in the characteristics of boys and girls; but in Japan only the correlations with cognitive performance were higher for boys than girls.

Forty-four of the Japanese children were followed up and retested at 11 years (Kashiwagi, Azuma, & Miyake, 1982). At this age, significant correlations were obtained between school achievement and *WISC-R* IQ (.51), also between SES and IQ (.46), and achievement (.67). These measures of 11-year-olds correlated with several cognitive measures obtained at preschool age. It was found that early nonverbal skills were more predictive of later development than verbal skills. Eleven-year-old IQ correlated −.48 with impulsivity and .41 with persistence, as rated by psychologists at age 4. Over half of the maternal variables at 4 years correlated significantly with cognitive performances both at 4 and 11 years. Clearly, then, maternal variables play an important part in children's mental development.

Conroy et al. (1980) also noted that in Japan maternal variables tended to be associated more strongly with the preschool child's nonverbal skills than with his or her verbal performance. At age 11, however, this tendency was reversed, and maternal factors became more strongly associated with the development of verbal abilities.

Cognitive styles

Witkin and his colleagues (1962) developed systematically the concepts of cognitive style and psychological differentiation. According to Witkin (1967, p. 233), "cognitive styles are the characteristic self-consistent modes of functioning found pervasively throughout an individual's cognitive, that is perceptual and intellectual activities." His work was mainly concerned with the contrast between "field-independent" and "field-dependent" styles. Vernon (1973) has traced the origin of the concept of cognitive styles to the Greeks and Romans, and concluded that "Witkin's field-dependence-independence is the most successful, and replicable style so far investigated" (p. 141). Many cross-cultural studies have tested the generality of Witkin's theory, using mainly the *Rod and Frame Test (RFT)* and the *Embedded Figures Test (EFT)*.

Kojima (1978) tested 312 Japanese children, aged 5 to 6, with the portable *RFT*, the darkroom *RFT*, and a new simplified version of the *EFT*. For the darkroom *RFT* there was a statistically significant sex difference, with girls making larger errors. But no sex difference occurred with the portable *RFT*. Mean absolute error in degrees from the true vertical was used as the *RFT* score, and a high reliability (alpha coefficient) of .91 was obtained. The correlation between the portable *RFT* and *EFT* was significant only for boys ($r = -.35$); but the correlation between the darkroom *RFT* and *EFT* was significant in both sexes ($-.46$ and $-.28$). Kojima noted that Japanese children generally scored higher on the *WPPSI* performance scales than their American counterparts. But the *EFT* did not correlate consistently with one of the Wechsler subtests, *Block Design,* as it does among older children. He suggested that field independence might be measured with speeded tests. Hilger, Klett, and Watson (1976) used Harris's revision of the *Goodenough Draw-a-Man Test*, which is also related to the disembedding skills involved in psychological differentiation, and tested a sample of Japanese 6-year-old boys, who scored significantly higher than did American boys of the same age.

Another popular cognitive style is Kàgan's reflective versus impulsive, which is measured by the *Matching Familiar Figures* test (Kagan, Rosman, Albert, and Phillips, 1964). Hatano (1974) gave this test to American and Japanese children, and found that the Japanese made fewer errors, and were more cautious and reflective before reaching decisions: That is, their latency times were longer. This was confirmed by Salkind, Kojima, and Zelniker (1978), who administered the *MFF* to large numbers of American, Japanese, and Israeli children, aged 5 to 12 years. The Japanese made fewest errors, and were about 2 years ahead of the other groups in cognitive development. However, in the measurement of latency, only 5- to 7-year-old Japanese scored better.

Hatano and Inagaki (1976) also gave the *MFF*, along with a tactual–visual matching test, and two concept formation tests, to 51 Japanese children aged 5–6 years. Children who were reflective on the *MFF* showed longer latencies, and tended to seek more information before they reached decisions on the other test items. Hatano and Inagaki (1982) explain the cultural differences in cognitive styles in terms of the perceived meaning of errors and latencies.

Witkin and Berry (1975) proposed a persuasive theory of culture and cognitive development, which has been supported by many researches on field independence–dependence in different parts of the world. Recently Werner (1979) reviewed studies in both western and developing countries on psychological differentiation, and concluded, in agreement with Witkin and Berry, that the more dependent cognitive style is widespread in structurally tight societies which enforce social conformity, whereas the more independent style is prevalent among societies which encourage autonomy. Japan is a tight, group-oriented culture, which stresses socialisation practices (Morsbach, 1980). If Werner's conclusion is true, it would imply that Japanese children are more field dependent than those in less group-oriented cultures. However, Kojima's subjects were found to be high scorers on his modified *EFT*. Using the original children's version (*CEFT*) of *EFT*, Bagley, Iwawaki, and Young (1983) tested English, Japanese, and Jamaican children, and gave them a questionnaire for assessing the authoritarianism of their parents. The *CEFT* failed to show any significant correlation with the parental authoritarian questionnaire in any of the groups, except Jamaican girls in rural Jamaica. Means for parental authoritarianism among Japanese children in both Japan and London were close to those of English children (aged about 10 years). Jamaican rural children showed much higher scores (boys 17.92, girls 15.58) than Japanese or English (mean 10.7). Yet the *CEFT* scores for Japanese were significantly higher than in any of the non-Japanese groups. The results disconfirm the hypothesis that Japanese children who are exposed to socialisation characterised by affection and dependence would have high levels of field dependence. The *CEFT* may be better interpreted as an ability test rather than a measure of socialised cognitive style.

Clark and Halford (1983) compared urban and rural Anglo-Australian and Aboriginal children (aged around 10 years) on reading and mathematics achievement. They were also tested for nonverbal intelligence, field independence, reflectivity–impulsivity, and styles of conceptualisation. Using multiple regression analysis, the authors showed that the style measures contributed insignificantly to achievement, when intelligence is held constant. Thus it is useless trying to explain cultural or urban–rural differences by means of cognitive style.

Table 14.1. *Mean standard scores on NX 9–15, and score gains in later samples*

| Author | Grade | 1954 | | 1963 | 1972 | | |
		Mean	σ	Mean	Mean	σ	Gain
Kaneko	Fifth	51.58		58.60			7.02
Sano	Fourth	52.70	7.49		65.20	7.36	12.50
	Fifth	53.31	7.05		65.01	7.21	11.70

Intelligence tests

In the 1950s and 1960s, Japanese psychologists carried out numerous studies of intelligence, using tests standardised in Japan. These were mostly published in academic journals written in Japanese. Egawa (1956) gave the *Tanaka Intelligence Test* (which was widely used for group testing at that time) to 334 rural and 483 urban children, aged 6–15 years. He found that the urban group was significantly superior on the verbal subscales. But there was little difference on the nonverbal subscales. Other confirmatory studies were reported by Nakajima (1954), Ohira (1962), and Agarie and Ohnishi (1964).

The *Kyodai (Kyoto University) NX 9–15 Group Intelligence Test* was standardised in 1954. Nine years later, it was given to fifth-grade children in three schools which had been used as part of the standardisation sample (Kaneko, 1971). One school was in a residential zone, and two were in shopping districts. One hundred subjects were selected at random from children of these schools in 1954 and 1963. The factor structure of the *NX 9–15 Test* was closely similar in both samples. However, the mean standard score increased by 7 points over the period. Sano (1974) replicated Kaneko's study in 1971, with fourth- and fifth-grade samples from five schools in Kyoto, and three rural schools near Kyoto. The urban schools scored higher than the rural. As shown in Table 14.1, there was an even larger score gain, averaging 12.1 points over the 18-year period. Here, too, the same schools were tested in the same month in both years, hence sampling bias was likely to be minimal. Both Kaneko and Sano interpreted such cross-generation shifts as the result of cultural changes in Japan. They found higher rises in the subscales which depended on acquired knowledge and skills, whereas there were only small rises on subscales which required higher thought processes.

A study of IQ by Takuma (1968) involved 426 pairs of identical twins (MZ) and 105 pairs of fraternal twins (DZ); all were in the sixth grade. They were judged to be MZ or DZ at the Brain Institute of the Medical School of Tokyo University. Takuma employed six kinds of group intelligence tests, commonly used in Japan at that time. The correlations for MZ twins were higher than those for DZ on all six tests. Heritability coefficients ranged from .78 to .32. Whether the twins were reared apart or together was not investigated in this paper. Sawa (1957) gave the Japanese version of *WISC* to 80 pairs of identical twins reared together (age range 6–12). He found intraclass correlations of .87 for the *Full Scale,* .77 for *Verbal* and .83 for *Performance* IQs. His study did not involve any fraternal twins.

From 370 pairs of 12-year-old MZ twins, Takuma (1966) selected 55 pairs who showed intrapair differences of 8 or more IQ points both on an individual and a group test. He found that the heavier twins showed higher scores, that the first-born were higher than the second, and that twins who were born with *asphyxia neonatorum* obtained below average mean IQs. These findings indicated that intrapair differences appear in the later development of intelligence when identical twins experience different physical conditions at birth; and that the twin born under better conditions shows superior mental development.

Many Japanese psychologists have factor-analysed Japanese subjects' performance on standardised tests. For example, Okuno (1969) found the General Reasoning factor (*G*) and three group factors – Verbal (*V*), Spatial (*S*), and Numerical (*N*) on the *Kyodai NX 9–15* test. Ichitani (1965) administered to schoolchildren 14 subscales selected from several IQ tests commonly used in Japan. He found the *G* factor and three group factors, which he called Intellectual (*I*), Relational (*R*), and Speed (*S*). The results of factor analyses are often affected by methodological assumptions, the subject population tested, and the tests and items chosen. Furthermore, the interpretation of the extracted factors is usually subjective to a large degree.

Some Japanese psychologists have tried to employ other statistical techniques in investigating changes in the structure of intellectual ability. Kano (1962) administered the *Suzuki–Binet Test* to the same group of 228 children in Tokyo every year from first to ninth grade. Correlations at adjacent ages were quite high, for example, test scores at the third grade correlated .92 with those at fourth grade. The relationship decreased at longer intervals; for example, IQs at fourth grade correlated .84 and .79 with those at sixth and ninth grade respectively.

Kano's longitudinal data were reanalysed later by Ikuzawa (1970) and Nishikawa (1975). Ikuzawa applied the latent class model of latent structure analysis, using Green's (1951) method of solution, to the percentage-correct scores for each item. He identified five latent classes in children aged 6–15 years. The characteristics of each latent class were interpreted on the basis of estimated values of latent parameters (probability of correct responses for each item). He suggested that his latent classes correspond to Piaget's stages of intelligence, which are divided by 4 critical points. Nishikawa (1975) also reanalysed Kano's data by means of cluster analysis of the tetrachoric item intercorrelations within each grade group from first to ninth. Some two or three distinctive clusters were obtained in each group; and the scores on these were correlated over the whole age range. The content of the clusters changed with increasing age, and Nishikawa showed that they resembled Piaget's preoperational stage of thought in the early years, concrete operations in the middle, and formal operations in the highest grade.

Another way of getting more information from tests which provide several subscores is to analyse the profiles of intrapersonal differences, as well as the overall IQs which indicate interpersonal differences. Sano (1979) applied a profile analysis technique in a developmental study of intellectual abilities. He found 13 or 14 types of representative profiles recognisable at different grade levels, and characterised the development of intellectual abilities on the basis of the profiles that appeared most frequently at each grade.

IQ disputes in Japan

Since the early 1970s the interest of Japanese psychologists in IQ studies has waned. It is said that the measurement of individual differences in intellectual abilities tends to promote the spread of inequality in schools, employment, and so on. The ideal of equality has penetrated deeply into Japanese thinking; for example, to the extent that over 90% of Japanese identified themselves as middle class. Tests are also criticised as imperfect instruments of measurement, by both professionals and nonpsychologists. This has reduced active research on IQ tests, particularly group intelligence tests in Japan. Japanese psychologists are generally unfavourable towards evidence that indicates a high degree of genetic determination of individual and group differences in intelligence (Eysenck, 1980; Jensen, 1980).

To compare the level of intellectual abilities across cultures it is insufficient to employ scores on tests which have been constructed in one culture. Psychologists should investigate the panhuman generalisability of the cognitive activities which underlie intellectual performance. Often there are cross-cultural differences in patterns of performance across different tasks. Thus the scores on ability tests may vary with the tasks selected for cross-cultural investigations. If there is no theory that unites universal cognitive processes and intellectual activities, cross-cultural differences are uninterpretable.

According to Lynn (1982), the mean IQ of Japanese children and adults is higher than that in the United States, and has been rising during the past 24 years. Lynn attributes the high rate of Japan's economic growth after World War II to this IQ advantage. His findings were brought to the notice of Japanese people through the Japanese press. A few psychologists published negative comments. Since the Wechsler tests are constructed on the basis of American culture, they said, it is not possible to compare people directly across cultures. In fact Lynn's figures are not derived from the Wechsler *Verbal Scales*, only from some of the *Wechsler Performance Tests* and *Digit Memory*. But, as will be shown below, Japanese-Americans consistently score at about IQ 110 on nonverbal and spatial tests, but only 100 on verbal intelligence tests. Hence, Lynn's findings add nothing to what was already known. Further criticisms of methodological weaknesses have been made by Flynn (1982), and of *both* Flynn and Lynn by Irvine (see Chapter 1). Finally, it is misleading to attribute economic growth to superiority in intelligence, when there are so many other cultural, geographic, and historical factors involved.

Japanese immigrants and their descendants in North America

The first Japanese emigrants came as labourers to Hawaii, the United States, and Canada from about 1884, at a time when there was much poverty and overcrowding in Japan itself. By 1900 there were some 85,000 in the United States and some 20,000 in British Columbia. But in the 20th century, due to legal restrictions on further immigration, the numbers had risen by 1941 only to 112,000 and 23,000 respectively. Soon after World War II, discriminatory legislation was abolished, and by the time of the 1980 census in the United States there were some 700,000 persons claiming to be of Japanese descent, of whom 24% lived in Hawaii and 37% in California (mainly Los Angeles). At the present time there are also some 45,000 in Canada. But there has been so much cross-cultural marriage in both countries that it is difficult to determine who should, or should not, be counted as Japanese.

From the earliest years of immigration, the Japanese were discriminated against, and persecuted, by the white majority in much the same way as the Chinese (Chan & Vernon, Chapter 13). Indeed, the Japanese were even more hated because they were more assertive and aggressive in the face of harassment. When their contracts as labourers expired, they quickly moved into market gardening, fishing, and other employment, where their industriousness and drive made them more successful than their white counterparts. They were also suspected of retaining allegiance to the Emperor of Japan rather than to their new country. Moreover, the political and naval power of Japan in the Pacific area was seen as a threat to white civilisation. After the Japanese attack on Pearl Harbor in 1941, almost all Japanese in the West Coast states and Canada (but *not* those resident in Hawaii) were forcibly evacuated to camps in the interior (Daniels, 1975; Vernon, 1982). They lost all their businesses and possessions, and at the end of the war received only about one-quarter of their value in compensation. The education of the second generation Nisei (as distinct from the original immigrants, the Issei) was also seriously affected.

In spite of these adversities, the Nisei, and the third generation of Sansei children, showed outstanding educational achievement in the late 1940s and 1950s; and a large proportion obtained middle-class employment as professionals or in business. By 1960, Japanese-Americans showed greater total years of education, more white-collar jobs, and higher mean incomes than American whites (Lyman, 1970; Schmid & Nobbe, 1965). However, part of their progress might be attributed to the above-average SES and education of a large proportion of postwar Japanese immigrants.

The acculturation of Japanese to American social norms, and their acquisition of the English language, made a slow start. Yet by the 1930s there were already frequent conflicts within Japanese families because the Nisei were regarded by their parents as too Americanised. Actually the relocation in 1942–1945 was of some benefit to Japanese-Americans because the Issei could give little leadership in this emergency, and the Nisei largely took over and made a fresh start. The Sansei and later generations regarded themselves as Americans rather than as Japanese, and they adopted most of the customs of their white peer groups. Nevertheless, they were still proud of their ancestry, and retained many of the values of their ancestors – the strong family cohesion, loyalty to authorities, methods of child rearing, adherence to social rituals, and strong motivation towards educational and occupational achievement (Lyman, 1970). Some of these qualities resemble white middle-class virtues, and this facilitated the acceptance of Japanese by American society, once the initial, and wartime, hostility had dissipated. Indeed, it was recognised in the 1920s that the Japanese were "good citizens." Their crime and delinquency rates were very low, and they made minimal demands on social welfare. Kitano (1969) gives figures for the numbers of arrests per 100,000 of the population. The Japanese figure was less than one-tenth that of the total U.S. population. Again it was frequently observed that Japanese children at school were extremely docile and compliant to teachers' demands; hence they have been called ideal pupils.

It is remarkable that this acculturation of Japanese abroad was so closely paralleled by the technological growth and partial westernisation of the Japanese in Japan, as just described.

Linguistic problems of Japanese immigrants

We have already seen that the Japanese and English languages are so different in their orthographies that the Japanese must have had many problems in learning to speak, read, and write English. An additional difference is that Japanese characters are usually written or printed in columns, and are read from top to bottom, starting on the right side of the page. However, some modern, and all technical, books in Japan are printed in horizontal lines, and read from left to right. Apparently this alteration in the required patterns of eye movements causes little or no difficulty.

It used to be thought that the acquisition of a second language caused such mental confusion that bilinguals became backward in their mother tongue as well as weak in the second language. However, recent investigations such as those of Peal and Lambert (1962) in Canada, have shown that progress depends mainly on the attitudes and motivation to learn the new language. Children of foreign-born parents are better taught in their own mother tongue in preschool and early school years, because this provides greater security, and reinforces their identification with their own culture. But when children realise the advantages of learning English, they can do so most readily by so-called immersion programmes, where they do not learn English as a foreign language but are taught other subjects in English, and are always spoken to in English by teachers and age-peers. Thus the continuing use of a foreign language at home, or attendance at a Japanese-language school outside ordinary school hours, does not necessarily handicap their progress in English, as would be expected. When the children live in segregated communities where they hear nothing but Japanese, and particularly if they attend Japanese schools only, they are slower in learning English. But when their homes are more dispersed in English-speaking areas, and the children interact with English-speaking friends in or out of school, they usually become reasonably fluent in a year or two. But it takes considerably longer for them to learn to comprehend English textbooks, and actually to think in English without having to translate back and forth into Japanese. Much depends on age: Children who speak nothing but a foreign language up to, say, 10 years have much greater difficulties, whereas those who have been exposed to English from an early age are more flexible.

These findings help to explain why up till the 1920s, Japanese children obtained low scores on verbal intelligence and achievement tests. But from 1950 onwards they were nearly equal, or even superior to Caucasians. Most postwar immigrant parents would have acquired some English in Japanese schools, and they often settled in English-speaking neighbourhoods. Hence their children adapted quickly. Third- and later-generation Japanese Americans were almost wholly English-speaking, unless they lived in homes with, say, grandparents who spoke little English.

Early studies with intelligence tests

We will now survey studies of the intelligence and other test scores of Japanese students, roughly in historical sequence. Several such studies in California or Hawaii were published in the 1920s.

Fukuda (1923) gave the *Stanford–Binet Test* in English to 43 Japanese children in Colorado, omitting or adapting some highly verbal items. He claimed an average IQ of 95. But his sample was atypical because one-third of the parents were professional or businessmen. In 1925, Murdoch gave the *National Intelligence Test (verbal)* and the *Army Beta (nonverbal)* to some 500 children, aged 12, of mixed ethnicity in Honolulu, including 61 urban and 56 rural Japanese. The urban group scored well below white Americans on the *National Test*; and the rural group was near the bottom of the list. But on the *Army Beta*, urban Japanese scored almost as highly as whites, although the rural children were still quite low. Very probably the latter came from entirely Japanese-speaking homes, and simply did not understand the instructions.

Wider-ranging work was carried out by Porteus and Babcock in Hawaii, and published in *Temperament and Race* in 1926. Six main ethnic groups were distinguished. On an abbreviated *Stanford–Binet* scale (omitting the most culture-biased items), Japanese and Chinese obtained the highest mean IQ of 93. But Porteus quite rightly regarded the *Binet* as unsuitable in this context, and preferred his *Porteus Mazes* performance test, which he gave to some 200 members of several ethnic groups. Japanese boys, with a mean *Mazes* IQ of 101.9, slightly exceeded white Americans (99.8), and Chinese boys averaged 95.3. However, Japanese and Chinese girls were 5 to 6 points lower. The numbers of children per thousand referred to the psychological clinic for mental retardation were ascertained. The Japanese figure was the lowest (0.64%), then Chinese and Hawaiian (1.9% to 2%), and other minorities with language difficulties ranged from 5% to 16.6%. Porteus was mainly interested in the "Social Efficiency" of the various minorities, that is, their social value to the community. He collected ratings of several personality traits by 25 persons with long experience in the islands. Again the Japanese were highest, averaging 85.5; Chinese obtained 82.6, and four other groups, 60.0 to 33.3 (presumably the possible maximum on this scale would be 100). Crime rates followed the reverse order, ranging from 0.6 per thousand Japanese and 1.6 Chinese, to 9.3 Puerto Rican. Porteus concluded that the Japanese had the greatest endowments of abilities and temperament, and were likely to become the leading group in the community, as in fact happened.

Sandiford and Kerr's (1926) study of performance test IQs among Oriental children in Vancouver, B.C. was mentioned in the previous chapter. Even at that early date the authors concluded that the Japanese were the most intelligent group in British Columbia. Several other investigations in the 1920s and 1930s gave similar results (Vernon, 1982), the Japanese scoring around 90 IQ on verbal intelligence and achievement tests, but equalling or surpassing the white norms in performance and visuospatial tests (for example, Goodenough's *Draw-a-Man*). E. K. Strong (1934) found the average grade placement of Japanese in California to be 4.5 months below that of whites. But they were superior in mathematics and spelling. Also, their English speech at that time was poor, although Chinese had acquired considerable fluency and accuracy. Another prewar study, by M. E. Smith (1939), examined the language development of ethnic-group children in Hawaii, aged 3–6 years. Smith showed that the percentage of English words used in ordinary conversation at home was only 52.4 among urban Japanese, and 33.1 among rural; whereas in other groups the figures ranged from 80.7 to 98.6. The Japanese also made most speech errors.

S. Smith (1942) gave tests of English achievement and nonverbal ability to quite large samples (aged 10–14 years) of ethnic groups in Hawaii in 1924, and to similar samples in 1938. Again the Japanese and Chinese were lower than whites in the English tests, but equalled them on nonverbal. All groups improved at the later date. The Japanese did gain more in English ability than other ethnic minorities (apart from the Filipinos). But their improvement of .39 sigma units was smaller than might have been expected.

Wartime and postwar studies

Studies of evacuated students were reported by Pusey (1945) and Portenier (1947). They had missed quite a lot of schooling, and showed some backwardness in verbal intelligence and reasoning, and arithmetical problem solving. However, Kitano (1962) noted that as early as 1935, Japanese high school students obtained 62% of A and B grades; and by 1941 this had risen to 91%. But the Sansei students in 1952 and 1955 dropped back to 81% and 70%. At the same time, Japanese students were beginning to increase in social participation. The numbers claiming membership of three or more high school clubs were 7% in 1952, but reached 26% in 1960. Kitano admits that the grading standards in California schools may have fluctuated over the periods discussed. But he attributes the apparent drop among Sansei to their being more acculturated, and thus performing scholastically more like white students. Meredith's (1965) and Watanabe's (1973) observations on weak English among Oriental students in American universities are described in Chapter 13. Some western writers have commented on the apparent unwillingness of Japanese college students to join in classroom discussions, or question the lecturer. But this is more a matter of social etiquette than of inability to express themselves in English.

In 1968, Werner and her colleagues published a follow-up study of over 600 children in the Hawaiian island of Kauai, from birth to 10 years. One-third of this sample were Japanese and one-quarter were Hawaiian, with smaller groups of Filipinos, Portuguese, and other whites. The Japanese infants obtained a mean *Cattell* IQ of 103 at 2 years, the whites, 98. But on the *Primary Mental Abilities* battery at 10 years, whites averaged 112, Japanese 109, and all other groups, 101 or less. The Japanese also showed the fewest errors in the *Bender Gestalt* test, and fewest emotional problems according to clinical ratings. However, 27% of the Japanese were found to have educational problems, as against 22% of whites and 40% upwards in the other groups. This classification was based on grades and teachers' ratings. A possible explanation is that the population of Kauai is more largely rural than that of Oahu; thus the Japanese families may still have been speaking a good deal of Japanese.

Relatively few publications on Japanese abilities or achievements were published in the 1970s, partly because of the difficulties in identifying representative samples. However, Schwartz (1971) reported a survey of 2,200 grades 6, 9, and 12 students in Los Angeles schools. He found that the Japanese showed the highest educational achievement, and other positive qualities, of all ethnic groups. Other studies of Oriental (largely Japanese) high school or college students, using factor tests, were summarised in Chapter 13 (Flaugher & Rock, 1972; DeFries, Vandenberg, et al., 1974; Hsia, 1980).

The specialisation of Oriental college students in different faculties or subjects is also outlined in Chapter 13. Like the Chinese, the Japanese tended to choose business, engineering, and science; but they were also more frequently found in education and medicine. McCarthy and Wolfle (1975) collected lists of all American doctoral degrees in 1969–1972 and classified them by race. (However, Orientals were not subdivided into Japanese, Chinese, or other Asians). When allowance is made for the total numbers in the U.S. population, Asians obtained 3 times as many doctorates as whites, and about 10 times as many as American blacks.

In Weyl's (1969) study of the professions favoured by different American ethnic groups, Japanese produced one and a half times as many professionals as expected from their numbers in the population. In particular there were twice or more times as many architects, artists and writers, natural scientists, and technicians. But there were fewer than average lawyers and clergymen. Because there do not seem to be any consistent differences in the test scores of Japanese and Chinese students, the somewhat smaller numbers of professionals among Japanese suggests that outstandingly able Japanese-Americans probably go in more for business, industry, politics, and so forth, whereas more Chinese become academics.

Final discussion: Japanese and Chinese at home and abroad[1]

It is reasonable to claim that the Japanese and Chinese both in their own countries and as immigrants abroad, provide a unique source of information on the effects of cultural changes on group differences in abilities and achievements. The peoples of the Orient represent almost the extreme range of humanity from one of the most, if not the most, technologically advanced nations in the world to some of the poorest peasant communities. True, as mentioned in Chapter 13, the inhabitants of mainland China are not accessible to scientific studies, although we have a lot of historical and sociological data. But comparative psychological studies of Chinese have been made in Taiwan, Hong Kong, and in Hawaii and North America, from the 1850s to the 1980s. Likewise, we know of the changes in Japan from 1868 to date, and in Hawaii, the United States, and Canada from 1885.

The content of Chapters 13 and 14 has been mainly "etic," that is, based on test results. Yet in the introduction to Chapter 13, the objections to comparing the scores of different cultural groups, and the difficulties of interpreting any differences, were emphasised. This stricture applies even when nonverbal tests such as *Raven's Progressive Matrices,* which are alleged to be "culture-fair," are used: although they have, in fact, yielded quite high

---

[1] This section was added by Professor Vernon at our request. We are most grateful. – Eds.

means among Orientals in Hawaii, Taiwan, and Hong Kong. However, we do not have to rely solely on measured IQs in comparing Oriental and western groups. Much the same differences are apparent in the educational and technological achievements of the various samples of Chinese and Japanese, at various dates. And such achievements do not involve imposing an entirely arbitrary or culture-bound metric (even though it does evaluate them in terms of western concepts of success). Moreover, sufficient historical and sociological data are available to justify "emic" generalisations about the samples. To take one example: Japanese and Chinese children in Hawaii have obtained very similar mean scores on verbal and nonverbal intelligence tests from about 1925 to the present time. Sometimes one, sometimes the other, has scored a little higher. Yet the Japanese remained backward in English-language capacities for a considerably longer time than the Chinese. Presumably this was because the Chinese tended to move from the plantations into Honolulu more rapidly, and to acquire English for commercial and business activities; whereas the Japanese were more concerned with maintaining their traditional culture and language in their own communities, and were slower to assimilate until after World War II. (Other writers, with more knowledge of cultural changes in these two minorities, would probably be able to give fuller explanations.)

The main finding of our surveys is that repression, discrimination, and persecution by the majority culture, even when combined with great poverty and other adverse conditions such as different mother tongues, do not necessarily result in retardation of intellectual, educational, and economic growth. For many years Oriental immigrants experienced hardships comparable to those of blacks in the southeastern United States, and native Indians in many parts of the United States and Canada; and yet their descendants won acceptance, and were eventually recognised as two of the most successful ethnic minorities. Their children are now scoring more highly on many tests devised by western psychologists for American children, whereas both black and native Indian children are still scoring about as much below white norms as they did, say, in the 1920s.

How has this come about? We have no good grounds for arguing that Japanese and Chinese inherit genes underlying intelligence that are superior to those of Caucasians. The original immigrants of both groups were poor, little-educated peasants; although some writers believe that the Japanese at least must have been above average in intelligence and resourcefulnes to wish to move to a foreign country. Any theory of racial or biological differences in abilities is rejected nowadays by almost all psychologists, although there is in fact no reason why such differences should not occur in mental traits as they do in physical traits. But it is admitted by Jensen (1980), and others who support genetic theories, that we just do not have any reliable means of proving or disproving the existence of such differences.

It should be noted that the situation in North America has altered considerably since World War II, when discriminatory legislation against Oriental immigrants was abolished (in 1954), and vast numbers of new immigrants arrived, most of them screened for acceptable vocational skills. Thus large proportions of recent Japanese, Chinese, Korean, and Vietnamese families are likely to be above average educationally, and many of them already have some acquaintance with the English language. Currently, in Canada, many wealthy Chinese from Hong Kong are applying for immigration because of their fears of the Chinese communist takeover in 1997. Thus, regardless of the extent to which socioeconomic class is dependent on genetic intelligence, this improvement in the educational and occupational qualifications of postwar immigrants must have contributed to the continuing rise in the overall status of Oriental parents and their children in North America. Further discussion of possible genetic differences between Orientals and Caucasians in North America is of little more than academic interest, because so much intermarriage is occurring that, apart from new immigrants, it is difficult to decide who is or is not racially different.

There is some stronger evidence of biological differences in temperament. Several investigators (e.g., Freedman, 1974; Kagan, Kearsley, & Zelazo 1978) show that Oriental babies are more placid and less excitable than Caucasian ones. This has been observed with infants who are too young to have learned from their parents. No doubt the mothers' handling and methods of rearing their children do tend to reinforce this placidity, and to promote the security and cooperativeness of Oriental children. Hence, by the time they go to school they are more motivated to learn and to behave obediently than white children. Freedman has reported very similar characteristics among American Indian babies, such as the Navajo. He suggests that North American Native peoples originated from the same mongoloid stock as the Japanese and Chinese. However, the cultural values and child-rearing practices of Native North Americans differ greatly from those of Japanese, so that their children are relatively lacking in motivation to learn and in adjustment to the majority culture. Their intellectual growth is adversely affected by the conflict between their values and those of Caucasians, by their resentment of past injustices, and the restriction of opportunities for growth and progress in their present environments.

In addition, differences between mongoloid groups in Asia and in North America may have arisen through genetic drift, which occurs when subgroups become isolated from one another for thousands of years, and are subjected to different ecological (e.g., climatic) or cultural pressures. Thus, the Inuit may be outstandingly high in visuospatial abilities (including stone carving) because their survival in the Arctic is so dependent on visual sensitivity.

Another feature in which Japanese, Chinese, and North American Native peoples are similar is the unusual patterning of their test scores. They have always scored less well in verbal abilities and achievements than in nonverbal reasoning and visuospatial abilities. An obvious explanation would be that all these mongoloid groups are handicapped in verbal development by speaking a non-English language in their home countries, and in North America. But this is negated by the fact that the Orientals in the United States and Canada have been speaking English at home, in school, and elsewhere for several generations. Yet they continue to score more highly on nonverbal and spatial tests. It is conceivable, therefore, that there is some genetic difference which might account for this "imbalance." It has been suggested that lateralisation of brain functions may be involved, the mongoloids making more use of the right hemisphere, Caucasians more use of the left. But this is quite speculative, and cannot be accepted unless confirmed by further neuropsychological research. The only relevant evidence at present is the apparently high level of visual-artistic talents in Japanese, Chinese, the Inuit, and some Native North American tribes, that is, talents which are commonly attributed to right-brain functions. It is of interest also that Hatta (1978) was able to show that the reading of Japanese kanji is mainly processed in the right hemisphere. In China the written or printed script is wholly pictographic. But North American Native peoples never had an indigenous script, so that we cannot compare their reading of the mother tongue with that of other cultures.

Another point of interest arises from the test results, and educational–technological growth of Orientals who did *not* emigrate to the intellectually stimulating climate of North America, but developed comparable abilities in other parts of Asia. Thus Stevenson's and Stigler's investigations showed the achievements of Taiwanese elementary school children in reading and arithmetic to equal or exceed those of Americans, and to be quite comparable to those of Japanese children. However, we would expect them to be more advanced than mainland Chinese, because their economy, industry, and education were modernised, first by the period of Japanese rule (1895–1945), and later by the migration of Chiang Kai-shek's Nationalist Chinese government in 1949. Presumably British colonial rule, and trade, similarly promoted intellectual growth in Hong Kong and Singapore.

Mainland China, however, is much more closely comparable with India. In both countries some 80% of the population are rural, as against less than 25% in Japan. In both, the standards of living of the great majority are extremely low and malnutrition is rife; and the education available to the masses is of poor quality. Yet several recent research studies have shown that Indian and Pakistani children whose parents have emigrated to the United Kingdom, and who have received all their education in that country, score very close to British norms in school achievement and in nonverbal intelligence tests. It would seem to follow that the peoples of mainland China are potentially as able as those of Japan, although obviously it will take a great many years for modern technology, better standards of living, and effective education to spread throughout China, and thus enable the potentiality to be realised. This prediction is also confirmed by the close resemblance of Chinese and Japanese immigrants and their descendants in North America, where they live and grow up in the same favourable environment.

Throughout this discussion, the similarities between Chinese and Japanese (outside their own countries) may have been overemphasised, and their differences ignored. Obviously there were, and are, personality differences. During the long period of oppression, the Chinese reacted mainly by stoicism and patience, whereas the Japanese were more assertive in seeking their rights, more innovative and adaptable. The social organisation of the two cultures in America differed considerably – the Chinese with their clans and tongs in the ghettos, the Japanese adapting more quickly to the Caucasian nuclear family structure. (This particular difference may have been largely due to the much smaller proportion of women and children among early Chinese immigrants.) Nowadays, although both are mainly employed in high-grade occupations, Chinese are more likely to stay in professional work, whereas more Japanese run business enterprises or enter politics.

Naturally there must have been many differences of social organisation between the two groups in Asia, and these probabaly persisted to some extent in their present-day, highly Americanised, culture. But at the same time socialisation practices and values were, and still are, sufficiently similar to bring about the same educational motivation and need for achievement of their children, which chiefly underlie their scholastic and occupational success.

References

Agarie, Y., & Ohnishi, S. (1964). A study on regional differences in the structure of intelligence: Comparisons of Okinawa and Kansai. *Japanese Journal of Educational Psychology, 12,* 28–36.

Akiyama, M. M., Brewer, W. F., & Shoben, F. J. (1979). The yes-no question answering system and statement verification. *Journal of Verbal Learning and Verbal Behavior, 18,* 365–380.

Akiyama, M., Takei, S., & Saito, K. (1982). Statement verification and question answering in children. *Japanese Journal of Educational Psychology, 30,* 265–272.

Bagley, C., Iwawaki, S., & Young, L. (1983). Japanese children: Group-oriented but not field dependent? In C. Bagley & G. K. Verma (Eds.), *Multicultural childhood: Education, ethnicity and cognitive styles* (pp. 27–37). Aldershot, U.K.: Gower.

Clark, L. A., & Halford, G. S. (1983). Does cognitive style account for cultural differences in scholastic achievement? *Journal of Cross-Cultural Psychology, 14,* 279–296.

Comber, L. C., & Keeves, J. F. (1973). *Science education in nineteen countries.* Stockholm: Almquist & Wiksell.

Conroy, M., Hess, R. D., Azuma, H., & Kashiwagi, K. (1980). Maternal strategies for regulating children's behavior: Japanese and American families. *Journal of Cross-Cultural Psychology, 11,* 153–172.

Cummings, W. K. (1980). *Education and equality in Japan.* Princeton, NJ: Princeton University Press.

Daniels, R. (1975). *The decision to relocate the Japanese Americans.* Philadelphia: Lippincott.

DeFries, J. C., Vandenberg, S. G., McClearn, G. E., et al. (1974). Near identity of cognitive structure in two ethnic groups. *Science, 183,* 338–339.

Egawa, R. (1956). Intellectual differences between rural children and city children: A factor analytic study. *Japanese Journal of Educational Psychology, 4,* 102–109.

Eysenck, H. J. (1980). *The structure and measurement of intelligence.* New York: Springer-Verlag.

Flaugher, R. L., & Rock, D. A. (1972). *Patterns of ability factors among four ethnic groups.* Research Memorandum No. 7. Princeton, NJ: Educational Testing Service.

Flynn, J. R. (1982). Lynn, the Japanese, and environmentalism. *Bulletin of the British Psychological Society, 35,* 409–413.

Freedman, D. G. (1974). *Human infancy: An evolutionary perspective.* New York: Wiley.

Fukuda, T. (1923). Some data on the intelligence of Japanese children. *American Journal of Psychology, 34,* 599–602.

Gensley, J. (1975). The most academically talented students in the world. *Gifted Child Quarterly, 19,* 185–188.

Green, B. F. (1951). A general solution for the latent class model of latent structure analysis. *Psychometrika, 16,* 151–166.

Hatano, G. (1974). The development of reflectivity. In *Development of children and education* (Report No. 2). Tokyo: National Institute for Educational Research.

Hatano, G., & Inagaki, K. (1976). Reflection-impulsivity in perceptual and conceptual matching tasks among kindergarten children. *Japanese Psychological Research, 18,* 196–203.

Hatano, G., & Inagaki, K. (1982). The cognitive style differences in the use of latency and the number of errors as cues for inferring personality characteristics. *Japanese Psychological Research, 24,* 145–150.

Hatta, T. (1978). Recognition of Japanese kanji and hirakana in the left and right visual fields. *Japanese Psychological Research, 20,* 51–59.

Hatta, T. (1981). Different stages of kanji processing and their relation to functional hemisphere asymmetries. *Japanese Psychological Research, 23,* 27–36.

Hayashi, T., Okamoto, N., & Habu, K. (1962). Children's achievement motivation and its relation to intelligence, school achievements, anxiety tendencies, and parent-child relations. *Bulletin of Kyoto Gakugei University, Series A, 21,* 16–20.

Hess, R. D., Kashiwagi, K., Azuma, H. et al. (1980). Maternal expectations for mastery of developmental tasks in Japan and the United States. *International Journal of Psychology, 15,* 259–271.

Hilger, M. I., Klett, W. G., & Watson, C. G. (1976). Performance of Ainu and Japanese six-year-olds on the Goodenough–Harris Drawing test. *Perceptual and Motor Skills, 42,* 435–438.

Hsia, J. (1980). *Cognitive assessment of Asian Americans.* Symposium on bilingual research. Los Alamitos, CA.

Husén, T. (1967). *International study of achievement in mathematics.* Stockholm: Almquist & Wiksell.

Ichitani, T. (1965). A factor analytic study on the development of intellectual abilities. *Bulletin of Kyoto Gakugei University, Series A, 27,* 1–21.

Ikuzawa, M. (1970). Latent class analysis of intellectual development from 6 to 15 years. *Jimbun Kenkyu: Studies in the Humanities, Osaka City University, 21,* 2–45.

Ishii, K. (1977). Backgrounds and suicidal behaviors of committed suicides among Kyoto University students, III. *Psychologia, 20,* 191–205.

Jensen, A. R. (1980). *Bias in mental testing.* New York: Free Press.

Kagan, J., Kearsley, R. B., & Zelazo, P. R. (1978). *Infancy: Its place in human development.* Cambridge, MA: Harvard University Press.

Kagan, J., Rosman, B. L., Albert, J., & Phillips, W. (1964). Information processing in the child: Significance of analytic and reflective attitudes. *Psychological Monographs, 78* (Whole No. 578).

Kaneko, S. (1971). Changes in intelligence test performance during ten years. *Bulletin of Niigata University–Takata Branch, 15,* 11–20.

Kano, H. (1962) *Studies on mental development of school children through nine years.* Tokyo: Institute for Science of Labor.

Kashiwagi, K., & Azuma, H. (1981). Sex-typing in the cognitive socialization processes in Japan and the U.S. *Japanese Journal of Psychology, 52,* 296–300.

Kashiwagi, K., Azuma, H., & Miyake, K. (1982). Early maternal influences upon later cognitive development among Japanese children: A follow-up study. *Japanese Psychological Research, 24,* 90–100.

Kimura, Y., & Bryant, P. (1983). Reading and writing in English and Japanese: A cross-cultural study of young children. *British Journal of Developmental Psychology, 1,* 143–154.

Kitano, H. H. L. (1962). Changing achievement patterns of the Japanese in the United States. *Journal of Social Psychology, 58,* 257–264.

Kitano, H. H. L. (1969). *Japanese Americans: The evolution of a subculture.* Englewood Cliffs, NJ: Prentice-Hall.

Kojima, H. (1978). Assessment of field dependence in young children. *Perceptual and Motor Skills, 46,* 479–492.

Kuraishi, S., Umemoto, T., Yasuhara, H., Okuno, S., et al. (1958). Psychological studies on learning of school subjects: The developmental study on the relations between achievement in arithmetic and intelligence factor. *Japanese Journal of Educational Psychology, 6,* 159–167.

Lyman, S. M. (1970). *The Asian in the West.* Reno: University of Nevada, Western Studies Center.

Lynn, R. (1982). IQ in Japan and the United States shows a growing disparity. *Nature, 297,* 222–223.

Maehr, M., & Nicholls, J. G. (1980). Cultural and achievement motivation: A second look. In N. Warren (Ed.), *Studies in cross-cultural psychology* (Vol. 2, pp. 221–267). New York: Academic Press.

Makita, K. (1968). The rarity of reading disability in Japanese children. *American Journal of Orthopsychiatry, 38,* 599–614.

McCarthy, J. L., & Wolfle, D. (1975). Doctorates granted to women and minority group members. *Science, 189,* 856–859.

Meredith, G. M. (1965). Observations on the acculturation of Sansei Japanese Americans in Hawaii. *Journal of Social Psychology, 8,* 41–49.

Morsbach, H. (1980). Major psychological factors influencing Japanese interpersonal relations. In N. Warren (Ed.), *Studies in cross-cultural psychology* (Vol. 2, pp. 316–344). New York: Academic Press.

Murdoch, K. (1925) A study of differences found between races in intellect and in morality. *School and Society, 22,* 628–632, 659–664.

Nakajima, T. (1954). Intellectual development of children and preadolescents in isolated villages. *Japanese Journal of Educational Psychology, 2,* 211–216.

Nishikawa, K. (1975). Analysis of structural change of intelligence and genetic relations: A nine year follow-up study. *Psychologia, 18,* 1–14.

Nomura, Y. (1981). Data-driven and conceptually-driven processing in the reading of kana and kanji script. *Psychologia, 24,* 65–74.

Ohira, K. (1962). A study on the intelligence and the language proficiency of city and farm-village children. *Japanese Journal of Educational Psychology, 10,* 107–112.

Okuno, S. (1969). A factorial study on the differentiation of intelligence. *Bulletin of Faculty of Education, Yamanashi University, 4,* 169–194.

Osaka, R. (1961). Intelligence tests in Japan. *Psychologia, 4,* 218–234.

Peal, E., & Lambert, W. E. (1962). The relation of bilingualism to intelligence. *Psychological Monographs, 76* (No. 546).

Portenier, L. G. (1947). Abilities and interests of Japanese-American high school seniors. *Journal of Social Psychology, 25,* 53–61.

Porteus, S. D., & Babcock, H. (1926). *Temperament and race.* Boston: Badger.

Pusey, H. C. (1945). Arithmetic achievement of Japanese Americans. *Mathematics Teacher, 38,* 172–174.

Saito, H., Inoue, M., & Nomura, Y. (1979). Information processing of kanji (Chinese characters and kana (Japanese characters): The close relationship among graphemic, phonemic, and semantic aspects. *Psychologia, 22,* 195–206.

Sakamoto, T., & Makita, K. (1973). Reading in Japan. In J. A. Downing (Ed.), *Comparative reading* (pp. 440–465). New York: Macmillan.

Salkind, N. J., Kojima, H., & Zelniker, T. (1978). Cognitive tempo in American, Japanese, and Israeli children. *Child Development, 49,* 1024–1027.

Sandiford, P., & Kerr, R. (1926). Intelligence of Chinese and Japanese children. *Journal of Educational Psychology, 17,* 361–367.

Sano, T. (1974). Changes in intelligence test performance during eighteen years. *Japanese Journal of Educational Psychology, 22,* 110–114.

Sano, T. (1979). Application of profile analysis to development of intellectual abilities. *Bulletin of Aichi University of Education, 28,* 171–178.

Sato, S. (Ed.). (1982). Growing up in Japan [Special issue]. *Japan Echo, 9.*

Sawa, H. (1957). An analysis of identical twins' intelligence. *Japanese Journal of Educational Psychology, 4,* 199–202.

Schmid, C. F., & Nobbe, C. E. (1965). Socioeconomic differentials among nonwhite races. *American Sociological Review, 30,* 909–922.

Schwartz, A. J. (1971). The culturally advantaged: A study of Japanese-American pupils. *Sociological and Social Research, 55,* 341–353.

Smith, M. E. (1939). Some light on the problem of bilingualism as found from a study of English among preschool children of non-American ancestry in Hawaii. *Genetic Psychology Monographs, 21,* 119–284.

Smith, S. (1942). Language and nonverbal test performance of racial groups in Honolulu before and after a fourteen-year interval. *Journal of General Psychology, 26,* 51–93.

Stevenson, H. W., Stigler, J. W., Lucker, G. W. et al. (1982). Reading disabilities: The case of Chinese, Japanese, and English. *Child Development, 53,* 1164–1181.

Stigler, J. W., Lee, S., Lucker, G. W., & Stevenson, H. W. (1982). Curriculum and achievement in mathematics: A study of elementary school children in Japan, Taiwan, and the United States. *Journal of Educational Psychology, 74,* 315–322.

Strong, E. K. (1934). *The second generation Japanese problem.* Stanford, CA: Stanford University Press.

Takuma, T. (1966). On the early physical conditions influencing the development of intelligence. *Japanese Journal of Psychology, 37,* 257–268.

Takuma, T. (1968). An experiment on heredity influence on intelligence. *Japanese Journal of Educational Psychology, 16,* 237–240.

Uemoto, T., & Haslerud, G. M. (1959). Response and attitude of American and Japanese children to number situation. *Bulletin of Kyoto University, Faculty of Education, 5,* 69–96.

Vernon, P. E. (1973). Multivariate approaches to the study of cognitive styles. In J. B. Royce (Ed.), *Multivariate analysis and psychological theory* (pp. 125–148). New York: Academic Press.

Vernon, P. E. (1982). *The abilities and achievements of orientals in North America.* New York: Academic Press.

Watanabe, C. (1973). Self-expression and the Asian-American experience. *Personnel and Guidance Journal, 51,* 390–396.

Werner, E. E. (1979). *Cross-cultural child development: A view from the planet earth.* Belmont, CA: Wadsworth.

Werner, E. E., Simonian, K., & Smith, R. S. (1968). Ethnic and socioeconomic status differences in abilities and achievement among preschool and school-age children in Hawaii. *Journal of Social Psychology, 75,* 43–59.

Weyl, N. (1969). Some comparative performance indexes of American ethnic minorities. *Mankind Quarterly, 9,* 106–119.

Witkin, H. (1967). Cognitive styles across cultures. *International Journal of Psychology, 2,* 233–250.

Witkin, H., & Berry, J. (1975). Psychological differentiation in cross-cultural perspective. *Journal of Cross-Cultural Psychology, 6,* 4–87.

Witkin, H., Dyk, R., Faterson, H. F., Goodenough, D., & Karp, S. (1962). *Psychological differentiation.* New York: Wiley.

Part III

Cultural limits upon human assessment

Minorities and enclaves

15   Native North Americans: Indian and Inuit abilities

Damian McShane and J. W. Berry

This chapter examines the abilities of a diverse group of peoples who are distributed from the Arctic to the northern border of Mexico, and who constitute the Native[1] sector of the contemporary populations. This population includes all Indian and Inuit (Eskimo) peoples and the Metis (those of mixed Native and other ancestry, who identify with and live as Native peoples). The geographical range includes Greenland but excludes Mexico (see McShane & Cook, 1985, for reviews of Hispanic literature).

The people of this region are far from homogeneous either culturally or genetically; moreover, acculturative influences from various sources (British, French, Spanish, Russian, African) have led to even greater diversity during the post-Columbian period. The justification for including such a range of peoples in a single chapter is thus a matter not so much of science as of convenience. Nevertheless, historically they have been categorised or even lumped together by non-Native writers (and hence much of the literature is organised in these terms). Furthermore, at the present time there are significant social, cultural, and political movements among the various Native groups toward Native collective identity and action.

Ecological and cultural perspective

We need some valid framework for arranging the available information on Native abilities which will allow internal cultural diversity to be represented while avoiding a situation where every distinct cultural group is considered as a separate entity. As Figure 15.1 shows, there are far too many cultural groups for all to be considered in a single chapter. Fortunately, the early work of Kroeber (1939), which was later extended by Driver and Massey (1957) and by Driver (1969), provides us with substantial evidence of *culture areas* (broad regions of relative internal cultural similarity) which permit us

The authors gratefully acknowledge major editorial revisions by S. H. Irvine in the final stages of manuscript preparation.

[1] Although adjectives such as *indigenous* or *aboriginal* would serve the descriptive purpose, and nouns such as *Amerindians* and *First Nations* might also be appropriate, the main concern here is simply to establish the focus of the chapter while avoiding peripheral, but emotive, terminological issues.

Figure 15.1. Cultural groups of Native North America (from Driver & Massey, 1957).

Figure 15.2. Culture areas of Native North America (from Driver & Massey, 1957).

to focus on a limited number of broader categories (see Fig. 15.2). Other evidence demonstrates the existence of ecological and linguistic factors which tend to correspond to (and provide supportive evidence for the validity of) these culture areas. Considerable supplementary evidence in the three works just mentioned further validates the existence of these culture areas; however, for the purposes of this chapter we need not proceed beyond the point of establishing that there are reasonable grounds for claiming the existence of 13 major culture areas:

1. Central and Eastern Arctic	7. Plateau
	8. Plains
2. Western Arctic	9. Prairies
3. Yukon Sub-Arctic	10. East
4. MacKenzie Sub-Arctic	11. California
5. Eastern Sub-Arctic	12. Great Basin
6. Northwest Coast	13. Southwest

Although they do not coincide exactly, there are clear similarities between these culture areas and the nature of the land they occupy. This observation by Kroeber (1939), along with the earlier general work of Forde (1934), gave a great stimulus to the "ecological perspective" in anthropology and subsequently in cross-cultural psychology. Avoiding the discredited position of "environmental determinism," Kroeber (1939, p. 1) argued that eschewing it should "not prevent the recognition of relations between nature and culture, nor the importance of these relations to the full understanding of culture."

Thus, in ecological anthropology there is a search for covariation between natural and cultural phenomena, whereas in ecological psychology there is a parallel consideration of relationships between natural and behavioural phenomena. Pulling these positions together, an ecological approach to cross-cultural psychology (Berry, 1975, 1976) searches for systematic relationships between natural, cultural, and behavioural variables. More specifically in this chapter, we will be searching for patterns of human abilities in culture areas which can be viewed as collective adaptations to particular ecological settings.

Certain habitats are likely to predispose a population toward hunting and gathering as an economic base (extreme temperatures, lack of water, etc.), and this in turn encourages a nomadic lifestyle, low population density, and a minimal level of social stratification in the traditional culture. We may then ask: "What sorts of psychological qualities are likely to prevail in such an ecological setting?" An answer to this question (which, as we shall see, may indicate the development of certain perceptual and cognitive abilities), provides a set of hypotheses about the behaviours and dispositional qualities likely to be encountered among groups of people who have similar habitats.

There is also the recognition that human behaviour is not only an outcome of adapting to one's eco-cultural setting, it is also influenced by factors which lie outside the setting. Acculturative influences in the form of schooling, wage employment, urbanisation, labour migration, and religious, linguistic, and political changes may all impinge upon and alter the behaviour of individuals (McShane, 1987a). Thus an account must be made of these acculturation factors; and then their influence on both the collective life of the group and the extant behaviour of individuals (acculturated behaviour) needs to be described and ultimately predicted (Berry, 1976).

Abilities within culture areas

Although the earlier discussion of the 13 culture areas of North America brought some sensible clustering to the vast array of cultural variation, it was developed primarily to serve the needs of anthropologists. For our purposes, we may reduce the number even further, reflecting the lesser interest of psychology in particular cultural variations. We propose to organise our material according to the following six regions: *Arctic* (including Western, Central, and Eastern Arctic culture areas), *Sub-Arctic* (including Yukon, MacKenzie, and Eastern Sub-Arctic culture areas), *West Coast and Mountain* (including Northwest, California, Plateau, and Great Basin culture areas), *Central* (including Plains and Prairies culture areas), *East*, and *Southwest*.

Arctic

Research in the Arctic culture area has been almost exclusively with the Inuit (formerly called Eskimo), although other groups (such as the Aleut) also inhabit the Western Arctic. Widespread public fascination with the Inuit seems to have been parallelled by scientific research attention. As early as 1961, Vallee proposed a number of "suggestions for psychological research among the Eskimo"; reviews a decade later (Berry, 1971; McElroy, 1971) documented a substantial research activity, and by 1980 (Forsius, 1980), many of the key features of behaviour in the Arctic had been examined by psychologists. Of course, not all projects dealt with abilities; however, reviews by Kleinfeld (1973), Bowd (1974), and Guilmet (1975) revealed a major interest in cognitive abilities by many researchers.

There are two identifiable paradigms to the study of abilities in the Arctic: One is the piagetian (Feldman, 1974; Dasen, 1975a, 1975b), and the other is broadly psychometric. Within the latter are those who have used tests to assess intelligence or general ability "levels" (e.g., Preston, 1964; Vernon, 1966, 1969) and those who have looked for "patterns" or "structure" of ability among specific tests (e.g., Berry, 1966; MacArthur, 1968a).

Whatever the approach taken, there seems to have been a common point of departure: the recognition of the adaptive value of visual, spatial, and practical abilities for hunter-gatherers in the Arctic. Because a similar argument has also been made for hunter-gatherer populations elsewhere in North America (e.g., Berry & Annis, 1974), in Australia (Kearins, 1976), and in Africa (van de Koppel, 1983), it is worth making the general line of argument explicit here. The first expression of the importance of this group of abilities was made by Vallee (1961), who argued that in the Arctic, "inhabitants must develop an exceptional sensitivity to minor variations in the perceptual field in order to survive" (p. 41); he also proposed that spatial and practical abilities may be well developed for similar functional reasons. Even earlier, ethnographic observations had indicated a well-developed cognitive representation of geographical space. For example, Galton (quoted in Werner, 1948), remarks on the almost geographical memory of an Eskimo whose feats were directly observed by a Captain Hall. With no aid except his memory, this Eskimo drew a map of a territory whose shores he had but once explored in his kayak. The strip of country was 1,100 miles long as the crow flies, but the coastline was at least six times this distance. A comparison of the Eskimo's rude map with an Admiralty chart printed in 1870 revealed a most unexpected agreement.

Similar skill has been found by Carpenter (1955, p. 131), who asked some present-day Inuit to "make sketches of the world as they conceived it"; the results were astonishingly accurate. Moreover, Bagrow (1948) has reported that the Inuit are capable of making depressions and elevations on their maps to represent the third dimension. The Inuit themselves consider the relief maps the more valuable, as giving a more accurate representation. Because the area is rugged and intersected by fjords and glaciers, relief maps help the nomadic Inuit more readily to survey and identify a given locality. Some of these maps have been estimated to cover areas as large as 250,000 square miles (Irwin, 1981), and anecdote has it that even British Admiralty charts were occasionally corrected on the basis of information contained in them. We are dealing here not with a rudimentary knowledge or ability but with a highly integrated conceptualisation of space and a sophisticated set of graphic conventions for representing this knowledge.

Actual testing for these visuospatial abilities was begun in the early 1960s by Berry (1966) and Vernon (1966), who independently administered a set of similar tests (*Witkin Embedded Figures*, *Kohs Blocks Designs*, *Raven's Progressive Matrices*, and various spatial tests). Results indicated a well-developed set of abilities in this domain (using as a criterion mean performance of European and African samples). There was also observed a pattern of intercorrelation among them (Berry, 1966), which suggested that they functioned as a cluster of abilities rather than discrete abilities independent from each other. This correlational pattern was identified as the "field-independent" cognitive style by Berry (1976), whereas Vernon (1969) preferred to interpret the correlations as one aspect of general intelligence. Subsequent work by MacArthur (1968a, 1968b, 1973, 1975, 1978) with Central (Canadian) Inuit and those in Greenland, and by Kleinfeld (1971) and

Forbes and Lonner (1980) in Alaska, confirmed this particular skill pattern among Inuit.

This generally high level of development of visuospatial abilities has usually been interpreted as a functional adaptation to the ecological situation in which they have developed. A corollary seems to be that in this very domain where sex differences are often found (Berry, 1975; Van Leeuwen, 1978), none appears to be present among the Inuit (Berry, 1966; MacArthur, 1967; Kleinfeld, 1971). It may be that ecological press is at work in such a pervasive way that all are culturally socialised and behaviourally trained so that these abilities are generally widespread in the population. Alternatively or, more likely, additionally, if at least some aspects of this ability cluster have some genetic links, the Inuit population may be biologically, as well as culturally and behaviourally, adapted to the Arctic habitat.

In contrast, Vernon (1969) and MacArthur (1975) have noted that verbal abilities seem to be developed to a lesser extent than the visuospatial abilities, again using performance relative to Eurocanadian norms as their criterion. This finding of lower verbal ability has not been replicated by Taylor and Skanes (1976) in a study of Inuit and Eurocanadians in Labrador. One must point out that in almost all of these studies, language abilities have been assessed in a second language (English). Hence, there is no clear-cut way to estimate *relative* differences in ability in the visual-spatial and verbal domains, either between cultural groups or within Native groups. Verbal test findings, though, correspond with both structured (e.g., Kleinfeld, 1974) and ethnographic observations of verbal production generally in the North (Hallowell, 1946; Honigmann, 1968), where words are often used sparingly, and a high verbal output is considered socially inappropriate (Cazden & John, 1969). Given that all tests of verbal ability were in a second language (English), we are left to infer from all the evidence what the ability findings might be in their first language. One exception to this general criticism (Mawhinney, 1983) was a vocabulary study with James Bay Cree that falls into the discussion of the Sub-Arctic culture area in the next section.

Within the piagetian tradition, Greenfield, Reich, and Olver (1966), Vernon (1969), Feldman (1974), and Dasen (1975a, 1975b) all employed various tasks related to the concrete operational stage. Although in Vernon's (1969) report, the Inuit schoolboys did not display conservation in 40% to 50% of the cases, Greenfield et al. (1966) reported levels of performance among Inuit that were equivalent to the "normal" performance of Eurocanadian schoolchildren. In the more extensive study of Dasen (1975a), a detailed examination was made of performance on a variety of conservation tasks (e.g., quantity and weight, seriation, reclassification, orders, rotation, horizontality) for 80 Canadian Inuit schoolchildren (10 in each group aged 6 to 14). A comparison was then made (Dasen, 1975b) between these results and those obtained by him in Australia and Africa on similar-size samples for each age. In this perspective, the Inuit children (as well as the hunting-based

Australian Aboriginal children) developed spatial operations earlier than the African sample; conversely at some (but not all) age levels, the African sample displayed conservation of quantity, weight, and volume (presumably ecologically adaptive for them) sooner than the Inuit and Aboriginal samples.

The picture for the Arctic area, then, generally is one in which one pattern of abilities seems to be well developed, relative to Euroamerican norms, and to the performance of other samples who have experienced a similar degree of exposure to acculturation from Euroamerican sources: The data includes a high performance on both piagetian and psychometric tests of visually based spatial, analytic, disembedding, and inductive abilities. Although there are some reports of lower levels of verbal ability, this has not been uniform and, as we have noted, represents second-language ability only. If this high spatial–low verbal difference proves valid for first language tests, the fact that it was predicated from an ecological analysis of life requirements, and that it corresponds to anthropological observations, lends some support for the concept of cultural differentiation.

Sub-Arctic

Many of the same ecological constraints we noted in the discussion of the Arctic region are also at work in the Sub-Arctic region: Hunting-and-gathering also predominates here, but now it is in the boreal forest rather than on the tundra and the sea. Only two language families (Athapaskan and Algonquian) are present in the region. Note, however, that one Algonquian group, the Plains Cree, have extended south and west into the Central Plains region, and other Algonquian speakers reside in the East region.

Represented in this region are the Algonquian-speaking peoples (Montagnais, the Naskapi of northern Quebec and Labrador, and the Cree, Ottawa, Algonquin, and Ojibwa in the midregions of Canada); among the Athapaskan speakers are the Chipewyan, Beaver, Carrier, Slave, Kaska, Dogrib, Hare, and Kutchin peoples (see Fig. 15.1). Given the common boreal forest habitat and the presence of only two extremely widespread language families, it is possible to attempt to make general statements about human abilities in this Sub-Arctic region, although it will be necessary to take local cultural and acculturational variations into account.

The Ojibwa (sometimes called Chippewa) are the largest Native group in North America (north of Mexico). Approximately 200,000 Ojibwa live in the Upper Great Lakes region, divided between the United States and Canada. In the United States, the Ojibwa are the third largest group of American Indians, numbering around 100,000 and 120,000 persons.

Between 60,000 and 100,000 Ojibwa live on more than 200 reserves and settlements in Canada, mainly in Ontario, but also in Manitoba and Saskatchewan. In addition, of 500,000 Metis (mixed blood) in Canada, approximately 100,000 (mostly Ojibwa-French) reside in Ontario (Frideres, 1974). In the United States the greatest concentrations of Ojibwa are in Minnesota, where about half (36,000) of the Indian population of the state live in the Twin Cities metro area (six counties encompassing Minneapolis–St. Paul), making it one of the largest urban concentrations of American Indians in the country.

Generally, Indian groups in this area seem to demonstrate unique *WISC* subtest profiles which reveal patterns unique to Indian groups. McShane and Plas (1982b, 1982c) applied the Bannatyne (1974) factor scheme to *WISC* scores of Ojibwa and Sioux children with school difficulties and found a pattern of performance different from that associated with samples of learning disabled children: Spatial scores were significantly greater than Sequential scores, which in turn exceeded Conceptual and Acquired Knowledge scores. The pattern was most evident within a subgroup of children (differentiated through use of the *Traditional Experience Scale* of McShane, 1980a) who experienced a more traditional Indian cultural heritage. Also focussing on discrete subtest patterns, Hollingshead and Clayton (1971a, 1971b) found that for Indian children in their study, male retarded readers scored lower on *Digit Span* and *Similarities* than did females; female retarded readers scored lower on *Block Design* than male counterparts; and all readers were weak in vocabulary and strong in *Block Design, Picture Completion*, and *Coding*. Following *WISC* assessments of 210 white and Indian children in Montana, Peck (1972) reported that the white sample scored significantly higher on all subtests except for *Block Design*. He also found that Indian males scored significantly higher than Indian females on *Picture Completion*. In a longitudinal study designed to identify specific intellectual and psycholinguistic skills related to the achievement gains of Ojibwa reservation children, McShane and Plas (1982c) found the mean Verbal scale score for a group of 35 Indian children to be 90.5 ($SD = 13.5$). Although certain subtest scores from the *Illinois Test of Psycholinguistic Abilities* (*ITPA*) were found to be more predictive of reading and mathematics achievement gains than were *WISC-R* subtest scores for this group, a six-variable combination of *WISC-R* subtest scores (*Block Design, Object Assembly, Vocabulary, Comprehension, Picture Arrangement, Information*) was able to capture a substantial portion of the variance associated with language achievement gains for these Indian children. The *Object Assembly* subtest score was also found to be predictive of reading achievement gain when used with *ITPA Visual Association* and *Auditory Closure* scores. The *WISC-R Picture Arrangement* subtest made a substantial contribution to predicting mathematics gain scores when used in combination with the *ITPA Grammatic Closure* and *Sound Blending* subtests. The fact that *Block Design* and *Object Assembly* can predict achievement gains in such verbally oriented subject areas as reading and language may be due to a tendency of Ojibwa children to overutilise spatial processing strengths.

In another Ojibwa study, McShane and Plas (1982a) reported that Ojibwa children with a history of frequent middle-ear disease involvement scored lower on *ITPA* auditory subtests than on visual subtests. Such uneven auditory–visual performance was not observed in Ojibwa children who had experienced fewer episodes of otitis media. Other specific *ITPA* subtest profile differences between the two groups of Ojibwa children were found to be significant. The same two authors (McShane and Plas, 1982c) completed another separate study with Ojibwa children using the *ITPA*. Analyses indicated high intercorrelations (.62 to .94) between specific *ITPA* subtests. Subjected to multiple regression, the subtests accounted for about 65% of the variance in *Wechsler Intelligence Scale* IQ. Three *ITPA* subtests accounted for 48% of the variance of yearly growth in language skills and 68% of the variance relating to changes in mathematics skills.

The only other reported speech and language work with the Ojibwa was by Larkin (1970) who compared 50 reservation and 50 urban Ojibwa kindergarten and second-grade students with 50 white pupils on the *Boehm Test of Basic Concepts (BTBC)*. Few differences were found in *BTBC* performance at kindergarten, but highly significant differences between all groups (urban Ojibwa–reservation Ojibwa, white–Ojibwa) were found at second grade.

In a cross-sectional study of 100 Cree and Ojibwa (Chippewa) children, 7 through 15 years of age, St. John, Krichev, and Bawman (1976) found *WISC Performance* IQs to be in the normal range for all ages while *Verbal* IQs were lower. *Performance-Verbal* IQ differences diminished with age; familiarity with the English language increased the *Verbal* IQ but had little effect on *Performance* IQ. A significant correlation between IQ and school grades was found only for 9- to 10-year-olds, a somewhat atypical result.

As we noted in the Arctic section, an ecological analysis can be made for the two regions (Arctic and Sub-Arctic), and similar predictions result. In the monograph by Berry (1976), three groups from the Sub-Arctic region were studied (James Bay Cree, Ojibwa, and Carrier). Generally high levels of visuospatial abilities were predicted, but some ability variation across groups was also expected due to eco-cultural variations (relative reliance on hunting, tightness of the social system, and socialisation practices). A fourth Amerindian contrast group included in the overall design was the Tsimshian, from the West Coast region, where these eco-cultural factors were such that they led to a prediction of lower visuospatial ability (minimal reliance on hunting). Results were complicated by variations in acculturation to Euro-canadian lifestyle (especially the presence of formal schooling). When this was controlled for, the hypotheses received general confirmation. Among the Sub-Arctic samples, visuospatial abilities were by Eurocanadian norms well developed (but not as high as among the Inuit), and within this particular study, the Cree scored higher than the Tsimshian and the Carrier.

The study in Alaska by Forbes and Lonner (1980) mentioned in the last section also showed ecologically consistent differences in test performance: Athapaskan children scored higher in spatial tests than the Tlingit and Haida children, who belong to the West Coast region and are not substantially involved in hunting activity. Supplementary evidence comes from Schubert and Cropley (1972), who found northern Cree to have high performance scores (including many visuospatial tests) on an intelligence test battery. Those with initial low performance scores showed substantial gain after brief training, a finding that confirms most cross-cultural experience with tests.

Concordant with the conclusions of Schubert and Cropley (1972) are persistent reports of a differential between performance, or "apparatus," measures and verbal measures among Amerindians (see McShane & Plas, 1984a, for a review). However, as noted in the Arctic section (and by Brandt, 1984, in commenting on McShane & Plas, 1984a), findings of lower verbal scores relative to performance scores mean little when verbal abilities are assessed in a second language and are calibrated by alien norms. The one published attempt to assess verbal ability in the mother tongue (Mawhinney, 1983) found a small (+ .28, N = 40) significant positive correlation between a *Cree Picture Vocabulary Test* and *Kohs Blocks* among the James Bay Cree. However, as an exploratory study on Cree vocabulary, it offers no evidence about the relative levels of achievement on verbal and performance tasks in the absence of a wider normative context. More important, perhaps, was Mawhinney's finding no sex differences in Cree vocabulary performance. Other work in the Sub-Arctic region includes a search by West and MacArthur (1964) for tests with the "least cultural bias," which may be suitable for assessing Indian and Metis students. The test recommended as exhibiting the least cultural bias is *Raven's Progressive Matrices*, while verbal measures were considered less suitable. A subsequent report by MacArthur (1968a) confirmed this view of less bias in performance (and "reasoning from nonverbal stimuli") measures than on verbal ones. Of course, "less bias" means in this case "less different" from Eurocanadian norms. Nowadays, *bias* is a technical term, as Poortinga and van der Flier demonstrate in Chapter 6. Further evidence for the relatively superior achievement on performance tests derives from the work of Knowles and Boersma (1968) with Cree, and of Cropley and Cardey (1975), also with Cree. However, one study with Cree (Wiltshire & Gray, 1969), while revealing good performance on the *Draw-a-Man* test, also revealed a lower performance on *Raven's Progressive Matrices*; no verbal measures were employed. In light of inconsistent evidence from a number of different sources, some caution is needed in evaluating any broad generalisation about the widespread differential development of verbal and spatial abilities from second-language versus performance test results in the Sub-Arctic region.

West Coast and Mountain

Little information appears to be available for this area; at least, studies attempting to relate abilities to the ecological and cultural context are sparse. We have already noted in earlier sections that for these largely sedentary and socially stratified peoples there is some evidence that performance test scores appear to be lower than in the Arctic and Sub-Arctic regions (Berry & Annis, 1974; Forbes & Lonner, 1980).

One study does address the visuospatial abilities of Northwest peoples (Coast Salish and Kwakiutl of British Columbia by Gaddes, McKenzie, & Barnsley, 1968). Based on the notion that their well-known art forms might give them a set of learning experiences conducive to high spatial performance, the authors administered four apparatus tests (*Wechsler Block Designs*, *Goodenough Draw-a-Man*, *Porteus Mazes*, and *Cattell Culture-Fair*, short form) to four groups of elementary school children (Eurocanadian rural, Eurocanadian urban, Salish suburban, and Kwakiutl rural isolated). Analyses of variance indicated significant variation across groups on all but the *Draw-a-Man* test; however, *t* tests revealed no significant group differences, except for the *Cattell Culture-Fair Test*. Thus, although the studies reviewed earlier revealed some test performance differences between Northwest groups and other Native groups, this study suggests that Northwest performance in apparatus, as distinct from paper-and-pencil, tests, approximates that of Eurocanadians.

Two studies by Bowd (1972, 1973) included a Northwest group (Bella Bella) of children in comparative studies of school achievement and mechanical aptitude. In the first study, performance on *Raven's Progressive Matrices* was notably lower than among other groups (e.g., Eurocanadian and Cree). In the second study, the Bella Bella group exhibited generally higher scores on a Verbal factor score, but lower scores on two Mechanical factor scores (one dealing with mechanical background and the other dealing with mechanical activities such as hobbies, Meccano, etc.). To the extent that mechanical aptitude rests on some underlying performance-domain abilities, it is possible to employ this pattern (high verbal, low mechanical) as further evidence in the general picture we have already noted for Northwest Coastal peoples.

Central

Psychological research with Central Indians has had a long history, beginning with early work by Telford (1932), who administered the *Goodenough Intelligence Test* to 225 Sioux pupils. The Indian mean (88) fell between white (100) and black (77–79) mean scores. However, on a second test, the *Mare and Foal* administered to 35 Sioux pupils, mean scores exceeded those of the other two groups, perhaps because of their greater familiarity with horses, the stimulus content of that test. Garth and Smith (1937), using a figural and a language test with the same subjects, found that the performance of Indian children was consistently closer to white performance on the *Pintner–Paterson* performance test than on the verbal test, and that IQ scores on the performance test were 10 to 14 points higher than those on the verbal test. Grace Arthur (1941) administered the *Arthur Test* and the *Stanford–Binet* to Central Indian children of elementary and high school age, and found the median IQ to be considerably higher on the *Arthur Test*. The *Grace Arthur Performance Test of Intelligence* (a battery of representational or so-called nonverbal tests), yielded, on a representative sample of Indian pupils from six tribes, an average IQ score of 100.2, slightly above the national average for whites. As part of this study, a group of 30 Sioux pupils on the Pine Ridge Reservation obtained an average IQ score of 102.8. Exactly the same group, however, tested a year later with the *Kuhlman–Anderson Test*, a verbal test requiring reading ability, obtained an average IQ score of 82.5. Cattell (1940) experimented with the *Stanford–Binet*, the *American Council on Education's Psychological Examination* (arithmetical section), the *Cattell Culture-Free Intelligence Test*, and the *Grace Arthur Point Performance Scale*. He concluded that the *Arthur* test was more "culture-free" than any of the others.

In more recent times, these early trends have been confirmed. Peck (1972) found differences between white and Indian children's scores on the *WISC* in Montana public schools. White children scored higher on all subtests except *Block Design* and *Object Assembly*, and Indian males scored significantly higher on *Picture Completion* and *Picture Arrangement* than Indian females. More specific to the Sioux are the studies of Dorsch (1980) and Wakefield (1982). The purpose of Dorsch's study was to examine the factor structure of the *WISC-R* for a reservation population to provide evidence for its construct validity. In accomplishing this, Dorsch also found that 90% of the Sioux reservation children had performance IQ scores greater than verbal IQ scores compared to a 50% occurrence among normative samples. Dorsch speculates that the scores his study reported may be related to a field-independent cognitive style. However, once again, we must remember that these verbal measures were taken in a second language, and that regression effects are embedded in these percentages.

Wakefield tested Indian children attending a Catholic boarding school to determine the relationship between scoring patterns on the *WISC-R* and the *Matching Familiar Figures Test*. A developmental trend was reported, but sex was not a category that produced significant mean differences. Wakefield concluded that reflectivity and fast-accurate problem-solving strategies are characteristic of these Indian children and that there was a 12-point or more performance score superiority compared to verbal scores on the *WISC-R*. Performance superiority on apparatus tests is again found in very recent studies of Sioux intelligence. Browne (1984) reported a study of *WISC-R* scoring patterns of approximately 200 Indian children (ages 6–16) representing all the nine tribes in South Dakota, one in North Dakota, and one in Nebraska. Analysis of subtest specificity, means profiles and subtest scatter, and factor structure revealed a pattern of *WISC-R* performance different from that of the standardisation population. Significant Performance–Verbal scale differences showed relative strength on performance subtests. However, these observed differences are difficult to interpret because *Picture Completion* and *Coding* seemed to hold a different position for these children in the factor structure of the *WISC-R* than for the standardisation population. *Picture Completion* showed a high degree of specificity rather than contributing to the Perceptual Organisation factor, and *Coding* did not contribute to the Freedom from Distractibility factor. Browne (1984) decided that the appearance of these two subtests in an inverse relationship in a fourth factor represents opposite ends of an information-processing continuum. She related her empiricism to a model of right–left hemisphere differential functioning.

Kaufman (1984) describes the results of two studies regarding the use of the *Kaufman Assessment Battery for Children* with American Indian students. The Sioux children in Brokenleg's (1983) sample were more integrated into American society, attended regular public schools, and spoke English well. Naglieri's (1982) group of Navajo children lived on a reservation in an isolated community of 1,700, the majority spoke primarily Navajo, and less than half lived in dwellings that had running water. All were tested by a Navajo examiner (Naglieri & Kamphaus, 1983). The Sioux and Native groups earned virtually identical mean standard scores on the simultaneous processing and nonverbal subscales, both scoring at about the normative mean of 100. Their subtest profiles on these scales were also highly similar, both groups scored above 10 on *Gestalt Closure*, *Triangles*, and *Spatial Memory*, and below 10 on *Matrix Analogies*, *Photoseries*, and *Hand Movements*. Their strength was in visual-spatial abilities. They showed less developed skill in integration of sequential and simultaneous processes and reasoning.

The Sioux children displayed no discrepancy in their habits of processing information, but the Navajo group scored a striking 12 points higher on "simultaneous" compared with "sequential" processing tasks. This discrepancy may be illusory, however, and may not necessarily reflect a superiority in simultaneous processing. Examination of the subtest profile reveals extremely depressed scores in three subtests: *Number Recall*, *Word Order*, and *Riddles*. All three involve auditory stimuli and demand good verbal comprehension skills. The low scores may well reflect a limited proficiency in English (see Keats & Keats, Chapter 11, for similar findings among migrants to Australia), and could be underestimates of their true ability. The only valid global scores for this group of Navajos were probably the simultaneous processing and the apparatus standard scores. Because answers given in Navajo are acceptable for subtests like *Gestalt Closure* or *Arithmetic*, and Navajo instructions can be used during the teaching items of mental-processing subtests, these children were not unduly penalised on most *KABC* tasks. However, their low scores on *Word Order*, *Number Recall*, and *Riddles*, and their *WISC-R* verbal IQ of 74.9 compared to a performance IQ of 102.8, might be interpreted primarily as an index of their skill in the English language, not as a measure of their intelligence or of ability differentials.

McAreavey (1975) studied 100 educationally handicapped South Dakota

Sioux children. They were administered the *WISC* and *Wide Range Achievement Test of Reading* (*WRAT*). The purpose of the study was to determine the extent of "fairness" or "bias" exhibited by selective intelligence and achievement tests when applied to a selective sample of educationally handicapped South Dakota Sioux Indian children. Results suggested that significant differences do exist between verbal and performance IQs, but again using second-language norms. Ordering discrepancies in the scaling of items occurred on five subtests, suggesting item bias. All *WISC* subtests correlated positively with *WRAT* reading scores. The findings revealed significant differences on IQ across age, and females at ages 9–11 did not show the same decline in performance as males on the verbal subtests. There was an important main effect of reading skill on both full verbal and performance IQ: As reading skill increased, significant differences emerged for full verbal and performance IQs. To conclude, when controls on language proficiency are built into experiments that assess performance and verbal IQ differences, variations in second-language skills are seen to mediate test performance.

East

As in the Central culture area, much of the psychological work on abilities in the East is unrelated to ecological or cultural factors; rather, there is a concern for general abilities and their possible relationships with the educational system introduced from Europe. This situation is probably a function of the very early (and in many cases overwhelming) acculturative influences in this region, which have rendered the original forms of eco-cultural adaptation somewhat irrelevant. Moreover, some studies group various Indian bands together in their samples, so that a number of cultural variables may be lost from view. Very early studies of this sort (e.g., Jamieson, 1928; Joblin, 1947) have not been reviewed in our analysis.

One published study (Turner & Penfold, 1952) was an examination of Oneida, Delaware, and Chippewa schoolchildren in southwestern Ontario, using three general tests (*Otis Quick-Scoring Mental Ability Test, Henmon–Nelson Test of Mental Ability*, and the *WISC* and the *Raven's Progressive Matrices*). In addition to the 240 Indian children, the study also included 215 Eurocanadian children. Generally all scores were lower (many significantly so) for the Indian children relative to the Eurocanadian children. However, on the *WISC*, Indian children did as well on the performance scale as the Eurocanadian children. Although the *Otis* is a figural test and the *Henmon–Nelson* is a verbal test, there is no report on a parallel difference on these tests (between verbal and figural performance) in the article.

A second study in the same general region (southwestern Ontario) was carried out by Dilling in 1965 with 357 Indian children (band unspecified) and more than 1,000 Eurocanadian children, using three tests (*Metropolitan Advanced Reading Test, Dominion Survey of Arithmetic Fundamentals*, and the *Terman Non-Language Multi-Mental Test*). Once again a general dif-

ference was found between Indian and Eurocanadian children, but there is
no report regarding relative performance on the tests within the Indian
sample.

A final study (Marjoribanks, 1972) included a sample of Iroquois (nation
not specified), in a comparative study of Canadian students (Protestant,
Jewish, French, and Indian) using *SRA Primary Mental Abilities*. Once
again, Indian children performed relatively poorly, and once again spatial
(and reasoning) scores tended to be higher than verbal (in English) and number scores.

In all three studies, these generally lower scores were explained in terms
of *social* factors (e.g., status, language at home, attitudes, degree of integration of the schools), but there was no attempt to relate performance to
traditional ecological or cultural factors, or to predict performance from an
analysis of them.

Southwest

The development of visual-motor perception, as measured by the *Bender
Gestalt Test*, has been examined for various Southwest Indian groups (Taylor & Thweat, 1972; Vincent, 1975). Taylor and Thweat, for example, discovered that 6- and 7-year-old Navajo children lagged behind a Euroamerican control group in visual-motor perception; however, by ages 11
to 12, the differences between the *Bender Test* performances of Indian and
white children had disappeared. Both groups had matured in the visual-motor
area and were able to copy the *Bender* designs with few, if any, errors.

The *Draw-a-Man (DAM)* is among the few tests for which fairly extensive
data are available for Native peoples. Since it was first described (Goodenough, 1926), the *DAM* test has become widely used to compare children
from various cultural groups. It is easily administered, requiring only a piece
of paper and a pencil; the instructions are "Draw a man, the best you can."
The test is scored by counting the number and accuracy of details in the
figure drawn. Aesthetic merit counts for very little, except that representation of correct proportions and evidence of good motor coordination earn
some points. The test might be described as one of perception, or attention
given to one's environment, and "production," or skill in drawing
conventions.

Havighurst (1944) thought that cultural environment affects the performance of children on the *DAM*. Dennis (1942), suggested that the remarkably
high *DAM* scores obtained by Hopi Indian boys derive from the emphasis
Hopi culture places on male art skills. In a later study, Dennis (1966) tried
to determine specific cultural factors influencing children's *DAM* performance. Goodenough and Harris (1950) observed that the test may not be
suited to comparing children across cultures but still may be useful in ranking
children within a culture.

Cundick (1970), using the *DAM* and *WISC*, tested about 100 Southwest

Indian schoolchildren from kindergarten to grade 6, concluding that the relatively normal performance IQs for this group on the *Wechsler Scales* and the *DAM*s commended their use for gathering normative data from children in the Southwest United States.

Beyond the Southwest area, there has been extensive use of the *DAM* as part of the National Study of American Indian Education in which 1,700 American Indian primary schoolchildren, representing 14 tribal groups living in 12 states, were surveyed (Levensky, 1970). In this important study children in grades 1–6 were pupils in Bureau of Indian Affairs, public, and private (parochial) day and boarding schools. Whole classrooms were tested at once. Analyses of the 1,700 *DAM* protocols were presented by sex, age, reservation, urban, and tribal group, and geographic area. Levensky concluded that between ages 6 and 8 years Indian *DAM* performance was superior to that of Euroamerican children, but was inferior between 8 and 13 years. Tribal group differences were evident; and *DAM* scores were positively correlated with teacher ratings of student scholastic performance.

Kirk (1972) reviewed several studies of Indian children's psycholinguistic abilities as measured by the *Illinois Test of Psycholinguistic Abilities (ITPA)*. One study involved first- and third-grade Papago Indian children (Lombardi, 1970); the second, 53 Navajo and Pueblo first-grade children (Garber, 1968); and the third, a group of mentally handicapped Sioux children together with 50 comparable non-Indian handicapped children. Indian group averages were compared with the means for black children and the original non-Indian standardisation sample. Kirk inferred from these mean comparisons that Indians possess superior ability in visual sequential memory ability compared to black and Anglo children. Moreover, these visual memory abilities were better developed in the Indian samples than the other abilities in the battery.

Along with several other intelligence tests, Peters (1963) administered the *WISC* to 59 Hopi Indian children. Scores on all tests significantly correlated with one another and a definite curvilinear relationship between age and IQ was obtained. Children aged 7 to 9 years obtained higher scores on all tests and subtests than younger and older Hopi children. Sachs (1974) obtained *WISC* protocols for 33 elementary and 38 junior high Mescalero Apache students. Younger females scored significantly lower than the older females and the younger males on all IQ scales. A variety of sex- and age-related differences were found for individual subtest scores. The author also found that these children obtained lower-scaled score means on the performance subtests and higher-scaled score means on the verbal subtests when compared to Cundick's (1970) Indian subjects.

Thurber (1976) tested 44 Navajo children in kindergarten to grade 3 using the *WISC*, and obtained differences in mean-scaled scores for boys and girls (VIQ = 66.3 and 67.6, PIQ = 97.5 and 88.2, respectively). However, Cundick (1970) reported that the Verbal scores of a group of Southwest Indian children did not increase significantly after grade 2. Sabatino, Hayden, and

Kelling (1972), using the *WISC*, reported that Navajo children ($N = 33$) referred for special class placement experienced school learning problems predominantly due to a lack of knowledge of the linguistic rules subserving the English language, rather than to perceptual difficulties. These results are constrained by small sample sizes.

Other studies utilising the *WISC* have reported normative performance IQs and poor internal consistency for Navajo and Apache on the *Vocabulary* subtest (Guilliams, 1975); variation in PIQ–VIQ differences based on reading, sex, and age (McAreavey, 1975); *WISC* achievement level congruence (Rohner, 1965) and interrelationships of *WISC* performance scores and independence, need achievement, and affiliation (Query, Query, & Singh, 1975; Davis & Cropley, 1976). Finally, Conrad (1974) in a "treatment" experiment, administered the *WISC* to 80 fourth- and fifth-grade Papago Indian children under a reinforcement condition and under standard administration, by Anglo and Papago examiners. Children scored significantly better with reinforcement. Type of examiner had no effect, nor were there sex effects. *Block Design* scores were significantly higher than other subtests.

Relatively few research studies report use of the *WISC-R* for research purposes with American Indian groups. In one study representative of this body of literature, Hynd, Kramer, Quackenbush, Conner, and Weed (1979) administered the *WISC-R* to 44 primary schoolchildren for whom Navajo rather than English was the primary language, and all of whom attended a reservation boarding school. Test means obtained were 64, 95, and 77 for the Verbal, Performance, and Full scales, respectively. The lowest scores occurred on the *WISC-R Verbal* subtests tapping receptive and expressive English skills. The authors suggested that Performance subtests (*Picture Completion*, *Block Design*, *Object Assembly*, and *Codes*) seemed to provide an adequate and generally nonbiased estimate of potential. Ertz (in press) administered the *WISC-R* to 24 age and sex matched pairs of Indian and non-Indian learning-impaired students with a mean age of $10\frac{1}{2}$ (*Digit Span* and *Codes* were not administered). Indian children scored lower on *Information*, *Similarities*, *Vocabulary*, and *Comprehension*, suggesting to the author a deficit in Verbal Comprehension skills for Indian learning-impaired youngsters. Ertz concluded that results from *WISC-R* studies did not provide sufficient data on construct validity in Indian groups to allow clinicians to interpret *WISC-R* profile configurations for individual American Indian students.

In comparing *WISC-R* domain study data produced by the standardisation sample with the intercorrelations of scores for blacks, Chicanos, and Papago Indians, Reschly (1978) found a two-factor solution to be sufficient for the Indian data. The first factor was composed of all Verbal Scale subtests except *Digit Span*, while all Performance Scale subtests except *Codes* were related to the second factor. When the Kaufman (1979) three-factor solution was applied to the Papago data, the first and second factors were related to the Verbal and Performance scale subtests, respectively, while the third factor contained only the Codes subtest.

Zarske, Moore, and Peterson (1981) analysed *WISC-R* factors derived from previously diagnosed samples of learning-disabled Navajo ($N = 192$) and Papago ($N = 50$) children. Two factor solutions for both groups closely resembled that found by Kaufman and Reschly, where Factor 1 was composed of Verbal Scale subtests and Factor 2 of Performance Scale subtests. The author concluded that *WISC-R* is an appropriate measure of general intelligence function for both learning-disabled groups.

In a more recent study using the *WISC-R*, Reynolds and Willson (1982) contrasted subtest performances for Mexican-Americans ($N = 243$), Native American Papagos ($N = 240$), and white children ($N = 252$) independent of overall differences in general ability level. The authors attempted to minimise the effect of the General Ability factor through use of a partial point-biserial correlation between race and individual subtest performance, where total performance was the controlling variable. This was done to evaluate the extent to which performance differences might have been because of specific ability factor differences rather than attributed to differences in a General Intelligence factor. On all subtests except *Mazes*, the absolute level of performance rank ordered whites, Mexican-Americans, and Papagos. When controlled for these overall differences, whites showed higher performance than the Papago on all verbal subtests. Once overall level of performance was equated, no white–Mexican-American differences appeared on any other subtests. The Papago, however, performed significantly higher than whites on *Block Design* and *Mazes*. The authors noted that both sets of results sharply contrast with black–white comparisons. These show, once overall level of performance is controlled, no difference between blacks and whites on the Verbal factor, whites exceeding blacks on the Spatial-Utilisation factor; blacks perform better on memory capacity tasks such as *Digit Span*.

Abilities and acculturation

The picture painted up to this point has been largely one of human abilities seen within geographic regions, as an adaptation to ecological and cultural influences. However, Native North Americans have been undergoing a process of acculturation to outside influences (mainly of European origin) for up to 500 years, depending on the group. This process has generally placed them in a position of being culturally dominated, to the extent that one can expect two consequences for human abilities. In one, acculturation creates a cultural situation in which abilities are likely to shift towards a pattern more like the Euroamerican dominant group; here, abilities actually "improve" in the ethnocentric sense of becoming closer to the norms of the larger society. In the other, acculturation can erode, and even destroy, the cultural and psychological functioning characteristic of a people prior to contact. A serious performance decline in many domains, including those sampled by psychological tests of ability, is the predictable outcome. Here, rather than "improvement" there may be a "decline" due to cultural disorganisation or disruption.

Moreover, Native ways of life have altered drastically with changing ecological conditions. Among historically recorded changes are deteriorated physical status due to disease, violence, and accident; physical containment and geographical limitation; alterations of sociopolitical structure and relationships; and transformations of some surface characteristics of family structure.

This remaking of the environment contrasts with the enduring of certain cultural structures and processes. These include the maintenance of some aspects of traditional structures of adult–adult and adult–child interactions, and some continuity of traditional forms of relations between mother and child. Some research also suggests that individual coping styles derive to a great extent from old cultural forms (McShane, 1980b, 1986a, 1987a).

From description to cause

In the task of regionally categorising the material on Native peoples, trends emerge. For example, most of the studies have been imposed from outside the culture context, and only a handful have begun with the culture as an element in the design of the study. One can reasonably interpret the frequency of test use in a community as an index of exposure to social change. The dysynchronous occurrence of social change and cultural continuity creates difficulties, and the act of administering a test is a microcosm of them. Individual testing, or the "no collaboration" instruction in group tests, isolates the subject from cultural norms, from the press of ethnohistory, and from the obligations of a traditional lifestyle.

Although this example may seem to be a parenthesis, it serves to dramatise the whole range of rationalisations of minority test results that are possible, on a scientific continuum from "straightforward" negative abnormality to "subtle" exotic difference that admits no explanation because the specimen cannot be classified. In the section that follows, we seek to establish ground rules for interpreting the findings that have already been sorted regionally. These causal explanations are recognisably psychological; and they have been imposed on the data by members of a culture whose theory of knowledge has developed without reference to the systems of thought that define Native cultures. Consequently, as the studies unfold for a second time and others are introduced, we are able to reveal and evaluate both their scientific utility and their social sensitivity. Although the first is the important criterion, the very nature of cross-cultural enquiry invalidates material that, in a quest for cause, is oblivious to important social variables.

Classes of explanation of Native abilities

The evidence for test performance variation that identified Native peoples as distinct cultural enclaves within North America appears to be substantial. The reasons for such differentiation have nevertheless been many and varied. To bring order to the discussion, a classification of the types of explanation offered by researchers for these differences was developed by McShane (1983a). He refers to them as "D" models. He distinguishes two qualitatively different types of model. The first is a *norm-referent* model that views Native performance as necessarily "deviant" from the Euroamerican standard, and by implication, is inferior. Generally, but by no means always, writers have blamed genetic or physiological deficit, social disadvantage, cultural deprivation and disorganisation, and intergenerational disruption for poor test performance. A distinct value system is expressed in the use of such explanations. They carry with them a form of stigmatisation of Native identity. A less value-oriented position is seen in two other ecologically consonant frameworks for causal attribution. These account for test performances in groups as *differences* in cultural contexts that affect the *development* of abilities.

Genetic deficit. To account for test score differences between groups by invoking genetic deficit in one of them is a long inference. It is such a big stride from the data when only external signs of genetic variation are the criteria, that it is today held to be unscientific, as Thoday's (1969) definitive paper articulated so well. No surprise accompanies the observation that most of the studies giving genetic reasons for test differences were published before 1948. These included work by Rowe in 1914, Paschal and Sullivan (1925), Fitzgerald and Ludeman (1926), Jamieson and Sandiford (1938), and Haught (1934).

Many of these sources used as an index of deficit the "amount of Indian blood" in the individual, by tracing the racial origins of parents and grandparents. Groups were then identified according to their "Indian blood" proportions, and test scores, the dependent variables, were compared. All the studies listed claimed that the more "Indian blood" in the individual, the greater the probability of a low test score. They typically administered English-language group tests or unmodified *Stanford–Binet* subtests to their subjects.

Not all early researchers encountered Indian groups that performed below white norms. Notable exceptions were Klineberg (1928), Garth and Smith (1937), and Arthur (1941). The common ground in these studies was the use of *apparatus* (performance) tasks, and figural rather than English-language tests. The unusual aspect among them was Grace Arthur's deliberate construction of intellective tasks that had origins in the observed daily experiences of the subjects. All produced consistent findings that led to a single conclusion: Given apparatus, and non-English context for problem solving,

Indian subjects produced scores that were not only equal to white norms but occasionally exceeded them. Moreover, scores showed no decline with increase of "Indian blood" in Klineberg's work; and he observed a speed-accuracy trade-off in the response patterns of the subjects. Such habitual strategies are, of course, transmitted from the Native culture, whereas speeded contexts in testing are inherited, willy-nilly, from the dominant culture.

Although the *hypothesis* of covariance between genetic programmes and mental functions is valid, the *evidence* presented as a test of it in Amerindian data is far less credible as a test of this hypothesis than it is of another, more plausible one. The key to understanding its diverse and inconsistent empirical findings lies not in pervasive, invariant functions in the subjects but in the choice and use of tools by psychologists. When these vary, so does the test performance of the subject, and in a predictable direction. Testing in a second language medium produces depressed scores. There is, indeed, nothing remarkable about that.

Physiological deficit. Dispositional qualities have traditionally been associated with differences on test performance, the most common being the sex of the subject. Some physiological impairments are more precise markers than others, so that inferences from their incidence in groups to causal influence are more secure than many. We assess the importance of firm evidence of specific physiological deficit in Native peoples. In turn we examine *otitis media*, *visual defects*, *fetal alcohol syndrome*, and *lead poisoning* as high-risk agents in the physiological impairment of cognitive functioning in Amerindian groups.

One of the most serious health problems affecting Natives is otitis media (middle-ear infection). In fact, in every year except one since 1961, when it was first recorded as a reportable disease, otitis media has been the most common disease among North American Indians. Stewart (1975) found that during the 7-year period for which complete data were available, first visits for otitis media increased from a rate of 5.7% to 12.3% of the Indian population. One in every five of the children seen on first visit progressed to the chronic state of the disease if left untreated; and there was a reservoir of more than 22,000 unoperated patients in potential need of otologic survey and 13,000 in need of hearing aids. McShane (1979b, 1982) reviewed the prevalence and etiology of otitis media in Native children. At the same time he evaluated the psychoeducational consequences of prevention and intervention in the disease. A number of variables (environmental, dispositional, and degree of exposure to risk) seemed to be implicated in its etiology among Native peoples. Schaefer's (1971) contribution to our understanding of the issues began with two observations. First, Inuit living in "acculturated" or Eurocanadian-like settlements suffered more from otitis media than "traditional" or isolated groups. Second, the generation born before World War I showed little or no incidence of middle-ear disease.

Through further epidemiological surveys he confirmed this higher infection rate among Inuit infants raised outside traditional encampments; and he isolated a possible cause in the availability of cows' milk, lacking possible protective elements in mothers' milk. Only acculturating groups bottle-fed their infants. The hypothesis of bottle-feeding as a precipitator of middle-ear disease in Indian children has additional visibility in the reports of Manning, Avery, and Ross (1974) and of Timmermans and Gerson (1980).

The high incidence of otitis media within Indian populations probably contributes to learning problems. McShane and Plas (1982a), and others (Ling, McCoy, & Levinson, 1969; Kaplan, Fleshman, Bender, Baum, & Clark, 1973; McShane, 1979a, 1979b, 1982), have linked episodes of otitis media and subsequent hearing loss to reductions in language ability, lower academic achievement in reading, mathematics, and language areas, and to other weaknesses in psycholinguistic skills.

Hearing loss following otitis media is another physiological condition occurring at almost epidemic rates among North American Indian and Inuit children aged 0 to 2 (Stewart, 1975; McShane, 1982; McShane & Plas, 1982a; Gottleib & Green, 1984). Research workers noting a relationship between dysfunctions in language development and a history of otitis media, have begun to suspect that the development of oral-linguistic processing skills may be retarded by recurrent bouts of the disease and the associated intermittent episodes of mild to moderate hearing loss (Holm & Kunze, 1969). We can now consider the evidence for this claim.

Otitis media is most common in Indian children during the first 2 years of life; and this is the critical period for language development. Kaplan et al. (1973) followed health charts for 489 Alaskan Inuit children from birth to the age of 12 months; 76% of them had experienced one or more episodes of otitis media. On the *WISC*, the total sample obtained a mean Verbal IQ of 77 and a mean Performance IQ of 98. Those with conductive hearing loss, or loss greater than 25 db, achieved significantly lower Verbal scores than did children with no history of otitis media and no hearing loss. Even more telling, the greater the number of infections suffered by the child, the less likelihood of a high Verbal score. Children sustaining fewer than four episodes during the first 2 years of life obtained a Verbal IQ of 77, while those with four or more episodes achieved a mean score of 71. Children who suffered hearing loss because of the disease were delayed significantly in school compared to unaffected children as measured by grade placement and achievement tests. This gap tended to widen as children proceeded through succeeding grade levels. In a related study using *WPPSI* and *WISC-R* data, McShane and Plas (1982a) divided a group of Ojibwa in half, based on the kind and number of otitis media episodes sustained in younger childhood. A significant correlation was found between group membership and *Weschler* Verbal–Performance scale *difference* scores; those who had a history of more than four episodes tended to produce larger difference scores than whose who had sustained fewer than four occurrences. With such evidence available, the influence of otitis media history on Indian *Wechsler Scale* performances needs to be systematically investigated and described. The impact of this most common Indian health problem on the developing language skills of Indian children is pertinent to *Wechsler Scale* performances and for educational achievement where listening is a critical skill.

Moreover, classroom coping skills are adversely affected by poor *vision*; and there is evidence that Indian groups are at risk in this domain. Hamilton (1976) found six times as many Indian children as non-Indian children entering the school system with a vision handicap (usually not detected before fourth grade). Even when their vision problems were detected and treated, the majority of Indian children (57%), compared to a minority of non-Indian children (22%), did not wear their glasses.

Finally, we consider physiological impairments that result from prolonged exposure to two quite different substances; *alcohol* and *lead*. Because alcoholism is widespread among many Indian groups (Wallace, 1973), *fetal alcohol syndrome* (FAS) cannot be overlooked as a possible physiological contributor to the learning difficulties experienced by many Indian children. May (1981), director of the Indian Health Service's FAS programme, described FAS as a pattern of malformations which is found in children born to mothers who drink excessively during pregnancy. May ranked FAS the number one cause of permanent mental retardation in the United States. Drinking by Indian children and adolescents also leads to impairment of intellectual abilities (Jones, 1975; Streissguth, 1977; Streissguth, Herman, & Smith, 1978).

Apart from self-induced and uterine physiological impairment, involuntary exposure to noxious materials in the environment can cause brain damage. For example, Gregory and Mohan (1977) reviewed nine studies examining the effect of asymptomatic lead exposure on childhood intelligence (Needleman, Gunnoe, & Leviton, 1979; Needleman, 1980; and Yule, Lansdown, Millar, & Urbanowitz, 1981). With data from the second United States National Health and Nutrition Examination Survey (Mahaffey, Amnest, Roberts, & Murphy, 1982) showing young children, the poor, rural residents, males, and blacks at higher risk for elevated blood lead levels, Indian children may be at risk on a number of criteria.

Disadvantage. Environmental variables have been shown to predict substantial amounts of variation in test performance. Earnings, nutrition, and health care vary greatly in North American society, and groups consistently at the bottom end of the range reveal depressed abilities and achievements. Indian populations are ranked low on all such indices of environmental support. Economic poverty, poor nutrition, and inadequate health care may place Native children at a disadvantage in the development of cognitive abilities. For instance, the Ojibwa suffer an unusually high frequency of malnutrition. Johnston (1976) measured height, weight, hematocrit, and the nutritional status of a sample of 1,000 urban Indian children in Minneapolis and compared these data with similar measures from a sample of Indian children on an Ojibwa reservation and with a large representative non-Indian sample. Using a method of relating height to weight called an "index of adiposity" (weight/height), these investigators found a high frequency of obesity and several interesting developmental trends across age and sex groups. Johnston's study provides valuable data in relation to obesity and other forms of malnutrition.

Poor housing and crowded living space, and access only to lower-quality education programmes and experiences have also enjoyed prominence as disabling factors in the learning process of Native children.

Deprivation. A combination of physiological and environmental disadvantage defines the interactive concept of deprivation. Poverty and poor health care lead to more illness, which increases absenteeism in school. Poor nutrition may mean less energy for learning. Inability to hear reduces the amount of information available to cope with learning tasks. The need to compete in a money economy may lead to migration and high mobility between families, communities, and schools (Chadwick & Strauss, 1975; Mohatt & Blue, 1982), causing loss of educational/learning continuity, probable social promotion, and deprivation of essential educational experience. The deprivation model lists negative abnormalities compared with white norms, stigmatising the target group without specifying cause (McShane, 1983a).

Cultural disorganisation. The concept of cultural disorganisation (or deculturation) is actually a societal form of the individual or small-group deprivation hypothesis. Children enmeshed in relations between two disparate cultures are caught up in complex and bewildering sets of forces pressuring them to assimilate (relinquish cultural identity and move into larger society); to integrate (maintain cultural integrity while becoming a part of larger society); to reject (by withdrawing from contact or influence, or by resisting passively or actively); or to experience marginality (a combination of cultural loss, deculturation, and exclusion from participation in dominant society [Berry, 1981]). Where a very strong surrounding culture actively rejects individuals from a nondominant culture, discrimination may also be a significant component of the cultural disorganisation hypothesis. Like the deprivation hypothesis, this model is incapable of producing more than a list of possible causes. It seems to have little scientific status, lacking the means to falsify all its possible components.

Disruption. A considerable body of evidence in anthropological and historical sources supports the use of the construct of uprooting or disruption from one generation to the next as a mechanism for emotional and cognitive maladjustment. To provide psychological referents for disruption as a cause of mental dysfunction in new generations, we cite normative indicators of adolescent pathology (McShane, in press, b; McShane & Adams, in press), and also quote some work on parent–child interaction patterns.

A number of research studies (Ogden, Spector, & Hill, 1970; Wintrob & Sindell, 1972; Beiser, 1974; Dlugokinski & Kramer, 1974; Forslund & Myers, 1974; Kleinfeld & Bloom, 1977; Attneave & Beiser, 1982) show Native adolescents to be at high risk for functional breakdown. From these sources the suicide rate is estimated at five times higher than for the rest of the population. Moreover, Inuit and Amerindian students drop out of school and enter the mental health treatment system in very large absolute numbers and in abnormally high proportions (Berry, 1971; Bank Street College, 1976). Finally adolescent alcoholism is reported (Cockerham, 1975; Jensen, Strauss, & Harris, 1977; Goldstein, Oetting, & Edwards, 1979) to be nearly three times the population figure.

Apart from surveys whose results point to coping failures in new generations, there are psychological essays in specifying disruption as a cause of such behaviours. These are thematically diffuse, and cover changes in family behaviour patterns among the Ojibwa (Boggs, 1956), differential internalisation of achievement motivation needs, a high need accompanying a strong degree of cultural identification (Kerckhoff, 1959), and the correlation of mothers' reports of traditional behaviour patterns with verbal-performance difference scores from the *WISC* (McShane, 1982). The evidence is nonprogrammatic; and at best it suggests rather than proves the case.

One other type of study ascribes introjective disruption as the cause of maladaptive behaviour. This deals with accidental or deliberate removal of the children from the influence of one or both parents. Work by Westermeyer (1977), by Green (1983), and by Long (1983) shows that between a quarter and one-third of all Indian children under 10 live outside the parental home; and that fostering is a practice that far exceeds the rate for whites. Green and Long, in particular, claim that repeated and sudden loss of care from parents is traumatic. While such family-based accidents may be inadvertent, much criticism has also been levelled at the policy of school provision that compels attendance at boarding schools. Such a policy of deliberate familial disruption invites mental health problems among Native peoples, according to several of the authors quoted at the beginning of this section.

Difference and developmental models

Thus far we have considered value-laden explanations that start by ascribing all Native test score averages that are below the published norms to deficits, or lack of "competence," as the Piagetians might express it. Difference models assume no lack of underlying competence, but assume instead that competence is expressed in a fashion that the tests may not always bring to the surface. Supporting such assumptions is the school of thought that languages differ not in their degree of demand on brain architecture but in their response to ecological demand. Equivalent cognitive capacity is required to process language of whatever origin. Moreover, the affective contexts of assessment in addition to the language of presentation have seldom allowed (Cole & Bruner, 1971) the conclusion that all performance differences described a direct path to competence distinctions.

Our example of the use of the difference explanation for test discrepancy is, ironically enough, the observed difference between Indian verbal and visual-spatial scores that may be an artifact of depressed second-language performance. Although we have been justifiably cautious in treating these scores as veridical, it is still possible to invoke two kinds of explanations that might account for the gap between verbal and spatial averages. The first is sociocultural in nature, the second is based on neurological evidence.

Sociocultural differences. The evidence for different language function in Indian groups once again covers a broad spectrum. Some literature (Boggs, 1956; Hickerson, 1970, 1971) concludes that Indian children who are relatively acculturated often appear unresponsive and passive. The literature also suggests that verbal interactions in acculturated families tend to be less frequent and less intense than in less acculturated families. This relative lack of interaction may retard the development of language skills among acculturated Indians.

Using a somewhat different approach, Black (1973) studied the sociolinguistic rules in Ojibwa-speaking communities. She discussed an ethnography of speaking that describes for a particular society a culturally specified social structure for speech: where, how, and to whom, and whether to talk. She has produced an Ojibwa etiquette manual for questioning and answering which is subtitled ''How to get information without asking questions and how to answer questions without giving any information.'' Black observed that an Ojibwa social role exists that produces contentless or deflected answers, or even silence, in response to a request for direct factual or personal information. Obviously, such cultural roles concerning question-and-answer behaviour are extremely relevant in the testing situation. Not so directly obvious, but equally pertinent, are discrepancies in emphasis on strategies of information processing that are imposed by different cultural contexts (Hallowell, 1955).

Schubert and Cropley (1972) have suggested that the conceptualisation of intelligence of the larger society places primary emphasis on information processing in abstract verbal terms and that Indian children, as a result of cultural training, do not consistently and automatically analyse experience in such abstract terms. Such a phenomenon may well represent cultural differences rather than deficit.

In considering sociocultural reinforcement of close attention to visual cues as a key to understanding the apparent spatial–verbal divide in Indian test performance, there are three relevant sources, all of which suggest emphasis on nonverbal communication. While Hall (1969) with Navajo children, and Darnell (1979) with Cree, noted lack of direct eye contact in face-to-face interactions, Guilmet (1978a, 1978b, 1978c) reported in his study of the gaze behaviour of young Indian children that they spent more time looking at teachers from a distance than did Caucasian children. In a classroom observation study, Guilmet (1981) found that Navajo children observed other students and teachers more, and spoke to them less, than did non-Indian children.

Neurological factors. Differences in language development and visual processing of information can be attributed in some degree to what one generation teaches the next. The concept of cultural differentiation also assigns variation in performance to factors that may be neurologically determined through inheritance or through habitual grooving of pathways by repeated learning. Such dispositional differences have been called upon to explain differential patterns of verbal and spatial acquisition in Indian groups. The rationale stems from work by Bogen (1969), who hypothesised two distinct modes of thought, *appositional* and *propositional* lateralised in the right and left hemispheres, respectively. The right hemisphere deals with logical relations involving simultaneous comparisons and contrasts, while the left is sequential, and language-oriented. The literature on cerebral specialisation and dominance in Indian groups is growing; and it seems to reveal consistent support for differences in the habitual use of right and left hemispheres for information processing.

Rogers, TenHouten, Kaplan, and Gardiner (1977) analysed the electroencephalographic records of Hopi children who had been asked to listen to stories told in both English and the Hopi language. Because there was a greater dyschronisation through the right hemisphere during stories presented in the Hopi language, the authors concluded that specialised modes of thought, either appositional or propositional, might be required for processing these different languages. After eliminating from the sample those Navajo children who experienced mild to moderate hearing loss, Hynd and Scott (1980) compared the performances of the Indian group with those of Anglo children on an auditory processing task that involved listening to 30 pairs of consonant–vowels through use of a two-channel headphone. The Navajo children favoured the left ear when reporting the paired stimuli, while Anglo children favoured the right ear. The authors interpreted their results using an appositional–propositional processing model, suggesting that the children used *different linguistic predispositions* in order to master the task. A similar dichotic listening task was required of older (mean 22.8 years) bilingual Navajos in a study reported by Hynd, Teeter, and Stewart (1980). Because these Indians tended to demonstrate left hemisphere reliance, as did Anglo subjects, the authors concluded that appositional–propositional preferences may be culturally influenced; older, successful Indian college students might have abandoned their culturally influenced earlier predispositions towards right hemisphere specialisation (cf. Thompson & Bogen,

1976; McKeever, 1981). Alternatively, they could be the Indian equivalent of "left-handers" in white groups; it is difficult to say at this point.

Witelson (1977) has suggested that bilateral neural involvement in spatial processing interferes with left hemisphere processing, and may result in deficit linguistic processing through overuse of the spatial, holistic mode. It is possible that the Indian child's assumed dependency on right hemisphere–related thought processes may affect the efficient acquisition of English language skills; for instance, Hier, LeMay, Rosenberger, and Perlo (1978) found that 45% of their adult developmental dyslexia sample produced computerised brain tomograms that revealed right parieto-occipital regions that were wider than the left regions. The patients with these reversed patterns of asymmetry (right hemisphere larger than left) obtained mean *Wechsler* Verbal IQs that were significantly lower than other patients, and lower than their own average Performance scale IQs.

In some cases a correlation between reversed asymmetry and a relative deficit in Verbal IQ also has been observed. Investigators have speculated that right hemisphere language dominance in individuals with reversed asymmetry may represent a risk factor for delayed or deficient language development (Hier et al., 1978; Rosenberger & Hier, 1980). Another group of investigators failed to find a correlation of Verbal IQ scores with patterns of hemispheric morphology, but did report proportionately more symmetric occipital widths than normally would be expected in a group of right-handed boys with developmental dyslexia (Haslam, Dalby, Johns, & Rademaker, 1981). Only one series (McShane, 1983b, 1986a; McShane, Risse, & Rubens, 1984; McShane & Willenbring, 1984) actually has found significant differences in patterns of cerebral asymmetry among white, black, Indian, and Oriental groups, as revealed by computerised brain tomograms.

This finding demonstrates physiological differences between ethnic groups. As such, it may imply correlation between performance and hemisphere differences; but it does not, of course, support the inference that hemisphere irregularities between ethnic groups can be inferred from performance differences, or can indeed cause these differences.

To conclude, difference models are not predicated on norm-related judgments of inferior performance. They regard data as a basis for hypothesis generation. Two of these hypotheses relate specifically to sociocultural and dispositional explanations.

Developmental. Another perspective concerns developmental change versus the stability of the mature organism. If we are more concerned with change as a function of process, rather than being concerned just with difference, do observed life-span changes in fixed attributes consist of differences in level only (quantitative change), or does the structure of attributes itself undergo developmental transformations (number of attributes, relationship among attributes) in the sense of structural change? If *change* is the object of study, it follows that measures must directly relate to aspects of change, hence the emphasis on the analysis of developmental functions. A further consequence of this focus on change is the need for longitudinal data, not only to take account of individual variations in the rate of patterning of development, but to provide direct measures of the parameters of developmental functions stipulated as the units of analysis, and of their relationships to other relevant variables. Unfortunately there is little developmental data available about Native abilities and achievements. Evidence for the hypothesis of structural change, calling for a developmental explanation of achievement and ability patterns among Native peoples, seems to rest in two kinds of material, both of which have already been outlined in the review of regional differences. The first (Peters, 1963; Coleman et al., 1966; McShane, in press, a) points to an apparent decline in school performance beginning at grade 2 and progressively worsening. The next, observable in studies by Saslow and Harrover (1968), Kleinfeld and Bloom (1977), and Attneave and Beiser (1982), concerns the high rates of adolescent breakdown that are associated with decline in academic performance, low self-esteem, and intergenerational conflict.

The whole picture is one of a developmental pattern in which Indian children, reared in nurturant surroundings, enter schools that expose them to cultural discrepancies. Under culture-alien conditions they exhibit, by maturity, behaviour that is perceived by the majority culture as *either* shy, withdrawn, and nonlearning *or*, at the opposite pole of the flight–fight continuum, as rude, aggressive, and destructive to self and others.

These behaviours, under a developmental umbrella, would be regarded as *normal* in the population, and a theory would be devised to predict poor performance on culture-alien tasks because of a progressive organismic response to anxiety-laden learning conditions. Such a theory is not immediately to hand because the evidence that would affirm it is not available, as our concluding remarks make clear. Just as there are uncertainties about what empiricism on Indian groups leads to, so in the cross-cultural field in general there is an unresolved debate about the validity of developmental theory formation. It is best witnessed in two recent sources: Cole and Scribner (1982) and Berry, Dasen, and Witkin (1982).

Summary, caveats, and conclusions

Summary

The amount of material dealing with groups of Native peoples who are widely dispersed in a large subcontinent, provoked a discussion of ecological adaptations that predicted the differential development of common skills. A presentation of data was accomplished for Arctic, Sub-Arctic, West Coast and Mountain, Central, East, and Southwest regions. The observed deviation of group performance from Euroamerican norms, and from the norms established within any one Native group, calls for explanation. A number of classes of explanation were examined. These included ecological press as a general "regional" model, and several competing "D" models (deficit, difference, and developmental). The questions that remain from these four different perspectives on the same database ask whether this conceptual structure has continuing potential for understanding and extending the database; and which of the competing classes of explanation account for more of the group variation than any of the others. Our concluding remarks are more concerned with the first question than the second, simply because answers to the second question are not possible until we understand the nature of the data we are given.

On the face of it, two general, and perhaps simplistic, conclusions emerge from the review. First, analysis of empirical results and ethnographic studies advance the hypothesis that some Native groups process information differently from Euroamericans, and also from other indigenous peoples in contrasting habitats. Although generalisations have centred on the configuration and level of performance in the visual and verbal domains, there is no evidence to confirm the validity of inferences from poor group performance in second-language verbal tests, or to suggest that specific differences lie exclusively in these areas.

Caveats

The reasons for our qualified statements are to be found in the evaluation of the data at hand. Without confidence in the material, little can be concluded. We now concentrate on the common criticisms levelled at studies of indigenous cognitive processes (McShane, 1986b). These serve as suitable disclaimers and as counsels to perfection.

Emic and etic distinction. An undisputable conclusion from the data is its inherently "etic" character. By this is meant the preponderance of scales and measures brought into Native contexts only after first establishing their use outside them. Such acts assume that stimuli remain universally applicable and interpretable. "Emic" studies make no assumptions about properties of stimuli, and seek to find unique cultural contexts where the assumption of cognitive competence may be vindicated (Berry, 1976). A preponderance of etic instrumentation in the body of the literature begs obvious questions of equivalence when comparisons are made. In general, Native studies have not established the various types of equivalence that are required before inferences for such comparisons are absolved from methodological caveats. The many and various meanings of equivalence can be pursued in Berry (1980) and Brislin (1980); Furnham and Henry (1980); Hui and Triandis (1983).

Construct validity. When the pursuit of equivalence is ignored, the fundamental requisite of comparisons, measurement validity (Straus, 1969) or more generally construct validity, is in question. Since the early 1960s, researchers have pointed out that the meaning of a test score depends on its susceptibility to a number of culture specifics. A more general barrier to the assumption that tests are universal vehicles for the same sources of variance is encountered whenever communication involves the use of one language or another. Phillips (1983) and Greenbaum and Greenbaum (1983) have recently enumerated challenges to construct validity issued by failures in communication. Olmedo (1981) asks that examiner variables be considered relevant to the evaluation of test scores. Apart from these explicit difficulties, a large number implicit, or covert, confounding social context variables have been listed by Malpass (1977), who regards many of them to be uncontrolled in almost all cross-cultural studies. From the strength of the protest, one might be surprised that any measurement research is still attempted, but the most compelling argument comes from Dana (1984), who asserts that there is a moral responsibility to determine construct validity in every study involving minorities, because minorities are seldom able to exert counterinfluence on highly technical reports that are beyond the comprehension of all but a privileged handful of scientists. Past and future databases are thereby called to account.

Design faults. What to use to assess abilities and achievements is the prime argument. There remains, though, the abiding problem of the design of psychological experiments that permit correct inferences from data. Several researchers have specified major structural faults. Among the more recent are Dinges, Trimble, and Hollenbeck (1979); Berry (1981); McShane and Plas (1984a, 1984b); McShane (1984); and McShane (in press, a). These weaknesses range from elementary inferential errors to major gaffes, such as those involving intergenerational comparison of cross-cultural data, as if social change had been held in abeyance. The centroid that explains most of the problems in study design is the lack of any systematic programme of work in which a plan of campaign is evident. The episodic and idiosyncratic nature of the legacy of data is the price paid, much of it being "one of a kind" and relatively valueless as a permanent contribution to the understanding of cognition among Native peoples.

Reprise

Conceptually, all the deficit models construing minority group performance that falls below a majority mean as evidence for pathology, are alike. On the other hand, difference and developmental explanations of the cause of such performance can be associated with a more normative framework. A choice of either general model would be systematically misleading, because that would prevent work that tested competing theories in the same set of experiments. The empiricism reviewed in this chapter allows no confidence in the great majority of inferences that have been made from Native performance on tests. Only by setting alternative explanatory models against each other, in longitudinal designs that consider level of analysis, life stage, and situational boundaries, can the questions that have been raised by this review be resolved. Years, rather than months, of patient work are indicated, because much of what has been done already in the name of scientific enquiry will have to be disavowed.

References

Arthur, G. (1941). An experience in testing Indian school children. *Mental Hygiene, 25,* 188–195.

Attneave, C. L., & Beiser, M. (1982). Mental disorders among native American children: Rates and risk periods for entering treatment. *American Journal of Psychiatry, 139*(2), 193–198.

Bagrow, L. (1948). Eskimo maps. *Imago Mundi, 5,* 92–93.

Bank Street College of Education (1976). *Young Native Americans and their families: Educational needs, assessment, and education.* New York: Bank Street College of Education Research Division.

Bannatyne, A. (1974). Diagnosis: A note on recategorization of the WISC scaled scores. *Journal of Learning Disabilities, 7,* 272–273.

Beiser, M. (1974). A hazard to mental health: Indian boarding schools. *American Journal of Psychiatry, 131,* 305–306.

Berry, J. W. (1966). Temne and Eskimo perceptual skills. *International Journal of Psychology, 1,* 207–229.

Berry, J. W. (1971). Psychological research in the North. *Anthropologica, 13,* 143–157.

Berry, J. W. (1975). An ecological approach to cross-cultural psychology. *Nederlands Tijdschrift voor de Psychologie, 30,* 51–84.

Berry, J. W. (1976). *Human ecology and cognitive style: Comparative studies in cultural and psychological adaptation.* New York: Sage-Halsted.

Berry, J. W. (1980). Introduction to *Methodology.* In H. C. Triandis & J. W. Berry (Eds.), *Handbook of cross-cultural psychology* (Vol. 2). Boston: Allyn & Bacon.

Berry, J. W. (1981). Native peoples and the larger society. In R. C. Gardner & R. Kalin (Eds.), *A Canadian social psychology of ethnic relations.* Toronto: Methuen.

Berry, J. W., & Annis, R. C. (1974). Ecology, culture, and psychological differentiation. *International Journal of Psychology, 9,* 173–193.

Berry, J. W., Dasen, P. R., & Witkin, H. A. (1982). Developmental theories in cross-cultural perspective. In L. Adler (Ed.), *Cross-cultural research at issue.* New York: Academic Press.

Black, M. B. (1973). Ojibwa questioning etiquette and use of ambiguity. *Studies in Linguistics, 23,* 13–19.

Bogen, J. E. (1969). The other side of the brain II: An appositional mind. *Bulletin of the Los Angeles Neurological Societies, 34,* 135–161.

Boggs, S. T. (1956). An international study of Ojibwa socialization. *American Sociological Review, 21,* 191–198.

Bowd, A. D. (1972). Some determinants of school achievement in several Indian groups. *Alberta Journal of Educational Research, 18,* 69–76.

Bowd, A. D. (1973). A cross-cultural study of the factorial composition of mechanical aptitude. *Canadian Journal of Behavioral Science, 5,* 13–23.

Bowd, A. D. (1974). Practical abilities of Indians and Eskimos. *Canadian Psychologist, 15,* 281–290.

Brandt, E. A. (1984). The cognitive functioning of American Indian children: A critique of McShane and Plas. *School Psychology Review, 13*(1), 74–82.

Brislin, R. W. (1980). Translation and content analysis of oral and written materials. In H. C.

Triandis & J. W. Berry (Eds.), *Handbook of cross-cultural psychology* (Vol. 2, pp. 389–444). Boston: Allyn & Bacon.

Brokenleg, M. (1983). *Sioux American Indian and White children: A comparison of hemispheric dominance using the K-ABC.* Unpublished doctoral dissertation, University of South Dakota, Vermillion.

Browne, D. B. (1984). WISC-R scoring patterns among native Americans of the Northern Plains. *White Cloud Journal, 3*(2), 3–16.

Carpenter, E. S. (1955). Space concepts of the Aivilik Eskimo. *Explorations, 5,* 131–145.

Cattell, R. B. (1940). A culture free intelligence test: 1. *Journal of Educational Psychology, 31,* 161–180.

Cazden, C. B., & John, V. P. (1969). Learning in American Indian children. In S. Ohannessian (Ed.), *Styles of learning among American Indians: An outline for research.* Washington: Centre for Applied Linguistics.

Chadwick, B. A., & Strauss, J. H. (1975). The assimilation of American Indians into urban society: The Seattle case. *Human Organization, 34,* 359–369.

Cockerham, W. C. (1975). Drinking attitudes and practices among Wind River Reservation Indian youth. *Journal of the Study of Alcohol, 36,* 321–326.

Cohen, H., Levy, J., & McShane, D. A. (in press). Functional illiteracy and hemisphere specialization for tactile information. *Neuroscience.*

Cohen, H., Levy, J., & McShane, D. A. (in press). Scholarisation et spécialisation hémisphérique dans le traitement d l'information. *Neuropsychologia.*

Cole, M., & Bruner, J. S. (1971). Cultural differences and inferences about psychological processes. *American Psychologist, 26,* 867–876.

Cole, M., & Scribner, S. (1982). Developmental theories applied to cross-cultural cognitive research. In L. Adler (Ed.), *Cross-cultural research at issue.* New York: Academic Press.

Coleman, J. S. et al. (1966). *Equality of educational opportunity.* Washington, DC: Government Printing Office.

Conrad, R. D. (1974). *Papago children's intelligence scores as influenced by tester ethnicity, reinforcement, and cultural fairness.* Unpublished doctoral dissertation (75-4136), University of Arizona, Tucson.

Cropley, A. J., & Cardey, R. M. (1975). Contact with the dominant culture and cognitive competence in Canadian Indians and Whites. *Canadian Journal of Behavioural Science, 7,* 328–338.

Cundick, B. P. (1970). Measures of intelligence on Southwest Indian students. *Journal of Social Psychology, 31,* 151–156.

Dana, R. H. (1984). Intelligence testing of American Indian children: Sidesteps in quest of ethical practice. *White Cloud Journal, 3*(3), 35–43.

Darnell, R. (1979). *Reflections on Cree interactional etiquette: Educational implications* (Working paper on sociolinguistics, No. 57). Austin, TX: Southwest Educational Development Laboratory.

Dasen, P. R. (1975a). Le développement des operations concrètes chez les Esquimaux canadiens. *International Journal of Psychology, 10,* 165–180.

Dasen, P. R. (1975b). Concrete operational development in three cultures. *Journal of Cross-Cultural Psychology, 6,* 156–172.

Davis, J. C., & Cropley, A. J. (1976). Psychological factors in juvenile delinquency. *Canadian Journal of Behavioural Science, 8*(1), 68–77.

Dennis, W. (1942). The performance of Hopi children on The Goodenough Draw-a-Man Test. *Journal of Comparative Psychology, 34,* 341–348.

Dennis, W. (1966). Goodenough scores, art experience, and modernization. *Journal of Social Psychology, 68,* 211–228.

Dinges, N. G., Trimble, J. E., & Hollenbeck, A. R. (1979). American Indian adolescent socialisation: A review of the literature. *Journal of Adolescence, 2,* 259–296.

Dlugokinski, E., & Kramer, L. (1974). A system of neglect: Indian boarding schools. *American Journal of Psychiatry, 13,* 670–673.

Dorsch, P. (1980). *An investigation of the construct validity of the WISC-R for a group of Sisseton–Wapeton Sioux children*. Unpublished doctoral dissertation, University of South Dakota, Vermillion.

Driver, H. E. (1969). *Indians of North America* (2nd ed.). Chicago: University of Chicago Press.

Driver, H. E., & Massey, W. C. (1957). *Comparative studies of North American Indians*. Philadelphia. American Philosophical Society.

Ertz, H. (in press). WISC-R scores among matched pairs of non-Indian and American Indian students who were displaying learning disorders. *White Cloud Journal*.

Feldman, C. (1974). *The development of adaptive intelligence*. San Francisco: Jossey-Bass.

Fitzgerald, J. A., & Ludeman, W. W. (1926). The intelligence of Indian children. *Journal of Comparative Psychology, 6,* 319–328.

Forbes, N. W., & Lonner, W. J. (1980). *Sociocultural and cognitive effects of commercial television on previously television-naive rural Alaskan children* (Final Report to NSF [BNS-78-25687]). Bellingham, WA.

Forde, D. (1934). *Habitat, economy, and society*. London: Methuen.

Forsius, H. (1980). Behavior. In F. A. Milan (Ed.), *The human biology of circumpolar populations*. Cambridge University Press.

Forslund, M. A:, & Myers, R. E. (1974). Delinquency among Wind River Indian Reservation youth. *Criminology, 12*(1), 97–106.

Frideres, J. S. (1974). *Canada's Indians: Contemporary conflicts*. Scarborough, Ontario: Prentice-Hall of Canada.

Furnham, A., & Henry, J. (1980). Cross-cultural locus of control studies: Experiment and critique. *Psychological Reports, 47,* 23–29.

Gaddes, W. H., McKenzie, A., & Barnsley, R. (1968). Psychometric intelligence and spatial imagery in two Northwest Indian and two White groups of children. *Journal of Social Psychology, 75,* 35–42.

Garber, M. (1968). *Ethnicity and measures of educability: Differences among Navajo, Pueblo, and rural Spanish American first graders on measures of learning style, hearing, vocabulary, entry skills, motivation and home environment processes*. Unpublished doctoral dissertation, University of Southern California, Los Angeles.

Garth, T. R., & Smith, O. D. (1937). The performance of full-blooded Indians on language and non-language intelligence tests. *Journal of Applied Psychology, 12,* 511–516.

Goldstein, G. S., Oetting, E. R., & Edwards R. (1979). Drug use among Native American young adults. *International Journal of Addiction, 14,* 855–860.

Goodenough, F. L. (1926). Measurement of intelligence of school children. *Journal of Experimental Psychology, 9,* 388–397.

Goodenough, F. L., & Harris, D. B. (1950). Studies in the psychology of children's drawings. *Psychological Bulletin, 47,* 369–433.

Gottlieb, N. H., & Green, L. W. (1984). Life events, social network, lifestyle and health: An analysis of the 1979 National Survey of Personal Health Practices and Consequences. *Health Education Quarterly, 11*(1), 91–105.

Green, H. J. (1983). Risks and attitudes associated with extracultural placement of American Indian children: A critical review. *Journal of the American Academy of Child Psychiatry, 11*(1), 63–67.

Greenbaum, P. E., & Greenbaum, S. D. (1983). Cultural differences, nonverbal regulation, and classroom interaction: Sociolinguistic interference in American Indian education. *Peabody Journal of Education, 61*(1), 16–33.

Greenfield, P. M., Reich, L. C., and Olver, R. (1966). On culture and equivalence II. In J. S. Bruner, R. Olver, & P. M. Greenfield (Eds.), *Studies in cognitive growth*. New York: Wiley.

Gregory, R. J., & Mohan, P. J. (1977). Effect of asymptomatic lead exposure on childhood intelligence: A critical review. *Intelligence, 1,* 381–400.

Guilliams, C. I. (1975). *Item analysis of American and Chicano responses on the vocabulary scales of the Stanford–Binet LM and Wechsler batteries* (Final report, 65 pp.). (ERIC Document Reproduction Service No. ED 032 174).

Guilmet, G. M. (1975). Cognitive research among the Eskimo: A survey. *Anthropologica, 17,* 61–84.

Guilmet, G. M., (1978a). Navajo and Caucasian children's verbal and nonverbal visual behavior in the urban classroom. *Anthropology and Education Quarterly, 9,* 196–215.

Guilmet, G. M. (1978b). Instructor reaction to verbal and nonverbal visual styles: An example of Navajo and Caucasian children. *Anthropology and Education Quarterly, 10,* 154–266.

Guilmet, G. M. (1978c). Maternal perceptions of urban Navajo and Caucasian children's classroom behavior. *Human Organization, 38,* 87–91.

Guilmet, G. M. (1981). Oral-linguistic and nonoral-visual styles of attending: Navajo and Caucasian children compared in an urban classroom and on an urban playground. *Human Organization, 40,* 145–150.

Hall, E. T. (1969). Listening behavior: Some cultural differences. *Phi Delta Kappan,* 379–380.

Hallowell, A. I. (1946). Some psychological characteristics of Northeastern Woodland Indians. In F. Johnson (Ed.), *Man in Northeastern North America.* New York: Peabody Foundation for Archaeology.

Hallowell, A. I. (1955). *Culture and experience.* Philadelphia: University of Pennsylvania Press.

Hamilton, J. E. (1976). Vision anomalies of Indian school children: The lame deer study. *Journal of the American Optometric Association, 47*(4), 479–487.

Haslam, R. H. A., Dalby, J. T., Johns, R. D., & Rademaker, A. W. (1981). Cerebral asymmetry in developmental dyslexia. *Archives of Neurology, 38,* 679–682.

Haught, B. F. (1934). Mental growth of the southwestern Indian. *Journal of Applied Psychology, 18,* 137–142.

Havighurst, R. J. (1944). The intelligence of Indian children as measured by a performance scale. *Journal of Abnormal and Social Psychology, 39,* 419–433.

Hickerson, H. (1970). *The Chippewa and their neighbors: A study in ethnohistory.* New York: Holt, Rinehart & Winston.

Hickerson, H. (1971). The Chippewa of the Upper Great Lakes: A study in sociopolitical change. In E. B. Leacock & N. O. Lurie (Eds.), *North American Indians in historical perspectives* (pp. 169–199). New York: Random House.

Hier, D., LeMay, M., Rosenberger, P., & Perlo, V. (1978). Developmental dyslexia: Evidence for a sub-group with a reversal of cerebral asymmetry. *Archives of Neurology, 35,* 90–92.

Hollingshead, M. C., & Clayton, C. (1971a). *Comparison of WISC patterns of retarded and non-retarded readers: Indian Youth.* (ERIC Document Reproduction Service No. 057931).

Hollingshead, M. C., & Clayton, C. (1971b). *Study of the relationship between the performance of Indian youth on the Wechsler Intelligence Scale for Children and the Chicago Non-Verbal.* (ERIC Document Reproduction Service No. 057932).

Holm, V. A., & Kunze, L. H. (1969). Effects of chronic otitis media on language and speech development. *Pediatrics, 43*(5), 833–839.

Honigmann, J. J. (1968). Interpersonal relations in atomistic societies. *Human Organization, 27,* 220–229.

Hui, C. H., & Triandis, H. C. (1983). Multistrategy approach to cross-cultural research: The case of locus of control. *Journal of Cross-Cultural Psychology, 14*(1), 65–68.

Hynd, G. W., Kramer, R., Quackenbush, R., Conner, & Weed (1979). Clinical utility of the WISC-R and the French Pictorial Test of Intelligence with Native American primary grade children. *Perceptual and Motor Skills, 4,* 480–482.

Hynd, G. W., & Scott, S. A. (1980). Propositional and appositional modes of thought and differential cerebral speech lateralization in Navajo Indian and Anglo children. *Child Development, 51,* 909–911.

Hynd, G. W., Teeter, A., & Stewart, J. (1980). Acculturation and the lateralization of speech in the bilingual Native American. *International Journal of Neuroscience, 11,* 1–7.

Irwin, C. (1981). *Inuit navigation.* Unpublished paper, Syracuse University.

Jamieson, E. (1928). *The mental capacity of Southern Ontario Indians.* Unpublished doctoral dissertation, University of Toronto.

Jamieson, E., & Sandiford, P. (1938). The mental capacity of southern Ontario Indians. *Journal of Educational Psychology, 29*, 317–328, 536–551.

Jensen, G. F., Strauss, J. H., & Harris, V. W. (1977). Crime, delinquency and the American Indian. *Human Organization, 36*(3), 252–257.

Joblin, E. M. (1947). *The education of Indians in Western Ontario* (Bulletin No. 13). Toronto: Ontario College of Education.

Johnston, B. (1976). *Ojibwa heritage.* New York: Columbia University Press.

Jones, K. L. (1975). Aberrant neuronal migration of the fetal alcohol syndrome. *Birth Defects: Original Article Series, 11*, 131–132.

Kaplan, G. J., Fleshman, J. K., Bender, T. R., Baum, C., & Clark, P. S. (1973). Longterm effects of otitis media: A ten-year cohort study of Alaskan Eskimo children. *Pediatrics, 52*, 577–585.

Kaufman, A. A. (1979). Cerebral specialization and intelligence testing. *Journal of Research and Development in Education, 12*(2), 96–107.

Kaufman, B. (1984). Styles of learning among Native children: A review of research. *Canadian Journal of Native Education, 11*(3), 27–37.

Kearins, J. (1976). Skills of desert Aboriginal children. In G. E. Kearney and E. W. McElwain (Eds.), *Aboriginal cognition: Retrospect and prospect.* Canberra: Australian Institute of Aboriginal Studies.

Kerckhoff, A. C. (1959). Anomie and achievement motivation: A study of personality development within cultural disorganization. *Social Forces, 37*, 196–202.

Kirk, S. A. (1972). Ethnic differences in psycholinguistic abilities. *Exceptional Children, 39*, 112–118.

Kleinfeld, J. (1971). Visual memory in village Eskimo and Urban Caucasian children. *Arctic, 24*, 132–138.

Kleinfeld, J. (1973). Intellectual strengths in culturally different groups: An Eskimo illustration. *Review of Educational Research, 43*, 341–359.

Kleinfeld, J. (1974). Effects of nonverbal warmth on the learning of Eskimo and White students. *Journal of Social Psychology, 92*, 3–19.

Kleinfeld, J., & Bloom, J. (1977). Boarding schools: Effects on the mental health of Eskimo adolescents. *American Journal of Psychiatry, 134*, 411–417.

Klineberg, O. (1928). An experimental study of speech and other factors in "racial" differences. *Archives of Psychology, 15*(93), 109.

Knowles, D., & Boersma, F. (1968). Optional shift performance of culturally-different children to concrete and abstract stimuli. *Alberta Journal of Educational Research, 14*, 165–177.

Kroeber, A. (1939). *Cultural and natural areas of Native North America.* Berkeley: University of California Press.

Larkin, K. A. (1970). *Performance of reservation American Indian, inner-city American Indian, and inner-city white children on the Boehm Test of Basic Concepts.* Unpublished master's thesis, University of Minnesota, Minneapolis.

Levensky, K. (1970). The performance of American Indian children on the Draw-a-Man test. In R. Havighurst (Ed.), *National study of American Indian education, 1*(2). Minneapolis: University of Minnesota.

Ling, D., McCoy, R. J., & Levinson, E. D. (1969). The incidence of middle ear disease and its educational implications among Baffin Island Eskimo children. *Canadian Journal of Public Health, 60*, 385–390.

Lombardi, T. P. (1970). Psycholinguistic abilities of Papago Indian school children. *Exceptional Children, 36*, 485–493.

Long, K. A. (1983). The experience of repeated and traumatic loss among Crow Indian children: Response patterns and intervention strategies. *American Journal of Orthopsychiatry, 53*, 116–126.

McAreavey, J. P. (1975). *An analysis of selected educationally handicapped South Dakota*

Sioux Indian children's responses to the Wechsler Intelligence Scale for Children and Wide Range Achievement Test of Reading. Unpublished doctoral dissertation, University of Colorado, Boulder. (University Microfilm Order No. 76-3655).

MacArthur, R. S. (1967). Sex differences in field dependence for the Eskimo: Replication of Berry's finding. *International Journal of Psychology, 2,* 139–140.

MacArthur, R. S. (1968a). Some cognitive abilities of Eskimo, white and Indian-Metis pupils aged 9–12 years. *Canadian Journal of Behavioural Science, 1,* 50–59.

MacArthur, R. S. (1968b). Some differential abilities of Northern Canadian Native youth. *International Journal of Psychology, 3,* 43–51.

MacArthur, R. S. (1973). Some ability patterns: Central Eskimos and Nsenga Africans. *International Journal of Psychology, 8,* 239–247.

MacArthur, R. S. (1975). Differential ability patterns: Inuit, Nsenga, and Canadian Whites. In J. W. Berry & W. J. Lonner (Eds.), *Applied cross-cultural psychology.* Lisse: Swets & Zeitlinger.

MacArthur, R. S. (1978). Ecology, culture, and cognitive development: Canadian Native youth. In L. Driedger (Ed.), *The Canadian ethnic mosaic.* Toronto: McClelland & Stewart.

McElroy, A. (1971). *A Survey of Psychological Studies of Canadian Eskimos.* Paper presented to Canadian Sociology and Anthropology Association.

McKeever, W. F. (1981). Note: Evidence against the hypothesis of right hemisphere language dominance in the Native American Navajo. *Neuropsychologia, 19,* 595–598.

McShane, D. A. (1979a). Bias in assessment of American Indian children. *Listening Post, 1*(4), 8–19. Albuquerque: Indian Health Service Mental Health.

McShane, D. A. (1979b, October). Middle ear disease, language, and educational delay in American Indian children. *Journal of American Indian Education, 19,* 7–11.

McShane, D. A. (1980a). A review of scores of American Indian children on the Wechsler Intelligence Scales. *White Cloud Journal, 1*(4), 3–10.

McShane, D. A. (1980b). The need for an internal, subjective, and relational approach to the cultural promotion of mental health within American Indian Communities. In *Research priorities in Native American mental health service delivery,* workshop report, Services for Minorities Program – National Institute of Mental Health, October 22–23, Albuquerque, NM.

McShane, D. A. (1982). Otitis media and American Indians: Prevalence, etiology, psychoeducational consequences, prevention, and intervention. In S. Manson (Ed.), *New directions in prevention among American Indian and Alaskan Native communities* (pp. 265–297). Portland: Oregon Health Sciences University Press.

McShane, D. A. (1983a). Cognition, affect, and behavior in American Indian children: A developmental perspective of a transcultural situation. *Peabody Journal on Education, 61*(1), 34–48.

McShane, D. A. (1983b). Neurocranial form: Differentiating four ethnic populations using a simple CT scan measure. *International Journal of Neuroscience, 21,* 137–145.

McShane, D. A. (1986a). Cerebral asymmetries using computed tomography: The effects of handedness, gender, age, and ethnicity. *Journal of Clinical and Experimental Neuropsychology, 8*(2), 148.

McShane, D. A. (1986b). Ojibwa adult-child interactions. *Canadian Journal of Native Studies, 13*(1), 72–87.

McShane, D. A. (1986c). Testing, assessment research, and increased control by Native communities. In H. McCue (Ed.), *Selected papers from the first Mokakit Conference,* July 25–27, 1984, Vancouver: Mokakit Research Association.

McShane, D. A. (1987a). Mental health and North American Indian/Native communities: Cultural transactions, education, and regulation. *American Journal of Community Psychology, 15*(1), 95–117.

McShane, D. A. (1987b). Undergraduate training in psychology for American Indians. In P. J. Woods (Ed.) *The Psychology Major: Training and Employment Strategies.* Washington, D.C.: American Psychological Association.

McShane, D. A. (in press, a). American Indian mental health research: Meta-review, synthesis and future priorities. In F. Cheung (Ed.), *Minority mental health research: A review monograph*. Maryland: National Institute of Mental Health.

McShane, D. A. (in press, b). A review and analysis: Mental health research and services to American Indian youth. *Journal of Adolescence*.

McShane, D. A. (Issue Ed.). (1983, Fall). The transcultural education of American Indian and Alaska Native children: Teachers and students in transition. *Peabody Journal of Education*, 61(1), 1–112.

McShane, D. A., & Adams, G. (Special Issue Ed.). (in press). The emotionally disturbed ethnic minority child. *Journal of Adolescence*.

McShane, D. A., & Cook, V. (1985). Transcultural intellectual assessment: Hispanic performance on the Wechslers. In B. Wolman (Ed.), *Handbook of intelligence: Theories, measurements, and applications*. New York: Wiley.

McShane, D. A., & Plas, J. M. (1982a). The relationship of otitis media frequency to the intellectual and psycholinguistic performances of American Indian children. *Journal of Preventive Psychiatry, 1*(3), 277–292.

McShane, D. A., & Plas, J. M. (1982b). WISC-R factor structures for Ojibwa Indian children. *White Cloud Journal, 2*(4), 18–23.

McShane, D. A., & Plas, J. M. (1982c). Wechsler scale performances of American Indian children. *Psychology in the Schools, 19*, 8–17.

McShane, D. A., & Plas, J. M. (1984a). The cognitive functioning of American Indian children: Moving from the WISC to the WISC-R. *School Psychology Review, 13*(1), 61–73.

McShane, D. A., & Plas, J. M. (1984b). Response to a critique of the McShane and Plas (1984a) review of American Indian performance on the Wechsler Intelligence Scales. *School Psychology Review, 13*(1), 83–88.

McShane, D. A., & Plas, J. M. (in press). The relationship of intellectual and psycholinguistic abilities to the achievement gains of American Indian children. *Canadian Journal of Native Studies*.

McShane, D. A., Risse, G. L., & Rubens, A. B. (1984). Cerebral asymmetries on CT scan for three ethnic groups. *International Journal of Neuroscience, 23*, 69–74.

McShane, D. A., & Willenbring, M. L. (1984). Alcohol use and cerebral asymmetries. *Journal of Nervous and Mental Disease, 172*(9), 529–532.

Mahaffey, K. R., Amnest, J. L., Roberts, J., & Murphy, R. S. (1982). National estimates of blood lead levels: United States, 1976–1980; Association with selected demographic and socioeconomic factors. *New England Journal of Medicine, 307*, 573–579.

Malpass, R. S. (1977). Theory and method in cross-cultural psychology. *American Psychologist, 32*(12), 1069–1079.

Manning, P., Avery, M. E., & Ross, A. (1974). Purulent otitis media: Differences between populations in different environments. *Pediatrics, 53*(2), 135–136.

Marjoribanks, K. (1972). Ethnic and environmental influences on mental abilities. *American Journal of Sociology, 78*, 323–337.

Mawhinney, T. A. (1983). A picture vocabulary test for the James Bay Cree. In S. H. Irvine & J. W. Berry (Eds.), *Human assessment and cultural factors*. New York: Plenum.

May, P. A. (1981). *FAS: Report on Outreach efforts and analysis of approach* (HSA Document 240-81-0002). Washington, DC: Government Printing Office.

Mohatt, G., & Blue, A. (1982). Primary prevention as it relates to traditionality and empirical measures of social demeanor. In S. Manson (Ed.), *New directions in prevention among American Indian and Alaskan Native communities* (pp. 91–115). Portland: Oregon Health Sciences University Press.

Naglieri, J. A. (1982). Does the WISC-R measure verbal intelligence for non-English-speaking children? *Psychology in the Schools, 19*, 479–480.

Naglieri, J. A., & Kamphaus, R. W. (1983, March). *Use of the Kaufman Battery for Children with culturally diverse children*. Paper presented at the meeting of the National Association of School Psychologists, Detroit.

Needleman, H. L. (1980). *Low level lead exposure: The clinical implications of current research.* New York: Raven Press.

Needleman, H. L., Gunnoe, C., & Leviton, A. (1979). Deficits in psychological and classroom performances of children with elevated dentine lead level. *New England Journal of Medicine, 300,* 688–695.

Ogden, M., Spector, M. H., & Hill, C. A. (1970). Suicides and homicides among Indians. *Public Health Reports, 85*(1), 75–80.

Olmedo, E. L. (1981). Testing linguistic minorities. *American Psychologist, 36*(10), 1078–1082.

Paschal, F. C., & Sullivan, L. R. (1925). Racial differences in the mental and physical development of Mexican children. *Complete Psychological Monographs, 3*(14), 76.

Peck, R. L. (1972). *A comparative analysis of the performance of Indian and white children from North Central Montana on the Wechsler Intelligence Scale for Children.* Unpublished doctoral dissertation, Montana State University, Bozeman.

Peters, H. (1963). Performance of Hopi children on four intelligence tests. *Journal of American Indian Education, 2,* 27–31.

Phillips, Susan (1983). *The invisible culture.* New York: Longman.

Preston, C. E. (1964). Psychological testing with Northwest coast Alaskan Eskimos. *Genetic Psychology Monographs, 69,* 323–419.

Query, J. M., Query, W. T., & Singh, D. (1975). Independence training need achievement and need affiliation: A comparison between white and Indian children. *International Journal of Psychology, 10,* 255–268.

Reschly, D. J. (1978). WISC-R factor structures among Anglos, Blacks, Chicanos, and Native American Papagos. *Journal of Consulting and Clinical Psychology, 46,* 417–422.

Reynolds, C. R., & Willson, V. L. (1982, August). *Intellectual differences among Mexican-Americans, Papagos, and Whites independent of "g."* Paper presented to the annual meeting of the American Psychological Association, Washington, DC.

Rogers, L., TenHouten, W., Kaplan, A. P., & Gardiner, M. (1977). Hemispheric specialization of language: An EEG study of bilingual Hopi Indian children. *International Journal of Neuroscience, 8,* 1–6.

Rohner, R. P. (1965). Factors influencing the academic performance of Kwakiutl children in Canada. *Comparative Education Review, 9,* 331–340.

Rosenberger, P. B., & Hier, D. B. (1980). Cerebral symmetrics and verbal intellectual deficits. *Annals of Neurology, 8,* 300–304.

Sabatino, D. A., Hayden, D. L., & Kelling, K. (1972). Perceptual language, and academic achievement of English, Spanish, and Navajo speaking children referred for special classes. *Journal of School Psychology, 10,* 39–46.

Sachs, D. A. (1974). The WISC and the Mescalero Apache. *Journal of Social Psychology, 92,* 303–304.

St. John, J., Krichev, A., & Bawman, E. (1976). Northwestern Ontario Indian children and the WISC. *Psychology in the Schools, 13,* 407–411.

Saslow, H. L., & Harrover, M. J. (1968). Research on psychosocial adjustment of Indian youth. *American Journal of Psychiatry,* 224–231.

Schaefer, O. (1971). Otitis media and bottle feeding: An epidemiological study of infant feeding habits and incidence of recurrent and chronic middle ear disease in Canadian Eskimos. *Canadian Journal of Public Health, 62,* 478–489.

Schubert, J., & Cropley, A. J. (1972). Verbal regulation of behavior and IQ in Canadian Indian and White children. *Developmental Psychology, 1,* 295–301.

Stewart, J. L. (1975). The Indian Health Service hearing program: An overview. *Hearing Instruments, 26,* 22–23.

Straus, M. A. (1969). Phenomenal identity and conceptual equivalence of measurement in cross-national comparative research. *Journal of Marriage and the Family,* 233–239.

Streissguth, A. P. (1977). Maternal drinking and the outcome of pregnancy: Implications for child mental health. *American Journal of Orthopsychiatry, 47,* 422–431.

Streissguth, A. P., Herman, C. S., & Smith, D. W. (1978). Intelligence, behavior, and dysmorphogenesis in the fetal alcohol syndrome: A report on 20 patients. *Journal of Pediatrics, 92*, 363–367.

Taylor, H. D., & Thweat, R. C. (1972). Cross-cultural developmental performance of Navajo children on the Bender-Gestalt Test. *Perceptual and Motor Skills, 35*(1), 307–309.

Taylor, L. J., & Skanes, G. (1976). Cognitive abilities in Inuit and White children from similar environments. *Canadian Journal of Behavioural Science, 8*, 1–7.

Telford, C. W. (1932). Test performance of full and mixed-blood North Dakota Indians. *Journal of Comparative Psychology, 14*, 123–145.

Thoday, J. M. (1969). Limits to genetic comparison of populations. *Journal of Biosocial Science (Supplement), 1*, 3–14.

Thompson, A. L., & Bogen, J. E. (1976). More on the question of cultural hemisphericity. *Bulletin of the Los Angeles Neurological Societies, 99*, 139–149.

Thurber, S. (1976). Changes in Navajo responses to the Draw-a-Man test. *Journal of Social Psychology, 99*, 139–140.

Timmermans, F., & Gerson, S. (1980). Chronic granulomatus otitis media in bottlefed Inuit children. *Canadian Medical Association Journal, 122*, 545–547.

Turner, G. H., & Penfold, D. J. (1952). The scholastic aptitude of the Indian children of the Caradoc reserve. *Canadian Journal of Psychology, 6*, 31–44.

Vallee, F. G. (1961). Suggestions for psychological research among the Eskimo. *Bulletin of Ontario Psychological Association, 14*, 39–45.

van de Koppel, J. M. H. (1983). *A developmental study of the Biaka Pygmies and the Bangandu.* Lisse: Swets & Zeitlinger.

Van Leeuwen, M. S. (1978). A cross-cultural examination of psychological differentiation in males and females. *International Journal of Psychology, 13*, 87–122.

Vernon, P. E. (1966). Educational and intellectual development among Canadian Indians and Eskimos. *Educational Review, 18*, 79–91, 181–195.

Vernon, P. E. (1969). *Intelligence and cultural environment.* London: Methuen.

Vincent, L. L. (1975). The performance of Navajo and Apache Indian children on the Bender-Gestalt Test using the Koppitz Developmental Scoring System for visual-motor perception. *Dissertation Abstracts International, 55.* (University of Northern Colorado Microfilms No. 75-11107).

Wakefield, L. E. (1982). *Relationships among selected scoring patterns on the Wechsler Intelligence Scale for Children–Revised and Quadrant classification on the Matching Familiar Figures Test.* Unpublished doctoral dissertation, University of South Dakota, Vermillion.

Wallace, H. M. (1973). The health of American Indian children. *American Journal of the Diseases of Children, 125*, 449–454.

Werner, H. (1948). *Comparative psychology of mental development* (rev. ed.). Chicago: Follet.

West, L. W., & MacArthur, R. S. (1964). An evaluation of selected intelligence tests for two samples of Metis and Indian children. *Alberta Journal of Educational Research, 10*, 17–27.

Westermeyer, J. (1977). Cross-racial foster home placement among native American psychiatric patients. *Journal of the National Medical Association, 69*(4), 231–236.

Wiltshire, E. B., & Gray, J. E. (1969). Draw-a-Man and Raven's Progressive Matrices (1938) intelligence test performance of reserve Indian children. *Canadian Journal of Behavioural Science, 1*, 119–122.

Wintrob, R., & Sindell, P. (1972). Culture change and psychopathology: The case of Cree students in Quebec. In J. W. Berry & G. J. S. Wilde (Eds.), *Social psychology: The Canadian context.* Toronto: McClelland & Stewart.

Witelson, S. F. (1977). Developmental dyslexia: Two right hemispheres and none left. *Science, 195*, 309–311.

Yule, W., Lansdown, R., Millar, I. B., & Urbanowitz, M. A. (1981). The relationship between blood lead concentration, intelligence, and attainment in a school population: A pilot study. *Developmental Medical Child Neurology, 23,* 567–576.

Zarske, J. A., Moore, C. L., & Peterson, J. D. (1981). WISC-R factor structures for diagnosed learning disabled Navajo and Papago children. *Psychology in the Schools, 18,* 402–407.

16 Aboriginal cognition and psychological nescience

L. Z. Klich

Introduction

The aim of this chapter is to focus attention on Australian Aboriginal cognitive skills in their cultural context. The intention is not to provide a review of all cognitive research findings about Aborigines: The total body of research work, with a few exceptions, has been assessed by psychologists themselves as "grossly inadequate" (Kearney & McElwain, 1976). In a more recent comprehensive summary, Watts (1982) tabulated research studies of Aboriginal cognitive abilities from 1967 onwards, and concluded that the majority had simply contributed to an overwhelming emphasis on "deficit" (compare McShane & Berry, Chapter 15).

The intent here is rather to assemble available research evidence relating to Aboriginal cognitive skills and expertise. Initially this will involve sifting or "noodling" through earlier research findings (in certain parts of central Australia, Aborigines, venturesome whites, and passing researchers are known occasionally to go noodling: This entails painstakingly searching through the deserted mullock heaps for small opals that may have been overlooked by the opal miners who originally created the mullock, or mining refuse). Such research noodling can sometimes yield gemlike evidence of value suggesting that Aboriginal cognitive proficiency may have been adequately sampled in certain circumstances but may not have been recognised as such within the interpretive framework of the time or of particular researchers.

More recent research studies which have specifically identified and analysed cognitive skills valued within Aboriginal contexts will then be considered. Such research has been characterised by recognition of Aboriginal

This chapter, in attempting to revise and integrate a range of materials, in part draws upon topics first addressed in "Redirections in cognitive research with Australian Aborigines," *Australian Aboriginal Studies* (1983), *1*, 38–42, and "Toward a recognition of Australian Aboriginal competence in cognitive functions," in J. Kirby, (Ed.), *Cognitive Strategies and Educational Performance* (New York: Academic Press, 1984). I am indebted to the University of New England and the Australian Institute of Aboriginal Studies for continued funding and support. I am particularly grateful to the Pitjantjatjara and Yankuntjatjara people of the northwest of South Australia for shared learning and frequent permission to stay on their lands; to the staff at Ernabella, Amata, Indulkana, and Fregon Aboriginal schools, especially Robert Lines and Geoff Higgins; and to Sue Maguire and Barry Jeromson for room to write and food for thought.

cognitive competence, in contrast to earlier perceptions of cognitive skill variations as intellectual deficits, and has also been due to the reconceptualisation of cognition in terms of context-sensitive processes or operations instead of inherent properties or capacities. It has also sought to identify and examine those situations in which that competence may be evident, and to comprehend the processes underlying the skills by which that competence is expressed.

Finally, I shall briefly discuss several issues with implications for methodology derived from ongoing research at the interdisciplinary workface which may help to signpost future directions in cognitive research with Australian Aborigines.

Background

The Australian human environment today comprises a cultural and linguistic patchwork quilt of increasing complexity. Some 40% of the population were born overseas or have at least one parent born overseas. Nearly 99% of Australians are immigrants or the descendants of immigrants who have landed during the last 200 years. Multiculturalism is a social fact of life; and the recognition of multiculturalism as a political ideal currently occupies centre stage in the build-up to the inevitable 1988 bicentenary birthday party.

Amid all this pluralistic euphoria, it is probably too easy to forget that 200 years ago without doubt, and possibly many thousands of years ago, the human environment in Australia was already multicultural and multilingual. The first Australians were Aborigines, and they constituted hundreds of different cultural groups with discrete languages and social norms, of which a surprising number endure today.

Ab origine, of course, means "from the very first," and although the name thus bestowed on the original inhabitants of Australia by European invaders with a classical education clearly recognised Aboriginal prior ownership of this island continent, it certainly did not bring with it concomitant legal acknowledgment, let alone respect for human dignity. Having mastered the complex skills needed to cope with the intractability of extreme environmental conditions, and then having survived even harsher treatments meted out in the process of subsequent European colonisation, it was not until 1967 that the descendants of the first Australians were legally given equal rights in Australia, and at present they number about 180,000, or a little over 1% of the population.

They may be living under deplorable conditions on the fringe of small country towns, or in northern islands and coastal communities set among the lush vegetation of a tropical climate. They may be travelling between remote settlements across the wilderness of central Australia, perpetuating ceremonial rituals steeped in mythical significance and linked to the visual features of an immense and apparently arid habitat, passing on an intricate set of beliefs and practices in response to environmental demand, and considering themselves the embodiment of those mythical ancestors who through their actions had given form and therefore meaning to the land around them. They are equally likely elsewhere to be living in metropolitan city suburbs and modern housing estates.

Whether the situation they presently find themselves in is urban or rural, contemporary or traditional, Aboriginal people in Australia share a cultural heritage that is unique (Elkin, 1974; Berndt & Berndt, 1981), with archaeological data confirming Aboriginal occupancy dating back at least 40,000 years, and probably longer. The available evidence suggests that, having come originally from Asia via the areas now known as Indonesia and New Guinea, once in Australia Aborigines remained relatively isolated before the influx of Europeans, apart from infrequent contact with Macassan traders on the northern coastline.

The first European encounters with Aborigines, judging by the harsh and disparaging comments in the journals of early Dutch and English navigators (with the notable exception of Captain Cook), established a protracted pattern of negative appraisal by immigrants towards the Aboriginal way of life. Instead of viewing the comparative lack of material possessions among Aborigines as the purposeful product of efficient adaptation by successful hunter–gatherers, Europeans instead interpreted it as symbolic of cultural impoverishment and intellectual inferiority.

Anthropologists and missionaries were not slow to follow convicts, soldiers, and pastoralists who arrived in the wake of Cook's visit, but greater contact and more frequent if not always more accurate observation during the first 150 years or so of European incursion were largely subject to the interpretive constraints of social evolutionary thinking. The notion of a general evolutionary scale in the biological domain and its colonially opportune extension into Spencer's doctrine of social evolution had become a core element of scientific thought and appraisal during the 19th century (Cole & Scribner, 1974), and its traces have persisted in popular and politically expedient terminology virtually to the present day. Assessments of Aboriginal cognitive functioning within such a framework typically characterised the first Australians as belonging on one of the lower rungs of the intellectual development ladder (Chase & von Sturmer, 1973), and often at its base.

Anthropological efforts focussed initially on the more obvious exotic features such as physical characteristics, but as realisation grew that Aboriginal social behaviour and kinship organisation were considerably more varied and more complex than had been originally appreciated, research was extended to encompass social anthropology. So much greater was the complexity in fact, that a noted modern anthropologist considered Aborigines to be so far ahead of the rest of humanity where the organisation of the family was concerned that westerners had to employ all the refinements of contemporary mathematics to record and understand the careful, deliberate systems of social rules they had developed (Lévi-Strauss, cited in Franklin, 1976).

Spasmodic gratuitous asides dealing with Aboriginal cognitive proficiency in the early commentaries often attested to displays of visual skills in hunting or tracking: For example, "All blacks can find their way through scrub or bush, or over plains for any distance, as if by instinct" (Palmer, 1884), or "the senses of the Australians, especially sight, are decidedly keener than ourselves" (Curr, 1886). It has been noted by Chase and von Sturmer (1973) that an evolutionary perspective inevitably led to the interpretation of such reports as evidence of indisputable proximity to the animal kingdom, because everyday reliance on highly developed senses, especially those of sight and smell, was also basic to brute survival.

The first systematic attempt to examine Aboriginal cognitive skills came at the turn of the century in what probably constituted the first occasion on which trained psychologists had worked among culturally different people in their natural surroundings (Haddon, 1935).

Early assessments

April 1898 saw the arrival on Thursday Island of the Cambridge Anthropological Expedition to the Torres Strait, whose members gathered ethnographic, linguistic, physiological, and psychological data in the area during a period of some seven months. Six visiting Australian Aborigines were tested for visual acuity on Mabuiag Island, and their mean result was higher than that of the local Torres Strait islanders. Attributing this to the comparative youth and health of the Aborigines, Rivers additionally remarked that "the ease with which most of them acquired the method and their general behaviour in connection with the testing gave me the impression that . . . they are far from being so low in the scale of intelligence as has sometimes been supposed" (Rivers, 1901, p. 41).

Drawing attention to widespread accounts of supposedly exceptional sharpness of vision among "natives," including Aborigines, Rivers's (1901) analysis of the Cambridge Expedition data showed that the visual acuity of the average islander was marginally superior to that of a normal European, but not what might be termed extraordinary. On the other hand, he considered their observational powers to be "equal to any of those which have excited the admiration and wonder of travellers elsewhere" (Rivers, 1901, p. 42), and ascribed this to particularised knowledge developed through exclusive attention to minute details of objects in their everyday environment.

The unsubtle penetration of the social evolutionary framework is clearly evident in Rivers's further conjecture that this apparent emphasis on "the sensory side of mental life" (i.e., the functional exercise of those perceptual skills required for efficient survival within specific environmental constraints) probably precluded access to "higher" mental functions (as defined in European or Cambridge culture), so that "the predominant attention of the savage to concrete things around him may act as an obstacle to higher mental development" (Rivers, 1901, p. 45).

If scientists are indeed expected to address their data, then this would seem to be one small example of straying well beyond such conversational limits, although perhaps not so surprising when viewed in conjunction with awareness that a popular proposal for scientific debate at the time was T. H. Huxley's idea that Aborigines constituted the missing links in the evolution of mankind (Kearney, 1966). In all fairness to Rivers, Kearins (1977) has pointed out that subsequent data collection with other cultural groups alongside the few major differences, and some confusing inconsistencies in the Torres Strait findings when compared with European performance norms, led Rivers many years later to question and appreciate the limitations of the evolutionary approach to understanding cultural differences in cognition.

Some years after the Cambridge expedition, Stanley Porteus was invited to South Australia as adviser on training programmes and facilities for the mentally handicapped. He expressed interest in learning about Aborigines and their culture, and was taken in 1915 to a mission station where he administered the *Porteus Maze Tests* to 28 Aboriginal children. Porteus had previously attempted in Melbourne to devise effective procedures for selecting from amongst supposed "mental defectives" those who could best profit from specialised instruction. He considered that the *Binet Tests* then commonly in use did not measure foresight, planning, and sustained attention, which in his opinion were essential components of intelligence, and therefore designed the *Porteus Maze Tests,* which he still claimed nearly 40 years later were the most effective measures of planning capacity (Porteus, 1950). This first testing of Aboriginal children with the *Maze* gave a mean mental age of 9 years, 9 months to children whose mean chronological age from mission records was 10 years, 2 months, a result Porteus thought to be unusually good in a racial group that was in his experience almost universally considered to be among the least intelligent of mankind (Porteus, 1950).

Later testing and more extensive exposure to Aboriginal skills in different environmental contexts expanded Porteus's interests beyond mere assessment of mental age and measurement of cranial capacity to include a wide range of cognitive functions evident in habitat-relevant intellectual skills. Thus, on the question of the relative efficiency of auditory versus visual memory skills he considered it was reasonable "to suppose that in a race such as the Australian, which is dependent largely for existence on keenness of visual observation, visual memory will be disproportionately developed" (Porteus, 1931, p. 390), and indeed Aboriginal performance on devised measures of the two processes showed that mean mental age scores on the visual memory task were more than 2 years ahead of auditory memory scores.

Porteus also developed a *Footprint Test* in order further to assess visual skills more appropriate to Aboriginal experiences. This required duplicate photographs of footprints to be matched with a series of eight original photographs, and norms for the test were established with a white high school sample from Hawaii. Aborigines faced with this task tended on average to deliberate for a few seconds longer before completion, but their mean performance score equalled that of the white students. Given the relative unfamiliarity of the Aborigines with the products of western technology such as photographs, Porteus (1931) considered their achievement to be exceptional, indicating that "with test material with which they are familiar the aborigines' ability to discriminate form and spatial relationships is at least equal to that of whites of high-school standards of education and of better than average social standing" (1931, p. 401).

In a discussion of the relative "degrees" of intelligence attributed to different groups of Aborigines resulting from an anthropologist's suggestion that relative intelligence may have simply reflected degrees of previous exposure to the use of the English language, Porteus (1933) placed considerable emphasis on what he called the "social intelligence" displayed by Aborigines in their own surroundings but refused to relinquish his expectations of Aboriginal inadaptability to white culture. He elaborated that Aborigines probably suffered from an earlier cessation of brain growth than occurred in Europeans, and that their inferior auditory rote memory indicated a "deficient capacity" to benefit from school instruction, so that continued poor scholastic achievement seemed inevitable.

The results of many further years of research on "australid mentality" using the *Maze Tests,* together with similar studies of other cultural groups from around the world, were summarised in Porteus (1965). The culmination was a tabular ranking of "comparative mentalities" as represented by mean *Maze* age-scores, thus grading 25 groups of "illiterate adults" on an intellectual ladder which further graphically illustrated the pervasive heritage of social evolutionary interpretation, and echoed its central premise disseminated some 80 years previously that "nineteenth century Englishmen were of the highest mentality and lived in the most advanced society, representing a standard against which other people could be measured" (Cole & Scribner, 1974, p. 15). Porteus clearly felt unable to jettison that core dogma, and we may note the intriguing juxtaposition this created, that although Porteus consistently advocated a high opinion of Aboriginal "social intelligence" as expressed in artistic, inventive, and general living skills within their own environment, he adamantly denied the effects of environmental influences such as contact with European culture when it came to evaluating cognitive test performance, preferring instead to promulgate belief in a "biologically determined inferiority" (Porteus, 1965, p. 164).

Overlapping with the latter efforts of Porteus, a substantial component in the study of Aboriginal cognition has come from the work of McElwain and his colleagues at the University of Queensland. McElwain had originally accompanied Fowler, who tested Aborigines of the Gascoyne River area of West Australia in 1940 with a number of performance measures including the *Ferguson Form Board* and the *Alexander Passalong Test*. They reported encouraging results emphasising the very wide range of individual results obtained, the large variation in scores between different tribal groups, and the considerably smaller difference between male and female scores than had been reported in previous studies. They declared that "if we can rely on our results, some natives have intelligence of a high degree" (Fowler, 1940, p. 127).

Under McElwain's supervision a variety of cognitive ability measures with established use in western cultures were over many years carefully trialled for validity with indigenous groups in Australia and Papua–New Guinea (Kearney, 1966), ultimately resulting in the construction of the *Queensland Test* (McElwain & Kearney, 1970), which attempted to minimise the effects of cultural background and educational experience on task performance and hence represents one of many efforts in psychology to devise a "culture-free" or "culture-fair" test. The *Queensland Test* is described as an individually administered performance test of general cognitive ability, particularly designed for use under conditions of reduced communication. The five subtests are nonverbal in administration and response, with the tester inviting the subject to reproduce arranged materials or to imitate manipulative procedures. The materials are nonrepresentational, the test goals are unambiguous, and all items gradually increase in difficulty.

In communities, settlements, and remote locations throughout Australia, more than 1,000 Aboriginal children and adults with a wide spectrum of European contact were tested and their achievement compared with European-descent performance (McElwain & Kearney, 1970). The findings signified that "Aboriginal groups are inferior to Europeans, and in approximately the same degree as they have lacked contact" (McElwain & Kearney, 1973, p. 47). In order to maximise confidence that the *Queensland Test* could be used with Aborigines as a measure of "cognitive ability" rather than an index of acculturation, three separate sets of test norms corresponding to three relative degrees of estimated contact with white majority culture were established and included in the test documentation.

If, however, the influences of language and formal educational experience as intervening variables are assumed to have been minimised in the *Queensland Test,* the question remains as to what are the reasons for consistently lower Aboriginal scores. Possible contributing factors listed by McElwain and Kearney (1973) were that Aboriginal children did not use symmetry as freely as European children in solving problems, that they tended to have difficulty in handling flat surface representations, and that Aboriginal language systems did not appear to have many quantitative components. An additional factor discussed by McElwain (1976) was that although the test goals may be quite clearly perceived by the testee, competent strategies for the solution of specific problems require appropriate selective attention. The Aboriginal child or adult may be utilising preferred learning or processing strategies that are contextually inefficient for a particular task, or may not have the necessary prior experience with similar problem-solving situations to deploy his or her attentiveness judiciously. Thus, in paying attention to all the perceived aspects of a given problem-solving context, the Aboriginal person may well be dealing with some or many features of the task that are simply irrelevant from the tester's or test designer's cultural vantage point.

Accordingly, in complete contrast to Porteus, McElwain and Kearney insisted that "there are no inborn or genetic limitations on the basic intelligence of Aborigines" (1973, p. 50), and argued instead that environmental experience was a major determinant of performance on measures of cognitive ability.

Testing deficits and differences

Psychological research with Aboriginal Australians proliferated in the period 1960–1980, producing two edited volumes of readings (Kearney, de Lacey, & Davidson, 1973; Kearney & McElwain, 1976) and a plethora of discrete investigations (Kearney & McElwain [1975] compiled an inventory of psychological research with Aboriginal Australians which itemised some 280 studies). Much of this research unfortunately does not survive more rigorous methodological scrutiny. Brislin (1976), for example, reviewed many of the studies published in the edited volume by Kearney, de Lacey, and Davidson (1973). Specifically addressing problems in the methodology of cognitive studies with Australian Aborigines, he discussed a range of plausible rival hypotheses that might equally well explain apparently lower performance scores among subjects without an established tradition of exposure to sophisticated western assessment procedures.

Watts (1982) has produced the most recent tabulation of cognitive research with aboriginal Australians, and in general terms three categories can be identified based on the use of similar instruments: studies which have used supposed measures of general intelligence; those which have tested psycholinguistic abilities; and those concerned with Piaget's theory of intellectual development. All three domains have produced consistent findings of inferior performance by Aboriginal children, and these findings have usually been interpreted as demonstrating that environmental factors have retarded the development of cognitive functions.

Testing intelligence

Within the parameters of this paper, studies by Money and Nurcombe (1974) and McIntyre (1976) represent positive efforts to sample Aboriginal cognitive proficiency utilising assessment procedures better aligned with Aboriginal cultural process and content. Applying the premise that graphic tasks were probably more compatible with the everyday cognitive demands of a culture in which painting, carving, totemic designs, and ceremonial decorations constituted a rich and revered artistic tradition, Money and Nurcombe (1974) used the nonverbal *Draw-a-Man Test* and the *Bender Visual-Motor Gestalt Test* with Aboriginal children from eastern Arnhem Land. They found that

Aboriginal female mean scores were slightly below the expected norm, but that Aboriginal male mean scores were consistently above, and attributed this to differential experience within a culture where a great deal of artistic endeavour was associated with the (supposedly predominant) male sphere of sacred knowledge embedded in ceremonial rituals.

McIntyre (1976) examined dimensions of cognitive style among urban and rural Aboriginal and non-Aboriginal children, and used the *Queensland Test* as one measure of general cognitive ability. She found some support for McElwain and Kearney's (1970) proposition that performance on the *Queensland Test* for Aboriginal children was related to degree of contact with European culture (or some variable connected with contact) because no significant difference appeared on the *Queensland Test* scores between cultural groups in the urban location, but white children performed significantly better in the more remote rural environment.

Using discriminant analysis to explore the nature of the performance differences among the four samples of upper primary schoolchildren, McIntyre found that after inclusion of standard and process-modified measures of field independence, reflectivity, conceptual style, and school achievement, no discriminant function differentiated between the groups simply on the basis of culture. The major function produced an urban–rural distinction (80% of the variance) and the next involved educational content variables (11% of the variance). Other analyses showed that field dependence and reflectivity were related to intelligence, whereas conceptual style was not, cognitive style measures were more related to school performance for Aboriginal than for white children, and rural Aborigines were more impulsive than the other groups. Overall, then, specific geographical location appeared to exert a more tangible influence on cognitive test performance than broad cultural background.

Psycholinguistic testing

A closer scrutiny of the psycholinguistic literature also suggests that some of the tasks involving visual processing produced relatively more favourable results for Aborigines; for instance, Bruce, Hengeveld, and Radford (1971) found that Aboriginal primary schoolchildren performed better than non-Aboriginal children on the *Illinois Test of Psycholinguistic Abilities* (*ITPA*) *Visual Closure Scale*, and Nurcombe and Moffitt (1970) found no significant difference on the same scale among white and Aboriginal preschoolers. Teasdale and Katz (1968) reported no differences among 5-year-old Aboriginal and white schoolchildren on *Visual Decoding* and *Visual-Motor Association Scales*, while Harries (1967) estimated that Aboriginal children of preschool age in northern New South Wales were "within the normal range" of scores on the *Visual Decoding* and *Visual-Motor Sequential* subtests. Watts (1982) suggests that given widely differing degrees of fluency in the English language between and within both rural and urban Aboriginal groups, the expectation of reliable familiarity with standard English as part of the *ITPA* administration is in many cases unreasonable, and depressed performance scores by Aborigines on subtests may therefore confidently be predicted.

Piagetian tasks

In the piagetian domain, De Lemos (1969) argued that according to Piaget's theory, the order of progression in cognitive development from a sensorimotor stage in infancy through to the stage of formal operations in adolescence should be invariant because it is biologically determined, but that the rate of advancement through the stages is a result of environmental interaction, and thus children exposed to different sociocultural influences could be expected to achieve the same order of stages, but not necessarily at similar ages.

Her own research focussed on the concept of conservation, and found that it developed much later in Aboriginal children than in European children, with some instances where it ostensibly did not develop at all (De Lemos, 1969). Where European children invariably acquired the conservation of quantity, weight, and volume, in that order, Aboriginal children appeared to develop conservation of weight before that of quantity. In addition, a statistically significant difference in performance favoured "part-Aboriginal" children over "full-blood" Aboriginal children, although both were living under identical conditions in the same community, and this result was later cited by Jensen (1973) in support of his rationale for genetic differences in intellectual capacity between racial groups.

Dasen (1973) attempted to replicate De Lemos's research with high and low contact Aboriginal groups and an urban European sample, while also assessing the comparative development of logico-mathematical operations related to concepts of number and measurement in contrast to spatial operations. The stages described in Piaget's theory did, indeed, occur in the same order in both Aboriginal and white children, but the rate of development among Aboriginal children was so "slow" that a reasonably large percentage of Aborigines were thought to be unlikely to develop some of the concrete operational concepts even in maturity.

Contrary to De Lemos's evidence, Dasen found no difference within the Aboriginal data in the performance of "part-Aboriginal" and "full-blood" Aboriginal children, but between the two cultural groups a major difference did appear in the sequence of operational acquisition. The urban white children acquired logico-mathematical operations earlier than spatial operations, while the process was reversed for the high and low contact Aboriginal groups (both from central Australia), who developed spatial concepts earlier than concepts related to number and measurement.

Dasen (1975) then attempted to extend Berry's eco-cultural model of behavioural adaptation to the piagetian cognitive domain. Berry (1976) had proposed an ecological framework for interpreting cultural and behavioural variation by arguing that no longer should cultural variables be viewed as antecedent and behavioural variables as consequent, but rather that the physical environment, the culture developed in response to environmental demand, and the range of individual behaviours evident in that cultural group were likely to be functionally interrelated. In terms of this model, Dasen predicted that spatial concrete operational concepts would necessarily develop more readily among groups such as the Eskimos, characterised by small group numbers, nomadic hunter–gatherer survival mechanisms, and low food accumulation, than among sedentary agriculturalist cultures with high food accumulation such as the West African Ebrie. He estimated that on the basis of their eco-cultural adaptive strategies, Australian Aborigines would show a rate of spatial operations development that would be intermediate between the other two groups, and this hypothesis was confirmed by the data.

Methodological concerns in the piagetian approach to the cross-cultural study of cognition have been elaborated by Dasen and Heron (1981) and Kamara and Easley (1977), and focus primarily on the tendency in cross-cultural piagetian research to collect data almost entirely through performance tests rather than through Piaget's own "method of critical exploration," which utilised probing clinical interviews. This may in part be the result in cross-cultural contexts of existing language barriers between interviewer and child, which perhaps do not permit a meaningful dialogue. Given also that the use of hypothetical, decontextualised, or impersonal queries within a question-and-answer routine has now been recognised as a verbal learning ritual characteristic of western cultures (Cole, Gay, Glick, & Sharp, 1971), and at odds with traditional Aboriginal communication strategies (Harris, 1977), it seems that the piagetian clinical interview technique to probe the reasoning underlying task performance is unlikely to be productive, at least with more traditionally oriented Aboriginal groups. This conclusion is generalised by Irvine and Berry, in Chapter 1, to all studies using interpreters.

The congruence of responses by subjects in one culture to the stimuli and procedures devised in another has also been the subject of criticisms concerned with cultural as well as linguistic obstacles to communication and the expression of competence in piagetian performance measures. Goodnow (1980), for example, considers that piagetian tasks usually contain a "perceptual trap" which may encourage inexperienced testees to follow misleading visual cues. Although the assumption behind such approaches (that a good way to assess intelligence or some other construct is to present people with an unfamiliar problem for which their past experience may not provide sufficient guidance) may arguably be valid in some sections of western cultures where psychological testing is a frequent occurrence, in the case of culturally different groups such as Australian Aborigines it is at best questionable, and the tasks may simply be measuring the extent to which individuals in that group are consciously acquainted with the rules and procedures of test-taking cultures.

The universality of the piagetian ideal of reasoning abstracted from practical content, context, and experience has been challenged in the writings
of Buck-Morss (1975) as originating from a culture in which learning and
schooling are customarily removed from ordinary life settings, often with
little immediate application to everyday skills. The ethnographic work of
Harris (1977) dealing with learning styles does indeed make it difficult to
locate the relevance of the piagetian ideal in the context of Aboriginal formal
and informal education. Harris described five major learning strategies
among traditionally oriented Aboriginal coastal people at Milingimbi: learning through real-life performance rather than practice in contrived settings;
the mastering of context-specific skills rather than abstract, generalisable
principles; learning through observation and imitation rather than through
oral or written verbal instruction; learning through personal trial-and-error
as opposed to verbally mediated demonstrations; and an evident orientation
towards people rather than tasks, information, or systems.

Like the results from measures of general intelligence and psycholinguistic
abilities, piagetian findings have been interpreted within a deficit framework
as evidence for the retarded development of basic cognitive functions due
to environmental influences, and that this cognitive "deficiency" can be
remedied or forestalled by compensatory education, often in the form of
early intervention programmes (de Lacey, 1970; Nurcombe & Moffitt, 1970).

One piagetian scholar reached a rather different conclusion: *Caveat interventor* was the specific warning issued by Seagrim (1977). Confronted
with the familiar pattern of inferior Aboriginal performance on piagetian
tasks from a long-term project in central Australia, he formally recognised
the logical endpoint of the interventionist approach as being that Aboriginal
children should be removed from their natural families as soon as possible
and for as long as possible if they were to achieve western cognitive competence (Seagrim & Lendon, 1976). This was manifestly unacceptable as an
educational goal, and an abhorrent prospect from any other point of view:
Not many years before, so-called part-Aboriginal children had already been
forcibly removed from their families by decree of government-appointed
European "protectors" in a shameful period of Australian history.

A plausible alternative, and one reminiscent of Cole and Scribner's ex-
hortation that "in the long run it will be more productive to direct our criticism at the deficiencies of our science rather than at the alleged deficiencies
of the people we study" (1974, p. 173), was to question the weighty assumption that cognitive competence in one culture necessarily precluded
competence in another. If language was indeed a crucial filter for interpreting
information and organising experience, as well as the major code for cultural
transmission – and enough evidence existed from bilingual programmes
around the world (including a far-sighted one among Pitjantjatjara Aborigines
at Ernabella, in Central Australia) to suggest that bilingual competence certainly could be achieved – then why not encourage dual cultural learning
systems where neither one emphasised the exclusion of situations or pro-

cedures which allowed for development in the other, and thus promote bi-cultural cognitive competence through bicultural learning? Seagrim and Lendon posited further that cognitive development appropriate for coping with the demands of white culture "may equally well be achieved by the persistence (or recovery) of Aboriginal culture in its richest and most fully integrated forms as by its complete destruction" (1976, p. 230).

Recognition of Aboriginal cognitive mastery by almost exclusively non-Aboriginal psychologists and educators may eventually lead to some understanding of the cognitive processes which underlie those skills, and so facilitate a wider realisation of such bicultural developmental goals. A handful of evidence so far exists from research which has explicitly sought to identify and analyse that mastery.

Aboriginal cognitive expertise

Cultures not only develop in response to environmental demand but also consequently systematise perceptions of it. The axiom that all human groups are competent to carry out the polytypic functions required by their physical environment and culture was a well-entrenched anthropological principle (Kroeber, 1948) at a time when theoretical assumptions and research methodology in western psychology were so permeated with ethnocentric myopia that where cross-cultural data were concerned, interpretations of them amounted to little more than an accretion of monocultural nescience and disciplinary xenophobia, often with some disastrous practical applications.

Even many years later it took a linguist (Labov, 1975) to push back at least one frontier of psychological ignorance and its unfortunate implementation. In Australia impoverished psychological interpretations transferred uncritically to learning contexts constitute the history of Aboriginal education and client-change programmes. In a trenchant review, McConnochie (1981) goes so far as to claim that psychological research consistently provided the strongest support for the affirmation among professional educators that well-documented failure of Aboriginal pupils in schools was caused by various deficits in the children. It is not surprising, therefore, that in order to gather evidence of Aboriginal cognitive expertise, research noodling needs to look beyond the "sterile pedantry" (Turner, 1973) of narrow disciplinary confines. In this section I shall attempt to assemble findings interrelating culture and cognition through Aboriginal perceptual and memory skills from research mostly conducted in more traditionally oriented Aboriginal contexts.

Exotic accounts by early travellers, and later intermittent anecdotal reinforcement by anthropological reports such as those earlier referred to by Rivers (1901), encouraged belief in remarkable powers of observation and supposedly exceptional memory skills among nonliterate cultural groups generally. In the absence of western forms of literacy, it was presumed that cultural demands for continuity and information transfer in an exclusively oral tradition require emphasis on memory skills (Reisman, 1956), and in attempting to explain "the reputation for excessively accurate and detailed memory which the more or less primitive group often possesses," Bartlett (1932, p. 264) suggested that manner of recall was a cultural predisposition determined by persistent and socially structured psychological schemata. It has also been argued that the development of specialised mnemonic devices such as epic poems, myths, and ceremonial verbal rituals constitutes an efficient, if not always conscious, procedural mechanism for the organisation, storage, and transmission of important cultural knowledge (Reisman, 1956; Havelock, 1963) and geographical information (Harwood, 1976; Hage, 1978).

These mechanisms undoubtedly also formed (and in many remote locations continue to form) an important part of the cultural cognitive environment of Aboriginal Australians, but evidence does exist that nonverbal methods for recording and transferring information were also in use. Basedow (1925) described message sticks on which stories involving the portrayal of symbolic animal tracks representing specific geographical terrain had been carved. Spencer and Gillen (1899) and Meggitt (1966) considered that the carrying of message sticks, sacred boards, and bullroarers by messengers to convene disparate groups for ceremonies was widespread throughout Australia, and Mountford's (1956) accounts clarify that highly detailed information such as the known position and number of visiting groups and expected times of arrival could be so marked and conveyed. A recent illustration with descriptive details of message stick use appears in Memmot (1979). Harris (1982) described a body-marking message system in which envoys could have their bodies decorated according to a system of 28 positions representing phases of the moon to indicate planned events within the lunar cycle. The technique was first described by Dawson in 1881, but Harris had recently had an Aboriginal co-worker who described just such a system.

Aboriginal skills in tracking, route finding, and geographical orientation similar to those cited in an earlier section have been discussed and analysed on several occasions in the literature (Strehlow, 1943; Lahiri, 1965). Some of the most detailed accounts of tracking skills are in unpublished fieldwork reports – for example, those by N. and P. Wallace – kept at the Australian Institute for Aboriginal Studies in Canberra.

Embedded in them is an amusing story recounted by members of mission staff from Ernabella at their own expense. A member of staff had thought to introduce the game "Who touched me?" at an Aboriginal women's meeting. In order to explain what it was about they had a trial run. Everyone sat in a large circle while one woman was blindfolded. At a nonverbal signal from a missionary another woman walked around the circle, touched the blindfolded one on the shoulder, and then returned to her original position. The blindfold was then removed and that woman was asked to guess who had touched her, by pointing. She simply looked behind her, named the woman whose fresh footprint was clearly visible in the sand, and said, "Is that all the game?'' The Aboriginal woman found it hard to believe that such a simpleminded task was considered to be entertaining by the mission staff.

Equally impressive are the accounts of how children and adults play at re-creating animal tracks in the sand with their hands. Precise hand movements involving the heel of the hand, the tips of the fingers pressed together, a single fingernail for a claw mark, the edges of two hands held closely together, the knuckles, and so on, are all utilised in exact sequences to produce vivid tracks seemingly indistinguishable from the real thing. To Wallace (1968) it seemed as if the sand was the blackboard, everyone was at once teacher and student, and such perfectly produced tracks were the elementary exercises in reading for meaning. When asking for someone's whereabouts it was noticeable also that whereas Europeans typically raised their heads and looked around, Aboriginal people were much more likely to look down for the appropriate tracks on the ground. Nor was it often merely a question of establishing identity with human footprints: The person's size, weight, gait, age, general health, possible load, likely destination, and urgency of movement were just as likely to be assessed from the reading.

Although I cannot say I have witnessed the same frequency of tracking activities among children that was reported by the Wallaces, I can certainly verify the extremely effective production of simulated animal and human tracks during the telling of stories among the Pitjantjatjara. I have been present at and have sometimes been given permission to videotape, for example, a number of occasions when *wati tjuta* (initiated Pitjantjatjara men) have recounted mythical stories accompanied by drawings in the sand illustrating journeys and places. These are often stylised depictions of relative locations significant within the story, and are interspersed with track prints used to elaborate narrative action.

Sometimes these abstracted geographical designs (essentially transposed cognitive maps) have imposed upon them track prints which may convey the species, the number, and the direction of beings moving through that country within the story. In other situations totemic body designs painted for or during rituals, designs on sacred boards and stones, or storytellers' simplified (almost shorthand) designs in the sand while recounting the making of an actual journey will contain necessary information on pertinent geographical locations. A highly detailed and well-illustrated structural analysis of graphic representation and cultural iconography among the Warlpiri can be found in Munn (1973).

Recall, recognition, and values

It is difficult to convey an appreciation of Aboriginal perceptual skills without some understanding of how Aborigines actually see their country. The actions of mythical ancestral beings are known to have created the physical features of the land, and hence the meaning of ancestral narratives is literally embodied in the topographical features perceived, that is, "spiritual" (for lack of a better word) scenarios are superimposed on the physical landscape, thus producing visible and, indeed, tangible beliefs. I may be looking at a collection of large, rather longish rocks: A Pitjantjatjara man in the same place sees bodies of men who died here when they were turned to stone. I can make out two indentations close together on the rocky slab: That's where a certain being knelt while copulating with a woman who came from that direction over there – look, you can see the marks on the hillside where she came down to meet him. That mountain is the embodiment of a gigantic lizard with its head up; that waterhole is where the sacred serpent emerges from the earth.

Munn (1973) suggests that major topographical features may be thought of as metamorphoses of parts of a mythical being's body, or due to bodily imprints, and as a result ancestral beings can be followed through their site associations. A typical ancestral narrative is built on a framework of site sequences, and at its most cursory level can be reduced almost to a listing of site names. But our notion of myth and ancestry does not adequately convey the immediacy of the interaction between person and belief: These events are constantly re-happening; you do not merely follow in the traditional ancestral footsteps, rather you are "keeping track of" that being. It is still the Dreaming now, not a Dreamtime long gone.

It is hardly surprising, then, to find accounts in the literature of exceptional Aboriginal skills in route finding, geographical orientation, and memory for locations. Spencer and Gillen's (1899) assessment that Aboriginal memory was "phenomenal" has been reiterated in the work of Lewis (1976), who reported that Aborigines with whom he travelled demonstrated "almost total recall of every topographical feature of any country they had ever crossed." Trying to understand how Aborigines were able to cover, without apparent error, enormous distances across the vast, arid, and to uneducated Western eyes seemingly featureless wilderness of Central Australia, Lewis tried plausible explanations derived from the navigational procedures in other cultures he had studied, for example, orientation by star positions at night, or use of the sun during the day. He found that Aborigines did occasionally rely on data such as the placing of the sun or the quality and direction of the wind, but only on those rare occasions when they were travelling in unfamiliar or, in their terms, "strange" country – strange because the mythical stories associated with it were not known, or not accessible to those individuals.

What became evident to Lewis was that Aborigines preferred to utilise a complex tographical schema which depended on detailed orientational awareness of important landmarks, familiarity with the mythical narratives interlinking those landmarks, and the ability continually to update dynamic mental maps. Aborigines were asked to point out the direction of distant places, and on 33 such occasions accuracy varied from absolutely correct to 67-degree error, with an average error of 13.7 degrees. The larger errors, however, always occurred when indicating European settlements or non-sacred places. The highest degree of accuracy related to the positions of mythically important locations. For six sacred sites, at least 200 kilometres distant in each case, the average error was 2.8 degrees, and the largest deviation recorded was 10 degrees.

Spiritually prominent landmarks were therefore critic~l components of Aboriginal geographical orientation, but such key bases are likely to be simply focal points within a more integrated corpus of mythical lore. Berndt (1959) depicted the whole Western Desert region as being crisscrossed with the meanderings of ancestral beings, often though not always linking known temporary and permanent waterholes. Access to invaluable route guiding information was therefore available through studied familiarity with the visibly marked ancestral activities.

Orientation and keeping track skills

Lewis (1976) observed a number of hunting incidents in which spatially oriented behaviour was impressively accurate but did not appear to have relied on external referents. From explanations offered by his Aboriginal guides, and later confirmatory observations, he believed that the Aborigines were able *constantly to update a dynamic mental map in terms of time, distance, and bearing, with radical realignments at each change of direction*. In this way hunters were able to remain at all times aware of the direction of their base and/or their objective. Lewis concluded that these exceptional Aboriginal visual-spatial orientation skills drew upon complex but flexible mental mapping processes made possible through intensive "terrestrial conditioning" which forged emotional and spiritual bonds with a data-filled environment.

It is then feasible to argue that visual memory for patterns of diverse features and the spatial relationships among them constitutes an acute survival requirement for desert-dwelling Aboriginal hunter–gatherer groups. The research of Kearins (1976, 1981) hypothesised just that, and was based on the premise that selection not only of the more obvious physical characteristics but also of sensory and cognitive adaptations was possible in response to environmental demand. Because these groups had been subject to genetic isolation for many generations, proficient performance on measures of visual-spatial memory could be expected.

In order to measure these skills, Kearins designed a spatial modification of Kim's game. The child was first asked to study a grid-marked array of either 12 or 20 objects for 30 seconds; then the objects were disarranged and the child was asked to replace the items in their original locations. The performance of an Aboriginal adolescent sample on all four such arrays was superior to that of a European-descent group. Aborigines performed equally well on all arrays, but the white children had significantly more difficulty with arrays of *same-name* objects to which differentiating verbal labels could not be easily applied.

The use of memory strategies relying primarily on visual-spatial memory seemed to be considerably more efficient within the task constraints of Kim's game than the verbal coding of information, but the suggestion that superior visual memory skills among Aborigines might be the results of genetic endowment generated controversy. Some five attempts at replication produced mixed and mostly nonsupportive results, and that research has been scrutinised by Klich and Davidson (1983).

It is worth noting, though, that in two of the replication attempts, the post hoc suggestion was made that the superior performance of Kearins's samples may have been due to previous experience with memory games (Drinkwater, 1978; Knapp & Seagrim, 1981). Both refer to a short account by Harney (1952), who described a memory game of the Warlpiri tribe. The game consists of a large circle drawn on the ground, along which the "head" of the game may place as many as 50 objects, while the other participants are not allowed to look. At a call from the "head," children look at the circle and attempt to memorise the objects. They then turn their backs to the circle, and the first player calls an object at a given point, and continues to call the objects along the line until a mistake is made, when the next player takes over. According to Harney, the children soon became experts at the game and could call the objects correctly.

Two points which have not previously been discussed seem pertinent. First, Harney makes it explicit that the objects represent other things, "pieces of sticks, stones, and odd bits of things to represent objects in that area. Should the people live near a highway, as at Phillips Creek settlement, the sticks would be bridges, the stones houses, bits of earth would be motor trucks, and so on" (Harney, 1952, p. 378). There is no more information on this aspect, since the whole game description occupies merely 15 lines, but if items can represent houses and bridges in settled areas, then they may equally well represent topographical features elsewhere; in which case the game is not unlike the recitation of place names and site locations by the older men during ancestral narratives, and may indeed be effective training for it. The game task clearly consists not of recalling the objects themselves, but of remembering what they represent and the sequential order of their occurrence (where position is determined by one object before and one after).

Second, the children stand with their backs to the circle and call out the list of names. In other words, no matter how the information may have been initially encoded, the reproduction is verbal. The two points taken together make the game a very different task from Kim's game, where visual memory for the location of objects relative to a number of others is critical, where some objects have been selected specifically because they cannot be easily verbally differentiated from one another, and where the child nonverbally replaces the items in their original locations.

A replication and extension of the initial Kearins study was reported by Klich and Davidson (1983), and presented some support for Kearins's original data, if not at the same time for an interpretation of them based on the argument of genetic advantage. Aboriginal children living in their own tribal areas did indeed exhibit superior visual memory skills as measured by Kim's game in that study. The significant difference in performance between Aboriginal and white children on a first presentation of the task, however, did not appear on a later presentation when preceded by an instructional and orienting procedure designed to optimise the use of visual memory strategies by all the children.

Attempts to examine temporal and spatial ordering with children have focussed on observed preferences for one type of contextual association over the other in free recall, usually with processing in the visual mode and with children of European urban origins. Davidson and Klich (1980) used two free recall tasks, one involving pictures and the other naturally occurring objects, to investigate temporal and spatial ordering among desert Aborigines. Their results showed that the majority of Aboriginal children preferred spatial over temporal order in the free recall of visual information, and this did not significantly decrease with age. The use of natural objects instead of picture stimuli also elicited significantly more changes in the direction of spatial rather than temporal order. In contrast to an earlier proposition by Freeman (1975), that as "normal" children got older they responded consistently to temporal, not spatial, patterning of stimuli, Davidson and Klich argued that continued preference for spatial order with increasing age was not necessarily due to the prolongation of an earlier developmental stage but was equally interpretable as a purposeful adaptive response to eco-cultural demand.

Cognitive scratch pads: Tallying and counting

A number of recent studies have been concerned with number systems and mathematical concepts in Aboriginal culture. Harris (1982) has stated that nonverbal counting techniques are still frequently used by Aboriginal people. Although this has tended in the past to be associated with inferences of cognitive inferiority, no such inferences have apparently been extended to the widespread use of identical tallying marks in such hallowed European contexts as scoring in cricket, or counting farm animals.

Sayers (1982) has applied to Aboriginal situations the precept that counting does not become necessary until objects are seen in such generalised form that their individually distinguishing properties are no longer perceived. She has contrasted, for example, the quantitative needs of a handcraft society in which tools and goods inevitably possess easily identifying characteristics with the numerical demands of a mass-production system, and has also demonstrated that the Wik–Mungkan people have rather different classification systems and modes of generalising concepts than those generally accepted as commonplace in white schools. Protein food, for example, may be classified according to its readiness to be eaten rather than in terms of number, colour, or shape.

Several researchers have examined Aboriginal card-playing techniques

(Berndt & Berndt, 1947; Holm & Japanangka, 1976); and Davidson (1979) has analysed the information-processing skills among Aborigines at Bamyili (now renamed Barunga). Where Europeans tend to rely exclusively on the numerical and suit symbols in the corner of each card in order initially to identify them and then on computational skills to calculate combinations and scores, Davidson considered that Aborigines instead utilise the large amount of other visual information on the rest of the card for pattern recognition and initial classification, and are able subsequently to maintain such visual information about their cards in a spatial memory array to be retrieved as required.

Sayers (1982) has confirmed that similar pattern recognition procedures seem to be used in card playing among the children at Aurukun, and cites an instance of children knowing or recognising the score value as soon as they saw the cards, well before the teacher had time to add up the appropriate numbers. The lack of conceptual equivalence between different adding or classifying systems, leading to problems in the transfer of skills across contexts, was illustrated by the fact that some of the children who had previously demonstrated skill in numerical addition at school began to have difficulties with it once they learned to play cards. In a counting system for some games where 10s are discounted, for example, $3 + 2 = 5$ is greater than $7 + 6 = 3$, and 10s, 20s, and 30s may be perceived as equally valueless.

Implications

Two relatively important elements for future Aboriginal cognitive research can, I believe, be identified from these diverse examples of cognitive expertise. The first is the need in cross-cultural cognitive research to incorporate interdisciplinary findings and techniques, especially from anthropology and linguistics. The second is the need to emphasise the study of contextual variables surrounding manifest behaviour.

Lewis's (1976) methods continually involved the collection and analysis of observational data from everyday contexts, research behaviours which are much more frequently found in the repertoire of ethnographers and anthropologists than of psychologists. Yet Lewis eventually employed what amounted to a quasi experiment: asking people to point to distant places. Although probably not conceived or construed as such, this certainly could be described as a cognitive task or test, for degrees of error or accuracy are in their own way performance test scores. But, given the necessary prior ethnographic knowledge which allowed this experiment to be located in a culturally familiar setting – because it drew upon the exercise of skills and behaviours which had already been observed in naturally occurring situations and attempted to vary culturally familiar and contextually appropriate information – not only were Aboriginal cognitive skills adequately sampled but the task provided invaluable evidence of what elements in it were critical to successful performance.

We can speculate in Lewis's case what a detailed linguistic analysis might have contributed to an understanding of how attention may be selectively deployed in the development of spatial orientation skills through particular language use. If a certain set of skills is consistently manifested within a specific cultural group, one might reasonably expect the language structures of that culture to facilitate the acquisition of those skills. Bodde (1939) drew attention, for example, to the fact that the Chinese were constantly being made aware of directional orientation not only by the layout of city streets along the compass axes, but by habitually referring to the movement of household objects in terms of their compass-point directions, even when the movement in question was only a few inches. One need not go so far as China: I daresay Adelaide mail carriers are aware of the north versus the south side of the street, and even New England graziers have been known to refer to "the west wall of the house" or "the south paddock." Kirton (1982) described how in learning the Yanyuwa Aboriginal language she was constantly prompted by her Yanyuwa teachers to remember that no statements concerning movement in the language were complete until the locative and/or directional information had been included: "The baby was crawling . . . on the east side"; "the plane had landed . . . on the south side"; and a dog that they watched run around the house had gone "southwards on the east side."

Among my notes on the work of Irving Hallowell, I find him referring to a case documented by de Silva (1931), who reported the strange (to western thinking) phenomenon of a 12-year-old boy with such an unusually accurate sense of spatial orientation that debate arose as to whether this might be an innate ability. Apparently, investigation of his personal history showed that his mother had consistently used cardinal directions in giving the boy instructions such as "Go sit in the chair on the east side of the porch." It is recorded that experiments showed he was dependent upon correct *initial* visual orientation, and was easily disoriented when rotated a few times in a dark room.

An interesting aspect of many of these reports is that use of direction information largely relates to or focusses on fixed features, such as a wall, a paddock, or a porch. But Laughren's (1978) work in the Warlpiri language indicates that directional terminology including the points of the compass and the positions of constantly moving features in relation to them are handled with ease by Warlpiri youngsters of less than 5 years: "A Warlpiri will ask a fellow passenger in a car to move north, south, east, or west rather than just 'move over.' He will refer to his right or left arm or leg as his north, south, east or west arm or leg, depending on his actual orientation" (Laughren, 1978, p. 2).

Kearins's research attempted to match experimental task requirements to long-term survival demands; and she insisted that if the tasks were devised to reflect the contextual parameters of a desert environment, then the social conditions surrounding the task administration should be equally representative of natural social conditions for valid results. Her contribution to future directions undoubtedly arises from her consistent emphasis on the importance of the social context of any interaction between researcher and Aboriginal people. The findings of others who have used the Kim's game demand that we comprehend the range of functional memorising strategies utilised across and within different cultures. To do this we need to examine much more closely those environmental, sociocultural, and even artificial situations which elicit the use of preferred memorising strategies that (possibly inconsequentially, from the user's point of view) may be contextually efficient or inefficient.

Interdisciplinary methodological exchange from anthropology and linguistics has contributed to the recent significant developments in the study of Aboriginal mathematical concepts and number systems. No longer are we likely to find Aboriginal cultures ethnocentrically classified as suffering from a paucity of numerical components, a proposition put forward many times in the past to rationalise low Aboriginal performance on psychological tests. Instead, as Harris (1982) explained, if the number terms do not appear, then either an appropriate functional context has not been identified, or the appropriate functional context may no longer exist. Where an existing context requires it, such as in the sharing of turtle eggs at certain times of the year, a complex and context-specific open-ended number system may be called upon (Sobek, 1981). This may become terminologically cumbersome and less meaningful at a numerical level beyond that perceived to be functional. The more cumbersome it becomes, the more of working memory it occupies, and the slower become mental calculations without recoding. The implications are obvious for any assessment of numbering "out of context."

In the study of spatial and temporal order preference, a change of stimulus type to one assumed to be more congruent with the naturalistic context of the behaviour under consideration produced a significant difference in that behaviour on an otherwise identical task. As alluded to in the earlier criticisms by Goodnow (1980) and Buck-Morss (1975), psychological testing situations have often required individuals to face an unexpected task in an unfamiliar context with completely novel materials. Price-Williams (1975) has placed this alongside the anthropological norm where task, materials, and context are all familiar, and has suggested a "graduating steps" design in which the three variables could be systematically varied from anthropological ease to psychological innovation.

Documenting the existence and the nature of traditionally oriented Aboriginal cognitive skills may well be a necessary but sadly insufficient aid for psychologists to move from nescience to some comprehension of the environment that Aborigines find themselves in today. Aboriginal remote contexts are changing quickly and dramatically amid a proliferation of intrusive but desirable, costly but entertaining, western technological artifacts. The first Australian communications satellite can now beam television programmes to the most far-distant Aboriginal community, should they wish to receive it. Travel across vast desert tracts for large ceremonial gatherings is, as often as not, in a four-wheel-drive vehicle. Video cassette recorders in Aboriginal communities can be used to record Aboriginal accomplishments, or to fast-forward the recycled images and advertisements of western culture.

If psychologists, garnering assistance from anthropology, linguistics, and education, and working in close cooperation with Aborigines themselves, cannot remedy some of the deficiencies in their science and provide a more comprehensive understanding of how cognitive expertise is learned and applied in Aboriginal contexts, then their science, like their nescience, may hold little value and less interest for Aborigines who wish to decide their own cognitive futures.

References

Bartlett, F. C. (1932). *Remembering*. Cambridge University Press.

Basedow, H. (1925). *The Australian Aboriginal*. Adelaide: Preece.

Berndt, R. M. (1959). The concept of the tribe in the Western Desert of Australia. *Oceania, 30*(2), 81–107.

Berndt, R. M., & Berndt, C. H. (1947). Card games amongst Aborigines in the Northern Territory. *Oceania, 17*, 248–269.

Berndt, R. M., & Berndt, C. H. (1981). *The world of the first Australians* (2nd ed.). Sydney: Landsdown Press.

Berry, J. W. (1976). *Human ecology and cognitive style*. Beverly Hills, CA: Sage.

Bodde, D. (1939). Types of Chinese categorical thinking. *Journal of the American Oriental Society, 59*, 201.

Brislin, R. (1976). Methodology of cognitive studies. In G. E. Kearney & D. W. McElwain (Eds.), *Aboriginal cognition*. Canberra: Australian Institute of Aboriginal Studies.

Bruce, D. W., Hengeveld, M., & Radford, W. C. (1971). *Some cognitive skills in Aboriginal children in Victorian Primary schools* (Progress Report No. 2). Melbourne: Australian Council for Educational Research.

Buck-Morss, S. (1975). Socio-economic bias in Piaget's theory and its implications for cross-cultural studies. *Human Development, 18*, 35–49.

Chase, A., & von Sturmer, J. (1973). Mental man and social evolutionary theory. In G. E. Kearney, P. R. de Lacey, & G. R. Davidson (Eds.), *The psychology of Aboriginal Australians*. Sydney: Wiley.

Cole, M., Gay, J., Glick, J., & Sharp, D. (1971). *The cultural context of learning and thinking*. London: Methuen.

Cole, M., & Scribner, S. (1974). *Culture and thought*. New York: Wiley.

Curr, E. M. (1886). *The Australian race* (Vol. 1). Melbourne: Government Printer.

Dasen, P. R. (1973). Piagetian research in Central Australia. In G. E. Kearney, P. R. de Lacey, & G. R. Davidson (Eds.), *The psychology of Aboriginal Australians*. Sydney: Wiley.

Dasen, P. R. (1975). Concrete operational development in three cultures. *Journal of Cross-Cultural Psychology, 6*(2), 156–172.

Dasen, P. R., & Heron, A. (1981). Cross-cultural tests of Piaget's theory. In H. C. Triandis & A. Heron (Eds.), *Handbook of cross-cultural psychology*, Vol. 4: *Developmental Psychology*. Boston: Allyn & Bacon.

Davidson, G. R. (1979). An ethnographic psychology of Aboriginal cognitive ability. *Oceania, 49*(4), 270–294.

Davidson, G. R., & Klich, L. Z. (1980). Cultural factors in the development of temporal and spatial ordering. *Child Development, 51*, 569–571.

de Lacey, P. R. (1970). A cross-cultural study of classificatory ability in Australia. *Journal of Cross-Cultural Psychology, 1*, 293–304.

De Lemos, M. M. (1969). The development of conservation in Aboriginal children. *International Journal of Psychology, 4*, 255–269.

de Silva, H. R. (1931). A case of a boy possessing an automatic directional orientation. *Science, 73*, 393–394.

Drinkwater, B. A. (1978). A reply to Kearins. *Australian Journal of Psychology, 30*, 33–56.

Elkin, A. P. (1974). *The Australian Aborigines* (rev. ed.). Sydney: Angus & Robertson.

Fowler, H. L. (1940). Report on psychological tests on natives in the north of Western Australia. *Australian Journal of Science, 2*, 124–127.

Franklin, M. A. (1976). *Black and white Australians*. London: Heinemann.

Freeman, N. H. (1975). Temporal and spatial ordering in recall by five- to eight-year-old children. *Child Development, 46*, 237–239.

Goodnow, J. J. (1980). Everyday concepts of intelligence and its development. In N. Warren (Ed.), *Studies in cross-cultural psychology* (Vol. 2). New York: Academic Press.

Haddon, A. C. (1935). *Reports of the Cambridge Anthropological Expedition to Torres Strait*, Vol. 1: *General Ethnography*. Cambridge University Press.

Hage, P. (1978). Speculations on Pulawatese mnemonic structure. *Oceania, 49*(2), 81–95.

Harney, W. E. (1952). Sport and play amidst the Aborigines of the Northern Territory. *Mankind, 4*(9), 377–379.

Harries, W. T. (1967). *The effect of attendance at a pre-school kindergarten on the level of intellectual functioning of mixed-blood Aboriginal children*. Unpublished thesis, University of New England, Armidale.

Harris, J. (1982). Facts and fallacies of Aboriginal number systems. In S. Hargraves (Ed.), *Language and culture* (Work papers of SIL-AAB, Series B), *8*, 153–181.

Harris, S. A. (1977). *Milingimbi Aboriginal learning contexts*. Unpublished doctoral dissertation, University of New Mexico, Albuquerque.

Harwood, F. (1976). Myth, memory, and the oral tradition: Cicero in the Trobriands. *American Anthropologist, 78*, 783–796.

Havelock, E. A. (1963). *Preface to Plato*. Cambridge University Press.

Holm, N., & Japanangka, L. (1976). The mathematics of card playing in an Aboriginal community. *The Aboriginal Child at School, 4*, 19–22.

Jensen, A. R. (1973). *Educability and group differences*. London: Methuen.

Kamara, A. I., & Easley, J. A. (1977). Is the rate of cognitive development uniform across cultures? In P. R. Dasen (Ed.), *Piagetian psychology*. New York: Gardner Press.

Kearins, J. (1976) Skills of desert Aboriginal children. In G. E. Kearney & D. W. McElwain (Eds.), *Aboriginal cognition*. Canberra: Australian Institute of Aboriginal Studies.

Kearins, J. (1977). *Visual spatial memory in Australian Aboriginal children of desert regions*. Unpublished doctoral dissertation, University of Western Australia, Perth.

Kearins, J. M. (1981). Visual spatial memory in Australian Aboriginal children of desert regions. *Cognitive Psychology, 13*, 434–460.

Kearney, G. E. (1966). *Some aspects of the general cognitive ability of various groups of Aboriginal Australians as assessed by the Queensland Test*. Unpublished doctoral dissertation, University of Queensland, Brisbane.

Kearney, G. E., de Lacey, P. R., & Davidson, G. R. (Eds.). (1973). *The psychology of Aboriginal Australians*. Sydney: Wiley.

Kearney, G. E., & McElwain, D. W. (1975). Psychological research in Aboriginal Australia. *A.I.A.S. Newsletter* (New Series No. 4).

Kearney, G. E., & McElwain, D. W. (Eds.). (1976). *Aboriginal cognition*. Canberra: Australian Institute of Aboriginal Studies.

Kirton, J. (1982). Some thoughts on Yanyuwa language and culture. In S. Hargrave (Ed.), *Language and culture* (Work papers of SIL-AAB, Series B), *8*, 1–18.

Klich, L. Z., & Davidson, G. R. (1983). A cultural difference in visual memory: On le voit, on ne le voit plus. *International Journal of Psychology, 18*, 189–201.

Knapp, P. A., & Seagrim, G. N. (1981). Visual memory in Australian Aboriginal children and children of European descent. *International Journal of Psychology, 16,* 213–231.

Kroeber, A. (1948). *Anthropology*. New York: Harcourt Brace Jovanovich.

Labov, W. (1975). Academic ignorance and black intelligence. In M. L. Maehr & W. M. Stallings (Eds.), *Culture, child and school*. Monterey, CA: Brooks/Cole.

Lahiri, T. K. (1965, December). Tracking as a fine art. *Citation,* 6–9.

Laughren, M. (1978). Directional terminology in Warlpiri. *Working papers in language and linguistics* (No. 8, pp. 1–16). Launceston: Tasmanian CAE.

Lewis, D. (1976). Observations on route-finding and spatial orientation among the Aboriginal peoples of the Western Desert region of Central Australia. *Oceania, 46,* 249–282.

McConnochie, K. (1981). White tests, black children: Aborigines, psychologists, and education. In B. Menary (Ed.), *Aboriginal schooling*. Adelaide: Adelaide College of the Arts and Education.

McElwain, D. W. (1976). Problems of problem solving. In G. E. Kearney & D. W. McElwain (Eds.), *Aboriginal cognition*. Canberra: Australian Institute of Aboriginal Studies.

McElwain, D. W., & Kearney, G. E. (1970). *Queensland test handbook*. Victoria: Australian Council for Educational Research.

McElwain, D. W., & Kearney, G. E. (1973). Intellectual development. In G. E. Kearney, P. R. de Lacey, & G. R. Davidson (Eds.), *The psychology of Aboriginal Australians*. Sydney: Wiley.

McIntyre, L. A. (1976). An investigation of the effect of culture and urbanisation on three cognitive styles and their relationship to school performance. In G. E. Kearney & D. W. McElwain (Eds.), *Aboriginal cognition*. Canberra: Australian Institute of Aboriginal Studies.

Meggitt, M. (1966). Gadjari among the Australian Aborigines of Central Australia. *Oceania Monograph No. 14,* University of Sydney.

Memmot, P. C. (1979). *Lardil properties of place*. Unpublished doctoral dissertation, University of Queensland, Brisbane.

Money, J., & Nurcombe, B. (1974). Ability tests and cultural heritage. *Journal of Learning Disabilities, 7,(5),* 297–303.

Mountford, C. P. (1956). *Art, myth, and symbolism. Records of the American–Australian Scientific Expedition to Arnhem Land* (Vol. 1). Melbourne: Melbourne University Press.

Munn, N. D. (1973). *Walbiri iconography*. Ithaca, NY: Cornell University Press.

Nurcombe, B., & Moffitt, P. (1970). Cultural deprivation and language deficit. *Australian Psychologist, 5(3),* 249–259.

Palmer, E. (1884). Notes on some Australian tribes. *Journal of the Anthropological Institute, 13,* 276–334.

Porteus, S. D. (1931). *The psychology of a primitive people*. London: Arnold.

Porteus, S. D. (1933). Mentality of Australian Aborigines. *Oceania, 4,* 30–36.

Porteus, S. D. (1950). *The Porteus Maze Test and intelligence*. Palo Alto, CA: Pacific Books.

Porteus, S. D. (1965). *Porteus maze tests: Fifty years of application*. Palo Alto, CA: Pacific Books.

Price-Williams, D. R. (1975). *Explorations in cross-cultural psychology*. San Francisco: Chandler & Sharp.

Reisman, D. (1956). *The oral tradition, the written word and the screen image*. Yellow Springs, OH: Antioch Press.

Rivers, W. H. R. (1901). *Reports of the Cambridge Anthropological Expedition to the Torres Strait,* Vol. 2: *Physiology and psychology*. Cambridge University Press.

Sayers, B. J. (1982). Aboriginal mathematical concepts. In S. Hargrave (Ed.), *Language and culture* (Work papers of SIL-AAB, Series B), *8,* 183–200.

Seagrim, G. N. (1977). Caveat interventor. In P. R. Dasen (Ed.), *Piagetian psychology*. New York: Gardner Press.

Seagrim, G. N., & Lendon, R. (1976). The settlement child and school. In G. E. Kearney &

D. W. McElwain (Eds.), *Aboriginal cognition*. Canberra: Australian Institute of Aboriginal Studies.

Sobek, V. C. (1981). The imposition of superimposition: The Gumatj number system of northeastern Arnhem Land exposed. Unpublished thesis, Darwin Community College, Darwin.

Spencer, B., & Gillen, F. (1899). *The native tribes of Central Australia*. London: Macmillan.

Strehlow, T. G. H. (1943). Black tracker, *SALT, Army Education Journal, 6*, 6.

Teasdale, G. R., & Katz, R. M. (1968) Psycholinguistic abilities of children from different ethnic and socio-economic backgrounds. *Australian Journal of Psychology, 20*(3), 115–160.

Turner, V. (1973). Foreword. In N. D. Munn, *Walbiri iconography*. Ithaca, NY: Cornell University Press.

Wallace, P. (1968). *Tracking ability*. Unpublished report to the Australian Institute of Aboriginal Studies. Canberra: A.I.A.S.

Watts, B. H. (1982). *Aboriginal futures* (Report No. 33). Canberra: Education Research and Development Committee.

17   Testing Bushmen in the Central Kalahari

Helmut Reuning

It is one of the ironies of the study of human populations that scientists turned their attention to the Bushmen[1] only when it was almost too late. About a hundred years had to pass after Wilhelm Bleek (1857) recognised their "great interest for the history of mankind in general" (Spohr, 1962), before this interest led to action and tangible results. A number of reports by explorers, missionaries, and traders about the Kalahari and its people were published before 1950, but relatively few investigations of Bushmen by scientists.[2] Intensive scientific studies have been initiated and conducted only during the last 30 to 40 years. During this time, the Bushmen were beginning to feel the pressure of neighbouring people who pushed into their territories in parts of the Kalahari and made their traditional mode of life difficult or impossible.

Today a great number of scholarly publications exists reporting many details about the Bushmen's way of life, their material and spiritual culture, knowledge and beliefs, the organisation of Bushman society, their social, economic, and artistic activities, their physical and health characteristics (e.g., Shapera, 1965; Silberbauer, 1965, 1972, 1981; Lee & DeVore, 1976; Marshall, 1976; Tobias, 1978; Lee, 1979). In the last three decades, there has been such a spate of reports and books on the Bushmen that one must hesitate to write about them again. However, the voices of psychologists are conspicuously absent in this chorus, with the exception of those of Porteus (1937), Minde (1937), both on a relatively small scale, of our own team, and of Katz (1973, 1976).

Avoiding as far as possible repetition of what we have said in previous publications, I want to give an account of the position of "our" Bushmen; of the simple theoretical background to our studies; of the development of

---

[1] I retain the name Bushman/Bushmen. It has been suggested that, because of its "derogatory" connotations (some even speak of "racist overtones"), this name should be dropped in favour of the new name "San" (cf. Lee & DeVore, 1976, p. 5; Marshall, 1976, p. xxi; Tobias, 1978, pp. 1–3; Lee, 1979, p. 30). The name San is by no means free from pejorative connotations (cf. Martin, 1926, p. 441; Silberbauer, 1981, pp. 3–4). We have *never* heard a Bushman referring to himself or his people as "San." But we have often obtained to our questioning the answer "I am Bushman"; and this was usually said proudly.

[2] A complete bibliography of the literature on Bushmen would comprise well over 300 titles; about one-eighth of these predate 1950.

453

suitable procedures; to describe some of the testing and highlights of test results; and – in retrospect nearly a quarter of a century later – to assess the value of our work and findings as I see it. It may well be that readers will attribute no other than historical value to our studies. For one cannot, due to the changed condition of the Bushmen, repeat or continue and improve them; except, perhaps, in the form of longitudinal studies of the effects of cultural change on the Bushmen. Changes in the Kalahari, even in the remoter parts of the Central Kalahari, have been rapid and drastic since 1966; and the situation of our Bushman testees as it had prevailed until then does not exist any longer, nor could it ever be restored. As George Silberbauer (1981, p. 1) says in respect of his own study of the G/wi in the same period (1958–1966), "the 'ethnographic present' is now the past."

Our findings are based on five fieldwork periods – 1958, 1959, 1962, 1963 and 1966 – each lasting 4 to 7 weeks. They were reported in a number of specific publications (Morgan, 1959; Reuning, 1959, 1971–1972, 1972; Fridjhon, 1961; Reuning & Wittmann, 1963; Van Wyk, 1964; Winter, 1964, 1967; Humphriss & Wortley, 1971) and, more comprehensively, in a monograph, "Psychological Studies of the Bushmen" (Reuning & Wortley, 1973; hereafter quoted as R & W 73).

The Bushmen

Differences between groups

Contrary to a widespread belief, the Kalahari Bushmen are *not* descendants of refugees from other areas of Southern Africa. Those Bushmen who had the bad luck to live outside the Kalahari and were forced to take a stand against white and black intruders into their life space either did not survive clashes with them or were absorbed into the populations of the immigrants. In the Kalahari, the Bushmen were left in peace until recent times – as long as other people were not interested in their arid environment. There is evidence that the Kalahari has been inhabited by the ancestors of present-day Bushmen for a very long time. Their adaptation to the environment is so perfect that it could not have been achieved in the span of a few hundred years. There is also archaeological material in parts of the Kalahari indicating Stone Age man's presence there long before the migrations of black people or colonisation by Europeans reached the area (Yellen, 1971; Cohen, 1974; Silberbauer, 1981, pp. 3, 7, et seq.).

The Bushmen are not a "dying race." They hold their numbers very well, showing either no decline in their population or else modest population increase. It seems, however, that they may not be able to hold on to their territories – in the Central Kalahari about 500 to 900 km^2 for a band of 50 Bushmen – against the pressure of other land-hungry people. They would then be forced to give up the hunting-and-gathering lifestyle and would eventually be absorbed into other population groups. A similar process has made the Bushmen of the northern Cape Province of South Africa "disappear" among the coloured and black peoples of that region. In the Kalahari, intermarriage (sometimes forced on Bush-women) is not only occurring already, its frequency is on the increase, particularly in "contact areas."

Although most of today's Bushmen live in an arid desert environment, there are considerable differences in living conditions and cultural adaptations of Bushman groups in different parts of the Kalahari (see Fig. 17.1). Changes in the composition of the soil or sand and, perhaps, small differences in rainfall may cause marked dissimilarities in plant growth and availability of water. For example, the Nyae Nyae[3] area in the northeast of South-West Africa and the Dobe–Duda[4] area in the northwest of Botswana have a number of permanent waterholes, and several semipermanent ones in addition. Except for a few boreholes established in recent years, no such waterholes existed in most parts of the Central Kalahari, where surface water is found for only 6 to 10 weeks of the year. The Central Kalahari has some fluid-storing plants as a substitute in normal years, for example, an abundance of *Tsama* melons, which are less frequent in the Nyae Nyae, Dobe, and Duda areas. In the latter, numerous *Mongongo* (*Ricinodendron rautanenii Schinz*) groves are found which provide *Mongongo* nuts, a highly nutritious food, in useful quantities, storable for months. *Mongongo* trees are not found in the central and southern parts of Botswana. Comparing the living conditions of the G/wi in the Central Kalahari with those of the northwestern areas, Lorna Marshall (1976, p. 78) says: "Compared to these G/wi, the Nyae Nyae !Kung, all of whom had access to a waterhole, seemed to me well off indeed." These divergent living conditions are seen in much the same way by Tanaka (1976, pp. 114–115). He estimates that the G/wi in the ≠Xade area (see the section on living conditions) have to spend about twice the time, in gaining their food, as the !Kung in the area of Dobe: namely, on average 32½ hours per week compared to 12–19 hours per week. Similar or greater differences can be assumed between the living conditions of present-day Central Kalahari Bushmen and those Bushmen who lived – and left their paintings – in the mountain regions of the Drakensberg and other parts of South Africa.

There is also a marked diversity among the languages spoken by Bushmen in different areas (Traill, 1978, esp. p. 147). We found to our astonishment, in 1958, that the members of two Bushman bands, the one living only about 50 km distant from the other, could not communicate with each other. Most of them could do so only with the help of a few men who were sufficiently bilingual to act as interpreters. The Bushmen's knowledge of other Bushman populations, beyond the range of their immediate neighbours, is rather limited (cf. Marshall, 1976, pp. 21, 52). We could not find anyone among the Bushmen at Motokwe who knew that about 90 km to the northwest of them lived another band of Bushmen who called themselves !Xõ.

[3] The main research area of the Marshall expeditions (Marshall, 1976).
[4] Research area of R. B. Lee, I. DeVore, and associates (Lee & DeVore, 1976; Lee, 1979).

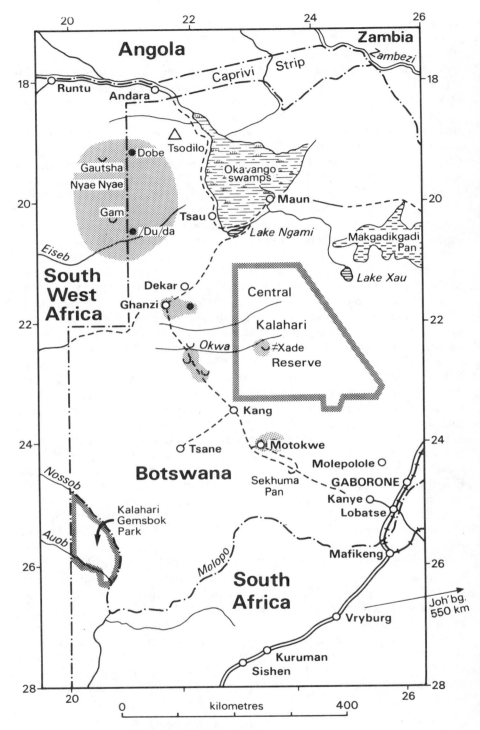

Figure 17.1. Kalahari Bushman research areas.

The range of variations of Bushman populations should be kept in mind if the following is to be understood correctly. As the sketch map (Fig. 17.1) shows, there is no overlap of the northern research areas of the Marshalls and of Lee and associates with the region of our own fieldwork near Ghanzi (21°41′ S, 21°39′ E), southeast of Ghanzi and around Motokwe. When we speak of our experiments with Bushmen, we mean those Bushmen in Botswana whom we encountered on farms around Ghanzi; at boreholes 30 km to 140 km to the east and southeast of Ghanzi; in the vicinity of the Kgalagari village Motokwe (24°03′ S, 23°18′ E); and in the western part of the Central Kalahari Game Reserve near ≠Xade pan (22°26′ S, 23°15′ E). Our subjects belonged mainly to the language groups of Nharo, !Xõ, G/wi, G//ana, and (probably) Tsase.[5] What we experienced with these groups may not be exactly the same as could be observed and said about Bushmen in other areas, such as the !Kung, who live about 120–150 km west of the Okavango Swamps, on both sides of the Botswana–South-West Africa border. What has been written about the !Kung in the northwest of Botswana (Lee, 1976, 1979) and in the northeast of South-West Africa (Marshall, 1976) is not necessarily in every respect valid for our subjects from the Ghanzi and Central Kalahari areas. The environmental stress, particularly in the gruelling early summer before the rainy season, is certainly greater for the Bushmen living in the Central Kalahari than for those in the northwest of Botswana. Consequently, the relative allocations of time to work and leisure, to such energy-demanding activities as hunting and dancing versus playing or just sitting and talking, are likely to be different too. For detailed information on topography, climate, flora and fauna, natural and social living conditions of the Central Kalahari, I refer the reader to the writings of Silberbauer (1965, 1972; 1981, chaps. 2–5) and Tanaka (1976). Descriptions of life in Ghanzi and the surrounding cattle farm area are given by Silberbauer (1965) and Guenther (1976, 1979, 1983), whose fieldwork was carried out in 1968–1970, some years later than ours.

The Bushman subjects of the present study

The sample of subjects participating in the tests and experiments described below was a heterogeneous one (R & W 73, pp. 31–38). Not only did they speak six or seven different languages, but some groups, especially those near Ghanzi, had fairly close contact with white and /or black people, others had less or no contact with people and cultures other than their own. In addition to these variations between groups or bands, individual members of the same group may or may not have done work on one of the Ghanzi farms or, in a few cases, on a gold mine in the Transvaal; near Motokwe,

---

[5] Tsase is a little-known Bushman language (Silberbauer, 1965, p. 15; Traill, 1978, p. 145) spoken by Bushmen living west and north of Molepolole (24°25′ S, 25°35′ E) and possibly including the Bushmen in the Motokwe area. These Bushmen have as yet not been studied extensively by anthropologists and linguists.

some Bushmen were "owned" by Kgalagari and had to work for them at times (cf. Silberbauer & Kuper, 1966).

Besides keeping the results of the different groups separate, we used the following classification:

Groups	Culture contact	N	%
(a) "Wild" Bushmen	No culture contact	40	8
(b) Borehole Bushmen	Little culture contact	123	24
(c) Bushmen living near Kgalagari village and borehole	Contact mainly with black people	92	18
(d) Cattle post and farm Bushmen	Contact with black and white people	257	50
	Total sampled Bushmen	512	100

For each individual, an identification number was issued, and the following information was recorded with the help of an interpreter: the Bushman's name and sex, his or her estimated age, the tribe to which he said he belonged, the name of the place where he said he was born, whether he was married and to whom, and details about familial relationships (parents, children, siblings, other relatives and their background and ages if possible). Also recorded were details about the subject's appearance, obvious personality characteristics, and anything noteworthy; clothing (traditional or European); the languages he or she was able to understand or speak; whether he or she had ever been to a big town, had seen, talked to, or dealt with people other than those of his or her and neighbouring bands (e.g., Kgalagari, Tswana, other black people, white people) and in what capacity. Taking all this information into account, the amounts of "black culture contact" and "European culture contact" were condensed into a rating (0 to 4) for each person tested.

The age of each individual was assessed, first by each tester independently; then these estimates were combined into one consensus assessment. The relative ages within the group or band, as they appeared in the information on family relationships and personal data obtained from the Bushmen themselves, were taken into account for the final age estimate. In addition, the age assessments of research workers from other disciplines were considered – those made during the multidisciplinary expeditions of 1958, 1959, and 1962 – in particular the ones based on medical and dental examinations. Such age determinations, in intervals of 5 years, from under 15 to 60 and over, are crude, but sufficiently accurate for the investigation of the relationship between age and other variables.

Living conditions of the Bushmen at the time of testing

Farm Bushmen. In spite of the closer "culture contact" of the farm Bushmen, their living conditions were similar to those of the "wild" Bushmen (cf. Guenther, 1983, pp. 77–78). Within the range of our research (with the exception of the Ghanzi prisoners), none of the testees lived in houses; all lived in the open or in their traditional grass huts and shelters, somewhere in a wooded part of the farm or vicinity of the borehole. The unemployed men, and occasionally the workers too, went hunting when game had been sighted or set traps for small buck or birds (e.g., guinea fowls), and caught springhares, porcupines, or ant bears. The women went on their excursions, daily or almost daily, to collect plant food and firewood. Living on or near a cattle farm has certain advantages for these Bushmen: relatively easy access to water, usually a diesel- or wind-operating pump next to a corrugated iron dam and watering trough; the availability of milk and staple food, such as mealie maize meal; an occasional share of a slaughtered animal as part of the farm worker's wages; the possibility of obtaining used clothes, blankets, tools, and utensils. The main disadvantage of the farm life is the scarcity of both animals and plant food, due to the introduction of domestic animals in the Bushmen's former hunting grounds, and of firewood, due to overutilisation.

Borehole Bushmen. The two categories (b) and (c) of borehole Bushmen took an intermediate position between the extremes of farm and "wild" Bushmen. In the one category (b), a few of the men had sporadic contact with travelling officials, for example, stock inspectors and veterinaries, and with transport drivers or traders, when these stopped or camped near the borehole. The other category (c) had more frequent contact with black cattle-owners and their relatives, especially those gathering around the watering point at the borehole. Both groups, (b) and (c), had access to water at any time; and both lived essentially on hunting and gathering plant food. With the first rains, in late November or December, the Bushmen would usually move away from the borehole, returning to it only when necessary, and live in the "wilds" for as long as possible, without intruding into the territory of another band. For such periods, the borehole Bushmen lived very much the traditional life of their forebears, little different from that of the "wild" Bushmen, but somewhat less stressful.

"Wild" Bushmen. The G/wi in the Central Kalahari Game Reserve, near ≠Xade pan, lived entirely as hunters and gatherers and were in every respect dependent on the natural products of their environment. They belonged to one band which, until 1959, had had hardly any contact with the outside world. They had never seen white people before George Silberbauer made contact with them in June 1959, and had only on very rare occasions seen black people who strayed into the region on hunting or bartering trips. Guided by George Silberbauer, we met this band of more than 50 Bushmen (including children and old people) in August 1963, after a drive of a day and a half cross-country from Ghanzi and a further day of searching for them. We

found them in a camp about 18 km east of ≠Xade, not easily accessible to our vehicles, and persuaded them to move to our campsite for a few days.

The season, the beginning of the hottest and driest period of the year, was not ideal for our purpose. The Bushmen felt the pinch of the meagre months, suffered from the dry heat, and were at times tired and listless. In spite of this, their cooperation and motivation were good.

Ghanzi prisoners. Some 28 Bushmen were tested while being held at the Ghanzi prison, mostly in connection with cattle thefts. The prison is a modern building, bright, clean, and "friendly"-looking. Testing was done in the patio inside the building. The prisoners were all males and almost all farm Bushmen of the (d) category. They were generally in good shape and healthy, being provided with food, clothes, sleeping quarters, and not too hard work (road repairs, gardening, etc.). Having water "on tap" was for them something of a marvel.

Diet and health

The popular belief that the Bushmen's food comes mainly from the produce of hunting animals is incorrect. Normally, the proportion of meat in the Bushmen's diet is about 15% to 30% by weight (on average 250 g per person per day); and in a good hunting season, it would hardly exceed 40% of the total food intake (Tanaka, 1976, pp. 112–13; Silberbauer, 1981, pp. 198–206). It has been stated that the G/wi at ≠Xade could survive without animal food, but not without vegetable food (Tanaka, 1976, p. 113). The mass of plant food gathered per day averages 3.5 to 5 kg per person (Silberbauer, 1981, p. 199); more than half of this is essentially fluid intake.

As the sufficiency of the Bushmen's diet varies seasonally, their health tends to vary too. In early summer and in periods of drought, the diet of those Bushmen who depend on hunting and gathering is not always adequate. It is often lacking in fat and fluids, and possibly in vitamin C and vitamins of the B-complex. Because of the temporary state of malnutrition and/or vitamin deficiency, there is a greater susceptibility to minor illnesses such as respiratory diseases, influenza, and skin trouble (e.g., "Witkop," or *favus*, an irritating fungus infection of the scalp, especially of children). These afflictions disappear or recede in times of normal food supplies and adequate diet.

In general, Bushmen are healthy. However, their resistance to imported diseases is low, and one cannot fail to observe a greater frequency of contagious diseases (tuberculosis, syphilis), and of alcoholism among those Bushmen who have frequent contact with strangers and with civilisation.

Techniques and tools for making a living

The following brief descriptions relate to the Bushmen's traditional way of life, familiar to all of them at the time of our fieldwork.[6]

---

[6] These are described in much greater detail by Silberbauer (1981) and Tanaka, (1976); for the northern regions by Marshall (1976); Lee and DeVore (1976); and Lee (1979).

Daily activities of women. The collection of food plants makes the greatest contribution to the Bushmen's economy. It is the woman's responsibility and the major part of her working time is spent in collecting the day's plant food supply for her family and dependents. Gathering is usually done in small parties of women and adolescent girls from families friendly with one another. Once the gathering area – within an 8-km radius of the camp – is reached, picking berries, nuts, and fruits, and digging out roots, tubers, and bulbs, are the two types of work required. Collecting trips, lasting from 1 or a few hours in autumn (April to June) to 6 hours in early summer (September to December), have to be made almost every day by the women. A load of considerable weight, up to 28 kg plus firewood, may have to be carried back to the camp.

A straight branch (of *Rhigozum brevispinosum*) peeled and trimmed, 90–120 cm long and about 2 cm in diameter, sharpened at the one end to a slanting plane, serves as a digging stick. It is also a kitchen tool, for mashing tubers, and so on, with the blunt end. The only other tool needed is a carrying container, usually the lower part of the woman's cloak of antelope hide knotted into a pouch, sometimes a leather bag or a net for larger items.

After the women's return to the camp, in the afternoon, the gathered food plants are prepared for eating and cooking. Other household work can now be done as far as time permits. There is, except during the favourable periods of late summer and autumn, little spare time for bead work, singing, games, and dancing. Older women who cannot stand the rigours of gathering excursions spend most of their time in the camp, supervising the children's playing, making beads out of ostrich eggshell pieces, and bead decorations. Meals are taken round the fire next to the family's shelter or sleeping place. They are very informal, and much eating takes place during all hours of the day.

Activities of men. The work of the men, who are not tied to a daily routine of food gathering and household tasks, is more varied than that of the women. Hunting, which is "entirely a male affair" (Marshall, 1976, pp. 130, 177),[7] is the most important activity for those men who are young and fit enough to do it, about one in five of the band's members. Meat is greatly desired as food and is a vital contributor of protein to the Bushmen's diet. By far the greater quantities of meat (about 80%) are obtained from large (eland, gemsbok, wildebeest) and medium-size (hartebeest, springbok) antelopes. These are hunted with bow and poisoned arrows, the hunters usually going out in pairs. Smaller mammals, birds, tortoises, and the like, are caught by various other means (e.g., snares), usually by men, occasionally by young boys and girls. To catch springhares in their underground warrens, the men use flexible probes, 4 m to 5 m long, with barbed tips. They are made of several lengths of straight peeled and smoothed raisin bush (*Grevia flava*,

---

[7] Cf. also Lee (1979, pp. 235, 450); for a very comprehensive description of hunting procedures and equipment of the Central Kalahari Bushmen, see Silberbauer (1981, pp. 204–217).

the same wood is used for making bows), tied together end to end, and fitted with a steenbok horn which forms a pointed hook. The rod is pushed into the springhare's warren and is moved about until it hooks the animal, which is then dug out. Although more frequently caught, small animals, including vertebrates, contribute relatively little (about 20%) to the total meat supply.

Even more time, than on the actual hunt, is spent by men on processing hides, making and maintaining tools, weapons, utensils (e.g., wooden bowls, dishes, mortars), ropes and strings. Curing animal hides for making clothes, straps, satchels, and other leather-pieces is time-consuming and tedious. Preparing sinew for making threads, and sewing leather clothes, also takes time. The construction of bows, arrows, quivers, and the preparation of poisoned arrows requires great skill and care. All this is men's work and occupies them during the greater part of waking hours in the camp. What may be left of daytime can be devoted to travel and amusement, visiting or dancing.

Common activities. Certain activities are not exclusively men's or women's tasks. Huts or shelters are built by women, but men assist in this work. Men also contribute to food collecting, when returning from an unsuccessful hunt, or in times unfavourable for hunting. Bushmen are very talkative and use every opportunity, during sedentary work, for talking, telling stories, and joking, but also for the exchange of important information, such as recounting incidents, successful actions or mishaps, information about movements of game animals, the planning of an intended hunt, or the discussion of social problems and conflicts (cf. Silberbauer, 1981, chaps. 3–6).

Bushmen love fun and games. Children play games almost all day and have a large repertoire of games and homemade toys. Adults, too, like to play games, sometimes between work periods, often in the late afternoon and evening (Marshall, 1976, chap. 10; Sbrzesny, 1976).

The Bushman parents' care for infants and children is exemplary. With very rare exceptions, they take their parental responsibilities seriously and never fail to do the best they can for their children. The children learn by make-believe playing and by emulating adults. Once they have outgrown their toddler stage, they play with one another, and the little ones learn from the older children. They are always under the benevolent supervision of an older person in the camp, or are at least within sight and hearing of the adults. Infants and children therefore grow up with a feeling that their life is secure and their environment predictable to a high degree, although their subculture is closely linked with the, at times precarious, world of the adults (Silberbauer, 1981, pp. 162–65).

Perhaps the strangest among the Bushmen's activities, and for the European the most difficult to understand, are the ritual dances, in particular the ritual curing dance and the role of the trance dancers or "healers" during these prolonged and strenuous group functions. Their frequency and importance vary, both regionally and seasonally, and reach a height during the times of plenty (late summer, autumn), when Bushman bands visit one another. The ritual dances give expression to the Bushmen's cosmological beliefs and religious feelings, and at the same time have important functions of conflict resolution and enhancement of group cohesion. I shall not attempt to go into details of the Bushmen's dances, which are only remotely related to our topic of ability assessment. Instead, I refer the interested reader to some relevant publications: Silberbauer (1981; see index, under "dances"); Sbrzesny (1976, under "Tanz-und Rhythmus-Spiele"); for the northern parts of the Kalahari: Katz (1976), Marshall (1976; see index, under "dances").

To conclude this necessarily very brief sketch of the "cultural context" in which we found our Bushmen, I should like to make an incidental remark: We had some but not all of the information summarised in the foregoing sections in our minds when we compiled our initial testing programme. This should be clear from the dates of the publications cited. The invitation to participate in the 1958 expedition came at short notice, in June 1958, and the psychology team consisted of only two persons.[8] From that moment, we studied all the relevant literature we could lay our hands on, including reports on work in progress, and learned from experience and by observation as we went along.

Pre-fieldwork considerations

In the beginning, we had no theory about the Bushmen's mental faculties. We could think of a number of good reasons *why* one should be interested in a "psychology of the Bushmen" (Reuning, 1971–1972; R & W 73), but we had not been able to formulate a hypothesis we could test. Nor did we have anything to take as a precedent for the design of experiments. The *Psychological Abstracts*, about 50 volumes of them, revealed under "Bushman" only one title: *A Bushman Dictionary*, by Dorothea F. Bleek (1956). The writings of our two forerunners in experimental psychology – Porteus (1937) and MacCrone (see Minde, 1937, p. 253) – were hidden under titles

---

[8] Barbara Pethick and myself. Of the colleagues who joined in the subsequent fieldwork and assisted in the data analysis, the late Wendy Wortley (née Winter) in particular contributed many good ideas and spared no effort – against personal odds – to systematise data and clarify our understanding of them. She had a great love for the indigenous peoples of Southern Africa and spent much of her leave and holiday time in the Kalahari with friends she had met there during our expeditions.

I had been interested in the Bushmen since my early school days in Swakopmund (South-West Africa), when I curiously inspected Bushman implements such as bows, arrows, bead chains, digging sticks, and many other objects my father had brought from his fieldwork as a geologist in South-West Africa; or when he told us of encounters with Bushmen in the southern Namib (near Aus and Lüderitz, from where they have long since disappeared). This interest was revived, and widened to include rock art, during my study years at the Psychology Department and the Frobenius-Institute (Ethnology) of Frankfurt University. Naturally, I grasped the opportunity of participating in the research projects of the "Kalahari Research Committee," formed jointly by the Witwatersrand University and the Institute for the Study of Man in Africa, and made full use of the support given by my own workplace, the National Institute for Personnel Research, Johannesburg.

not obviously related to the study of Bushmen; and we got to know them only later. This was perhaps fortunate, because their main instrument, the *Porteus Maze Test*, did not appear suitable when we tried it, even after recasting the paper-and-pencil version in the form of solid models (R & W 73, p. 60).

However, from what I knew about the Bushmen, one question forced itself upon my mind: What kind of people must the Bushmen be if on the one hand they persist in an extremely simple economy and technology, not taking any hints from their more "advanced" neighbours, and on the other they produce an intriguingly lively and complex, though strange (to us), folklore? And what cognitive complexities and skills fostered a visual art that is judged to be both exemplary and unique?

Of two plausible answers that we could frame, 30 years ago – "They are intellectually not capable of making progress" and "They are not motivated to do so" – the second seemed the more likely to me. But no one could be sure until more was known about these aspects of the Bushman mind, and about their psychological makeup generally (Reuning, 1959).

We were at that time convinced, perhaps somewhat naively, that basic mental processes are "universal," the same for Bushmen as for us, or at least similar for both. If this were not so, the talk of "one mankind" and of "equal opportunities for all" would not make sense. It must be possible, we thought, to demonstrate this by suitable experiments, including cognitive performance tests. Intelligence, too, as far as it is not preconditioned by particular beliefs and traditions, or programmed in a language very different from ours, should have a similar basic structure, although not necessarily developed in every facet to the same performance level. The first stage for us would mainly be to establish common ground, psychological functions common to all human beings. The next step would be to look at individual differences within the Bushman population. At all times we would have to be sensitive to the question of the applicability of our methods. Only when we found these acceptably free from ethnic or cultural bias, could we consider comparing Bushman performance with that of other groups.

The first expedition and the initial test battery (1958)

In selecting the tests for the first expedition, I let myself be guided by the thinking of contemporary "developmental psychology" and focussed on drawing ability, perceptual and conceptual performance tests using visual stimulus materials. It goes without saying that only relatively simple arrangements and clear situations, which did not require lengthy verbal explanations, appeared to be suitable. We could not expect to have an interpreter familiar with the administration of psychological tests. And we could not assume that the Bushmen would have had any practice in the use of pencil and paper (at that stage we did not know what we found out later, that they could use these things very well without prior practice). The necessity to work without laboratory facilities (electricity, etc.), in the open, further restricted the experimental repertoire. This had its advantages: One may imagine the feelings of a Kalahari dweller not only put into an examlike situation by strange people, but moreover in a closed room, if only a tent. We used at best a small folding table, an empty food box, or the like to support the test material, sitting next to it on jerry cans. As often as not, we would place our materials and ourselves on the ground, using a ground sheet to keep things clear of sand and dust. These simple arrangements helped to leave the Bushmen's normal environment almost unimpaired.

The first sample of instruments taken into the field, after some trial applications to illiterates, consisted of nine different tasks or tests:

1. *Sand Drawing* (Reuning, 1959; R & W 73). A square black board (75 cm × 75 cm) with a 1-centimetre-high border is covered with a thin layer of medium-coarse sand. It is placed flat on the ground before the kneeling or squatting testee and tester. Through the interpreter, the testee (or a group of them, to save time) is instructed that he (she) should draw, using his finger, a man or an animal (springbok) in the sand. If necessary, the tester demonstrates the task by drawing the outline of a tree. If the testee is at a loss to draw a man or an animal, he is allowed to draw any other simple object he can think of. After completion, the testee's drawing is photographed, by a camera mounted above the board in a fixed position, for later evaluation.

2. *Pattern Completion: bilateral symmetry* (Hector, 1958, 1959, 1966). Each item of this test consists of an arrangement of one black and two coloured (red or grey) oblongs (60 mm × 15 mm) within a black frame (210 mm × 148 mm). By the correct placement, within the frame, of another cut-out black oblong, the pattern of four oblongs can be made into a bilaterally symmetric configuration. There is only one solution, one correct position, for each item. In order to find it, the testee has to recognise the symmetry line and, relative to it, the correct place and orientation of the fourth oblong. The "correctness" of the response, its symmetry or lack of it, is obvious to the testee, thus providing feedback. Two practice and 11 test items were used, combined in a booklet. Each response to an item was scored on a 4-point scale, 3 = correct; 2 = correctly located but not exactly placed; 1 = correctly placed after warning; 0 = "incorrectly located and/or wrongly placed."

3. *Object Relations Test (ORT)* (Zilian, 1956). The test material consists of a test board (346 mm × 220 mm) on which a ring-shaped field of 24 positions is printed; and a supply of 200 rubber pieces, half of them square (20 mm × 20 mm × 10 mm) half of them round (20 mm diameter × 10 mm high); and half of each shape black, half of them white. In addition, one of the square or round surfaces is smooth, the other patterned; and by using single pieces or two on top of one another, 16 different categories of objects can be used. The tester sets the beginning of a sequence of objects, for example (all smooth side up, single) black square (*bs*) – white square (*ws*)

– black round (*br*) – white round (*wr*). Then the tester indicates that the testee should continue in this way until the 24 positions of the ring have been filled. The testee has to abstract the rule inherent in the sequence and apply it to the repetition or continuation. Three relatively easy tasks were given: (a) To make the subjects aware of the different materials, one each of the above-mentioned four types of pieces is set at the beginning of each quadrant of the field, the remaining five positions of the quadrant to be filled with the same sort of pieces. (b) Two pairs of objects, for example, round–square, round–square (all white or all black, all smooth and single) are set, and the ring has to be completed with this alternation of round and square. (c) The example given above (*bs*, *ws*, *br*, *wr*) is set over two cycles, and has to be completed over four cycles. To score this first application of the *ORT*, a rating on a 4-point scale was given: 3 = correct; 2 = understands the rule, but makes mistakes; 1 = grasps principle after some assistance, but can't solve problem; 0 = no understanding of the task. The sum of the three ratings made the total score.

4. *Colour Vision* (Tests for Colour-Blindness, Ishihara, 1951). The seven charts for illiterates, one practice and six test items, are shown one at a time to the testee, who has to trace the winding path of related colours through the background of random patches varying in colour and saturation. The testee uses a blade of grass or a thin twig for the tracing. Each item is scored *correct* or *wrong*; notes are made of difficulties experienced or careless errors made by the testee. (Because I am slightly "red–green blind," this test was always given by my colleague, B. Pethick.) The results were handed to the Anatomy Department of the Witwatersrand University, to be evaluated in the context of other genetically determined characteristics of the Bushmen. We found only one young man among 127 Bushmen who failed on all six Ishihara test charts.

5. *Geometric Illusions* (Herskovits, Campbell, & Segall, 1956). This series of six geometric illusions – *Müller–Lyer*, *Horizontal-Vertical* in two forms, *Sander Parallelogram*, *Poggendorff*, and *Perspective Illusion* – had been used widely in cross-cultural studies undertaken by the authors, Herskovits et al., and their collaborators. We had to omit the *Sander Parallelogram*, which was too complex and bewildering for our subjects; and the *Poggendorff* illusion, because the required responses did not allow a clear distinction to be made between testees who understood and those who did not understand the problem (cf. Morgan, 1959). The responses to the four illusion figures which we found applicable were recorded for and handed over to Mrs. P. Morgan for analysis and incorporation in the comprehensive investigation of Herskovits et al. (cf. Morgan, 1959; Segall, Campbell, & Herskovits, 1966).

6. A variable *Model of the Müller–Lyer Illusion* was applied a few times, but was found wanting. The metal slide by means of which the illusion figure could be presented as a continuous variable (over the range from "very strong illusion susceptibility" to "no susceptibility") was precision-made

by Dr. D. R. de Wet of the National Institute for Personnel Research (NIPR), Johannesburg. However, the ever-present fine Kalahari sand and dust got into it and made the smooth operation of the model impossible. Reluctantly, we had to give up using it.

7. *Complex Sorting Test* (Reuning, after Abels, 1954). This was a modification of *Abels's KVT* (*Konzentrations-Verlaufs-Test*) for use with illiterates. Instead of the 60 cards with number matrices, cards with 4 × 4 matrices of small chequered squares were used. There are 126 possible variations of such figures, two of them, A and B, standing out by their maximal symmetry (4 symmetry axes *and* rotational symmetry). The cards had to be sorted into 4 labelled compartments of a tray depending on whether the one (A), the other (B), both (A + B), or none of them was contained in the matrix. One selected testee found this task difficult and very trying. For this reason, we did not apply this test on a larger scale.

8. *Recognition of Shapes* (Reuning, 1951). Stimulus cards with geometric shapes of constant area (4 cm^2, in black silhouette on white) were pushed into frames (60 mm × 60 mm) forming the lids of small wooden boxes. These were distinguishable only by the inserted stimulus figures. One box with the "critical figure," that is, the one to be recognised later, was placed before the testee, whose attention was drawn to the figure on the lid. A small object (e.g., a match) was put into the box before the subject's eyes, with the instruction that he should find this again. The box was then removed and, 20 seconds later, together with three additional boxes as "distractors," presented again. The difficulty of recognising the critical figure depended on the similarity between it and the distractors. The procedure was learned quickly by practice items with dissimilar figures (e.g., triangle, square, star, and circle). This was an exploratory setup and, when applied to eight Ghanzi prisoners, found to function satisfactorily. (It was used again in 1966.)

9. *Cube Construction* (Hudson, 1953). This is one of the subtests of the NIPR's *General Adaptability Test Battery* (*GAB*), used in the mining industry for the placement of recruits into different job categories. The test instruction is normally given by a silent film demonstration. Without the instruction film, the administration of this test in the Kalahari was unsatisfactory. It was, after a few trials, not applied any further.

Of the tests described above, numbers (2), (3), (4), and (8) could be administered language-free, by mime and demonstration, without the help of an interpreter. The sand drawing (1) required a brief verbal instruction ("make a picture of a man or an animal") and an explanation of the testee's response if it was not recognisable. For the illusion experiments, a short general instruction ("you must indicate the longer of the two lines" [5]; or "say when the lines are equal" [6]) was in most cases sufficient. However, the Herskovits material had instances in which the subjects, paying attention to small detail, were misled and, for example, pointed to the apparently protruding end of a line instead of to one of the lines as a whole. In such cases, the interpreter had to explain the task once more. Tests (7) and (9) required more elaborate verbal instructions and were, for that reason and because of their difficulty, the first to be omitted.

First results and observations: Test construction principles

In general, the Bushmen were cooperative and willing to participate in our experiments and undergo testing. None of them refused to respond. They had, as a group, been told through the interpreter that there would be mealie meal and tobacco for those who made themselves available at our camp, as compensation for the loss of time for their own food-seeking activities. There was evidence that the Bushmen found our programme of psychological experiments on the whole enjoyable. They regarded the testing as "nice games" for which, however, one had to think very hard. Some Bushmen, when called by the tester, were nervous and exhibited a kind of "stage fright" (as most of us would under corresponding circumstances). This subsided, however, when we were sitting down by the sand-drawing board and the interpreter[9] gave the instructions. The rather informal and not too unfamiliar situation of sand drawing was very effective in setting the subjects at ease and giving them an opportunity to see the testers at close range. Nervousness was still noticeable at the beginning of the subsequent tests with less familiar materials. Some Bushmen showed marked hand tremor when they manipulated the oblong in *Pattern Completion* or the rubber pieces in the *Object Relations Test*. We were struck, however, by the great care which they all applied to test materials. One single oblong, cut out of thin cardboard, lasted without damage through 81 test sessions, being shifted about on 1,053 test patterns. Apart from such common characteristics, the behaviour of the testees varied greatly, from very shy and timid, through calm, matter-of-fact, to talkative, loud, and boisterous.

Performances varied widely too. In all age groups, some Bushmen laboured even with easy items, others grasped almost immediately what was required and made few errors. In the two tests, *Pattern Completion* and *Object Relations*, which from the beginning functioned surprisingly well, the responses covered almost the full range of possible scores, 0 to 29 (out of 0 to 33) and 2 to 9 (out of 0 to 9), respectively. The score distributions were close to normal, and the responses to the two tests correlated positively ($r = .53$), an indication of substantial proportions of "true" variance in both tests. Of the *Pattern Completion*, a test designed only a few weeks earlier and still in a preliminary form, one item seemed too difficult and was solved correctly only once. Items which were structured with a more or less vertical symmetry line and had vague resemblances to faces of living beings, were

---

[9] Usually Magwe Thamae, a young Bushman, about 24 years of age and going to school in Ghanzi at the time. He speaks, besides his native Nharo, G/wi and Tswana fluently, Afrikaans well, and English reasonably well, We were fortunate to have his assistance on all expeditions, except our work near Motokwe.

most readily solved – apparently a consequence of our mimed instruction/ demonstration in which the experimenter pointed to the symmetry of a human face as an analogy (cf. Fridjhon, 1961). From these and similar observations we gained an inkling of the complexities of some of our tests and items, and of the multifarious experimental and environmental influences which could affect responses to them.[10] Clear examples of cultural factors could also be seen in the Bushmen's sand drawings. We analysed them by means of classifications in terms of some selected aspects. Obvious differences occurred in the type of object chosen and its orientation in the drawing field, upright (70%), upside-down (20%), and sideways or mixed (10%); and in the "point of view" chosen, side view, front view, plan or top view (looking from above), twisted perspective, and perspective. Men tended to draw more often in plan view (relevant male activities are tracking of spoor, butchering large animals, curing animal skins), women drew more often in elevation. It was also possible to distinguish between naturalistic, schematic (e.g., plan view), and symbolic drawings. However, because we allowed the testee a choice in drawing an animal, a man, *or* a simple object, the evaluation of the drawings was complicated by the divergent "levels of aspiration." Over 40% (34/80) of the subjects preferred to draw simple objects, for example, an egg, a stick or pot, or "spoor" of an animal – not easily comparable to more ambitious animal or man drawings. None of these Bushmen had had any previous experience in seeing or making pictures.

Looking at the results in general, we were encouraged to improve the existing tests and to develop new ones for an enlarged repertoire, which we intended to apply on later occasions. The experiences made with the application of the first test selection, especially the distinction between tests which proved problematic (containing unfamiliar, delicate detail and necessitating much verbal explanation) and those which functioned well (clear, simple instructions to situations that "spoke for themselves") were utilised for this work. We could now formulate some requirements for ability testing with unsophisticated people, under difficult field conditions, and with imperfect means of communication:

1. The principle of the test, i.e., its purpose or what it demands of the testee, should be understandable without any (or at least with a minimum of) verbal explanation.

---

[10] Questions arising from the *Pattern Completion*, in particular, led to a number of specific experiments investigating such factors, external influences as well as those inherent in the structure of single items and item sequences (learning !) (see Grobler, 1959; Roberts, MacQuarrie, & Shepherd, 1959; Fridjhon, 1961; Tekane, 1961, 1963; Mundy-Castle & Nelson, 1962; von Mayer, 1963; Reuning & Wittmann, 1963; Crawford-Nutt, 1974, 1977a, 1977b; Steingrüber, 1974).

Important among the findings was that *Pattern Completion* can be used as a reliable instrument for the assessment of intelligence at the lower levels of cognitive development and among preliterate groups.

2. The test situation, as it presents itself to the testee, must contain some "desideratum" which *invites* a response. Looking at a test problem, the testee should know without further instruction what he is supposed to do. In other words, items must possess *Aufforderungscharakter* (literally: "character of inviting action"; a term of Gestalt psychology, usually translated as "valence" [cf. Lewin, 1926]).

3. The stimulus material must be equally familiar or equally unfamiliar to all subjects (or groups of subjects, if comparisons are to be made). Where necessary, a minimum of familiarity must be established by demonstration and practice items.

4. The response to the test problems must be given by the testee in the form of action, i.e., not in verbal terms which have to be back-interpreted to the tester.

It is not always possible to meet these requirements,[11] and approximation will often have to be sought. Our tests *Pattern Completion* and *Object Relations* conform fairly closely to all four desiderata.

In addition, it is desirable that the first test, or the first few tests, should not put the subjects into an altogether unfamiliar situation. At least the situation should contain some familiar elements or elements easily associated with familiar activities. Our sand drawing, and to some extent *Object Relations* as well as *Size Constancy* (see section entitled "Some results: Successful tests") were useful starters. *Bead stringing* (below, discussed under "Successful tests") contains familiar elements and activity, but it does not fulfill the first of the four requirements set out above.

Subsequent expeditions: Test modifications and further tests

On subsequent expeditions, new experiments were added to the initial selection of tests, and these were improved by the modification or addition of items to those tests which were found promising, although not yet in an optimal format. The scoring procedures were improved, ratings replaced by objective scores. Wherever it seemed feasible, the individual test version was changed into a group test version, by the construction of special demonstration boards or posters, and by the addition of suitable practice items. Following the guidelines set out above, we selected, designed, or modified, between 1958 and 1966, a total of 36 different tests for application to Kalahari Bushmen. Because it is impossible to describe and discuss all of these within the space of this chapter, we must refer to the detailed descriptions, illustrations, and references in R & W 73 (pp. 13–30). As indicated by the examples of the first series of tests in this chapter, about half of all experiments functioned very satisfactorily; some were still acceptable but were too de-

---

[11] Of course, our requirements are not the same as the demands of "functional equivalence," "item equivalence," and "score equivalence" expounded by Poortinga (1971, 1983) as conditions of cross-cultural comparability. Functional equivalence is implied here. In my opinion, these equivalences can only be investigated and established, once the tests of a battery "function" for all groups to be compared, in the sense intended here. Comparison of the Bushmen with other populations was *not* a primary concern of our work.

manding in terms of time or technical requirements. A few yielded doubtful or unreliable responses, called for further improvements, or had to be regarded as failures.

Some results: Unsuccessful tests

Among the instruments which produced unreliable and therefore inconclusive results was the series of perceptual illusions by Herskovits et al. (1956). This material was applied by us again to 100 Bushmen in 1959; and by P. Silberbauer to 21 of the Bushmen at ≠Xade in 1964, including in the latter case the *Sander Parallelogram*. The proportions of individuals who responded consistently (perfect Guttman scales, no errors) were mostly low, ranging from 34/100 and 9/21 with the *Müller–Lyer illusion* to 59/100 with the first *Horizontal–Vertical illusion* (⌐) and to 18/21 with the *Sander Parallelogram*. In other words, about one-half of the response sets were marred by inconsistencies. It is difficult to reconcile our findings with the high coefficients of "reproducibility" reported by Segall et al. (1966). Apart from the unknown test reliability of these illusion figures (cf. Gregor & McPherson, 1965), the theoretical interpretations given to cross-cultural experiments with these materials appear to be fraught with unsolved problems. The Bushmen's responses on average fell between those of black and white South African adults and were not as extreme as might be expected from their "uncarpentered" and "open vista" environment. Experience in and adaptation to a certain environment and culture *do* affect the perception of visual phenomena, but reference to this fact is not sufficient to explain the observed cross-cultural differences in illusion perception, for a number of reasons (cf. Révész, 1934; Metzger et al., 1970; Metzger, 1975, chap. 6): (1) The illusions operate not only on line drawings but also on real things and objects of corresponding shape; (2) they are experienced not only in visual but also in haptic perception; (3) illusions occur strongly in phenomenal situations in which the dimensions "carpentered, rectangular" versus "natural, irregular," "open vista" versus "enclosed environment" and "habituation to see depth in two-dimensional drawings" are all irrelevant.[12] It seems necessary and desirable to extend and refine experiments with illusion perception before their results can be interpreted conclusively in cross-cultural contexts (Taylor, 1974).

Some of our experiments failed to produce useful results because we did not, probably, put our question in a form understandable to the Bushmen. Examples are an experiment on *Similarities* of simple configurations (after Goldmeier, 1937); and an *Embedded Figures* test (R & W 73, pp. 15–16, 47–49). The latter type of test has been used in cross-cultural studies as one measure of "cognitive style," related to the distinction of "field dependent"

---

[12] To experience one example, the reader may try to match – without measurement – the height of a pile of equal coins to the diameter of one such coin lying next to it. If he does not "see" the horizontal–vertical illusion, he must be a rare individual.

and "field independent" (Witkin et al., 1962; Berry, 1971; Witkin & Berry, 1975). Our impression was that the Bushmen's inability to cope with our – we thought relatively easy – embedded figures was due not so much to their field dependence but rather to a high demand on perceptual analysis and cognition in *unfamiliar* percepts. A test like the *African Embedded Figures Test* (van de Koppel, 1977, p. 287) might have been more suitable, but we cannot do more than speculate about this.

Such tests as *Stereovision* (R & W 73, p. 16), the *Seashore Tests* of acoustic abilities (R & W 73, pp. 17, 55–57), or *Cube Construction* (discussed in the section on the initial test battery) could not be conducted properly because our testing locality and equipment were too primitive.

Some results: Successful tests

Clear-cut results were obtained, in spite of poor testing conditions, with tests of *Visual Acuity* (VA) and *Hearing*.

VA testing was done with the *E-Chart for Illiterates*, developed by the American Optical Company, and an *E* cut out of Masonite board. The superior eyesight popularly attributed to the Bushmen was confirmed (Humphriss & Wortley, 1971; R & W 73, pp. 51–52). The Bushmen's superiority in VA might not be as great as it appears from the numerical results. On clear nights they can see, with unaided eyes, the four Galilean moons of the planet Jupiter. However, after a week or two in the Kalahari, some members of the expedition staff, including the writer, could also recognise correctly these celestial bodies and their positions relative to Jupiter, without any optical assistance.

Hearing tests were conducted with a battery-operated portable audiometer. The Bushmen's hearing sensitivity, in comparison to European norms, was below the (ASA) normal threshold of hearing; that is, their hearing, between frequencies of 750 Hz and 6,000 Hz, was better than normal. Deterioration of hearing with age (*presbyacusis*) was much less pronounced than in Europeans (R & W 73, pp. 53–55).

Particularly interesting results were obtained in an experiment on *Size Constancy*: and some attention is now given to them. It is a characteristic of human (and animal) perception that objects are seen as having a constant size, irrespective of the varying size of their images on the eye's retina. The size of the retinal image is a function of the viewing distance and of perspective. A small child nearby and a tall man farther away may be projected the same size on the retina, yet we "see" that the child is small, the man tall. However, the tendency to retain "size constancy" is not equally strong in all individuals and groups of individuals. We measured it with a simple device of one "standard disk" (20 cm in diameter) propped up and seen at a standard distance of 6 metres; and a set of 11 disks (varying in diameter from 15 cm to 25 cm, in steps of 1 cm). The "variables" were shown in a random sequence twice at 3 m (= short observation distance) and twice at

12 m (= long observation distance). The subject has to say each time whether the variable is larger or smaller than the standard. The 2 × 22 responses yield two threshold values (i.e., variable sizes which appear to be equal to the size of the standard), one for the short and one for the long observation distance. The difference between the two threshold values (each based on 22 judgments) is a measure of size constancy: It is high when the difference is small, low or weak when the difference is large.

The task was readily understood by the Bushmen. Comparing their scores and those of four other contrast groups – (1) black mineworkers, locomotive drivers; (2) white research workers, NIPR; (3) black researchers, NIPR; (4) white optometric students – we found that the Bushmen, besides showing less uncertainty in their judgments, had significantly better size constancy than all other groups (Winter, 1967; R & W 73, pp. 14–15, 49–50).

Size constancy implies that the observer takes the viewing distance correctly into account. In the case of the Bushmen, this could be explained as a consequence of cultural and environmental pressure. It is essential for a young Bushman to prove that he is a good hunter. Hunting the larger game animals with bow and arrows requires, besides stamina and many other skills, an accurate assessment of the proper shooting distance, because the range and accuracy of the light bow is limited to about 30 metres. It can be expected that a man practising this kind of hunting frequently should be able to estimate distances correctly, and as a corollary have perception characterised by high size constancy. This is, perhaps, not the whole story: Bushwomen are also superior in size constancy, although they *do not hunt* and their daily activities – scanning the bushveld and the sand for the presence of food plants and for signs of their growth under the surface – demand and perfect different aspects of perception. It may be that in addition to the direct ecological pressure and learning, there is also genetic selection involved. The Bushmen's marriage customs make it likely that a good hunter has a better chance to marry and have surviving children than a poor one. As in all human development, both cultural and genetic factors probably operate jointly and supplement each other towards optimal adaptation to the given ecological situation.

Among the perceptual-cognitive tests were two which make similar demands and are positively correlated (r ≈ .6): *Fret Repetition and Continuation* and *Squares Detection* (R & W 73, pp. 22–23, 59–60). In the former, a given pattern has to be repeated or continued, that is, copied after the model given on the same page, by drawing short lines between the appropriate dots of a printed grid. In *Squares Detection*, an apparently random agglomeration of dots is presented on each page which shows in the top left corner a model, that is, four dots connected by straight lines to form a square. The quadruples of dots which make the corners of a square of the same size have to be found and shown by drawing the four lines between the corner dots.

The Bushmen found the *Fret Repetition and Continuation* relatively difficult, and *Squares Detection* less so, although in the former the model shows *which* dots are to be connected, whereas in the latter they have to be identified by the testee. Yet, the testees performed relatively better in *Squares Detection*, and a young boy of about 13 years completed every one of 70 squares correctly and neatly, as if he had the "idea" (Plato, *Phaidros*) of a square clearly in his mind. In the visual environment of the Bushmen there are many naturally regular forms, in leaves, flowers, fruits, eggs, and so forth, and their artifacts and decorations l ̇ ̇ ̇ circles, zigzag, and triangular patterns; but we have not seen any square ⸲ the Kalahari, except in structures of European origin, and in our test material.

Pattern Completion (Patco) part *I* (bilateral symmetry) was, in 1962–1963, supplemented by part *II* (rotational symmetry), and, in 1966, both parts were converted to group test format called *Symmetry Completion (Symco): I*, bilateral; *II*, rotational symmetry. Whereas the bilateral *Patco/Symco I* appeared to be one of the most "culture-fair" tests we have ever used, the rotational symmetry completion of *Patco/Symco II* is strongly influenced by familiarity or experience with *rotation, as mediated by formal, especially technical education* (Reuning & Wittmann, 1963). The Bushmen obtained relatively high scores on rotational symmetry, in spite of the absence of any formal education. Traditional Bushman culture, like that of their black neighbours, does not know the use of the wheel. However, rotation plays a role in a number of Bushman games and dances; and several of the toys Bushman children make and play with, have dominant rotating elements (Marshall, 1976; Sbrzesny, 1976). Thus, rotation is a phenomenon which the Bushmen know and use. We have seen children at ≠Xade making functional models of motor vehicles and playing with them, rolling the profiled "tires" over a smoothed patch of sand, so that they leave behind realistic-looking miniature "tracks of lorries" (R & W 73, p. 58). *Pattern Completion* and *Symmetry Completion* are consistently correlated, and invariably in a positive direction, with all other cognitive tests, $r = .23$ to $r = .78$; on the average $r = .57$ for the bilateral, $r = .48$ for the rotational part.

As a test of *work behaviour*, we used a continuous work test (Reuning, 1983), namely *Continuous Bead Stringing* (R & W 73, pp. 27–28, 62–68). Small beads of several different colours had to be strung on a length of fuse wire, changing colour after every third bead; as a time marker, one white bead had to be inserted at a gong signal given every 3 minutes. The work was done continuously for 20 three-minute periods, or for 1 hour. Principal components analysis of the test responses yielded four components which corresponded to similar aspects of other continuous work tests, applied to other groups of testees: accuracy, speed of work, increase, and fluctuations over testing time.

The Bushmen, sitting on a large ground sheet, worked much more slowly and less accurately than groups of students of education, teacher trainees, who did the same bead stringing in a lecture room. The Bushman average was 652 beads/hour with 6% errors; that of the teacher trainees was 1,300 beads/hour with 0.3% errors. The difference is only partly attributable to the vastly different testing conditions. The main reason for it is a different concept of time and a different attitude towards speeded work. Bead stringing correlated with sex, females working faster ($r = .35$; $p < .05$); and with performance in *Mazes* ($r = .31$; $p < .05$). *Accuracy* of bead stringing was positively correlated with performance in *Symmetry Completion* (rotational), *Object Relations*, the *Fret Tests*, and *Squares Detection*. *Fluctuations* in bead stringing were correlated *negatively* with tests which demanded concentration, for example, *Kohs Blocks*, the *Fret Tests*, *Pattern Completion*: That is, few fluctuations were associated with high scores in tests where persistence was needed.

It was possible to establish and compare variability percentages (100 × $SD/\overline{X}$) in speed of work for students (17.3%) and Bushmen (16.7% to 31.6% in four groups; 21.2% in the largest group of 42 Bushmen). The fastest compared to the slowest Bushman performance had a ratio of 4.3:1 in *number of beads strung*; and the most and least accurate results were 0 errors and 34% errors. For the students, the corresponding figures were 2.4:1; and 0 errors and 1.1% errors. Thus, the variability of the Bushman performances was not smaller but, if anything, greater than that of the white students. The significance of this will be discussed in the section on test reliabilities and intercorrelations.

Representing the physical world: Words

Enumeration of Words (R & W 73, p. 68) was a kind of structured interview. It needed the help of a good interpreter continuously and could therefore be conducted with only 25 of the Bushmen. It was introduced by the question "Suppose I want to learn your language, *which words* would you teach me *first*?" Without exception, the first words, about 10 to 12, were *animal* names. A second group of words usually consisted of *verbs* (I run, I sit, sleep, shoot, fetch water, etc.); in a few cases, parts of the body; and in others, celestial bodies (sky, sun, moon) were named, following the animals. The activities indicated by the verbs often revealed what was on the testee's mind: "I sleep" seemed to mean that he or she felt tired; "I am not hungry," a subtle hint that he or she *was* hungry; and so forth. A third, and usually final, group of words would consist of words designating things the testee would see when looking around: sand, grass, trees, and the like. This gave the impression that he or she was about to "run dry," often made explicit by the remark "It is enough." This experimental procedure seemed a worthwhile one. However, the material we could collect was too limited to allow a more comprehensive analysis.

Representing the physical world: Drawing

As stated in the section on pre-fieldwork considerations, the nature of the Bushmen's artistic abilities was one of our key questions. This part of our programme consisted of the tasks *Mosaic Construction, Sand Drawing, Pencil Drawings, Free Drawing* with poster paints, and *Clay Modelling* (R & W 73, pp. 69–78). A few remarks about the drawings obtained from the Bushmen must suffice here.

Sand Drawing was conducted (1959 and later) in two parts: (1) drawing a "bottle" (a 1-gallon plastic bottle was placed on the far side as a model); (2) drawing a "man" and a "springbok," the latter from memory (people were, of course, always visible). The drawing was introduced by the tester, who drew a simple side view of a "jerry can," also placed on the far side of the drawing board, and pointed to corresponding elements of the model can and its representation. The bottle drawing could always, that of man and springbok could often, be administered without the interpreter.

As observed already in 1958, a large proportion of sand drawings were made as if looking down from above, or in "plan view." The bottle in 61/213 cases (28.6%), in spite of the side view example given before and although the model was seen from the side (none of the Bushmen ever attempted to look at it from above). The man was in 42/193 cases (22%) drawn as if stretched out on the ground – the springbok in 74/195 cases (38%). The top or plan view did not occur in any other sample of sand drawings, collected by the same procedure from whites and blacks, except in one sample of illiterate black mineworkers, and less frequently: the bottle 2/58 (3.4%); the man, 0/57; the animal (a cow), 2/57 (3.5%). The choice of this view, to some extent perhaps suggested by the low position of the drawing board, seems natural, especially to people who often work on the ground and live without furniture. Because the plan view does not occur in the drawing of literates, its use is probably "extinguished" by the conventions of visual representation learned through formal education. One group of farm Bushmen, who had access to a trading store (walking distance one way about 14 km), where they may have seen pictures (advertisements), drew only the man, schematic "stick figures," a few times in plan view, 3/26 (11.5%).

The majority of man drawings (60%) and animal drawings (74%) were rendered by Bushmen as stick figures. In contrast, blacks (mineworkers, 76% of them illiterates) drew mostly "outline" or "mixed" (e.g., body in outline, with linear limbs) figures. These differences were highly significant in 3 × 2 tables: $\chi^2 = 61.58$ p < .001 for "man"; $\chi^2 = 67.45$ p < .001 for "animal" drawings ($df = 2$).

Related to this is the extreme simplicity of the Bushman sand drawings: Structural characteristics only, no details (fingers, toes, hair, eyes, etc.) were represented. This is in keeping with the coarseness of the medium, finger drawings in sand. And it contrasts again with the tendency of the blacks to include much small detail in their drawings (buttons, hair, fingers, toes, a pipe, etc.), which causes the images to become clumsy, less well proportioned. In this respect, intelligent high school girls also failed to adapt their style to the coarse medium of sand; they included in man and animal drawings details which could not easily be shown in sand and distorted the proportions.

Another characteristic, occurring in about 40% of animal *side view* drawings of Bushmen, but not of others, is the *omission* of those body parts which in the open grassland are not clearly visible and blend with the light-coloured background of the Kalahari sand: for example, the light-coloured face and belly of the springbok. In rock paintings, these parts are usually rendered in white, here in the sand they are implied by untouched drawing space.

In style, the poster-paint drawings resemble the sand drawings. Almost always the first figures drawn are animals, often in strikingly arbitrary colours (e.g., a springbok in blue, although light brown or ochre was within reach). The naming of freely chosen objects was very casual too: A "man" drawing that did not come up to expectation or looked deformed was quickly relabelled "a ghost," and so forth.

On the whole, most of these drawings indicate that the Bushmen are competent observers of their environment, and some of them possess a latent ability for pictorial representation. We gave ratings for, besides other properties, "representational goodness" (recognisability) of drawings. These ratings were significantly correlated with perceptual performance test scores, and with the same type of rating applied to the Bushmen's clay models.

Test reliabilities and intercorrelations

Because of successive test revisions and changes in the composition of our test batteries, and because of the Bushmen's mobility – some were present one day, gone the next – it was impossible for us to administer one test battery (e.g., of a factorial design) to *all* of a large enough sample of Bushmen. We had to look at different tables of intercorrelations for each of the 1959, 1962, 1963, and 1966 data.

Estimates of test *reliability* were made on the basis of correlations between test halves or test parts which were separately scorable. They were very satisfactory. Of 28 tests, 22 had reliabilities of .70 or higher: 17 had reliabilities in excess of .80, and 3 reached .90 or more. Only one test was below .5. Such reliability coefficients are possible only if the tests are capable of fine performance differentiations or if the variance between individuals is large. We have found that the latter is true to some extent: Where we could establish variability percentages, these were as high as or higher than the corresponding values found in other groups of testees, South African whites and blacks. Our subjective impressions of test behaviour corroborated the finding of high variability.

This large individual variance was contrary to our expectations. For two reasons we had expected significantly smaller performance variances between Bushmen, compared to those obtained in other populations: (1) The small numbers of people in Bushman bands which have contact with and know each other restrict the choice of eligible mates for marriage. One should expect some inbreeding, a "limited gene pool" and reduced genetic variance. (2) Variations in the Bushmen's eco-cultural environment, "milieu differences," within and between bands, seem to be smaller than corresponding variations prevailing in other South African populations. Differences in personal circumstances which we often hold responsible for differences in intellectual development (person A has travelled widely, has access to a variety of educational and entertainment institutions; person B, living in a small village, has few or none of such opportunities) are virtually absent in Bushman society, both according to what *we* saw and to what *they* told us in response to personal data enquiries.

Yet neither of these two limiting factors seems to have a noticeable effect on performance variations. In particular, our data provide little evidence of negative effects of a limited environment on mental development. The only shortcomings were in tests of "conceptual reasoning" (*Object Relations, Form Series Test, Concept Identification*), in which the scores tended to be in the lower parts of the scales. But we have to remember that the concepts used – regular shapes, colours and their interrelations – were unfamiliar or strange to the Bushmen.

Age and *sex* were not strongly correlated with test performances. In a few cases, younger persons obtained higher scores on speeded tests, older ones on measures of accuracy. Men performed slightly better in drawing and in tests requiring attention to detail; women were faster, men more accurate in *Continuous Bead Stringing*. Men were on average rated higher on "culture contact." This rating, especially contact with Europeans, was positively correlated with most perceptual and cognitive tests ($r = .3$), more so with speed scores ($r = .4$) and with quality of artistic performances ($r = .4$). The correlations, however, do not tell us whether culture contact makes the Bushmen respond more quickly and/or intelligently; or whether the bright and alert Bushmen *seek* culture contact more often or more readily. In the 1966 table of intercorrelations, the correlations with culture contact, with both whites and blacks, are all low, possibly a sign that we succeeded in making the tests if not "culture-fair," then "context congruent."

When variables are ordered in terms of similarity of test *contents*, say, cognitive as distinct from artistic, speed as distinct from accuracy, and so on, the intercorrelations form patterns. The different categories of tests tend to be positively correlated with one another, but *less* strongly than tests *within* categories. However, some confounding influences must be taken into account: (1) A great deal of *learning* took place during most test sessions, making some testees "different persons" before and after. Thus, different sequences of test administration, unavoidable due to the Bushmen's mobility, could affect the relative difficulty of some tests for some subjects. (2) The numbers of testees varied from one test session to another and therefore the sample of subjects is not identical for all tests within one correlation table. (3) Our tests were experimental, still somewhat crude and not standardised. (4) Improvements made between one application of a certain test and the next may have changed the test contents. These defects tend to blur the clarity of the structure that may exist in a correlation table.

The patterns of intercorrelations (R & W 73, Tables 10–13) suggest that a fairly strong general intellectual factor is operative in all sets of data. The cognitive and perceptual tests – *Pattern Completion, Fret Repetition and Continuation, Squares Detection, Kohs Blocks, Object Relations, Form Series Test*, and *Concept Identification* – are all positively correlated ($r = .2$ to .78). In addition, there appear to be more specific factors: One of them is related to artistic abilities. A Speed of Perception or Speed of Reaction factor is suggested by correlations between speed measures derived from different tests (*Object Relations, Mazes, Squares Detection, Tapping, Beadstringing*). This and, independent of it, a factor of Accuracy or Meticulousness may be due to temperamental differences. These are also indicated by distinct preferences, in the mosaic construction task, for either compact and/or circular, or dispersed and straight-line arrangements.

Validity and the concept of intelligence

We could not carry out a direct systematic validation study, to establish what exactly our tests, or at least some of them, measure. An external criterion for this could only be provided by the Bushmen themselves, and it would have been necessary to ask them that they rate or rank themselves in respect of, say, "cleverness," "hunting ability," or some such characteristic which would make sense to them. We have not made such a request, to avoid interfering with their social life, which is based more on cooperation than on competition. Silberbauer (1981, p. 133) states that the language of the G/wi has "no structural device for expressing elaborate ranked comparisons." We found this confirmed in an experiment on stylistic pictorial preferences (1959). When the Bushmen were asked to put four pictures of a hunting scene (silhouettes in four different styles) in a rank order from most to least preferred, they could not do this. All they could say was "I like this," implying that the remaining pictures were all not preferred, none more, none less (R & W 73, p. 68). It is thus likely that a rank order as a validity criterion would have failed.

There were, however, incidents which made us think that the Bushmen's concept of "intelligence" was not too different from ours. Some of them showed keen interest in *our* reactions to the performance of a spouse, a relative, or a friend. When the tester at the end of a test had praised a good performance, they let us know, through the interpreter; "We could have told you so, he [or she] is clever." On such an occasion an old Bushman called Ducy (age 50) said with a broad grin: "Ducy jolly good"; he had learned a few English words when helping with cattle droves.

A young Bushman, about 19 years of age, who grew up as an orphan and was retarded, hence nicknamed "Blesbok," was frequently teased because, as Magwe Thamae explained, he was "so stupid." He performed consistently poorly on all tests, in spite of being well motivated.

On the other hand, there were certain Bushmen who were pushed forward by the others, when we needed a guide or some information. After some palaver, they would say: "Take him with you, he will show you" or "Ask him, he knows." These persons, male or female, singled out by their fellows as knowledgeable, usually obtained above-average scores in our tests; but whether by accident of experimenter expectation or by cognitive design of the subject, we cannot say.

On the basis of the Bushmen's reactions to our testing, we observe, perhaps contrary to popular opinion, that a "radical cultural relativism" (Berry, 1972) is not always necessary for the investigation of cognitive competence. We seemed to achieve good domain consistency with "standard" tests, thoughtfully chosen by the reseach team.

In a very readable and penetrating essay on the concept of intelligence, Hofstätter (1966, p. 241) proposes a definition of "intelligence." He says it is the "ability to discover redundancy" ("Intelligenz ist die Befähigung zur Auffindung von Redundanz"). Redundancy in this sense means "surplus information," regularity, predictability in situations which contain a higher degree of "order" than is obvious. By perceptual and cognitive analysis, this high degree of order can be made explicit. The experiments in our category of "cognitive tests" are all intelligence tests in terms of the foregoing definition. In order to assess the Bushmen's average intelligence, in comparison with "IQs" of other people, our tests would first have to be standardised with one or more reference groups. A statement about the absolute level of intelligence, the "power of the mind" (Biesheuvel, 1959) of the Bushmen, is not, therefore, feasible. In line with Hofstätter's concept, the "maximum complexity of order which the testees are still able to grasp" could provide such a yardstick (Hofstätter, 1966, p. 237). To my knowledge, psychology has not yet been able to develop an absolute measure of intellectual capacity.

Criticism and critical evaluation

Our experimental approach to the study of the Bushmen's psychological makeup has recently been stigmatised by Berland (1983, pp. 143–144). He calls it "test-and-run strategy," and sees our research as an example of "interpreting performance measures when investigators are not familiar with the ecocultural content and social organizations of task settings."

Berland quotes only from the summary report on our work (Reuning, 1972), and not the comprehensive monograph (R & W 73), which he lists in his references, but has, perhaps, not been able to obtain. It seems to us improbable that a thorough reading of R & W 73 could sustain a charge of ignorance of the subjects of our research and their background. He grants us extenuating circumstances by saying that during our fieldwork period, we did not "have the extensive ethnographic record on Kalahari gatherers and hunters available" which is now available to him. However, as I have shown in the section on group differences, not all of this record would have helped to assess the situation of the Bushmen of *this* investigation.

Many different methods can be and are used to gain knowledge about marginal people like the Bushmen. Among the methodological possibilities are general ethnographic studies, "participant observation" by the social anthropologist, and various specific studies of biological, physiological, eco-logical, ethological, psychological, social, linguistic, and other aspects of the target population. The aim of our research was to establish a "psychology of the Bushmen" – more ambitious than realistic, as it turned out. This is not entirely dissimilar to the aim of the participant observer, although dif-ferences in emphasis exist. Anthropologists focus on what their subjects do, what they know, feel, and want, there and then, in order to understand their sociocultural system. Psychologists studying motivation, coping, and problem solving, are interested not only in explaining present behaviour, but also in their subjects' potential and in predicting possible future behav-iour of individuals, per se and as members of the group.

If psychologists cover an optimally wide range of skills and cognitive functions, their method can approximate to the more comprehensive and penetrating, but also more time-consuming, method of participant obser-vation. In some respects, these two methods are complementary. The ob-serving anthropologist has to learn the language of the people to be studied. If the language is mastered, this is both an advantage and a limitation: It provides access to the most important verbal and language-based thinking, to folklore and many features of social life; but it restricts the investigation to speakers of this language. In the case of the Kalahari peoples with their linguistic diversity, this could be a severe restriction. Experimental psy-chologists, if they are not linguists as well, have to restrict their investiga-tions to nonverbal facets of abilities and skills – a severe limitation too; but they can easily include in their research speakers of different languages when language is thought to be an intervening variable in cognitive performance.

I should like, by way of constructive comment, to point out one weakness of ethnographic methods, for which the experimental psychological method could provide a corrective. Because the latter has an objective "historical anchor" in the form of concrete and repeatable tasks and task situations confronting large numbers of subjects, it is to a lesser extent "subject to an unavoidable and uncertain degree of selectivity and refraction induced by the idiosyncrasies of personality and prior experience of both the fieldworker and his or her informants." (Silberbauer, 1981, p. xv). The risk of subjective selectivity is particularly great in fieldwork done by the "participant ob-server."[13] Not every publication about Bushmen maintains an awareness of the risk of such bias from cover to cover as does Silberbauer's, and some

---

[13] Margaret Mead's early ethnographic work on the Samoans has been shown to be a classical example of failing in this respect; cf. Freeman (1983).

are noticeably biased. Naturally, experimental psychologists can be prejudiced too; but because of the factual experimental underpinning of their research, bias is always defined by what they include among their experimental tasks and by what they leave out.

Reprise

We have learned a great deal about what Bushmen can do and what they cannot do when confronted with new situations and problems. Our general impression is that they are astonishingly adaptable and seem to be less tied to rigid rules and taboos than other so-called economically backward people. That they have remained in this state is their choice rather than the result of any lack of cognitive competence.

On the basis of our findings, we made recommendations about the direction which future training of the Kalahari Bushmen could take, to secure for them an acceptable position among the people living in their neighbourhood (R & W, 1973, pp. 103–105). One can only wish that their fate may be better than "belonging to the past" within a few generations from now.

Due to political and social changes in Botswana, our fieldwork came to an abrupt end in 1966. As far as our programme of experiments and tests is concerned, it remained incomplete. The sampling of behaviours and skills was broad, but not comprehensive enough: Besides excluding verbal tests, we did not include any tests of number abilities. Because the need to count rarely arises in the Bushmen's normal life, their arithmetic ability is likely to be "underdeveloped." It would also have been of particular interest to observe the initial potential and learning process in Bushman adults and children in their approaches to numeracy as a form of cognitive innovation.

As is often the case with scientific work, our research has raised more questions than it has answered. Our great regret is that the Bushman ecology is all but destroyed, so that they may always remain just what they are – unanswerable questions.

Glossary of tribal and place names

Ethnic groups of Bushmen and their languages

    G//ana
    G/wi
    !Kung
    Nharo
    !Xõ
    Tsase

Places, usually around a "pan" (a shallow expanse containing water temporarily)

    Dobe
    /Du/da

Gautsha
Gam
Nyae Nyae (pronounced nĩ nĩ)
≠Xade

"Click" consonants and symbols

/	indicates a voiceless dental click (~ *ts*)
G/ or g/	indicates a voiced dental click
//	indicates a voiceless lateral click (as used in urging on horses)
!	indicates a voiceless palatal click
≠	indicates a voiceless alveolar click
~	indicates nasalisation of the vowel over which it is placed
X, x	is pronounced like *ch* in Scots or German *Loch*.

References

Abels, D. (1954). *K-V-T. Konzentrations-Verlaufs-Test* [Concentration-over-time test]. Stuttgart: Testverlag S. Wolf.

Berland, J. C. (1983). Dress rehearsals for psychological performance. In S. H. Irvine & J. W. Berry (Eds.), *Human assessment and cultural factors* (pp. 139–154). New York: Plenum.

Berry, J. W. (1971). Ecological and cultural factors in spatial perceptual development. *Canadian Journal of Behavioural Science, 3*, 324–336.

Berry, J. W. (1972). Radical cultural relativism and the concept of intelligence. In L. J. Cronbach & P. J. D. Drenth (Eds.), *Mental tests and cultural adaptation* (pp. 77–88). The Hague: Mouton.

Berry, J. W., and Dasen, P. R. (Eds.). (1974). *Culture and cognition: Readings in cross-cultural psychology*. London: Methuen.

Biesheuvel, S. (1959). The nature of intelligence: Some practical implications of its measurement. *Psygram, 1*(6), 78–80. Reprinted (1974) in J. W. Berry & P. R. Dasen (Eds.), *Culture and cognition: Readings in cross-cultural psychology* (pp. 221–224). London: Methuen.

Bleek, D. F. (1956). *A Bushman dictionary*. New Haven, CN: American Oriental Society.

Cohen, G. (1974). Stone Age artefacts from Orapa Diamond Mine, Central Botswana. *Botswana Notes and Records, 6*, 1–4.

Crawford-Nutt, D. H. (1974). Symmetry Completion Test (Symco): Development of a scoring method. *Psychologia Africana, 15*, 191–202.

Crawford-Nutt, D. H. (1977a). The effect of educational level on the test scores of people in South Africa. *Psychologia Africana, 17*, 49–59.

Crawford-Nutt, D. H. (1977b). The Symco Test as a test of ability. *Psychologia Africana, 17*, 79–98.

Cronbach, L. J., & Drenth, P. J. D. (Eds.). (1972). *Mental tests and cultural adaptation*. The Hague: Mouton.

Freeman, D. (1983). *Margaret Mead and Samoa: The making and unmaking of an anthropological myth*. Cambridge, MA: Harvard University Press.

Fridjhon, S. H. (1961). The Patco Test, symmetry and intelligence. *Journal of the National Institute for Personnel Research, 8*, 180–188.

Goldmeier, E. (1937). Ueber Aehnlichkeit bei gesehenen Figuren [On similarity in visually perceived figures]. *Psychologische Forschung, 21*, 146–208.

Gregor, A. J., & McPherson, D. A. (1965). A study of susceptibility to geometric illusion among cultural subgroups of Australian Aborigines. *Psychologia Africana, 11*, 1–13.

Grobler, J. (1959). *Artistic ability, judgment and interest as a source of influence on Patco Test performance*. Unpublished master's thesis, University of South Africa, Pretoria.

Guenther, M. G. (1976). From hunters to squatters: Social and cultural change among the Farm San of Ghanzi, Botswana. In R. B. Lee & I. DeVore (Eds.), *Kalahari hunter-gatherers: Studies of the !Kung San and their neighbors* (pp. 120–134). Cambridge, MA: Harvard University Press.

Guenther, M. G. (1979). *The farm bushmen of the Ghanzi district, Botswana*. Stuttgart: Hochschul Verlag.

Guenther, M. G. (1983). Buschmänner (Nharo). In K. E. Müller (Ed.), *Menschenbilder früherer Gesellschaften* (pp. 75–107) Ethnologische Studien zum Verhältnis von Mensch und Natur. Gedächtnisschrift für Hermann Baumann. Frankfurt: Campus Verlag.

Hector, H. (1958). A new Pattern Completion Test. *Journal of the National Insitute for Personnel Research, 7,* 132–134.

Hector, H. (1959). A coloured version of the Pattern Completion Test. *Journal of the National Institute for Personnel Research, 7,* 204–205.

Hector, H. (1966). Intelligenzstudien mit dem Symmetrieprinzip [Intelligence studies with the principle of symmetry]. *diagnostica, 12,* 127–132.

Herskovits, M. J., Campbell, D. T., & Segall, M. H. (1956). *Materials for a cross-cultural study of perception*. Program of African Studies. Evanston, IL.: Northwestern University.

Hofstätter, P. R. (1966). Zum Begriff der Intelligenz [On the concept of intelligence]. *Psychologische Rundschau, 17,* 229–248.

Hudson, W. (1953). *The occupational classification of Africans*. Unpublished doctoral dissertation, University of the Witwatersrand, Johannesburg.

Humphriss, D., & Wortley, W. L. (1971). Two studies of visual acuity. *Psychologia Africana, 14,* 1–19.

Irvine, S. H., & Berry, J. W. (Eds.). (1983). *Human assessment and cultural factors*. New York: Plenum.

Ishihara, S. (1951). *Tests for Colour-Blindness* (10th ed.). Tokyo: Kanehara; London: H. K. Lewis.

Katz, R. (1973). *Preludes to growth: An experimental approach*. New York: Free Press.

Katz, R. (1976). Education for transcendence: !Kia-healing with the Kalahari !Kung. In R. B. Lee & I. DeVore (Eds.), *Kalahari hunter-gatherers: Studies of the !Kung San and their neighbors* (pp. 227–301). Cambridge, MA: Harvard University Press.

Lee, R. B. (1979). *The !Kung San. Men, women and work in a foraging society*. Cambridge University Press.

Lee, R. B., & DeVore, I. (Eds.). (1976). *Kalahari hunter-gatherers: Studies of the !Kung San and their neighbors*. Cambridge, MA: Harvard University Press.

Lewin, K. (1926). Vorbemerkungen über die seelischen Kräfte und Energien und über die Struktur des Seelischen. (Preliminary remarks about the psychic forces and energies and on the structure of the mind) *Psychologische Forschung, 7,* 294–329.

Marshall, L. (1976). *The !Kung of Nyae Nyae*. Cambridge, MA: Harvard University Press.

Martin, R. (1926). Zur Anthropologie der Buschmänner [On the anthropology of the Bushmen]. In E. Kaiser, *Die Diamantenwüste Südwest-Afrikas* (pp. 436–490). Berlin: Dietrich Reimer.

Metzger, W. (1975). *Gesetze des Sehens* [Laws of seeing] (3rd ed.). Frankfurt am Main: Verlag W. Kramer.

Metzger, W., Vukovich-Voth, O., & Koch, I. (1970). Ueber optisch-haptische Masstäuschungen an dreidimensionalen Gegenständen [On optic-haptic measurement of illusions with three-dimensional objects]. *Psychologische Beiträge, 12,* 329–366.

Minde, M. (1937). *In search of happiness*. London: Frederick Muller.

Morgan, P. (1959). A study in perceptual differences among cultural groups in Southern Africa, using tests of geometric illusions. *Journal of the National Institute for Personnel Research, 8,* 39–43.

Mundy-Castle, A. C., & Nelson, G. K. (1962). A neuropsychological study of the Knysna forest workers. *Psychologia Africana, 9,* 240–272.

Poortinga, Y. H. (1971). Cross-cultural comparison of maximum performance tests: Some methodological aspects and some experiments with simple auditory and visual stimuli. *Psychologia Africana* (Monograph Supplement No. 6).

Poortinga, Y. H. (Ed.). (1977). *Basic problems in cross-cultural psychology.* Selected papers from the 3rd International Conference of the International Association for Cross-Cultural Psychology. Lisse: Swets & Zeitlinger.

Poortinga, Y. H. (1983). Psychometric approaches to intergroup comparison: The problem of equivalence. In S. H. Irvine & J. W. Berry (Eds.), *Human assessment and cultural factors* (pp. 237–257). New York: Plenum.

Porteus, S. D. (1937). *Primitive intelligence and environment.* New York: Macmillan.

Reuning, H. (1951). *Wiedererkennen in Wahlversuchen mit Kindern* [Recognition in choice experiments with children]. Inaugural-Dissertation, Naturwissenschaftliche Fakultät, Johann Wolfgang Goethe-Universität, Frankfurt am Main.

Reuning, H. (1959). Psychologische Versuche mit Buschleuten der Kalahari. (Psychological experiments with Bushmen of the Kalahari) *Umschau in Wissenschaft und Technik, 59,* 520–523.

Reuning, H. (1971–72). Experimentell-psychologische Buschmann-Studien in der zentralen Kalahari [Experimental psychological Bushman studies in the Central Kalahari]. *Journal of the South-West Africa Scientific Society, 26,* 17–43.

Reuning, H. (1972). Psychological studies of Kalahari Bushmen. In L. J. Cronbach & P. J. D. Drenth (Eds.), *Mental tests and cultural adaptation* (pp. 171–181). The Hague: Mouton.

Reuning, H. (1983). Continuous Work Tests: Their scope in cross-cultural contexts. In S. H. Irvine & J. W. Berry (Eds.), *Human assessment and cultural factors* (pp. 303–318). New York: Plenum.

Reuning, H., & Wittmann, G. (1963). Relative difficulty of two kinds of symmetry in the Patco Test. *Psychologia Africana, 10,* 89–107.

Reuning, H. & Wortley, W. L. (1973). Psychological studies of the Bushmen. *Psychologia Africana* (Monograph Supplement No. 7.).

Révész, G. (1934). System der optischen und haptischen Raumtäuschungen [System of the optic and haptic spatial illusions]. *Zeitschrift für Psychologie, 131,* 296–375.

Roberts, A. O. H., MacQuarrie, M. E., & Shepherd, J. M. (1959). Some aspects of the Pattern Completion Test. *Journal of the National Institute for Personnel Research, 8,* 59–64.

Sbrzesny, H. (1976). *Die Spiele der !Kõ-Buschleute* unter besonderer Berücksichtigung ihrer sozialen und gruppenbindenden Funktion [The games of the !Kõ Bushmen with special consideration of their social and group-binding function]. *Monographien zur Humanethologie,* vol. 2, ed. I. Eibl-Eibesfeld. München: R. Piper.

Segall, M. H., Campbell, D. T., & Herskovits, M. J. (1966). *The influence of culture on visual perception.* Indianapolis, IN: Bobbs-Merrill.

Shapera, I. (1965). *The Khoisan peoples of South Africa.* London: Routledge.

Silberbauer, G. B. (1965). *Bushman survey.* Report submitted to the Government of Bechuanaland, Gaberones.

Silberbauer, G. B. (1972). The G/wi Bushmen. In M. G. Bicchieri (Ed.), *Hunters and gatherers today* (271–326). New York: Holt, Rinehart & Winston.

Silberbauer, G. B. (1981). *Hunter and habitat in the Central Kalahari desert.* Cambridge University Press.

Silberbauer, G. B., & Kuper, A. (1966). Kgalagari masters and Bushman serfs. *African Studies, 25,* 171–179.

Spohr, O. H. (1962). *Wilhelm Heinrich Immanuel Bleek: A biobibliographical sketch.* (Varia Series No. 6). Cape Town: University of Cape Town Libraries.

Steingrüber, H. (1974). *Analyse und Modifikation eines sprachfreien Tests zur Erfassung der unteren IQ-Bereiche unter dem Aspekt zweier verschiedener testtheoretischer Modelle* [Analysis and modification of a language-free test for the assessment of lower IQ ranges, using two different test-theoretical models]. Inaugural-Dissertation, Mathematisch-Naturwissenschaftliche Fakultät, Universität Düsseldorf.

Tanaka, J. (1976). Subsistence ecology of Central Kalahari San. In R. B. Lee & I. DeVore

(Eds.), *Kalahari hunter-gatherers: Studies of the !Kung San and their neighbors* (pp. 98–119). Cambridge, MA: Harvard University Press.

Taylor, T. R. (1974). A factor analysis of 21 illusions: The implications for theory. *Psychologia Africana, 15,* 137–148.

Tekane, I. (1961). An error analysis of responses to the Patco Test by Bantu industrial workers. *Journal of the National Institute for Personnel Research, 8,* 189–194.

Tekane, I. (1963). Symmetrical pattern completions by illiterate and literate Bantu. *Psychologia Africana, 10,* 63–68.

Tobias, P. V. (Ed.). (1978). *The Bushmen: San hunters and herders of Southern Africa.* Cape Town: Human & Rousseau.

Traill, A. (1978). The languages of the Bushmen. In P. V. Tobias (Ed.). *The Bushmen: San hunters and herders of Southern Africa* (pp. 137–147). Cape Town: Human & Rousseau.

van de Koppel, J. M. H. (1977). A preliminary report on the Central African differentiation project. In Y. H. Poortinga (Ed.), *Basic problems in cross-cultural psychology* (pp. 282–288). Lisse: Swets & Zeitlinger.

Van Wyk, I. (1964). EEG in the Kalahari. *Psygram, 6,* 17–22.

Von Mayer, B. (1963). The Patco Test, intelligence and closure. *Perceptual and Motor Skills, 17,* 890.

Winter, W. L. (1964). Recent findings from the application of psychological tests to Bushmen. *Psygram, 6,* 42–55.

Winter, W. L. (1967). Size constancy, relative size estimation and background: A cross-cultural study. *Psychologia Africana, 12,* 42–58.

Witkin, H. A., & Berry, J. W. (1975). Psychological differentiation in cross-cultural perspective. *Journal of Cross-Cultural Psychology, 6,* 4–87.

Witkin, H. A., Dyk, R. B., Faterson, H. F., Goodenough, D. R., & Karp, S. A. (1962). *Psychological differentiation: Studies of development.* New York: Wiley.

Yellen, J. E. (1971). Archaeological excavations in Western Ngamiland. *Botswana Notes and Records, 3,* 276.

Zilian, E. (1956). Ueber einen sprachfreien Intelligenztest [On a language-free intelligence test]. In *Bericht über den 20. Kongress der deutschen Gesellschaft für Psychologie, Berlin 1955* (pp. 198–200). Göttingen: Verlag für Psychologie, Hogrefe.

18   Caste and cognitive processes

J. P. Das and Amulya Kanti Satpathy Khurana

Caste is not a birthmark; it so happens that a Hindu in India is accidentally born into a certain caste. It is not a genetically defined category, such as mental retardation can sometimes be, nor is it as distinct as membership in a specific ethnic group. Caste can best be compared to being in a religious sect, like Protestants and Catholics, whose members may have the same ethnicity. The priests, warriors, merchants, and the service castes share the same genetic pool.

Why do we then search for cognitive markers which would be associated with castes? The best reason a researcher in this field can give is that caste represents a conglomerate of surrogate variables. A search for cognitive competencies among high-versus low-caste groups leads to educational and economic disparities between the two castes which must influence intellectual performance. Caste, like age, can be regarded as an empty variable. The experiential history of low-caste children, in general, is relatively disadvantageous for developing cognitive competence; it is that history of experiences in which we are really interested while comparing low-versus high-caste performance.

How unique are these experiences? What are the major variables which go into this nebulous notion of "experiences"? We suggest that they are the same nonhereditary factors which influence intellectual performance anywhere in the world. The variables, then, are environmental, such as parental expectation regarding the child's educational achievement, the quality of education, and physical factors associated with poverty, such as malnutrition and childhood diseases. If we assume that caste is a salient factor for cognitive competence because it represents these environmental variables, then we have extended the usefulness of studying the relationship between caste and cognition. We can then compare our findings to those of all others who study group and individual differences in cognitive competence. Caste ceases to be an exotic variable; its study can make a valid contribution to understanding cognitive competence.

Caste, nevertheless, has been regarded as an exotic variable by European and North American researchers. It has remained an engaging topic of conversation in cross-cultural psychology meetings, and, in fact, when interest is waning in these meetings, ask two psychologists from India to explain the

487

caste system. The ensuing debate will be lively because of "unresolvable" differences in the Indian psychologists' interpretations of the caste system.

The caste system

An acceptable definition of caste as traditionally construed is as follows: "A caste may be defined as a collection of families or groups of families bearing a common name; claiming common descent from a mythical ancestor, human or divine; professing to follow the same hereditary calling; and regarded by those who are competent to give an opinion as forming a single homogeneous community. The name generally denotes or is associated with a specific occupation. A caste is almost invariably endogamous in the sense that a member of the large circle denoted by the common name may not marry outside of that circle, but within the circle, there are usually a number of smaller circles each of which is also endogamous" (Risley, cited in Cox, 1948, p. 4).

Difficult as it is to describe the essence of caste, we make a brief presentation of the origin and contemporary practices of the caste system. The word *caste* has two terms in Sanskrit, and therefore in all northern Indian languages, which are derived from Sanskrit. The terms are *varna* and *jati*. Apparently, from very ancient times, since the Aryans came through the northwestern part of India to settle in the river valleys of the Indus and Ganges, there were four varnas, each attached to an occupation. These were *brahmana,* whose occupation was scholarly activity, including the knowledge and recitation of scriptures; *kshatriya,* the caste of kings and warriors; *vaishya*, the merchants; and *shudra,* which was associated with anyone who performed services, such as public cleaning of roads and sewers, hairdressing, laundry, and shoemaking. Apart from these four varnas, some authorities think that there was the category of untouchables. These were the people who were engaged in dirty work including cleaning lavatories and tanning leather. However, the word *varna* literally meant colour. It is believed by many in India that the top three castes were of a lighter skin colour than the fourth caste. It is also believed that the untouchables are outside the caste system of Hindus; probably they were the native people, who were conquered by the invading Aryans. No one knows when the occupations became encrusted into an inflexible hierarchy of castes.

The Brahmins (brahmana) were regarded as the highest of the four castes, and the shudras were the lowest. The warriors were lower than the Brahmins and higher than the merchants. The Brahmins wore a sacred thread, which is often the distinguishing mark of their superiority. They are called *dwija* (literally, twice born) because all Brahmins go through an initiation ceremony in their childhood in order to learn the traditional religious practices of their high caste. In recent times, the two lower castes, merchants and service people, have tried to model themselves after Brahmins, adopting many of their ways. This movement toward identification with Brahmins is described as "Sanskritization" (Srinivas, 1962).

However, one must understand that each of these four distinct varnas has numerous subcastes, and very often it is impossible to decide whether subcastes in adjacent varnas go with the upper or the lower caste. Perhaps it would be right to say that the subcastes are the social reality of the Hindu caste system, and are referred to as *jati*. The subcaste divisions are hardly isomorphic with occupation. Instead, they represent conventionally accepted divisions, and the conventions are by no means universal across the states or linguistic regions.

What are the distinguishing marks of a caste? The traditional features of the caste system, according to Ghurye (1961), are as follows: endogamy, which restricts the marriage between people of different castes; hierarchy; restrictions on community relations between castes; restrictions on choice of occupation; civil and religious privileges and disadvantages; and untouchability. Of all these characteristics, perhaps endogamy is still the strongest one, which has resisted change (Paranjpe, 1970). The other characteristic which remains in force is community relations, perhaps most clearly manifested in ritual status. However, no racial differences between castes based on endogamy can be supported. As Nesfield (1885) points out, the restrictions of marriage which are imposed by rules of caste did not, in contemporary Hindu society, exist until at least a thousand years after the Aryans had come into the country, and by that time the Aryan blood had been absorbed beyond recovery into the indigenous. Not till the time of Manu, that is, about 200 B.C. or later, did the caste rules in regard to marriages come into force. Even then, as Manu's own writings show, they were not universally accepted by the Brahmins themselves. It is clear, then, that after the Aryan invader had set foot on Indian soil, a Brahmin, or professional priest, could marry any woman he liked (see Cox, 1948, chap. 1, for further discussion).

Paranjpe, citing Stevenson, makes the distinction between secular status and ritual status. Whereas secular status is determined by wealth, education, occupation, and the like, ritual status is based on the concept of purity and pollution. The practices of purity and pollution are rather mystical in origin; however, the hierarchical relationship between different castes can often be defined by these practices. One of the most prominent ones is the sharing of cooked versus uncooked food between castes. If the two castes regard each other as more or less of equal hierarchical status, then they might share cooked food. However, if a caste is thought to be distinctly below the referent caste, then only uncooked food may be exchanged between them.

The practice of purity and pollution takes an extreme form in the relationship between the three higher castes, and the so-called untouchables. Even 50 years ago, the shadow of a person from an untouchable caste could not fall on the food a Brahmin was eating. Untouchability, of course, is an illegal practice in post-independent India. There have been several *positive discrimination* measures enacted since independence in 1947, which give the untouchables special privileges in school (scholarship funds) and preferential status in employment (in the civil service of state and federal governments). The abolition of untouchability was the result of a prolonged social revolution, spearheaded by Mahatma Gandhi. The former untouchables were renamed Harijan, literally, "God's people," and Gandhi vowed to make a Harijan the first president of independent India. However, he died a few months after India gained independence, and his influence on Indian society in regard to treating Harijans as at least equal to other caste Hindus has not taken root. The different levels of government in India treat them as better than equal, and practise positive discrimination toward the Harijans, which inevitably has led to resentment among high-caste Hindus. In spite of the special privileges enjoyed by Harijan students in schools and colleges, a vast majority of them still do not complete high school. Most Harijan families live below the poverty line, and continue to be the most disadvantaged section of the society.

The research to be reviewed in this chapter concerns children from high and low castes. In most of the studies that have been published on caste and cognitive competence, the low caste usually consists of *scheduled caste* children, which is a government term for Harijan children. The high caste usually entails the top two castes. They are the advantaged castes, with a disproportionately large representation among professionals. They outnumber any other castes in professions practising medicine and law, college and university teaching, and high-ranking civil services. Children from these caste groups have high academic standing in school and compete easily for entrance into prestigious technical and nontechnical post-secondary institutions. In contrast, the Harijan children in most parts of India may not go beyond six years of elementary schooling. In fact, in most of the research reported on the cognitive performance of Harijan children, one observes that the samples are from grade 6 or lower in elementary school.

The rest of the chapter considers the cognitive performance of advantaged and disadvantaged children. We explain in the next section why these terms are preferred to high- and low-caste children. The foregoing introduction to the caste system provides a context in which the difference between the performance of the two groups of children can be understood.

Research on caste, social disadvantage, and cognition: A perspective

A quick survey of studies relating caste to cognitive competence revealed that only a handful of papers mention caste as a major variable. Most others have confounded caste and poverty, and the "new" label is either cultural deprivation or cultural disadvantage (see Sinha, Tripathi, & Misra, 1982, for a sample of papers). There are at least two reasons for avoiding a focus on caste – one is academic and the other, we think, is political.

The lowest castes are also economically disadvantaged, living in relatively unsanitary conditions and lacking good schooling. Because caste does not promote cognitive incompetence due to hereditary factors, and because poverty and its consequences are the major factors which contribute to the lower cognitive competence of the Harijan (or "scheduled caste") children, it is accurate to label the primary variable to be disadvantage or deprivation, rather than caste.

What we think to be the political reason is quite transparent to those who live in India. We have unpleasant associations with "caste." Zealous support for one's own caste group, casteism, has been a negative and somewhat disruptive element, obstructing social progress in India. Those who do academic research do not wish to involve themselves, at least overtly, with the tradition of denigration of the so-called lower castes. Consider the comment of the ancient lawgiver of the Hindus, Manu (see Cox, 1948, p. 7), who wrote that the person from the lowest caste (shudra) was created to be a slave of a Brahmin. A shudra emancipated by his master is not really released from servitude; because that is innate in him, who can set him free from it? The academic psychologists in India like to dissociate themselves from such views. The attitude is analogous to North American racism – most academics are reluctant to study racial differences in intellectual competence between the whites and the blacks, mainly because of guilt, as the blacks have a history of being victimised by the whites.

Cross-cultural analogies like this provide a reason to present another perspective – that of emic versus etic approaches (Berry, 1974) to the study of caste and cognitive processes. The review of research presented in this chapter may appear to be emic at first glance. The researchers contrast high caste *and* high socioeconomic status with low caste *and* low socioeconomic status. They are studying one culture but different subpopulations. Because all researchers are also Indian, studying Indian cultural influences, an insider's view is presented in their research papers. The above are the principal characteristics of the emic orientation.

In spite of the emic orientation, an etic element must emerge when groups are being compared within the mosaic of cultures in India. Berry (1974) has suggested a term, *derived etic,* to describe the integration of emic studies for the purpose of comparability. Thus, an etic element is inherent, often in the objectives, and almost always in the conclusions, of the papers. The findings are usually related to universal issues in cross-cultural psychology – to the concept of deprivation derived from animal research on sensory deprivation, to the role of schooling problems of minority assessment, and to research on major cognitive domains of perception, memory, and thinking.

Thus, the research on caste and cognition does not exemplify an ummixed emic approach. Besides, even if the research is carried out by Indian scientists, the scientists are not giving an insider's point of view. First, they should distance themselves from the specific cultures they are studying in order to maintain objectivity. Second, the scientists *are* outsiders to many of the cultural groups they study. For instance, rarely would the scientist be a Harijan, or reside in a rural culture as a landless labourer; yet these

Table 18.1. *Acquisition and reversal in four subcultural groups generated by caste and class*

	Groups (N = 29 in each group)			
	Rich, high caste	Poor, high caste	Rich low caste	Poor, low caste
Verbal				
Acquisiton	14.31	20.48	25.41	23.45
	(6.55)	(13.82)	(11.65)	(11.84)
Reversal	7.03	8.96	12.59	10.48
	(5.16)	(4.57)	(6.78)	(7.17)
Nonverbal				
Acquisition	22.69	25.62	22.65	20.21
	(11.98)	(14.81)	(9.44)	(15.21)
Reversal	3.24	3.90	3.62	4.34
	(1.13)	(1.77)	(1.71)	(1.84)

Note: Trials taken to learn: Means and standard deviations (in parentheses).

are the cultural groups which are studied. We may then conclude that the etic element is not obvious in the emic approach, but it is implicit. All emic research by scientists from the same culture is *crypto-etic*.

Caste, SES, and cognitive processes: Fifteen years of research

The first set of studies, which are summarised in the following paragraph, were done in the state of Orissa by J. P. Das and his former students and colleagues. In the first study we asked two questions: Does birth in a higher caste hold absolute advantage over birth in a lower caste in terms of cognitive skills seen at the elementary school stage? Second, does birth in a rich rather than a poor family confer similar benefits? In fact, these are the major questions asked in four of the five studies. Only the tasks and samples varied from one study to the other.

Verbal and nonverbal processes. Since verbal and nonverbal processes may provide contrasts between the caste and class samples, in the first study (Panda & Das, 1970) we examined the acquisition and reversal of responses in both a verbal and a nonverbal conditioning task (Table 18.1). The samples were rich and poor Brahmin children and Harijan children, all of whom lived in a city. Using these samples, in one study we considered the effect of urban versus rural residence. Our experiment demonstrated clearly that the Brahmin children conditioned faster as well as reversed their responses faster in the verbal conditioning task. Economic prosperity was not a significant variable. However, the caste differences disappeared in nonverbal

Table 18.2. *Cultural deprivation and cognitive growth*

	Mean scores		
	Raven's Progressive Matrices	Word-reading time (in sec)	Short-term memory
Brahmin (high caste)			
Rich	21.22	74.27	5.48
Poor	19.30	74.12	5.60
Harijan (low caste)			
Rich	19.38	87.75	—
Poor	17.22	89.64	4.25
t *test significant between*	Rich Brahmin & Poor Harijan	Brahmin & Harijan	Brahmin & Harijan

conditioning. This might have been expected because the Brahmin families are supposed to have a verbal and articulate culture, reciting and reading scriptures. Verbal superiority of the Brahmins over that of the Harijans is commonly recognised. What is of interest here is that the Harijans did not show a general deficit in conditioning or learning.

Probing memory sets. This becomes clear in the next study (Das, Panda, & Jachuck, 1970), where a memory task was given (Table 18.2). As before, rich and poor children from both castes were involved. However, the gap in the income between the rich and poor was greater. The task for the children was to listen to a series of nine digits randomly arranged, and then recognise a pair of probe digits presented by the experimenter as an instance of a pair presented in the series. The probe digits has a 50–50 chance of being true or false instances. The results showed again that Brahmin children had a greater number of correct recognitions than the Harijan children. We had suspected that apart from a disadvantage in "memory," the Harijan children may have difficulty in simply coding auditorially presented digits into written form; that is, a difficulty in putting down on paper as they heard the digits being presented once per second. Thus, in a separate test, we looked at this performance. The poor Harijan children made significantly more errors in simply copying the digits which they heard, nearly three times as many. This skill is particularly important in early school years; for taking dictation, the skill is a critical one.

Reading skills: Degree of orthodoxy as a context variable. In the next study (Das & Singha, 1975) we wished to look at the effect of orthodox Brahmin

Table 18.3. *Caste, class, and cognitive competence*

Group	Word reading (sec)	STM (total digits)
1 Poor Harijan	35.37	83.20
2 Poor orthodox Brahmin	30.00	93.60
3 Poor nonorthodox Brahmin	30.60	91.60
4 Rich nonorthodox Brahmin	28.90	96.00
Total	31.22	91.10
Significant mean differences	1 vs 2 $p < .05$	1 vs 2 $p < .01$
	1 vs 4 $p < .01$	1 vs 4 $p < .01$

Note: Rich Harijan and rich orthodox Brahmins are quite infrequent.

culture on children's cognitive performance (Table 18.3). We reasoned that if the culture of the Brahmin home influences the development of verbal skills, the orthodox home would have a stronger influence. At the time of the experiment, it seemed reasonable to assume that the parents, especially the father, in an orthodox Brahmin home spends a great deal of time reciting and reading the scriptures because he makes his living by offering ritual worship in the temples and at the homes of lower castes. The nonorthodox Brahmin, who may be as poor as the orthodox Brahmin, earns a livelihood as a petty civil servant; thus, he does not have any demands for reciting scriptures. He does as much as he enjoys doing. We took three groups of Brahmin children, the rich urban and the poor urban, and the poor orthodox Brahmin children who live only in rural areas. We also had a group of urban Harijan children for comparison purposes with the Brahmins. One of the tasks was reading off the names of the four primary colours – red, green, yellow, and blue – each written 10 times in a random order on a chart. The words were written in 8 lines, 5 words to a line. We were gratified to find that the orthodox Brahmin children read the chart in a shorter time than the nonorthodox Brahmin children, and, as expected, in a shorter time than the Harijan children.

Urban and rural contexts for successive processing. Reading names of colours is hardly a representative verbal task. By the time we came around to do our fourth study, we had also begun to consider tasks such as recognising digit pairs, copying digits which are aurally presented, and word reading, all of which were examples of successive coding. Our attention had been also drawn to the difference between urban and rural children. We had noticed in a previous study that the urban Harijan children were not generally inferior to urban Brahmin children in many cognitive tasks; both groups of children came from poor families. Thus, in the next study (Das & Pivato, 1976), we are going to report how rural Harijan and rural Brahmin children (not particularly chosen from orthodox families) compared with each other.

Table 18.4. *Caste (Brahmin–Harijan) and cumulative effect of malnutrition (short–tall height): Summary of 2 (heights) × 2 (castes) analyses of variance (N = 60)*

Tests	F ratios		
	Caste main effect	Height main effect	Interaction
Raven's Progressive Matrices	<1	3.32[a]	<1
Figure Copying	<1	<1	<1
Memory for Designs	2.28	3.05[a]	<1
Cross Modal Coding	10.62[b]	3.17[a]	<1
Serial Recall	9.39[b]		
Digit Span	21.12[c]	<1	<1
Visual STM	15.62[c]	<1	<1
Word Reading	6.76[b]	<1	<1
Colour Naming	<1	<1	<1

[a] $p < .10$.
[b] $p < .01$.
[c] $p < .001$.

Because the cognitive tasks were differentially sensitive to caste differences, as will be seen from the results, we are going to describe this study in some detail.

Both social class and caste were varied in this larger project on the effect of malnutrition on cognitive competence. Only a portion of the research which relates to the performance of Brahmin and Harijan children is reported here. The specific design of the study should be discussed in some detail. It examines four groups of children, divided on *caste* and *height*; which were the tall and short Brahmin children, and the tall and short Harijan children. Without going into details about the effect of continuous malnutrition on the height of children, suffice it to say that the short children are more likely to have a continuous history of malnourishment in early childhood than the tall children, all other factors being equal. Rural children from Brahmin and Harijan castes were to be compared on a series of cognitive tasks. We have noticed in the previous study that urban Harijan children were not very different in their performance than urban Brahmin children. Therefore, we thought that the high-caste children would perform better on cognitive tasks than the Harijan children, when both groups lived in the villages.

Several cognitive tasks, including *Raven's Progressive Matrices,* were given. It was clear from the results presented in Table 18.4 that the Harijan children were not inferior to the Brahmins in their performance in the first three tasks. Incidentally, these tasks represented what we have called simultaneous processing, in contrast to *serial recall, digit span* and *visual short-term memory,* which require successive processing (Das, Kirby, & Jarman, 1975, 1979). One of the first three tasks is *Raven's Progressive*

Matrices, often regarded as an adequate test of nonverbal intelligence. Thus, it is heartening to see that the Brahmin children were not found to be superior to the Harijans on the *Progressive Matrices*. However, as far as the remaining tasks are concerned, the Harijan children were poorer in their performance. They were also inferior to the Brahmin children in *Cross-Modal Coding* tasks, which have a split loading on both Simultaneous and Successive factors, as well as in the *Speed of Reading 40 Words – red, green, blue,* and *yellow*, written in a random sequence, each for 10 times.

What do the caste differences reflect? One could speculate that they reflect the micro-environments of the children's homes, their ways of life. We can guess that the Brahmin household affords development of linguistic skills which require successive processing. All the tasks in which the Harijan children did poorly were instances of successive processing. Therefore, we could only speculate that in the Brahmin homes, this type of processing must be inherent in the experience of the Brahmin children. Their parents read scriptures aloud, and sing prayers in the morning and in the evening, and this would have facilitated the acquisition and use of successive processing in Brahmin children. Now, successive processing is crucial to early stages of reading. At this stage, decoding skills are required, and we have shown that decoding relates closely to successive processing (Cummins & Das, 1977). In the first few years of school, number work and reading both depend on decoding, and thus the facility with which the child uses successive processing must play an important role. The two – successive processing and early schoolwork – obviously interact with each other and accelerate successive processing, which in turn leads to better performance in reading and arithmetic. Thus, the role of schooling in improving cognitive skills is a crucial one. If the Harijan children are not actively involved in schoolwork, their cognitive processes would not develop satisfactorily.

Nutrition and cognition: Some evidence. At this point, we wish to report a complementary study on malnutrition as it relates to some personological factors (Dutta & Das, 1981). A sample of 240 Harijan boys reading in grades 4 and 5 in 100 schools of Orissa were subdivided into four groups on the basis of their height (below 25th percentile was short and above 75th percentile was tall). The sample was also divided on the basis of rural and urban residence. The height was considered to be an indication of malnourishment.

This chapter argues that whenever the malnourished and the less malnourished children have been compared, the former are shown to be inferior in cognitive tasks. Part of the reason may be in noncognitive personological factors of the type considered here. If this is valid, it needs to be shown as an initial step in this hypothetical model that the two groups can indeed be ordered hierarchically on these variables. Poor parental expectancy and self-concept are found to characterise the malnourished group. The malnourished children did show poor self-concept and lower parental expectations, as predicted. If the malnourished child is not as responsive as a less malnourished child, he or she is not likely to receive as much attention from parents or other caregivers at home, and later in school. Parental expectancy will be lower for a malnourished child who from infancy appears to be apathetic and relatively unresponsive. This situation becomes more obvious when the child enters school; his or her performance is poor, which in turn influences the parent's aspirations about the child's academic achievement. What is interesting is that children perceive their relative lack of competence and evaluate it correctly, which in turn provides a basis for their poor self-concept. The tall children, who were taken as controls in the present study, were also poor. But their parents might have provided relatively better nutrition within the restrictions of poverty by reallocating their meagre resources.

The caste factor has been further diluted in the following series of studies by different authors. Probably they represent the "garden variety" of research reports, involving socioeconomic status, minority religion, disadvantages associated with rural residence, poor schooling, and, of course, membership in the lower castes. This second set of studies were not exclusive to Orissa; they were done in several other states.

A persistent reference in the following set of studies is to cultural disadvantage. Thus the concept should be discussed before we present an "anthology" of abstracts of recent reports relating to the psychological and educational problems of disadvantaged children.

Understanding cultural disadvantage

The context in which the term *cultural disadvantage,* or *deprivation*, is used is environmental. Cultural deprivation refers to a complex set of conditions which favours intellectual retardation in a child. Two of these conditions are an unstimulating environment in which a child grows up and a lack of verbal commerce with adults. The impetus for work on cultural disadvantage has come from the research on early experience and sensory deprivation in comparative psychology. Following the work of Hebb on animals who were raised in restricted environments and were found to have retarded sensory and perceptual development, a number of psychologists have maintained that the single contributing factor to cultural disadvantage is the poor verbal and intellectual environment in the early life of the disadvantaged child. Numerous studies on animals showing the effect of an enriched early environment on the later growth of discrimination learning and problem-solving abilities have been conducted, and these in turn have been duplicated with the human infant.

However, in recent years there has been a reexamination of the animal data on restricted environment and their application or extension to humans. The inference from animal models is now less acceptable. But even in animal studies, rehabilitation following initial sensory deprivation is a critical factor. For example, when an animal is brought up in a lighted environment and not in a dark one, all other conditions being constant, the animal typically does not show the ill effects of sensory deprivation. Second, animals reared in a restricted environment do show initial disadvantages in discrimination learning, but such disadvantages gradually disappear with exposure to a normal environment. In other words, the gap between the sensory-deprived animals and those who are reared normally begins to narrow as the deprived animal is increasingly exposed to a normal environment following its early exposure to a restricted one.

A modified view of the psychological effects of early environmental experience advocates that it is not stimulation per se but the quality of stimulation that is important. The middle-class child most often has a superior quality of both verbal and nonverbal stimulation. These stimulations are distinct. The reinforcement systems in a middle-class home are of a delayed kind which is congruent to adult life; and certainly the verbal milieu in which the middle-class child grows up corresponds much more closely to that found in academic textbooks and in school learning situations. All in all, language is given a very important role as a determinant for the growth of intellect. However, there are even disturbing facts about this explanation. Das (1973) has advanced a modified threshold hypothesis to understand the effect of cultural disadvantage. The antidote to environmental deprivation may not be intensive stimulation – it may be simply the restoration of the environmental conditions prevailing for the majority of nondeprived children, allowing the potpourri of experience which exists for a child of that age. Such a view is essentially similar to those held by Lenneberg regarding language development. Provided that a child has normal intelligence, (above IQ 85), an enriched environment beyond the usual one may not be useful; but below this IQ threshold, enrichment would have a beneficial effect on intellectual development. All that a child from an extremely disadvantaged home needs is his removal to an ordinary environment. This could be provided by schooling, teacher's encouragement, and the positive attitude of parents towards the child's education.

A sample of recent research associated with caste and culture

Some recent studies in India are reported in this section. Caste and cultural disadvantage are frequently confounded in these research papers which, as a group, may be characterised as high in statistical sophistication, low on formulated hypotheses, and still lower on a theoretical focus.

Disadvantage studies. Rao (1979) investigated the development of seriation and numerical abilities in disadvantaged children. Children between 4 and 7 years of age belonging to labour-class families in slum areas and not attending school were sampled. From each age level, 72 children, equally divided into boys and girls, were selected. A similar number of subjects from each age level were selected from the school-going children to serve as a control group. The subjects were tested for discrimination, seriation, and numeration skills employing piagetian types of tests. The tests were given using three types of materials: (a) sticks – unidimensional; (b) slats – bidimensional; and (c) blocks – three-dimensional. All the materials were of wood, painted orange. The experimental design used was factorial design with schooling (2) × tests (3) × materials (3) × age levels (4). The data were analysed with ANOVA. The F ratios for the factors Age, Operations, Materials, and Schooling were found to be significant beyond the .01 level. The subjects' performance was examined in terms of their SES background. They were classified using the Socio-economic Rating Scale (Rao, 1973). The results corroborate the findings obtained in the first part of this study. Deprivation, socioeconomic factors or nonschooling adversely affect cognitive development in young children.

Sahu (1979) investigated the effect of social disadvantage on verbal competence and language achievement. Socially advantaged and disadvantaged subjects were drawn from three grade levels (2, 3, and 4), with 35 subjects in each of the six resulting subgroups. Scores on the *Indian Adaptation of the WISC* verbal subscales, with necessary reordering, and *Language Achievement Test Battery* scores were higher for advantaged subjects. *WISC* verbal scores were significantly correlated with *Word Reading, Spelling* scores, *Passage Comprehension* scores, and *Word Fluency* scores. Similar relationships were also present for word comprehension scores of advantaged subjects, but not for disadvantaged subjects. In a subsequent study along the same lines, Sahu (1981) examined 210 subjects drawn from advantaged and disadvantaged groups. *WISC* scale items were rearranged according to the difficulty level in the Oriya sample, which resulted in choosing four subscales. These were (1) Rearranged Information subscale; (2) Arithmetic subscale; (3) Rearranged Similarities subscale; and (4) Digit Span subscale. Results showed again that the social dimension factor significantly contributed to the variance on *WISC* verbal subscales, and not to the performance subscales. Thus, there were significant interaction effects between the social dimension and *WISC* subscales.

Ahmad (1980) examined the effect of sociocultural disadvantage on creative thinking. Children from advantaged and disadvantaged families who were in grades 7, 9, and 11 were selected from five types of institutions – extremely advantaged schools, slightly advantaged schools, average schools, slightly disadvantaged schools, and extremely disadvantaged schools. A total of 150 subjects participated in the study. Sahu's scale of cultural deprivation was administered to select the sample. Verbal and nonverbal tests of creativity by Baquer Mehdi were used. Using a 3 × 2 × 5 factorial design, the main effects of grade, schooling, and home backgrounds were found to be significant on verbal and nonverbal tests of creative thinking. None of the interactions, except for grade and school, were insignificant. Ahmad (1982) used the same design for investigation into the interactional effect of the home and school disadvantage on intellectual ability. The sample consisted of 120 subjects belonging to enriched and deprived home environments, studying in four categories of schools – extremely advantaged, extremely disadvantaged, slightly advantaged, and slightly disadvantaged educational institutions. Sahu's *Cultural Deprivation Scale,* an adaptation of Deutsch's (1967), was used to distinguish between advantaged and disadvantaged homes. A *School Deprivation Scale* constructed by the author was used to determine types of schools. A *General Mental Ability Test* by Joshi, and Baquer Mehdi's verbal and nonverbal tests of creative thinking, were also administered. Cross-comparison of verbal general mental ability scores of various groups of subjects revealed that verbal intelligence scores, as was found in the case of verbal creativity, were affected greatly by the enriched school environment only – which dominates not only all the categories of institutions but also the home background – while nonverbal creativity scores were affected by both home and environment.

Mohanty (1980) investigated the effects of sociocultural disadvantage on intelligence and short-term memory. The sample consisted of 200 boys (50 subjects, socioculturally advantaged and disadvantaged, in grades 3 and 4, in a 2 × 2 factorial design). *Raven's Progressive Matrices* (Coloured Form) test and short-term memory tests were used. Sociocultural dimension variances and grade variances were found to be significant for *Raven's,* short-term memory, clustering, and Ratio of Repetition Index (RRI) scores. The scores on all these four measures of cognitive abilities showed favourable trends for advantaged subjects. The results are interpreted as generally supporting a cumulative deficit hypothesis. However, the nature of obtained group differences was considered to be sociocultural rather than genetic.

Kaul (1981) conducted a study of some cognitive and socioemotional variables in socioeconomically disadvantaged children. The sample included 300 students from grade 5, distributed equally into three groups (middle, high, and the disadvantaged groups). It was found that the disadvantaged were significantly more field dependent as compared to the middle and high SES groups. They also demonstrated a stronger preference for visual modality as compared to the control groups. On creativity, the disadvantaged had an edge over the middle class in three of the four dimensions. On the fluency dimension, the disadvantaged did not differ significantly from either the middle or high SES groups. However, the disadvantaged were found to be significantly more cooperative than the high SES group.

Srivastava (1982) conducted a study of creative abilities in relation to socioeconomic status and culture. *Parsi's Creative Test* and *Kulshreshtha's SES Scale* were administered to students in eight high schools. It was found that culture and socioeconomic status exerted a significant effect upon creative abilities. Urban students did better. Subjects of middle SES scored higher than those of lower SES. However, the interaction was not significant.

Deprivation research. Recent studies of the effect of impoverished environment or prolonged deprivations in natural settings have unequivocally shown that deprivation of various kinds, such as sensory, motor, social, parental, cultural, economic, and so forth, result in deficient cognitive functioning, especially in complex perceptual tasks and conceptualisation. However, a close scrutiny of the studies reveals that meagre attempts have been made to crystallise comprehensively and quantify adequately the characteristics of deprivation variables. Tripathi and Misra (1976) have considered deprivation as a multidimensional and quantifiable variable operative over long periods. They conducted a study to discover the quantitative relationship between deprivation and relative efficiency in various types of cognitive processes such as depth perception, perceptual identification, and conceptualisation. The study was conducted on a large sample of 645 subjects drawn from an urban setting. *Prolonged Deprivation Scale* (Misra & Tripathi, 1975, 1977), *Pictorial Depth Perception Test, Perceptual Identification Task, Categorisation Task,* and *Kohs Block Design Test* were used. Results showed a negative relationship between deprivation and cognitive efficiency.

In an earlier study, Tripathi and Misra (1975) investigated cognitive activities as a function of prolonged deprivation on a sample of 50 males 16 to 25 years of age, residing in a background rural area. They were classified into high, medium, and low deprivation groups. The sample was subjected to six tests of cognitive functions and mental ability. The results demonstrate that less deprived subjects do better as compared to more deprived subjects. Further analysis of the data obtained from the medium deprivation group indicated that the results cannot be attributed to the caste of the subject. Despite certain methodological limitations and a small sample, the data obtained in this investigation support the view that the degree of deprivation is a prime determinant of psychological functioning.

Misra and Shahi (1977) conducted a study on prolonged deprivation and development of form perception. The sample consisted of 100 children from a rural area, between the ages of 4 and 7 years. They were classified into three deprivation groups – that is, high, middle, and low – on the basis of their scores on the *Prolonged Deprivation Scale* (Misra and Tripathi, 1975). The comparison of mean correct recognition of letter-like forms indicated significant detrimental effects of deprivation.

Differentiation and its social contexts. Sandeep (1978) examined the relationship between classroom interaction and cognitive development in 463 primary school children. Part of his analysis included children's responses on the *Picture Ambiguity Test* and *Picture Integration Test* as related to caste. The findings of caste for reorganisation may be summarised as follows: 1. Kshatriya (kings and warrior caste) group of children were highly figure-oriented and least ground-oriented. These children were the lowest in whole and part orientation and highest in part–whole orientation. 2. Brahmin children were more ground-oriented than other caste groups. 3. Vaishya (merchant caste) children were more part-oriented and to a lesser extent whole-oriented. They were the least part–whole oriented.

Majeed and Ghosh (1981) studied the effect of ethnicity and social class on cognitive differentiation. Their "ethnic" factor referred to Muslim and Hindu samples. Out of 150 grades 11 and 12 students of a rural college near Allahabad, 60 students were selected for the study on the basis of their socioeconomic status. Witkin's *Embedded Figures Test (EFT)* was administered individually. Results showed that subjects belonging to a low SES obtained a significantly higher score on the cognitive differentiation scale. Ethnicity – that is, high caste, Muslims, and scheduled caste – was not found to be related with *EFT* scores. Interactions were also insignificant. Later, Majeed and Ghosh (1983) conducted two studies to find out the effect of caste and religion ("ethnicity," as the authors name it), social class, and residential background on cognitive differentiation, again using Witkin's *Embedded Figures Test* score as the dependent variable. The first study involved 45 subjects from three groups (high-caste Hindus, scheduled castes, and Muslims) and two residential backgrounds (rural and urban). The result indicated a main effect of rural–urban background and a significant interaction between ethnicity and residential background. The second study completed on a total sample of 60 subjects indicated a significant effect of social class. However, the main effect of ethnicity was not obtained. Ethnicity and residential background appeared to be jointly operating as a significant influence on cognitive differentiation as measured by *EFT* tasks.

Although urban subjects would be expected to show higher differentiation scores than rural subjects, the ethnic membership disadvantage of Harijan subjects tends to be moderated more effectively in urban environments, where they displayed higher cognitive differentiation, in comparison to high-caste Hindu and Muslim subjects. On the other hand, the Harijans in the rural ecology appear to be influenced by a situation of double disadvantage. A unique feature of the Majeed and Ghosh research is that it considered Muslims along with Hindus on the dimension of social class. The above findings seem to point out that cognitive differentiation skills are not clearly contingent upon any single eco-cultural effect. Although social class and rural–urban differences turned out to be the strongest independent variables, socially generated intergroup relations resulting in social disadvantage also appear to moderate environmental enrichment or deprivation effects. It is a pity that the study was conducted on a fairly small sample.

The next paper we wish to review is perhaps the most unusual one because it contrasts not only high- and low-caste Hindus but also two Muslim groups, Shia and Suni. The instrument used was a verbal intelligence test. Although the subjects in each group numbered only 25 (and the results are almost incomprehensible because of suspected, statistical errors judging from the data in the tables), it is still interesting to observe that the Shia were some 12 IQ points lower than the Suni (112 and 124). No explanation, however, is given for the observed inferiority of the Shia Muslim group in verbal intelligence (Dharakan, 1978). Some intriguing prospects may be in store for those who pursue differences in test performance among Muslim sects.

In the concluding part of this review of Indian studies on caste and socioeconomic status, we shall discuss three significant papers in some detail. Sinha (1982) has reported the results of a well-executed research on school-age children. He gave tests of perceptual skills to three different age groups (5- 8- and 10-year olds). Half of the children were studying in superior schools, and the other half in ordinary, ill-equipped schools. There was a third variable of high and low caste. Sinha anticipated that the low-caste children in ordinary schools would be less efficient in his perceptual tasks, compared to high-caste children, but that with good schooling, the difference should disappear. In other words, the critical term in the analysis of variance design would be the interaction between school and caste. Development of perceptual skills with age was also anticipated.

One of his perceptual tasks was pictorial representation. Each picture was presented on a black and white card. It had certain objects which could not be visible to some of the characters in the picture, due to the interposition of other objects between them. However, all pictures were visible to the subject, who was asked to indicate whether or not a certain object was hidden from a particular character in the picture because of an interposition. Although the source of the task is not given, from the description it appears like one of the Witkin tasks. The other perceptual task was picture arrangement. Four pictures were given to the children to be put in order, so that the sequence would tell a story. Sinha's results show significant effect for age, type of schooling, and caste, but no interactions. He highlights some of the findings, among them that the scheduled caste (low-caste or Harijan) children were inferior in their performance to higher caste children, not only in ordinary schools but also in the superior schools. Thus, it is really remarkable that the low-caste children, in spite of their education in select schools of good quality in the city, were inferior to high-caste children in the same schools. Sinha does not seem to be especially sensitive to this finding; rather, he alerts the reader to the fact that scheduled caste children in good schools were superior to their counterparts in ordinary schools. The results may not come as a surprise to the reader, because of the selection process which operates in getting children to superior versus ordinary schools; for one thing, those scheduled caste children who can get admitted to the elitist schools either have to be quite brilliant to win scholarships or must have enough wealth to support the high tuition.

The next paper discussed is by Misra (1982), who starts out with a review of the concepts of deprivation, caste, and cognitive competence. He makes a strong plea for considering the extent of deprivation, rather than caste membership, as the salient variable for studying cognitive competence. He describes the cumulative effect of disadvantage as prolonged deprivation, constructs a scale to measure it, and relates it to cognitive tasks such as pictorial depth perception, categorisation, *Cattell's Culture Fair Test*, and *Kohs Block Design Test*. Children distinguished on the deprivation scale as low, medium, or highly deprived had correspondingly good, average, and low scores on almost all of the cognitive measures. Misra argues that birth in a specific caste is not associated with a specific level of cognitive competence but rather is the cumulative experiential base which makes a person cognitively more or less competent (Misra, 1982). It is difficult to contradict that statement. However, he also observes that caste has an important role, because high-caste children are still likely to be found in the highly deprived group. Again, the confounding association of caste and deprivation is in evidence as determinants of cognitive competence.

The last article reviewed in some depth considers *caste membership as a social frame of reference which influences learning and forgetting of adjectives* (Kanungo & Das, 1961). The experiment required college students from the first and second caste groups to remember adjectives ascribed to the two castes. Half of the adjectives were favourable and half were unfavourable to each caste. It was hypothesised that the favourable adjectives for one's own caste group and the unfavourable adjectives for the other caste group would be better recalled than favourable adjectives for the other caste group and unfavourable adjectives for one's own caste group.

The college students did not know they were being chosen for their membership in the first two castes, and they were unaware of the purpose of the experiment. Twenty-five students from each caste group were tested. Analysis of variance was used and the result of importance is the interaction between favourable and unfavourable adjectives, on the one hand, and adjectives relating to one's own versus the other group, on the other hand. More unfavourable than favourable adjectives were recalled, and the expected interaction was obtained. In explaining the results, the authors suggested that the first and second castes considered each other as rivals and were in constant competition for the highest positions in the professions as well as the community. Caste membership will influence selectivity in recall; that is why the interaction was expected to be significant. This study is quite different from all others in that it demonstrates the powerful influence of caste membership as a critical variable affecting memory.

Concluding remarks

It is easy to separate caste hierarchy from economic status. One needs simply to state that Brahmins, the highest caste, are not necessarily the richest; in fact, the business caste is traditionally the richest. It is also acceptable to say that each caste has its own culture, that the traditions and rituals practised in one caste set it apart from another. But these are sociological rather than psychological variables; they cannot influence the cognitive processes on which the castes may be distinguished. They have to be linked to psychological variables. Their path of influence must be charted through psychological domains.

When we start doing the charting, however, we discover that there are some other sociological territories to traverse, especially in regard to economic status. We find that both economic and cultural factors can be maximally separated by contrasting Brahmins with the lowest caste; the majority among them are Harijans. There are rich and poor Brahmins, but the Harijans are predominantly poor. A strategy for matching Brahmins with Harijans in economic status while comparing their cognitive competence has been followed in some of our studies reported here. The "cultural" advantages of Brahmins over Harijans, both groups being poor, then becomes a variable which may influence cognitive competence. By further contrasting the two caste groups in urban versus rural settings, we not only delineate the role of another powerful sociological variable but also show that the hypothesised influence of the "superior" Brahmin culture is not observed in urban communities. The studies reviewed in this chapter show that both economic and cultural factors can be related to cognitive competence, and that poverty and membership in the lowest caste are disadvantageous for the growth of cognitive competence. Sometimes their effects are additive, but sometimes they are interactive.

But what exactly are the mediating psychological variables? The question is implicit in each one of the studies cited. The micro-environment at home has been identified as a salient variable which entails a host of psychological factors. Parental expectation of a child's educational achievement and parental involvement in early acquisition of linguistic skills are one set of psychological variables which has been frequently mentioned in research. Peer group in and outside the school is a well-known factor which influences the academic competence of school children. Modelling family members at home, and friends in the school as well as in the community, are associated variables. These may, on occasion, become the most significant factors in shaping the cognitive development of children. Role models also influence the child's motivation for excellence.

Turning now to identify some "hard" variables, we face the difficult problem of understanding innate ability as a major element which distinguishes the high from low caste children. We have argued before that an innate ability difference will be hard to prove, even if we assume that the Brahmins and Harijans have retained their distinct genetic pools (Das & Singha, 1975). Each would have recaptured the normal range of variation in intelligence during the last 2,000 years. Ability differences can be looked at as differences in types of cognitive processing; according to one model, in simultaneous and successive processing and planning and judgment (Das, Kirby, & Jarman, 1979). The Harijan children were found to be as good in simultaneous processing (for example, in *Raven's Progressive Matrices*) as the Brahmins, but were poor in language skills. Their relative incompetence was traced to inadequate linguistic stimulation and modelling at home. Additionally, they

. may sometimes have the necessary skill but may not use it appropriately. Failure in utilisation of successive strategies rather than a deficiency in successive processing can be the critical factor. As far as the superiority of Brahmin children in *some* cognitive tests on *some* occasions is concerned, it seems to result from an efficient use of cognitive strategies.

There is, of course, another, even more obvious, antecedent to the superior performance of high-caste children – it has to do with knowledge base. The importance of knowledge base in explaining some part of developmental changes is well recognised in the research literature. Its role in contributing to cognitive competence differences between high and low caste or advantaged versus disadvantaged children should be readily recognisable. Children from advantaged or high-caste families are likely to acquire knowledge through osmosis, by merely being a part of the family, which helps them to do relatively better in cognitive tasks. They are also more likely to go to better schools. Even when they go to the same school, they are likely to get a better instruction from the teacher compared to the Harijan children in the same class. Thus, whenever research, as reviewed in this chapter, reveals that high-caste advantaged children are superior to the Harijan in some specific test or task, let us ask about the extent to which that performance is influenced by direct teaching, besides the informal education provided by the family.

Last, the role of physical factors associated with poverty and malnutrition cannot be ignored (Das & Soysa, 1978). Permanent changes in the nervous system can result from chronic malnutrition. Long periods of physical illness caused by various kinds of infections certainly retard the learning capacity of the disadvantaged children, partly through direct decrement in number of "healthy" days available for learning, and partly by isolating the children from social contacts because of long and frequent sickness.

To return to our original notion about caste as a proxy or surrogate variable, we have listed some powerful determiners which contribute to the observed incompetence of Harijan children in some cognitive tasks. We have tried to link these determinants to psychological variables. These variables are nomothetic ones in as much as they are operative in milieus unrelated to the caste system.

References

Ahmad, S. (1980). Effect of socio-cultural disadvantage on creative thinking. *Journal of Psychological Researches, 24*(2), 96–106.

Ahmad, S. (1982). Interactional effect of the home and school disadvantage on intellectual ability. *Psychologia, 25,* 65–69.

Berry, J. W. (1974). Radical cultural relativism and the concept of intelligence. In J. W. Berry & P. R. Dasen (Eds.) *Culture and cognition: Readings in cross-cultural psychology* (pp. 225–229). London: Methuen.

Berry, J. W. (1979). Research in multicultural societies. *Journal of Cross-Cultural Psychology, 10,* 415–434.

Cox, O. C. (1948). *Caste, class and race.* New York: Monthly Review Press.

Cummins, J. P., & Das, J. P. (1977). Cognitive processing and reading difficulties. *Alberta Journal of Educational Research, 23,* 245–255.

Das, J. P. (1973). Cultural deprivation and cognitive competence. In N. R. Ellis (Ed.), *International review of research in mental retardation* (Vol. 6, pp. 1–53). New York: Academic Press.

Das, J. P., Kirby, J. R., & Jarman, R. (1975). Simultaneous and successive synthesis: An alternative model for cognitive abilities. *Psychological Bulletin, 82,* 87–103.

Das, J. P., Kirby, J. R., & Jarman, R. (1979). *Simultaneous and successive cognitive processes.* New York: Academic Press.

Das, J. P., Panda, T. P., & Jachuck, K. (1970). Cultural deprivation and cognitive growth. In H. C. Haywood (Ed.), *Social-cultural aspects of mental retardation.* East Norwalk, CT: Appleton-Century-Crofts.

Das, J. P., & Pivato, E. (1976). Malnutrition and cognitive functioning. In N. R. Ellis (Ed.), *International review of research in mental retardation* (Vol. 8). New York: Academic Press.

Das, J. P., & Singha, P. S. (1975). Caste, class and cognitive competence. *Indian Educational Review, 10,* 1–18.

Das, J. P., & Soysa, P. (1978). Late effects of malnutrition. *International Journal of Psychology, 13,* 295–303.

Deutsch, M., et al. (1967). *The disadvantaged child.* New York: Basic.

Dharakan, P. N. O. (1978). Relationship between intelligence and religious group differences. *Indian Psychology Review, 16,* 37–39.

Dutta, T., & Das, J. P. (1981). Noncognitive correlates of malnutrition. *Social Change,* 9–12.

Ghurye, G. S. (1961). *Caste, class and occupation.* Bombay: Popular Book Depot.

Kanungo, R., & Das, J. P. (1961). Differential learning and forgetting as a function of the social frame of reference. *Journal of Abnormal and Social Psychology,* 82–86.

Kaul, V. (1981). *Some cognitive and socioemotional variables in socio-economically disadvantaged children.* Unpublished doctoral dissertation, ITT, Delhi.

Majeed, A., & Ghosh, E. S. K. (1981). Effect of ethnicity and social class on cognitive differentiation. *Journal of Psychological Researches, 25,* 84.

Majeed, A., & Ghosh, E. S. K. (1983). Effects of ethnicity, social class and residential background on cognitive differentiation. *Psychological Studies, 28*(3), 13–17.

Misra, G. (1982). Deprivation and cognitive competence. In D. Sinha, R. C. Tripathi, & G. Misra (Eds.), *Deprivation: Its social roots and psychological consequences.* New Delhi: Concept Publishing.

Misra, G., & Shahi, B. P. (1977). Prolonged deprivation and development of form perception. *Journal of Educational Research, 21*(3), 185.

Misra, G., & Tripathi, L. B. (1975). *Development of an objective tool to measure prolonged deprivation in Indian setting.* Unpublished paper, Psychology Department, Gorakhpur University.

Misra, G., & Tripathi, L. B. (1977) *Manual of prolonged deprivation scale.* Agra: National Psychological Corporation.

Mohanty, B. (1980). Effects of socio-cultural disadvantage on intelligence and short term memory. *Indian Psychological Review, 19*(4), 17–24.

Nesfield, J. C. (1885). *The caste system of north-western provinces & Oudh.* Cited in O. C. Cox (Ed.), *Caste, class & race.* New York: Monthly Review.

Panda, K. C., & Das, J. P. (1970). Acquisition and reversal in four subcultural groups generated by caste and class. *Canadian Journal of Behavioural Sciences, 2,* 267–273.

Paranjpe, A. C. (1970). *Caste, prejudice and the individual.* Bombay: Lalvani Publishing House.

Rao, S. N. (1973). The socio-economic status rating scale. *Indian Journal of Social Sciences, 11*(4).

Rao, S. N. (1979) Development of discrimination, seriation and numeration abilities in disadvantaged children. *Journal of Indian Education, 5,* 11–18.

Risley, H. H. *The people of India*. Cited in O. C. Cox (1948), *Caste, class and race*. New York: Monthly Review Press.

Sahu, S. (1979). Effect of social disadvantage on verbal competence and language achievement. *Psychological Studies, 24*(1), 66–72.

Sahu, S. (1981). Verbal competence of social disadvantaged children. *Journal of Social and Economic Studies, 9*(1), 59–65.

Sandeep, P. (1978). *Classroom-interaction and cognitive development in primary school children*. Unpublished doctoral dissertation, Osmania University, Hyderabad.

Sinha, D. (1982). Some social disadvantages and development of certain perceptual skills. In D. Sinha, R. C. Tripathi, & G. Misra (Eds.), *Deprivation: Its social roots and psychological consequences*. New Delhi: Concept Publishing.

Sinha, D., Tripathi, R. C., & Misra, G. (Eds.) (1982). *Deprivation: Its social roots and psychological consequences*. New Delhi: Concept Publishing.

Srinivas, M. N. (1962). *Caste in modern India and other essays*. Bombay: Asia Publishing House.

Srivastava, E. (1982). A study of creative abilities in relation to socio-economic status and culture. *Perspectives in Psychological Research, 5*(2), 37–40.

Tripathi, L. B., & Misra, G. (1975). Cognitive activities as a function of prolonged deprivation. *Psychological Studies, 20*(2), 54–61.

Tripathi, L. B., & Misra, G.. (1976). Some cognitive processes as functions of prolonged deprivation. *Indian Journal of Psychology, 51*(2), 129–143.

19 Educational adaptation and achievement of ethnic minority adolescents in Britain

Gajendra K. Verma

Introduction

Access to education, once confined to a small privileged section of the population, is now a right for all. Indeed, children in most countries are required to attend school until a determined age. Consequently, schools have to cater for a child population coming from a wide variety of social backgrounds and experiences. As a result, the educational system is constantly subject to pressures, internal and external, arising from the diversity of often competing demands that society makes upon it. Solutions to these pressures take many forms, embracing a spectrum from specific operations in classrooms to blind faith at policy levels. Policy statements express these beliefs: in education as a process that maximises individual potential; and, at the other end of the scale, faith in the power of education to change society for the better.

One of the many elements in the debate about priorities in such a heterogeneous system of beliefs is the adequacy of existing provision to a particular type of child. One such type is the "ethnic minority child"; others include the "gifted child" and the "educationally subnormal child." Although such labels tend to reduce children to ciphers and to discount the uniqueness of the individual's experience, categorisation is perhaps an inevitable consequence of seeking to emphasise the need for one particular aspect of educational provision. That type of concern is nevertheless consistent with the terms of the British 1944 Education Act, which marked the beginning of the operationalisation of the ideal of providing education for each child according to age, aptitude, and ability.

The explicit objectives of formal education vary in emphasis from society to society. Broadly speaking, they serve two interrelated functions. The first of these centres on *individual* development in terms of the acquisition of skills and knowledge considered as important by that society. These range from the basics of literacy and numeracy to the more sophisticated ones that will enable a particular career path or channel of employment to be followed by an individual. The second function centres around the needs, expectations, and requirements of *society* as a whole if it is to operate effectively. The dominant ideologies and values of that society will determine the conception of those needs, aspirations and requirements, and the resources,

509

both human and material, that are to be made available to operate the educational system. A detailed system of rewards – whether in terms of wealth and/or status – is offered, commensurate with the proficiency acquired in particular levels of skills regarded essential for the effective functioning of that society. The dominant culture of society will also determine the degree of freedom of access to acquire particular skills, thus establishing a particular societal hierarchy.

Nevertheless, the concept of equality of opportunity is an attractive model offered to society's young people and their parents. It is also an important focal point, particularly in a democratic society, in the debate and dialogue about the role and values to be placed on formal education, and in terms of its accessibility to all sections of the population. One of the issues of that debate in Britain and elsewhere is the place of ethnic minorities. Ethnic identity has become a potent force, carrying with it considerable implications for society in all its dimensions. Not the least of these is education. How have the children of ethnic minorities fared in British schools?

Ethnic minority children, although not a new phenomenon in British schooling, came to feature prominently in the classrooms of postwar Britain, as their numbers increased in the wake of postwar migration to this country. It brought many people from the New Commonwealth in search of prosperity and in response to the need for an increased workforce to man British industries and services in the postwar expansion.

At first, provision for ethnic minority children consisted primarily of equipping them to cope with life in British society; for many of these children provision began with teaching them English. Later, the numbers of ethnic minority children in classrooms increased as immigrant groups established themselves. However, because the patterns of settlement tended to result in concentration in areas where manufacturing industry flourished, ethnic minority children became a distinctive feature of particular schools. Then issues began to shift away from pure survival to ones of whether the structures of the education system could offer these children the same chance of academic success as that sought by the population at large. What factors weighed against minority children? Were they inferior to "proper" English ones, in terms of potential or merely because of disadvantage of one sort or another?

Issues like these in addition to questions raised about the ethnocentric stance of the school curriculum have steadily come to the fore. The process has been accelerated by the increasing proportion of ethnic minority children in schools. Another contributing factor has been the number of ethnic minority youngsters reaching school-leaving age and faced with the reality of the world of work. In a shrinking youth employment market that reality has been soured and has dramatised how ill-equipped some of them are to advance their aspirations.

Having sketched the broad educational background to the issue of the achievements and abilities of ethnic minorities in British schools, we now turn to the definition of ethnicity, a category that is commonly used as if it were an independent variable that caused, or could cause, variation in achievement measures.

The classification variable: Ethnicity

Within the social sciences a variety of approaches have been devised for analysing ethnicity, and numerous definitions have been proposed. Common to most definitions are the elements of shared cultural values and social structures. Its essential characteristics have been summarised by Glazer and Moynihan (1975): "Ethnicity is a new social category . . . [marked by] a pronounced and sudden increase in the tendencies by people in many countries and in many circumstances to insist on the significance of their group distinctiveness and identity and on new rights that derive from this group character."

Since the 1960s this phenomenon has had a marked impact on education, because of the gradual consciousness of their ethnicity among minority groups throughout the world. The ethnic identity movement has asserted itself in western countries and in Australia. For example, ethnicity in the United States seemed to emerge from urban deprivation and poverty. The successes of Welsh and Scottish nationalists in the 1970s, a surprise to many English people, pointed to a new ethnic political consciousness in Britain. More recently, ethnic awareness amongst Afro-Caribbean and Asian communities in Britain has emerged in opposition to the manifest racism which these minorities face in schools and wider society.

Ethnicity indicates membership of a group which is distinctive in terms of cultural identity, language, religion, physical features perhaps, and lifestyles. The fundamentally distinctive feature of an ethnic group is not physical appearance, however, but cultural values. It can be argued that it is possible, for example, for social classes to be ethnic groups in a "racially" homogeneous society if they have distinctive lifestyles and values, and if mobility between different social class groups is restricted. Ethnic groups can be identified not only in terms of cultural values, but through endogamy (finding marriage partners from within one's own ethnic group).

Intermarriage causes a blurring of "racial" boundaries; often in reaction to these trends, dominant racist forces assign individuals arbitrarily to particular racial groups. This is often the case in America where people with more Caucasian than Negro ancestry are nevertheless assigned to the black ethnic group, that is, defined loosely by colour of the skin. It is ironical that a person who is black in North America would be white in Puerto Rico, and in cultures like America, being "black" or "white" is based on the symbolic definitions of different power structures (Montagu, 1977). In Britain for many people ethnicity includes physical appearance or skin colour and this belief has been the salient factor in discrimination against and social rejection of New Commonwealth ethnic minorities.

In Britain the terms *black* and *Asian* are used to describe people of Caribbean, African, and South Asian origin or ancestry. The term "British" is also used to refer to all people of Britain, whatever their cultural orientation, or country of birth. Within this broad framework we refer to different ethnic groups by national labels – "English" implies that an individual is white or mixed race with English ancestry; "West Indian" and "Asian" again refer to British groups, but ones with a differing ancestry. This situation is further compounded by the anger and frustration of the Welsh, Scots, and Northern Irish. They resent being described as English, and they are justified in maintaining their separate identity.

In the British context acts of overt racism have forced minority groups to define and defend their own ethnicity. This situation is well documented by Jeffrey (1976) in a study of "migrants and refugees." Pakistani Christian immigrants came to Britain from a preponderantly Muslim country which had not, by and large, respected their Christian identity. They had hoped that in Britain, nominally a Christian country, they would receive more equitable treatment. However, their Christian identity was ignored or denigrated. Increasing polarisation of ethnic groups in Britain could explain why some "Asian" groups with distinctive religious and linguistic identities tended to be highly endogamous. The picture for West Indians is, in contrast, still one of increasing intermarriage.

A more recent approach to defining the concept of ethnicity is that of cultural pluralism. This model stresses the distinct attributes of ethnic groups and the need for them to live in separate – yet equal – harmony. The pluralist approach to ethnicity is based on an appreciation of cultural diversities. This movement of the 1980s has two broad aspects: (a) equality of opportunity relating to educational, social, occupational, and political matters; (b) retention and maintenance of ethnic identity and distinct culture.

In summary, ethnicity is not an all-or-nothing classification; it is more an amorphous conglomeration of cultural indicators with which the individual identifies. In countries such as Australia and Canada, one finds a complex diversity of competing loyalties in ethnic groups, a lack of uniform social patterns, and a high degree of internal socioeconomic stratification. Such diverse patterns clearly suggest that there is no unanimity among members of ethnic groups as to whether they wish to retain either their ethnicity or their own culture. In a country such as Britain with increasing rates of intermarriage, ethnicity is defined in political terms, and radical, pluralistically oriented white people have multiple ethnic affinities with white, black, and Asian people. Ethnicity is not a permanent attribute of one's identity. Yet, ethnicity has all too frequently been a fixed treatment in studies of test performance: a quasi-permanent and unchanging influence.

Ethnicity and educational achievement

The issue of the educational achievement of ethnic minority youngsters has been central to the "race and education" debate over the last two decades.

During this period a number of research studies have examined achievement levels among the various ethnic groups – both in Britain and internationally. The findings of these studies have often been contradictory and/or inconclusive.

"Category" research

Much confusion emanates from the fact that when differential achievement is being looked at, the argument often rests heavily on the "average" or mean performance for the different groups. Take, for example, the widely publicised assertion that in Britain children of West Indian and Asian origins perform less well than their white counterparts. Such a statement, although warranted by the evidence presently available, can lead to misattributions, as do other "findings." The fact that a set of data shows that group X's performance is inferior to that of another group does not mean that the performance of all individuals from group X is inferior to that of all individuals from the other group.

A study by Craft and Craft (1983) showed that West Indian pupils were underrepresented among high achievers, and overrepresented among low achievers. The category "West Indian" can be misleading because this contains children from different cultural and social backgrounds. Similarly, data on the educational achievement of "Asians" are likely to mask considerable variations in the achievement of different subcultural–ethnic groups within this blanket term. More recent studies (Scarr, 1984; Verma, with Ashworth, 1986) indicate greater differences in achievement within groups than between groups, irrespective of ethnic origin.

Other researchers have also pointed out that there are greater differences within than between ethnic groups. For example, Driver (1980) and Tomlinson (1983) have shown that West Indian girls perform at higher levels than West Indian boys. Figueroa (1984) has pointed out that many pupils of West Indian origin do very well in the British educational system. Studies have also treated South Asians as a uniform group and have ignored the important religious, cultural, and ethnic differences to be found among them. Furthermore, existing studies vary considerably in size and scale, and in methodological and ideological orientation. Mortimore (1981) in a recent review of the literature in this area, has argued that current research findings are inadequate to explain differences in performance between different ethnic groups. Some researchers, studying the area in depth, have identified a wide range of factors involved in the achievement process; they have also emphasised the complexity of the issue (Mabey, 1981; Tomlinson, 1983; Verma, with Ashworth, 1986).

The result of a study (Verma, with Ashworth, 1986) concerning the examination performance of ethnic minority youngsters in comparison with their white peers showed no significant differences between ethnic groups in terms of the number of examinations they expected to take (see Table

Table 19.1. *Examination entry by ethnic group (in percentages)*

		No exams at all	G.C.E. "0" level		C.S.E.'s		Others	
			1–4	5–9	1–4	5–9	1–2	3–6
All	(N = 394)	14.2	29.4	18.4	42.7	31.2	20.9	19.6
White	(N = 143)	14.3	29.5	18.4	38.1	33.6	15.1	21.6
Pakistani	(N = 73)	16.9	22.1	23.7	57.6	15.3	38.9	6.8
Bangladeshi	(N = 44)	26.7	20.1	13.4	20.1	19.3	20.0	20.0
Indian	(N = 67)	4.7	46.4	9.4	48.9	32.7	32.5	30.5
West Indian	(N = 65)	10.5	30.0	20.0	80.0	10.0	10.0	15.0

Source: Verma, with Ashworth, 1986.

19.1). Analysis of variance was computed which showed no significant interaction between ethnic groups.

Despite the fact that the evidence available is inconclusive or even incomplete, the explanations offered, however tentative, have often been used for political and ideological purposes. It might have been better, given the present state of knowledge, if it had been utilised exclusively for the promotion of a balanced debate on how research on achievement might be improved, and on how the educational process might best assist the progress of all ethnic minority children.

In another respect the present approach to an explanation of achievement research is unsatisfactory. Educational achievement is not simply the fulfillment of intellectual potential as measured by performance in public examinations. Such an indicator overlooks the performance of a considerable part of the school population, particularly in the later stages of compulsory schooling. In Britain public examinations are designed to cater for approximately the top 60% of 16-year-olds. Thus examination performance itself is too simplistic a measure of educational achievement. In our recent writings we have argued that educational achievement is the outcome of a complex process involving personal, educational, social, and institutional factors (Verma & Bagley, 1984; Verma, with Ashworth, 1986). Whatever criteria are used to assess pupil performance, they are bound to reflect (apart from the methodological or ideological stance of the researchers) certain qualities of both the school and the pupil, and to a greater extent the quality of the relationship between the school and its pupils.

A considerable range of psychological and educational factors have been suggested in the literature to characterise the differential achievement of ethnic groups in British schools. Among the most widely used ones are: testing and assessment; the attitudes of teachers; self-esteem and identity; and curriculum. The following examination of these factors indicates the complexity of the issues bearing on differential achievement.

The dependent variables: Tests and assessments

Testing and/or assessment has been an area of controversy in British education for over three decades, although traditionally tests have been used as a major tool for selection and placement purposes within the formal education system. Critics have expressed concern primarily over issues such as the principles and assumptions underlying test construction, test administration, and the interpretation of test results. Another major issue debated in many parts of the world today is the impact of testing and assessment procedures on the life chances of young people from certain ethnic, cultural and social groups. These issues apply with particular force within the context of a plural society. Thus, in recent years, widespread scepticism has developed about testing and about the validity and reliability of such tests. The rigid use of tests may form the basis of a life sentence upon a child. Such concerns are not altogether unjustified nor trivial.

There is sufficient evidence in the literature to suggest that the development and use of tests in America and Britain were geared to protect and sustain class interests (Karier, 1976; Kamin, 1977). In Britain tests were promoted as part of the educational selection procedures (11 + selection)[1] on the naive assumption that there was cultural and social homogeneity in society. The 11 + selection system was official British educational policy for nearly 20 years until 1965, when the then Labour government announced its intention to end selection at 11 +.

Before World War II, European and North American countries tended to foster and encourage a philosophy of education which was essentially ethnocentric. Attitudes, values, standards of behaviour, languages, and folkways of the dominant cultural groups were considered as the norm; minority groups were expected to conform to that set of norms as reflected in testing and assessment procedures. Even after the war, standardised testing continued to be used in the United States as the vehicle for ascertaining the differences in basic ability and in school achievement among pupils. In short, familiarity with the Anglo-Saxon culture was accepted as the standard for participation in the social, economic, occupational, and political life of western societies. Furthermore, the early testing movement stressed the assumptions behind the assimilationist ethnocentric view of society. It also reflected the dominant elitist values of the test designers and their cultural and ideological stance; test designers themselves were white, middle-class academics who had little, if any, understanding of the values and backgrounds of social and ethnic minority groups.

In the field of western education the testing movement gave rise to massive discrimination between various racial and ethnic groups (Karier, 1976). Policies governing test use on minority groups not only discriminated against

---

[1] The 11 + examination made use of intelligence tests, standardised papers in English and arithmetic. They were administered to children during the school year in which they became 11 years old – hence, 11 +.

children in their education, but also restricted employment opportunities and access to higher education for the underprivileged. Furthermore, using "standardised" tests helped to develop and perpetuate the myth of "scientific objectivity." Sometimes it was argued that the tests measured a genetic component in intelligence. This myth was reinforced by the strong conviction of such people as Terman in the United States, and Cyril Burt in the United Kingdom (see Kline, Chapter 7).

The work of Karier (1976) and Kamin (1977) in particular indicates that even today many ability and achievement tests widely used in schools reflect the elements peculiar to one particular culture and which may not be reflected in that of minority children. Human behaviour can neither develop in a cultural vacuum nor can it be sampled without culturally based assumptions. In the last 20 years some test designers have attempted to introduce culturally broadly based tests; some claim to have succeeded in designing culture-free or culture-fair tests! The reasoning which underlies this belief is easy to refute. Furthermore, this belief also indicates their failure to understand the meaning of culture.

Although in the last decade, some sophistication has been introduced in the process of testing, many of the issues have remained unresolved. In Britain a large number of tests, published by agencies such as the National Foundation for Educational Research (NFER) and Moray House, contain culturally embedded assumptions which discriminate against cultural–ethnic minorities, providing an unreliable estimate of their abilities. For example, many tests, which depend heavily on speed, do not have the same meaning for certain ethnic minority children. Their lifestyles, built on different cultural bases, may not have conditioned them to academic pursuits and to "working against the clock"; and their concept of speed is one of relative unimportance to them. Scarr (1981) comments that standardised test scores only measure past learning of information and skills that are sampled by tests and the schools. Furthermore, the majority of existing tests are technically defective and are difficult to adapt for ethnically mixed populations such as are to be found in the United Kingdom. Above all, the ethnocentrism of many tests is a well-known and persistent problem that seems incapable of resolution so long as traditional procedures continue to be employed in test construction.

The issues in testing and assessment are no longer matters of purely academic debate. During the late 1960s and early 1970s a fairly widespread anti-testing movement developed, particularly in the United States. Some school boards banned testing on the basis of invasion of privacy and invalid application to some minority groups. In 1969 the American Association of Black Psychologists expressed its concern about test bias by calling for a moratorium on all testing of black people until more equitable tests are available. Although this call was contested by some educationalists and researchers on the grounds that the absence of normative checks, however crude, would lead to increased discrimination and consequent disadvantage, the movement has had considerable success. Many test developers and educators have begun, only slowly, to become aware that the nurturance of behaviour, and the assessment of behaviour, are all culture-specific.

In Britain, even today, the 11+ is not quite dead. There are many Local Education Authorities (LEAs) which still use 11+ or similar testing and assessment procedures. A recent survey of LEAs by Gipps, Steadman, Blackstone, and Stierer (1983) showed that although between 1972 and 1980 there had been a dramatic decline in standardised testing for selection purposes, there had been an equally dramatic rise in testing for screening, monitoring, assisting transfer, and allocating resources. That means, in effect, testing for selection has now become testing to "aid transfer" within schools. Unfortunately, in some LEAs the two are synonymous. The same authors also comment that they were surprised at the extent to which ability or IQ-type tests of verbal and nonverbal reasoning were still in use. More LEAs tested IQ than tested mathematics. There was a belief among LEAs and teachers that these (IQ) tests can supply measures of "potential." This leads us to the question of intelligence and IQ as an indicator of educational achievement.

The central constructs: Intelligence, achievement, and minority status

The concept that commonly comes to people's minds when considering educational achievement is that of intelligence. Studies have suggested that there is a relationship between intelligence and public examination results; perhaps because the two types of tests are not dissimilar. Both types of tests require the ability to solve problems within given time limits, assume a certain level of required knowledge and attempt to sample cognitive behaviour at a certain point in time. Thus, it would not be surprising to find that similar factors affect both intelligence test scores and examination results.

However, *intelligence* is now a suspect term in the field of education unless its usage is carefully qualified. The main reason why it has fallen into disrepute is its equation with the IQ test score itself. Despite obvious limitations, scores in IQ tests have long been regarded as measures of academic potential. The term *IQ* is seen by many teachers as broadly synonymous with educability. Furthermore, knowledge of a pupil's IQ score can play a significant part in determining the expectations not only of the teacher but of the education system as a whole about the pupil's potential achievement.

As pointed out earlier, overall trends of achievement research in Britain show that children from certain minority communities (for example, West Indian and Asian) tend to perform less well at school compared to their white peers. Studies (e.g., in the Swann Report, Department of Education & Science, 1985) have also shown that children from lower socioeconomic backgrounds, within *each* ethnic group, do less well academically than children from middle-class backgrounds. Do these patterns of deficit necessarily imply that such children are on average less intelligent? Various explanations have been offered for the differential achievement between different ethnic–cultural groups. A view widely accepted throughout history is that certain ethnic and racial groups are inherently less able than others, and are, in fact, genetically inferior. In effect, such a view implies that observed inferiorities – whether in terms of culture, language, or achievement – are in fact heritable deficits (Edwards, 1981). This position has been attributed to Jensen (1969, 1973) and Eysenck (1971) in particular.

Although genetic variation within groups is well known, the problem has been well defined by Thoday (1969): which is what may be inferred from observations between groups reared in different environments. He argues that the scientific problem is insoluble, and that persons who reach one conclusion or the other on existing evidence are expressing attitudes or beliefs, nothing more nor less. It is therefore both surprising, and disturbing, that scientists in the 1980s should conclude from observations on tests that average differences are functions of genetic variations between ethnic groups. Flynn (1980) points out that it is an interesting question as to why scientists have a continuing need to produce empirical evidence, given the irrationality of their case. He provides a discussion of Jensen's data and arguments, and other work in the field (see also Scarr, 1984). Recent material, more broadly based, indicates that genetic factors have a much smaller impact on human performance than has hitherto been alleged (Fischbein, 1980; Plomin & De Fries, 1980).

A whole range of assumptions underlies the arguments put forward by those who assert that there is something called "intelligence" which can be accurately measured by IQ tests applied in standard form in every ethnic group. The theory that children can be divided into different groups of differing mental capacities is clearly derived from the theory and practice of intelligence testing. The most vigorous attack on the whole concept of IQ has been the publication by Kamin (1977). His main conclusion was that there existed no data that would lead a prudent man to conclude that IQ scores were heritable.

Another criticism of the Jensen findings emerged from Jencks's (1973) work, in which he estimates that about half of the variance on intelligence test scores is attributable to genetic factors; and that environmental factors therefore exert powerful influence on individual performance. In accounting for test score variability, cross-cultural research on IQ tests shows that they are notoriously culture-specific; even the so-called culture-free ones among them have been developed within a particular setting. Thus, whatever their source, IQ tests contain "loaded" assumptions about intelligence. The suggestion that genetic differences derived from IQ test results among ethnic, cultural, and class groups account in large measure for differential educational achievement is not only of questionable validity, it also tends to divert attention away from more important issues related to the whole educational process.

Most of these controversies arise out of American data; but what empiricism has emerged from British studies has proved no less controversial. A recent review by Mackintosh (1985), however, is an indication of the current ethos. On the IQ score itself, Mackintosh considers that too much importance has been attached to it. It certainly is no mark of a person's true worth, and it predicts life success no better than other indices of attainment. His comparisons hinge on the existence of a fairly common occurrence, the depressing effects of low family status on test performance. Several correlates of IQ scores are traced in the white population. These include familial status as measured by occupation, income, family size, index of overcrowding, and place of residence. He finds that these same indices of family status and nurturance are also correlated with minority IQ scores. Observed differences between British-born West Indian and population IQ means are 5 to 10 points. When these differences are adjusted for family status differentials between West Indians and the rest of the population, the gap narrows to between 3 and 5 points. He concludes that such findings belie any fundamentalist, or genetic, explanation of test performance differences.

Views of intelligent behaviour and social competence as attributes strongly influenced by environment have emerged in important research studies (Zigler & Trickett, 1978; White, Kaban, & Attanucci, 1980). Of the new approaches, Lewis and Mercer's (1978) system of multicultural pluralistic assessment (SOMPA) is probably the best known. This method adjusts pupils' scores for the influence of sociocultural condition, and may be appropriate for distinguishing disadvantaged from nondisadvantaged pupils. However, it provides little in the way of diagnostic information that is of use for classroom practices involving remediation.

Given the various issues and shortcomings associated with testing and assessment procedures, there is a strong case for concluding that the whole process of assessment is in need of careful evaluation and revision. It is clear that there are ethnic, cultural, and class biases in the development and use of conventional tests which vary from the subtle and implicit to the obvious and explicit. However, the total abandonment of testing and assessment is not desirable. What is being argued is that the deficiencies require a more radical response in a fresh conceptualisation of its role. A radical approach might be to view and compare individuals within their own sociocultural and ethnic backgrounds. The strategy will then be to assess the ability of each person only in relation to others who come from similar sociocultural backgrounds and who have had approximately similar opportunity to acquire the knowledge and skills needed to answer questions on an achievement test. This, of course, is a solution that requires ethical, as well as scientific, justification.

Intervening variables: Teacher attitudes

The context of achievement includes the leadership of instructors in groups. How the attitudes of teachers may affect the motivation of ethnic minority students in Britain is an important question in assigning cause to an outcome. Evidence of prejudice can be found in three studies. Brittan (1976) conducted a survey of 510 teachers from 25 schools in various parts of England and showed that over 75% held negative opinions about the ability and social behaviour of West Indian pupils. Giles (1977) concluded from observational studies in classrooms that ethnic stereotyping was subtle and overt. Verma and Bagley (1982) showed that a quarter of a group of randomly sampled teachers in Britain displayed highly conservative attitudes; and that approximately 1 in 10 manifested a marked degree of racial prejudice. Such evidence implies that the processes of stereotyping and labelling that affect all our percepts function strongly in teachers' interactions with ethnic minorities. These processes may intervene to determine the relationship between teachers and minority pupils, and hence their achievements as measured in subject areas taught by these teachers. This line of argument is well defined in the research of Rosenthal and Jacobsen (1968), Nash (1976), and Rubovitz and Maehr (1973).

Pioneer work in this field was initiated by Rosenthal and Jacobsen (1968), who showed that teachers' expectations of pupils may be powerful determinants of pupils' performance. Since the publication of the findings in America, a host of studies have been conducted to investigate the various aspects of labelling effects on the achievement of children in a variety of situations. By 1973, Rosenthal had located 242 studies of labelling which had utilised all sorts of subjects and situations. Of these, about one-third strongly supported the labelling effect. But some researchers have remained unconvinced about it (Elashoff & Snow, 1971). However, on balance, the evidence shows that teachers' expectations may have a significant effect on pupils' school performance, and thus the "Pygmalion effect" can be said to exist. It should be pointed out, in fairness, that Rosenthal and Jacobsen's finding that IQ scores may also be expectancy-determined has not been replicated in any subsequent study (Crane & Mellon, 1978). Hence, although teachers' attitudes may be a contributory factor in the generally depressed performance of ethnic minority pupils, there is hardly any research evidence to support the view that negative attitudes of teachers are responsible for their low IQ scores.

Achievement test and IQ scores are educational *products,* but is there evidence of differential *process* in classrooms that would affect outcomes? Rubovitz and Maehr (1973), in a study entitled "Pygmalion Black and White," studied teachers' expectations in multiracial classrooms. They tested the hypothesis that white teachers would interact differently with white and black students labelled (in both cases) as "gifted" and "nongifted" in ways which would affect their school performance. They concluded that teachers gave preferential treatment to students labelled as "gifted," but that the pattern of treatment depended to some extent on the race of students. In general, they found that black students were treated less positively than whites. Furthermore, if blacks were labelled "gifted," they were subjected to *more* discrimination than those labelled "nongifted"! One point should be mentioned here. Teachers may not label *all* black children as low achievers, but only particular kinds of black children. In a study by Bagley, Bart, and Wong (1979), teachers were asked to rate the potential of children they taught. Some black children were rated as being of low potential while others were rated as being of high potential. The low potential children, as rated by their teachers, tended to be from homes which were materially handicapped, where the father might be absent, and where Creole rather than standard English was spoken.

However, teacher attitudes can seriously affect the progress and achievement of ethnic minority children in two main ways: by explicitly prejudiced interaction with them; and by holding low predictions of those pupils' abilities and achievement. Both are found among teachers of the dominant culture in British schools (Giles, 1977). Adults may fail to realise that children and young people are extremely perceptive and are capable of understanding the meaning of these attitudes; many South Asian and West Indian children in schools build up resentment and develop behavioural problems and severe emotional blocks in learning (Giles, 1977). When this happens, the self-fulfilling prophecy has been enacted.

Teacher attitudes that influence predictions of future success or failure, and prescriptions for skill acquisition, affect the achievements of pupils. The force of this conclusion is borne out in the data drawn from the National Child Development Survey on West Indian children. Bagley's (1982) analysis shows that if highly negative views of children were held by teachers, by the time the child was 7 years old, these opinions were accompanied by a marked degree of underachievement in the children concerned. More serious, perhaps, were the consequences of such views. They resulted in a substantial number of black children being recommended for placement in schools for the educationally subnormal.

A more subtle form of the expectancy phenomenon, where predictions lead to prescriptions for success in *limited* areas, has been identified for certain ethnic minorities in Britain, particularly older pupils of West Indian origin. The Rampton enquiry (Department of Education & Science, 1981) believes that this form of selective enhancement of potential may be damaging, because it serves to perpetuate a stereotype of academic weakness.

Many teachers feel that West Indians are unlikely to achieve in academic terms but may have high expectations of their potential in areas such as sport, dance, drama and art. If these particular skills are unduly emphasised there is a risk of establishing a view of West Indian children that may become a stereotype and teachers may be led to encourage these pupils to pursue these subjects at the expense of their academic studies.

In short, some teachers hold stereotyped attitudes and some do not; it is also true that sometimes the teacher expectancy effect works and sometimes it does not. The educational process involves a complicated interaction between teacher and pupil; teacher attitudes and stereotypes vary greatly, as do pupil attitudes. This is a complex and ill-understood phenomenon.

In the 1980s teachers are less likely to ignore the issue of ethnicity so far as the formal curriculum is concerned. Nevertheless, bias in teacher perception of ethnic minority pupils is a major problem for educational practice. Elaborate curriculum models can be set out, courses and materials designed, all of which recognise and enhance their personal, social, and cultural aspirations. These will come to nothing if teachers are not convinced of the need to develop, and to demand, training in the social skills that lead to high achievement motivation in children from minority groups. Little awareness of this need identifies either modern textbooks in educational methods, or initial training courses in the colleges of education.

Internalised variables: Self-esteem in minorities

Earlier American studies (reviewed by Pettigrew, 1964) concluded that many black children had to a large degree internalised the negative stereotypes which the dominant white culture held about them and as a result had poorer self-esteem than whites. Some researchers have explained the poor self-esteem of ethnic minority groups on the basis of their ethnic identity and socioeconomic status; such evidence has primarily come from the United States, where black and white differences are still of paramount importance. It has also been shown that ethnicity is a relevant factor in the poor self-esteem found in certain cultural and ethnic groups (Ausubel, 1958; Clarke, 1974).

Recent research on children and adolescents in America has contradicted the earlier patterns, showing that blacks do not have significantly poorer self-esteem than whites (Coopersmith, 1975; Bagley, Verma, Mallick, & Young, 1979). Some studies have even shown that blacks have significantly better self-esteem than whites (Goldman & Mercer, 1976).

Various explanations have been put forward to account for changed patterns in self-esteem in blacks: There has been a major paradigmatic shift not only in the assessment proceduures but also in the way results are interpreted; the emergence of the "black power" movement in America of the 1960s and 1970s might have changed their consciousness (Goldman, 1974); and the effects of changing reference groups in which black children evaluate themselves according to the standards of their black peers, and of black rather than white reference groups (Rosenberg & Simmons, 1973).

Research in Britain of self-esteem among ethnic minority pupils has also provided findings which have been both diverse and contradictory. Much of the early research concentrated on ethnic minority children's attitudes toward their "colour," and found that West Indian and Asian children identified negatively with their colour and ethnic characteristics (Milner, 1975). Such findings have been explained in terms of confusion and of a crisis of identity among ethnic minority children. Bagley, Mallick, and Verma (1979) in a study found that differences in self-esteem between West Indians and whites were confined to boys; West Indian girls were as self-confident as their white counterparts. Similarly, Louden (1978) found that although overall there were no statistically significant differences in self-esteem between ethnic groups, West Indian girls had higher levels of self-esteem than white girls. He found that in general, the higher the concentration of the blacks in a school, the higher the levels of self-esteem in the black pupils. Louden explained these findings in terms of the ethos and social climates of schools that influence self-esteem in various ethnic minority groups, including the degree to which minority groups are insulated from various types of racism.

Louden (1978) also found that pupils of South Asian origin had a higher mean self-esteem score than either West Indian or white adolescents, although this trend did not reach statistical significance. Verma (1981) also obtained small but consistent differences in self-esteem between South Asian and white adolescents, specifically on certain subscales of the *Coopersmith Self-Esteem Inventory* (Coopersmith, 1967). He explained the results of high self-esteem among South Asian youngsters in terms of the family structure: ". . . higher self esteem in spite of their educational and social disadvantage, is perhaps due to the fact that the adaptation processes of South Asians are mediated through the networks of family and friends, and to some extent through community based self-help systems" (Verma, 1981).

A more recent study (Verma, with Ashworth, 1986) showed that there were no statistically significant inter-ethnic differences in the levels of self-esteem as assessed by the *Coopersmith Self-Esteem Inventory*. The inventory yields measures of self-esteem derived from interactions at home, at school, and with peer groups, in addition to the general self-esteem component. It was possible, therefore, to assess the proportion of self-esteem derived from each of the possible sources. Because of the nature of the *Self-Esteem Inventory*, the comparison criteria of each source were as follows: 50% general–self; 16.67% school–academic; 16.67% social–self–peers; 16.67% home–parents. The results are presented in Table 19.2 in terms of the actual percentages for each of the sources according to ethnicity.

The evidence available so far in this area of research is somewhat inconclusive. This is in part because the attitudes of ethnic minority pupils are likely to have changed over the last decade. Another contributory factor may be imperfections in the instruments used to measure self-esteem. As was suggested earlier, attainment tests were prone to being "culture-blind." There is the risk that this may be inherent in measures of self-esteem, particularly when these are used in cross-cultural settings.

However, it is clear from evidence that self-esteem is culturally grounded, and therefore it is often meaningless to suggest that a particular ethnic group has "better" or "worse" self-esteem than any other (Verma, 1984). Self-esteem, as part of an individual's complex identity structure, has different bases and different meanings in different ethnic groups. For example, black identity has special components which reflect the particular experience of

Table 19.2. *Mean percentage of total self-esteem from subscales by ethnic group*

		General–self	Social–self–peers	Home–parents	School–academic
Whole sample	(N = 410)	54.203	17.686	15.673	12.439
White	(N = 154)	54.609	17.846	15.508	12.023
Pakistani	(N = 75)	53.809	17.377	16.072	12.750
Bangladeshi	(N = 45)	53.401	15.647	16.400	14.552
Indian	(N = 70)	51.998	17.695	16.171	14.135
West Indian	(N = 66)	54.905	18.502	15.854	10.738

Source: Verma, with Ashworth, 1986.

being black and surviving in a white-dominated society. In a plural society, different ethnic groups have different social–psychological orientations; these differences have to be mutually understood and tolerated if a successful multiculturalism is to emerge (Triandis, 1976).

There is evidence both from theoretical conceptualisation and research findings that schools can play an important part in enhancing the self-concept and self-esteem of all pupils. Pupils from the dominant culture are in an advantageous position because their norms, lifestyles, language, religion, and social patterns are reflected both explicitly and implicitly in all aspects of the school system and in society at large. On the other hand, ethnic minority pupils suffer from disadvantages both in school and in the wider society. Comparisons between majority and minority groups on self-esteem measures may then simply describe social contexts that are entrenched. As such, the measures run the risk of being a form of self-fulfilling prophecy.

Self-esteem and achievement

Having outlined the theoretical structure of self-esteem and its patterns among ethnic groups, it is most important to point out that the concept of black self-esteem should not invade the scientific literature in the way that IQ has done. There is a danger that now the IQ measure has been shown to be of little relevance (except in clinical settings to assess environmental changes), "scientific" racists may attempt to use self-esteem as a deterministic substitute. For example, some research findings show that self-esteem of certain ethnic groups is lower than whites', and that motivation is equally low; therefore it is assumed that this *causes* school failure. If such notions gain currency, there is the risk they will find their way into teachers' judgments on the educability of such pupils. Thus could be set off another damaging chain of stereotypes that can have such a powerful and adverse effect on the achievement of pupils.

Ethnic minority pupils in Britain have different identity structures from whites (Coleman, Hartzberg, & Norris, 1977). They have a more difficult struggle in educational, social, and personal aspects of life than their parents; yet many of them are successful in both achievement and identity development. They develop positive views of themselves as they grow older. Louden (1978) has argued that with the growth in numbers in minority communities the setting of their locus of control changes favourably. In schools where blacks or Asian groups are in the majority or even a substantial minority, they can more successfully guard against the demeaning slights of racism. A more recent research (Verma, with Ashworth, 1986) has failed to find any differences in levels of self-esteem between white, West Indian, and South Asian pupils in British schools.

Teachers sometimes seek to explain the behavioural and academic difficulties of ethnic minority pupils as a consequence of their having a poor self-concept and an identity problem. As a result a number of related pseudo-explanatory terms such as *low self-esteem* and *identity crisis* have been used by educators to rationalise low academic achievement of ethnic minority pupils. In Britain some writers have suggested that West Indian pupils in particular lack confidence in their own abilities, have low aspirations or depressed self-esteem: and that these "cause" poor achievement. They also believe the converse to be true: that West Indian pupils who perform less well at school are likely to have low self-esteem. The American evidence (Coopersmith, 1975), on the other hand, indicates that black children do not necessarily have low perceptions of themselves when they perform badly at school. In such evidence what is perhaps important is the reference group which a pupil, as an individual or a member of a group, has established. If the pupil is oriented towards "black culture," then his or her lack of achievement in terms of "teacher's culture" may be of no great concern personally. Nevertheless, the long-term consequences of underachievement are most likely to have a serious impact on feelings of competence and self-worth of black adults.

One British study (Bagley, Bart, & Wong, 1979) identified a group of West Indian pupils whose scores on standardised reading tests were as satisfactory as those of white, middle-class pupils. Evidence showed that their family background and attitudes were markedly more independent, self-reliant, and, indeed, hostile towards white society than those of other West Indian families. The two groups of West Indian families also differed in terms of social class – the former were distinctly more middle class than the latter. Therefore, it is at least possible that other attributes of middle-class family patterns, *including high motivation to achieve,* were responsible for the better performance of their children.

There is some evidence in the British literature that achievement and self-esteem are positively related. That is to say, pupils who perform less well at school tend to have poor self-esteem. Studies have also indicated that self-esteem is significantly related to educational achievement for "disad-

Table 19.3. *Correlation coefficients: Elements of self-esteem and examination results*

	White (N = 143)	Pakistani (N = 73)	Bangladeshi (N = 44)	Indian (N = 67)	West Indian (N = 65)
General–self	.119	.225	.091	.338	.410
Social–self–peers	.091	.279	.065	.228	.228
School–academic	.195	.035	.416	.389	.181
Home–parents	.075	.216	.202	.023	.309

Source: Verma, with Ashworth, 1986

vantaged'' as well as other pupils (Coard, 1971; Milner, 1975). The implication of such findings is that success or failure at school significantly influences the ways in which pupils view themselves. On the basis of the evidence, it would be wrong to conclude that poor self-esteem is the *cause* of poor achievement. It could equally be argued that low self-esteem is simply a result of that performance. For example, the pupil not doing well at school is more likely than one doing better, to agree with statements in a self-esteem questionnaire, such as ''I'm not doing as well in the school as I'd like to'' (item from the *Coopersmith Self-Esteem Inventory* [Coopersmith, 1967]).

Some writers suggest that the relationship between pupil and teacher in the multicultural classroom is a major contributor to the growth of a positive or negative self-concept (Verma & Bagley, 1982). Awareness of the teacher's feelings, assimilated into the pupil's self-concept, may operate as a mediator of educational achievement. The findings of various studies summarised by LaBenne and Greene (1969) show that ''poor'' self-concepts derived from school experiences tend to result in underachievement or poor performance. The school whose pupils see themselves as potential successes rather than as academic failures could be said to be succeeding to some extent. Similarly, pupils whose educational experiences help them to understand themselves and the society in which they function could be said to have gained something useful from that education.

A recent study (Verma, with Ashworth, 1986) examined the relationship between self-esteem and educational achievement among various ethnic groups in British schools. An analysis *within* each ethnic group was conducted to elicit the aspects of self-esteem in that particular group relating to achievement. The results are given in Table 19.3.

The results showed that certain measured components of self-esteem were correlated with achievement in some ethnic groups, but not in others. For example, self-esteem factors (except that derived from interaction in the home) accounted for variations in the performance of white and West Indian pupils, but not for variations among pupils of South Asian origin (Pakistani,

Bangladeshi, and Indian). "General-self" self-esteem was implicated in the achievement process for West Indian pupils. In brief, the findings suggest that the impact of the processes relating to educational achievement may be culture-dependent; factors affecting the achievement of one ethnic group may not necessarily affect the achievement of any other. Mackintosh's (1985) study notwithstanding, it may be fallacious always to explain achievement and underachievement of a particular ethnic minority group from the knowledge and understanding of the achievement processes of the majority group. Finally, Table 19.3 shows that the proportion of common variance between measures of self-esteem and examination results is as low as 1% and never exceeds 16%. In such circumstances sweeping generalisations are unwarranted.

Curriculum

In any discussion in the literature of the issues associated with educational achievement of pupils it has been repeatedly suggested that an inappropriate curriculum does play a major part in underachievement of pupils, particularly those from ethnic minority groups (Jeffcoate, 1979; Lynch, 1983). Some theorists have even focussed on the curriculum as the primary vehicle for attaining equality of educational opportunity and consequently equality of outcome. In fact, for them a changed curriculum has become synonymous with multicultural education, although they have been little concerned with the nature and process of such knowledge.

Writing about the pluralist dilemma in education, Bullivant (1981b) observes that conceptual models of the curriculum compete with one another and that a large part of the curriculum itself is in disarray. A six-country study of cultural pluralism shows that the curriculum is as much an ideological and political product as it is a vehicle for skill acquisition. Our concern for the curriculum is its central position in the definition of what shall count as achievement and ability in schools. If it is, as Bullivant suggests, part of the psychology of the school system, representing its values, beliefs, and ideology, then our concern parallels that of Irvine and Berry in Chapter 1, who perceive tests as rationalisations and defence mechanisms for those who assess ethnic groups.

In response to the changed social, cultural, and demographic characteristics of postwar Britain the curriculum reform movement was first conceived as a way of eliminating bias in curriculum materials and of countering ethnocentric stereotypes. Such a view was based to a large extent on studies which revealed relationships between the poor academic performance of ethnic minority pupils – particularly Afro-Caribbeans and Asians – and an inappropriate curriculum (Verma & Bagley, 1979, 1982).

During the 1970s the need was felt by some teachers that significant modifications of the curriculum were needed which would reflect the changed sociocultural characteristics of British society. Their main emphasis, therefore, has been on ethnic minority traditions, cultural heritage, religion, and other aspects relating to the country of origin of ethnic minority pupils. Such an approach attempted to develop a "multicultural curriculum" policy. What it amounted to was, broadly speaking, a limited and largely ineffective rationalisation directed at the accommodation of ethnic minority aspirations. It should be said, however, that individual schools, individual teachers, embarking on such initiatives had all too often to fall back on their own resources, in the absence of any policy directives or curriculum guidelines from the Department of Education and Science.

It was not until the late 1970s that specific criticisms were made about the trivialisation of the idea of a multicultural curriculum by many British educational writers and practitioners (Verma & Bagley, 1984). Jeffcoate (1979), for example, expressed concern about the relationships between the idea of a multicultural curriculum and the kind of classroom practice that would implement it. His scepticism about the usefulness of existing curriculum theories and models is centred around their relevance to practitioners. He argues for the creation of curriculum models founded on cultural pluralism. This would require the adoption of a more internationalist dimension to the curriculum. It would signal a shift away from the traditional conception of knowledge and the world, usually couched in the norms and standards of a particular culture, towards one more in keeping with today's plural societies, and a world in which societies are increasingly interdependent. The British government's latest thinking also includes concern for utilising a greater international perspective into the curriculum; this view appeared in the 1977 Green Paper "Education in Schools" (Department of Education & Science, 1977). Although the Green Paper refers to the needs of a new Britain which should be reflected in school curricula, such curricular aims have not been realised so far. An apparent difficulty in designing a curriculum model based on international material and experience is the actual identification of the common core of values and aspirations of the groups involved (Smolicz, 1979).

A major purpose of the school curriculum is the achievement of two broad goals – respect for others and respect for self (Jeffcoate, 1976). How this is to be achieved, however, is a matter of controversy. The school not only reflects the symbolic stereotyping and the stratification system of the wider society but imposes its own hierarchies and reference system; this may have a significant and negative impact both on pupils' self-concepts and their respect for others (Bagley et al., 1979). Bronfenbrenner (1974), writing about the social tactics of schooling, declares that:

The potentialities of the classroom group . . . [are] one of the most promising and least exploited areas for effecting behavioural change. Although modifications of classroom composition in terms of social class and race can have salutary effects, they by no means represent the most powerful resources at our disposal. Indeed, their potential is realised only to the extent that they facilitate development of the motivating processes (modelling, reinforcement, group commitment, involvement in superordinate goals etc.) . . . Such development need not be left to chance.

In this statement, Bronfenbrenner stipulates motivating processes that appear valid in task group formation: As such, they transfer to the context of what to assess, not in examinations of pupils but in the social skills of teachers who are vehicles for the transmission of curriculum content.

Has this specificity been evident in statements of goals and aims for curriculum change? There has been much public endorsement of an ideology where curriculum change is *believed* to alter the processes of education to enhance the life chances of minorities. Many find the logic of such statements debatable. Nevertheless, the Schools Council (1982) translated this change model into practices that were not psychological in nature, but were confined to employing materials and examination questions that demand knowledge of a wide range of cultures, thus avoiding an Anglocentric world view. Such assumptions, and such means of putting them into practice, are common in the prescriptions for multicultural education. There is little scientific evidence to support the view that minor curricular revisions can change fundamental aspects of classroom contexts, or of the structure of society at large in whose hands the life chances of minorities rest. Nevertheless, the results of one large-scale survey (Stenhouse, Verma, Wild, & Nixon, 1982) showed that such content changes can be positive. But these must be accompanied by support and reform in other "hidden curriculum" areas of classroom status of minorities and school organisation. There seems little point, for example, in introducing new curriculum materials and textbooks that are designed to alter attitudes and behaviour in any school where the majority of black students are assigned to the lowest stream. In that cultural context, changing the content will be seen as part of a process of ego defence, heavily dependent on rationalisation needed to avoid conflict with harsh social reality.

Another aspect of the psychology of curriculum provision is evident in criticisms of attempts to modify the traditional curriculum specifically to cater for minority groups. Bullivant (1981a) argues that multicultural education programmes could be perceived as strategies for keeping ethnic minorities in their place, for controlling their aspirations rather than enhancing their self-determination. A similar critique has come from Stone (1981), who warns that teachers may well dismiss any belief that underachievement has any genetic or racial basis, but may subscribe to a model of cultural deprivation that is equally damaging to the self-esteem of minority students. She advocates the traditional curriculum taught by formal methods of the highest quality as the route to equivalent outcomes for minorities.

These arguments for and against special curricula to accommodate the presence of minority groups in British schools are neither original nor empirically based. They are best understood as part of the ethos, or psychology, of the assessment of minorities. In general, the solutions they represent are simplistic in their assumptions of psychological cause and effect, and they suffer badly when compared with Bronfenbrenner's modest specification of what is needed at the classroom level. They also ignore completely the whole social fabric that makes use of the skills of school leavers, or that, in the case of minorities in Britain, leaves them in greatly disproportionate numbers in the dole queue.

Reflections

In any analysis of educational achievement concerning ethnic minority groups it is often difficult to separate the strands of political ideology, educational reality, and the science of psychology. For example, some critics interpret the recognition of and provision for cultural diversity within the educational system as a threat to the dominant culture. With so many ideologies and counterideologies, some with vested interests in pluralist education, it is not surprising to find considerable confusion both in the literature and at the grass-roots level over how to make appropriate provision for ethnic groups to accommodate other features of pluralism, and to measure the outcomes. It is not clear at the present time which direction the current move towards multicultural education will take. However, there appears to be a positive commitment and response on the part of a section of the British population to the idea of cultural pluralism. In recent years there has also been increased awareness among many teachers and educators which has brought about curricular change in the environments of many schools.

The aim of education in a plural society must be to facilitate the academic and social development of young people who have a cognitively complex view of the world in which they live (Bagley & Verma, 1983). Although they should retain a sense of pride in their personal and cultural identity, children of all ethnic groups should also develop a sufficient degree of empathetic awareness of the personal and cultural identities of others and should feel no need to retreat behind alienating barriers of cultural protectionism. This approach should meet the cultural, affective, and cognitive needs of groups and individuals from all ethnic groups in society. It must also have an inbuilt flexibility in response to changing circumstances; like culture, cultural pluralism is not a static entity, it is a continuous and dynamic process.

The achievements of minority groups and of the white majority in Britain might well be measured from such a cognitive map in future. The problems of constructing the tests and tasks that would operationally define the aims of the last paragraph may be severe; but they are problems that many psychologists might welcome. In the present conventional definitions of achievement and ability, minorities in Britain are at one with minorities in America, Canada, Australia, and Africa. They are invariably presented, on tests constructed by psychologists and educators, as subnormal, or failures, or losers. Medical models of man observe differences that are not necessarily deficits, in their measurements of functions, and they have acceptance within minorities and majorities. Equally rational, utilitarian theories of mental measurement have yet to emerge. Until they do, psychology has to be perceived as a discipline that is primarily ethnocentric. A social-scientific discipline that allows no self-esteem to its subjects cannot object if they reject its claims.

References

Ausubel, D. P. (1958). Ego development among segregated Negro children. *Mental Hygiene, 42,* 362–369.

Bagley, C. (1973). *The Dutch plural society: A comparative study in race relations.* London: Oxford University Press.

Bagley, C. (1982). Achievement, behaviour disorder and social circumstances in West Indian children and other ethnic groups. In G. K. Verma & C. Bagley (Eds.), *Self-concept, achievement and multicultural education.* London: Macmillan.

Bagley, C., Bart, M., & Wong, J. (1979). Antecedents of scholastic success in West Indian ten-year-olds in London. In G. K. Verma & C. Bagley (Eds.), *Race, education and identity.* London: Macmillan.

Bagley, C., Mallick, K., & Verma, G. K. (1979). Pupil self-esteem: A study of black and white teenagers in British schools. In G. K. Verma & C. Bagley (Eds.), *Race, education and identity.* London: Macmillan.

Bagley, C., & Verma, G. K. (Eds.). (1983). *Multicultural childhood: Education, ethnicity and cognitive styles.* Aldershot, Gower.

Bagley, C., Verma, G. K., Mallick, K., & Young, L. (1979). *Personality, self-esteem and prejudice.* Farnborough: Saxon House.

Brittan, E. (1976). Multiracial education II: Teacher opinion on aspects of school life – pupils and teachers. *Educational Research, 18*(3), 182–192.

Bronfenbrenner, U. (1974). *The two worlds of childhood: U.S. and U.S.S.R.* Harmondsworth: Penguin.

Bullivant, B. (1981a). *Race, ethnicity and curriculum.* Sydney: Macmillan.

Bullivant, B. (1981b). *The pluralist dilemma in education: Six case studies.* London: Allen & Unwin.

Clarke, A. S. (1974). An analysis of students' self-esteem and students' attitudes towards culture in secondary schools in Trinidad. *Dissertation Abstracts International, 34,* 12A, *1,* 7637.

Coard, B. (1971). *How the West Indian child is made educationally sub-normal in the British school system.* London: New Beacon.

Coleman, J., Hartzberg, J., & Norris, M. (1977). Identity in adolescence: Present and future self-concepts. *Journal of Youth and Adolescence, 6,* 63–75.

Coopersmith, S. (1967). *The antecedents of self-esteem.* New York: Freeman

Coopersmith, S. (1975). Self-concept, race and education. In G. K. Verma & C. Bagley (Eds.), *Race and education across cultures.* London: Heinemann Educational Books.

Craft, M., & Craft, A. (1983, February). The participation of ethnic minority pupils in further and higher education. *Educational Research, 25*(1), 10–19.

Crane, W. D., & Mellon, P. M. (1978). Causal influences of teachers' expectations of children's academic performance: A cross-lagged panel analysis. *Journal of Educational Psychology, 70,* 39–49.

Department of Education and Science. (1977). *Education in schools: A consultative document* (CMND 6869). London: H.M.S.O.,

Department of Education and Science. (1981). *West Indian children in our schools – Interim report of the Committee of Inquiry into the Education of Children from Ethnic Minority Groups* (CMND 8273). London: H.M.S.O.

Department of Education and Science. (1985). *Education for all* (CMND 9453). London: H.M.S.O.

Driver, G. (1980). *Beyond underachievement.* London: Commission for Racial Equality.

Edwards, J. R. (1981). Psychological and linguistic aspects of minority education. In J. Megarry,

S. Nisbet, & E. Hoyle (Eds.), *World yearbook of education 1981: Education of minorities*, London: Kogan Page.

Elashoff, J. D., & Snow, R. E. (1971). *Pygmalion reconsidered*. Arden: NC: Jones.

Erikson, E. (1959). Identity and the life cycle. *Psychological Issues, 1*(1), 1–171.

Eysenck, H. J. (1971). *Race, intelligence and education*. London: Temple Smith.

Figueroa, P. (1984). Minority pupil progress. In M. Craft (Ed.), *Education and cultural pluralism*. London: Falmer Press.

Fischbein, S. (1980). I.Q. and social class. *Intelligence, 4,* 51–63.

Flynn, J. R. (1980). *Race, I.Q. and Jensen*. London: Routledge & Kegan Paul.

Giles, R. (1977). *The West Indian experience in British schools*. London: Heinemann Educational Books.

Gipps, C., Steadman, S., Blackstone, T., & Stierer, B. (1983). *Testing children*. London: Heinemann Educational Books.

Glazer, N., & Moynihan, D. P. (Eds.). (1975). *Ethnicity – theory and experience*. Cambridge, MA: Harvard University Press.

Goldman, P. (1974). *The death and life of Malcolm X*. London: Gollancz.

Goldman, R. K., & Mercer, B. (1976). Self-esteem and self-differentiation: A comparison between black and white children in follow-through and non follow-through classes. *Educational Research Quarterly, 1*(3), 49–53.

Jeffcoate, R. (1976). Curriculum planning in multiracial education. *Educational Research, 18,* 192–200.

Jeffcoate, R. (1979). *Positive image towards a multicultural curriculum*. London: Chameleon.

Jeffrey, P. (1976). *Migrants and refugees: Muslim and Christian Pakistani families in Bristol*. Cambridge University Press.

Jencks, C. (1973). *Inequality*. Harmondsworth: Penguin.

Jensen, A. R. (1969). How much can we boost I.Q. and scholastic achievement? *Harvard Educational Review, 39,* 1–123.

Jensen, A. R. (1973). *Educability and group differences*. London: Methuen.

Kamin, L. J. (1977). *The science and politics of I.Q.* Harmondsworth: Penguin.

Karier, C. (1976). Testing for order in the corporate liberal state. In R. Dale, G. Esland, & M. MacDonald (Eds.), *Schooling and capitalism*. London: Routledge & Kegan Paul.

LaBenne, W., & Greene, B. (1969). *Educational implications of self-concept theory*. Santa Monica, CA: Goodyear.

Lewis, J., & Mercer, J. (1978). The system of multicultural pluralistic assessment: SIMPA. In W. Coulter & H. Morrow (Eds.), *Adaptive behaviour: Concepts and measurements*. New York: Grune & Stratton.

Louden, D. M. (1978). Self-esteem and locus of control: Some findings in immigrant adolescents in Britain. *New Community, 6,* 218–234..

Lynch, J. (1983). *The multicultural curriculum*. London: Batsford Academic and Educational.

Mabey, C. (1981). Black British literacy: A study of reading attainment of London black children from 8 to 15 years. *Educational Research 23*(2), 83–95.

Mackintosh, N. (1985). The I.Q. question. In C. Bagley & G. K. Verma (Eds.), *Personality, cognition and values*. London: Macmillan.

Milner, D. (1975). *Children and race*. Harmondsworth: Penguin.

Montagu, A. (1977) On the non-perception of "Race" differences. *Current Anthropology, 18,* 743–744.

Mortimore, P. (1981). *Achievement in schools* [Occasional paper]. Research and Statistics, ILEA.

Nash, R. (1976). *Teacher expectations and pupil learning*. London: Routledge & Kegan Paul.

Pettigrew, T. (1964). *A profile of the Negro American*. New York: Van Nostrand.

Plomin, R., & De Fries, J. (1980). Genetics and intelligence: Recent data. *Intelligence, 4,* 14–15.

Rosenberg, M., & Simmons, G. (1973). *Black and white self-esteem: The urban school child*. Washington, DC: American Sociological Association.

Rosenthal, R. (1973). The Pygmalion effect lives. *Psychology Today, 7,* 56–63.

Rosenthal, R., & Jacobsen, L. (1968). *Pygmalion in the classroom.* New York: Holt, Rinehart & Winston.

Rubovitz, P., & Maehr, M. L. (1973). Pygmalion black and white. *Journal of Personality and Social Psychology, 25,* 210–218.

Scarr, S. (1981). Testing for children: Assessment and the many determinants of intellectual competence. *American Psychologist, 36,* 1159–1167.

Scarr, S. (1984). *Race, social class and individual differences in I.Q.* Hillsdale, NJ: Erlbaum.

Schools Council (1982). *Multicultural education.* London: Schools Council.

Smolicz, J. (1980). *Culture and education in a plural society.* Adelaide: Curriculum Development Centre.

Stenhouse, L., Verma, G. K., Wild, R. D., & Nixon, J. (1982). *Teaching about race relations: Problems and effects.* London: Routledge & Kegan Paul.

Stone, M. (1981). *The education of the black child in Britain.* London: Fontana.

Thoday, J. M. (1969). Limits to genetic comparison of populations. *Journal of Biosocial Science Supplement, 1,* 3–14.

Tomlinson, S. (1983). *Ethnic minorities in British schools.* London: Heinemann Educational Books.

Triandis, H. (1976). The future of pluralism. *Journal of Social Issues, 32,* 179–208.

Verma, G. K. (1979). Attitude measurement in a multiethnic society. *Bulletin of the British Psychological Society, 32,* 460–462.

Verma, G. K. (1981) *Problems of vocational adaptation of South Asian adolescents in Britain, with special reference to the role of the school.* Unpublished Report, University of Bradford.

Verma, G. K. (1984). Self-esteem and educational achievement in young South Asians in Britain. *BPS Educational and Child Psychology, 1*(1), 35–45.

Verma, G. K., with Ashworth, B. (1986). *Ethnicity and educational achievement.* London: Macmillan.

Verma, G. K., & Bagley, C. (Eds.). (1979). *Race, education and identity.* London: Macmillan.

Verma, G. K., & Bagley, C. (1982). *Self-concept, achievement and multicultural education.* London: Macmillan.

Verma, G. K., & Bagley, C. (Eds.). (1984). *Race relations and cultural differences.* London: Croom Helm.

Verma, G. K., & Mallick, K. (1982). Tests and testing in a multiethnic society. In G. K. Verma & C. Bagley (Eds.), *Self-concept, achievement and multicultural education.* London: Macmillan.

Vetta, A. (1977). Genetical concepts and I.Q. *Social Biology, 24,* 166–169.

White, B., Kaban, B., & Attanucci, J. (1980). *The origins of human competence: Final Report of the Harvard Pre-school Project.* Boston: Lexington Press.

Zigler, E., & Trickett, P. (1978). I.Q., social competence, and evaluation of early childhood intervention programmes. *American Psychologist, 33,* 789–798.

20 The diminishing test performance gap between English speakers and Afrikaans speakers in South Africa

J. M. Verster and R. J. Prinsloo

Psychometric tests have been in use in South Africa for over half a century now in the context of personnel selection, educational assessment, and related research. The ethnocultural, linguistic, and socioeconomic heterogeneity of the South African population has afforded a rare opportunity for studying the effects of such variables on test performance. At the same time this diversity has posed daunting problems for psychometric methodologists, test constructors, and test users.

Innovative South African research on test development and use amid such diversity has attracted favourable international attention in relation to many important psychometric themes. Some of the most noteworthy contributions include Biesheuvel's (1972) work, initiated around 1950, on the construction of the *General Adaptability Battery* for classifying black mining recruits; Hudson's (1960, 1962) work on pictorial depth perception; studies by Mundy Castle and Nelson (1962) and Nelson (1969) involving neuropsychological assessment in an isolated community of forest workers; Reuning's (1972; Reuning & Wortley, 1973) studies on the Bushmen of the Kalahari; research by Grant (1972) and Kendall (1972) on ability structures of ethnic groups in cultural transition; Poortinga's (1971, 1972) methodological contributions to cross-cultural comparability; and J. M. Verster's (1983a) entry into computerised assessment and structural analysis of cognitive processes in different groups. But for want of space, there are many other excellent studies that could be mentioned here; as well as a large number of more routine, applied, or empirical projects involving test construction and application for a wide variety of purposes.

The aim in this chapter is to review the findings of South African psychometric research on a relatively unpublicised but potentially important theme, the comparison of test scores in the country's two main white subgroups: English speakers and Afrikaans speakers. The contrast implied here is a subtle one, between nonexclusive groups that share a national ecological context yet differ in terms of mother tongue, social history, and certain values, norms, and practices in their respective cultural lives. The

The views expressed in this chapter are those of the authors and do not necessarily reflect those of the Human Sciences Research Council or other institutions whose work is referred to in the text.

534

groups are sufficiently similar to each other, and to others with an Anglo-European heritage, to enable the use of common measuring procedures and familiar instruments with a view to testing the generality and robustness of established psychometric theories and constructs. At the same time, the opportunity avails itself for identifying such intergroup test score differences as may obtain with a limited range of independent variables on which the groups concerned are known to differ. The work reviewed here accordingly has the potential to reflect on the meaning of test scores and test score differences.

The importance of this issue has gained increasing recognition in the psychometric literature, and is critically highlighted in contributions from a cross-cultural (Irvine & Berry, 1983) or life-span developmental (Honzik, 1984) perspective in particular. Recent advances in adjacent research fields, notably experimental cognition, information processing, and psychobiology, have similarly called attention to the predicament in psychometrics arising from its persistent failure to establish the meaning of tests in scientifically acceptable terms.

Irvine (1983) has suggested a useful paradigm for construct validation in psychometrics and has shown, through its application to test data from North America and black Africa, that the once confident predictions of North American test theory are not supported in the African data. This chapter calls traditional test theory further into question by examining the extent to which it can account for the pattern of test score differences in the two white South African subgroups that differ from each other, and from the modal western pattern only in marginal terms.

The chapter starts by presenting a brief description of the two language groups, attempting to contrast them in historical and psychosocial perspective. It then goes on to discuss comparative test data from empirical studies over three and a half decades, representing generational cohorts spanning nearly a century. Attention is focussed, in particular, on the diminishing test performance gap between English speakers and Afrikaans speakers in association with the progressive cultural convergence of the two language groups. Next, commentary is offered on the methodological problem of data comparability. This chapter concludes with a section on the interpretation of empirical findings and their relevance to the issue of establishing the meaning of test scores in terms of current psychometric theory.

A brief description of the populations

English-speaking South Africans, currently constituting some 40% of the total white population of about 4.53 million, are descended chiefly from 1820s British settler stock. Through their language and politics they have retained strong cultural affinities with the wider English-speaking world. Their institutions of socialisation, education, and employment are modelled on Anglo prototypes and their value system has traditionally embodied liberal-democratic elements in association with materialism and pragmatism. Until recently, English speakers were the undisputed leaders in the nation's economic life, having gained early control of the mineral wealth and taken the lead in developing commerce and industry. Their way of life, for several generations, has been essentially urban, middle class, and Anglo-oriented rather than nationalistic.

A numerical majority (60%) of the white population are Afrikaans speakers who are descended mainly from Dutch, German, Belgian, and French Huguenot immigrants to the country between about 1650 and 1800. Unlike their English-speaking counterparts, they severed close bonds with their West European origins at an early stage. They have concentrated on forging an independent national character of their own, exemplified in their own unique language. Historically, their social development proceeded from an impoverished rural base, guided by a conservative religious value system and a political ideology emphasising their separateness from all other groups. Only in recent generations have they experienced significant social change, in association with large-scale urbanisation, improved quality and levels of education, consolidation of political influence, and increasing material prosperity. Although they have become progressively more urban and middle class, child-rearing practices would still appear to foster greater conservatism, authoritarianism, and ethnocentrism than in the case of English speakers (Mynhardt, Plug, Tyson, & Viljoen, 1979).

Early empirical evidence of test score differences

The first systematic evidence of test score differences between the two white language groups in South Africa came to light in the early 1950s. Olckers (1950) administered a battery, including the *S.A. Group Test,* to the total population of Afrikaans- and English-speaking standard 5 (grade 7) pupils in the Johannesburg central area. He noted very unequal mean IQ distributions for the English and Afrikaans schools in his study (see Table 20.1). The mean IQ of the total English group was some 7.41 points higher than for the Afrikaans group, representing a difference of approximately three-fourths of a standard deviation. At about the same time, Morkel (1950) found a significant difference in the performance of 502 English-speaking and 500 Afrikaans-speaking young men seeking enlistment in the then Union Defence Forces, on a test of mental alertness. The difference was of a similar order of magnitude and again favoured English speakers. It was argued that the difference could not be accounted for simply by differences in the two language versions of the tests. This view was supported by the work of Biesheuvel (1952), who presented data based on the figural *Raven's Progressive Matrices* test. He found consistent mean differences of around half a standard deviation favouring English speakers across a range of adult occupational and educational categories. Langenhoven (1957) showed that in the large and representative samples used in the standardisation of the *New*

Table 20.1. *Distribution of mean IQs of schools, in Olckers's (1950) sample*

Mean IQ per school	English schools	Afrikaans schools
96–100	0	4
101–105	8	8
106–110	11	6
111–115	9	2
116–120	9	1
121–125	2	0
Total	39	21
Mean IQ .	112.2	104.79
Standard deviation	10.18	9.48

Note: $z = 15.99$, $p < 0.01$.

South African Group Test (NSAGT), English-speaking pupils were better at all age and education levels by an average of 9.9 IQ points, or nearly one standard deviation, on the nonverbal part of the test.

In 1959, Biesheuvel and Liddicoat published data from the national standardisation of the *South African Wechsler Adult Intelligence Scale (SAWAIS)* in which consistent differences favouring English speakers were again found. This paper represents the first systematic attempt to account for the intergroup differences, using a series of carefully designed analyses.

In the first analysis the mean IQs of English-speaking (ES) and Afrikaans-speaking (AS) samples were compared across five levels of socioeconomic status (SES), leaving age and sex uncontrolled. Findings bore out the expectation that differences in favour of ES would be greatest in the intermediate SES categories and smallest at the upper and lower extremes of SES. This was interpreted as implying that developmental conditions are likely to converge for ES and AS under extreme SES conditions. In fact, the difference between ES and AS did not reach statistical significance for the lowest SES category, comprising only unskilled labourers, presumably because "lack of responsiveness due to low intelligence and an environment catering for little more than the necessities of life, would leave little scope for differential cultural development" (Biesheuvel & Liddicoat, 1959, p. 5).

In another analysis the three subtests considered most likely to contain different cultural associations for the two language groups (*Information, Comprehension,* and *Similarities*) and the three thought least likely to contain culturally biased content (*Block Design, Digit-Symbol Substitution,* and *Arithmetic Reasoning*) were selected for analysis. ES and AS samples matched for age, sex, and education were compared on these two sets of subtests at each of three SES levels, namely high (A), intermediate (C), and low (E). The main hypothesis under investigation, that differences between the language groups would be greater in tests with ample scope for specific cultural associations than in those with a more generalised cultural content, was only partially borne out. Seven out of nine comparisons yielded differences significant at 5% or better in the case of the former, as against four out of nine significant differences (all at 1%) in the case of the latter.

The most consistent result occurred in the case of *Arithmetic Reasoning,* on which ES and AS were virtually equal in all three SES categories. Biesheuvel & Liddicoat noted the significance of this, pointing out that "arithmetic is a subject in which all scholars are drilled alike, and in which a specific cultural effect is therefore least likely to occur" (p. 8). In the upper (A) and intermediate (C) SES categories, ES performed significantly better than AS on *Block Design* and *Digit-Symbol* despite an apparent absence of cultural bias in these tests. The authors offered a tentative explanation for this by referring to the possibility of different attitudes in the language groups towards the speed requirements in the tests, particularly *Digit-Symbol.* They considered it more likely, however, that the differences might result from a lesser ability of AS to perceive new relations in unfamiliar, nonverbal materials. This would imply a difference in the levels of fluid intelligence (g_f) between English- and Afrikaans-speaking samples, in keeping with the earlier findings of Biesheuvel (1952), Langenhoven (1957), and others.

Independent support for this interpretation was found in a comparison of item easiness vectors for ES and AS across all *SAWAIS* subtests. After accounting for the effects of differential cultural associations in the item content of certain tests, persistent language group differences favouring ES were considered to point to "a more general and fundamental influence, operative in all the tests" (Biesheuvel & Liddicoat, 1959, p. 11). Although the authors identified this influence with Spearman's g, it would seem more precisely specified in terms of the Cattell–Horn construct, g_f. In another analysis, the possibility that the persistent performance differences might be attributable to differences in the urban–rural status of the samples was clearly discounted, at least for subjects in the intermediate SES category (C) that was used in this analysis.

Biesheuvel and Liddicoat (1959) did not analyse their data in terms of verbal and performance subscale differences between ES and AS. Nor did they offer a systematic analysis of differences between the language groups stratified in terms of age. Supplementary analyses along these lines, using the original standardisation data of the 1950s, have been carried out for the purpose of this chapter.

In Tables 20.2, and 20.3, results of the separate analyses carried out on males and females respectively are summarised. In all 36 comparisons, a difference favouring ES can be seen, with only 3 differences failing to reach statistical significance at the 5% level or beyond. In the case of males, the difference favouring English speakers is consistently greater on the *Performance Scale* than on the *Verbal Scale,* indicating greater differentiation in g_f than g_c abilities between the language groups. A somewhat modified pattern is found for females, with differences being greater for *Performance*

Table 20.2. *Comparison of SAWAIS Verbal and Performance scale scores by age category: English- and Afrikaans-speaking males tested in 1950s*

Age	English verbal			Afrikaans verbal				English performance			Afrikaans performance			
	N	$\bar{X}$	s	N	$\bar{X}$	s	Diff.	N	$\bar{X}$	s	N	$\bar{X}$	s	Diff.
18–19	76	111.66	16.71	120	102.76	18.16	8.9***	76	110.42	14.63	120	99.49	15.34	10.93***
20–24	80	106.96	18.74	120	103.05	18.14	3.9	80	108.63	16.04	120	100.35	15.47	8.28***
25–29	76	108.36	17.16	114	102.49	17.44	5.87*	76	109.13	16.25	114	99.29	16.69	9.84***
30–34	74	109.00	15.96	111	102.15	17.33	6.85***	76	106.87	15.57	111	98.37	16.80	8.5***
35–39	76	109.57	16.37	114	104.59	15.54	4.98**	76	107.24	16.96	114	98.67	15.53	8.57***
40–44	60	107.12	18.83	90	103.43	17.06	3.69	60	106.45	18.56	90	98.24	18.03	8.21**
45–49	49	112.16	16.67	71	102.11	16.46	10.05***	49	112.74	17.51	71	96.58	16.70	16.16***
50–54	44	113.14	14.31	59	102.34	17.00	10.08***	44	109.14	15.01	59	97.70	15.99	11.44***
55–59	40	109.75	16.27	31	99.36	18.64	10.39*	40	113.70	15.59	31	95.52	17.35	18.18***

Note: * $p < .05$; ** $p < .01$; *** $p < .001$.

Table 20.3. *Comparison of SAWAIS Verbal and Performance scale scores by age category: English- and Afrikaans-speaking females tested in 1950s*

Age	English verbal			Afrikaans verbal				English performance			Afrikaans performance			
	N	X̄	s	N	X̄	s	Diff.	N	X̄	s	N	X̄	s	Diff.
18–19	80	103.73	17.78	120	96.78	15.12	6.95**	80	106.14	17.27	120	98.66	14.26	7.48**
20–24	80	106.49	14.97	120	97.21	16.17	9.28***	80	107.18	14.42	120	97.93	16.17	9.25***
25–29	76	103.49	13.91	113	98.80	16.76	4.69*	76	105.84	13.43	113	99.67	15.37	6.17**
30–34	74	107.00	16.61	111	95.93	15.68	11.07***	74	109.64	16.99	111	100.59	14.44	9.05***
35–39	73	104.01	15.03	112	94.34	16.09	9.67***	73	108.06	15.22	112	100.28	17.15	7.78**
40–44	60	105.18	13.54	85	97.08	15.65	8.1**	60	104.88	12.21	85	101.38	14.36	3.50
45–49	50	106.08	17.42	67	95.49	15.23	10.63***	50	108.90	14.58	67	99.16	15.51	9.74**
50–54	42	107.69	14.20	51	93.10	17.15	14.59***	42	107.36	14.99	51	95.06	15.07	12.30***
55–59	28	114.21	11.46	14	95.21	13.25	19.0***	28	113.96	11.90	14	98.07	10.27	15.89***

Note: * $p < .05$; ** $p < .01$; *** $p < .001$.

than *Verbal* scores in the lower but not in the higher age categories. For both sexes, there is a clear indication of an increase in the magnitude of the difference, for both *Verbal* and *Performance* scores, from the age of 45 years onwards. This results not only from a progressive decrease in scores with age in the Afrikaans sample, but from an increase in scores with increasing age in the English sample, particularly in the case of *Performance* tests (cf. Cattell, 1983). It seems probable that this phenomenon is less due to differential ageing effects on intelligence in the two language groups than to differential cohort experiences. The cultural distance between the two populations is likely to be greater in the older cohorts than in the younger.

Because the data on which these analyses are based were collected during the decade of the 1950s, subjects in the oldest age category (55–59 years) would have been born as early as the 1890s and would have had their formative experiences at a time when English and Afrikaans speakers in South Africa were exposed to very different kinds of influences in many spheres of life. As adults at the time of testing, they are likely to have differed more from one another in terms of lifestyle, occupational history, and intellectual pursuits than in the case of younger cohorts.

Data in Tables 20.2 and 20.3 are consistent with the general proposition of a gradual convergence of the two white subcultures in South Africa over time, but less so with regard to influences on g_f than on g_c abilities. Subsequent sections of this chapter will follow evidence bearing on this proposition through more recent generations, right up to the cohort of contemporary preschool children.

Project TALENT survey

The data cited thus far refer to the situation in South Africa some 30 years ago. The question may be asked whether this pattern of language group differences in test performance has persisted to the present, or whether it represents merely a cohort-specific phenomenon reflected in the early data.

To pursue this question, we turn now to data from the large-scale Project TALENT Survey,[1] initiated in South Africa by the Institute of Manpower Research of the Human Sciences Research Council (HSRC) in 1965. In that year all white standard 6 (grade 8) pupils in South Africa ($N = 69,908$) were assessed on a battery of intelligence, aptitude, interest, personality, and scholastic achievement tests. These pupils were tested again in 1967 when in standard 8 and in 1969 when they were in standard 10 (the final high school year in South Africa, known as "matriculation"). As a result of the very large groups that were tested, statistically reliable results were obtained. Furthermore, it should be noted that all the tests used in the Project TALENT Survey were constructed and standardised with great precision

[1] The assistance of the Institute for Manpower Research of the Human Sciences Research Council, and in particular Dr. W. L. Roos, is acknowledged for supplying data from the Project TALENT Survey. Interpretation of the data is the responsibility of the authors alone.

Table 20.4. *Scores of English- and Afrikaans-speaking pupils on the New South African Group Test*

	English Stand. 6 – 1965			Afrikaans Stand. 6 – 1965			
	N	X̄	s	N	X̄	s	Difference
Nonverbal IQ	21,129	108.24	15.12	40,900	100.80	14.71	7.44**
Verbal IQ	21,129	104.76	15.47	40,900	99.59	15.66	5.17**
Total IQ	21,129	106.21	14.39	40,900	99.87	14.39	6.34**
	English Stand. 8 – 1967			Afrikaans Stand. 8 – 1967			
	N	X̄	s	N	X̄	s	Difference
Nonverbal IQ	16,908	107.91	13.92	30,964	102.30	13.78	5.61**
Verbal IQ	16,908	103.88	13.73	30,964	100.90	14.16	2.98**
Total IQ	16,908	106.28	13.28	30,964	101.93	13.44	4.35**
	English Stand. 10 – 1969			Afrikaans Stand. 10 – 1969			
	N	X̄	s	N	X̄	s	Difference
Nonverbal IQ	3,728	115.99	16.29	4,964	111.18	15.45	4.81**
Verbal IQ	3,728	110.58	13.60	4,964	109.81	13.98	0.77**
Total IQ	3,728	114.23	14.82	4,964	111.44	14.61	2.79**

Note: ** $p < 0.01$.

by the HSRC. Care was taken to ensure that no items were included that were obviously biased against either of the language groups; and that the item discrimination values and difficulty values of items were more or less uniform. This implies also that the rank orders of the items according to their difficulty values were the same for both language groups; and that the reliability and validity coefficients were of acceptable standards in the two groups. In Table 20.4 the Total IQ, Verbal IQ, and Nonverbal IQ means on the *New South African Group Test (NSAGT)* are presented for the Project TALENT population tested in 1965, 1967, and 1969.

In all comparisons the English sample mean is greater than the Afrikaans sample mean ($p < .01$). On each of the three test occasions, the difference between English and Afrikaans means is greater for nonverbal IQ (g_f abilities) than for verbal IQ (g_c abilities). The relative difference favouring nonverbal IQ increases from one test-year to the next, although the absolute difference in nonverbal IQ diminishes over the high school years. This would suggest that the common school curriculum to which pupils of both language groups are exposed progressively diminishes the disparity in intellectual per-

Table 20.5. *Stanine scores (1965) of English- and Afrikaans-speaking standard 6 pupils on the Junior Aptitude Tests*

Tests	English			Afrikaans			
	N	X̄	s	N	X̄	s	Difference
Classification	21,083	5.22	1.99	40,767	4.92	1.99	0.30**
Reasoning	21,083	5.45	1.88	40,767	4.71	1.97	0.74**
Number ability	21,083	5.33	1.99	40,767	4.66	1.97	0.67**
Synonyms	21,083	4.67	1.88	40,767	5.05	1.96	0.38**
Comparison	21,083	4.69	1.61	40,767	5.08	2.06	0.39**
Spatial 2D	21,083	5.25	1.97	40,767	4.71	1.93	0.54**
Memory (paragraph)	21,083	5.41	1.94	40,767	4.75	1.87	0.66**
Memory (words and symbols)	21,083	5.39	1.98	40,767	4.75	1.93	0.64**
Mechanical insight	21,083	4.97	1.88	40,767	4.97	1.89	0.00

Note: ** $p < 0.01$.

formance, through both selection and stimulation, but that the effect of schooling is greatest in the area of verbal intellectual skills. The absolute difference in total IQ between the language groups decreases over the high school period from just over 0.44 SD units to about 0.14 SD units. Note that although some 17.64% of English-speaking pupils tested in 1965 progressed through to standard 10, only 12.14% of Afrikaans pupils survived the same scholastic selection process. The differential selection rates would imply that if the subjects had been stratified on the basis of age irrespective of school standard and had been tested over the same period, a greater test score differential between the language groups would have been evident after 4 years.

In Tables 20.5 to 20.7 Project TALENT data are presented for English- and Afrikaans-speaking pupils tested on scholastic aptitude batteries in 1965, 1967, and 1969. English sample means are significantly higher in 13 out of a total of 19 comparisons. In 2 comparisons no difference is found: *Mechanical Insight* (standard 6) and *Disguised Words* (standard 10). In 4 comparisons the Afrikaans group has a significantly higher mean, *Synonyms and Comparison* (standard 6), *Disguised Words* (standard 8), and *Calculations* (standard 10). Note that all the group mean differences are within the range noted above in the case of IQ scores, with none exceeding half a standard deviation. Where the Afrikaans group mean is higher, the difference lies in the range 0.17 to 0.23 SD units, or about one-fifth of a standard deviation. Data in Tables 20.5 to 20.7 are consistent with the general interpretation applicable to findings in Table 20.4. Among English- and Afrikaans-speaking high school pupils of approximately one generation ago (± 20 years ago), a difference in favour of the former of up to half a standard deviation in ability

Table 20.6. *Stanine scores (1967) of English- and Afrikaans-speaking standard 8 pupils on the Senior Aptitude Tests*

Tests	English			Afrikaans			Difference
	N	$\overline{X}$	s	N	$\overline{X}$	s	
Verbal comprehension	4,719	5.59	1.88	7,071	4.68	1.93	0.91**
Calculations	4,719	5.35	1.97	7,071	4.83	1.95	0.52**
Disguised words	4,719	4.74	1.64	7,071	5.16	2.03	0.42**
Comparison	4,719	5.40	2.03	7,071	4.84	1.98	0.56**
Pattern completion	4,719	5.37	1.96	7,071	4.86	1.89	0.51**

Note: ** $p < 0.01$.

Table 20.7. *Stanine scores (1969) of English- and Afrikaans-speaking standard 10 pupils on the Senior Aptitude Tests*

Tests	English			Afrikaans			Difference
	N	$\overline{X}$	s	N	$\overline{X}$	s	
Verbal comprehension	3,715	5.48	1.98	4,960	4.89	2.05	0.59**
Calculations	3,715	4.13	1.95	4,960	4.80	1.88	0.33**
Disguised words	3,715	4.49	1.89	4,960	4.98	1.91	0.01
Comparison	3,715	5.17	2.09	4,960	4.54	2.04	0.63**
Pattern completion	3,715	5.35	2.01	4,960	4.75	1.92	0.60**

Note: ** $p < 0.01$.

and aptitude test scores is the rule. Differences are smallest, or even in the reverse direction, in the case of tests closely based on the school curriculum (g_c measures) and greatest on tests calling for abstract, nonverbal reasoning and problem solving (g_f measures). The average magnitude of the difference shows evidence of a decrease compared with data from earlier cohorts. As noted earlier in the chapter, Olckers (1950), for example, found a difference of three-fourths of a standard deviation among the standard 5 pupils he tested, whereas the reanalysis of *SAWAIS* standardisation data presented in Tables 20.2 and 20.3 shows a difference of up to 1.5 SD units for the cohort born in the 1890s and tested at age 55–59 years. Naturally these are crude comparisons, based on different measuring instruments administered at different stages in the life span. Nonetheless, the general pattern in the results thus far is consistent with the hypothesis of *a progressive decrease in ability score discrepancies with increasing cultural convergence over successive generations of white South Africans.* English–Afrikaans differences appear more persistent over successive cohorts in the case of g_f measures

Table 20.8. *Distribution of English- and Afrikaans-speaking pupils by IQ category*

Language group and sex	Superior IQ N	%		Average IQ N	%		Total N	%
English								
Boys	506	30.5		486	16.4		992	21.5
% in category			51.0			49.0		
Girls	435	26.2		486	16.4		921	19.9
% in category			47.2			52.8		
Total	941	56.7		972	32.8			
Afrikaans								
Boys	338	20.4		958	32.4		1,296	28.1
% in category			26.1			73.9		
Girls	380	22.9		1,026	34.8		1,406	30.5
% in category			27.0			73.0		
Total	718	43.3		1,984	67.2			
Total	1,659			2,956			4,615	
N		100.0			100.0			100
%			35.9			64.1		

than g_c measures. This is presumably because the former assess intellectual skills fostered within the microsystem of the home and immediate community, where there is greater resistance to or inertia in the face of pressures towards cultural convergence than in the school and work environment, where g_c abilities are chiefly fostered.

In the analyses presented thus far, attention has been focussed exclusively on the issue of central tendency or mean performance levels in the two groups. Roos (1983) conducted an interesting analysis of Project TALENT data focussing on a different distribution characteristic, namely the incidence of intellectual superiority in the two language groups. Using the population of standard 6 pupils tested in 1965, he identified a group of superior IQ pupils and a group of average IQ pupils, regardless of language affiliation. The former group comprised all pupils who obtained a *NSAGT* stanine 9 (IQ > 127), the latter all those obtaining a stanine 5 (IQ = 97–103). The distribution of English and Afrikaans pupils between these categories is indicated in Table 20.8. Here it can be seen that the representation of English and Afrikaans pupils in the two categories is very uneven. Of pupils classified as superior IQ, 56.7% are English-speaking and 43.3% are Afrikaans-speaking. Conversely, in the average IQ category, 67.2% are Afrikaans-speaking and only 32.8% are English-speaking.

Hence data from the large-scale Project TALENT Survey, conducted among high school pupils from 1965 to 1969, bear further testimony to test performance differences favouring English speakers over Afrikaans speakers. There is some evidence that the gap has narrowed in comparison with earlier cohorts tested in the 1950s, particularly on measures of so-called crystallised intellectual skills. In the following section data bearing on this trend is reviewed in more recent studies, up to and including the contemporary cohort of preschool children in the 1980s. Thereafter, consideration is given to the difficult methodological problem of data comparability, which has been set aside in the discussion thus far. No attempt can be made to explain or interpret the meaning of intergroup test score differences until the equivalence of data has been established.

Recent comparisons of English and Afrikaans test scores

In 1971, Verster (1974) collected data for a comparative study of the intellectual characteristics of English- and Afrikaans-speaking personnel at the upper end of the ability distribution in South Africa. His samples were carefully drawn from the population of graduate research personnel employed by the Council for Scientific and Industrial Research (CSIR), stratified according to seniority and research field. Although the focus of his attention was on structural and stylistic similarities and differences between the language groups, a comparison of mean performance levels was made as well. For the purpose of this study a battery of 14 high-level tests was specially compiled, with a view to referencing factors of Deduction, Induction, Space, and Verbal Meaning. Tests of the Verbal Meaning factor were not considered in the analysis of mean differences because different language versions had to be used. Of the remaining 11 tests, 6 gave rise to statistically significant differences favouring the English sample, with differences on the remaining 5 tests being in the same direction but not significant at the 5% level of confidence (see Table 20.9). Of the 6 tests on which significant differences were found, 5 defined a common reasoning factor, akin to g_f, in which inductive and deductive variance merged. The sixth test, *Cube Comparison,* loaded as intended on a factor of Spatial Reasoning in the English sample, but shared its variance between Space and Reasoning in the Afrikaans sample.

Working with the same samples, Süssenguth (1972) administered an additional battery of self-report questionnaire measures of problem-solving styles. His results show, inter alia, evidence of higher scores for the Afrikaans sample on such dimensions as rigidity versus versatility in thinking, ideational conformity versus ideational independence, and low performance potential versus high performance potential. Although the measurement scales used were exploratory only, they provide valuable pointers to stylistic differences in approach to intellectual tasks, including ability tests, between the language groups. These differences seem compatible with differences between the populations, found in other studies, on personality dimensions

Table 20.9. *Scores of English- and Afrikaans-speaking scientists tested on Verster's (1974) battery*

	English (N = 88)		Afrikaans (N = 72)		
	X̄	s	X̄	s	Difference
Locations	8.66	2.41	7.75	2.49	0.91*
Deductive reasoning	33.19	8.14	30.07	7.80	3.12*
Card rotation	21.14	4.53	20.28	4.91	0.86
H. L. vocabulary	—	—	—	—	—
Letter sets	23.22	3.61	21.85	4.63	1.37*
Inference	16.90	2.79	12.19	2.85	4.71***
Cube comparison	33.66	6.21	30.60	7.39	3.06*
Reading comprehension	—	—	—	—	—
Figure classification	140.55	33.74	129.49	30.10	11.06*
Blox	35.17	3.97	34.06	5.09	1.11
Reasoning ability	12.34	2.49	11.50	3.01	0.84
Pattern completion	18.65	5.79	17.46	6.26	1.19
Figure series	21.67	5.57	20.22	5.03	1.45
Adv. vocabulary	—	—	—	—	—

Note: * $p < 0.05$; *** $p < 0.001$

such as overregimentation (Steyn, 1971) and conservatism, authoritarianism, and ethnocentrism (Mynhardt et al., 1979).

In a more detailed analysis of test variance in the CSIR research scientist population, de Jager and Boeyens (1981) analysed the effects of various independent variables, including home language (English or Afrikaans), age, sex, and field of research (scientific discipline) on performance differences on a routinely used general ability selection test, *Mental Alertness*. Using Automatic Interaction Detection (AID) analysis with the test score as the dependent variable, they found that home language accounted for only 1% of total test variance, whereas field of research, for example, accounted for 21.3%. This would suggest that experiential factors other than language per se are likely to lie at the heart of English and Afrikaans subgroup differences in test performance.

Working at a different stratum in the adult population, this time with trainee engineering technicians, J. M. Taylor (1978) also found evidence of mean differences favouring English speakers over Afrikaans speakers. Although the differences were not statistically significant on the versions of *Mental Alertness* and *Gottschaldt Figures* used in this study, significant differences were found on tests of spatial reasoning, deductive reasoning, scientific knowledge, and technical reading comprehension. The samples were equated on such criteria as age and level of education, but they were found to differ on a number of background variables. In particular, Afrikaans subjects had on average more siblings, and parents with lower education levels, and a greater proportion had been educated at schools in rural areas. Interestingly, the average school achievement in the Afrikaans sample was higher, yet their college achievement as trainee engineering technicians was poorer, particularly in mathematics. These findings point to the likelihood that a variety of independent variables, from the category described by Irvine (1983) as high inference variables, underlie differences between English and Afrikaans subcultures in South Africa and covary with test performance.

In a study of structural invariance, Cudeck and Claasen (1983) presented means and standard deviations for carefully selected samples of English- (N = 319) and Afrikaans-speaking pupils (N = 171) on the revised *NSAGT–G*. The samples are drawn from the very recent cohort defined by the national population of standard 5 pupils in 1981. Although they do not test for mean differences, subsequent analysis of their published data shows persistent differences in the expected direction on tests of *Figure Analogies* ($p <$ .01) and *Pattern Completion* ($p <$ .01). No significant differences occur, however, on tests of *Number Series, Verbal Reasoning,* and *Word Analogies,* while the Afrikaans sample has a small but significant edge on a test called *Word Pairs*. These findings suggest that although the English-language group retains a long-established advantage on measures of the g_f type, the gap has narrowed over successive cohorts, to the point of closure in the rising school generation on measures of the g_c type. These are measures linked closely to formal schooling. The magnitude of the differential in the case of g_f measures has shrunk to between one-third and one-fourth of a standard deviation in this analysis.

With the recent introduction of computerised psychometric assessment at the National Institute for Personnel Research (NIPR) in Johannesburg (J. M. Verster, 1982; T. R. Taylor, 1983), it has become possible to analyse individual and intergroup differences in terms of measures other than the traditional, opaque total score in which separate contributions of accuracy, speed, persistence, and other characteristics are inextricably confounded. In one version of NIPR's entry to the computerised testing field, conventional paper-and-pencil tests are adapted for computer presentation using the PLATO software system (Taylor, Gerber, & Rendall, 1981). A number of prototype tests in this programme have been administered experimentally to a range of technical and administrative personnel recruited to a large public corporation in South Africa which is sponsoring the project. Although the total numbers tested thus far are not very large, an attempt was made to select comparable English- and Afrikaans-speaking samples for analysis, with a view to inclusion in this chapter. Tests on which data are presently available include a *High Level* and an *Intermediate Level Mental Alertness Test,* a spatial reasoning test called *Rotate and Flip,* and a clerical aptitude test called *Error Checking*. Since recruitment to different job categories is known to involve sex biases, data are analysed separately for males and females within each language group. Because sample cells are, at present, large enough for statistical reliability only in the case of the *Intermediate Level Mental Alertness Test,* only data for this test are presented here in tabular form. Results of analyses in the case of the other tests are referred to without detailed presentation.

Data describing test performance on the *Mental Alertness Test* are available in a number of separate measures, including Total Score (number of items correct within time limit), Total Time (cumulative time spent working on test items, excluding time on instructions, practice items, and intervals between test items), Item Reached (farthest item reached in the test on expiry of available time), Number Attempted (number of items answered), and Proportion Correct (Number Attempted divided by Total Score). In Table 20.10, data on these variables are presented for English- and Afrikaans-speaking male and female job applicants tested on the PLATO *Intermediate Mental Alertness* in 1984. All applicants had completed the South African matriculation examination (standard 10) but had not yet undergone tertiary training.

In Table 20.10 it can be seen that in the case of males the language groups differ significantly only on one performance variable, Proportion Correct, where the estimated English population mean is approximately 0.25 SD units higher. In the case of females, English speakers again achieve a significantly better score on Proportion Correct (0.63 SD units) as well as on Total Score (0.46 SD units). Afrikaans females, however, do better on the measures reflecting rate of work, including Total Time (0.36 SD units) and Number Attempted (0.36 SD units). The general pattern in these results is not contradicted in the case of other PLATO computerised tests. The English samples consistently have the edge on power measures, the greatest difference being in the case of spatial reasoning, measured by the *Rotate and Flip* test where the estimated population means differ by 0.56 SD units on Total Score (number correct) in the case of males. Differences in rate of work measures on the other tests are generally small or nonexistent and reflect no consistent pattern. Where differences occur, these never exceed one-third of a standard deviation and may favour either language group. No group differences were found on any measure in the case of *Error Checking,* which assesses speed and accuracy on a simple clerical–perceptual task.

Findings from the analysis of PLATO test data in the contemporary cohort of young adult job applicants are interesting since they cast the first light on a fundamentally important issue raised originally by Biesheuvel and Liddicoat (1959). This has to do with the relative importance of speed and power in determining intergroup differences between English- and Afrikaans-speaking South Africans. The modern findings, although based on imperfect speed measures, support the earlier researchers' surmise that differences are more likely to reflect power variance, identified with the ability to perceive and apply new relations, than speed variance from diverse sources including motivation and attitudes as well as inherent capacity. Although Biesheuvel and Liddicoat (1959) tentatively identified the power component with *g*, it

Table 20.10. Scores of English- and Afrikaans-speaking job applicants tested on PLATO Intermediate Mental Alertness, 1984

	English males			Afrikaans males				English females			Afrikaans females			
	N	X̄	s	N	X̄	s	Difference	N	X̄	s	N	X̄	s	Difference
Total score	192	19.94	5.06	254	19.17	4.88	0.77	70	18.5	4.34	139	16.01	5.19	2.49*
Total time	192	1,586.0	272.3	254	1,574.0	225.3	12.00	70	1,568.0	271.1	139	1.465.0	298.0	103.00***
Item reached	192	29.07	2.83	254	28.99	2.09	0.08	70	28.6	2.85	139	29.35	1.72	−0.75*
Num. attempted	187	28.1	3.64	240	28.47	2.60	−0.37	70	27.91	3.26	125	28.87	2.39	−0.96***
Prop. correct	187	0.72	0.17	240	0.67	0.17	0.05**	70	0.67	0.15	125	0.56	0.19	0.11*

Note: * $p < .05$; ** $p < .01$; *** $p < .001$.

seems likely in the light of subsequent work to be more precisely charac-terised in terms of the Cattell–Horn notion of g_f (Cattell, 1963, 1971; Horn & Cattell, 1966; Horn, 1978, 1980).

The last set of data to be presented here with regard to group mean com-parisons between English speakers and Afrikaans speakers comes from a battery developed at the HSRC and known as the *Junior South African Intelligence Scale (JSAIS)* (Madge, 1981). This battery comprises 22 subtests constructed according to a neo-Guilfordian model. Of the subtests, 12 pro-vide a composite Global IQ (GIQ), while further subsets of 5 tests each provide a Verbal IQ (VIQ) and a Performance IQ (PIQ). Other subscales, including memory, number, and reasoning, can be formed as well from sub-sets of tests grouped on a rational basis. Empirical verification of construct validity for such scales has yet to be published. The *JSAIS* is intended for individual administration to very young children in the age range 3 to 7 years. Suitably translated, standardised, and equated versions are available for use in English- and Afrikaans-speaking samples.

An analysis of language-group differences on the *JSAIS* in large, repre-sentative, contemporary samples of preschool and junior school children was undertaken with a view to inclusion in this chapter. The following pattern of results emerged: Among very young children in the age range 36 to 59 months, no group mean differences between English speakers and Afrikaans speakers were found. In the age range 60 to 77 months, no difference was found on GIQ, but differences favouring English speakers were found for PIQ and a memory scale, both significant at the 5% confidence level. A difference significant at 1% and favouring Afrikaans speakers was found in the case of VIQ. In the age range 78 to 95 months, Afrikaans speakers had a significantly higher mean on VIQ ($p < .05$) with no other variable yielding a significant difference.

These results seem consistent with the trend that might have been pre-dicted from earlier studies involving more mature subjects. Absolute dif-ferences are generally nonsignificant or small, never exceeding one-third of a standard deviation. In the case of children with no formal schooling (36 to 59 months) no differences are found, suggesting the possibility of a close convergence between the language groups with regard to qualitative influ-ences in the home on the early intellectual development of the most recent cohort. In the older age groups (5 to $6\frac{1}{2}$ years and $6\frac{1}{2}$ to 8 years) where 1 or 2 years of school exposure may be assumed, a small difference in the cur-riculum-based abilities tapped by VIQ (g_c) begins to appear in the favour of Afrikaans-speaking children, whereas a slight advantage favouring En-glish-speaking children is evident in the case of abilities tapped by PIQ (g_f) that depend more on incidental, informal learning opportunities.

It is tempting to speculate that according to the data presented thus far, it has taken some four or five generations of social, economic, and cultural development for the Afrikaans segment of the population in South Africa to bridge a gap in measured abilities of just over one standard deviation in relation to their English-speaking counterparts. During this period, Afrikaners have experienced what might be considered a social revolution. Having come from early beginnings as pioneer farmers in the Cape, a significant number joined the hazardous Great Trek northward into an unknown interior to escape continuing conflicts with colonial powers and Xhosa pastoralists. Their descendants endured many skirmishes with indigenous tribes, two wars with England, a major rebellion, and the difficult period of World War I, during and after which extreme poverty prevailed and cultural life was minimal. Thereafter, the Afrikaner entered a period of rapid urbanisation, and the challenge of adapting to metropolitan life after generations of agrarian existence. It has been only in the last three or four decades that Afrikaans speakers have had the opportunity to concentrate their energy on cultural advancement, coupled with major strides in political, economic, and intellectual life. Recent cohorts have experienced significant changes in lifestyle, values, and child-rearing practices with increasing exposure to western, mainly American, norms and standards. The effects of this process of rapid and far-reaching acculturation and socioeconomic upward mobility appear to be accompanied by changes in psychometric test performance data. The consistent trend is a closing of the gap between Afrikaans and English test score distributions. Yet the convergence of means cannot be assumed to denote equality of ability, any more than differences in means can be accepted as evidence of differences in ability, until the comparability of test data obtained in the different groups has been established.

The issue of data comparability

At the centre of the methodological controversy over the problem of test data comparability is the question whether (and to what extent) the same meaning can be attached to the test scores of groups from different cultural backgrounds. As van der Flier (1982) observes, many kinds of factors can influence the meaning of a test: instructions, problem-solving strategy, familiarity with test materials and concepts, previous experience with the test task or similar tasks, the need to work under time pressure, and attitudinal or motivational factors. A great deal of effort has been devoted to the problem of formulating psychometric criteria for the comparison of test scores (Irvine, 1969, 1983; Poortinga 1971, 1975, 1983; Mellenbergh, 1972, 1983; van de Vijver & Poortinga, 1982). These attempts share two limitations. First, as pointed out by van der Flier (1982), they are based on groups distinguished in advance. More seriously, they provide no basis for inferring the meaning of test scores (or difference scores) in terms of psychological theory. Hence, at best, intergroup differences can be established, but not interpreted.

In the South African context Verster (1983a) has made a start in addressing the latter limitation by constructing tests on the basis of cognitive theory and attempting to fit scores from different groups to a common, theoretically predicted model using confirmatory structural modelling techniques (Browne, 1982). Although this work has not yet been addressed to the problem of English and Afrikaans test performance differences, encouraging progress has been made in identifying theoretically meaningful cognitive process variables, assessed by latency measures on computerised tests, which have equivalent construct validities in relatively dissimilar groups of black and white South Africans. Extension of this work to more subtly contrasted groups is likely to yield useful results.

Using empirical methods similar to the above, although with the limitation that theory was ignored as both a basis for test construction and statistical modelling, Cudeck and Claasen (1983) provide powerful evidence for the structural equivalence of test data for the English and Afrikaans samples included in their study. Referred to in a previous section, this study used data from the six subtests of the *NSAGT–G* administered to carefully selected nationally representative samples of English- and Afrikaans-speaking standard 5 pupils, tested in 1981. Although a Box (1949) test indicated that the covariance matrices for the two groups were not equal, testing of successive restricted factor-analysis models following Jöreskog's (1971) procedures provided a good fit for the strictest factor model examined, in which all parameters were constrained to be equal in the two samples. This finding is a useful step towards establishing the comparability of English and Afrikaans test data, but it does not go far enough because the two factors in the final solution are purely empirical and may lack psychological meaning. Although it is tempting to identify them with the familiar constructs, g_f and g_c, even post hoc inferential interpretation would seem unwise, because only six tests and two factors are involved, two tests share variance between the factors, the factors are extracted in a first-order analysis and correlate above .8 in both samples, and all tests have significant residual variances.

Investigations in other South African samples have found similar empirical evidence of factorial invariance between English- and Afrikaans-speaking groups. Working with data collected in 1967 and 1969 as part of the HSRC's Project TALENT Survey, Vorster (1978), for example, found moderate to high congruency coefficients between ability factors for English- and Afrikaans-speaking pupils analysed separately by sex and school standard. The three orthogonally rotated factors extracted by analytic procedures in each of the subsamples could be loosely labelled Reasoning, Space, and Verbal. Fluctuations in patterns of loadings across subsamples and the fact that virtually all 12 tests in the battery proved to be factorially complex, and differentially so in different subsamples, suggests that these labels are, at best, very gross taxonomic descriptors. They do not necessarily signify theoretically meaningful latent psychological dimensions, nor do they provide a basis for inferring the nature of the mental operations or processes that might underlie group mean differences on particular tests.

In Verster's (1974) study of CSIR research scientists, referred to earlier, analytic factoring procedures (Jöreskog, 1963) with oblique (direct quartimin) rotation also produced three factors, labelled Reasoning, Space, and Verbal in each of the two language groups, although an entirely different battery of tests was used to that in Vorster's (1978) study. Despite fairly high coefficients of congruence between factors in the two language groups, interesting variations in the pattern of factor loadings were observed. Certain tests – for example, *Deductive Reasoning* based on verbal syllogisms and *Figure Classification* from the ETS reference kit (French, Ekstrom, and Price, 1963) – had markedly different loadings in the two samples. In the analysis of English data, they had substantial loadings (.52 and .68 respectively) on the Space factor, with nonsignificant loadings on Reasoning, while in the Afrikaans data a reverse pattern was found. Here *Deductive Reasoning* correlated .66 and *Figures Classification* .78 with the Reasoning factor while their loadings on Space were zero-order. Supplementary information gained from protocol analysis and selected interviews following the lead of French (1965) suggested that English and Afrikaans scientists differed in their approach to the tests in terms of a stylistic dimension, Global versus Analytic thinking. English speakers apparently adopted a more global, opportunistic approach to the tests, using visual representations where appropriate, such as Venn diagrams to solve verbal syllogisms. In the Afrikaans sample a more sequential analytic style was favoured, at least by a significant subgroup. Certain tests, for example, *Cube Comparison,* gave rise to a bipolar distribution in the Afrikaans sample and produced moderate loadings (.38 and .35, respectively) on both the Space and Reasoning factors, indicating the use of different stylistic approaches within this group. In the English sample *Cube Comparison* correlated only with Space (.64).

Inconclusive as they are, these findings suggest the need for extreme caution when wishing to infer equivalence of psychological meaning in tests when psychometric criteria for equivalence have been met. Mean population differences on ability tests are at least as likely to reflect stylistic or other differences in approach to the tests as differences on the presumed underlying "ability."

The meaning of test scores

This brings us full cycle to the problem underlying all psychometric work, namely, what do the test scores mean? Has test development and related research in the context of white English- and Afrikaans-speaking South Africans over a period of more than three decades failed to advance our understanding in relation to this question? Certainly, a wealth of empirical support has been found for the local applicability of grossly described ability classifications from elsewhere, as in Irvine's (1979) logically constructed taxonomy, or the work of Hakstian and Vandenberg (1979) on empirically derived structures at the second-order level in a variety of cultures. The general agreement between white South African ability patterns and test data from other cultures is encouraging for those who would see the pursuit of universals as a worthwhile enterprise. There is the danger, however, that in subscribing to the common "culture" of psychometric practice, researchers working in different national or cultural populations are simply imposing a common set of constraints on the behaviour of their subjects and are being rewarded with common empirical artifacts as a result. Scientific understanding about the nature of human cognitive capabilities cannot be said to have advanced when, say, answers to sets of questions about the meaning of words are found to be similarly correlated in different populations, in keeping with the hypothesis that they all relate to a common underlying factor of "verbal ability."

Yet this is the kind of sterile tautology to which classical psychometric research has succumbed in the past. The need to transcend this form of research has been well recognised in the international literature of the past decade (Verster, 1983b) and the search for new paradigms is well underway (e.g., Posner, 1978; Sternberg & Detterman, 1979; Carroll, 1980; Eysenck, 1982; Hunt, 1982). Irvine (1979) has emphasised the widely endorsed view among contemporary researchers that the products of traditional psychometric research, namely, "ability" factors, are not, in themselves, explanatory constructs. They are, at best, pointers to underlying sources of explanation in terms of information-processing parameters. These, in turn, require classification with the aid of independent experimentation, guided by cognitive theory from beyond the realm of factor analysis.

Experimental work along these lines has been initiated in South Africa, following the lead by Verster (1983a) at NIPR. Current projects include an attempt to specify different processing parameters that might help to explain differences in test performance between subgroups of the population, including white English speakers and Afrikaans speakers. Regrettably, results of this work are not yet ready for inclusion in this discussion.

Conclusions

Meanwhile, it would seem instructive to attempt to summarise what has been learned about the meaning of test scores from this review of psychometric research among English- and Afrikaans-speaking subgroups in South Africa.

First, it would seem that the gradual convergence of mean scores between English- and Afrikaans-speaking samples over successive cohorts spanning four or five generations, although only imperfectly indicated, corresponds well with the more general process of cultural convergence between the populations. This is consistent with the uncontested view that culture, in its widest sense, somehow plays a significant role in shaping the nature and level of intellectual abilities.

More information is added when a crude distinction is made between scores on so-called fluid (g_f) (nonverbal) and crystallised (g_c) (verbal–number) ability measures. Evidence has been presented suggestive that the rate of convergence between *population* means is greater in the case of g_c than

g_f test scores. A plausible (if partial) source of explanation would seem to be that skills needed to perform on verbal and number tests are significantly influenced by formal schooling and to the extent that pupils of both language groups are subject to a common formal curriculum at school, convergence of scores would be expected. In the case of nonverbal and performance tests that are less obviously related to schooling, differences between the *population* means are greater and more persistent over generations. It could be that skills required to do these tests are more closely dependent on early intellectual experiences, and stimulation over the life span from within the informal context of home, family, and community life. If so, it would appear that qualitative cultural differences between influences and opportunities obtain at this level, identifiable with Bronfenbrenner's (1979) notion of microsystem.

An important contradiction is apparent between these findings and the views of Cattell (1983) based on g_f–g_c theory. Assuming the identity usually made in his writings between verbal–number tests and g_c on the one hand and nonverbal–performance tests and g_f on the other, his prediction would be that when there is no known difference in genetic makeup between populations, but identifiable cultural differences exist, population means should differ noticeably on g_c but not on g_f measures. More specifically, he intimates that when population means for different cultural groups are found to differ on general intelligence, an even greater difference would be predicted for g_c measures, but a relatively smaller difference for g_f measures (*cf.* Cattell, 1983, p. 249).

In the comparison of test data obtained in English- and Afrikaans-speaking South African cultures, a different pattern has been observed. Here the indications are that both g_f and g_c measures are responsive to *cultural* influences, but in different ways. Moreover, g_f measures have proved more sensitive to the subtle differences between the cultures in the South African context than g_c measures. These findings call for a revision of the conceptualisation of these constructs and the theory from which they stem, which has been a dominant force in the psychometric literature of past decades. The more general psychometric construct of "ability," as a source of explanation for intergroup and individual differences, likewise is in need of careful reappraisal. Although it may continue to have utility in applied settings, it may well have outlived its usefulness in psychological theory.

References

Biesheuvel, S. (1952). The nation's intelligence and its measurement. *South African Journal of Science, 39*, 120–138.

Biesheuvel, S. (1972). Adaptability: Its measurement and determinants. In L. J. C. Cronbach & P. J. D. Drenth (Eds.), *Mental tests and cultural adaptation*. The Hague: Mouton.

Biesheuvel, S., & Liddicoat, R. (1959). The effects of cultural factors on intelligence test performance. *Journal of the National Institute for Personnel Research, 8*, 3–14.

Box, G. E. (1949). A general distribution theory for a class of likelihood criteria. *Biometrika, 36,* 317–346.

Bronfenbrenner, U. (1979). *The ecology of human development. Experiments by nature and design.* Cambridge, MA: Harvard University Press.

Browne, M. W. (1982). Covariance structures. In D. M. Hawkins (Ed.), *Topics in applied multivariate analysis.* Cambridge University Press.

Carroll, J. B. (1980). *Individual difference relations in psychometric and experimental cognitive tasks* (Report No. 163, AD A086057). Chapel Hill: University of North Carolina.

Cattell, R. B. (1963). Theory of fluid and crystallized intelligence: A critical experiment. *Journal of Educational Psychology, 54*(1), 1–22.

Cattell, R. B. (1971). *Abilities: Their structure, growth and action.* Boston: Houghton Mifflin.

Cattell, R. B. (1983). The role of psychological testing in educational performance: The validity and use of ability predictions. *Mankind Quarterly, 23*(3–4), 227–273.

Cudeck, R., & Claasen, N. (1983). Structural equivalence of an intelligence test for two language groups. *South African Journal of Psychology, 13*(1), 1–5.

de Jager, J. J., & Boeyens, M. (1981). *Gedifferensieerde norme vir die Hoëvlakbattery/Verstandelike Helderheid en Deduktiewe Redeneer-vermoë-toets: gegradueerdes* [Differentiated norms for the *High Level Battery Mental Alertness and Deductive Reasoning Test:* Graduates] (PERS 309). Pretoria: National Institute for Personnel Research.

Eysenck, H. J. (Ed.). (1982). *A model for intelligence.* New York: Springer-Verlag.

French, J. W. (1965). The relation of problem-solving styles to the factor composition of tests. *Educational and Psychological Measurement, 25,* 9–28.

French, J. W., Ekstrom, R. B., & Price, L. A. (1963). *Manual for kit of reference tests for cognitive factors.* Princeton, NJ: Educational Testing Service.

Grant, G. V. (1972). The organization of intellectual abilities of an African ethnic group in cultural transition. In L. J. C. Cronbach & P. J. D. Drenth (Eds.), *Mental tests and cultural adaptation.* The Hague: Mouton.

Hakstian, A. R., & Vandenberg, S. G. (1979). The cross-cultural generalizability of a high-order cognitive structure model. *Intelligence, 3,* 73–103.

Honzik, M. P. (1984). Life-span development. *Annual Review of Psychology, 35,* 309–332.

Horn, J. L. (1978). Human ability systems. *Life-span Development and Behaviour, 1,* 211–256.

Horn, J. L. (1980). Concepts of intellect in relation to learning and adult development. *Intelligence, 4,* 285–317.

Horn, J. L., & Cattell, R. B. (1966). Refinement and test of the theory of fluid and crystallized general intelligence. *Journal of Educational Psychology, 57*(5), 253–270.

Hudson, W. (1960). Pictorial depth perception in sub-cultural groups in Africa. *Journal of Social Psychology, 52,* 183–208.

Hudson, W. (1962). Pictorial perception and educational adaptation in Africa. *Psychologia Africana, 9,* 226–239.

Hunt, E. (1982). Towards new ways of assessing intelligence. *Intelligence, 6,* 231–240.

Irvine, S. H. (1969). Factor analysis of African abilities and attainments: Constructs across cultures. *Psychological Bulletin, 71,* 20–32.

Irvine, S. H. (1979). The place of factor analysis in cross-cultural methodology and its contribution to cognitive theory. In L. Eckensberger, W. Lonner, & Y. Poortinga (Eds.), *Cross-cultural contributions to psychology.* Lisse: Swets & Zeitlinger.

Irvine, S. H. (1983). Testing in Africa and America: The search for routes. In S. H. Irvine & J. W. Berry (Eds.), *Human assessment and cultural factors.* New York: Plenum.

Irvine, S. H., & Berry, J. W. (Eds.) (1983). *Human assessment and cultural factors.* New York: Plenum.

Jöreskog, K. G. (1963). *Statistical estimation in factor analysis.* Uppsala: Alungvist & Wiksell.

Jöreskog, K. G. (1979). Statistical analysis of sets of congeneric tests. *Psychometrika, 36,* 409–426.

Kendall, I. M. (1972). *A comparative study of the organization of mental abilities of two matched ethnic groups: The Venda and the Pedi.* (PERS 171). Johannesburg: National Institute for Personnel Research.

Langenhoven, H. P. (1957). *Vergelyking van prestasies van Afrikaanse en Engelse groepe wat gelyk gemaak is t.o.v. nie-verbale roupunttelling in die Nuwe Suid-Afrikaanse Groeptoets (NSAGT)* [Comparison of performance of Afrikaans and English groups equated in terms of nonverbal raw score on the *New South African Group Test (NSAGT)*]. Pretoria: National Bureau for Educational and Social Research.

Madge, E. M. (1981). *Manual for the Junior South African Individual Scales.* Pretoria: Human Sciences Research Council.

Mellenbergh, G. J. (1972). An investigation of the applicability of the Rasch model in different cultures. In L. J. C. Cronbach & P. J. D. Drenth (Eds.), *Mental tests and cultural adaptation.* The Hague: Mouton.

Mellenbergh, G. J. (1983). Conditional item-bias methods. In S. H. Irvine & J. W. Berry (Eds.), *Human assessment and cultural factors.* New York: Plenum.

Morkel, P. (1950). *The A(G) mental alertness test: The reliability, difficulty, and grading of the forms.* Unpublished master's thesis, University of Stellenbosch.

Mundy Castle, A. C., & Nelson, G. K. (1962). A neuropsychological study of the Knysna forest workers. *Psychologia Africana, 9,* 240–272.

Mynhardt, J. C., Plug, C., Tyson, G. A., & Viljoen, H. G. (1979). Ethnocentrism, authoritarianism and conservatism among two South African student samples: A two-year follow-up study. *South African Journal of Psychology, 9*(1–2), 23–26.

Nelson, G. K. (1969). A neuropsychological study of the children of the Knysna forest workers. *Psychologia Africana, 12,* 143–171.

Olckers, P. J. (1950). Skoolpunte en standaarde [School grades and standards]. *Journal for Social Research, 1,* 172–182.

Poortinga, Y. H. (1971). Cross-cultural comparison of maximum performance tests: Some methodological aspects and some experiments with simple auditory and visual stimuli. *Psychologia Africana Monograph Supplement* (No. 6).

Poortinga, Y. H. (1972). A comparison of African and European students in simple auditory and visual tasks. In L. J. C. Cronbach & P. J. D. Drenth (Eds.), *Mental tests and cultural adaptation.* The Hague: Mouton.

Poortinga, Y. H. (1975). Limitations on intercultural comparison of psychological data. *Nederlands Tijdschrift voor de Psychologie, 30,* 23–29.

Poortinga, Y. H. (1983). Psychometric approaches to intergroup comparison: The problem of equivalence. In S. H. Irvine & J. W. Berry (Eds.), *Human assessment and cultural factors.* New York: Plenum.

Posner, M. I. (1978). *Chronometric explorations of mind.* Hillsdale, NJ: Erlbaum.

Reuning, H. (1972). Psychological studies of Kalahari Bushmen. In L. J. C. Cronbach & P. J. D. Drenth (Eds.), *Mental tests and cultural adaptation.* The Hague: Mouton.

Reuning, H., & Wortley, W. (1973). Psychological studies of the Bushmen. *Psychologia Africana Monograph Supplement* (No. 7).

Roos, W. L. (1983). *Die intellektueel superieure leerling – 'n vergelykende studie* [The intellectually superior pupil – a comparative study] (Report MT-52). Pretoria: Human Sciences Research Council.

Sternberg, R. J., & Detterman, D. K. (Eds.). (1979). *Human intelligence: Perspectives on its theory and measurement.* Norwood, NJ: Ablex.

Steyn, D. W. (1971). *The construction and evaluation of a South African scale of authoritarianism* (PERS 152). Johannesburg: National Institute for Personnel Research.

Süssenguth, C. O. E. (1972). *Problem-solving styles of research scientists* (PERS 184). Pretoria: National Institute for Personnel Research.

Taylor, J. M. (1978). *Short-term validation of a selection battery for trainee engineering technicians* (PERS 270). Johannesburg: National Institute for Personnel Research.

Taylor, T. R. (1983). Computerized testing. *South African Journal of Psychology, 13*(1), 23–31.

Taylor, T. R., Gerber, N., & Rendall, M. E. (1981). *The programming of psychological tests on the PLATO system* (C/PERS 303). Johannesburg: National Institute for Personnel Research.

van der Flier, H. (1982). Deviant response patterns and comparability of test scores. *Journal of Cross-Cultural Psychology, 13,* 267–298.

van de Vijver, F. J. R., & Poortinga, Y. H. (1982). Cross-cultural generalization and universality. *Journal of Cross-Cultural Psychology, 13*(4), 387–408.

Verster, J. M. (1974). A study of intellectual structure in two groups of South African scientists. *Psychologia Africana, 15*(3), 169–190.

Verster, J. M. (1982). *A cross-cultural study of cognitive processes using computerized tests.* Unpublished doctoral dissertation, University of South Africa, Pretoria.

Verster, J. M. (1983a). The structure, organization, and correlates of cognitive speed and accuracy: A cross-cultural study using computerized tests. In S. H. Irvine & J. W. Berry (Eds.), *Human assessment and cultural factors.* New York: Plenum.

Verster, J. M. (1983b). *Human cognition and intelligence: Towards an integrated theoretical perspective* (PERS 350). Johannesburg: National Institute for Personnel Research.

Vorster, J. F. (1978). The invariance of the factor structure of the intermediate and senior forms of the NSAGT. *Humanitas, 3,* 409–417.

Author index

Subject index